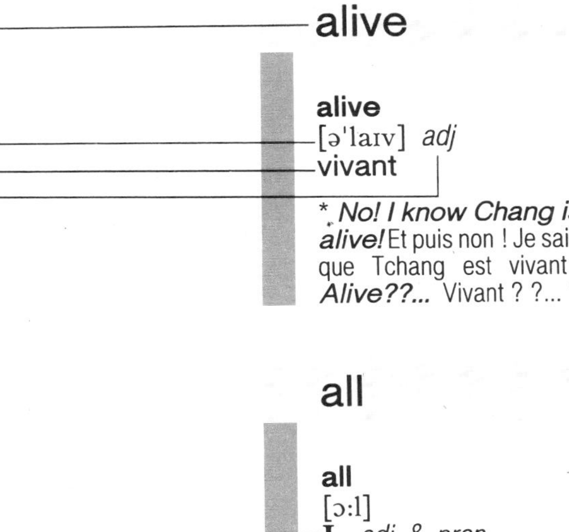

alive

alive
[ə'laɪv] *adj*
vivant

* ***No! I know Chang is alive!*** Et puis non ! Je sais que Tchang est vivant ! ***Alive??...*** Vivant ? ?... *

all

all
[ɔ:l]
I. *adj & pron*

...all

tout, toute, tous, toutes

don't eat all (of) the cake ne mangez pas tout le gâteau 9 11

all the guards are armed tous les gardes sont armés

* ***They've been walking all day...*** Ils ont marché toute la journée... * 10

II. *adv*
1. tout, tout à fait, complètement

rire

rire
[rir]
I. *vi*
1. to laugh

* ***Ha ! ha ! ha ! laissez-moi rire !...*** Ha! ha! ha!... You make me laugh!... ***Je dirais même plus : Ha ! ha ! ha !...*** To be precise : Ha! ha! ha!... *

2. Loc
j'ai dit ça pour rire I was only joking when I said that

II. *n m*
laughter

risquer

risquer
[riske] *vt* 3
to risk 5
8

▸ **risque**
[risk] *n m*
risk

prendre des risques 9
to take risks 11

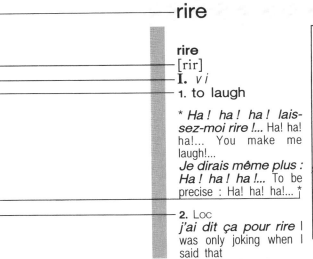

HOW TO USE THE DICTIONARY

1. Headword.
2. Pronunciation (see table).
3. Part of speech.
4. Figures I., II., etc. show the different parts of speech of a headword.
5. Translation of the headword.
6. Figures 1., 2., etc. show the different meanings of the word.
7. Idiom (Loc, for locution, in French) introduces idiomatic expressions.
8. Sub-entry. The main derivatives are given as sub-entries beneath the headword. The structure of the sub-entries is identical to that of the main entries.
9. Example.
10. Asterisks show that the example is illustrated. The example is identical to the text in the speech bubble.
11. Translation of example.

COMMENT UTILISER LE DICTIONNAIRE

1. Entrée.
2. Prononciation (voir tableau).
3. Catégorie grammaticale.
4. Les chiffres I., II., etc. indiquent les différentes catégories grammaticales d'un même mot.
5. Traduction du mot.
6. Les chiffres 1., 2., etc. indiquent les différentes traductions du mot.
7. Loc (en anglais Idiom) indique que le mot entre dans une expression idiomatique (ou dans plusieurs).
8. Sous-entrée. Sous le mot d'entrée ont été regroupés ses principaux dérivés. La structure de cette sous-entrée est la même que la structure de l'entrée principale.
9. Exemple.
10. L'astérisque indique que l'exemple est illustré. Le texte de l'exemple est celui qui figure dans la bulle.
11. Traduction de l'exemple.

TINTIN
AU PAYS DES MOTS

TINTIN
ILLUSTRATED DICTIONARY

Anglais-Français / Français-Anglais
English-French / French-English

Hélène HOUSSEMAINE-FLORENT • David JONES
Sur une idée de / Based on an idea by
BOOKMAKER

Images de / Cartoons by
HERGÉ
Choisies par / Chosen by
Patrick MICHEL-DANSAC

HARRAP

avec la coopération de / in co-operation with
METHUEN CHILDREN'S BOOKS

CONCEPTION ET RÉALISATION/PLANNED AND PRODUCED BY
BOOKMAKER

DIRECTION ÉDITORIALE/EDITORIAL DIRECTION
Marie Garagnoux • Patrick Michel-Dansac

ASSISTÉS DE/WITH
Françoise Avril

RÉDACTION/COMPILED BY
Hélène Houssemaine-Florent • David Jones

AVEC LA COLLABORATION DE/WITH
Marc Martinez
Professeur agrégé d'anglais
Ray Jones, BA
Teacher of French
Peter Weisman
Conseiller américain/American consultant

CHOIX DES ILLUSTRATIONS/ILLUSTRATIONS CHOSEN BY
Patrick Michel-Dansac

LETTRAGE/LETTERING
Anne Delobel

MAQUETTE/LAYOUT
Conception/Design :
Claire Forgeot • DOS CARRÉ
Réalisation/Produced by :
Michèle Andrault • Monique Michel-Dansac

AUTRES COLLABORATEURS/OTHER CONTRIBUTORS :
Jean Grobla • Béatrice Leroy • Françoise Paicher
Marie-Pierre Kappes • Richard Northcott

Edition publiée par/First published by
HARRAP BOOKS Ltd, Chelsea House, 26 Market Square, Bromley, Kent BR1 1NA

« Les Aventures de Tintin » sont publiées en anglais par

"The Adventures of Tintin" are published in English by

METHUEN CHILDREN'S BOOKS LTD

ISBN 0-245-54961-7

Réimpression/Reprinted 1989, 1990 (three times), Juin 1992

FOREWORD

TINTIN ILLUSTRATED DICTIONARY works like a traditional bilingual dictionary. It contains the basic vocabulary of French and English, covering most of the words that learners are likely to come across in the first few years of studying a foreign language.

The meanings treated and the translations given are the most common ones; they are given in order of frequency of occurrence. Examples show how the words are used in context. The different meanings are followed, if necessary, by the most important idiomatic expressions in which the headword is found.

Wherever possible, we have illustrated our examples with drawings from Hergé's Adventures of Tintin. The text of the speech bubbles has been rewritten to adapt the drawings to the examples chosen by the authors. In this way, language is put into context in a striking and lively fashion, sometimes with very amusing results. Consulting this dictionary is a way to learn while having fun.

We have made every effort to remain faithful to Hergé's world, by keeping the personalities and mannerisms of his characters. Tintin fans will recognize their heroes, and for others, who have forgotten them or who never knew them well, this dictionary will be the opportunity to rediscover them.

AVERTISSEMENT

TINTIN AU PAYS DES MOTS se consulte comme un dictionnaire bilingue traditionnel. Il présente le vocabulaire de base. Le choix des mots s'est fait à partir des grilles de vocabulaire établies pour les quatre premières années de l'enseignement secondaire.

Les sens et les traductions retenus sont les plus usuels ; ils sont présentés dans l'ordre de leur fréquence d'emploi. Les exemples montrent les utilisations typiques du mot. Les différents sens du mot sont suivis, quand il y a lieu, des principales expressions idiomatiques dans lesquelles il apparaît.

Chaque fois que cela était possible, nous avons illustré ces exemples avec des vignettes extraites des albums de Tintin. Le texte des bulles a été refait à partir des exemples proposés par les auteurs. La langue est ainsi mise en situation de façon vivante et souvent très drôle mais avec toute la précision grammaticale et lexicographique nécessaire. Consulter ce dictionnaire est donc un moyen efficace et divertissant d'enrichir ses connaissances.

Nous nous sommes efforcés de respecter l'univers d'Hergé en conservant à tous les personnages leurs caractéristiques et leurs « tics ». Les passionnés de Tintin y retrouveront tous leurs héros et, pour ceux qui les auraient oubliés ou qui ne les connaîtraient pas très bien, ce livre sera l'occasion de les redécouvrir.

The dictionary takes British English as its base. When a word or its spelling is different in American English, this is indicated by the abbreviation *Am*.

Each entry is marked off by a horizontal grey rectangle containing the headword and a vertical grey rectangle to the left of the text. When an entry is more than one column long, the horizontal rectangle is repeated and the headword preceded by suspension points. The structure of the entries is presented in diagram form on the endpapers (together with pronunciation tables and a list of abbreviations used in the dictionary).

Irregular French and English plurals are shown as well as irregular English verb forms, comparatives and superlatives.

The dictionary is in two parts: English-French and French-English. These two parts are separated by an appendix giving the basic grammatical rules of each language, plus a list of English irregular verbs, a French verb conjugation table and a numbers table.

Hergé's style of lettering has been followed in the illustrations. Below is a table of the capital letters, to help our English-speaking users who might be unaccustomed to this style of handwriting.

C'est l'anglais britannique qui est présenté ici ; quand l'orthographe ou le mot lui-même est différent en américain, c'est l'abréviation *Am* qui l'indique.

Chaque mot fait l'objet d'un article délimité par un rectangle gris horizontal où s'inscrit le mot d'entrée, et par un rectangle gris vertical qui s'aligne sur le texte à gauche. Quand l'article comporte plus d'une colonne, le rectangle gris horizontal est repris, et le mot d'entrée répété et précédé de points de suspension. Pour la structure des articles, voir les croquis présentés sur les pages de garde (voir également sur ces pages les tableaux des signes phonétiques et des abréviations utilisés dans le dictionnaire).

Les pluriels irréguliers en français et en anglais sont indiqués, ainsi que les comparatifs, les superlatifs et les verbes irréguliers anglais.

Le dictionnaire comporte deux parties : anglais-français, français-anglais. Ces deux parties sont séparées, au milieu de l'ouvrage, par un appendice grammatical qui présente les règles de base des deux langues et où figurent la liste des verbes irréguliers anglais, le tableau de conjugaison des verbes français et celui des nombres.

•A *A*	•B *B*	•C *C*	•D *D*	•E *E*	•F *F*
•G *G*	•H *H*	•I *I*	•J *J*	•K *K*	•L *L*
•M *M*	•N *N*	•O *O*	•P *P*	•Q *Q*	•R *R*
•S *S*	•T *T*	•U *U*	•V *V*	•W *W*	•X *X*
•Y *Y*	•Z *Z*				

a

a
[ə] *art*
an [æn] *devant une voyelle*
1. un, une

is it a boy or a girl? est-ce que c'est un garçon ou une fille ?

2. le, la l'
they cost $2 a kilo ils coûtent 2 dollars le kilo

3. par
four times a year quatre fois par an

able

able
['eɪbl] *adj*
Idiom
to be able to pouvoir

* *Don't be sad, Mrs Wang, we'll be able to cure him... I promise you!... He'll soon be better!...* Ne soyez pas triste, madame Wang, on pourra le guérir... Je vous le promets !... Il sera bientôt guéri !... *

I'll never be able to swim like her je ne pourrai jamais nager comme elle

about

about
[ə'baʊt]
I. *adv*
1. environ, à peu près

I'll be back in about two hours je serai de retour dans deux heures environ

2. partout
don't leave your things lying about! ne laisse pas tes affaires traîner partout !

3. Idiom
to be about to do something être sur le point de faire quelque chose

* *Rrrring* Dring
Captain! That's funny! I was about to call you! Capitaine ! C'est drôle, j'étais sur le point de vous téléphoner ! *

II. *prep*
1. à propos de, au sujet de, sur

a book about butter-

...about

flies un livre sur les papillons

2. Idiom
what about a game of tennis? si on jouait au tennis ?

what about me? et moi ?

above

above
[ə'bʌv] *prep*
1. au-dessus de

...above

* *They are flying above the clouds.* Ils volent au-dessus des nuages. *

2. plus de
children above the age of 10 les enfants de plus de 10 ans

3. Idiom
above all surtout

abroad

abroad
[ə'brɔːd] *adv*
à l'étranger

don't forget your passport, we're going abroad n'oubliez pas votre passeport, nous partons à l'étranger

absent

absent
['æbsənt] *adj*
absent

...absent

* ***I'd like to speak to the director.*** Je voudrais parler au directeur. ***The director is absent, Sir!*** Le directeur est absent, monsieur ! *

accelerate

accelerate
[æk'seləreɪt] *vi*
accélérer

* *Accelerate, or we'll never catch them up!*

...accelerate

Accélérez, ou nous ne les rattraperons jamais ! *

accent

accent
['æksənt] *n*
1. accent *m*

he has a strong foreign accent il a un fort accent étranger

2. accent *m*
an acute/grave accent un accent aigu/grave

accept

accept
[ək'sept] *vt*
accepter

all right, I accept your invitation d'accord, j'accepte votre invitation

accident

accident
['æksɪdənt] *n*
accident *m*

we nearly had an accident on a failli avoir un accident

according to

according to
[ə'kɔ:dɪŋ tʊ] *prep*
selon

* ***Meanwhile...*** Pendant ce temps... ***According to the pendulum, it's this way...*** Selon le pendule, c'est par ici... *

across

across
[ə'krɒs] *prep*
1. à travers, d'un côté à l'autre de

we walked across the fields nous avons marché à travers champs

2. de l'autre côté de
they live just across the road ils habitent juste de l'autre côté de la rue

3. Idiom
to go across a road/a river traverser une route/une rivière

to swim across a river traverser une rivière à la nage

act

act
[ækt]
I. *n*
acte *m*

II. *vi*
1. agir

* ***We'll have to act fast!*** Il faut que nous agissions vite ! *

2. jouer
he's acting in a play by Shakespeare il joue dans une pièce de Shakespeare

► **actor**
['æktəʳ] *n*
acteur *m*

► **actress**
['æktrɪs] *n*
actrice *f*

she's a film actress elle est actrice de cinéma

actual

actual
['æktjʊəl] *adj*
véritable, réel

I've never seen an actual ghost je n'ai jamais vu de véritable fantôme

► **actually**
['æktjʊəlɪ] *adv*
1. vraiment, réellement

I don't believe it actually happened! je ne

crois pas que cela soit vraiment arrivé !

2. en fait
what are you doing? – actually, I've forgotten qu'est-ce que vous faites ? – en fait, j'ai oublié

add

add
[æd] *vt*
1. additionner

what do you get if you add 9 and 27? qu'obtient-on si on additionne 9 et 27 ?

2. ajouter
add a little sugar ajoutez un peu de sucre

► **add up**
additionner

I'm trying to add up all these figures j'essaie d'additionner tous ces chiffres

address

address
[ə'dres] *n*
adresse *f*

write down your name and address écrivez votre nom et votre adresse

admire

admire
[əd'maɪəʳ] *vt*
admirer

* ***Oh, Snowy, I admire your courage... But for you, that lion would have eaten me...*** Oh, Milou, j'admire ton courage... Sans toi, ce lion m'aurait dévoré... ***You know, that lion wasn't as nasty as he looked.*** Tu sais, ce lion n'était pas aussi méchant qu'il en avait l'air. *

admit

admit
[əd'mɪt] *vt*
1. admettre, avouer

admit it, you're working for Müller! avouez-le, vous travaillez pour Müller !

2. laisser entrer
she opened the door to admit them elle a ouvert la porte pour les laisser entrer

adventure

adventure
[əd'ventʃəʳ] *n*
aventure *f*

* ***Billions of blue blistering barnacles!... I've had enough of these adventures...*** Mille milliards de mille sabords !... J'en ai assez de ces aventures... *

advertise

advertise
['ædvətaɪz]
I. *vt*
faire de la publicité pour

they advertise their brand on television ils font de la publicité pour leur marque à la télévision

II. *vi*
1. faire de la publicité

every company has to advertise toutes les entreprises doivent faire de la publicité

2. passer une annonce
they advertised in the paper for a secretary ils ont passé une annonce dans le journal pour une secrétaire

► **advertisement**
[əd'vɜːtɪsmənt] *n*
1. publicité *f*

2. annonce *f*

* ***Read the advertisement they've put in the newspaper!*** Lisez l'annonce qu'ils ont passée dans le journal ! *

advice

advice
[əd'vaɪs] *n*
conseil(s) *m (pl)*

* ***Take my advice and leave!*** Suivez mon conseil, partez ! *

aeroplane

aeroplane
['eərəpleɪn] *n*
(*Am:* **airplane)**
avion *m*

afford

afford
[ə'fɔ:d] *vt*
avoir les moyens de s'acheter, pouvoir payer

we can't afford a new car nous n'avons pas les moyens de nous acheter une nouvelle voiture

afraid

afraid
[ə'freɪd] *adj*
Idiom
he's afraid of the dark il a peur du noir

Tintin, I'm afraid! Tintin, j'ai peur !

* ***Later at the Bristol...*** Plus tard, au Bristol...
I'm afraid we have no rooms, Sir. Je regrette, monsieur, nous n'avons plus de chambre. *

after

after
['ɑ:ftəʳ] *prep*
1. après

what shall we do after lunch? que ferons-nous après le déjeuner ?

2. Idiom
after all après tout

the police are after him la police le recherche

► **afternoon**
[ɑ:ftə'nu:n] *n*
après-midi *m* or *f*

at 2 o'clock in the afternoon à 2 heures de l'après-midi

► **afterwards**
['ɑ:ftəwədz] *adv*
après, ensuite

what are you going to do afterwards? qu'est-ce que vous allez faire après ?

again

again
[ə'geɪn] *adv*
1. de nouveau, encore

it's raining again! il pleut de nouveau !

2. Idiom
to start again recommencer

against

against
[ə'geɪnst] *prep*
1. contre

* ***Hurry up!*** Dépêchez-vous !
The ladder's against the wall... L'échelle est contre le mur... *

all the evidence is against him toutes les preuves sont contre lui

2. Idiom
it's against the law c'est illégal

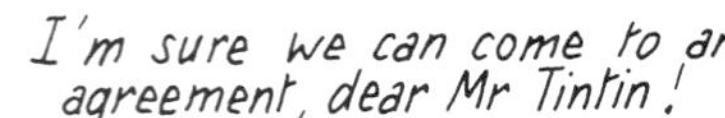

it's against the rules c'est interdit par le règlement

age

age
[eɪdʒ] *n*
1. âge *m*

children of all ages les enfants de tous âges

...age

2. Idiom
she's ten years of age elle a dix ans

I've been waiting for ages! ça fait une éternité que j'attends !

ago

ago
[ə'gəʊ] *adv*
il y a

Tintin went out ten minutes ago Tintin est sorti il y a dix minutes

...ago

fifty years ago il y a cinquante ans

agree

agree
[ə'gri:] *vi*
être d'accord

we ought to get out of here! – I agree! nous devrions partir d'ici ! – je suis d'accord !

...agree

► **agreement**
[ə'gri:mənt] *n*
accord *m*

* ***I'm sure we can come to an agreement, dear Mr Tintin!*** Je suis sûr que nous pouvons arriver à un accord, cher monsieur Tintin ! *

ahead

ahead
[ə'hed] *adv*
devant, en avant

you go ahead, I'll stay here partez devant, je vais rester ici

air

air
[eəʳ] *n*
air *m*

...air

there's no air in this room on manque d'air dans cette pièce

* ***Quick, some air, I'm stifling!*** Vite, un peu d'air, j'étouffe ! *

► **airport**
['eəpɔ:t] *n*
aéroport *m*

► **airplane** (*Am*)
→ AEROPLANE

...air

Quick, some air, I'm stifling!

alive

alive
[ə'laɪv] *adj*
vivant

* *No! I know Chang is alive!* Et puis non ! Je sais que Tchang est vivant ! *Alive??...* Vivant ? ?... *

all

all
[ɔ:l]
I. *adj & pron*

...all

tout, toute, tous, toutes

don't eat all (of) the cake ne mangez pas tout le gâteau

all the guards are armed tous les gardes sont armés

* *They've been walking all day...* Ils ont marché toute la journée... *

II. *adv*
1. tout, tout à fait, complètement

...all

They've been walking all day ...

she was dressed all in red elle était habillée tout en rouge

I forgot all about Snowy! j'ai complètement oublié Milou !

do you mind if I smoke? – not at all! est-ce que cela vous dérange si je fume ? – pas du tout !

2. Idiom
I'm aching all over! j'ai mal partout !

we had a good time all the same nous nous sommes bien amusés quand même

allow

allow
[ə'laʊ] *vt*
1. permettre

allow me to help you permettez-moi de vous aider

...allow

2. Idiom
parking/smoking isn't allowed here il est interdit de stationner/de fumer ici

all right

all right, alright
[ɔ:l'raɪt]
I. *adj*
bien

are you all right, Captain? vous allez bien, capitaine ?

...all right

II. *adv*
d'accord

* *Do you mind if I have a quick look?* Vous permettez que je jette un coup d'œil ? *All right...* D'accord... *

almost

almost
['ɔ:lməʊst] *adv*
presque

Do you mind if I have a quick look?
All right...

...almost

what time is it? – it's almost five o'clock quelle heure est-il ? – il est presque cinq heures

alone

alone
[ə'ləʊn] *adj*
seul

* *Don't go alone, Captain, I'm coming with you...* N'y allez pas

...alone

Don't go alone, Captain, I'm coming with you ...

seul, capitaine, je viens avec vous... *

along

along
[ə'lɒŋ]
I. *prep*
le long de

...along

there are lampposts, all along the street il y a des réverbères tout le long de la rue

* *He's walking along the river...* Il marche le long du fleuve... *

II. *adv*
Idiom
come along! venez donc !

come along with me venez avec moi

He's walking along the river...

I'll be along in a few minutes je serai là dans quelques instants

how are you getting along? comment ça va ?

aloud

aloud
[ə'laʊd] *adv*
à haute voix

to read aloud lire à haute voix

alphabet

alphabet
['ælfəbet] *n*
alphabet *m*

already

already
[ɔ:l'redɪ] *adv*
déjà

have you already finished? avez-vous déjà fini ?

also

also
['ɔ:lsəʊ] *adv*
aussi

delightful evening: it's raining, and it's also very cold charmante soirée : il pleut, et il fait très froid aussi

although

although
[ɔ:l'ðəʊ] *conj*
bien que, quoique

...although

although he's tired he can't sleep bien qu'il soit fatigué, il n'arrive pas à dormir

always

always
[ɔ:lweɪz] *adv*
toujours

* *Why do you always repeat what I say?* Pourquoi répètes-tu toujours ce que je dis ? *

...always

Why do you always repeat what I say?

ambulance

ambulance
['æmbjʊləns] *n*
ambulance *f*

America

America
[ə'merɪkə] *n*
Amérique *f*

▶ **American**
[ə'merɪk(ə)n]
I. *n*
Américain *m*,

...America

Américaine *f*

II. *adj*
américain

among

among
[ə'mʌŋ] *prep*
parmi, entre

I can see him among the crowd je le vois parmi la foule

and

and
[ænd]
I. *conj*
et

look, there are Thompson and Thomson regardez, voilà Dupond et Dupont

II. Idiom
one hundred and one cent un

three thousand and twenty trois mille vingt

angry

angry
['æŋgrɪ] *adj*
angrier, angriest
fâché, en colère

are you still angry with me, Tintin? êtes-vous toujours fâché contre moi, Tintin ?

animal

animal
['ænɪməl] *n*

...animal

animal *m*

* *Hurray!* Hourrah ! *Llamas are very touchy animals...* Les lamas sont des animaux très susceptibles... *

ankle

ankle
['æŋk(ə)l] *n*
cheville *f*

Hurray!

Llamas are very touchy animals...

announce

announce
[ə'naʊns] *vt*
annoncer

hurry up, our flight has been announced dépêchez-vous, notre vol a été annoncé

another

another
[ə'nʌðəʳ] *adj & pron*
1. un/une autre

...another

Would you like another cup of tea?

I'll do it another day je le ferai un autre jour

2. encore un, encore une
* *Would you like another cup of tea?* Voulez-vous encore une tasse de thé ? *

* *Several hours later...* Plusieurs heures après... *Another one, that makes the seventh pair of tracks...* Encore une, ça fait la septième trace... *

Several hours later...
Another one, that makes the seventh pair of tracks...

answer

answer
['ɑ:nsəʳ]
I. *vi*
répondre

* *What about the skeleton, Wolff, was that you?* Et le squelette, Wolff, c'était vous ?
Yes, skeleton, were you the Wolff? Come on, answer! Oui, squelette, c'était vous le Wolff ? Allons, répondez ! *

...answer

What about the skeleton, Wolff, was that you?
Yes, skeleton, were you the Wolff? Come on, answer!

II. *vt*
répondre à

answer the following questions répondez aux questions suivantes

III. *n*
réponse *f*

that's the right answer c'est la bonne réponse

any

any
['enɪ]
I. *adj*
1. n'importe quel, n'importe quelle

you can get them in any supermarket on peut les trouver dans n'importe quel supermarché

2. du, de la, des *(in questions)*
have you got any stamps? avez-vous des timbres ?

3. de, d' *(in negatives)*
* *Great snakes! I haven't got any money!* Sapristi ! je n'ai pas d'argent ! *

II. *pron*
1. n'importe lequel, n'importe laquelle

which one would you like? – I don't mind, give me any of them lequel voulez-vous ? – cela m'est égal, donnez-moi n'importe lequel

Great snakes! I haven't got any money!

...any

2. en
I haven't got any left je n'en ai plus

III. *adv*
Idiom
are you feeling any better? est-ce que vous vous sentez mieux ?

* *Accelerate or they'll catch up with us!* Accélérez ! Ils vont nous rattraper ! *Impossible! This car can't go any faster!* Impossible ! Cette voiture ne peut pas aller plus vite ! *

Accelerate or they'll catch up with us!
Impossible! This car can't go any faster!
20510·Z05

▸ **anybody, anyone**
['enɪbɒdɪ], ['enɪwʌn]
pron
1. n'importe qui

it's easy, anybody can do it c'est facile, n'importe qui peut le faire

2. quelqu'un
is there anyone in? y a-t-il quelqu'un (à la maison) ?

3. personne
it's a secret, don't tell anybody c'est un secret, ne le dites à personne

▸ **anything**
['enɪθɪŋ] *pron*
1. n'importe quoi

what would you like to eat? – anything! que voulez-vous manger ? – n'importe quoi !

2. quelque chose
can I do anything to help you? puis-je faire quelque chose pour vous aider ?

3. rien
I can't see anything je ne vois rien

▸ **anyway**
['enɪweɪ] *adv*
de toute façon

...any

I didn't like it much ***anyway*** de toute façon, je ne l'aimais pas beaucoup

► **anywhere**
['enɪweəʳ] *adv*
1. n'importe où

where shall I put this? – ***anywhere*** où voulez-vous que je mette ceci ? – n'importe où

2. quelque part
* *Is there anywhere we can talk in private?* Pouvons-nous discuter en privé quelque part ?
Certainly. Over there, we won't be disturbed... Certainement. Là-bas, nous serons tranquilles !... *

3. nulle part
I can't find my glasses ***anywhere*** je ne trouve mes lunettes nulle part

Is there anywhere we can talk in private ?
Certainly. Over there, we won't be disturbed...

apart

apart
[ə'pɑ:t] *adv*
1. éloigné

the houses aren't very far ***apart*** *(from each other)* les maisons ne sont pas très éloignées (les unes des autres)

2. en morceaux
my watch has fallen ***apart*** ma montre est tombée en morceaux

► **apart from**
prep
à part, sauf

everybody's here ***apart from*** *Tintin* tout le monde est là sauf Tintin

appear

appear
[ə'pɪəʳ] *vi*
1. apparaître

a plane appeared in the sky un avion est apparu dans le ciel

2. avoir l'air, sembler
* *Tuesday* Mardi
He appears to be busy. Il a l'air occupé. *

15
TUESDAY

He appears to be busy.

apple

apple
['æp(ə)l] *n*
pomme *f*

That's a big apple !...
BOUM

* *That's a big apple!...* Cette pomme est énorme !... *

appointment

apppointment
[ə'pɔɪntmənt] *n*
rendez-vous *m*

I'd like to see Mr Jones – do you have an ***appointment****?* J'aimerais voir M. Jones – vous avez un rendez-vous ?

apricot

apricot
['eɪprɪkɒt] *n*
abricot *m*

April

April
['eɪprəl] *n*
avril *m*

the first/second of April (Am: April first/second) le premier/deux avril

area

area
['eərɪə] *n*
1. région *f*

The research centre is in the Klow area ...
КЛОВ
KLOW
7.5

* *The research centre (Am: center) is in the Klow area...* Le centre de recherche est dans la région de Klow... *

2. quartier *m*
residential ***area*** quartier résidentiel

3. surface *f*, superficie *f*
to measure the ***area*** *of a room* mesurer la surface d'une pièce

arm

arm
[ɑ:m] *m*
bras *m*

► **armchair**
[ɑ:m'tʃeəʳ] *n*
fauteuil *m*

arm

arm
[ɑ:m] *vt*
armer

* *Look out, they're armed!* Attention, ils sont armés ! *

▶ **arms** *n pl*
armes *f pl*

their only arms were knives and swords leurs seules armes étaient des couteaux et des épées

Look out, they're armed!

army

army
['ɑ:mɪ] *n*
pl armies
armée *f*

around

around
[ə'raʊnd]
I. *prep*
1. autour de

...around

they all gathered around Calculus ils se sont tous rassemblés autour de Tournesol

2. environ
it cost around £100 cela a coûté environ 100 livres

II. *adv*
autour

there are mountains all around il y a des montagnes tout autour

arrange

arrange
[ə'reɪndʒ] *vt*
1. organiser

* *It was such a good idea to arrange this party!... I love dressing up!* Quelle bonne idée d'avoir organisé cette fête !... J'adore me déguiser !
So do I!... Moi aussi !... *

2. ranger, arranger
the books are all arranged in alphabeti-

...arrange

It was such a good idea to arrange this party!... I love dressing up!
So do I!...

cal order les livres sont tous rangés par ordre alphabétique

▶ **arrangement**
[ə'reɪndʒmənt] *n*
1. préparatif *m*, disposition *f*

I have made all the arrangements for the trip j'ai fait tous les préparatifs en vue du voyage

2. disposition *f*, arrangement *m*

you've changed the arrangement of the furniture vous avez changé la disposition des meubles

arrive

arrive
[ə'raɪv] *vi*
arriver

* *What time does the plane arrive in New York?* A quelle heure

...arrive

What time does the plane arrive in New York?
At six o'clock.
LAS DO

l'avion arrive-t-il à New York ?
At six o'clock. A six heures. *

▶ **arrival**
[ə'raɪv(ə)l] *n*
arrivée *f*

art

art
[ɑ:t] *n*
art m

do you like modern art? aimez-vous l'art moderne ?

article

article
['ɑ:tɪk(ə)l] *n*
1. article *m*

all the articles in the

...article

Look! There's an article about Red Rackham's treasure in the paper!

window are reduced Tous les articles en vitrine sont soldés

2. article *m*
* *Look! There's an article about Red Rackham's treasure in the paper!* Regardez ! Il y a un article sur le trésor de Rackham le Rouge dans le journal ! *

3. article *m*
"the" is the definite article « the » est l'article défini

artist

artist
['ɑ:tɪst] *n*
artiste *m f*

as

as
[æz]
I. *conj*
1. puisque, comme

...as

as the weather's bad, let's stay in puisqu'il fait mauvais, restons à la maison

2. pendant que, comme
they attacked me as I was sleeping ils m'ont attaqué pendant que je dormais

3. comme
do as the Captain tells you faites comme le capitaine vous le dit

...as

4. Idiom
* *As for me, I'm going for a walk in the park...* Quant à moi, je vais faire un tour dans le parc... *

as from next Monday dès lundi prochain

he was shivering as if he were cold il tremblait comme s'il avait froid

it looks as if it's going to rain on dirait qu'il va pleuvoir

As for me, I'm going for a walk in the park...

II. *adv*
aussi, si

he's not as tall as me il n'est pas aussi grand que moi

* *When you go in, mind...* Faites attention en entrant...
The step?... A la marche ?...
No, the door... Non, à la porte...
Thomson is as absent-minded... as

When you go in, mind...
The step?...

Thomson is as absent-minded...

...as

No, the door...

... as Thompson.

Thompson. Dupont est aussi étourdi... que Dupond. *

ashamed

ashamed
[ə'ʃeɪmd] *adj*
Idiom
to be ashamed of avoir honte de

ask

ask
[ɑ:sk] *v t*
1. demander

* *I'll ask a passer-by the way to the station. Provided there is a station, of course!* Je vais demander le chemin de la gare à un passant. A condition qu'il y ait une gare, bien sûr ! *

2. poser
may I ask you a question? puis-je vous

I'll ask a passer-by the way to the station. Provided there is a station, of course!
REDSKINCITY

...ask

poser une question ?

3. inviter
they have asked us to a party ils nous ont invités à une fête

► **ask for**
demander

he asked for a cup of tea il a demandé une tasse de thé

asleep

asleep
[ə'sli:p] *adj*
Idiom
to be asleep dormir

to fall asleep s'endormir

assign

assign (*Am*)
→ SET

astonish

astonish
[ə'stɒnɪʃ] *v t*
étonner

I was astonished to see her there j'étais étonné de la voir là

► **astonishing**
[ə'stɒnɪʃɪŋ] *adj*
étonnant

at

at
[æt] *prep*
1. à

I'll wait for you at the corner of the street je vous attendrai à l'angle de la rue

2. à
at five o'clock à cinq heures

3. Idiom
he's looking at me il me regarde

is she good at geography? est-elle bonne en géographie ?

attack

attack
[ə'tæk] *v t*
attaquer

* *Who's he attacking?* Qui attaque-t-il ? *

...attack

Who's he attacking?

attend

attend
[ə'tend] *vt*
assister à

they attended the meeting ils ont assisté à la réunion

* *Come on, Captain, you must attend the meeting. It's very important...* Allons, capitaine, vous devez assister à la réunion. C'est très important... *

Come on, Captain, you must attend the meeting. It's very important...

attention

attention
[ə'tenʃ(ə)n] *n*
attention *f*

pay attention to what I'm saying! faites attention à ce que je dis !

August

August
['ɔ:gəst] *n*
août *m*

Australia

Australia
[ɒ'streɪlɪə] *n*
Australie *f*

▸ **Australian**
[ɒ'streɪlɪən]
I. *n*
Australien *m*, Australienne *f*

II. *adj*
australien, ne

author

author
['ɔ:θəʳ] *n*
auteur *m*

who is the author of this book? qui est l'auteur de ce livre ?

automatic

automatic
[ɔ:tə'mætɪk] *adj*
automatique

autumn

autumn ['ɔ:təm] *n* (*Am:* **fall**)
automne *f*

average

average
['ævərɪdʒ]
I. *n*
moyenne *f*

temperatures will be above average les températures seront au-dessus de la moyenne

...average

II. *adj*
moyen

the average temperature la température moyenne

avoid

avoid
[ə'vɔɪd] *vt*
éviter

...avoid

* *I would have liked to come with you, but the doctor told me to avoid going out.* J'aurais aimé venir avec vous, mais le médecin m'a dit d'éviter de sortir. *

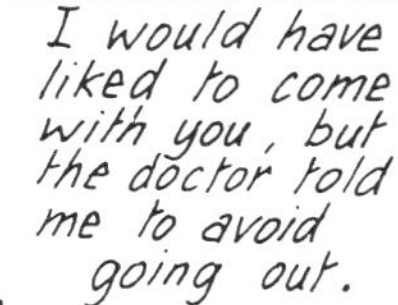
I would have liked to come with you, but the doctor told me to avoid going out.

awake

awake
[ə'weɪk] *adj*
réveillé, éveillé

...awake

What's the matter, Captain? Are you awake?

* *What's the matter, Captain? Are you awake?* Que se passe-t-il, capitaine ?... Etes-vous réveillé ? *

away

away
[ə'weɪ] *adv*
1. absent

I'll be away for a few days je serai absent quelques jours.

...away

2. Idiom
to go away s'en aller

put your toys away range tes jouets

to run away se sauver

to throw away jeter

it's long way away c'est loin d'ici

it's 5 kilometres (Am: kilometers) away c'est à 5 kilomètres

awful

awful
['ɔ:fʊl] *adj*
affreux

what awful weather! quel temps affreux !

▸ **awfully**
['ɔ:fʊlɪ] *adv*
vraiment, terriblement

I'm awfully sorry! je suis vraiment désolé !

baby

baby
['beɪbɪ] *n*
pl babies
bébé *m*

she's expecting a baby elle attend un bébé

* ***Why is this baby crying?*** Pourquoi ce bébé pleure-t-il ? ***Wooaaah!*** Wouaaah ! *

back

back
[bæk]
I. *n*
1. **dos** *m*

ouch! I've hurt my back! aïe ! je me suis fait mal au dos !

2. **arrière** *m*
sit in the back of the car assieds-toi à l'arrière de la voiture

II. *adj*
arrière, de derrière

we went in by the back door nous sommes entrés par la porte de derrière

III. *adv*
1. **en arrière**

I stepped back j'ai fait un pas en arrière

2. Idiom
to come back revenir

to go back retourner

to pay back rembourser

...back

to give somebody something back rendre quelque chose à quelqu'un

▸ **background**
['bækgraʊnd] *n*
arrière-plan *m*

there is a ship in the background il y a un navire à l'arrière-plan

▸ **backwards**
['bækwədz] *adv*
1. **en arrière**

to walk backwards marcher en arrière

2. **à l'envers**
* ***Thundering typhoons! What a lovely ship!*** Tonnerre de Brest ! Quel beau navire ! ***The Captain has put his pullover on backwards.*** Le capitaine a mis son pull à l'envers. *

The Captain has put his pullover on backwards.

bacon

bacon
['beɪk(ə)n] *n*
bacon *m*

they have bacon and eggs for breakfast ils mangent des œufs au bacon au petit déjeuner

bad

bad
[bæd] *adj*
worse [wɜ:s],
worst [wɜ:st]

...bad

I hope this bad weather won't last!

1. mauvais
* *I hope this bad weather won't last!* J'espère que ce mauvais temps ne durera pas ! *

2. méchant
you bad dog, Snowy! tu es méchant, Milou !

3. gros
I've got a bad cold j'ai un gros rhume

► **badly**
['bædlı] *adv*
mal

Abdullah is behaving very badly Abdallah se conduit très mal

bag

bag
[bæg] *n*
sac *m*

* *They've put Snowy into a bag!* Ils ont mis Milou dans un sac ! *

...bag

They've put Snowy into a bag!

baker

baker
['beıkəʳ] *n*
1. boulanger *m*, boulangère *f*

2. Idiom
at the baker's à la boulangerie

balance

balance
['bæləns] *n*
équilibre *m*

...balance

Tintin can't keep his balance. He's going to fall!

* *Tintin can't keep his balance. He's going to fall!* Tintin n'arrive pas à garder l'équilibre, il va tomber ! *

ball

ball
[bɔ:l] *n*
1. balle *f*

a tennis ball une balle de tennis

...ball

2. ballon *m*
a rugby ball un ballon de rugby

banana

banana
[bə'nɑ:nə] *n*
banane *f*

band

band
[bænd] *n*
1. orchestre *m*

he plays the trumpet in a band il joue de la trompette dans un orchestre

2. bande *f*, ruban *m*
the letters were tied together with a red band les lettres étaient attachées avec un ruban rouge

3. Idiom
a rubber band un élastique

► **band-aid** (*Am*)
→ STICKING PLASTER

bank

bank
[bæŋk] *n*
1. banque *f*

take this money to the bank apportez cet argent à la banque

...bank

2. bord *m*, rive *f*
we had a picnic on the river bank nous avons pique-niqué au bord de la rivière

bar

bar
[bɑ:ʳ] *n*
1. barreau *m*

* *I've got nothing to saw through the bars*

...bar

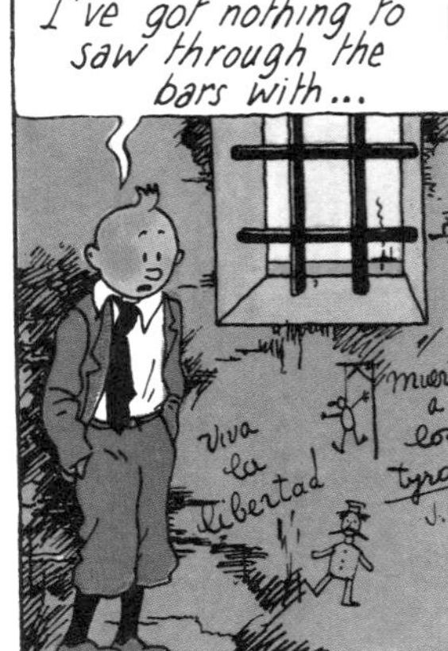
I've got nothing to saw through the bars with...
Viva la Libertad

with... Je n'ai rien pour scier les barreaux... *

2. bar *m*
he had a glass of beer in a bar il a bu un verre de bière dans un bar

3. Idiom
a bar of soap un savon

a bar of chocolate une tablette de chocolat

bargain

bargain
['bɑ:gın] *n*
bonne affaire *f*, occasion *f*

bark

bark
[bɑ:k] *v i*
aboyer

* *Why is Snowy barking like that?* Pourquoi Milou aboie-t-il ainsi ?

...bark

Why is Snowy barking like that?
Woof! Woof!

...bark

Woof! Woof! Wouah ! Wouah ! *

basket

basket
['bɑ:skɪt] *n*
panier *m*, corbeille *f*

* *Oh dear!... These baskets are quite heavy...* Oh là là !... Ces paniers sont bien lourds... *

...basket

Oh dear!... These baskets are quite heavy...

bath

bath
[bɑ:θ] *n*
1. bain *m*

I have (Am: take) a bath every morning je prends un bain tous les matins

2. baignoire *f*
don't forget to clean the bath (Am: bathtub) n'oubliez pas de nettoyer la baignoire

► **bathroom**
['bɑ:θru:m] *n*
salle *f* de bains

be

be
[bi:]
I. *v i*
1. être

Haddock is a sailor Haddock est un marin

...be

Tintin! where are you? Tintin ! où êtes-vous ?

2. avoir
my little brother is five mon petit frère a cinq ans

I'm hungry j'ai faim

are you cold? avez-vous froid ?

* *This tower is twenty metres (Am: meters) high!* Cette tour a vingt mètres de haut ! *

...be

This tower is twenty metres high!

II. *v aux*
1. *Note : pour former le présent continu et le passé continu*
what are you doing? que faites-vous ?

I was talking to Professor Calculus je parlais avec le professeur Tournesol

2. être
Note : pour former le passif

has the Captain been injured? le capitaine a-t-il été blessé ?

beach

beach
[bi:tʃ] *n*
plage *f*

* *They're landing on the beach.* Ils débarquent sur la plage. *

...beach

They're landing on the beach.

bean

bean
[bi:n] *n*
haricot *m*

bear

bear
[beəʳ] *n*
ours *m*

a polar bear un ours polaire

bear

bear
[beəʳ] *v t*
bore [bɔ:ʳ], borne [bɔ:n]
supporter

stop that noise! I can't bear it! arrêtez ce bruit ! je ne le supporte pas !

beard

beard
[bɪəd] *n*
barbe *f*

beat

beat
[bi:t]
beat, beaten
['bi:t(ə)n]
I. *v t*
1. battre

* *He beat Snowy with a stick!* Il a battu Milou avec un bâton ! *

2. battre
our team was beaten by two goals to one notre équipe a été battue par deux buts contre un

!
He beat Snowy with a stick!

II. *v i*
battre

my heart was beating faster and faster mon cœur battait de plus en plus vite

beautiful

beautiful
['bju:tifʊl] *adj*
beau *m*, belle *f*

...beautiful

what a beautiful day! quelle belle journée !

because

because
[bɪ'kɒz] *conj*
parce que

we stayed in because it was raining nous sommes restés à la maison parce qu'il pleuvait

...because

▶ **because of**
prep
à cause de

we stayed in because of the rain nous sommes restés à la maison à cause de la pluie

become

become
[bɪ'kʌm] *vi*
became [bɪ'keɪm], become [bɪ'kʌm]

...become

The sea's becoming very rough! I don't know whether our boat will hold out...

devenir

* *The sea's becoming very rough! I don't know whether our boat will hold out...* La mer devient très mauvaise ! Je ne sais pas si notre barque résistera... *

she wants to become a doctor elle veut devenir médecin

bed

bed
[bed] *n*
lit *m*

come on, it's time to go to bed! allez, il est l'heure d'aller au lit !

* *You should go to bed...* Vous devriez vous mettre au lit... *

▶ **bedroom**
['bedru:m] *n*
chambre *f* (à coucher)

...bed

!
You should go to bed...

beef

beef
[bi:f] *n*
bœuf *m*

we had roast beef for lunch nous avons mangé du rôti de bœuf au déjeuner

beer

beer
[bɪəʳ] *n*
bière *f*

before

before
[bɪ'fɔ:ʳ]
I. *prep*
avant

he'll get there before us il arrivera avant nous

II. *adv*
1. avant, déjà, devant

* *I've been here before...* Je suis déjà venu ici...
Thundering typhoons! Tonnerre de Brest ! *

...before

I've been here before...
Thundering typhoons!

2. Idiom
the day before la veille

III. *conj*
avant que, avant de

as I was saying before you interrupted me comme je disais avant que vous ne m'interrompiez

switch the lights out before you leave éteignez les lumières avant de partir

beg

beg
[beg]
begged, begged
I. *vi*
mendier

they were begging in the streets ils mendiaient dans les rues

II. *vt*
1. prier

we begged him to stay nous l'avons prié de rester

2. Idiom

I beg your pardon je vous demande pardon

begin

begin
[bɪ'gɪn]
I. *vi*
began [bɪ'gæn], begun [bɪ'gʌn]
commencer

I'm beginning to understand je commence à comprendre

...begin

II. *vt*
we can begin the lesson nous pouvons commencer la leçon

► **beginner**
[bɪˈgɪnəʳ] *n*
débutant *m*, débutante *f*

► **beginning**
[bɪˈgɪnɪŋ] *n*
début *m*, commencement *m*

behind

behind
[bɪˈhaɪnd]
I. *prep*
derrière

* ***Stay here... I'll go and see what's behind that door...*** Reste ici... Je vais voir ce qu'il y a derrière cette porte... ***OK.*** D'accord. *

II. *adv*
en arrière, derrière

you go on, I'll stay behind continuez, moi je resterai en arrière

Stay here... I'll go and see what's behind that door...
OK.

Belgium

Belgium
[ˈbeldʒɪəm] *n*
Belgique *f*

► **Belgian**
[ˈbeldʒɪən]
I. *n*
Belge *m f*

II. *adj*
belge

believe

believe
[bɪˈliːv]
I. *vt*
croire

it's not true! I don't believe you! ce n'est pas vrai ! je ne vous crois pas !

II. *vi*
I don't believe in ghosts! moi, je ne crois pas aux fantômes !

bell

bell
[bel] *n*
1. cloche *f*

the church bells are ringing les cloches de l'église sonnent

2. sonnette *f*

belong

belong
[bɪˈlɒŋ] *vi*
1. appartenir

...belong

who does this hat belong to? à qui appartient ce chapeau ?

* ***That scarf belongs to Chang!*** Cette écharpe appartient à Tchang ! *

2. être membre de
he belongs to several clubs il est membre de plusieurs clubs

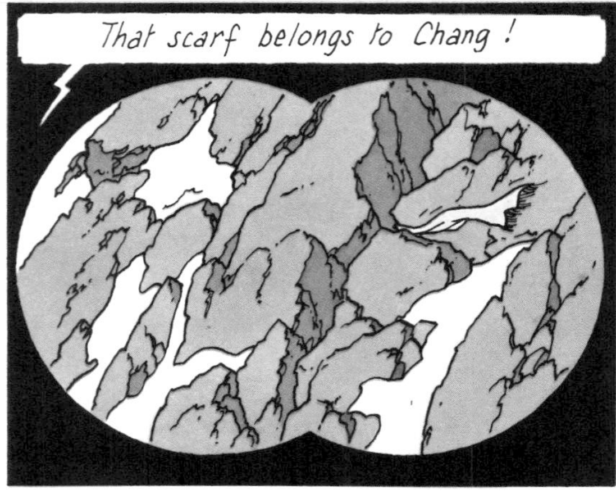

That scarf belongs to Chang!

below

below
[bɪˈləʊ]
I. *prep*
au-dessous de

all this land is below sea level toutes ces terres sont au-dessous du niveau de la mer

II. *adv*
au-dessous

they are in the valley below ils sont dans la vallée au-dessous

belt

belt
[belt] *n*
ceinture *f*

fasten your safety belts attachez vos ceintures de sécurité

bend

bend
[bend]
I. *n*
virage *m*

...bend

There are a lot of bends in this road!

* ***There are a lot of bends in this road!*** Il y a beaucoup de virages sur cette route ! *

II. *vt*
bent, bent [bent]
plier

I'll try to bend the bars in the window je vais essayer de plier les barreaux de la fenêtre

III. *vi*
1. se pencher

he bent (down) to pick up the coin il s'est penché pour ramasser la pièce

2. tourner
the road bends to the left la route tourne à gauche

beside

beside
[bɪˈsaɪd] *prep*
à côté de

come and sit beside me venez vous asseoir à côté de moi

► **besides**
[bɪˈsaɪdz]
I. *prep*
à part, en dehors de

nobody knows besides Tintin and the Captain personne n'est

...beside

Come on, get up, Captain! We're off!...
It's too far... besides, I'm tired... ZZZ...ZZZ..

au courant à part Tintin et le capitaine

II. *adv*
1. en outre, en plus

they've got three cars, and a motorcycle besides ils ont trois voitures, et une moto en plus

2. du reste, d'ailleurs
* *Come on, get up, Captain! We're off!...* Allons debout, capitaine ! Nous partons !...
It's too far... besides, I'm tired... ZZZ... ZZZ... C'est trop loin... du reste, je suis fatigué... RRR... RRR... *

best

best
[best]
I. *adj*
(le) meilleur, (la) meilleure

...best

it's the best film I've ever seen c'est le meilleur film que j'aie jamais vu

II. *n*
1. meilleur *m*, meilleure *f*

well done, Tintin, you're the best! bravo, Tintin, vous êtes le meilleur !

2. mieux *m*
do your best faites de votre mieux

III. *adv*
le mieux, la mieux

she's the best dressed woman I know c'est la femme la mieux habillée que je connaisse

bet

bet
[bet] *v t*
bet, bet [bet]
parier

...bet

I bet Rastapopoulos is behind this! je parie que Rastapopoulos est derrière cela !

better

better
['betəʳ]
I. *adj*
1. meilleur

she's better at English than at geography elle est meilleure en anglais qu'en géographie

...better

2. mieux
are you feeling better today? vous sentez-vous mieux aujourd'hui ?

yes, thank you, I'm a lot better oui, merci, je vais beaucoup mieux

3. Idiom
I hope you get better soon j'espère que vous serez bientôt remis

* *Take this medicine,*

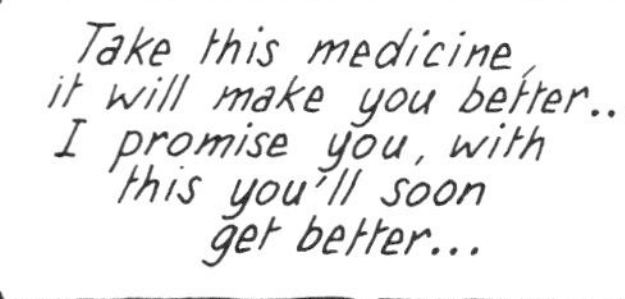

Take this medicine, it will make you better... I promise you, with this you'll soon get better...

it will make you better... I promise you, with this you'll soon get better... Prends ce médicament, il va te guérir... Je t'assure, avec ça, tu vas vite guérir... *

the weather should get better le temps devrait s'améliorer

II. *adv*
mieux

she sings a lot better than you elle chante beaucoup mieux que vous

it's late, we'd better go il est tard, il vaudrait mieux que nous partions

between

between
[bɪ'twi:n] *prep*
1. entre

what were you doing between five o'clock and seven thirty?

...between

que faisiez-vous entre cinq heures et sept heures et demie ?

2. Idiom
between now and next week d'ici à la semaine prochaine

beyond

beyond
[bɪ'jɒnd] *prep*
au-delà de

...beyond

there is a village beyond this mountain il y a un village au-delà de cette montagne

bicycle

bicycle
['baɪsɪk(ə)l] *n*
bicyclette *f*

she goes to school by bicycle elle va à l'école à bicyclette

big

big
[bɪg] *adj*
bigger, biggest
grand, gros

* *Oh! What a big elephant!* Oh ! Quel gros éléphant ! *

bike

bike
[baɪk] *n*
vélo *m*

Oh! What a big elephant!

bill

bill
[bɪl] *n*
1. facture *f*

have you paid the electricity bill? avez-vous payé la facture d'électricité ?

2. addition *f*
waiter, the bill (Am: check), please! garçon, l'addition s'il vous plaît !

3. *Am:* billet *m*
a ten-dollar bill un billet de dix dollars

bird

bird
[bɜ:d] *n*
oiseau *m*

* *Wooaaah!* Wouaaah ! *The bird's carrying Snowy away.* L'oiseau emporte Milou. *

The bird's carrying Snowy away.

birth

birth
[bɜ:θ] *n*
naissance *f*

what is your date of birth? quelle est votre date de naissance ?

▶ **birthday**
['bɜ:θdeɪ] *n*
anniversaire *m*

happy birthday! joyeux anniversaire !

bit

bit
[bɪt] *n*
1. morceau *m*

do you want a bit of cake? voulez-vous un morceau de gâteau ?

2. peu *m*
* *I feel a bit better today!* Je me sens un peu mieux aujourd'hui ! *

bit by bit peu à peu

bite

bite
[baɪt] *vt*
bit [bɪt], bitten ['bɪtn]
mordre

* *Ouch!* Aïe ! *Snowy got angry and bit him!* Milou s'est fâché et il l'a mordu ! *

bitter

bitter
['bɪtəʳ] *adj*
amer

Snowy got angry and bit him!

it tastes very bitter cela a un goût très amer

black

black
[blæk]
I. *adj*
noir

Haddock is dressed in black.

follow that black car! suivez cette voiture noire !

II. *n*
noir *m*

* *Haddock is dressed in black.* Haddock est habillé en noir. *

▶ **blackboard**
['blækbɔ:d] *n*
tableau *m* (noir)

blame

blame
[bleɪm]
I. *n*
responsabilité *f*, faute *f*
they're trying to put the blame on me ils essaient d'en rejeter la responsabilité sur moi

II. *vt*
1. accuser
he blamed me for breaking his toy il m'a accusé d'avoir cassé son jouet

2. Idiom
I don't blame you for running away je crois que vous avez bien fait de vous enfuir

blanket

blanket
['blæŋkɪt] *n*
couverture *f*

blazer

blazer
['bleɪzəʳ] *n*
blazer *m*

bleed

bleed
[bli:d] *vi*
bled, bled [bled]
saigner
Tintin, you're bleeding, are you hurt? Tintin, vous saignez, est-ce que vous êtes blessé ?

blind

blind
[blaɪnd] *adj*
aveugle

a blind man un aveugle

blood

blood
[blʌd] *n*
sang *m*

blow

blow
[bləʊ]
I. *n*
coup *m*

where am I? I must have had a blow on the head où suis-je ? j'ai dû recevoir un coup sur la tête

II. *vi*
blew [blu:], blown [bləʊn]
souffler

the wind is blowing very hard le vent souffle très fort

► **blow out**
souffler

* *Ah!... At last!...* Ah !... Enfin !...
We can't see anything, the wind has blown out the candle!... On ne voit rien, le vent a soufflé la bougie... *

...blow

► **blow up**
1. gonfler

they are blowing up balloons ils gonflent des ballons

2. faire sauter
they've blown up the bridge! ils ont fait sauter le pont !

blue

blue
[blu:]
I. *adj*
bleu

the sky is blue le ciel est bleu

II. *n*
bleu *m*

he's dressed in blue il est habillé en bleu

board

board
[bɔ:d] *n*
1. planche *f*

ironing board planche à repasser

2. tableau *m*
come and write the answer on the board venez écrire la réponse au tableau

► **notice** (*Am:* **bulletin) board** tableau d'affichage

3. bord *m*
all the passengers are on board tous les passagers sont à bord

* *Come on, Captain, you must come on board.* Allez, capitaine, il faut monter à bord.
I'm coming, I'm coming... J'arrive, j'arrive... *

4. pension *f*
a room with full board une chambre en pension complète

...board

► **boarding school** *n*
pension *f*

* *Stop it or I'll tell your father to send you to boarding school!...* Arrête ou je dis à ton père de te mettre en pension !...
No!... Non !... *

boat

boat
[bəʊt] *n*
bateau *m*

* *Good grief! A boat is chasing me!* Tonnerre ! Un bateau me poursuit ! *

body

body
['bɒdɪ] *n*
pl bodies ['bɒdɪz]
1. corps *m*

he has a body like an athlete il a un corps d'athlète

2. cadavre *m*
where did the murderer bury the body? où le meurtrier a-t-il enterré le cadavre ?

boil

boil
[bɔɪl]
I. *vi*
bouillir

the water's boiling l'eau bout

II. *vt*
1. faire bouillir

I'll boil some water to make tea je vais faire bouillir de l'eau pour le thé

2. Idiom
a boiled egg un œuf à la coque

boiled potatoes pommes de terre à l'eau

bone

bone
[bəʊn] *n*
1. os *m*

* *Where did you find that bone?* Où as-tu trouvé cet os ? *

2. arête *f*

...bone

I've swallowed a fish bone j'ai avalé une arête de poisson

book

book
[bʊk]
I. *n*
1. livre *m*

be quiet, I'm trying to read my book! taisez-vous, j'essaie de lire mon livre !

...book

2. cahier *m*
write this in your (exercise) books (Am: notebooks) écrivez ceci dans vos cahiers

3. carnet *m*
a book of stamps un carnet de timbres

II. *vt*
réserver, retenir

I've booked two seats for Signora Castafiore's concert j'ai réservé deux places

...book

pour le concert de la Castafiore

► **bookcase**
['bʊkkeɪs] *n*
bibliothèque *f*

* *Oh! They have completely emptied my bookcase!...* Oh ! Ils ont entièrement vidé ma bibliothèque !... *

boot

boot
[bu:t] *n*
botte *f*

* *Let me put my boots on and I'll come!* Laissez-moi mettre mes bottes et j'arrive !
OK! D'accord !
Quick... Hurry up, Tintin! Vite... Dépêche-toi, Tintin ! *

rubber boots bottes en caoutchouc

border

border
['bɔ:dər] *n*
frontière *f*

* *Tintin is going to cross the border.* Tintin va passer la frontière. *

bored

bored
[bɔ:d] *adj*
Idiom
to be bored s'ennuyer

Tintin is going to cross the border.

...bored

I'm bored, what shall we do? je m'ennuie, qu'est-ce qu'on peut faire ?

► **boring**
['bɔ:rɪŋ] *adj*
ennuyeux

what a boring story! quelle histoire ennuyeuse !

born

born
[bɔ:n] *adj*
1. né

she was born in 1977 elle est née en 1977

2. Idiom
to be born naître

borrow

borrow
['bɒrəʊ] *vt*
emprunter

...borrow

can I borrow your pen? puis-je emprunter votre stylo ?

I borrowed some money from a friend j'ai emprunté de l'argent à un ami

both

both
[bəʊθ]
I. *adj & pron*
(les) deux, tous (les) deux

...both

* *The Thompsons are both sick.* Les Dupondt sont tous les deux malades. *

milk or sugar? – both, please du lait ou du sucre ? – les deux, s'il vous plaît

he took both his shoes off il a enlevé ses deux chaussures

II. *adv*
et, à la fois

???
???

The Thompsons are both sick.

both you and I vous et moi

she is both intelligent and beautiful elle est à la fois intelligente et belle

bother

bother
['bɒðəʳ]
I. *n*
ennuis *m pl*

...bother

I hope I've not caused you too much bother j'espère que je ne vous ai pas créé trop d'ennuis

II. *v t*
déranger, embêter

don't bother her, she's busy ne la dérangez pas, elle est occupée

III. *v i*
Idiom
don't bother to lock the door ce n'est pas la peine de fermer la porte à clé

IV. *interj*
zut, flûte

bottle

bottle
['bɒt(ə)l] *n*
bouteille *f*

a bottle of milk une bouteille de lait

bottom

bottom
['bɒtəm] *n*
1. fond *m*

* *The wreck was at the bottom of the sea.* L'épave était au fond de la mer. *

2. derrière *m*
Snowy bit his bottom Milou lui a mordu le derrière

The wreck was at the bottom of the sea.

bound

bound
[baʊnd] *adj*
1. sûr, certain

he was bound to come c'était sûr qu'il viendrait

2. Idiom
it was bound to happen cela devait arriver

box

box
[bɒks] *n*
boîte *f*

boy

boy
[bɔɪ] *n*
garçon *m*

brain

brain
[breɪn] *n*
cerveau *m*

branch

branch
[brɑ:ntʃ] *n*
1. branche *f*

* *Tintin's hanging from a branch.* Tintin est suspendu à une branche. *

2. succursale *f*
the firm has several branches l'entreprise a plusieurs succursales

Tintin's hanging from a branch.

brave

brave
[breɪv] *adj*
courageux, brave

* *I was sure I'd find you in the end, Chang!...* J'étais sûr que je finirais par te retrouver, Tchang !...
You've saved my life! You are very brave! Tu m'as sauvé la vie ! Tu es très courageux ! *

I was sure I'd find you in the end, Chang!...
You've saved my life! You are very brave!

bread

bread
[bred] *n*
pain *m*

a loaf of bread un pain

break

break
[breɪk]
I. *n*
1. pause *f*

we take a coffee break at 11 o'clock nous faisons une pause-café à 11 heures

2. récréation *f*
the boys play football during break (Am: recess) les garçons jouent au football pendant la récréation

II. *v t*
broke [brəʊk], broken ['brəʊk(ə)n]
casser

to break one's arm/leg se casser le bras/la jambe

III. *v i*
casser, se casser

the bottle fell off the table and broke la bouteille est tombée de la table et s'est cassée

► **break down**
tomber en panne

* *The car's broken down. Let's get closer, without making any noise!* La voiture est tombée en panne... Approchons-nous sans faire de bruit. *

The car's broken down. Let's get closer, without making any noise!

► **break out**
1. éclater

a fire broke out in the warehouse un incendie a éclaté dans l'entrepôt

2. s'évader
two men have broken out of prison deux hommes se sont évadés de prison

► **break up**
Idiom
school breaks up (Am: lets out) tomorrow les vacances scolaires commencent demain

► **breakdown**
['breɪkdaʊn] *n*
panne *f*

breakfast

breakfast
['brekfəst] *n*
petit déjeuner *m*

what did you have for breakfast? qu'est-ce que tu as mangé au petit déjeuner ?

bridge

bridge
[brɪdʒ] *n*
pont *m*

Quick, let's dive off the bridge!...

* *Quick, let's dive off the bridge!...* Vite, plongeons du haut du pont !... *

briefcase

briefcase
['bri:fkeɪs] *n*
serviette *f*

I have your passport in my briefcase j'ai votre passeport dans ma serviette

bright

bright
[braɪt] *adj*
1. brillant, vif

bright red rouge vif

2. intelligent
she's a very bright girl c'est une fille très intelligente

bring

bring
[brɪŋ] *v t*
brought, brought
[brɔ:t]
1. apporter

* *It's a good thing I remembered to bring a picnic!* Heureusement que j'ai pensé à apporter un pique-nique !
Oh yes! Oh oui ! *

2. amener
can I bring a friend with me? puis-je amener un ami avec moi ?

It's a good thing I remembered to bring a picnic!
Oh yes!

► **bring up**
élever

she was brought up by her grandparents elle a été élevée par ses grands-parents

Britain

Britain
['brɪt(ə)n] *n*
Grande-Bretagne *f*

Scotland is in (Great)

...Britain

Britain l'Ecosse est en Grande-Bretagne

► **British**
['brɪtɪʃ]
I. *n*
Britanniques

II. *adj*
britannique

brother

brother
['brʌðəʳ] *n*
frère *m*

she has two brothers and two sisters elle a deux frères et deux sœurs

brown

brown
[braʊn]
I. *adj*
1. brun, marron

who is that man with brown hair? qui est cet homme aux cheveux bruns ?

2. bronzé
you're very brown, have you been in the sun? vous êtes très bronzé, êtes-vous allé au soleil ?

II. *n*
marron *m*, brun *m*

dressed in brown habillé en marron

brush

brush
[brʌʃ]
I. *n*
1. brosse *f*

use this brush to clean the carpet utilisez cette brosse pour nettoyer la moquette

2. pinceau *m*
she was painting with a very fine brush elle peignait avec un pinceau très fin

II. *vt*
1. brosser

to brush one's teeth se brosser les dents

2. balayer
he is brushing the floor il balaie le parquet

build

build
[bɪld] *vt*
built, built [bɪlt]
construire

bullet

bullet
['bʊlɪt]
balle *f*

* *He's been hit in the shoulder by a bullet...* Il a reçu une balle dans l'épaule... *

bulletin

bulletin (*Am*)
→ BOARD

He's been hit in the shoulder by a bullet...

bump

bump
[bʌmp]
I. *n*
1. coup *m*, choc *m*

I got a bump on the elbow j'ai reçu un coup au coude

2. bosse *f*
there are a lot of bumps in the road il y a beaucoup de bosses sur la route

II. *vt*
cogner

be careful not to bump your head on the ceiling faites attention de ne pas vous cogner la tête contre le plafond

► **bump into**
1. heurter, rentrer dans

we bumped into another car nous sommes rentrés dans une autre voiture

...bump

2. rencontrer par hasard
I bumped into an old friend j'ai rencontré un vieil ami par hasard

burgle

burgle
['bɜːg(ə)l] *vt*
cambrioler

* *Good grief!... I've been burgled!...* Ma

Good grief!... I've been burgled!...

...burgle

parole !... On m'a cambriolé !... *

► **burglar**
['bɜːgləʳ] *n*
cambrioleur *m*

► **burglary**
['bɜːglərɪ] *n*
pl burglaries
['bɜːglərɪz]
cambriolage *m*

burn

burn
[bɜːn] *vi & t*
burned, burned ou burnt, burnt [bɜːnt]
brûler

Snowy, come here, you'll burn yourself Milou, viens ici, tu vas te brûler !

* *The prairie is burning!* La prairie est en train de brûler ! *

The prairie is burning!

burst

burst
[bɜːst] *v i*
burst, burst [bɜːst]
éclater

the bubble burst la bulle a éclaté

he burst out laughing il a éclaté de rire

the child burst into tears l'enfant a éclaté en sanglots

bus

bus
[bʌs] *n*
1. bus *m*, autobus *m*

I'm waiting for the bus j'attends le bus

2. *Am:*
→ COACH

▸ **busstop** *n*
arrêt *m* de bus

bush

bush
[bʊʃ] *n*
buisson *m*

quick, let's hide behind that bush! vite, cachons-nous derrière ce buisson !

business

business
[ˈbɪznɪs] *n*
1. affaires *f pl*

...business

are you here on business? êtes-vous ici pour affaires ?

2. commerce *m*
he runs a small business il a un petit commerce

busy

busy
[ˈbɪzɪ] *adj*
busier, busiest
occupé

...busy

12
SATURDAY

He's very busy.

...busy

* *Saturday* Samedi
He's very busy. Il est très occupé. *

▸ **busy** (*Am*)
→ ENGAGED

but

but
[bʌt]
I. *conj*
mais

I don't know what they're doing, but I don't like it! je ne sais pas ce qu'ils font, mais ça ne me plaît pas !

II. *prep*
sauf

* *Everybody's here but Snowy.* Tout le monde est là sauf Milou. *

Everybody's here but Snowy.

butcher

butcher
[ˈbʊtʃəʳ] *n*
boucher *m*, bouchère *f*

at the butcher's à la boucherie

butter

butter
[ˈbʌtəʳ] *n*
beurre *m*

button

button
[ˈbʌt(ə)n] *n*
bouton *m*

what happens if you press this button? qu'est-ce qui se passe si on appuie sur ce bouton ?

buy

buy
[baɪ] *v t*
bought, bought [bɔːt]
acheter

...buy

I've bought you a present je t'ai acheté un cadeau

by

by
[baɪ]
I. *prep*
1. par

she has been kidnapped by the rebels

...by

elle a été kidnappée par les rebelles

2. en, par
* *Tintin came by train.* Tintin est venu en train.
Way out Sortie *

3. près de
come and sit by me venez vous asseoir près de moi

4. de
prices have increased by 20% les prix ont augmenté de 20 %

5. avant
if I'm not back by 6 o'clock, call the police si je ne suis pas de retour avant 6 heures, appelez la police

II. *adv*
Idiom
time goes by le temps passe

by and large de façon générale, en gros

Tintin came by train.

cabbage ...cabin

cabbage
['kæbɪdʒ] *n*
chou *m*

cabin

cabin
['kæbɪn] *n*
1. cabine *f*

* *Police: we must search your cabin.* Police : nous devons fouiller votre cabine. *

Police : we must search your cabin.

2. cabane *f*
they built a log cabin ils ont construit une cabane en rondins

café

café
['kæfeɪ] *n*
café *m*

we met in a café nous nous sommes rencontrés dans un café

cage ...cake

cage
[keɪdʒ] *n*
cage *f*

the lion has escaped from its cage le lion s'est échappé de sa cage

cake

cake
[keɪk] *n*
gâteau *m*

another piece of cake, Captain? encore un morceau de gâteau, capitaine ?

call

call
[kɔ:l]
I. *n*
1. appel *m* (téléphonique)

have there been any calls for me? y a-t-il eu des appels pour moi ?

2. visite *f*
to pay a call on somebody rendre visite à quelqu'un

II. *vt*
1. appeler

* *Quick, call a doctor! I'm in pain!* Vite, appelez un médecin ! Je souffre ! *

Quick, call a doctor! I'm in pain!

2. appeler, nommer
to be called s'appeler

what is your dog called? comment s'appelle votre chien ?

3. téléphoner à, appeler
I tried to call you but you weren't in j'ai essayé de te téléphoner, mais tu n'étais pas là

4. traiter de
he called me a fool il m'a traité d'imbécile

III. *vi*
1. appeler, crier

I can hear somebody calling for help j'entends quelqu'un qui appelle au secours

2. appeler, téléphoner

I'm calling from the station j'appelle de la gare

3. passer
I called at your house, but you weren't in je suis passé chez toi, mais tu n'étais pas là

► **call off**
annuler

the match has been called off le match a été annulé

...call

► **call for**
passer prendre

I'll call for you at 5 o'clock je passerai vous prendre à 5 heures

► **call up**
téléphoner à, appeler

call me up when you arrive téléphonez-moi quand vous arriverez

calm

calm
[kɑːm] *adj*
calme

the sea is calm la mer est calme

keep calm, Captain! restez calme, capitaine !

► **calm down**
se calmer

* *So! I play the fool!...* Aaah ! je fais le zouave !... *Now, now, calm down...* Allons, calmez-vous... *

camera

camera
['kæmrə] *n*
appareil *m* photo

he took a picture of me with his new camera il m'a pris en photo avec son nouvel appareil

► **(movie) camera**
caméra *f*

television camera caméra de télévision

camp

camp
[kæmp]
I. *n*
camp *m*, campement *m*

II. *vi*
camper

* *The next evening...* Le lendemain soir... *We'll camp here.* Nous camperons ici. *There is where the snow starts.* Voilà les premières neiges. *

► **camping**
['kæmpɪŋ] *n*
camping *m*

camping is forbidden here le camping est interdit ici

to go camping faire du camping

► **campsite**
['kæmpsaɪt] *n*
(terrain *m* de) camping *m*

there's a campsite near the river il y a un camping près de la rivière

can

can
[kæn] *v aux*
Note : forme négative **cannot** ; *forme négative abrégée* **can't**
1. pouvoir

* *I'm too tired, Snowy. I can't go any further!* Je suis trop fatigué, Milou. Je ne peux pas aller plus loin ! *

...can

can you hear me? m'entendez-vous ?

can I come with you? est-ce que je peux venir avec vous ?

2. savoir
help! I can't swim! au secours ! je ne sais pas nager !

3. Idiom
I can't see anything! je ne vois rien !

can

can
[kæn] *n*
1. bidon *m*

* *A can of petrol (Am: gas)!...* Un bidon d'essence !... *

2. boîte *f*
a can of peas une boîte de petits pois

Canada

Canada
['kænədə] *n*
Canada *m*

▶ **Canadian**
[kə'neɪdɪən]
I. *n*
Canadien *m*, Canadienne *f*

II. *adj*
canadien

candle

candle
['kænd(ə)l] *n*
bougie *f*

a birthday cake with 13 candles un gâteau d'anniversaire avec 13 bougies

candy

candy (*Am*)
→ SWEET

cap

cap
[kæp] *n*
1. casquette *f*

take your cap off enlève ta casquette

2. capuchon *m*
put the cap back on the pen remettez le capuchon sur le stylo

3. amorce *f*
a cap gun un pistolet à amorce

capital

Here we are in Sanaa, the capital of North Yemen!

...capital

capital
['kæpɪt(ə)l] *n*
1. capitale *f*

* ***Here we are, in Sanaa, the capital of North Yemen!*** Nous voilà à Sanaa, capitale du Yémen du Nord !... *

2. majuscule *f*
write your name in capitals écrivez votre nom en majuscules

captain

captain
['kæptɪn] *n*
capitaine *m*

I'm the captain of this ship! c'est moi le capitaine de ce navire !

he's the captain of our football team c'est le capitaine de notre équipe de football

car

Another car has caught fire!
841201

car
[kɑːʳ] *n*
1. voiture *f*

* ***Another car has caught fire!*** Encore une voiture qui a pris feu ! *

2. *Am:*→ CARRIAGE

caravan

caravan
['kærəvæn] *n*
caravane *f*

...caravan

In the desert...
The caravan of camels is leaving the fort...

* ***In the desert...*** Dans le désert...
The caravan of camels is leaving the fort... La caravane de chameaux quitte le fort... *

card

card
[kɑːd] *n*
carte *f*

...card

what about a game of cards? si on faisait une partie de cartes ?

she got a lot of birthday cards elle a reçu beaucoup de cartes d'anniversaire

cardigan

cardigan
['kɑːdɪgən] *n*
gilet *m* de laine

care

care
[keəʳ]
I. *n*
1. attention *f*, soin *m*

take care not to break it faites attention de ne pas le casser

...care

* *Goodbye, Tintin, and take care of yourself! If there's the slightest problem, just use your radio...* Au revoir, Tintin, et faites attention à vous ! S'il y a le moindre problème, utilisez votre radio... *

2. souci *m*
he hasn't a care in the world il n'a pas le moindre souci

II. *vi*

1. se soucier

she doesn't care about what people say elle ne se soucie pas de ce que disent les gens

2. Idiom
I don't care! ça m'est égal !

I couldn't care less! je m'en fiche !

► **care for**
1. soigner

they care for the sick ils soignent les malades

2. aimer
* *Would you care for a cup of tea, Tintin?* Aimeriez-vous une tasse de thé, Tintin ?
Certainly. Oui, volontiers. *

► **careful**
['keəf(ə)l] *adj*
1. prudent

he's a very careful driver c'est un conducteur très prudent

2. Idiom
to be careful faire attention

be careful, that vase is worth a fortune! faites attention, ce vase vaut une fortune !

► **careless**
['keəlɪs] *adj*
négligent

Freddy is rather careless in his work Freddy

...care

est un peu négligent dans son travail

► **caretaker**
['keəteɪkəʳ] *n*
1. concierge *m f*

2. gardien *m*, gardienne *f*
he's the new caretaker at the castle c'est le nouveau gardien du château

carpet

carpet
['kɑ:pɪt] *n*
tapis *m*,
moquette *f*

I'll vacuum the carpet je vais passer l'aspirateur sur la moquette

* *Ah, bliss! I'll be able to sleep comfortably on this carpet!* Ah, quel bonheur ! je vais pouvoir dormir confortablement sur ce tapis ! *

carriage

carriage
['kærɪdʒ] *n*
(*Am:* **car**)
wagon *m*, voiture *f*

* *Crash crack* Boum crac
Over there, the carriage is falling... We jumped just in time Oh ! là-bas, le wagon dégringole... Il était temps que nous sautions... *

* *It's funny... All the compartments in this carriage are empty...* C'est curieux... Tous les compartiments de cette voiture sont vides... *

carrot

carrot
['kærət] *n*
carotte *f*

carry
['kærɪ] *v t*
(carried, carried)
1. porter

* *Would you like some help?* Voulez-vous de l'aide ?
Certainly not. This crate is heavy but we can carry it ourselves!... Sûrement pas ! Cette caisse est lourde, mais nous pouvons la porter nous-mêmes !... *

2. transporter
the lorry (Am: truck) is carrying sand le camion transporte du sable

▶ **carry (*Am:* go) on** continuer

carry on reading continuez à lire

▶ **carry out** exécuter

I have carried out your orders, Captain j'ai exécuté vos ordres, capitaine

cartoon

cartoon
[kɑ:'tu:n] *n*
1. dessin *m* animé

there is a cartoon on television il y a un dessin animé à la télévision

2. dessin *m* humoristique, caricature *f*
* *It's a cartoon of General Alcazar...* C'est une caricature du général Alcazar... *

...cartoon

case

case
[keɪs] *n*
1. valise *f*

pack your cases (Am: bags), we're leaving immediately faites vos valises, nous partons tout de suite

2. étui *m*
a violin case un étui à violon

case

case
[keɪs] *n*
cas *m*

in that case, we'll have to take a taxi dans ce cas, il faudra que nous prenions un taxi

take an umbrella in case it rains prenez un parapluie, au cas où il pleuvrait

in any case en tout cas

castle

castle
['kɑ:s(ə)l] *n*
château *m*

who lives in that castle? qui habite ce château ?

cat

cat
[kæt] *n*
chat *m*

catch

catch
[kætʃ] *v t*
caught [kɔ:t]
caught,
1. attraper

he caught the ball il a attrapé la balle

look out, I'll throw the rope, try and catch it! attention, je lance la corde, essayez de l'attraper !

to catch a fish pêcher un poisson

...catch

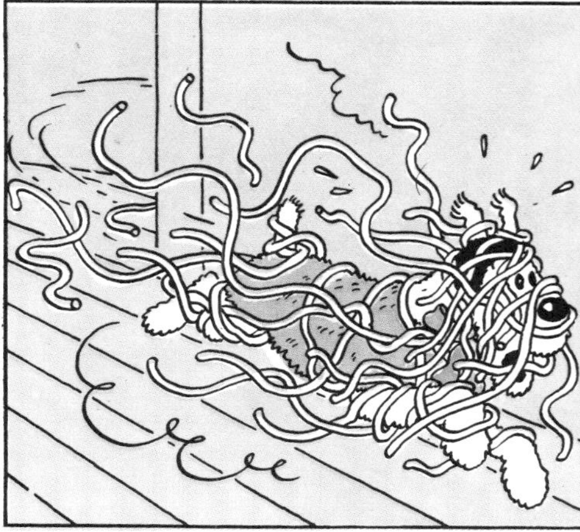

2. surprendre, attraper
* *If I catch that dog stealing food again!...* Si je surprends ce chien en train de voler encore de la nourriture !...
That's what happens when you leave doors open! Voilà ce qui arrive quand on laisse les portes ouvertes ! *

3. prendre, arriver à l'heure pour
do you think we'll catch the train? pensez-vous que nous arriverons à l'heure pour le train ?

4. attraper
* *I can't stop sneezing, I've caught a cold!* Je n'arrête pas d'éternuer, j'ai attrapé un rhume ! *

5. comprendre, saisir
I'm sorry, I didn't catch what you said

...catch

excusez-moi, je n'ai pas compris ce que vous avez dit

► **catch up**
rattraper

they're catching up with us/they're catching us up ils nous rattrapent

cause

cause
[kɔ:z]

...cause

Don't drive so fast, you might cause an accident!
MI-2051

I. *n*
cause *f*

II. *v t*
causer, provoquer

* *Don't drive so fast, you might cause an accident!* Ne conduisez pas si vite, vous pourriez provoquer un accident ! *

ceiling

ceiling
['si:lɪŋ] *n*

...ceiling

plafond *m*

the ceiling is painted white le plafond est peint en blanc

cellar

cellar
['sɛləʳ] *n*
cave *f*

* *Professor Topolino has been locked in the cellar...* Le profes-

...cellar

?
CLANG CLANG
Professor Topolino has been locked in the cellar...

seur Topolino a été enfermé dans la cave... *

cent

cent
[sent] *n*
cent *m*

it costs two dollars and fifty cents ça coûte deux dollars et cinquante cents

centimetre

centimetre
['sentɪmi:təʳ]) *n*
(*Am:* **centimeter**)
centimètre *m*

centre

centre
['sentəʳ] *n*
(*Am:* **center**)
centre *m*

* *Could you tell me how to get to the town centre (Am: cen-*

...centre

Could you tell me how to get to the town centre?
I certainly could, Sir.

...centre

ter of town)? Pourriez-vous me dire comment faire pour aller dans le centre de la ville ?
I certainly could, Sir. Volontiers, monsieur. *

cereal

cereal
['sɪərɪəl] *n*
céréale *f*

we always have cereal for breakfast

...cereal

nous mangeons toujours des céréales au petit déjeuner

certain

certain
['sɜ:tn] *adj*
1. sûr, certain

* *It's Sakharine who did it! I'm absolutely certain!* C'est Sakharine qui a fait le coup ! J'en suis absolument sûr !...

...certain

It's Sakharine who did it! I'm absolutely certain!
It's very likely!...

It's very likely!... Il y a de grandes chances !... *

2. certain
it takes a certain courage to do that il faut un certain courage pour faire ça

► **certainly**
['sɜ:tənlɪ] *adv*
1. certainement, assurément

our team is certainly going to win notre équipe va certainement gagner

2. bien sûr
could you give me a hand? – certainly pourriez-vous me donner un coup de main ? – bien sûr

chair

chair
[tʃeəʳ] *n*
chaise *f*

* *I'm sorry, Mr Baxter... That chair wasn't very strong... I'll give you another one...* Excusez-moi, M. Baxter... Cette chaise n'était pas très solide... Je vais vous en donner une autre... *

chalk

chalk
[tʃɔːk] *n*
craie *f*

champion

champion
['tʃæmpɪən] *n*
champion *m*, championne *f*

chance

chance
[tʃɑːns] *n*
1. hasard *m*

I met him by chance this morning je l'ai rencontré par hasard ce matin

2. chance *f*, possibilité *f*
we've got no chance of arriving before them! nous n'avons aucune chance d'arriver avant eux !

3. occasion *f*
if ever you have the chance to see him... si jamais vous avez l'occasion de le voir...

change

change
[tʃeɪndʒ]
I. *n*
1. changement *m*

* *The forecast announced a change in the weather. The storm will soon be over...* La météo a annoncé un changement de temps. La tempête sera bientôt finie... *

2. monnaie *f*
they've given me the wrong change! ils se sont trompés en me rendant la monnaie !

3. Idiom
for a change pour changer

II. *v i*
1. changer

there's no direct train, you have to change in Paris il n'y a pas de train direct, il faut changer à Paris

the Captain will never change! le capitaine ne changera jamais !

2. se changer
she changed into an evening dress elle s'est changée et a mis une robe du soir

III. *v t*
1. changer de

she's changed her dress elle a changé de robe

can I change places with you? est-ce que je peux changer de place avec vous ?

I've changed my mind j'ai changé d'avis

2. changer, transformer
the witch changed him into a toad la sorcière l'a transformé en crapaud

3. faire la monnaie de
can you change a 10 dollars? pouvez-vous faire la monnaie de 10 dollars ?

channel

channel
['tʃæn(ə)l] *n*
1. chaîne *f*

this programme's (Am: program's) boring, what's on the other channels? cette émission est ennuyeuse, qu'est-ce qu'il y a sur les autres chaînes ?

2. bras *m* de mer
a narrow channel separates the island from the mainland un étroit bras de mer sépare l'île du continent

3. Idiom
the (English) Channel la Manche

* *Tintin crossed the Channel by boat.* Tintin a traversé la Manche en bateau.
Way out sortie *

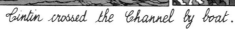

Tintin crossed the Channel by boat.

chapter

chapter
['tʃæptəʳ] *n*
chapitre *m*

character

character
['kærəktəʳ] *n*
1. caractère *m*, tempérament *m*

he has a very strong character il a beaucoup de caractère

...character

2. personnage *m*
all the characters in the play tous les personnages de la pièce

charge

charge
[tʃɑ:dʒ]
I. *n*
1. accusation *f*

he denies all charges of cheating il nie toutes les accusations d'avoir triché

2. frais *m pl*
the delivery charge les frais de livraison

3. Idiom
this is for you: there is no charge for delivery ceci est pour vous, la livraison est gratuite

in charge responsable

who is in charge here? qui est le responsable ici ?

II. *vt*
1. faire payer

how much did they charge you for it? combien vous l'ont-ils fait payer ?

2. accuser

* *You are charged with murder!...* Vous êtes accusé de meurtre !... *

III. *vi*
charger

...charge

the cavalry charged la cavalerie a chargé

charming

charming
['tʃɑ:mɪŋ] *adj*
charmant

what a charming village! quel charmant village !

chase

chase
[tʃeɪs] *vt*
poursuivre

* *Wooah! Wooah!* Woof ! Woof !
Snowy is chasing the cat... Milou poursuit le chat... *

Snowy is chasing the cat...

cheap

cheap
[tʃi:p] *adj*
pas cher, bon marché

I'm looking for a cheap hotel je cherche un hôtel pas cher

cheat

cheat
[tʃɪ:t] *vi*
tricher

don't play cards with him, he cheats ne jouez pas aux cartes avec lui, il triche

check

check
[tʃek] *vt*
vérifier

* *A trifling correction, I think... But we'd better just check my figures once more, we mustn't make a mistake.* Correction minime, me semble-t-il... Mais vérifions tout de même mes calculs encore une fois, nous ne devons pas nous tromper. *

...check

► **check in**
se présenter à l'enregistrement

all passengers on flight 505 please check in tous les passagers du vol 505 sont priés de se présenter à l'enregistrement

► **check** (*Am*)
→ BILL

cheek

cheek
[tʃi:k] *n*
1. joue *f*

she has red cheeks elle a les joues rouges

2. culot *m*, insolence *f*
* *He called me a fool! What a cheek! He won't get away with it!* Il m'a traité d'imbécile ! Quel culot ! Il ne va pas s'en tirer comme ça ! *

cheer

cheer
[tʃɪəʳ] *vt*

Idiom
to cheer somebody up remonter le moral à quelqu'un

...cheer

his jokes cheered us up ses plaisanteries nous ont remonté le moral

cheer up, Captain, we've still got a chance! courage, capitaine, nous avons encore une chance !

► **cheerful**
['tʃɪəfʊl] *adj*
gai, de bonne humeur

* *Too-ra... loor-ra... loor-ra-lay!...* Tralalaouti ! Tralalaouti !... *Tintin looks very cheerful.* Tintin a l'air très gai. *

Tintin looks very cheerful.

cheese

cheese
[tʃi:z] *n*
fromage *m*

chemist

chemist
['kemɪst] *n*
(*Am:* **druggist)**
1. pharmacien *m*, pharmacienne *f*

the chemist gave me some ointment le pharmacien m'a donné de la pommade

2. chimiste *m f*
* *Who were we talking about?* De qui parlions-nous ? *We were talking about that famous chemist, Professor Smith.* Nous parlions de ce célèbre chimiste, le professeur Smith. *

► **chemistry**
['kemɪstrɪ] *n*
chimie *f*

...chemist

cherry

cherry
['tʃerɪ] *n*
pl cherries
cerise *f*

chest

chest
[tʃest] *n*
1. poitrine *f*

* *Slap-bang, a punch in the chest!* Et vlan ! un coup de poing dans la poitrine ! *

...chest

Slap-bang, a punch in the chest!

2. coffre *m*
the treasure is in that chest le trésor est dans ce coffre

chicken

chicken
['tʃɪkɪn] *n*
poulet *m*

chief

chief
[tʃi:f] *n*
I. *n*
chef *m*

take me to your chief conduisez-moi à votre chef

II. *adj*
principal

the chief reason la raison principale

child

child
['tʃaɪld] *n*
pl children
['tʃɪldrən]
enfant *m f*

when I was a child quand j'étais enfant

chimney

chimney
['tʃɪmnɪ] *n*
cheminée

...chimney

the chimney of the ship is black la cheminée du bateau est noire

chin

chin
[tʃɪn] *n*
menton *m*

* *He hit Haddock on the chin!* Il a frappé Haddock au menton ! *

...chin

He hit Haddock on the chin!

chip

chip
[tʃɪp] *n*
(*Am:* **French fry)**
frite *f*

fish and chips poisson avec des frites

chocolate

chocolate
['tʃɒklɪt] *n*
chocolat *m*

...chocolate

this chocolate cake is delicious! ce gâteau au chocolat est délicieux !

choice

choice
[tʃɔɪs] *n*
choix *m*

* *We have no choice...* Nous n'avons pas le choix...
We must kill him!... Il faut le tuer !... *

...choice

choose

choose
[tʃu:z] *vt*
chose [tʃəʊz],
chosen ['tʃəʊzn]
choisir

I don't know which one to choose je ne sais pas lequel choisir

chop

chop
[tʃɒp]
I. *n*

...chop

côte *f*, côtelette *f*

a pork chop une côte de porc

II. *vt*
chopped, chopped
couper

I'll chop some wood je vais couper du bois

► **chop down**
abattre

to chop down a tree abattre un arbre

Christmas

Christmas
['krɪsməs] *n*
Noël *m*

Happy Christmas! Joyeux Noël !

we got a lot of Christmas cards nous avons reçu beaucoup de cartes de Noël

Father Christmas le Père Noël

church

church
[tʃ3:tʃ] *n*
église *f*

they go to church every Sunday ils vont à l'église tous les dimanches

cigarette

cigarette
[sɪgə'ret] *n*
cigarette *f*

...cigarette

► **cigare**
[si'gɑ:ʳ] *n*
cigare *m*

cinema

cinema ['sɪnəmə] *n*
cinéma *m*

let's go to the cinema (Am: movies) tonight si on allait au cinéma ce soir ?

circle

circle
['s3:k(ə)l] *n*
cercle *m*

stand in a circle around me mettez-vous en cercle autour de moi

circus

circus
['s3:kəs] *n*
cirque *m*

...circus

* *So you didn't know that there was a circus on the Moon, did you? I even heard that they needed two clowns... You two would do nicely!* Ah, vous ignoriez qu'il y avait un cirque sur la Lune ? J'ai même appris qu'ils avaient besoin de deux clowns... Vous feriez parfaitement l'affaire ! *

...circus

city

city
['sɪtɪ] *n*
(grande) ville *f*
pl cities

I wouldn't like to live in this city je n'aimerais pas habiter cette ville

class

class
[klɑ:s] *n*
1. classe *f*, cours *m*

...class

Damian arrived late for the French class Damian est arrivé en retard au cours de français

2. classe *f*
I like travelling (Am: traveling) first class j'aime voyager en première classe

► **classroom**
['klɑ:sru:m] *n*
classe *f*, salle *f* de classe

clean

clean
[kli:n]
I. *adj*
propre

let me see your hands, are they clean? montre-moi tes mains, sont-elles propres ?

II. *vt*
1. nettoyer

* *I'm going to clean the furniture...* Je vais nettoyer les meubles... *

...clean

2. Idiom
to clean one's teeth se laver les dents

clear

clear
[klɪəʳ]
I. *adj*
1. dégagé

the sky is clear le ciel est dégagé

2. transparent, clair

the water is perfectly clear l'eau est parfaitement transparente

3. clair, évident
it's clear that they want to kill us il est clair qu'ils veulent nous tuer

II. *vt*
débarrasser, dégager

I'll clear the table je vais débarrasser la table

► **clear off**
s'en aller, filer

clear off! I'm busy! va-t'en ! je suis occupé !

► **clear up**
1. éclaircir

* *We'll clear up this mystery...* Nous allons éclaircir ce mystère... *

2. s'éclaircir
the weather will clear up tomorrow le temps s'éclaircira demain

3. ranger
go and clear up your room va ranger ta chambre

► **clearly**
['klɪəlɪ] *adv*
1. clairement, distinctement

* *I can't hear you, could you speak more clearly?* Je ne vous entends pas, pourriez-vous parler plus clairement ? *

...clear

2. manifestement, de toute évidence
they're clearly afraid manifestement, ils ont peur

clerk

clerk
[klɑ:k] (*Am :* [klɜ:k])
employé *m,* employée *f* (de bureau)

he's a bank clerk il est employé de banque

clever

clever
['klevəʳ] *adj*
1. intelligent

she's the cleverest pupil in the class c'est l'élève la plus intelligente de la classe

2. adroit, habile
* *He's not very clever!* Il n'est pas très adroit ! *

He's not very clever!

climb

climb
[klaɪm] *vi & t*
grimper, monter

I'll climb (up) this tree, perhaps I'll be able to see them je vais grimper à cet arbre, peut-être pourrai-je les voir

clinic

clinic
['klɪnɪk] *n*
clinique *f*

* *What are you doing?* Mais que faites-vous ?
I'm better: I'm leaving the clinic... Je vais mieux : je quitte la clinique... *

...clinic

clock

clock
[klɒk] *n*
horloge *f,* pendule *f*

it's half past six by the church clock il est six heures et demie à l'horloge de l'église

close

close
[kləʊs] *adv*

...close

près

stay close to me restez près de moi

close

close
[kləʊz] *vi & t*
fermer

don't forget to close the windows n'oubliez pas de fermer les fenêtres

...close

* *And now, Mrs Yamilah, close your eyes...* Et maintenant, madame Yamilah, fermez les yeux... *

at what time do the shops (Am: stores) close? à quelle heure ferment les magasins ?

cloud

cloud
[klaʊd] *n*
nuage *m*

▶ **cloudy**
['klaʊdɪ] *adj*
cloudier, cloudiest
nuageux

it's very cloudy today le ciel est très nuageux aujourd'hui

club

club
[klʌb]
I. *n*
1. club *m*

are you a member of the club? êtes-vous membre du club ?

2. gourdin *m*
* *He hit Tintin with a club...* Il a frappé Tintin avec un gourdin... *

II. *n pl*
trèfle *m*
the ace of clubs l'as de trèfle

He hit Tintin with a club...

coach

coach
[kəʊtʃ] *n* (*Am:* **bus**)
1. car *m*, autocar *m*

* *Do you see that? They're taking the coach... There can't have been any seats left in the train...* Tu as vu, ils prennent le car... Il n'y avait sans doute plus de places dans le train... *

Do you see that? They're taking the coach... There can't have been any seats left in the train...
CAFE DES

2. wagon *m*, voiture *f*
the train only had two coaches le train

...coach

n'avait que deux voitures

3. entraîneur *m*
he's a football (Am: soccer) coach il est entraîneur de football

coal

coal
[kəʊl] *n*
charbon *m*

put some more coal on the fire remettez du charbon sur le feu

coast

In Kiltoch, the coast is rocky.

coast
[kəʊst] *n*
1. côte *f*

* *In Kiltoch the coast is rocky.* A Kiltoch la côte est rocheuse. *

2. Idiom
the coast is clear le champ est libre

coat

coat
[kəʊt] *n*
1. manteau *m*

put your coat on, it's cold mettez votre manteau, il fait froid

2. couche *f*
a coat of paint une couche de peinture

cocoa

cocoa
['kəʊkəʊ] *n*
cacao *m*

coffee

coffee
['kɒfɪ] *n*
café *m*

black coffee café noir

white coffee (Am: coffee with milk) café au lait

coin

coin
[kɔɪn] *n*
pièce *f*

how much is this coin worth? combien vaut cette pièce ?

cold

cold
[kəʊld]
I. *adj*
froid

this soup is cold! cette soupe est froide !

brr! I'm cold! brr ! j'ai froid !

* *Hurry up, Snowy, it's terribly cold!* Dépêche-toi, Milou, il fait terriblement froid ! *

Hurry up, Snowy, it's terribly cold!

II. *n*
rhume *m*

atchoo! – bless you! have you got a cold? atchoum ! – à vos souhaits ! vous avez un rhume ?

* *Tchooo!* Atchoum ! *The Captain's caught a cold.* Le capitaine a attrapé un rhume. *

...cold

TCHOOO
The Captain's caught a cold.

collect

collect
[kə'lekt] *vt*
1. collectionner

she collects stamps elle collectionne les timbres

2. aller chercher
I'll collect you at the station j'irai vous chercher à la gare

► **collection**
[kə'lekʃ(ə)n] *n*
collection *f*

would you like to see my stamp collection? aimeriez-vous voir ma collection de timbres ?

colour

colour
['kʌləʳ] *n*
(*Am :* **color**)
couleur *f*

what colour is her dress? de quelle couleur est sa robe ?

...colour

a colour television un téléviseur couleur

come

come
[kʌm] *vi*
came [keɪm], come [kʌm]
1. venir

can I come with you? est-ce que je peux venir avec vous ?

...come

March comes before April mars vient avant avril

* *These cigarettes come from Borduria, look at the pack, Captain...* Ces cigarettes viennent de Bordurie, regardez le paquet, capitaine... *Good grief!...* Ça alors !... *

2. arriver
hurry up! – I'm coming! dépêchez-vous ! – j'arrive !

...come

These cigarettes come from Borduria, look at the pack, Captain...
Good grief!...

► **come along**
1. venir

why don't you come along with us? pourquoi ne venez-vous pas avec nous ?

2. se dépêcher
* *Come along, we're going to be late!* Dépêchez-vous, nous allons être en retard !
I'm coming... Je viens... *

Come along, we're going to be late!
I'm coming...

► **come back**
revenir, rentrer

* *No, Sir, the Captain hasn't come back from his trip!* Non, monsieur, le capitaine n'est pas revenu de voyage ! *I'm telling you that nobody's in. The Captain hasn't come back from his trip!* Je vous dis qu'il n'y a personne. Le capitaine n'est pas revenu de voyage ! *

No, Sir, the Captain hasn't come back from his trip!

I'm telling you that nobody's in. The Captain hasn't come back from his trip!

...come

► **come in**
entrer

knock knock – come in! toc toc – entrez !

► **come on**
1. venir, se dépêcher

come on, we'll miss the train! viens, nous allons manquer le train !

2. Idiom
come on, it's only a game! allons, ce n'est qu'un jeu !

comfortable

comfortable
['kʌmftəbl] *adj*
1. confortable

there's nothing better than a comfortable armchair and a good pipe! il n'y a rien de mieux qu'un fauteuil confortable et une bonne pipe !

2. Idiom
come in and make yourself comfortable entrez et mettez-vous à l'aise

comic

comic
['kɒmɪk] *n*
journal *m* de bandes dessinées

he buys a comic every week il achète un journal de bandes dessinées toutes les semaines

► **comic strip** *n*
bande *f* dessinée

* *For goodness' sake Tintin, do you take me for a character*

For goodness' sake Tintin, do you take me for a character out of a comic strip or what?
Wait for me!

...comic

out of a comic strip or what? Enfin, Tintin ! Vous me prenez pour un personnage de bande dessinée ou quoi ?
Wait for me! Attendez-moi ! *

command

command
[kə'mɑ:nd] *n*
1. ordre *m*

they refuse to obey

...command

my commands ils refusent d'obéir à mes ordres

2. Idiom
* *Billions of blue blistering barnacles! I'm in command of this ship!* Mille milliards de mille sabords ! C'est moi qui commande ce navire ! *

common

common
['kɒmən] *adj*
1. commun

these butterflies are not very common ces papillons ne sont pas très communs

2. fréquent
drive slowly, accidents are common here conduisez lentement, les accidents sont fréquents ici

► **common sense** *n*
bon sens *m*

* *If you had any common sense, you wouldn't have got the time wrong!... Do you hear?* Si vous aviez un peu de bon sens, vous ne vous seriez pas trompé d'heure !... Vous entendez ? *

...common

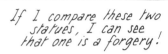

company

company
['kʌmpənɪ] *n*
pl companies
1. société *f*, compagnie *f*

he works for a shipping company il travaille pour une compagnie de navigation

2. compagnie *f*
I'll come with you to keep you company je viendrai avec vous pour vous tenir compagnie

compare

compare
[kəm'peəʳ] *vt*
comparer

* *If I compare these two statues, I can see that one is a forgery!* Si je compare ces deux statues, je vois bien que l'une est fausse ! *

competition

competition
[kɒmpɪ'tɪʃ(ə)n] *n*
compétition *f*, concours *m*

a swimming competition une compétition de natation

complain

complain
[kəm'pleɪn] *vi*
se plaindre

...complain

he's complaining about your cheek il se plaint de ton insolence

complete

complete
[kəm'pli:t]
I. *adj*
complet

the complete works of Shakespeare les œuvres complètes de Shakespeare

...complete

II. *vt*
terminer

how long will it take you to complete the repairs? combien de temps vous faut-il pour terminer les réparations ?

► **completely**
[kəm'pli:tlɪ] *adv*
complètement

* *Come on, stand up, Captain!* Allons, debout, capitaine !
I can't go on, I'm completely exhausted! Je ne peux pas aller plus loin, je suis complètement épuisé ! *

compulsory

compulsory
[kəm'pʌlsərɪ] *adj*
obligatoire

it is compulsory to wear a safety belt la ceinture de sécurité est obligatoire

computer

computer
[kəm'pju:təʳ] *n*
ordinateur

* *There are several computers in the rocket to assist with the piloting...* Il y a plusieurs ordinateurs dans la fusée pour faciliter le pilotage... *

concern

concern
[kən'sɜ:n] *vt*

...concern

concerner

what I have to say doesn't concern you ce que j'ai à dire ne vous concerne pas

► **concerning**
[kən'sɜ:nɪŋ] *prep*
à propos de, au sujet de

* *I have a question to ask you concerning Snowy.* J'ai une question à vous poser à propos de Milou. *

concert

concert
['kɒnsət] *n*
concert *m*

conclusion

conclusion
[kən'klu:ʒ(ə)n] *n*
conclusion *f*

don't go jumping to conclusions n'en tirez pas de conclusions trop hâtives

condition

condition
[kən'dɪʃ(ə)n] *n*
1. condition *f*

you can go on one condition tu peux y aller à une condition

2. état *m*
* *This boat doesn't seem to be in very good condition!* Ce bateau n'a pas l'air en très bon état !... *

conductor

conductor
[kən'dʌktəʳ] *n*
1. chef *m* d'orchestre

the conductor bowed to the audience le chef d'orchestre a salué le public

2. receveur *m* (d'autobus)

► **conductress**
[kən'dʌktrɪs] *n*
receveuse *f* (d'autobus)

confidence

confidence
['kɒnfɪdəns] *n*
confiance *f*

I have no confidence in him je ne lui fais pas confiance

confuse

confuse
[kən'fju:z] *vt*
embrouiller

...confuse

the issue is quite clear, don't try to confuse things l'affaire est très claire, n'essayez pas d'embrouiller les choses

► **confused**
[kən'fju:zd] *adj*
1. perplexe, déconcerté

you look confused tu as l'air perplexe

2. confus
my memories are very confused mes souvenirs sont très confus

► **confusing**
[kən'fju:zɪŋ] *adj*
déroutant

oh dear, how confusing! mon Dieu, que c'est déroutant !

congratulate

congratulate
[kən'grætjʊleɪt] *vt*
féliciter

► **congratulations**
[kəngrætjʊ'leɪʃ(ə)nz] *n pl*
félicitations *f pl*

* *Let me shake your hand, Tintin... Congratulations!... Well done!... Thanks to you, we've arrested the culprits...* Laissez-moi vous serrer la main, Tintin... Toutes mes félicitations !... Bravo... grâce à vous, nous avons arrêté les coupables... *

consider

consider
[kən'sɪdəʳ] *vt*
1. examiner, réfléchir à

...consider

we must consider the problem carefully il nous faut examiner ce problème en profondeur

2. considérer
I consider him to be a fool je le considère comme un imbécile

► **considerable**
[kən'sɪdərəbl] *adj*
considérable

* *All this has cost a considerable sum of money and called for an awful lot of work...* Tout cela a coûté une somme considérable et nécessité énormément de travail... *

All this has cost a considerable sum of money and called for an awful lot of work...

consist

consist
[kən'sɪst] *vi*
1. consister
our job will consist in keeping watch notre travail consistera à faire le guet

2. comporter
the committee consists of ten members le comité comporte dix membres

contain

contain
[kən'teɪn] *vt*
contenir

The casket only contains old documents !...
Old documents ?... It was a waste of time to go to all that trouble !

* *The casket only contains old documents!... Le coffret ne contient que de vieux documents !... *Old documents?... It was a waste of time to go to all that trouble!* De vieux documents ?... C'était bien la peine de se donner tant de mal ! *

continent

continent
['kɒntɪnənt] *n*
continent *m*

Australia is a continent l'Australie est un continent

there are some English people who have never been to the continent il y a certains Anglais qui n'ont jamais visité le continent

continue

continue
[kən'tɪnju:] *vi & vt*
continuer

it will continue to rain all day il continuera à pleuvoir toute la journée

control

control
[kən'trəʊl]
I. *n*
1. contrôle *m*

Heavens ! The plane is out of control !

* *Heavens! The plane is out of control!* Grands Dieux ! J'ai perdu le contrôle de l'avion ! *

2. commande *f*
* *I must reach the controls...* Il faut absolument que j'arrive aux commandes... *

3. autorité *f*
he has no control over his pupils il n'a aucune autorité sur ses élèves

WOOUUIIIIIII

TRIII
I must reach the controls ...

II. *vt*
1. maîtriser

he can't control his horse il n'arrive pas à maîtriser son cheval

2. contrôler
the government controls prices le gouvernement contrôle les prix

convenient

convenient
[kən'vi:nɪənt] *adj*
1. commode

this isn't a very convenient place to talk ce n'est pas un lieu très commode pour parler

2. Idiom
the house is very convenient for the school la maison est très bien située pour se rendre à l'école

conversation

conversation
[kɒnvə'seɪʃ(ə)n] *n*
conversation *f*

this is a private conversation! ceci est une conversation privée !

convince

convince
[kən'vɪns] *vt*
convaincre, persuader

* *Captain, we must*

...convince

Captain, we must convince them that we are innocent...

convince them that we are innocent... Capitaine, nous devons les convaincre de notre innocence... *

cook

cook
[kʊk]
I. *n*
cuisinier *m*, cuisinière *f*

...cook

Ah, here's the cook! What nice little dish have you made us for lunch?
Spaghetti, Captain.

* *Ah, here's the cook...! What nice little dish have you made us for lunch?* Ah ! voilà le cuisinier !... Qu'est-ce que vous nous avez préparé de bon pour le déjeuner ?
Spaghetti, Captain. Des spaghetti, capitaine. *

II. *vt*
cuire, faire cuire

I'll cook the potatoes je ferai cuire les pommes de terre

...cook

III. *vi*
1. faire la cuisine

where did you learn to cook? où avez-vous appris à faire la cuisine ?

2. cuire
the stew takes several hours to cook le ragoût doit cuire plusieurs heures

► **cooker**
['kʊkəʳ] *n*
(*Am:* **stove**)
cuisinière *f*

a gas cooker une cuisinière à gaz

► **cooking**
['kʊkɪŋ] *n*
cuisine *f*

do you like English cooking? aimez-vous la cuisine anglaise ?

cool

cool
[ku:l] *adj*
frais

I'd like a nice cool drink j'aimerais boire quelque chose de bien frais

it's a lot cooler today il fait beaucoup plus frais aujourd'hui

► **cool down**
refroidir

wait for your soup to cool down attends que ta soupe refroidisse

* *Well, now we must let the engine cool down!* Bon, maintenant il faut laisser refroidir le moteur !
To be precise, we must let the engine cool down! Je dirais même plus, il faut laisser refroidir le moteur ! *

Well, now we must let the engine cool down!
To be precise, we must let the engine cool down!

copy

copy
['kɒpɪ] *vt*
copied, copied
copier

he copied his homework from another pupil il a copié son devoir sur un autre élève

corn

corn
[kɔ:n] *n*
1. blé *m*

...corn

they grow corn and other cereals ils cultivent du blé et d'autres céréales

2. *(Am)* maïs *m*
we had corn on the cob nous avons mangé des épis de maïs

► **cornflakes**
['kɔ:nfleɪks] *n pl*
corn flakes *m pl*, flocons *m pl* de maïs

corner

He's not going to pop up on the street corner like that...

!

...corner

cough ...

corner
['kɔ:nəʳ] *n*
coin *m*

** He's not going to pop up on the street corner like that...* Il ne va quand même pas surgir comme ça au coin de la rue... *

correct

correct
[kə'rekt]
I. *adj*
1. correct, bon

that is the correct answer c'est la bonne réponse

2. exact
** Eight o'clock sharp! But that is not the correct time... This clock is definitely slow...* Huit heures juste !... Mais ce n'est pas

Eight o'clock sharp! But that is not the correct time ... This clock is definitely slow...

l'heure exacte !... Cette pendule retarde, c'est certain ! *

II. *vt*
corriger

the teacher had corrected our homework le professeur avait corrigé nos devoirs

► **correction**
[kə'rekʃ(ə)n] *n*
correction *f*

the teacher's corrections are in red ink les corrections du professeur sont à l'encre rouge

corridor

corridor
['kɒrɪdəʳ] *n*
couloir *m*

his office is at the end of this corridor son bureau est au fond de ce couloir

cost

cost
[kɒst]
I. *vt*
cost, cost
coûter

** How much does that boat cost?* Combien coûte ce bateau ? *

II. *n*
coût *m*

the cost of living le coût de la vie

How much does that boat cost?

cottage

cottage
['kɒtɪdʒ] *n*
1. petite maison *f* (de campagne)

the fishermen live in these cottages les pêcheurs habitent dans ces petites maisons

2. Idiom
thatched cottage chaumière *f*

cotton

cotton
['kɒt(ə)n] *n*
coton *m*

a cotton shirt une chemise en coton

cough

cough
[kɒf]
I. *n*
toux *f*

I've caught a bad cough j'ai attrapé une mauvaise toux

II. *vi*
tousser

could

could
[kʊd] *v aux*
pouvoir

could I borrow your binoculars? pourrais-je emprunter vos jumelles ?

I'm sorry, I couldn't help laughing je suis désolé, je n'ai pas pu m'empêcher de rire

** Tintin still hasn't come back, he could have warned me...* Tintin n'est toujours pas revenu. Il aurait pu me prévenir... *

Tintin still hasn't come back, he could have warned me ...

count

count
[kaʊnt] *vi & vt*
compter

try to count how many men there are essayez de compter combien il y a d'hommes

there were six of us, not counting the children nous étions six, sans compter les enfants

► **count on**
compter sur

good luck, Tintin, we're counting on you! bonne chance, Tintin, nous comptons sur vous !

counter

counter
['kaʊntəʳ] *n*
1. comptoir *m*

the butcher was behind his counter le

...counter

boucher était derrière son comptoir

2. jeton *m*
the game is played with counters le jeu se joue avec des jetons

country

country
['kʌntrɪ] *n*
pl countries
1. pays *m*

...country

Do you prefer to live in a town or in the country?

he is the president of this country c'est le président de ce pays

2. campagne *f*
* *Do you prefer to live in a town or in the country?* Préférez-vous habiter en ville ou à la campagne ? *

county

county
['kaʊntɪ] *n*
pl counties
comté *m*

couple

couple
['kʌpl] *n*
1. couple *m*

a young couple un jeune couple

...couple

2. Idiom
a couple of deux ou trois

I'll be back in a couple of hours je serai de retour dans deux ou trois heures

course

course
[kɔːs] *n*
1. cours *m*

I'm going to do a French course je vais suivre un cours de français

2. cours *m*
in the course of the last few months au cours de ces derniers mois

3. cap *m*
set a course for this island mettez le cap sur cette île

4. Idiom
of course bien sûr, naturellement

* *Well, of course, it's them over there, hiding behind their newspapers... Thomson and Thompson!* Mais bien sûr, ce sont eux, là-bas, cachés derrière leurs journaux... Dupont et Dupond ! *

Well, of course, it's them over there, hiding behind their newspapers...
Thomson and Thompson!

of course not bien sûr que non

cousin

cousin
['kʌzən] *n*
cousin *m*, cousine *f*

Sheila is my cousin Sheila est ma cousine

cover

cover
['kʌvəʳ]
I. *vt*
couvrir

the streets are covered with snow les rues sont couvertes de neige

II. *n*
1. couverture *f*

the book with the blue cover le livre avec la couverture bleue

2. couvert *m*
* *Take cover!* Mettez-vous à couvert ! *Bang Bang* Pan Pan *

...cover

Take cover!
BANG BANG

cow

cow
[kaʊ] *n*
vache *f*

* *Where on earth is this cow taking me?... Woof! Woof!* Mais où cette vache va-t-elle me conduire ?... Wouah ! Wouah ! *

...cow

Where on earth is this cow taking me?...
WOOF! WOOF!

crash

crash
[kræʃ]
I. *vi*
s'écraser

II. *n*
1. accident *m*

there has been a terrible plane crash il y a eu un terrible accident d'avion

2. fracas *m*
a loud crash woke me up j'ai été réveillé par un grand fracas

▸ **crash into**
heurter, rentrer dans

the car crashed into a lamppost la voiture a heurté un réverbère

crate

crate
[kreɪt] *n*
caisse *f*

crazy

crazy
['kreɪzɪ] *adj*
crazier, craziest
fou *m*, folle *f*

* *What are you doing, Captain? Have you gone crazy?* Qu'est-ce que vous faites, capitaine ? Vous êtes devenu fou ? *

cream

cream
[kri:m] n
crème *f*

strawberries and cream fraises à la crème

put some suntan cream on mets de la crème solaire

creep

creep
[kri:p] *vi*

...creep

crept, crept [krept]
se glisser

* *Let's try to creep up behind the guards and surprise them...* Essayons de nous glisser derrière les gardes pour les surprendre... *

crew

crew
[kru:] *n*
équipage *m*

cricket

cricket
['krɪkɪt] *n*
cricket *m*

to play cricket jouer au cricket

crime

crime
[kraɪm] *n*
1. crime *m*, délit *m*

what crime has he

...crime

committed? quel délit a-t-il commis ?

2. criminalité *f*

cross

cross
[krɒs]
I. *vt*
traverser

be careful when you cross the road faites attention en traversant la rue

...cross

II. *n*
croix *f*

* *It's a cross, isn't it?* C'est bien une croix, n'est-ce pas ?... *

III. *adj*
fâché

I'm sorry, Tintin, are you cross with me? je suis désolé, Tintin, êtes-vous fâché contre moi ?

▸ **cross out**
barrer

several words have been crossed out plusieurs mots ont été barrés

▸ **crossroads**
['krɒsrəʊdz] *n*
carrefour *m*

turn left at the crossroads tournez à gauche au carrefour

crowd

crowd
[kraʊd] *n*
foule *f*

I don't want to lose Snowy in the crowd je ne veux pas perdre Milou dans la foule

cry

cry
[kraɪ]
I. *n*
cri *m*

* *Aaaaaah! They heard a cry...* Aaaaaah Ils ont entendu un cri... *

II. *vi*
cried, cried
1. pleurer

don't cry, Abdullah we'll meet agair soon ne pleure pas, Ab

...cry

They heard a cry...

dallah, nous nous reverrons bientôt

2. crier
somebody is crying for help quelqu'un crie au secours

► **cry out**
pousser un cri

she cried out in surprise elle a poussé un cri de surprise

cup

cup
[kʌp] *n*
1. tasse *f*

would you like a cup of tea? voulez-vous une tasse de thé ?

2. coupe *f*
our football team won the cup notre équipe de football a gagné la coupe

cupboard

cupboard
['kʌbəd] *n*
placard *m*

the plates are in the cupboard les assiettes sont dans le placard

curious

curious
['kjʊərɪəs] *adj*
1. curieux

* *Is that it?* Ça y est ? *Yes, that's it! That will teach you to be curious, Snowy!* Ça y est, oui ! Ça t'apprendra à être curieux, Milou ! *

2. bizarre, curieux
what's that curious smell? quelle est cette odeur bizarre ?

...curious

curtain

curtain
['kɜːt(ə)n] *n*
(*Am:* **drape**)
rideau *m*

draw the curtains, it's dark fermez les rideaux, il fait nuit

cushion

cushion
['kʊʃ(ə)n] *n*
coussin *m*

customer

customer
['kʌstəməʳ] *n*
client *m*, cliente *f*

customs

customs
['kʌstəmz] *n pl*
douane *f*

they searched our bags at customs on a fouillé nos bagages à la douane

cut

cut
[kʌt] *vt*
cut, cut [kʌt]
1. couper

...cut

ouch, I've cut my hand! aïe ! je me suis coupé la main

you should get your hair cut! vous devriez vous faire couper les cheveux !

2. réduire, diminuer
we have cut all our prices nous avons réduit tous nos prix

► **cut down**
1. abattre

all the trees have been cut down tous les arbres ont été abattus

2. réduire
we must cut down our expenses nous devons réduire nos dépenses

► **cut off**
1. couper

you nearly cut my ear off vous avez failli me couper l'oreille

2. couper

the telephone is cut off le téléphone est coupé

► **cut out**
1. découper

she was cutting out pictures from magazines elle découpait des photos dans les magazines

2. Idiom
to cut out drinking/smoking arrêter de boire/fumer

cycle

cycle
['saɪk(ə)l]
I. *n*
bicyclette *f*, vélo *m*

II. *vi*
aller à bicyclette

she cycles to school elle va à l'école à bicyclette

dad

dad, daddy
[dæd, 'dædɪ] *n*
papa *m*

* *My daddy will be very cross with you!... And he'll cut your head off!...* Mon papa va être très fâché contre toi !... Et il te coupera la tête !... *

daily

daily
['deɪlɪ] *adj*
quotidien

daily paper journal quotidien

dairy

dairy
['deərɪ] *n*
pl dairies
laiterie *f*

damage

damage
['dæmɪdʒ]
I. *n*
dégâts *m pl,*
dommages *m pl*

That explosion must have caused an enormous amount of damage cette explosion a dû causer des dégâts énormes

II. *vt*
endommager,
abîmer

it's all right, the ca is hardly damage ça va, la voiture est peine endommagée

dance

dance
[dɑ:ns]
I. *n*
danse *f*

I'll teach you thi dance je vous appren drai cette danse

...dance

II. *vi & vt*
danser

* *Let's dance! Let's dance!* Dansons ! Dansons !
Hurray! Hourra !
Let's dance! Dansons !
Look! That's the way white men dance! Regarde ! C'est comme ça que dansent les hommes blancs ! *

danger

danger
['deɪndʒəʳ] *n*
danger *m*

I'm out of danger je suis hors de danger

▸ **dangerous**
['deɪndʒərəs] *adj*
dangereux

don't go in there, it's dangerous! n'entrez pas, c'est dangereux !

dare

dare
[deəʳ]
I. *v i*
1. oser

* *Who's there?* Qui est là ?
He daren't move. Il n'ose pas bouger. *

Captain! how dare you? capitaine ! comment osez-vous ?

2. Idiom
I dare say she'll come tomorrow je suppose qu'elle viendra demain

II. *v t*
défier

I dare you to jump off the roof! je te défie de sauter du toit !

He daren't move.

dark

dark
[dɑ:k]
1. *adj*
1. sombre, noir
it's very dark in here il fait très sombre là-dedans

2. foncé
he's wearing a dark blue jacket il porte une veste bleu foncé

3. brun
is she fair or dark? est-ce qu'elle est blonde ou brune ?

II. *n*
noir *m*

I'm afraid of the dark j'ai peur du noir

► **darkness**
['dɑ:knɪs] *n*
obscurité *f*

the house is in darkness la maison est plongée dans l'obscurité

darling

darling
['dɑ:lɪŋ] *n*
chéri *m*, chérie *f*

are you all right, darling? tu vas bien, ma chérie ?

date

date
[deɪt] *n*
1. date *f*

what date is it today?

...date

quelle est la date d'aujourd'hui ?

2. rendez-vous *m*
let's make a date for next week prenons rendez-vous pour la semaine prochaine

3. Idiom
he asked her out for a date il l'a invitée à sortir avec lui

up to date moderne

out of date démodé

daughter

daughter
['dɔ:təʳ] *n*
fille *f*

they have two sons and a daughter ils ont deux fils et une fille

day

day
[deɪ] *n*
1. jour *m*

what day is it today? quel jour sommes-nous aujourd'hui ?

we'll have to walk ten hours a day nous devrons marcher dix heures par jour

2. journée *f*
I've been working all day j'ai travaillé toute la journée

...day

* *Forward, Snowy! We'll have to walk all day!...* En avant, Milou ! Il va falloir marcher toute la journée !... *

3. Idiom
the day before yesterday avant-hier

the day after tomorrow après-demain

dead

dead
[ded] *adj*
mort

* *Dead?* Mort ?
No, he's breathing, he's not dead! Non, il respire, il n'est pas mort ! *

deaf

deaf
[def] *adj*
sourd

you'll have to speak louder, he's deaf! il faut que vous parliez plus fort, il est sourd !

deal

deal
[di:l]
I. *n*
1. marché *m*, affaire *f*

I'll make a deal with you je vais faire un marché avec vous

2. Idiom
a great deal beaucoup

we haven't got a great deal of food nous n'avons pas beaucoup de nourriture

...deal

II. *v t*
dealt, dealt [delt]
donner, distribuer

it's your turn to deal the cards c'est à toi de donner les cartes

▶ **deal with**
se charger de, s'occuper de

I'll deal with the cooking je me chargerai de faire la cuisine

dear

dear
[dɪəʳ] *adj*
1. cher

dear Mrs Hancock chère madame Hancock

a very dear friend un ami très cher

2. cher
this hotel is too dear (Am: expensive) cet hôtel est trop cher

3. Idiom
oh dear! oh mon Dieu !

death

Tintin and the Captain have been sentenced to death...

...death

death
[deθ] *n*
mort *f*

* *Tintin and the Captain have been sentenced to death...* Tintin et le capitaine ont été condamnés à mort... *

December

December
[dɪ'sembəʳ] *n*
décembre *m*

...December

the first/second of December (Am: December first/second) le premier/deux décembre
come on the 6th of December (Am: on December 6) venez le 6 décembre

decide

decide
[dɪ'saɪd] *v t*
décider

...decide

what have you decided to do? qu'est-ce que vous avez décidé de faire ?

▶ **decision**
[dɪ'sɪʒən] *n*
décision *f*

we still haven't come to a decision nous ne sommes toujours pas arrivés à une décision

deck

deck
[dek] *n*
pont *m*

* *The waves are covering the deck...* Les vagues recouvrent le pont... *

declare

declare
[dɪ'kleəʳ] *v t*
déclarer

...declare

* *War has been declared!... War has been declared!* La guerre est déclarée !... La guerre est déclarée ! *

deep

deep
[di:p] *adj*
profond

* *The river is really*

...deep

deep!... La rivière est bien profonde !...
Splash Plouf *

defend

defend
[dɪ'fend] *v t*
défendre

several armed men are defending the entrance plusieurs hommes armés défendent l'entrée

definite

definite
['defɪnɪt] *adj*
1. précis, déterminé

he didn't give a definite answer il n'a pas donné de réponse précise

2. sûr, certain
they're coming tomorrow, it's definite ils viennent demain, c'est certain

...definite

► **definitely**
['defɪnɪtlɪ] *adv*
1. certainement, sans aucun doute

they're definitely leaving tomorrow ils partent certainement demain

2. nettement, de loin
this one is definitely better celui-ci est nettement meilleur

3. absolument
do you agree? – definitely! êtes-vous d'accord ? – absolument !

degree

degree
[dɪ'gri:] *n*
1. degré *m*

the temperature is over forty degrees il fait plus de quarante degrés

...degree

2. licence *f*
she has a degree in biology elle a une licence de biologie

delay

delay
[dɪ'leɪ]
I. *n*
retard *m*

we are sorry for the delay nous sommes désolés pour le retard

...delay

II. *vt*
retarder

I hope I haven't delayed you too much j'espère que je ne vous ai pas trop retardés

delicious

delicious
[dɪ'lɪʃəs] *adj*
délicieux

this cake is delicious,

...delicious

can I have some more? ce gâteau est délicieux, puis-je en reprendre ?

delight

delight
[dɪ'laɪt] *n*
joie *f*, plaisir *m*

to my delight, all my friends were there à ma plus grande joie, tous mes amis étaient là

...delight

► **delighted**
[dɪ'laɪtɪd] *adj*
ravi, enchanté

* *Tintin!... Captain!... I am delighted to see you again!...* Tintin !... Capitaine !... Je suis ravi de vous revoir !... *

► **delightful**
[dɪ'laɪtfʊl] *adj*
charmant

thank you for a delightful evening merci,

nous avons passé une soirée charmante

deliver

deliver
[dɪ'lɪvəʳ] *vt*
livrer

these flowers were delivered this morning ces fleurs ont été livrées ce matin

dentist

dentist
['dentɪst] *n*
dentiste *m f*

I have to go to the dentist's tomorrow je dois aller chez le dentiste demain

department

department
[dɪ'pɑ:tmənt] *n*
1. rayon *m*

where is the toy department? où est le rayon des jouets ?

2. service *m*
she works in the sales department elle travaille au service des ventes

departure

departure
[dɪ'pɑ:tʃəʳ] *n*
départ *m*

I didn't notice his departure je n'ai pas remarqué son départ

depend

depend
[dɪ'pend] *vi*
dépendre

...depend

* *Tharkey, will we be able to leave tomorrow?* Tharkey, pourrons-nous partir demain ?
It depends on the weather; we'll decide tomorrow morning... Cela dépend du temps ; nous déciderons demain matin... *

depth

depth
[depθ] *n*
profondeur *f*

describe

describe
[dɪs'kraɪb] *vt*
décrire

* *Can you describe the car?* Pouvez-vous décrire la voiture ?
Yes, it's a beige car

...describe

...describe

with a sunroof. Oui, c'est une voiture beige avec un toit ouvrant. *

► **description**
[dɪs'krɪpʃ(ə)n] *n*
description *f*

desert

desert
['dezət]
I. *n*
désert *m*

...desert

* *We're lost in the middle of the desert...* Nous sommes perdus au milieu du désert... *

II. *adj*
1. désertique

a desert region une région désertique

2. Idiom
a desert island une île déserte

We're lost in the middle of the desert...

► **deserted**
[dɪ'zɜ:tɪd] *adj*
désert

a deserted street une rue déserte

deserve

deserve
[dɪ'zɜ:v] *vt*
mériter

they got what they deserved! ils ont eu ce qu'ils méritaient !

design

design
[dɪ'zaɪn] *vt*
1. concevoir

the architect who designed this building l'architecte qui a conçu cet immeuble

2. créer
she designs children's clothes elle crée des vêtements pour enfants

desk

desk
[desk] *n*
1. pupitre *m*

all the pupils are sitting at their desks tous les élèves sont assis à leurs pupitres

2. bureau *m*
* *These are the plans... Voici les plans... Thank you, Professor. Put them on my desk.* Merci, professeur. Posez-les sur mon bureau. *

These are the plans...
Thank you, Professor. Put them on my desk.

dessert

dessert
[dɪ'zɜ:t] *n*
dessert *m*

that was very nice, what's for dessert? c'était très bon, qu'est-ce qu'il y a comme dessert ?

destroy

destroy
[dɪ'strɔɪ] *vt*
détruire

...destroy

The fire has destroyed everything!...

* *The fire has destroyed everything!...* l'incendie a tout détruit !... *

detail

detail
['dɪ:teɪl] *n*
détail *m*

tell me all the details racontez-moi tous les détails

detective

detective
[dɪ'tektɪv] *n*
détective *m*

* *We've asked two famous detectives to investigate this case.* Nous avons demandé à deux détectives célèbres d'enquêter sur cette affaire... *

We've asked two famous detectives to investigate this case.

develop

develop
[dɪ'veləp] *vt*
développer

our scientists have developed a new product nos scientifiques ont développé un nouveau produit

have you had your photos developed? avez-vous fait développer vos photos ?

* *Very interesting, Professor, could you*

...develop

Very interesting, Professor, could you develop your idea?... I'm listening to you...

develop your idea?... I'm listening to you... Très intéressant, professeur, pouvez-vous développer votre idée ?... Je vous écoute... *

dial

dial
['daɪəl]
I. *n*
cadran *m*

the dial reads 1500! le cadran indique 1500 !

...dial

II. *v t*
composer

* *No, it's not Mr Cutts the butcher, you dialled* (*Am:* dialed) *the wrong number!...* Non, ce n'est pas la boucherie Sanzot, vous avez composé un mauvais numéro !... *

No, it's not Mr Cutts the butcher, you dialled the wrong number!...

diamond

diamond
['daɪəmənd] *n*
diamant *m*

a diamond necklace un collier de diamants

dictate

dictate
[dɪ'kteɪt] *v i & v t*
dicter

I am going to dictate a passage in French

...dictate

to you je vais vous dicter un passage en français

► **dictation**
[dɪk'teɪʃ(ə)n] *n*
dictée *f*

dictionary

dictionary
['dɪkʃənrɪ] *n*
pl dictionaries
dictionnaire *m*

...dictionary

I looked the word up in my dictionary j'ai cherché le mot dans mon dictionnaire

die

die
[daɪ] *v i*
mourir

* *Don't miss him!... He must die!...* Ne le

...die

Don't miss him!... He must die!...

rate pas !... Il faut qu'il meure !... *

difference

difference
['dɪfərəns] *n*
différence *f*

* *What's the difference between Thompson and Thomson?* Quelle est la

...difference

What's the difference between Thompson and Thomson?

différence entre Dupond et Dupont ? *

► **different**
['dɪfərənt] *adj*
différent

difficult

difficult
['dɪfɪkəlt] *adj*
difficile

it's difficult to see in

...difficult

this fog c'est difficile de voir dans ce brouillard

* *The cave is difficult to reach: shall we try all the same?* La grotte est difficile d'accès, essayons-nous quand même ?
Of course! Bien sûr ! *

► **difficulty**
['dɪfɪkəltɪ] *n*
pl difficulties
difficulté *f*

The cave is difficult to reach: shall we try all the same?
Of course!

dig

dig
[dɪg] *v i & v t*
dug, dug [dʌg]
creuser

Snowy has dug a hole to bury his bone Milou a creusé un trou pour enterrer son os

dining room

dining room
['daɪnɪŋru:m] *n*
salle *f* à manger

dinner

dinner
['dɪnəʳ] *n*
1. dîner *m*

come on, dinner's ready venez, le dîner est prêt

2. Idiom
dinner's ready! à table !

direct

direct
[daɪ'rekt]
I. *adj*
direct

is there a direct flight? est-ce qu'il y a un vol direct ?

* ***Zorrino, what is the most direct route to get to the Temple of the Sun?*** Zorrino, quel est le chemin le plus direct pour atteindre le Temple du Soleil ? ***We must cross over the mountain.*** Il faut passer par la montagne. *

II. *vt*
diriger

he directs a large company il dirige une grande société

▶ **direction**
[daɪ'rekʃ(ə)n] *n*
direction *f*

* ***Let's follow him! He went in that direction!*** Poursuivons-le! Il est parti dans cette direction! *

▶ **directly**
[daɪ'rektlɪ] *adv*
1. directement

go directly home allez directement à la maison

2. immédiatement, tout de suite
he'll be here directly il arrive tout de suite

...direct

dirty

dirty
['dɜ:tɪ] *adj*
dirtier, dirtiest
sale

* ***Really, Snowy, you haven't only been drinking but you're dirty too!...*** Vraiment Milou, non seulement tu as bu, mais en plus tu es sale !...
Dirty... You think... hic... that... hic... I'm dirty... hic... Sale... Tu penses... hic... que... hic... je suis sale... hic... *

Really, Snowy, you haven't only been drinking but you're dirty too!...
Dirty... You think... hic... that... hic... I'm dirty... hic...

disagree

disagree
[dɪsə'gri:] *vi*
1. ne pas être d'accord

* ***I completely disagree with you!...*** Je ne suis pas du tout d'accord avec vous !...
For goodness' sake, Captain, let me explain to you... Mais enfin, capitaine, laissez-moi vous expliquer... *

2. Idiom
oysters disagree with me les huîtres ne me réussissent pas

...disagree

I completely disagree with you!...
For goodness' sake, Captain, let me explain to you...

disappear

disappear
[dɪsə'pɪəʳ] *vi*
disparaître

where's Tintin? he's disappeared! où est Tintin ? il a disparu !

disappoint

disappoint
[dɪsə'pɔɪnt] *vt*
décevoir

it disappointed me cela m'a déçu

▶ **disappointment**
[dɪsə'pɔɪntmənt] *n*
déception *f*

disaster

disaster
[dɪ'zɑ:stəʳ] *n*
désastre *m*, catastrophe *f*

* ***This is where the air disaster took place...*** C'est ici que s'est produit la catastrophe aérienne... ***Let's go!*** Allons-y ! *

This is where the air disaster took place...
Let's go!

discover

discover
[dɪs'kʌvəʳ] *vt*
découvrir

Professeur Calculus has discovered a new molecule le professeur Tournesol a découvert une nouvelle molécule

► **discovery**
[dɪs'kʌvərɪ] *n*
pl discoveries
découverte *f*

discuss

discuss
[dɪs'kʌs] *vt*
discuter, parler de

* *I'd like to discuss something with you!* J'aimerais vous parler de quelque chose ! *

► **discussion**
[dɪs'kʌʃ(ə)n] *n*
discussion *f*

disgusting

disgusting
[dɪs'gʌstɪŋ] *n*
dégoûtant

ugh! it's disgusting! beurrk ! c'est dégoûtant !

dish

dish
[dɪʃ] *n*
plat *m*

I need a large dish to serve the vegetables

...dish

in j'ai besoin d'un grand plat pour servir les légumes

► **dishes**
n pl
vaisselle *f*

sit down, I'll wash the dishes asseyez-vous, je vais faire la vaisselle

distance

distance
['dɪstəns] *n*
1. distance *f*

* *The distance between us is narrowing.* La distance entre nous se réduit. *

2. lointain *m*
can you see that house in the distance? voyez-vous cette maison dans le lointain ?

► **distant**
['dɪstənt] *adj*

lointain, éloigné

in the distant past dans un passé lointain

district

district
['dɪstrɪkt] *n*
1. région *f*

this district is mountainous cette région est montagneuse

...district

2. quartier *m*
they live in a nice district of town ils habitent un joli quartier

* *Professor Fan-Hsi-Ying's house is in this district...* C'est dans ce quartier qu'est la maison du professeur Fan Se Yeng... *

...district

disturb

disturb
[dɪs'tɜ:b] *vt*
déranger

Tintin is asleep, do not disturb him Tintin dort, ne le dérangez pas

dive

dive
[daɪv] *vi*
plonger

...dive

...dive

* *I must dive in and rescue Snowy!...* Je dois plonger pour sauver Milou !...
Careful, Tintin! Careful! There are lots of sharks!... Attention, Tintin ! Attention ! Il y a beaucoup de requins !... *

divide

divide
[dɪ'vaɪd] *vt*
1. partager

we'll divide the money between us nous partagerons l'argent entre nous

2. diviser
the room is divided in two by a partition la pièce est divisée en deux par une cloison

56 divided by 8 is 7 56 divisé par 8 égale 7

do

do
[du:]
did [dɪd], done [dʌn]
I. *vt*
faire

* *Tintin, stop! What are you doing?* Arrêtez, Tintin ! Qu'est-ce que vous faites ? *

I've done my homework j'ai fait mes devoirs

I'll do my best je ferai de mon mieux

...do

II. *vi*
1. faire

do as you're told! faites ce qu'on vous dit !

2. marcher, aller
the company is doing very well l'entreprise marche très bien

how are you doing? comment ça va ?

3. Idiom
how do you do? enchanté (de faire votre connaissance)

...do

* *This is Tintin, Sir...* Voici Tintin, mon lieutenant...
Fine! How do you do! I hope everything went off all right... Très bien ! Enchanté ! J'espère que tout s'est bien passé... *

that will do! ça suffit !

that's got nothing to do with it! cela n'a rien à voir !

it has nothing to do with you cela ne vous regarde pas

III. *v aux*
do you speak English? – yes, I do parlez-vous anglais ? – oui

did you see the western last night? – no, I didn't as-tu vu le western hier soir ? – non

I don't like fish – neither do I je n'aime pas le poisson – moi non plus

you know Professor Calculus, don't you? vous connaissez le professeur Tournesol, n'est-ce pas ?

don't touch that button! ne touchez pas à ce bouton !

► **do up**
fermer, attacher

he did up his buttons il a fermé ses boutons

do your shoelace up attache ton lacet

► **do without**
se passer de

the captain will have to do without whisky le Capitaine devra se passer de whisky

dock

dock
[dɒk] *n*
dock *m*

the ship is still in dock le navire est toujours au dock

doctor

doctor
['dɒktəʳ] *n*
médecin *m*,
docteur *m*

...doctor

quick, call a doctor! vite, appelez un médecin !

document

document
['dɒkjʊmənt] *n*
document *m*

* *This document is of vital importance...* Ce document est d'une importance capitale... *

...document

dog

dog
[dɒg] *n*
chien *m*

* *Well done, Snowy!... You're a very clever dog!...* Bravo, Milou !... Tu es un chien très intelligent !... *

dollar

dollar
['dɒlər] *n*
dollar *m*

...dollar

how much is it? – twenty-five dollars combien est-ce ? – vingt-cinq dollars

door

door
[dɔːr] *n*
porte *f*

* *Blistering barnacles!!... The door's locked!... They've locked us in!...* Mille

...door

sabords ! !... La porte est fermée à clé !... Ils nous ont enfermés !... *

doubt

doubt
[daʊt]
I. *vt*
douter

I doubt if we can do it alone je doute que nous puissions le faire seuls

...doubt

II. *n*
doute *m*

down

down
[daʊn]
I. *prep*
1. en bas de

* *The monastery is just down the mountain...* Le monastère est juste en bas de la montagne... *

...down

The monastery is just down the mountain...

...down

2. Idiom
to go down the stairs/the hill descendre l'escalier/la colline

he ran down the stairs/the hill il a descendu l'escalier/la colline en courant

she fell down the stairs elle est tombée dans l'escalier

they live down the street ils habitent un peu plus loin dans cette rue

II. *adv*
Idiom
to go down descendre

the lift (Am: elevator) is going down l'ascenseur descend

put your bags down posez vos valises

sit down asseyez-vous

I wrote down her address j'ai noté son adresse

► **downstairs**
[daʊn'steəz] *adv*
en bas

the family who live downstairs la famille qui habite en bas

come downstairs to the kitchen venez en bas à la cuisine

dozen

dozen
['dʌz[ə]n] *n*
douzaine *f*

a dozen eggs, please une douzaine d'œufs, s'il vous plaît

draw

draw
[drɔː]
I. *n*
match *m* nul

the match ended in a draw ils ont fait match nul

II. *vt*
drew [druː],
drawn [drɔːn]
1. dessiner

he drew a picture of the church il a dessiné l'église

* *He's quite a big*

...draw

He's quite a big man with dark hair... I'll try and draw him for you...

man with dark hair... I'll try and draw him for you... C'est un homme assez gros avec des cheveux noirs... Je vais essayer de vous le dessiner... *

2. tirer
draw the curtains, it's dark tirez les rideaux, il fait nuit

III. *vi*
1. dessiner

she draws very well elle dessine très bien

2. faire match nul
the two teams drew les deux équipes ont fait match nul

► **draw up**
1. s'arrêter

a car has drawn up outside the house une voiture s'est arrêtée devant la maison

2. dresser

to draw up a list dresser une liste

► **drawer**
[drɔːʳ] *n*
tiroir *m*

the cutlery is in the top drawer les couverts sont dans le tiroir du haut

► **drawing**
['drɔːɪŋ] *n*
dessin *m*

show me your drawing of the house montre-moi le dessin que tu as fait de la maison

dreadful

dreadful
['dredfʊl] *n*
affreux

what dreadful weather! quel temps affreux !

dream

dream
[driːm]
I. *n*
rêve *m*

I had a dream last night j'ai fait un rêve cette nuit

* *They are definitely Incan flowers...* Oui, oui, ce sont bien des fleurs d'Inca...
Tintin is having a strange dream... Tintin fait un rêve étrange... *

They are definitely Incan flowers...
Tintin is having a strange dream.

II. *vi*
dreamt, dreamt
[dremt]
or dreamed, dreamed
1. rêver

I dreamt I was drowning j'ai rêvé que je me noyais

2. Idiom
I wouldn't dream of lying to you! jamais il ne me viendrait à l'idée de vous mentir !

dress

dress
[dres]
I. *n*
1. robe *f*

she was wearing a long black dress elle portait une longue robe noire

2. tenue *f*
he was wearing evening dress il était en tenue de soirée

II. *vt*
habiller

who's that man dressed in black? qui est cet homme habillé de noir ?

to get dressed s'habiller

III. *vi*
s'habiller

I got up and dressed je me suis levé et je me suis habillé

drill

drill
[drɪl] *n*
1. perceuse *f*

he made a hole in the wall with the drill il a fait un trou dans le mur avec la perceuse

2. roulette *f*
the dentist took his drill le dentiste a pris sa roulette

3. exercice *m*
a grammar drill un exercice de grammaire

drink

drink
[drɪŋk]
I. *n*
1. boisson *f*

they sell hot and cold drinks ils vendent des boissons chaudes et froides

2. Idiom
would you like a drink? voudriez-vous boire quelque chose ?

II. *vi & vt*
drank [dræŋk],
drunk [drʌŋk]
boire

the Captain has given up drinking le capitaine a arrêté de boire

drive

drive
[draɪv] *vt*
drove [drəʊv],
driven ['drɪv(ə)n]

...drive

1. conduire

* *I can't drive this vehicle!...* Je ne sais pas conduire cet engin !... *

2. Idiom
that noise is driving me mad! ce bruit me rend fou !

► **driver**
['draɪvəʳ] *n*
conducteur *m*,
conductrice *f*

I can't drive this vehicle!...

drop

drop
[drɒp]
I. *n*
1. goutte *f*

a drop of rain une goutte de pluie

more coffee? – just a drop, please encore du café ? – juste une petite goutte, s'il vous plaît

2. baisse *f*
there's been a drop in the temperature il y a eu une baisse de température

3. Idiom
be careful, there's a sheer drop here! attention, ça descend à pic ici !

II. *vt*
dropped, dropped
laisser tomber

don't drop that vase ne laissez pas tomber ce vase

► **drop in**
passer

he dropped in to see us yesterday il est passé nous voir hier

► **drop off**
1. s'endormir

* *He dropped off in front of the fire.* Il s'est endormi devant le feu... *

2. déposer
drop me off at the next corner dépose-moi au prochain coin de rue

drown

drown
[draʊn] *vi*
se noyer

* *Oh, no, Snowy, we're going to drown! Help!* Mon Dieu, Milou, nous allons nous noyer ! Au secours ! *

...drown

drunk

drunk
[drʌŋk] *adj*
ivre

druggist

druggist (*Am*)
→ CHEMIST

dry

dry
[draɪ]

...dry

I. *adj*
drier, driest
sec *m*, sèche *f*

I'll lend you some dry clothes je vous prêterai des vêtements secs

II. *vi & vt*
dried, dried
sécher

* *How can we dry our clothes!* Comment sécher nos vêtements ! *

duck

duck
[dʌk] *n*
canard *m*

dull

dull
[dʌl] *adj*

1. gris, sombre
the weather is dull again today il fait encore gris aujourd'hui

...dull

2. ennuyeux
what a dull book! quel livre ennuyeux !

3. terne
this wall is a dull colour la couleur de ce mur est terne

during

during
['djʊərɪŋ] *prep*
pendant

have you brought

...during

anything to read during the flight? avez-vous apporté de quoi lire pendant le vol ?

dust

dust
[dʌst] *n*
poussière *f*

the furniture is covered with dust les meubles sont couverts de poussière

...dust

► **dustbin**
['dʌstbɪn] *n*
(*Am:* **garbage can)**
poubelle *f*

► **dustman**
['dʌstmən] *n*
pl dustmen [dʌstmɪn]
(*Am:* **garbage collector)**
éboueur *m*

► **dusty**
['dʌstɪ] *adj*
dustier, dustiest

poussiéreux, couvert de poussière

the books are dusty les livres sont couverts de poussière

duty

duty
['dju:tɪ] *n*
pl duties
1. devoir *m*

...duty

it is my duty to help them il est de mon devoir de les aider

2. Idiom
duty-free shop boutique hors taxe

on duty de service

each

each
[i:tʃ]
I. *adj*
chaque

each cabin has two beds in it il y a deux lits dans chaque cabine

II. *pron*
1. chacun, chacune

they have each scored two points ils ont marqué deux points chacun

Easy does it! Each of you will get one!...

I'll give you two pounds each je vous donnerai deux livres chacun

* *Easy does it! Each of you will get one!...* Doucement ! Vous en aurez chacun un !... *

2. pièce
they cost 50 pence each ils coûtent 50 pence pièce

► **each other**
pron
se, l'un l'autre

they hate each other ils se détestent

we should all help each other nous devrions tous nous aider les uns les autres

eager

eager
['i:gəʳ] *adj*
1. désireux

they aren't very eager to help us ils ne sont pas très désireux de nous aider

2. impatient
are you eager to leave? êtes-vous impatient de partir ?

ear

ear
[ɪəʳ] *n*
oreille *f*

!?
Snowy pricks up his ears.

* *Snowy pricks up his ears...* Milou dresse les oreilles... *

early

early
['ɜ:lɪ]
earlier, earliest
I. *adj*
1. tôt

hello, you're early! bonjour, vous êtes arrivé tôt !

2. Idiom
in the early afternoon/evening en début d'après-midi/de soirée

II. *adv*
1. tôt, de bonne heure

we have to get up early tomorrow il faut que nous nous levions tôt demain matin

2. Idiom
* *Early in the morning.* De bon matin. *

Early in the morning.

earn

earn
[ɜ:n] *vt*
gagner

how much do you earn a month? combien gagnez-vous par mois ?

earth

earth
[ɜ:θ] *n*
1. terre *f*

...earth

the earth is very rich in this region la terre est très riche dans cette région

2. Terre *f*
I can see the Earth from here! je vois la Terre d'ici !

* *Hello... Hello... This is Tintin... We're moving away from the Earth!...* Allô... Allô... Ici Tintin... Nous nous éloignons de la Terre !... *

east

east
[i:st]
I. *n*
est *m*

they live in the east of England ils habitent dans l'est de l'Angleterre

II. *adj*
est

the east coast la côte est

East Germany l'Allemagne de l'Est

III. *adv*
à l'est, vers l'est

there's a village just east of here il y a un village tout près d'ici vers l'est

Easter

Easter
['i:stəʳ] *n*
Pâques *m*

are you going on vacation at Easter? est-ce que vous partez en vacances à Pâques ?

Easter egg œuf de Pâques

easy

easy
['i:zɪ] *adj*
easier, easiest
facile

* *... but I can't drive this vehicle...* ... mais je ne sais pas piloter cet engin...
Yes you can, it's very easy!... Mais si, c'est très facile !... *

eat

...eat

eat
[i:t] *vt*
ate [eɪt],
eaten ['i:t(ə)n]
manger

* *Come and have a look, I've found something to eat...* Venez voir, j'ai trouvé de quoi manger... *

educate

educate
['edjʊkeɪt] *vt*
1. éduquer

2. Idiom
he was educated in England il a fait ses études en Angleterre

▶ **education**
[edjʊ'keɪʃ(ə)n] *n*
éducation *f*,
enseignement *m*

effect

effect
[ɪ'fekt] *n*
effet *m*

* *Has the medicine had any effect on you? Are you feeling better?...* Est-ce que le médicament vous a fait de l'effet ? Vous sentez-vous mieux ?... *

effort

effort
['efət] *n*
effort *m*

make an effort faites un effort

egg

egg
[eg] *n*
œuf *m*

we had bacon and eggs for breakfast

...egg

nous avons mangé des œufs au bacon au petit déjeuner

eight

eight
[eɪt]
I. *adj*
huit

my brother is eight mon frère a huit ans

...eight

II. *n*
huit *m*

▸ **eighteen**
[eɪ'ti:n]
I. *adj*
dix-huit

II. *n*
dix-huit *m*

▸ **eighty**
['eɪtɪ]
I. *adj*
quatre-vingts

his grandfather is eighty son grand-père a quatre-vingts ans

eighty-one quatre-vingt-un

II. *n*
pl eighties
quatre-vingts *m*

in the eighties dans les années quatre-vingts

Eire

Eire
['eərə] *n*
Eire *f*, la République d'Irlande

either

either
['aɪðəʳ]
I. *adj*
1. l'un ou l'autre, n'importe lequel

* *You can take either*

...either

You can take either road, they both lead to the village...
Thank you, I'll take the shortest...

road, they both lead to the village... Vous pouvez prendre l'une ou l'autre route, elles mènent toutes les deux au village... *Thank you, I'll take the shortest...* Merci, je vais prendre la plus courte... *

2. chaque
on either side of the road de chaque côté de la route

II. *pron*
l'un ou l'autre, n'importe lequel

I don't like either of them je n'aime ni l'un ni l'autre

III. *adv*
non plus

I don't speak Italian, and I don't speak French either je ne parle pas italien, et je ne parle pas français non plus

IV. *conj*
either... or ou... ou

either Snowy comes with us or I won't go! ou Milou vient avec nous, ou je n'y vais pas !

elbow

elbow
['elbəʊ] *n*
coude *m*

take your elbows off the table! enlève tes coudes de la table !

elder

elder
['eldəʳ] *adj*
aîné

my elder sister ma sœur aînée

▸ **eldest**
['eldɪst] *adj*
aîné

Paul is their eldest child Paul est l'aîné de leurs enfants

electric

electric
[ɪ'lektrɪk] *adj*
électrique

he's playing with his electric train il joue avec son train électrique

▸ **electricity**
[ɪlek'trɪsɪtɪ] *n*
électricité *f*

it works by electricity cela marche à l'électricité

elephant

elephant
['elɪfənt] *n*
éléphant *m*

eleven

eleven
[ɪ'levn]
I. *adj*
onze

my sister is eleven ma sœur a onze ans

...eleven

II. *n*
onze *m*

else

else
[els] *adv*
1. d'autre, autre

what else could I have done? qu'est-ce que j'aurais pu faire d'autre ?

* *Is there anybody*

...else

Is there anybody else?... No?... Let's go then!...

else?... No?... Let's go then!... Y a-t-il quelqu'un d'autre ?... Non ?... Alors, allons-y !... *

something else autre chose

how else? de quelle autre façon ?

2. Idiom
somewhere else ailleurs

or else ou bien, sinon

emergency

emergency
[ɪ'mɜ:dʒənsɪ] *n*
pl emergencies
Idiom
in an emergency, break the glass en cas d'urgence, briser la vitre

* *Hurry up! Don't you understand that this is an emergency?* Dépêchez-vous ! Vous ne comprenez pas qu'il y a urgence ? *

we'll have to make an emergency landing! il

...emergency

faudra faire un atterrissage forcé !

emergency exit sortie de secours

empty

empty
['emptɪ]
I. *adj*
emptier, emptiest
vide

the bottle is empty la bouteille est vide

* *It's a good thing it's empty!...* Heureusement qu'il est vide !... *

II. *vt*
emptied, emptied
vider

empty your pockets onto the table videz vos poches sur la table

encourage

encourage
[ɪn'kʌrɪdʒ] *vt*
encourager

end

end
[end]
I. *n*
1. fin *f*

the end of the story is disappointing la fin de l'histoire est décevante

2. bout *m*
I can't find the end of this piece of string je ne trouve pas le bout de cette ficelle

II. *vi*
finir, se terminer

* *Everything ended well, as usual, didn't it, Snowy?* Tout s'est bien terminé, comme d'habitude, n'est-ce pas Milou ?
It certainly did! Oui ! Oui ! *

III. *vt*
finir, terminer

I don't know how to end my story je ne sais pas comment terminer mon histoire

enemy

enemy
['enəmɪ]
I. *n*
pl enemies
ennemi *m*, ennemie *f*

* *It's Tintin, our old enemy!...* C'est Tintin, notre vieil ennemi !... *

II. *adj*
ennemi

the enemy army l'armée ennemie

engaged

engaged
[ɪn'geɪdʒd] *adj*
1. occupé

I tried to call them, but the line's engaged (Am: busy) j'ai essayé de les appeler, mais la ligne est occupée

2. fiancé
Gillian is engaged to my brother Gillian est fiancée à mon frère

engine

engine
['endʒɪn] *n*
moteur *m*

* *When we've blown up the tyres we'll check the engine.* Quand nous aurons gonflé les pneus, nous réviserons le moteur. *

► **engineer**
[endʒɪ'nɪəʳ] *n*
ingénieur *m*

England

England
['ɪŋglənd] *n*
Angleterre *f*

they live in England ils habitent en Angleterre

I'd like two tickets to England, please j'aimerais deux billets pour l'Angleterre, s'il vous plaît

▶ **English**
['ɪŋglɪʃ]
I. *adj*
anglais

he has an English accent il a un accent anglais

II. *n*
1. *the English* les Anglais

2. anglais *m*
do you speak English? est-ce que vous parlez anglais ?

▶ **Englishman, Englishmen**
['ɪŋglɪʃmən, mɪn] *n*
Anglais *m*

she married an Englishman elle a épousé un Anglais

▶ **Englishwoman, Englishwomen**
['ɪŋglɪʃwʊmən, wɪmɪn] *n*
Anglaise *f*

enjoy

enjoy
[ɪn'dʒɔɪ] *vt*
1. aimer

did you enjoy the play? est-ce que tu as aimé la pièce ?

2. Idiom
to enjoy oneself s'amuser

did you enjoy yourselves at the circus? est-ce que vous vous êtes amusés au cirque ?

enough

I can't go fast enough!

...enough

enough
[ɪ'nʌf]
I. *adv & pron*
assez

* *I can't go fast enough!* Je ne vais pas assez vite ! *

have you had enough to eat? est-ce que vous avez assez mangé ?

II. *adj*
assez de

we haven't got enough time! nous n'avons pas assez de temps !

enquire

enquire
→ INQUIRE

enter

enter
['entəʳ]

...enter

I. *vi*
entrer

* *You may enter now...* Vous pouvez entrer maintenant... *

II. *vt*
entrer dans

he entered the room il est entré dans la pièce

You may enter now...

entertain

entertain
[entə'teɪn] *vt*
amuser

he entertained us by telling funny stories il nous a amusés en racontant des histoires drôles

▶ **entertainment**
[entə'teɪnmənt] *n*
distraction *f*

there's not much entertainment here in the evening il n'y a pas

...entertain

beaucoup de distractions ici le soir

entire

entire
[ɪn'taɪəʳ] *adj*
entier

the entire country is in chaos le pays entier est plongé dans le chaos

...entire

▶ **entirely**
[ɪn'taɪəlɪ] *adv*
entièrement, complètement, tout à fait

* *I entirely agree with you!* Je suis tout à fait d'accord avec vous ! *Just as well!!!* Vous avez intérêt ! ! ! *

I entirely agree with you!
Just as well!!!

envelope

envelope
['envələʊp] *n*
enveloppe *f*

don't forget to put a stamp on the envelope n'oubliez pas de mettre un timbre sur l'enveloppe

escape

escape
[ɪs'keɪp]
I. *vi*

...escape

s'échapper

Tintin managed to escape Tintin a réussi à s'échapper

II. *n*
1. évasion *f*

after their escape from prison après leur évasion de prison

2. Idiom
we had a narrow escape! nous l'avons échappé belle !

especially

especially
[ɪ'speʃ(ə)lɪ] *adv*
spécialement, particulièrement

* *It's especially hot today!* Il fait particulièrement chaud aujourd'hui ! *

Europe

Europe
['jʊərəp] *n*
Europe *f*

It's especially hot today!

...Europe

part of Turkey is in Europe une partie de la Turquie est en Europe

► **European**
[jʊərə'pɪən]
I. *n*
Européen *m*, Européenne *f*

II. *adj*
européen

even

even
['i:v(ə)n]
I. *adv*
même

* *It's the end of the world!...* C'est la fin du monde !...
Everybody was frightened, even Tintin... Tout le monde avait peur, même Tintin... *

II. *adj*
1. pair

8 is an even number 8 est un nombre pair

2. plan, uni
the surface must be absolutely even la surface doit être absolument plane

3. Idiom
to get even with someone se venger de quelqu'un

...even

It's the end of the world !...

Everybody was frightened, even Tintin...

evening

evening
['i:vnɪŋ] *n*
1. soir *m*

goodbye, I'll see you tomorrow evening! au revoir, à demain soir !

2. soirée *f*
we spent the evening watching television nous avons passé la soirée à regarder la télévision

event

event
[ɪ'vent] *n*
événement *m*

ever

ever
['evəʳ] *adj*
1. jamais

nothing ever happens here! il ne se passe jamais rien ici !

2. déjà

...ever

Have you ever seen such a storm ?

* *Have you ever seen such a storm?* Avez-vous déjà vu une tempête pareille ? *

3. Idiom
for ever pour toujours

ever since depuis

every

every
['evrɪ] *adj*

...every

chaque, tous les

we go to school every day nous allons à l'école tous les jours

► **everybody**
['evrɪbɒdɪ],
everyone
['evrɪwʌn]
pron
tout le monde

is everybody ready? est-ce que tout le monde est prêt ?

► **everything**
['evrɪθɪŋ] *pron*
tout

where am I? I've forgotten everything! où suis-je ? j'ai tout oublié !

► **everywhere**
['evrɪweəʳ] *adv*
partout

* *Snowy, Snowy!... Where on earth is he?* Milou, Milou !... Où est-il donc ? *

...every

I've looked everywhere... J'ai cherché partout...
Snowy!... Milou !...
Snowy!... Milou !... *

exact

exact
[ɪg'zækt] *adj*
exact

have you got the exact time? avez-vous l'heure exacte ?

...exact

► **exactly**
[ɪg'zæktlɪ] *adv*
exactement

thank you, that's exactly what I wanted! merci, c'est exactement ce que je voulais !

exam

exam, examination
[ɪg'zæm],
[ɪgzæmɪ'neɪʃ(ə)n] *n*
examen *m*

...exam

I've got a French exam tomorrow j'ai un examen de français demain

► **examine**
[ɪg'zæmɪn] *vt*
examiner

examine these documents carefully examinez ces documents avec attention

example

example
[ɪg'zɑ:mpl] *n*
exemple *m*

her kindness is an example to us all sa gentillesse est un exemple pour nous tous

for example par exemple

excellent

excellent
['eksələnt] *adj*
excellent

* *That's an excellent idea, Calculus!* C'est une idée excellente, professeur ! *

except

except
[ɪk'sept] *prep*
sauf, à part

...except

* *Everybody's here except Tintin...* Tout le monde est là sauf Tintin...
Yes, he hasn't come... Oui, il n'est pas venu... *

exchange

exchange
[ɪks'tʃeɪndʒ]
I. *vt*
échanger

they exchanged insults/blows ils ont échangé des insultes/des coups

...exchange

* *Let's exchange our hats!...* Echangeons nos chapeaux !...
Let's try... Essayons... *

II. *n*
1. échange *m*

and what will you give me in exchange? et qu'est-ce que vous me donnerez en échange ?

...exchange

2. change *m*
what is the exchange rate of the dollar? quel est le taux de change du dollar ?

excited

excited
[ɪk'saɪtɪd] *adj*
excité, surexcité

the crowd is excited la foule est surexcitée

...excited

► **exciting**
[ɪk'saɪtɪŋ] *adj*
excitant, passionnant

* ***What an exciting story!*** Quelle histoire passionnante! *

excuse

excuse
I. *n*
[ɪk'skju:s]
prétexte *m*,

...excuse

excuse *f*

he says he's ill, but it's just an excuse il dit qu'il est malade, mais ce n'est qu'un prétexte

II. *vt*
[ɪk'skju:z]
excuser

Excuse me, could you tell me what you're doing here? excusez-moi, pourriez-vous me dire ce que vous faites là ?

exercise

exercise
['eksəsaɪz] *n*
exercice *m*

a French exercise un exercice de français

* ***So, I don't get enough exercise, do I!... You'll see!*** Ah, je ne fais pas assez d'exercice ! Vous allez voir !
Hup! Hop !
Great! Magnifique ! *

...exercise

► **exercise book (*Am:* notebook)** *n*
cahier *m*

exit

exit
['egzɪt] *n*
sortie *f*

emergency exit sortie de secours

* ***The exit must be this way...*** La sortie doit être par là... *

expect

expect
[ɪk'spekt] *vt*
s'attendre à

* ***General Alcazar! What a surprise, I didn't expect to meet you here!...*** Général Alcazar ! Quelle surprise, je me m'attendais pas à vous rencontrer ici ! ***Why not?...*** Pourquoi pas ?... *

expensive

The equipment for the expedition to the Moon was very expensive, but everything's ready now...

expensive
[ɪk'spensɪv] *adj*
cher

* *The equipment for the expedition to the Moon was very expensive, but everything's ready now...* Le matériel pour l'expédition sur la Lune a coûté très cher, mais maintenant tout est prêt... *

experiment

Come, Captain, come and have a look!...
Broken glass!... Calculus must have carried out an experiment!...

experiment
[ɪk'sperɪmənt] *n*
expérience *f*

* *Come, Captain, come and have a look!...* Venez, Capitaine, venez voir!...
Broken glass!... Calculus must have carried out an experiment!... Des éclats de verre !... Tournesol a dû faire une expérience ! *

explain

explain
[ɪk'spleɪn] *v t*
expliquer

I can explain everything to you je peux tout vous expliquer

▸ **explanation**
[eksplə'neɪʃ(ə)n] *n*
explication *f*

extra

extra
['ekstrə] *adj*
supplémentaire, de plus

set an extra place at the table mettez un couvert de plus à la table

extraordinary

extraordinary
[ekstrə'ɔ:dɪnərɪ] *adj*
extraordinaire

* *The Thompsons! What an extraordinary coincidence!* Les Dupondt ! Quelle coïncidence extraordinaire ! *

?
?
The Thompsons! What an extraordinary coincidence!

extremely

extremely
[ɪk'stri:mlɪ] *adv*
extrêmement

* *It's extremely hot tonight, don't you think, Snowy?...* Il fait extrêmement chaud ce soir, tu ne trouves pas, Milou ?... *

It's extremely hot tonight, don't you think, Snowy?...

eye

eye
[aɪ] *n*
1. œil *m*

close your eyes! fermez les yeux !

2. Idiom
* *Keep your eye on him!* Surveille-le de près !

Keep your eye on him!
All right!

All right! D'accord !

▸ **eyebrow**
['aɪbraʊ] *n*
sourcil *m*

▸ **eyelash**
['aɪlæʃ] *n*
cil *m*

▸ **eyesight**
['aɪsaɪt] *n*
vue *f*

she has very good eyesight elle a une très bonne vue

face

face
[feɪs] *n*
1. visage *m*

* *His face is dirty.* Son visage est sale. *

2. grimace *f*
the Captain's making funny faces le capitaine fait des grimaces

3. cadran *m*
the clock face le cadran de l'horloge

His face is dirty.

fact

fact
[fækt] *n*
fait *m*

Idiom
in fact en fait, en réalité

in fact, I wanted Mr Cutts the butcher en réalité, je voulais la boucherie Sanzot

factory

factory
['fækt(ə)rɪ] *n*
pl factories
usine *f*

a car factory une usine d'automobiles

fail

fail
[feɪl] *v t*
échouer, rater

he failed the exam il a échoué à l'examen

fair

fair
[feəʳ] *adj*
1. blond

who's that boy with fair hair? qui est ce garçon aux cheveux blonds ?

2. juste, bien
he's got more than me, it's not fair! il en a plus que moi, ce n'est pas juste !

3. passable
your homework is fair ton devoir est passable

...fair

► **fairly**
['feəlɪ] *adv*
assez, un peu

I'm fairly tired je suis un peu fatigué

fall

fall
[fɔ:l]
I. *n*
1. chute *f*
Snowy had a fall Milou a fait une chute

2. *Am:*
→ **autumn**

II. *v i*
fell [fel], fallen ['fɔ:l(ə)n]
1. tomber

hold on, Tintin don't fall! accroche-toi Tintin, ne tombe pas !

* *Captain Haddock fell off his chair.* Le capitaine Haddock est tombé de sa chaise. *

2. baisser
the temperature has fallen la température a baissé

► **fall over**
tomber (par terre)
he slipped on the ice and fell over il a glissé sur la glace et il est tombé

Captain Haddock fell off his chair.

family

family
['fæmɪlɪ] *n*
pl families
famille *f*

* *Here's my nice little family!* Voici ma petite famille ! *

Here's my nice little family !

famous

famous
['feɪməs] *adj*
célèbre

Tintin, the famous reporter Tintin, le célèbre reporter

far

far
[fɑːʳ] *adv*
farther, farthest/further, furthest
1. loin

* *Cheer up, Snowy, the village can't be*

very far... Courage, Milou, le village n'est plus très loin... *

Cheer up, Snowy, the village can't be very far...

2. beaucoup
you drink far too much, Captain! vous buvez beaucoup trop, capitaine !

3. Idiom
how far is it from London to Paris? combien y a-t-il de kilomètres de Londres à Paris ?

so far we've had no problems jusqu'ici nous n'avons pas eu de problèmes

fare

fare
[feəʳ] *n*
1. (prix *m* du) billet *m*

how much is the fare to Paris? combien coûte un billet pour Paris ?

2. Idiom
the return (Am: round-trip) fare is very expensive l'aller-retour est très cher

farm

farm
[fɑːm] *n*
ferme *f*

► **farmer**
['fɑːməʳ] *n*
agriculteur *m*,

agricultrice *f*,
fermier *m*,
fermière *f*

fashion

fashion
['fæʃ(ə)n] *n*
mode *f*

she keeps up with fashion elle suit la mode, elle est toujours à la mode

in fashion à la mode

fast

fast
[fɑːst]
I. *adj*
rapide

a fast car une voiture rapide

Ten thousand thundering typhoons! Don't drive so fast!

II. *adv*
1. vite

* *Ten thousand thundering typhoons! Don't drive so fast!* Mille millions de mille tonnerres ! Ne roulez pas si vite ! *

2. Idiom
fast asleep profondément endormi

fat

fat
[fæt] *adj*
fatter, fattest
gros

what a fat man! qu'est-ce qu'il est gros, ce monsieur !

father

father
['fɑːðəʳ]
père *m*

favour

favour
['feɪvəʳ] *n*
(*Am:* **favor**)
service *m*, faveur *f*

* *Will you do me a favour? Keep an eye on the car while I go*

Will you do me a favour? Keep an eye on the car while I go hunting.
Yes Tintin.
1385

hunting. Veux-tu me rendre un service ? Garde la voiture pendant que je vais chasser.
Yes Tintin. Oui Tintin. *

favourite

favourite
(*Am:* **favorite**)
['feɪvərɪt] *adj*
favori, préféré

yum yum, my favourite food! miam miam, mon plat préféré !

fear

fear
[fɪəʳ]
I. *n*
peur *f*

I couldn't move from fear! j'étais paralysé de peur !

II. *vt*
craindre, avoir peur de

I fear the worst, Captain! je crains le pire, capitaine !

▶ **fearful**
['fɪəfʊl] *adj*
1. peureux

* *Mice, mice!... It's crawling with mice in here!...* Des... des souris !... C'est plein de souris, ici !...

Thompson and Thomson are fearful... Dupond et Dupont sont peureux... *

2. affreux
what fearful weather! quel temps affreux !

feather

feather
['feðəʳ] *n*
plume *f*

Mice, mice! ... It's crawling with mice in here!...
Thompson and Thomson are fearful ...

February
['febrʊərɪ] *n*
février *m*

the first/second of February (Am: February first/second) le premier/deux février

come on the 6th of February (Am: on February 6) venez le 6 février

fed up

fed up
['fedʌp] *adj*

Idiom
* *I'm fed up with waiting!* J'en ai assez d'attendre !
Yes, I'm getting bored! Oui, je commence à m'ennuyer ! *

I'm fed up with waiting!
Yes, I'm getting bored!

feed

feed
[fi:d] *vt*
fed, fed [fed]
donner à manger à, nourrir

* *Come on, Snowy, I'm going to feed you!...* Viens, Milou, je vais te donner à manger !...
Good idea!... Bonne idée !... *

Come on, Snowy, I'm going to feed you!...
Good idea!...

feel

feel
[fi:l]
I. *vt*
felt, felt [felt]
1. sentir

...feel

I felt a pain in my arm... I hope it's not serious...
Let me see, Tintin, don't move...

* *I felt a pain in my arm... I hope it's not serious...* J'ai senti une douleur dans le bras... J'espère que ce n'est pas grave...
Let me see, Tintin, don't move... Montre-moi, Tintin, ne bouge pas... *

2. toucher, tâter
feel his forehead, it's very hot touche son front, il est très chaud

3. penser, avoir l'impression

I feel that something's strange here j'ai l'impression qu'il y a quelque chose d'étrange ici

II. *vi*
1. se sentir

* *She doesn't feel very well...* Elle ne se sent pas très bien... *

2. Idiom
I feel hungry/cold j'ai faim/froid

!

She doesn't feel very well...

the walls feel damp les murs sont humides (au toucher)

I don't feel like going out je n'ai pas envie de sortir

I feel like a cup of tea je prendrais bien une tasse de thé

▸ **feeling**
['fi:lɪŋ] *n*
1. sentiment *m*

...feel

I have a feeling somebody's watching us j'ai le sentiment que quelqu'un nous observe

2. sensation *f*
I had a feeling of cold j'ai eu une sensation de froid

feet

feet
[fi:t] → FOOT

fellow

fellow
['feləʊ] *n*
1. individu *m*

I wonder who that fellow can be je me demande qui est cet individu

2. camarade *m f*
schoolfellow camarade de classe

fence

fence
[fens] *n*
clôture *f*, barrière *f*

fetch

fetch
[fetʃ] *v t*
aller chercher

* *Go and fetch that bone, Snowy!...* Va chercher cet os, Milou !... *

...fetch

Go and fetch that bone, Snowy!...

fever

fever
['fi:vəʳ] *n*
fièvre *f*

Tintin is running a high fever Tintin a beaucoup de fièvre

few

few
[fju:]
I. *adj*
peu de

...few

* *I have very few clues in this case...* J'ai vraiment très peu d'indices dans cette affaire... *

II. *pron*
a few quelques

a few people quelques personnes

I have very few clues in this case...

field

field
[fi:ld] *n*
1. champ *m*

look, Captain, the plane is landing in the field! Regardez, capitaine, l'avion se pose dans le champ !

2. terrain *m*
football/rugby field terrain de football/de rugby

fifteen

fifteen
[fɪf'ti:n]
I. *adj*
quinze

II. *n*
quinze *m*

▸ **fifth**
[fɪfθ] *adj & n*
cinquième

▸ **fifty**
['fɪftɪ]
I. *adj*
cinquante

...fifteen

II. *n*
pl fifties
cinquante *m*

in the fifties dans les années cinquante

fight

fight
[faɪt]
I. *vi*
fought, fought [fɔːt]
se battre, lutter

...fight

II. *n*
bagarre *f*, lutte *f*

figure

figure
['fɪgəʳ] *n*
chiffre *m*

a three-figure number un nombre de trois chiffres

fill

fill
[fɪl] *vt*
remplir

* *Don't fill my glass!* Ne remplissez pas mon verre ! *

film

film *n*
[fɪlm]
(*Am:* **movie**)

...film

1. film *m*
they're watching a film ils regardent un film

2. pellicule *f*
I must buy a film for my camera il faut que j'achète une pellicule pour mon appareil photo

finally

finally
['faɪnəlɪ] *adv*
enfin, finalement

find

find
[faɪnd] *vt*
found, found [faʊnd]
trouver

I can't find my hat je ne trouve pas mon chapeau

...find

* *How did you find the film (Am: movie)?* Comment avez-vous trouvé le film ? *Most interesting!...* Très intéressant... ! *

fine

fine
['faɪn]
I. *adj*
1. beau

...fine

...fine

* *What a fine day!* Quelle belle journée ! *

the weather is fine il fait très beau

2. bien
how are you? – I'm fine, thank you comment allez-vous ? – très bien, merci

3. fin
this pen has a very fine point ce stylo a une pointe très fine

II. *n*
amende *f*

* *I'm sorry, you'll have to pay a fine.* Je suis désolé, mais vous devrez payer une amende. *

finger

finger
['fɪŋgəʳ] *n*
doigt *m*

...finger

I think I've broken my finger! je crois que je me suis cassé le doigt !

finish

finish
['fɪnɪʃ]
I. *vt*
finir, terminer

...finish

have you finished your homework? as-tu fini tes devoirs ?

II. *vi*
finir

call me when you've finished appelez-moi quand vous aurez fini

have you finished with the newspaper? as-tu fini de lire le journal ?

...finish

Snowy's finished up nearly all the sausages...

► **finish up**
Idiom

* *Snowy's finished up nearly all the sausages...* Milou a mangé presque toutes les saucisses... *

fire

fire
['faɪəʳ] *n*
1. feu *m*

...fire

they are sitting in front of the fire ils sont assis devant le feu

2. incendie *m*, feu *m*
the firemen are putting the fire out les pompiers éteignent l'incendie

* *The house is on fire.* La maison est en feu. *

the plane's caught fire! l'avion a pris feu !

The house is on fire.

► **fire engine** *n*
voiture *f* de pompiers

► **fireman**
['faɪəmæn] *n*
pl firemen
pompier *m*

► **fireplace**
['faɪəpleɪs] *n*
cheminée *f*

the fire is burning in the fireplace le feu brûle dans la cheminée

firm

firm
[fɜ:m]
I. *n*
firme *f*, entreprise *f*

he works for a large firm il travaille dans une grande entreprise

II. *adj*
ferme

the ground doesn't look very firm le sol n'a pas l'air très ferme

first

first
[fɜ:st]
I. *adj & n*
premier, première

it's the first time we've met c'est la première fois que nous nous rencontrons

Charles the First Charles Premier

the first of May (*Am: May first*) le premier mai

II. *adv*
1. d'abord

untie me first, then I'll explain détachez-moi d'abord, je vous expliquerai ensuite

2. pour la première fois
when did you first go to France? quand êtes-vous allé en France pour la première fois ?

fish

fish
[fɪʃ]
I. *n*
poisson *m*

II. *vi*
pêcher

I'm fishing for mackerel je pêche le maquereau

fit

fit
[fɪt]
fit, fit
I. *vt*
aller à

these shoes don't fit me! ces chaussures ne me vont pas !

II. *vi*
1. aller

take my shoes if they fit prends mes chaussures si elles te vont

...fit

2. tenir
we won't all fit in the lifeboat nous ne tiendrons pas tous dans le canot de sauvetage

III. *adj*
fitter, fittest
en forme

you have to be fit to climb this mountain pour escalader cette montagne, il faut être en forme

five

five
[faɪv]
I. *adj*
cinq

II. *n*
cinq *m*

fix

fix
[fɪks] *vt*
1. réparer

* *Well?* Alors ?
That's it!... The engine's fixed... Ça y est !... Le moteur est réparé... *

2. attacher, fixer
fix it to the post with string attachez-le au poteau avec de la ficelle

Well?
That's it!... The engine's fixed...

flag

flag
[flæg] *n*
drapeau *m*
pavillon *m*

look, a British flag! regarde, un drapeau britannique !

flame

flame
[fleɪm] *n*
flamme *f*

flash

flash
[flæʃ]
I. *n*

1. flash *m*
the photographer used a flash le photographe a utilisé un flash

2. Idiom
a flash of light une lueur

a flash of lightning un éclair

3. flashlight
(Am) → **torch**

II. *v i*
clignoter

* *Look over there, Captain!...* Regardez là-bas, capitaine !...
Yes, there's a light flashing... Oui, il y a une lumière qui clignote... *

flat

flat
[flæt]
I. *adj*
flatter, flattest
1. plat

the land is very flat le terrain est très plat

...flat

2. Idiom
we've got a flat tyre (Am: tire) nous avons crevé

the tyres are flat les pneus sont crevés

II. *n*
(*Am:* **apartment)**
appartement *m*

flavour

flavour
['fleɪvə^r] *n*
(*Am:* **flavor)**
1. goût *m*

this food has a strange flavour ce plat a un drôle de goût

2. parfum *m*
what flavour ice cream do you want? à quel parfum veux-tu ta glace ?

flight

flight
[flaɪt] *n*
1. vol *m*

flight 714 to Sydney le vol 714 pour Sydney

2. Idiom
a flight of stairs un escalier *m*

float

float
[fləʊt] *v i*
flotter

...float

The raft is floating on the sea.

...float

* *The raft is floating on the sea.* Le radeau flotte sur la mer. *

floor

floor
[flɔː^r] *n*
1. plancher *m*

I swept the floor j'ai balayé le plancher

2. étage *m*
* *Mr Tintin?* Monsieur Tintin ?

...floor

First floor (Am: second floor). Premier étage. *

3. Idiom
sit on the floor! asseyez-vous par terre !

flour

flour
['flaʊə^r] *n*
farine *f*

...flour

mix the eggs and flour mélangez les œufs et la farine

flower

flower
['flaʊə^r] *n*
fleur *f*

what pretty flowers! quelles jolies fleurs !

flu

flu
[fluː] *n*
grippe *f*

I've got the flu j'ai la grippe

fly

fly
[flaɪ]
I. *v i*
flew [fluː], flown [fləʊn]
voler

...fly

We're flying too low!...
It's true, wait, we're going to land...

* *We're flying too low!...* Nous volons trop bas !...
It's true, wait, we're going to land... C'est vrai, attendez, nous allons atterrir... *

2. Idiom
are you flying or going by train? est-ce que vous y allez en avion ou en train ?

II. *n*
pl flies
mouche *f*

fog

fog
[fɒg] *n*
brouillard *m*

the flight was delayed because of fog le vol a été retardé à cause du brouillard

► **foggy**
['fɒgɪ] *adj*
foggier, foggiest
1. brumeux

a foggy day une journée brumeuse

2. Idiom
it's foggy il y a du brouillard

I haven't the foggiest (idea) je n'en ai aucune idée

follow

follow
['fɒləʊ] *vt*
suivre

* *I have a feeling we're being followed...* J'ai l'impression que nous sommes suivis...
That's for sure, somebody's following us... C'est sûr, on nous suit... *

...follow

I have a feeling we're being followed...
That's for sure, somebody's following us...

fond

fond
[fɒnd] *adj*

Idiom
Captain Haddock is fond of whisky le capitaine Haddock aime le whisky

are you fond of dancing? aimez-vous danser ?

food

food
[fu:d] *n*
1. nourriture *f*

* *It's dog food.* C'est de la nourriture pour chiens. *

2. cuisine *f*
do you like French food? aimes-tu la cuisine française ?

It's dog food.

fool

fool
[fu:l] *n*
idiot *m*
idiote *f*

foot

foot
[fʊt] *n*
pl feet [fi:t]
1. pied *m*

* *Ouch, my foot!* Aïe ! mon pied ! *

he's got big feet il a de grands pieds

2. pied *m* (= 30,5 cm)
the room is ten feet long la pièce fait trois mètres de long

he's 6 foot tall il mesure 1,83 m

OUCH, my foot!

football

football
['fʊtbɔ:l] *n*
(*Am:* **soccer**)
1. football *m*

they're playing football ils jouent au football

a football match un match de football

2. ballon *m* de football
the boys are playing with a plastic football les garçons jouent avec un ballon en plastique

► **football ground**
n
terrain *m* de football

for

for
[fɒʳ]
I. *prep*
1. pour

what did you get for your birthday? qu'est-ce que tu as eu pour ton anniversaire ?

...for

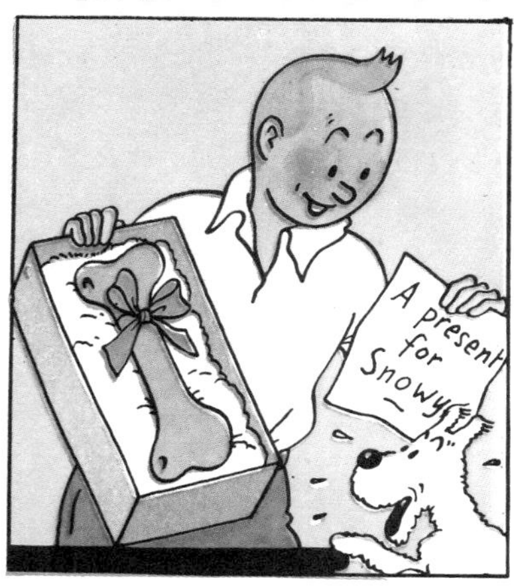

* *A present for Snowy.* Un cadeau pour Milou. *

2. depuis
he's been waiting for hours! il attend depuis des heures !

3. pendant
she lived in England for two years elle a habité en Angleterre pendant deux ans

4. Idiom
what's this lever for? à quoi sert ce levier ?

II. *conj*
car

I'm worried, for we've lost Snowy je suis inquiet, car nous avons perdu Milou

forbidden

forbidden
[fə'bɪdən] *adj*
interdit

it's forbidden to go any further il est interdit d'aller plus loin

smoking is forbidden il est interdit de fumer

forecast

forecast
['fɔ:kɑ:st]
I. *n*
1. prévision *f*

2. Idiom
* *The weather forecast, Captain!* La météo, capitaine ! *

II. *v*
prévoir

...forecast

foreground

foreground
['fɔ:graʊnd] *n*
premier plan *m*

* *Tintin is in the foreground.* Tintin est au premier plan. *

Tintin is in the foreground.

foreign

foreign
['fɒrən] *adj*
étranger

...foreign

foreign languages langues étrangères

► **foreigner**
['fɒrənə^r] *n*
étranger *m*
étrangère *f*

forest

forest
['fɒrɪst] *n*
forêt *f*

forget

forget
[fə'get] *vt*
forgot [fə'gɒt], forgotten [fə'gɒt(ə)n]
oublier

* *I've forgotten Snowy!* J'ai oublié Milou ! *

forgive

forgive
[fə'gɪv] *vt*

...forgive

forgave [fə'geɪv], forgiven [fə'gɪv(ə)n]
pardonner

* *I'm sorry, Tintin, won't you forgive me? Please, forgive me!* Je suis désolé, Tintin, pourrez-vous me pardonner ? Pardonnez-moi, je vous en prie !
That's all right! N'en parlons plus ! *

forgive me for being late pardonnez-moi d'être en retard

fork

fork
[fɔ:k] *n*
fourchette *f*

fortnight

fortnight
['fɔ:tnaɪt] *n*
deux semaines *f pl*
quinzaine *f* (de jours)

I'll be back in a fortnight je serai de retour

...fortnight

dans une quinzaine de jours

fortunately

fortunately
[ˈfɔ:tʃənɪtlɪ] *adv*
heureusement

fortunately you warned me! heureusement que tu m'as prévenu !

fortune

fortune
[ˈfɔ:tʃu:n] *n*
1. fortune *f*

it will cost a fortune cela va coûter une fortune

2. bonne aventure *f*
fortune teller diseuse de bonne aventure

she told his fortune elle lui a dit la bonne aventure

forty

forty
[ˈfɔ:tɪ]
I. *adj*
quarante

II. *n*
pl forties
quarante *m*

in the forties dans les années quarante

forward(s)

forward(s)
[ˈfɔ:wəd(z)] *adv*
1. en avant

forward, men! en avant, tous !

Tintin stepped forward Tintin a fait un pas en avant

2. Idiom
people were running backwards and forwards des gens couraient dans tous les sens

four

four
[ˈfɔ:ʳ]
I. *adj*
quatre

II. *n*
quatre *m*
* *Tintin is walking on all fours...* Tintin marche à quatre pattes... *

► **fourteen**
[fɔ:ˈti:n]
I. *adj*
quatorze

...four

Tintin is walking on all fours...

II. *n*
quatorze *m*

► **fourth**
[fɔ:θ] *adj & n*
quatrième

frame

frame
[freɪm] *n*
cadre *m*
* *The frame was too heavy and the picture fell down.* Le cadre était trop lourd et le tableau est tombé. *

...frame

The frame was too heavy and the picture fell down.

bicycle frame cadre de bicyclette

France

France
[frɑ:ns] *n*
France *f*

Pierre lives in France Pierre habite en France

...France

we went to France last summer nous sommes allés en France l'été dernier

France is a republic la France est une république

free

free
[fri:] *adj*
1. libre

...free

I'm not free tonight je ne suis pas libre ce soir

* *Never do that again!...* Ne fais plus jamais ça !...
You're free, Snowy... Are you better? Te voilà libre, Milou... Tu es content ? *

is this seat free? cette place est-elle libre ?

2. gratuit
two free toothbrushes with every alarm clock you buy! pour tout réveil acheté, deux brosses à dents gratuites !

Never do that again !...
You're free, Snowy... Are you better?

children are admitted free entrée gratuite pour les enfants

► **freedom**
[ˈfri:dəm] *n*
liberté *f*

* *Stranger! If you value your freedom... Make the sun shine again!* Etranger si tu

Stranger ! If you value your freedom... Make the sun shine again !

...free

tiens à ta liberté... Fais réapparaître le soleil ! *

freeze

freeze
[fri:z] *v i et v t*
froze [frəʊz], frozen ['frəʊz(ə)n]
geler

I'm freezing! je gèle !

the lake is frozen le lac est gelé

French

French
[frentʃ]
I. *adj*
français

Marie is French Marie est française

my French teacher mon professeur de français

French people Les Français

II. *n*
français *m*

do you speak French? parlez-vous français ?

► **Frenchman**
['frentʃmən] *n*
pl Frenchmen
Français *m*

the French les Français

► **Frenchwoman**
['frentʃwʊmən]
pl Frenchwomen
Française *f*

► **French fry**
(Am) → chip

frequent

frequent
['fri:kwənt] *adj*
fréquent

the train makes frequent stops le train fait des arrêts fréquents

► **frequently**
['fri:kwəntlɪ] *adv*
fréquemment

it frequently rains here il pleut fréquemment ici

fresh

fresh
[freʃ] *adj*
1. frais, fraîche

* *Look!* Regardez !
This crab isn't fresh! Ce crabe n'est pas frais !
But my crab is fresh, I promise you... Mais si, il est frais mon crabe, je vous assure... *

I need some fresh air j'ai besoin d'un peu d'air frais

...fresh

2. nouveau, nouvelle
give me a fresh piece of paper donnez-moi une nouvelle feuille de papier

Friday

Friday
['fraɪdɪ] *n*
vendredi

come and see me on Friday viens me voir vendredi

...Friday

they don't work on Fridays ils ne travaillent pas le vendredi

fridge

fridge [frɪdʒ]
(*Am:* refrigerator) *n*
frigo *m*, réfrigérateur *m*

the fridge is empty le frigo est vide

friend

...friend

friend
[frend] *n*
ami *m*, amie *f*

* *My dear Hercules, let me introduce you to two old friends of mine...* Mon cher Hippolyte, je vous présente deux de mes vieux amis...
Pleased to meet you, gentlemen... Enchanté, messieurs, enchanté !... *

he's my best friend c'est mon meilleur ami

he made friends with her il est devenu son ami

► **friendly**
['frendlɪ] *adj*
amical, amicale

they don't look very friendly! ils n'ont pas l'air très amicaux !

► **friendship**
['frendʃɪp] *n*
amitié *f*

frighten

frighten
['fraɪt(ə)n] *v t*
1. faire peur à, effrayer

oh, you frightened me! oh ! tu m'as fait peur !

2. Idiom
Snowy is frightened Milou a peur

from

from
[frɒm] *prep*
de

* *A telegram for you, Sir...* Un télégramme pour vous, Monsieur...
For me? Who can this telegram be from? Pour moi ? De qui peut être ce télégramme ? *

from London to Paris de Londres à Paris

where do you come from? d'où venez-vous ?

...from

he died from pneumonia il est mort de pneumonie

front

front
[frʌnt]
I. *n*
1. devant *m*

the front of the house le devant de la maison

...front

2. Idiom
in front of devant

II. *adj*
1. avant

the front seat le siège avant

* *Meanwhile...* Pendant ce temps...
Your front leg is broken, Snowy... Ta patte avant est cassée, Milou... *

Meanwhile ...
Your front leg is broken, Snowy...

2. premier
his photo was on the front page sa photo était en première page

frost

frost
[frɒst] *n*
1. givre *m*

there's frost on the windows il y a du givre sur les fenêtres

...frost

2. Idiom
there was a frost last night il a gelé cette nuit

► **frosty**
['frɒstɪ] *adj*
frostier, frostiest
gelé

fruit

fruit
[fru:t] *n*
fruit(s) *m (pl)*

...fruit

I've bought some fruit j'ai acheté des fruits

a piece of fruit un fruit

fruit juice/salade jus/salade de fruits

fry

fry
[fraɪ] *vt*
fried, fried
faire frire, frire

...fry

I'll fry the fish je ferai frire le poisson

fried potatoes (Am: french fries) pommes frites

fuel

fuel
[fjʊəl] *n*
carburant *m*

full

full
[fʊl]
plein *adj*

the cinema (Am: movie theater) is nearly full le cinéma est presque plein

* *At full moon...* A la pleine lune... *

At full moon ...

fun

fun
[fʌn] *n*
divertissement *m*

we had fun nous nous sommes amusés

this is fun! c'est amusant !

we did it for fun nous l'avons fait pour rire

don't make fun of Professor Calculus! ne vous moquez pas du professeur Tournesol !

...fun

That's funny, there's nobody here...

► **funny**
['fʌnɪ] *adj*
funnier, funniest
1. drôle, amusant

ha ha, that's very funny! hi ! hi ! c'est très drôle !

2. bizarre
* *That's funny, there's nobody here...* C'est bizarre, il n'y a personne... *

fur

fur
[fɜ:ʳ] *n*
fourrure *f*

what a nice fur coat! quel joli manteau de fourrure !

furious

furious
['fjʊərɪəs] *adj*
furieux

furniture

furniture
['fɜ:nɪtʃəʳ] *n*
meubles *m pl*

further

further, furthest
→ FAR

future

future
['fju:tʃəʳ] *n*
1. avenir

I promise I'll be more careful in future je promets qu'à l'avenir je ferai plus attention

2. futur
what is the future (tense) of this verb? quel est le futur de ce verbe ?

G

game

game
[geɪm] *n*
1. jeu *m*

it's only a game, Captain! ce n'est qu'un jeu, capitaine !

2. partie *f*
let's have a game of cards faisons une partie de cartes

3. gibier *m*
he's a big-game hunter c'est un chasseur de gros gibier

garage

garage
['gærɑ:(d)ʒ] *n*
garage *m*

garden

garden
['gɑ:d(ə)n] *n*
jardin *m*

* *What a lovely day!* Quelle belle journée !
In the garden... Dans le jardin... *

...garden

What a lovely day!
In the garden...

► **gardening**
['gɑ:dnɪŋ] *n*
jardinage *m*

gas

gas
[gæs] *n*
1. gaz *m*

I can smell gas! ça sent le gaz !

2. *Am:*
→ **petrol**

...gas

a gas cooker (Am: stove) une cuisinière à gaz

gate

gate
[geɪt] *n*
barrière *f*, grille *f*

* *The car has gone through the gate.* La voiture a franchi la grille. *

...gate

The car has gone through the gate.

gather

gather
['gæðəʳ]
I. *v t*
1. cueillir

they're gathering mushrooms ils cueillent des champignons

2. comprendre, déduire
I gather that you're leaving tomorrow? je crois comprendre que vous partez demain ?

3. prendre
the car's beginning to gather speed! la voiture commence à prendre de la vitesse !

II. *v i*
1. se rassembler, se réunir

* *Why have all those people gathered around that cow?...* Pourquoi tous ces gens se sont-ils rassemblés autour de cette vache ?... *

2. Idiom
gather round, ladies

Why have all those people gathered around that cow ?...

and gentlemen! approchez-vous, mesdames et messieurs !

general

general
['dʒenərəl]
I. *adj*
général

there was general panic ce fut la panique générale

II. *n*
général *m*

General Alcazar le général Alcazar

► **generally**
['dʒenrəlɪ] *adv*
généralement

gentle

gentle
['dʒent(ə)l] *adj*
doux

be gentle with the baby sois doux avec le bébé

► **gently**
['dʒentlɪ] *adv*
doucement

gentleman

gentleman
['dʒent(ə)lmæn] *n*
pl gentlemen
1. monsieur *m*

ladies and gentlemen! mesdames et messieurs !

who's that gentleman in a black hat? qui est ce monsieur au chapeau noir ?

2. gentleman *m*
he's a perfect gentleman c'est un vrai gentleman

geography

geography
[dʒɪ'ɒgrəfɪ] *n*
géographie *f*

geography is my favourite (Am: favorite) subject la géographie est ma matière préférée

a geography book un livre de géographie

get

get
[get]
got, got [gɒt]
I. *v t*
1. recevoir, avoir

I got a letter this morning j'ai reçu une lettre ce matin

he's going to get a surprise! il va avoir une surprise !

2. chercher
go and get the map allez chercher la carte

A-TISHOO !...
I'm getting the flu!

3. attraper
* *A-tishoo!... I'm getting the flu!* Atchoum !... je suis en train d'attraper la grippe ! *

4. faire
I got the Captain to help me je me suis fait aider par le capitaine

he should get his hair cut il devrait se faire couper les cheveux

5. réussir à, arriver à

On the ocean...

Have you got the radio repaired?
No!...

* *On the ocean...* Sur l'océan...
Have you got the radio repaired? Avez-vous réussi à réparer la radio ?
No!... Non !... *

I can't get these boots off je n'arrive pas à enlever ces bottes

6. comprendre
I don't get the joke je ne comprends pas cette plaisanterie

do you get it? tu comprends ?

II. *v i*
1. aller

how do you get to the castle from here? comment fait-on pour aller d'ici, au château ?

2. arriver
* *I hope I'll get there in time...* J'espère que je vais arriver à temps... *

3. devenir

I hope I'll get there in time...

I'm getting old je deviens vieux

* *Oh! The weather's getting stormy!...* Oh ! Le temps devient orageux !... *

4. Idiom
get ready! préparez-vous !

to get dressed s'habiller

► **to have got**
→ HAVE

BRROM
Oh! The weather's getting stormy!...

...get

► **get in**
1. monter

get in quick, we're leaving! monte vite (dans la voiture), nous partons !

2. arriver
what time does the train get in? à quelle heure arrive le train ?

► **get off**
descendre

he got off his bicycle il est descendu de son vélo

► **get on**
1. monter dans

quick, get on the bus! vite, montez dans l'autobus !

2. monter sur
she got on the bike/on the horse elle est montée sur le vélo/sur le cheval

3. aller
how are you getting on? comment allez-vous ?

4. s'entendre
I don't get on with the new boss je ne m'entends pas avec le nouveau patron

5. continuer
* *Get on with your work !... Blistering barnacles... Don't stop!* Mais, continuez vo-

...get

tre travail !... Mille sabords !... Ne vous arrêtez pas ! *

6. Idiom
to be getting on vieillir

I'm getting on, you know, Tintin je ne suis plus tout jeune, vous savez, Tintin

he's getting on for fifty il approche de la cinquantaine

► **get out**
1. sortir

* *Get out of here at once!* Sortez d'ici tout de suite ! *

get your exercise books out sortez vos cahiers

2. sortir, descendre
who's that getting out of plane? qui est en train de sortir de l'avion ?

► **get up**
se lever

get up, Captain! levez-vous capitaine !

he got up to offer her his seat il s'est levé pour lui offrir sa place

ghost

ghost
[gəʊst] *n*
fantôme *m*

gift

gift
[gɪft] *n*
1. cadeau *m*

there's a free gift in every packet (Am: package) chaque paquet contient un cadeau

2. don *m*
she has a gift for music elle a un don pour la musique

girl

girl
[gɜːl] *n*
fille *f*

they have two boys and a girl ils ont deux garçons et une fille

give

give
[gɪv] *vt*
gave [geɪv], given [ˈgɪv(ə)n]
donner

* *We're going to give this Tintin a good hiding...* Nous allons lui donner une bonne correction à ce Tintin...
Shh! Silence! Chut ! Silence ! *

...give

► **give up**
1. abandonner, laisser tomber

it's too difficult, I give up! c'est trop difficile, j'abandonne !

2. renoncer à, arrêter
* *Er... No thank you, Lieutenant... I've given up drinking whisky...* Heuh... non merci, lieutenant... J'ai arrêté de boire du whisky...

All right, I won't insist, then... Ah bon, je n'insiste pas alors !... *

glad

glad
[glæd] *adj*
gladder, gladdest
content, heureux

I'm glad to see you, Tintin! je suis content de te voir, Tintin !

glass

glass
[glɑ:s] *n*
verre *m*

have a glass of whisky, Captain prenez un verre de whisky, capitaine

the walls are made of glass les murs sont en verre

► **glasses** *n pl*
lunettes *f pl*

...glass

where are my glasses? où sont mes lunettes ?

glove

glove
[glʌv] *n*
gant *m*

put your gloves on, it's cold mets tes gants, il fait froid

go

go
[gəʊ]
went [went], gone [gɒn]
I. *vi*
1. aller

where are you going? où vas-tu ?

2. partir
it's late, I must be going il est tard, je dois partir

3. marcher
my watch isn't going ma montre ne marche pas

4. devenir
you've gone pale, Tintin vous êtes devenu pâle, Tintin

5. se passer
* *Hello gentlemen, how did your trip go?* Bonjour, messieurs, comment s'est passé votre voyage ?
Very well, thank you. Très bien, merci. *

I hope everything goes well j'espère que tout se passera bien

...go

6. Idiom
it's going to rain il va pleuvoir

he's going to cry il va pleurer

* *Tintin is going upstairs...* Tintin monte l'escalier... *

the cases won't all go into the car les valises n'entreront pas toutes dans la voiture

to go down descendre

Tintin is going upstairs...

to go up monter

to go across traverser

II. *n*
Idiom
it's my/your go c'est à moi/à toi de jouer

► **go away**
s'en aller

go away, I'm busy! va-t-en, je suis occupé !

► **go on**
1. continuer

go on with your work continuez votre travail

2. se passer
* *What's going on here?* Qu'est-ce qui se passe ici ?
I wonder!... Je me le demande !... *

► **go out**
1. sortir
I'm going out tonight je sors ce soir

he's going out with my sister il sort avec ma sœur

...go

What's going on here?
I wonder!...

2. s'éteindre
don't let the fire go out ne laisse pas le feu s'éteindre

► **go without**
se passer de

I had to go without my breakfast j'ai dû me passer de petit déjeuner

goal

goal
[gəʊl] *n*
but *m*

he scored a goal il a marqué un but

god

god
[gɒd] *n*
dieu *m*

do you believe in God? croyez-vous en Dieu ?

my God! mon Dieu !

gold

gold
[gəʊld] *n*
or *m*

is that a gold watch? est-ce que cette montre est en or ?

► **goldfish**
[ˈgəʊldfɪʃ] *n*
poisson *m* rouge

good

good
[gʊd]
I. *adj*
better, best
1. bon, bonne

this meal is very good! ce repas est très bon !

good morning, Captain! bonjour, capitaine !

good afternoon bonjour

good evening bonsoir

good night bonne nuit

2. fort, doué
he's very good at maths (Am: math) il est très fort en maths

3. sage
* *Be good, Snowy!* Sois sage, Milou ! *Woof! Woof!* Wouah ! Wouah ! *

II. *n*
1. bien *m*

Be good, Snowy!
Woof! Woof!

* *This tea's going to do me a lot of good...* Ce thé va me faire beaucoup de bien... *

2. Idiom
has he gone away for good? est-il parti pour de bon ?

► **goods** *n pl*
marchandises *f pl*

* *Have the goods been delivered?* Les marchandises ont-elles été livrées ?

This tea's going to do me a lot of good...

...good

I don't know. Ask the Captain... Je ne sais pas. Demandez au capitaine... *

a goods (Am: freight) train un train de marchandises

► **goodbye**
[gʊdˈbaɪ] *interj*
au revoir, adieu

say goodbye to Tintin! dites au revoir à Tintin !

Have the goods been delivered?
I don't know. Ask the Captain...

govern

govern
[ˈgʌvən] *vt*
gouverner

the man who governs this country l'homme qui gouverne ce pays

► **government**
[ˈgʌvənmənt] *n*
gouvernement *m*

grandchildren

grandchildren
[ˈgræntʃɪldrən] *n pl*
petits-enfants *m pl*

► **granddaughter**
[ˈgrændɔːtə^{r}] *n*
petite-fille *f*

► **grandfather**
[ˈgrænfɑːðə^{r}] *n*
grand-père *m*

► **grandmother**
[ˈgrænmʌðə^{r}] *n*
grand-mère *f*

...grandchildren

► **grandparents**
['grænpeərənts] *n pl*
grands-parents *m pl*

► **grandson**
['grænsʌn] *n*
petit-fils *m*

grape

grape
[greɪp] *n*
raisin *m*

...grape

a bunch of grapes une grappe de raisin

grapefruit

grapefruit
['greɪpfru:t] *n*
pamplemousse *m*

grass

grass
[grɑ:s] *n*
1. herbe *f*

I ought to cut the grass je devrais tondre l'herbe

2. pelouse *f*
keep off the grass pelouse interdite

grateful

grateful
['greɪtfʊl] *adj*
reconnaissant

* *Ah, Tintin! I'm very grateful to you for coming...* Ah, Tintin ! Je vous suis reconnaissant d'être venu... *

great

great
[greɪt] *adj*
1. grand, énorme

what's that great building? quel est cet énorme bâtiment ?

2. grand, important
Signora Castafiore is a great singer la Castafiore est une grande chanteuse

► **Great Britain** *n*
Grande-Bretagne *f*

green

green
[gri:n]
I. *adj*
vert

the Professor has turned green le professeur est devenu vert

we painted the door green nous avons peint la porte en vert

II. *n*
vert *m*

He's dressed in green.

* *He's dressed in green.* Il est habillé en vert. *

greengrocer

greengrocer
['gri:ngrəʊsəʳ]
(*Am:* **fruit-and-vegetable dealer**) *n*
marchand *m*, marchande *f* de fruits et légumes

...greengrocer

at the greengrocer's chez le marchand de fruits et légumes

greeting

greeting
['gri:tɪŋ] *n*
1. salut *m*

greetings, old friend! salut, vieux frère !

2. Idiom
birthday greetings bon anniversaire

grey

grey
[greɪ]
(*Am:* **gray**)
I. *adj*
gris

the sky is very grey le ciel est tout gris

II. *n*
gris *m*

he was dressed in grey il était habillé en gris

grocer

grocer
['grəʊsəʳ] *n*
épicier *m*, épicière *f*

at the grocer's chez l'épicier

grocer's shop épicerie *f*

ground

ground
[graʊnd] *n*
1. sol *m*, terre *f*

...ground

* *The milk has spilt on the ground...* Le lait s'est répandu sur le sol... *

let's sit on the ground asseyons-nous par terre

2. terrain *m*
a football/rugby ground (Am: field) un terrain de football/rugby

► **ground floor**
(*Am:* **first floor**) *n*
rez-de-chaussée *m*

The milk has spilt on the ground ...

group

group
[gruːp] *n*
1. groupe *m*

Tintin is in that group of men Tintin est parmi ce groupe d'hommes

2. groupe *m*
orchestre *m*
a pop group un groupe pop

grow

grow
[grəʊ]
grew [gruː], grown [grəʊn]
I. *vi*
1. pousser

* *Nothing grows in this desert!* Rien ne pousse dans ce désert ! *

2. grandir
hasn't your son grown! comme votre fils a grandi !

3. augmenter
their numbers are growing leur nombre augmente

4. devenir
the weather's growing colder and colder le temps devient de plus en plus froid

II. *vt*
cultiver

they grow cabbages is cultivent les choux

▶ **grow up**
grandir, devenir adulte

* *What do you want to be when you grow up? Que veux-tu faire quand tu seras grand ? *Reporter, sir.* Reporter, monsieur. *

...grow

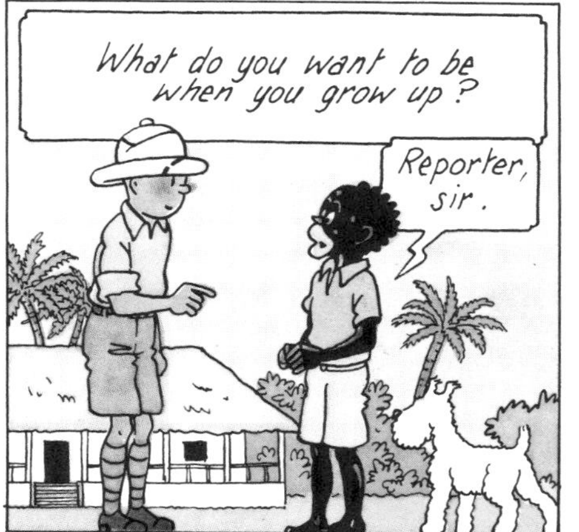

grown-up

grown-up
['grəʊnʌp]
I. *n*
adulte *m f*, grande personne *f*

the grown-ups are talking les grandes personnes sont en train de parler

II. *adj*
adulte

guess

guess
[ges] *vt*
deviner

* *And guess who I've invited? Signora Castafiore! Isn't that funny?...* Et devinez qui j'ai invité ? La Castafiore ! C'est drôle, non ?... *

guest

guest
[gest] *n*
invité *m*, invitée *f*, hôte *m f*

be polite to our guests! sois poli avec nos invités !

guilty

guilty
['gɪltɪ] *adj*
guiltier, guiltiest
coupable

I plead not guilty je plaide non coupable

gun

gun
[gʌn] *n*
1. pistolet *m*, revolver *m*, fusil *m*

2. Idiom
* *Look out, Captain, he's got a gun!* Faites attention, capitaine, il est armé !
Blistering barnacles! Mille sabords ! ! !... *

habit

habit
['hæbɪt] *n*
habitude *f*

I've got into the habit/out of the habit of watching television j'ai pris/j'ai perdu l'habitude de regarder la télévision

hair

hair
[heəʳ] *n*
1. cheveux *m pl*

* ***Well, we'll have to cut their hair then!...*** Eh, bien ! Il va falloir leur couper les cheveux !... *

he's having his hair cut il se fait couper les cheveux

2. cheveu *m*
there's a hair in my soup il y a un cheveu dans ma soupe

3. poil *m*
my coat is covered with dog hairs mon manteau est couvert de poils de chien

► **hairdresser** *n*
coiffeur *m*, coiffeuse *f*

half

half
[hɑ:f]
I. *n*
pl halves [hɑ:vz]
moitié *f*, demi *m*, demie *f*

I've read half of the book j'ai lu la moitié du livre

five and a half cinq et demi

cut the cake in half coupez le gâteau en deux

II. *adj*
demi

* ***Now watch... First I take half a glass of water... I say : half a glass...*** Et maintenant regardez bien... Je commence par prendre un demi-verre d'eau... Je dis bien : un demi... *

half an hour une demi-heure

III. *adv.*
1. à moitié

I'm half asleep je suis à moitié endormi

it's half past two/three il est deux/trois heures et demie

► **half term** *n*
vacances de milieu de trimestre

hall

hall
[hɔ:l] *n*
1. entrée *f*, hall *m*

leave your coats in the hall laissez vos manteaux dans l'entrée

2. salle *f*
a concert hall une salle de concerts

hallo

hallo → HELLO

ham

ham
[hæm] *n*
jambon *m*

a ham sandwich un sandwich au jambon

hand

hand
[hænd] *n*
1. main *f*

* *Hands up!* Haut les mains ! *

he shook hands with me il m'a serré la main

2. aiguille *f*
the hands of the clock les aiguilles de l'horloge

the hour/minute hand la petite/grande aiguille

3. Idiom
on the other hand d'autre part

I bought a second-hand car j'ai acheté une voiture d'occasion

handkerchief

handkerchief
['hæŋkətʃɪf] *n*
pl handkerchieves [-vz]
mouchoir *m*

hang

hang
[hæŋ]
hung, hung [hʌŋ]
I. *vt*
suspendre

hang your jacket in the wardrobe suspendez votre veste dans l'armoire

II. *vi*
pendre

pictures hang on the walls des tableaux pendent aux murs

happen

happen
['hæpən] *vi*
1. se passer, arriver, avoir lieu

what's happening? qu'est-ce qui se passe ?

when did the accident happen? quand l'accident a-t-il eu lieu ?

2. Idiom
I happened to be there je me suis trouvé là par hasard

would you happen to have a tin-opener (Am: can opener)? auriez-vous par hasard un ouvre-boîte ?

happy

happy
['hæpɪ] *adj*
happier, happiest
1. content, heureux

* *Hurray! I'm happy! Tintin has succeeded!* Hourra ! Je suis heureux ! Tintin a réussi !

...happy

2. joyeux
happy birthday! joyeux anniversaire !

▸ **happiness**
['hæpɪnɪs] *n*
bonheur *m*

harbour

harbour
['hɑ:bər] *n*
(*Am:* **harbor**)
port *m*

hard

hard
[hɑ:d]
I. *adj*
1. dur

this mattress is really hard! ce matelas est vraiment dur !

2. difficile, dur
his accent is hard to understand son accent est difficile à comprendre

II. *adv*
1. fort

knock hard! frappez fort !

2. Idiom
to work hard travailler beaucoup
you don't work hard enough tu ne travailles pas assez

to try hard faire un gros effort

▸ **hardly**
['hɑ:dlɪ] *adv*
à peine

* *Speak up, I can hardly hear you...* Parlez plus fort, je vous entends à peine... *

harm

harm
[hɑ:m] *n*
mal *m*

a little walk won't do us any harm une petite promenade ne nous fera pas de mal

hat

hat
[hæt] *n*
chapeau *m*

hate

hate
[heɪt] *vt*
détester

I hate getting up in the morning je déteste me lever le matin

have

have
[hæv]
had, had [hæd]
I. *vt*
1. avoir

she has a gold ring elle a une bague en or

* *I haven't any money...* Je n'ai pas d'argent... *

2. prendre
I have a shower every morning je prends une douche tous les matins

have you had your lunch? avez-vous pris votre déjeuner ?

II. *v aux*
1. avoir, être

have you heard the news? avez-vous entendu la nouvelle ?

Captain Haddock has arrived le capitaine Haddock est arrivé

2. faire
I must have my hair cut je dois me faire couper les cheveux

▸ **have got**
avoir

I haven't got any money je n'ai pas d'argent

▸ **have to**
have got to
devoir

...have

* *It's late, I have (got) to go.* Il est tard, je dois partir.
Goodbye. Au revoir. *

he

he
[hi:] *pron*
il

wherever is he? mais où est-il donc ?

head

head
[hed] *n*
1. tête *f*

* *Have you hurt your head?* Vous êtes-vous fait mal à la tête ?
Yes, a little... Un peu oui...
Just a little... Un tout petit peu... *

2. chef *m*
who's the head of this firm? qui est le chef de cette entreprise ?

3. directeur *m*,

directrice *f*
the head of the school le directeur de l'école

▸ **headache**
['hedeɪk] *n*
mal *m* de tête

I've got a headache j'ai mal à la tête

▸ **headmaster, headmistress**
[hed'mɑ:stəʳ, mɪstrɪs] *n*
directeur *m*, directrice *f*

health

health
[helθ] *n*
santé *f*

...health

▸ **healthy**
['helθɪ] *adj*
healthier, healthiest
en bonne santé

* *Snowy doesn't look very healthy, Doctor, what do you think?* Milou n'a pas l'air en très bonne santé, docteur, qu'en pensez-vous ?
Quite right, let's see... Oui, en effet... je vais voir... *

heap

heap
[hi:p] *n*
tas *m*

a heap of dirty clothes un tas de vêtements sales

hear

hear
[hɪəʳ] *vt*
heard, heard [hɜ:d]
1. entendre

...hear

* *Speak up, I can't hear you!...* Parlez plus fort, je ne vous entends pas !... *

2. entendre dire, apprendre
I hear Signora Castafiore is giving a concert here j'apprends que la Castafiore donne un concert ici

heart

heart
[hɑ:t] *n*
1. cœur *m*

his heart is very slow son cœur bat très faiblement

the five of hearts le cinq de cœur

2. cœur *m*, centre *m*
in the heart of the forest au cœur de la forêt

3. Idiom
to learn a poem by heart apprendre un poème par cœur

his heart isn't in it il n'a pas le cœur à ça

heat

heat
[hi:t]
I. *n*
chaleur *f*

* *Poor old Snowy, you can't stand this heat... The flower is thirsty too...* Mon pauvre Milou, tu ne supportes pas cette chaleur... La fleur aussi a soif... *

...heat

II. *vt*
chauffer, faire chauffer

I'll heat some soup je ferai chauffer de la soupe

brr! is this house heated? brr ! cette maison est-elle chauffée ?

► **heating**
['hi:tɪŋ] *n*
chauffage *m*

central heating chauffage central

heavy

heavy
['hevɪ] *adj*
heavier, heaviest
1. lourd

oh! it's really heavy! oh ! c'est vraiment lourd !

2. fort, gros
a heavy shower une grosse averse

hello

hello
[hə'ləʊ] *interj*
bonjour, allô

hello, Tintin, how are you? I am delighted to see you again! bonjour Tintin, comment allez-vous ? je suis ravi de vous revoir !

help

help
[help]
I. *vt*
1. aider

* *Help me open this box...* Aidez-moi à ouvrir cette boîte... *

2. s'empêcher
they couldn't help laughing ils n'ont pas pu s'empêcher de rire

3. Idiom
to help oneself se servir

...help

help yourself to vegetables servez-vous de légumes

II. *interj*
au secours

help! au secours !

► **helpless**
['helplɪs] *adj*
1. désemparé

2. Idiom
* *Chuff Chuff Chuff Chuff* Tchouk Tchouk Tchouk Tchouk

They've tied Tintin up: he's helpless... Ils ont ligoté Tintin, il ne peut rien faire... *

her

her
[hɜ:ʳ]
I. *pron*
1. la

they're going to kill her ils vont la tuer

CHUFF CHUFF CHUFF CHUFF

They've tied Tintin up: he's helpless...

...her

2. lui
give her a book donnez-lui un livre

II. *adj*
1. son, sa, ses

she came with her brother/her sister/her parents elle est venue avec son frère/sa sœur/ses parents

2. le, la, les
she's washing her face elle se lave le visage

► **hers**
[hɜ:z] *pron*
1. le sien, la sienne, les siens, les siennes, à elle

my car's faster than hers ma voiture est plus rapide que la sienne

that book is hers ce livre est à elle

2. Idiom
a friend of hers un de ses amis

...her

▸ **herself**
[hɜːˈself] *pron*
1. se

she is looking at herself in the mirror elle se regarde dans la glace

2. elle-même
she says she can do it herself elle dit qu'elle peut le faire elle-même

3. Idiom
(all) by herself toute seule

here

here
[hɪəʳ] *adv*
1. ici

* *Oh! I thought I'd put my pen down here...* Tiens ! Je croyais que j'avais posé mon stylo ici... *

Oh! I thought I'd put my pen down here...

2. Idiom
here is/are voici

here I am! me voici !

here you are! tenez !

can I borrow your pen? – yes, here you are puis-je emprunter votre stylo ? – oui, tenez

hero

hero
[ˈhɪərəʊ] *n*
pl heroes
héros *m*

hi

hi
[haɪ] *interj*
salut, bonjour

hi, old chum, how are you? salut, mon vieux comment vas-tu ?

hide

hide
[haɪd]
hid [hɪd], hidden [ˈhɪd(ə)n]

...hide

I. *vt*
cacher

where have they hidden the treasure? où ont-ils caché le trésor ?

II. *vi*
se cacher

* *Quick, hide behind the trees...* Vite, cachez-vous derrière les arbres... *

Quick, hide behind the trees...

Idiom
hide-and-seek cache-cache *m inv*

high

high
[haɪ]
I. *adj*
1. haut

2. élevé
the price is too high for me le prix est trop élevé pour moi

II. *adv*
haut

the plane is flying very high l'avion vole très haut

hill

hill
[hɪl] *n*
colline *f*

the village is up a hill le village est en haut d'une colline

him

Where's Tintin? I can't see him!

him
[hɪm] *pron*
1. le

* *Where's Tintin? I can't see him!* Où est Tintin ? Je ne le vois pas ! *

2. lui
throw him this rope jetez-lui cette corde

▸ **himself**
[hɪmˈself] *pron*
1. se

* *The Professor must have hurt himself!...* Le professeur a dû se faire mal !... *

2. lui-même
he wants to do it himself il veut le faire lui-même

3. Idiom
(all) by himself tout seul

The Professor must have hurt himself!...

hire

hire
['haɪəʳ]
(*Am:* **to rent)**
I. *vt*
louer

I'd like to hire a car, please j'aimerais louer une voiture, s'il vous plaît

II. *n*
1. location *f*

a car-hire (Am: car-rental) firm une firme de location de voitures

2. Idiom
for hire à louer

his

his
[hɪz]
I. *adj*
1. son, sa, ses

he came with his brother/his sister/ his parents il est venu avec son frère/sa sœur/ ses parents

...his

2. le, la, les
* *A few moments later...* Quelques instants plus tard...
Hurray! He's opening his eyes!... Victoire ! Il ouvre les yeux !... *

II. *pron*
1. le sien, la sienne, les siens, les siennes, à lui

your jacket is like his ta veste est comme la sienne
that book is his ce livre est à lui

...his

2. Idiom
a friend of his un de ses amis

history

history
['hɪstərɪ] *n*
histoire *f*

we study history at school nous étudions l'histoire à l'école

hit

hit
[hɪt] *vt*
hit, hit
1. frapper

he's hitting Snowy il frappe Milou

2. heurter
the car hit a tree la voiture a heurté un arbre

3. toucher
I've been hit by a bullet j'ai été touché par une balle

hobby

hobby
['hɒbɪ] *n*
pl hobbies ['həbɪz]
passe-temps *m*

hold

hold
[həʊld] *vt*
held, held [held]
1. tenir

hold the rail tenez la rampe

...hold

they are holding hands ils se tiennent par la main

* *Hold tight, Captain hold tight!* Tenez bon, capitaine, tenez bon ! *

2. contenir
the tank holds fifty litres (*Am: liters*) le réservoir contient cinquante litres

3. tenir, organiser
they're holding a meeting ils tiennent une réunion

...hold

► **hold on**
1. tenir bon

hold on Captain I'll throw you a rope! tenez bon, capitaine, je vous lance une corde !

2. attendre
hold on while I get my coat attendez un instant, je vais chercher mon manteau

3. ne pas quitter
* *Meanwhile...* Pendant ce temps...

Hello! Mr Tintin?... Hold on, I'll fetch him... Allô ! M. Tintin ?... Ne quittez pas, je vais le chercher... *

hole

hole
[həʊl] *n*
trou *m*

you've got a hole in your trousers (*Am:*

...hole

pants) vous avez un trou à votre pantalon

holiday

holiday
['hɒlɪdeɪ]
(*Am:* **vacation)**
vacances *f pl*

it's nice to be on holiday! c'est bien d'être en vacances !

...holiday

where did you go on holiday? où avez-vous passé vos vacances ?

the school holidays les vacances scolaires

home

home
[həʊm]
I. *n*
1. maison *f*

this is Marlinspike, my home voici Moulinsart, ma maison

at home à la maison

2. maison *f*, institution *f*
an old people's home une maison de retraite

3. Idiom
make yourself at home faites comme chez vous

II. *adv*
chez soi, à la maison

I want to go home je veux rentrer chez moi

► **homework**
['həʊmwɜ:k] *n*
devoirs *m pl*

honest

honest
['ɒnɪst] *adj*
honnête

honey

honey
['hʌnɪ] *n*
miel *m*

hope

hope
[həʊp] *vt*
espérer

* *I hope that with this disguise I won't be recognized...* J'espère qu'avec ce déguisement, on ne me reconnaîtra pas... *

is the Professor coming? – I hope so/ I hope not est-ce que le professeur vient ? – je l'espère/j'espère que non

I hope that with this disguise I won't be recognized...

horrible

horrible
['hɒrɪbl] *adj*
horrible, affreux

a horrible monster un monstre horrible

horrid

horrid
['hɒrɪd] *adj*
affreux, horrible

what horrid weather! quel temps affreux !

horse

horse
[hɔ:s] *n*
cheval *m*

to ride a horse monter à cheval

hospital

hospital
['hɒspɪt(ə)l] *n*
hôpital *m*

he's in hospital (*Am: in the hospital*) il est à l'hôpital

hot

hot
[hɒt] *adj*
hotter, hottest
chaud

* *It's ever so hot today!...* Qu'est-ce qu'il fait chaud aujourd'hui !... *

I'm hot! j'ai chaud !

ouch! the water's too hot! aïe ! l'eau est trop chaude !

It's ever so hot today!...

hotel

hotel
[həʊ'tel] *n*
hôtel *m*

hour

hour
['aʊəʳ] *n*
heure *f*

* *Tintin's been waiting for hours...* Tintin attend depuis des heures... *

...hour

Tintin's been waiting for hours...

house

house
[haʊs] *n*
maison *f*

* *Look what's happened to my house...* Regardez ce qu'est devenue ma maison... *

Look what's happened to my house...
!

how

how
[haʊ] *adv*
1. comment

...how

how can we get over the river? comment pourrons-nous franchir la rivière ?

2. comme
how cold it is! comme il fait froid!
how interesting! comme c'est intéressant !

3. Idiom
how are you? comment allez-vous ?

...how

how do you do? bonjour !

how big is the room? quelles sont les dimensions de la pièce ?

how far is it to Moscow? combien y a-t-il de kilomètres jusqu'à Moscou ?

how long have you been waiting? depuis combien de temps attendez-vous ?

how many people? combien de personnes ?

how much money? combien d'argent ?

► **however**
[haʊ'evəʳ]
I. *adv*
1. si... que

I'm not afraid of you yeti however big you are! je n'ai pas peur de toi yéti si grand que tu sois !

2. Idiom
however hard I tried I couldn't do it j'ai eu beau essayer, je n'ai pas pu le faire

however did they do it? comment ont-ils bien pu faire ça ?

II. *conj*
pourtant, cependant, toutefois

I don't think it'll work, however I'll try je ne pense pas que ça marchera, pourtant je vais essayer

huge

huge
[hju:dʒ] *adj*
énorme

* *Oh dear, what a huge shark!... It's going to catch me!...* Oh, quel énorme requin !... Il va m'attraper !... *

hullo

hullo → HELLO

human

human
['hju:mən] *adj*
humain

a human being un être humain

human nature la nature humaine

humour

humour
['hju:məʳ] *n*
(*Am:* humor)

...humour

humour *m*

he's got no sense of humour il n'a aucun humour

hundred

hundred
['hʌndrəd]
I. *adj*
cent

a hundred pounds cent livres

...hundred

II. *n*
centaine *f*

hundreds of spectators des centaines de spectateurs

hungry

hungry
['hʌŋgrɪ] *adj*
hungrier, hungriest
Idiom

* *Snowy is hungry.* Milou a faim. *

...hungry

Snowy is hungry.

hunt

hunt
[hʌnt]
I. *vt*
chasser

are you enjoying hunting lions with me? Es-tu content de chasser les lions avec moi ?

II. *vi*
chercher

I've hunted everywhere, but I can't find it! j'ai cherché partout, mais je ne le trouve pas !

...hunt

he's hunting for his pen il cherche son stylo

hurry

hurry
['hʌrɪ]
I. *vi*
hurried, hurried
se presser, se dépêcher

we'll have to hurry or we'll miss the plane il faut nous dépêcher ou nous allons manquer l'avion

II. *n*
1. hâte *f*, précipitation *f*

what's all the hurry? pourquoi toute cette précipitation ?

2. Idiom
to be in a hurry être pressé

► **hurry up**
se dépêcher

...hurry

* *Hurry up!* Dépêchez-vous ! *

hurt

hurt
[hɜ:t]
hurt, hurt
I. *vt*
faire mal à, blesser

Snowy's hurt his paw Milou s'est fait mal à la patte

...hurt

are you hurt? êtes-vous blessé ?

II. *vi*
faire mal

don't do that, it hurts! ne faites pas ça, ça fait mal !

husband

husband
['hʌzbənd] *n*
mari *m*

I

I
[aɪ] *pron*
je, j'

I want je veux

I love j'aime

ice

ice
[aɪs] *n*
glace *f*

...ice

** Oh, dear!... I must be careful not to slip on the ice. It's very...* Oh là là ! !... Il faut que je fasse attention à ne pas glisser sur la glace ! C'est très...
... dangerous!... dangereux... ! *

▸ **ice cream**
[aɪskrɪːm] *n*
glace *f*

I like strawberry ice cream j'aime la glace à la fraise

idea

idea
[aɪ'dɪə] *n*
idée *f*

** Great snakes! A leopard!... Oh, I've got an idea!...* Sapristi ! Un léopard !... Oh, j'ai une idée !...
What a horrible animal!... Quelle horrible bête !... *

...idea

if

if
[ɪf] *conj*
si

if I'm not back in an hour, carry on without me si je ne suis pas de retour dans une heure, continuez sans moi

ill

ill
[ɪl] *adj*
malade

you look ill vous avez l'air malade

▸ **illness**
['ɪlnɪs] *n*
maladie *f*

illustrated

illustrated
['ɪləstreɪtəd] *adj*
illustré

* *This illustrated dictionary is really remarkable!...* Ce dictionnaire illustré est vraiment remarquable !... *

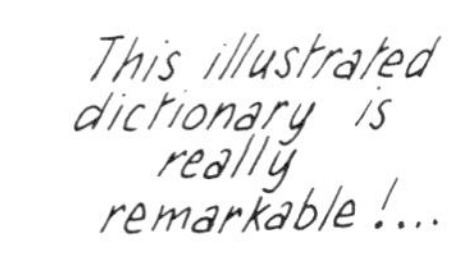

imagine

imagine
[ɪ'mædʒɪn] *vt*
imaginer, s'imaginer

try to imagine the scene essayez d'imaginer la scène

► **imagination**
[ɪmædʒɪ'neɪʃ(ə)n] *n*
imagination *f*

imitate

...imitate

imitate
['ɪmɪteɪt] *vt*
imiter

* *Stop imitating me, you wretched creature.* Arrête de m'imiter, sale bête.
Stop imitating me, you wretched creature. Arrête de m'imiter, sale bête. *

immediate

immediate
[ɪ'mi:dɪət] *adj*
immédiat

► **immediately**
[ɪ'mi:dɪətlɪ] *adv*
immédiatement, tout de suite

* *Captain, you must come immediately!... yes... yes... immediately...* Capitaine, il faut que vous veniez immédiatement !... oui... oui... immédiatement... *

immigrant

immigrant
['ɪmɪgrənt] *n*
immigré *m*, immigrée *f*

impatient

impatient
[ɪm'peɪʃ(ə)nt] *adj*
impatient

I'm impatient to leave je suis impatient de partir

important

important
[ɪm'pɔ:tənt] *adj*
important

I must talk to you, Mr Tintin, it's very important je dois vous parler, M. Tintin, c'est très important

impossible

impossible
[ɪm'pɒsəb(ə)l] *adj*
impossible

* *It's impossible to go any further... We are stuck in the seaweed...* C'est impossible de continuer... Nous sommes bloqués par les algues... *

impressive

impressive
[ɪm'presɪv] *adj*
impressionnant

* *Oh!... What an impressive sight!* Oh !... Quel spectacle impressionnant ! *

improve

improve
[ɪm'pru:v]
I. *vi*
s'améliorer

...improve

* *I hope the weather will improve, otherwise...* J'espère que le temps va s'améliorer, sinon... *

II. *vt*
améliorer

exercises to improve your spelling des exercices pour améliorer votre orthographe

► **improvement**
[ɪm'pru:vmənt] *n*
amélioration *f*

I hope the weather will improve, otherwise...

in

in
[ɪn]
I. *prep*
1. dans

what's in that crate? qu'y a-t-il dans cette caisse ?

put it in your pocket mettez-le dans votre poche

2. en, à, au, aux
in England/France en Angleterre/France

in Portugal au Portugal

in the United States aux États-Unis

in London/Paris à Londres/Paris

3. dans, en
I'll be back in five minutes je serai de retour dans cinq minutes

in 1989 en 1989

4. en
who's that woman dressed in green? qui est cette femme habillée en vert ?

II. *adv*
1. à l'intérieur, dedans

* *He opened the door and looked in.* Il a ouvert la porte et regardé à l'intérieur. *

2. à la maison
good morning, is Tintin in? bonjour, est-ce que Tintin est à la maison ?

3. à la mode
hats are in this year les chapeaux sont à la mode cette année

...in

?
He opened the door and looked in.

inch

inch
[ɪntʃ] *n*
pl inches ['inʃɪz]
pouce *m* (= 2,54 cm)

it's about six inches long c'est long d'à peu près quinze centimètres

twelve inches make one foot douze pouces font un pied

increase

increase
[ɪn'kri:s]
I. *vt*
augmenter

they've increased the price ils ont augmenté le prix

II. *vi*
* *The temperature's increasing!... I can't stand it any more...* La température augmente !... Je n'en peux plus !... *

The temperature's increasing!... I can't stand it any more...

III. ['ɪnkri:s] *n*
1. augmentation *f*

an increase in salaries une augmentation des salaires

2. Idiom
on the increase en hausse

indeed

indeed
[ɪn'di:d] *adv*
1. vraiment, en effet

* *I'm very tired indeed!... I just can't get up!...* Je suis vraiment très fatigué... Je n'arrive pas à me lever... *

2. Idiom
yes indeed! oui, bien sûr !

thank you very much indeed merci mille fois

I'm very tired indeed!... I just can't get up!...

independent

independent
[ɪndɪ'pendənt] *adj*
indépendant

Indian

Indian
['ɪndɪən]
I. *n*
Indien *m*, Indienne *f*

II. *adj*
indien *m*, indienne *f*

industry

industry
['ɪndəstrɪ] *n*
pl industries
['ɪndəstrɪz]
industrie *f*

influence

influence
['ɪnflʊəns] *n*
influence *f*

I'll try to use my

...influence

influence with the police j'essaierai d'utiliser mon influence auprès de la police

inform

inform
[ɪn'fɔ:m] *vt*
informer, avertir

we ought to inform the police nous devrions avertir la police

...inform

► **information**
[ɪnfə'meɪʃ(ə)n] *n*
information *f*, renseignement *m*

I'd like some information about flight times, please je voudrais un renseignement sur les horaires des vols, s'il vous plaît

inhabitant

inhabitant
[ɪn'hæbɪtənt] *n*
habitant *m*, habitante *f*

injure

injure
['ɪndʒəʳ] *vt*
blesser

* *Captain, are you injured?* Capitaine, êtes-vous blessé ? *

...injure

inn

inn
[ɪn] *n*
auberge *f*

let's have lunch at this inn déjeunons dans cette auberge

inquire

inquire
[ɪn'kwaɪəʳ] *vi*
1. se renseigner

you'll have to inquire about train times at the next station il faudra vous renseigner sur les horaires des trains à la prochaine gare

2. demander
"is everything all right?" she inquired « est-ce que tout va bien ? », demanda-t-elle

► **inquiry**
[ɪn'kwaɪrɪ] *n*
pl inquiries
1. demande *f* de renseignements

we've already received several inquiries nous avons déjà reçu plusieurs demandes de renseignements

2. Idiom
to make inquiries faire une enquête

inside

inside
[ɪn'saɪd]
I. *adv*
à l'intérieur, dedans

* *Come inside, it's cold out there! We're coming...* Venez à l'intérieur, il fait froid dehors ! Nous arrivons... *

II. *prep*
dans, à l'intérieur de

there was nothing inside the envelope il n'y avait rien à l'intérieur de l'enveloppe

III. *n*
intérieur *m*

the inside of the house l'intérieur de la maison

insist

insist
[ɪn'sɪst] *vi*
insister

the Thompsons insisted on coming with us les Dupondt ont insisté pour venir avec nous

instead

instead
[ɪn'sted] *adv*
1. plutôt

...instead

there is no tea, would you like coffee instead? il n'y a pas de thé, aimeriez-vous plutôt du café ?

2. à ma / ta / sa / notre / votre / leur place
if you don't want to go, I'll go instead si vous ne voulez pas y aller, j'irai à votre place

3. Idiom
instead of me à ma place

instead of au lieu de

* *Thundering typhoons! What are you doing there, instead of pumping?* Tonnerre de Brest ! Que faites-vous là au lieu de pomper ?
Us? We're resting... it's tiring work, you know... Nous ? On se repose... c'est fatigant, vous savez... *

intelligent

intelligent
[ɪn'telidʒənt] *adj*
intelligent

Snowy is a very intelligent dog Milou est un chien très intelligent

intend

intend
[ɪn'tend] *v i*
avoir l'intention

* *What do you intend to do now, Captain?* Qu'avez-vous l'intention de faire maintenant, capitaine ?
I don't know... Je ne sais pas... *

interest

interest
['ɪnt(ə)rɪst]
I. *v t*
intéresser

this film doesn't interest me ce film ne m'intéresse pas

II. *n*
1. intérêt *m*

his interests are reading and sports la lecture et le sport sont ses centres d'intérêt

2. Idiom
to take an interest in s'intéresser à

he takes no interest in what I do il ne s'intéresse pas à ce que je fais

► **interested**
['ɪnt(ə)restɪd] *adj*
intéressé

are you interested in football? est-ce que tu t'intéresses au football ?

...interest

► **interesting**
['ɪnt(ə)rɪstɪŋ] *adj*
intéressant

* *This is an interesting case...* Voilà une affaire intéressante...
To be precise: very interesting... Je dirais même plus : très intéressante... *

into

into
['ɪntu:] *prep*
1. dans

* *Follow me. Let's go into the Professor's laboratory...* Suivez-moi. Entrons dans le laboratoire du professeur... *

2. en
he cut the cake into four pieces il a coupé le gâteau en quatre

tadpoles change into frogs les têtards se changent en grenouilles

introduce

introduce
[ɪntrə'dju:s] *v t*
présenter

* *Let me introduce you to Captain Haddock...* Permettez-moi de vous présenter le capitaine Haddock...
How do you do, Captain. Enchanté, capitaine. *

invent

invent
[ɪn'vent] *v t*
inventer

► **invention**
[ɪn'venʃ(ə)n] *n*
invention *f*

* *And this is my latest invention...* Et voici ma dernière invention... *

invisible ...invite ...Ireland

invisible

invisible
[ɪn'vɪzəb(ə)l] *adj*
invisible

invite

invite
[ɪn'vaɪt] *vt*
inviter

* *Thank you for inviting us to dinner!* Je vous remercie de nous avoir invités à dîner !

... Cheers! ... A votre santé !
... Cheers! ... A votre santé ! *

► **invitation**
[ɪnvɪ'teɪʃ(ə)n] *n*
invitation *f*

Ireland

Ireland
['aɪələnd] *n*
Irlande *f*

► **Irish**
['aɪrɪʃ]
I. *n*
irlandais *m*

do you speak Irish? parlez-vous l'irlandais ?

II. *adj*
irlandais

► **Irishman, Irishwoman**
['aɪəriʃmæn, 'aɪəriʃwumən] *n*
pl Irishmen, Irishwomen
['aɪəriʃmen, 'aɪəriʃwɪmɪn]
Irlandais *m*, Irlandaise *f*

the Irish les Irlandais

iron ...island

iron

iron
['aɪən] *n*
1. fer *m*

the bridge is made of iron le pont est en fer

an iron bar une barre de fer

* *Take this iron bar to open the chest...* Prenez cette barre de fer pour ouvrir le coffre... *

2. fer *m* à repasser
the iron's too hot, it's burnt my shirt le fer à repasser est trop chaud, il a brûlé ma chemise

island

island
['aɪlənd] *n*
île *f*

* *There's Black Island...* Voici l'Ile Noire... *

it

it
[ɪt] *pron*
1. il, elle

where's my umbrella? – it's in the hall où est mon parapluie ? – il est dans l'entrée

where's your car? – it's at the garage où est votre voiture ? – elle est au garage

2. le, la
where's my umbrella? – I can't see it où est mon parapluie ? – je ne le vois pas

where's your car? – I've taken it to the garage où est votre voiture ? – je l'ai mise au garage

3. il
it's raining/snowing il pleut/neige

* *It's eleven o'clock.* Il est onze heures. *

It's eleven o'clock.

it's hot/cold out today il fait chaud/froid dehors aujourd'hui

4. ce, cela
it's very difficult c'est très difficile

► **its**
[ɪts] *adj*
son, sa, ses

the dog has lost its bone le chien a perdu son os

► **itself**
[ɪt'self] *pron*
1. se

the cat is washing itself le chat se lave

2. lui-même, elle-même
there's nothing wrong with the motor itself le moteur lui-même n'a rien

3. Idiom
(all) by itself tout seul

jacket

jacket
['dʒækɪt] *n*
veste *f*

jam

jam
[dʒæm] *n*
1. confiture *f*

2. Idiom
traffic jam embouteillage *m*

January

January
['dʒænjʊərɪ] *n*
janvier *m*

the first/second of January (Am: January first/second) le premier/deux janvier

come on the 20th of January (Am: on January 20) venez le 20 janvier

jar

jar
[dʒɑːʳ] *n*
bocal *m,* pot *m*

jet

jet, jet plane
[dʒet], ['dʒetpleɪn] *n*
avion *m* à réaction

I've never flown a jet je n'ai jamais piloté un avion à réaction

jewel

jewel
['dʒuːəl] *n*
bijou *m*

► **jewellery** (*Am:* **jewelry)**
['dʒuːəlrɪ] *n*
bijoux *m pl*

job

job
[dʒɒb] *n*
1. travail *m,* tâche *f*

...job

have you got any jobs you want doing? avez-vous des travaux à faire ?

2. emploi *m,* poste *m*
she's got a job in a bank elle a un emploi dans une banque

3. Idiom
* *I had a job to find the house.* J'ai eu du mal à trouver la maison. *

it's a good job Tintin was there! heureusement que Tintin était là !

...job

I had a job to find the house.

join

join
[dʒɔɪn] *vt*
1. relier, joindre

* *Once I've joined these two wires the radio will work...* Une fois que j'aurai relié ces deux fils, la radio fonctionnera... *

2. adhérer à
he wants to join the club il veut adhérer au club

Once I've joined these two wires the radio will work...

3. s'engager dans
to join the army s'engager dans l'armée

joke

joke
[dʒəʊk]
I. *n*
1. plaisanterie *f,* blague *f*

* *Ha! Ha! Ha! Ha!... Really, Calculus, your*

...joke

jokes are as funny as ever... Ha Ha! Ha! Ha! They are!... Ha! Ha! Ha Ha!... Ha ! Ha ! Ha Ha ! Vraiment, Tournesol, vos plaisanteries sont toujours aussi drôles... Ha Ha ! Ha ! Ha ! Vraiment !... Ha ! Ha Ha ! Ha !... *

...joke

2. farce *f*
let's play a joke on the Captain! faisons une farce au capitaine !

II. *vi*
plaisanter

don't worry, I was only joking ne vous inquiétez pas, je plaisantais

journalist

journalist
['dʒɜːnəlɪst] *n*
journaliste *m f*

journey

journey
['dʒɜːnɪ] *n*
voyage *m*

* ***Well, Cuthbert, are you going on a journey?*** Eh bien, Tryphon, vous partez en voyage ?

...journey

...journey

No, I'm not, I'm going on a journey. Non, non, je pars en voyage. *

judge

judge
[dʒʌdʒ]
I. *n*
juge *m*

II. *vt*
juger

...judge

she's judging the competition c'est elle qui juge le concours

July

July
[dʒuː'laɪ] *n*
juillet *m*

the first/second of July (Am: July first/second) le premier/deux juillet

...July

come on the 10th of July (Am: on July 10) venez le 10 juillet

jump

jump
[dʒʌmp]
I. *vi*
1. sauter

* ***Woooah!*** Wouah! ***That's it, he's jumped out of the aeroplane (Am: airplane). I hope his parachute will open!...*** Ça y est, il a sauté de l'avion. J'espère que son parachute va s'ouvrir !... *

...jump

2. sursauter
oh, it's you! you made me jump! oh, c'est vous ! vous m'avez fait sursauter !

3. Idiom
to jump the queue (Am: line) passer avant son tour

II. *n*
saut *m*

long/high jump saut en longueur/en hauteur

▸ **jumper (*Am:* sweater)** ['dʒʌmpəʳ] *n*
pull-over *m*, pull *m*

June

June
[dʒuːn] *n*
juin

...June

the first/second of June (Am: June first/second) le premier/deux juin

come on the 10th of June (Am: on June 10) venez le 10 juin

junior

junior
['dʒuːnɪəʳ] *adj*
1. cadet, junior

...junior

William Brown, Junior William Brown junior

2. primaire
junior (Am: primary) school école primaire

just

just
[dʒʌst] *adv*
1. juste

...just

what time is it? – it's just four o'clock quelle heure est-il ? – il est quatre heures juste

we were just talking about you! nous étions juste en train de parler de vous !

2. juste, seulement
I've just met her once je l'ai rencontrée une fois seulement

3. juste, de justesse

...just

I just caught the train j'ai attrapé le train de justesse

4. Idiom
to have just done something venir (juste) de faire quelque chose

* *Look, the helicopter has just landed...* Regardez, l'hélicoptère vient d'atterrir... *

just a minute! un instant !

keen

keen
[ki:n] *adj*
1. enthousiaste

all the pupils are very keen tous les élèves sont très enthousiastes

2. vif, fin
* *Fortunately you have a keen sense of smell, Snowy, you'll be able to follow their trail...* Heureusement que tu as l'odorat fin, Milou, tu vas pouvoir suivre leur piste... *

...keen

3. Idiom
to be keen on something aimer quelque chose

I'm not very keen on dancing je n'aime pas beaucoup danser

keep

keep
[ki:p]
kept, kept [kept]
I. *vt*

...keep

1. garder

* *You can keep it, it might be useful...* Tu peux le garder, cela pourra peut-être te servir... *

to keep a secret garder un secret

we've kept some cake for you nous avons gardé du gâteau pour toi

2. tenir
this coat will keep you warm ce manteau te tiendra chaud

3. retenir
you're very late, what kept you? vous êtes très en retard, qu'est-ce qui vous a retenu ?

4. Idiom
to keep an eye on something surveiller quelque chose

II. *vi*
1. continuer, ne pas arrêter

* *Hurry up, they're coming!* Dépêchez-vous, il arrivent ! *Keep running... Quick!...* N'arrêtez pas de courir... Vite !... *

2. rester
keep calm! restez calme !

keep to the left restez à gauche

3. Idiom
how are you keeping? comment allez-vous ?

...keep

to keep fit se maintenir en forme

kettle

kettle
['ket(ə)l] *n*
bouilloire *f*

I'll put the kettle on for tea je vais mettre la bouilloire à chauffer pour le thé

key

key
[ki:] *n*
1. clé *f*, clef *f*

the key is in the door la clé est sur la porte

2. touche *f*
the keys of the piano/of the typewriter les touches du piano/de la machine à écrire

kick

kick
[kɪk]
I. *vt*
donner un coup de pied à/dans

that man tried to kick Snowy cet homme a essayé de donner un coup de pied à Milou

II. *n*
coup *m* de pied

kill

kill
[kɪl] *vt*
tuer

kind

kind
[kaɪnd]
I. *adj*
gentil, aimable

* *Take this, it's for you, it's a present.* Prends ça, c'est pour toi, je te le donne.
It's very kind of you! C'est très gentil de ta part ! *

II. *n*
1. sorte *f*, genre *m*

all kinds of toys toutes sortes de jouets

2. marque *f*
what kind of car is that? c'est quoi comme marque de voiture ?

► **kindness**
['kaɪndnɪs] *n*
gentillesse *f*, bonté *f*

king

king
[kɪŋ] *n*
roi *m*

kiss

...kiss

kiss
[kɪs]
I. *n*
baiser *m*

give me a kiss donne-moi un baiser

II. *vt*
embrasser

* *Let me kiss you!* Laissez-moi vous embrasser ! *

III. *vi*
s'embrasser

kitchen

kitchen
['kɪtʃɪn] *n*
cuisine *f*

knee

knee
[ni:] *n*
genou *m*

► **kneel**
[ni:l] *vi*
knelt, knelt [nelt]
s'agenouiller

knife

knife
[naɪf] *n*
pl knives [naɪvz]
couteau *m*

* *Heavens! my knife!* Ciel ! mon couteau ! *

knock

knock
[nɒk]
I. *n*
coup *m*

...knock

II. *vt*
frapper, cogner

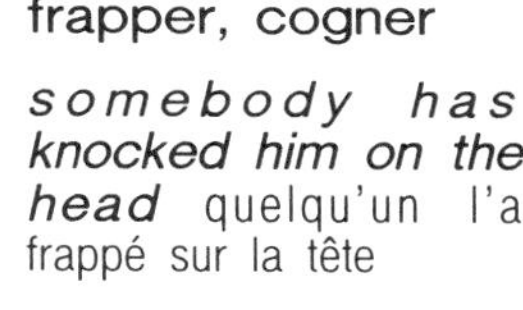

somebody has knocked him on the head quelqu'un l'a frappé sur la tête

III. *vi*
frapper, cogner

somebody's knocking at the door on frappe à la porte

I knocked against the table je me suis cogné contre la table

...knock

The blow must have knocked him out...

► **knock down**
renverser

he was knocked down by a car il a été renversé par une voiture

► **knock out**
assommer

* *The blow must have knocked him out...* Le coup a dû l'assommer... *

► **knock over**
renverser

I knocked my cup of coffee over j'ai renversé ma tasse de café

know

know
[nəʊ]
knew [nju:], known [nəʊn]
I. *vt*

...know

1. savoir
do you know why he's angry? savez-vous pourquoi il est en colère ?

2. connaître
do you know Signora Castafiore? connaissez-vous la Castafiore ?

II. *vi*
savoir

what are they doing? – I don't know qu'est-ce qu'ils font ? je ne sais pas

► **knowledge**
['nɒlɪdʒ] *n*
connaissance *f*

lack

lack
[læk] *n*
manque *m*

he failed through lack of experience il a échoué par manque d'expérience

ladder

ladder
['lædəʳ] *n*
1. échelle *f*

...ladder

* *Woooah!* Wouah !
He's climbing the ladder... Il grimpe à l'échelle... *

2. Idiom
you've got a ladder (Am: run) in your tights ton collant est filé

Woooah!
He's climbing the ladder...

lady

lady
['leɪdɪ] *n*
pl ladies
dame *f*

there's a lady who wants to see you il y a une dame qui veut vous voir

ladies and gentlemen mesdames et messieurs

lake

lake
[leɪk] *n*
lac *m*

lamp

lamp
[læmp] *n*
lampe *f*

land

land
[lænd]
I. *n*
1. terre *f*

we can see the land from the boat nous apercevons la terre du bateau

2. pays *m*
people from different lands des gens de pays différents

3. terrain *m*,
terres *f pl*

what's the price of this land? quel est le prix de ce terrain ?

II. *v i*
atterrir

the plane will be landing in five minutes l'avion va atterrir dans cinq minutes

lane

lane
[leɪn] *n*
chemin *m*

* *In Tibet...* Au Tibet...
... Yes, definitely, this lane is too narrow, a lorry (Am: truck) couldn't get through... ... C'est sûr, ce chemin est trop étroit, un camion ne pourrait pas passer... *

In Tibet...
...Yes, definitely, this lane is too narrow, a lorry couldn't get through...

language

language
['læŋgwɪdʒ] *n*
1. langue *f*

what language are they speaking? quelle langue parlent-ils ?

2. langage *m*
mind your language! surveille ton langage !

large ...last

large
large
[lɑ:dʒ] *n*
grand

last
last
[lɑ:st]
I. *adj*
1. dernier

he left at the last minute il est parti à la dernière minute

last week/year la semaine/l'année dernière

last Monday lundi dernier

2. Idiom
the week before last il y a deux semaines

II. *adv*
1. dernier

to come last in a race arriver dernier dans une course

2. pour la dernière fois

When did you last see him?
Yesterday evening, I think...

* *When did you last see him?* Quand l'avez-vous vu pour la dernière fois ?
Yesterday evening, I think... Hier soir, je crois... *

3. Idiom
at last enfin

Tintin! you've arrived at last! Tintin ! vous êtes enfin arrivé !

III. *v i*
durer

How long will this storm last?

...last ...late

* *How long will this storm last?* Combien de temps cette tempête va-t-elle durer ? *

late
late
[leɪt]
I. *adj*
1. en retard

* *Hurry up, we're late!* Dépêchez-vous, nous sommes en retard ! *

Hurry up, we're late!

2. tard
it's late, we must go il est tard, il faut que nous partions

in the late afternoon tard dans l'après-midi

3. Idiom
the train is twenty minutes late le train a vingt minutes de retard

II. *adv*
en retard

he arrived late, as usual il est arrivé en retard, comme d'habitude

► **lately**
['leɪtlɪ] *adv*
dernièrement, récemment

I have seen him lately je l'ai vu dernièrement

► **later**
[leɪtəʳ] *adv*
1. plus tard

I'll be back later (on) je serai de retour plus tard

2. Idiom
see you later! à tout à l'heure !

► **latest**
['leɪtɪst] *adj*
dernier

* *Have you heard the latest news?... A plane has crashed in Nepal...* Connaissez-vous la dernière nouvelle ?... Un avion s'est écrasé au Népal... *

...late laugh ...law ...lawn

Have you heard the latest news?... A plane has crashed in Nepal...

laugh
laugh
[lɑ:f]
I. *v i*
1. rire

that story made us laugh till we cried cette histoire nous a fait rire aux larmes

2. se moquer
you mustn't laugh at her il ne faut pas sè moquer d'elle

II. *n*
1. rire *m*

he has a loud laugh il a un rire bruyant

2. Idiom
to do something for a laugh faire quelque chose pour rire

law
law
[lɔ:] *n*
1. loi *f*

2. Idiom
it's against the law c'est illégal

► **lawyer**
['lɔ:jəʳ] *n*
avocat *m*

lawn
lawn
[lɔ:n] *n*
pelouse *f*

to mow the lawn tondre la pelouse

lay
lay
[leɪ] *v t*
laid, laid [leɪd]
1. poser, mettre

he laid the tray down carefully on the table il a posé avec précaution le plateau sur la table

...lay

2. mettre
to lay the table mettre la table

3. pondre
the hen has laid an egg la poule a pondu un œuf

lazy

lazy
['leɪzɪ] *adj*
lazier, laziest
paresseux

lead

lead
[li:d]
led, led [led]
I. *vt*
1. conduire, mener

he led us to our room il nous a conduits à notre chambre

2. être à la tête de, diriger
he leads a large company il est à la tête d'une grande entreprise

II. *vi*
1. mener, être en tête

they are leading by three goals to one ils mènent par trois buts à un

2. mener, conduire
this path leads to the castle ce chemin mène au château

III. *n*
1. laisse *f*

* *Dogs must be kept on a lead (Am: leash)*

Dogs must be kept on a lead so that they don't run away ...
?

...lead

so that they don't run away... Les chiens doivent être tenus en laisse pour qu'ils ne se sauvent pas... *

2. Idiom
to be in the lead être en tête

to take the lead mener

► **leader**
['li:dəʳ] *n*
chef *m*

leaf

leaf
[li:f] *n*
pl leaves [li:vz]
feuille *f*

the leaves are falling off the trees les feuilles tombent des arbres

lean

Tintin, don't lean out !...

lean
[lɪ:n] *vi*
leaned, leaned/leant, leant [lent]
1. s'appuyer

he was leaning against the wall il s'appuyait contre le mur

2. se pencher
do not lean out of the window ne pas se pencher par la fenêtre

* *Tintin, don't lean out!...* Tintin, ne te penche pas !... *

3. pencher
the wall is leaning dangerously le mur penche dangereusement

learn

learn
[lɜ:n] *vt*
learned, learned/learnt, learnt [lɜ:nt]
apprendre

...learn

we learn French at school nous apprenons le français à l'école

leather

leather
['leðəʳ] *n*
cuir *m*

a leather jacket un blouson en cuir

leave

leave
[li:v]
left, left [left]
I. *vi*
partir, s'en aller

what time does the boat leave? à quelle heure part le bateau ?

II. *vt*
1. partir de, quitter

it's late, I have to leave you il est tard, il faut que je vous quitte

LEAVE ME ALONE!...

2. laisser
leave some for me! laissez-en pour moi !

I left my umbrella in the bus j'ai laissé mon parapluie dans le bus

* *Leave me alone!...* Laissez-moi tranquille !... *

3. Idiom
there's only one cake left il ne reste qu'un seul gâteau

...leave

I've still got some money left over il me reste encore de l'argent

► **leave out**
sauter, omettre

you've left a word out vous avez sauté un mot

left

left
[left]
I. *n*
gauche *f*

they drive on the left here ils roulent à gauche ici

* *Captain Haddock is sitting on Tintin's left...* Le capitaine Haddock est assis à la gauche de Tintin... *

II. *adj*
gauche

Captain Haddock is sitting on Tintin's left...

my left hand ma main gauche

III. *adv*
à gauche

turn left at the crossroads tournez à gauche au carrefour

► **left-hand** *adj*
gauche

on the left-hand side sur le côté gauche

leg

leg
[leg] *n*
1. jambe *f*

she's got long legs elle a de longues jambes

2. patte *f*
* *Come on, Snowy, show me your leg... I must see whether it's broken!...* Allez, Milou, montre-moi ta patte... Il faut que je voie si elle est cassée !... *

lemon

lemon
['lemən] *n*
citron *m*

► **lemonade**
[lemə'neɪd] *n*
limonade *f*

lend

lend
[lend] *vt*
lent, lent [lent]
1. prêter

...lend

* *Can you lend me your car? Yes, of course!...* Pouvez-vous me prêter votre voiture ? Oui, bien sûr !... *

2. Idiom
to lend a hand donner un coup de main

can you lend us a hand? peux-tu nous donner un coup de main ?

less

less
[les]
I. *adj*
moins de

we've got less time than we thought nous avons moins de temps que nous ne pensions

II. *pron*
moins

in less than an hour en moins d'une heure

you should drink less, Captain vous devriez moins boire, capitaine

III. *adv*
moins

this film is less interesting than the other one ce film est moins intéressant que l'autre

* *I'm getting used to walking on the moon... It's less and less difficult...* Je m'habitue à marcher sur la Lune... c'est de moins en moins difficile... *

lesson

lesson
['les(ə)n] *n*
leçon *f*

let

let
[let]
let, let
I. *vt*
1. laisser

...let

my parents won't let me go mes parents ne me laisseront pas y aller

here, let me show you how to do it tenez, laissez-moi vous montrer comment le faire

2. louer
flats to let (Am: apartments for rent) appartements à louer

3. Idiom
to let go of something lâcher quelque chose

...let

hold on Tintin! don't let go! tenez bon, Tintin ! ne lâchez pas prise !

let somebody know prévenez quelqu'un

II. *v aux*
let's see voyons

let's go! allons-y !

* *Let's go!... I hope you aren't too heavy!...* Allons-y !... J'espère que tu n'es pas trop lourd !... *

let's have a game of chess si on faisait une partie d'échecs ?

► **let in**
laisser entrer, faire entrer

the butler let us in le maître d'hôtel nous a fait entrer

► **let off**
1. faire partir

boys were letting off bangers (Am: firecrackers) des garçons faisaient partir des pétards

2. ne pas punir
the teacher was kind, he let me off le professeur a été gentil, il ne m'a pas puni

► **let out**
laisser sortir

* *Let me out!... Let me out!... Blistering barnacles!...* Laissez-moi sortir !... Laissez-moi sortir !... Mille sabords !...

letter

letter
['letəʳ] *n*
1. lettre *f*

write in small/capital letters écrivez en lettres minuscules/majuscules

2. lettre *f*
* *A few days later...* Quelques jours après... *Tintin, you've got a letter from Cuthbert Calculus!...* Tintin, vous avez une lettre de Tryphon Tournesol !... *

level

level
['lev(ə)l] *n*
niveau *m*

library

library
['laɪbrərɪ] *n*
pl libraries ['laɪbrərɪz]
bibliothèque *f*

lending library bibliothèque de prêt

lie

lie
[laɪ] *v i*
lay [leɪ], lain [leɪn]
s'étendre, se coucher, s'allonger

I think I'll go and lie on the bed je crois que je vais m'allonger sur le lit

he is lying on the floor Il est couché par terre

► **lie down**
se coucher

lie down, Snowy! couché, Milou !

lie

lie
[laɪ]
I. *v i*
mentir

you lied to me! vous m'avez menti !

...lie

II. *n*
mensonge *m*

to tell lies dire des mensonges

life

life
[laɪf] *n*
pl lives [laɪvz]
vie *f*

...life

you saved my life, Tintin vous m'avez sauvé la vie, Tintin

is there life on Mars? la vie existe-t-elle sur Mars ?

he got life imprisonment il a été condamné à la prison à vie

lift

lift
[lɪft]
(*Am:* **elevator)**
I. *n*
1. ascenseur *m*

2. Idiom
to give somebody a lift emmener quelqu'un (en voiture)

* *Hello, Mr Calculus... would you like a lift to the village?* Bonjour, monsieur Tournesol... Voulez-vous que je vous emmène au village ? *

II. *v t*
soulever, lever

it's so heavy I can't lift it! c'est tellement lourd que je n'arrive pas à le soulever !

light

light
[laɪt] *adj*
léger

...light

this box is very light cette boîte est très légère

he was wearing a light jacket il portait une veste légère

a light meal un repas léger

light

light
[laɪt]
I. *n*

...light

1. lumière *f*

* *Blistering barnacles!... The power has been cut off: there's no light...* Mille sabords !... Le courant est coupé : il n'y a plus de lumière... *

turn the lights on/off allumez/éteignez les lumières

2. feu *m*
can you give me a light? pouvez-vous me donner du feu ?

Blistering barnacles!... The power has been cut off: there's no light...

II. *vt*
lit, lit [lɪt]
allumer

she lit the candles elle a allumé les bougies

III. *adj*
clair

she has light brown hair elle a des cheveux châtain clair

it's not light enough to read il ne fait pas assez clair pour lire

► **lightning**
['laɪtnɪŋ] *n*

a flash of lightning un éclair

like

like
[laɪk] *vt*
1. aimer

do you like garlic? aimez-vous l'ail ?

...like

I don't like Janet je n'aime pas Janet

2. aimer, vouloir
would you like to come with us? aimeriez-vous venir avec nous ?

take as many as you like prenez-en autant que vous voulez

like

like
[laɪk] *prep*
1. comme

a town like London une ville comme Londres

you behaved like a fool! tu t'es conduit comme un idiot !

2. Idiom
to look like ressembler à

* *Thomson looks like Thompson...* Dupont ressemble à Dupond... *

it looks like rain on dirait qu'il va pleuvoir

► **likely**
['laɪklɪ] *adj*
1. probable

it's likely that she'll come il est probable qu'elle viendra

2. Idiom
they are likely to arrive tomorrow ils arriveront probablement demain

Thomson looks like Thompson ...

limit

limit
['lɪmɪt]
I. *n*
1. limite *f*

2. Idiom
speed limit limitation de vitesse

II. *vt*
limiter

line

line
[laɪn] *n*
1. ligne *f*

draw a straight line tracez une ligne droite

* *The first lines are illegible...* Les premières lignes sont illisibles... *

2. ligne *f*
the railway (Am: railroad) line la ligne de chemin de fer

3. queue *f*, file *f*
to stand in line faire la queue

The first lines are illegible...

lip

lip
[lɪp] *n*
lèvre *f*

list

list
[lɪst] *n*
liste *f*

listen

listen
['lɪs(ə)n] *vi*
écouter

listen to me! écoutez-moi !

litre

litre
['li:təʳ] *n*
(*Am:* **liter**)
litre *m*

little

little
['lɪtl] *adj*
petit

little

little
['lɪtl]
less [les],
least [li:st]
I. *adj*
peu de

...little

Later, in the rocket...
Hello, hello, this is Tintin... hello... we have very little oxygen left... hello... hello... we're stifling... hello... hello...

* *Later, in the rocket...* Plus tard, dans la fusée...
Hello, hello, this is Tintin... hello... we have very little oxygen left... hello... hello... we're stifling... hello... hello... Allô, allô, ici Tintin... allô... il nous reste très peu d'oxygène... allô... allô... nous étouffons... allô... allô... *

II. *pron*
a little un peu

would you like some cheese? – just a little, please voudriez-vous du fromage ? – un petit peu, s'il vous plaît

I'm feeling a little better je me sens un peu mieux

III. *adv*
à peine

I met him little more than a week ago je l'ai rencontré il y a à peine une semaine

live

live
[lɪv] *v i*
1. habiter, vivre, loger

where do you live? où habitez-vous ?

2. vivre
he lived to the age of 90 il a vécu jusqu'à (l'âge de) 90 ans

live

live
[laɪv] *adj*
1. en direct

a live concert un concert transmis en direct

2. sous tension
don't touch that cable, it's live ne touchez pas à ce câble, il est sous tension

lively

lively
['laɪvlɪ]
adj
1. plein de vie

she is a very lively girl c'est une fille pleine de vie

2. animé
the party is very lively la fête est très animée

living

living
['lɪvɪŋ] *n*
vie *f*

to earn a living gagner sa vie

▸ **living room**
['lɪvɪŋru:m] *n*
salle *f* de séjour, séjour *m*, salon *m*

load

load
[ləʊd]
I. *v t*
charger

* *Are these the last ones?* Ce sont les dernières ?
No, we still have to load these two crates. Non, il faut encore charger ces deux caisses. *

II. *n*
chargement *m*

Are these the last ones?
No, we still have to load these two crates.

loaf

loaf
[ləʊf] *n*
pl loaves [ləʊvz]

a loaf of bread un pain

local

local
['ləʊk(ə)l] *adj*
local, du coin

the local shops les magasins du coin

lock

lock
[lɒk]
I. *n*
1. serrure *f*

2. mèche *f*
a lock of blond hair une mèche de cheveux blonds

II. *v t*
fermer à clé

* *Heavens!... He's locked the door!...* Grands dieux !... Il a fermé la porte à clé !... *

Heavens!... He's locked the door!...

London

London
['lʌndən] *n*
Londres *m*

▸ **Londoner**
['lʌndənəʳ] *n*
Londonien *m*, Londonienne *f*

lonely

lonely
['ləʊnlɪ] *adj*
lonelier, loneliest

...lonely

seul

I feel lonely without Snowy je me sens seul sans Milou

long

long
[lɒŋ]
I. *adj*
1. long

the corridor is six metres (Am: meters)

...long

Goodbye, Tintin ...
So long!

long le couloir fait six mètres de long

let's go for a long walk allons faire une longue promenade

2. Idiom
have you been waiting for a long time? est-ce que vous attendez depuis longtemps ?

it's a long way c'est loin

II. *adv*
1. longtemps

I can't stay long je ne peux pas rester longtemps

have you been waiting long? est-ce que vous attendez depuis longtemps ?

it happened long ago cela s'est passé il y a longtemps

2. Idiom
he doesn't live here any longer il n'habite plus ici

all day/night long toute la journée/la nuit

* *Goodbye, Tintin...* Au revoir, Tintin... *So long!* A bientôt ! *

as/so long as pourvu que

you can come as long as you're good tu peux venir pourvu que tu sois sage

look

look
[luk]
I. *n*
1. regard *m*

an inquiring look un regard interrogateur

2. air *m*
this fellow has a fishy look cet individu a l'air louche

3. Idiom
to have a look at something regarder quelque chose

...look

let me have a look laissez-moi regarder

she's famous for her good looks elle est célèbre pour sa beauté

II. *vi*
1. regarder

look, it's General Alcazar! regardez, c'est le général Alcazar !

2. chercher
* *I can't find my pipe, I've looked everywhere!* Je ne trouve pas ma pipe, j'ai cherché partout ! *

3. avoir l'air
you look tired vous avez l'air fatigué

► **look after**
s'occuper de

can you look after the children? peux-tu t'occuper des enfants ?

I can't find my pipe, I've looked everywhere!
?

► **look at**
regarder

look at the blackboard regardez le tableau (noir)

► **look for**
chercher

I'm looking for my umbrella je cherche mon parapluie

► **look forward to**
1. attendre avec impatience

the children are looking forward to Christmas les enfants attendent Noël avec impatience

2. Idiom
I am looking forward to seeing you again il me tarde de vous revoir

► **look out**
faire attention

* *Look out, Tintin, he's got a gun! Stay hidden!* Faites attention, Tintin, il est armé ! restez caché ! *

...look

Look out, Tintin, he's got a gun! Stay hidden!

► **look round** (*Am:* **around)**
visiter

we looked round the museum nous avons visité le musée

► **look up**
1. lever les yeux

I looked up and saw an aeroplane (Am: airplane) J'ai levé les yeux et j'ai vu un avion

2. chercher
look the word up in your dictionary cherche le mot dans ton dictionnaire

loose

loose
[lu:s] *adj*
1. desserré

the screws are loose les vis sont desserrées

2. défait
* *Oh! my shoelace is loose.* Oh! mon lacet est défait. *

Oh! my shoelace is loose.

lord

lord
[lɔ:d] *n*
1. seigneur *m*

2. lord *m*
the House of Lords la Chambre des lords

lorry

lorry
[ˈlɒrɪ] *n*
pl lorries (*Am:* **truck**)
camion *m*

lose

lose
[lu:z]
lost, lost [lɒst]
I. *vt*
1. perdre

* *Thompson, I've lost my wallet!* Dupond, j'ai perdu mon portefeuille ! *

2. Idiom
to lose one's way se perdre

II. *vi*
perdre

we lost three nil (Am: nothing) nous avons perdu trois à zéro

lot

lot
[lɒt] *n*
Idiom
a lot of/lots of beaucoup de
she's got a lot of money elle a beaucoup d'argent

loud

loud
[laʊd]
I. *adj*
fort, bruyant

the music is too loud la musique est trop forte

II. *adv*
fort

Signora Castafiore is singing too loud la Castafiore chante trop fort

love

love
[lʌv]
I. *n*
1. amour *m*

his love for his country son amour pour son pays

my love mon amour

2. Idiom
to fall in love tomber amoureux

lots of love from Karen grosses bises, Karen

give my love to your sister embrasse ta sœur pour moi

II. *vt*
1. aimer

I love you! je t'aime !

2. adorer
* *Is that you, Tintin? I just love these bones the birds left behind!* C'est toi, Tintin ? J'adore ces os que les oiseaux ont laissés ! *

► **lovely**
[ˈlʌvlɪ] *adj*
lovelier, loveliest
adorable, ravissant

low

low
[ləʊ]
I. *adj*
bas

in a low voice à voix basse

...low

temperatures will remain very low les températures resteront très basses

II. adv
bas

the plane's flying too low l'avion vole trop bas !

luck

luck
[lʌk] *n*

...luck

chance *f*

what a piece/stroke of luck! quelle chance !

* *Goodbye, and good luck! I hope everything goes well for you!* Au revoir et bonne chance ! J'espère que tout se passera bien pour vous ! *

► **luckily**
[ˈlʌkɪlɪ] *adv*
heureusement

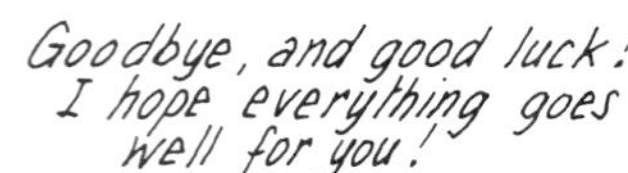

► **lucky**
[ˈlʌkɪ] *adj*
to be lucky avoir de la chance
Idiom
it's my lucky number c'est le chiffre qui me porte bonheur

luggage

luggage
[ˈlʌgɪdʒ] *n*
bagages *m pl*

lump

lump
[lʌmp] *n*
morceau *m*

two lumps of sugar, please deux morceaux de sucre, s'il vous plaî

lunch

lunch
[lʌntʃ] *n*
déjeuner *m*

MMMM

machine

machine
[mə'ʃiːn] *n*
machine *f*

* *Cuthbert Calculus has invented an amazing machine...* Tryphon Tournesol a inventé une machine extraordinaire... *

washing/sewing machine machine à laver/à coudre

Cuthbert Calculus has invented an amazing machine...

► **machinery**
[mə'ʃiːnərɪ] *n*
machines *f pl*

what's that strange machinery for? à quoi servent ces machines bizarres ?

mad

mad
[mæd] *adj*
madder, maddest
1. fou, folle

...mad

he's gone mad il est devenu fou

that noise is driving me mad ce bruit me rend fou

2. furieux
my father will be mad at me mon père sera furieux contre moi

3. passionné
he's mad about football il est passionné de football

mail

mail
[meɪl] *n*
1. poste *f*

I'll send it by mail je l'enverrai par la poste

2. courrier *m*
* *Some mail for me? My word, how can anyone know that I'm here?...* Du courrier pour moi ? Ça par exemple, comment sait-on que je suis ici ?... *

main

main
[meɪn] *adj*
principal

why can't we take the main road? pourquoi ne pouvons-nous pas prendre la route principale ?

make

make
[meɪk]
I. *n*
marque *f*

...make

what make is that car? quelle est la marque de cette voiture ?

II. *v t*
made, made [meɪd]
1. fabriquer

I've made this submarine j'ai fabriqué ce sous-marin

what do they make in that factory? que fabriquent-ils dans cette usine ?

...make

2. faire
I make my bed every morning je fais mon lit tous les matins

I'll make some tea je vais faire du thé

3. faire
seven and four make eleven sept et quatre font onze

4. rendre
this music makes me sad cette musique me rend triste

5. faire
to make somebody do something faire faire quelque chose à quelqu'un

the Professor makes me laugh le professeur me fait rire

6. Idiom
make yourself at home faites comme chez vous

what time do you make it? quelle heure avez-vous ?

make sure the lights are all out assurez-vous que toutes les lumières sont éteintes

▸ **make up**
1. inventer

* *Hello!... Come quick! I've just arrested a young boy who's making up a whole story...* Allô !... Venez vite ! Je viens d'arrêter un jeune garçon qui invente toute une histoire... *

Hello!... Come quick! I've just arrested a young boy who's making up a whole story...

2. se maquiller
she makes up in front of the mirror elle se maquille devant la glace

3. Idiom
to make up one's mind se décider

▸ **make-up** *n*
maquillage *m*

man

man
[mæn] *n*
pl men [mɛn]
homme *m*

* *Tintin is following a man.* Tintin suit un homme. *

Tintin is following a man.

manage

manage
['mænɪdʒ]
I. *vi*
1. réussir à

...manage

how did you manage to persuade him? comment avez-vous réussi à le convaincre ?

2. se débrouiller
she's old enough to manage on her own elle est assez grande pour se débrouiller toute seule

II. *vt*
diriger, gérer

she manages a large firm elle dirige une grande entreprise

▸ **manager**
['mænɪdʒəʳ] *n*
directeur *m*, directrice *f*, gérant *m*, gérante *f*

manner

manner
['mænəʳ] *n*
manière *f*, façon *f*

...manner

▸ **manners**
manières *f pl*

* *Thundering typhoons!... I'll teach you good manners, Abdullah!...* Tonnerre de Brest !... Je vais t'apprendre les bonnes manières, Abdallah !... *Waaah! Waaah!...* Wouin ! Wouin !... *

Idiom
it's bad manners to talk with your mouth

...manner

Thundering typhoons!... I'll teach you good manners, Abdullah!...
Waaah! Waaah!

full c'est mal élevé de parler la bouche pleine

many

many
['menɪ]
more [mɔːʳ], most [məʊst]
I. *adj*
1. beaucoup de

she has many friends elle a beaucoup d'amis

...many

2. Idiom
as many autant de

I've got as many toys as you j'ai autant de jouets que toi

how many combien de

how many people are there in the room? combien de gens y a-t-il dans la pièce ?

too many trop de

don't eat too many strawberries! ne mange pas trop de fraises !

II. *pron*
1. beaucoup

I haven't got many je n'en ai pas beaucoup

2. Idiom
as many autant

I've got as many as you j'en ai autant que toi

how many combien

too many trop

map

map
[mæp] *n*
1. carte *f*

I can't find where we are on the map je ne trouve pas l'endroit où nous sommes sur la carte

2. Idiom
city map plan (d'une ville)

March

March
[mɑːtʃ] *n*
mars *m*

the first/second of March (Am: March first/second) le premier/deux mars

come on the 5th of March (Am: on March 5) venez le 5 mars

mark

mark
[mɑːk]
I. *n*
1. note *f*

her marks (Am: grades) in French are excellent ses notes en français sont excellentes

2. marque *f*
* *I thought as much!... He's got a mark on his neck... The poor man's been hit by a dart...* Je m'en doutais !... Il porte une marque au cou... Le malheureux a reçu une fléchette... *

3. tache *f*
I've got an ink mark on my sleeve j'ai une tache d'encre sur la manche

II. *vt*
marquer
it's this one, I've marked it with a cross c'est celui-ci, je l'ai marqué d'une croix

I thought as much!... He's got a mark on his neck... The poor man's been hit by a dart...

market

market
[ˈmɑːkɪt] *n*
marché *m*

to go to market aller au marché

* *They are at the flea market...* Ils sont au marché aux puces... *

...market

They are at the flea market...

marmalade

marmalade
[ˈmɑːməleɪd] *n*
confiture *f* (d'oranges)

marry

marry
[ˈmærɪ]
married, married
I. *vt*
1. épouser, se marier avec

...marry

she married her director elle a épousé son directeur

2. Idiom
to get married se marier

II. *vi*
se marier

the Captain never married le capitaine ne s'est jamais marié

► **marriage**
[ˈmærɪdʒ] *n*
mariage *m*

mass

mass
[mæs] *n*
1. masse *f*

a mass of metal une masse de métal

2. tas *m pl*
I've got masses of things to do j'ai des tas de choses à faire

3. messe *f*
they go to Mass every Sunday ils vont à la messe tous les dimanches

match

match
[mætʃ]
I. *n*
1. match *m*

a rugby/boxing match un match de rugby/de boxe

2. allumette *f*
a box of matches une boîte d'allumettes

II. *vt*
aller avec

that blouse doesn't match that skirt ce chemisier ne va pas avec cette jupe

III. *vi*
aller ensemble

that blouse and that skirt don't match ce chemisier et cette jupe ne vont pas ensemble

material

material
[məˈtɪərɪəl] *n*
1. tissu *m*

I'd like some material to make curtains j'aimerais du tissu pour faire des rideaux

2. matière *f*
raw materials matières premières

3. matériau *m*
building materials matériaux de construction

mathematics

mathematics
[mæθˈmætɪks] *n*
mathématiques *f pl*

mathematics is my favourite (Am: favorite) subject les mathématiques sont ma matière préférée

► **maths** (*Am:* **math)**
[mæθs] *n*
maths *f pl*

our maths teacher notre professeur de maths

matter

matter
[ˈmætəʳ]
1. affaire *f*, question *f*

that's a different matter c'est une autre affaire

2. Idiom
what's the matter? Qu'est-ce qu'il y a ?

* *Hurray!... Hurray!... Come here, Tintin, and rejoice with me!...* Victoire !... Vic-

...matter

toire !... Venez Tintin, réjouissez-vous avec moi !... ***For goodness' sake, Captain, what is the matter?*** Mais enfin, capitaine, qu'est-ce qu'il y a ? *

what's the matter with him? qu'est-ce qu'il a ?

there's nothing the matter with me je n'ai rien

there's something the matter with the engine il y a quelque chose qui ne va pas dans le moteur

as a matter of fact à vrai dire

mattress

mattress
['mætrɪs] *n*
matelas *m*

* *Everyone is lying on his mattress...* Chacun

Everyone is lying on his mattress...

...mattress

est couché sur son matelas... *

May

May
[meɪ] *n*
mai *m*

the first/second of May (Am: May first/second) le premier/deux mai

...May

come on the 7th of May (Am: on May 7) venez le 7 mai

may

may
[meɪ] *v aux*
might [maɪt]
1. pouvoir

you may leave now vous pouvez partir maintenant

...may

may I come in? – yes, you may puis-je entrer ? – oui, bien sûr

2. Idiom
it may snow il va peut-être neiger

he said that it might snow il a dit qu'il allait peut-être neiger

where are they? – they may have missed the train où sont-ils ? – ils ont peut-être manqué le train

► **maybe**
['meɪbɪ] *adv*
peut-être

* *Maybe he isn't at home, he's not answering the door!...* Peut-être est-il sorti, il ne répond pas !... *

me

me
[mi:] *pron*
1. me, m'

...me

can you see/hear me? est-ce que vous pouvez me voir/m'entendre ?

2. moi
give it to me donnez-le moi

meal

meal
[mi:l] *n*
repas *m*

mean

mean
[mi:n] *adj*
1. avare

he's too mean to buy presents il est trop avare pour acheter des cadeaux

2. méchant
don't be mean to the poor dog! ne sois pas méchant avec ce pauvre chien !

mean

mean
[mi:n] *v t*
meant, meant [ment]
1. vouloir dire

what does this word mean? que veut dire ce mot ?

do you see what I mean? est-ce que vous voyez ce que je veux dire ?

2. Idiom
you're meant to be at school tu es censé être à l'école

meanwhile

meanwhile
['mi:nwaɪl] *adv*
pendant ce temps

measure

measure
['meʒəʳ]
I. *v t*
mesurer

we must measure the table to see if it's big

...measure

enough il faut mesurer la table pour voir si elle est assez grande

the room measures five metres (Am: meters) by three la pièce mesure cinq mètres sur trois

II. *n*
mesure *f*

the gramme (Am: gram) is a measure of weight le gramme est une mesure de poids

meat

meat
[miːt] *n*
viande *f*

medicine

medicine
['medsɪn] *n*
1. médicament *m*

* ***Well, gentlemen, do you have any medicine to cure him quickly?*** Alors, mes-

sieurs, avez-vous des médicaments pour le guérir rapidement ? *

2. médecine *f*
she is studying medicine elle étudie la médecine

Well, gentlemen, do you have any medicine to cure him quickly?
? ? ? ?
? ? ? ?

meet

meet
[miːt]
met, met [met]
I. *vt*
1. rencontrer

I met a stranger in the corridor j'ai rencontré un inconnu dans le couloir

2. retrouver
I said I'd meet them at the station j'ai dit que je les retrouverais à la gare

3. faire la connaissance (de)
pleased to meet you enchanté de faire votre connaissance

4. Idiom
have you met Mr Thompson? connaissez-vous M. Dupond ?

II. *vi*
1. se rencontrer

we first met in Paris nous nous sommes rencontrés pour la première fois à Paris

Ah, my dear Captain Padlock, I'll never forget our first meeting!
Haddock, Madam, Captain Haddock.

2. se retrouver
let's meet at the station retrouvons-nous à la gare

► **meeting**
['miːtɪŋ] *n*
1. rencontre *f*

* ***Ah, my dear Captain Padlock, I'll never forget our first meeting!*** Ah, cher capitaine Karbock, je n'oublierai jamais notre première rencontre !
Haddock, Madam, Captain Haddock. Haddock, madame, capitaine Haddock. *

2. réunion *f*
the meeting will take place in the staff room la réunion aura lieu dans la salle des professeurs

memory

memory
['memərɪ] *n*
pl memories

1. mémoire *f*
you've got a very good memory, Tintin vous avez très bonne mémoire, Tintin

2. souvenir *m*
childhood memories souvenirs d'enfance

men

men
[mɛn] → MAN

mend

mend
[mend] *vt*
raccommoder, réparer

mention

mention
['menʃ(ə)n] *vt*
1. parler de

don't mention it to the Professor n'en parlez pas au professeur

he mentioned your name il a parlé de vous

2. Idiom
* ***I don't know what would have become of me without you. Thank you ever so much...*** Je ne sais pas ce que je serais devenu sans vous. Merci beaucoup...
Don't mention it! Il n'y a pas de quoi ! *

I don't know what would have become of me without you. Thank you ever so much...
Don't mention it!

menu

menu
['menjuː] *n*
menu *m*

what's on the menu? qu'est-ce qu'il y a au menu ?

merry

merry
['merɪ] *adj*
merrier, merriest
joyeux

Merry Christmas! Joyeux Noël !

mess

mess
[mes] *n*
1. désordre *m*

2. Idiom
to make a mess of something gâcher quelque chose

message

message
['mesɪdʒ] *n*
message *m*

metal

metal
['metl] *n*
métal *m*

midday

midday
[mɪd'deɪ] *n*
midi *m*

middle

middle
['mɪdl] *n*
milieu *m*

midnight

midnight
['mɪdnaɪt] *n*
minuit *m*

might

might
[maɪt] *v aux*
pouvoir *(au conditionnel)*

it might snow il pourrait neiger

* *Well! You are lucky!* Eh bien ! Vous avez de la chance !
You might have broken your neck!... Vous auriez pu vous rompre le cou !...
Be quiet! Thundering typhoons! Silence ! Tonnerre de Brest ! *

Note : might *est également le passé de* may.

mile

mile
[maɪl] *n*
mile *m* (= 1,6 km)

it's 50 miles from here c'est à 80 kilomètres d'ici

milk

milk
[mɪlk] *n*
lait *m*

coffee with milk café au lait

▶ **milkman**
['milkmən] *n*
pl milkmen
laitier *m*

million

million
['mɪlɪən]
I. *n*
million *m*

it must be worth millions of dollars cela doit valoir des millions de dollars

II. *adj*
million

fifty million inhabitants cinquante millions d'habitants

mind

mind
[maɪnd]
I. *n*
1. esprit *m*

you showed great presence of mind, Tintin! vous avez fait preuve d'une grande présence d'esprit, Tintin !

2. Idiom
what do you have in mind? que pensez-vous faire ?

* *What's on your mind, Tintin?* Qu'est-ce qui vous préoccupe, Tintin ?
I wonder how we're going to find Zorrino... Je me demande comment nous allons faire pour retrouver Zorrino... *

he's out of his mind! il a perdu la tête !

to make up one's mind se décider

to change one's mind changer d'avis

II. *v t*
1. faire attention à

mind the step! faites attention à la marche !

2. Idiom
do you mind if I open the window? – I don't mind est-ce que cela vous dérange si j'ouvre la fenêtre ? – cela ne me gêne pas

never mind! ça ne fait rien !

he should mind his own business il devrait s'occuper de ce qui le regarde

▶ **mind out**
(*Am:* **watch out**)
faire attention

mind out, it's hot! faites attention, c'est chaud !

mine

mine
[maɪn] *pron*
1. le mien, la mienne, les miens, les miennes

her car is faster than mine sa voiture est plus rapide que la mienne

2. Idiom
a friend of mine un de mes amis

minute

minute
['mɪnɪt] *n*
1. minute *f*

* *Hello, Nestor, is the Captain in?* Bonjour, Nestor. Le capitaine est-il là ?
Yes, Mr Tintin, he'll see you in a few minutes... Oui, monsieur Tintin, il va vous recevoir dans quelques minutes.... *

it's twelve minutes past eight il est huit heures et douze minutes

...minute

Hello, Nestor, is the Captain in?
Yes, Mr Tintin, he'll see you in a few minutes...

2. instant *m*, minute *f*
just a minute un petit instant

mirror

mirror
['mɪrəʳ] *n*
miroir *m*, glace *f*

* *Would you like a comb as well?* Voulez-vous aussi un peigne ?

...mirror

No, thank you, just the mirror. Non merci, seulement le miroir.
Yes, just the mirror, thank you... Oui, seulement le miroir, merci... *

miserable

miserable
['mɪzərəbl] *adj*
triste, malheureux

Would you like a comb as well?
No, thank you, just the mirror.
Yes, just the mirror, thank you...

...miserable

you look miserable vous avez l'air triste

miss

miss
[mɪs] *n*
mademoiselle *f*

Miss Smith mademoiselle Smith

please, Miss, may I leave the room? s'il vous plaît, mademoiselle, puis-je sortir ?

miss

miss
[mɪs] *vt*
1. manquer, rater

I missed the target j'ai manqué la cible

* *Thomson has missed the train...* Dupont a manqué le train... *

...miss

2. Idiom
I miss you tu me manques

▸ **miss out**
omettre, sauter

you missed out a word vous avez omis un mot

Thomson has missed the train...

mistake

mistake
[mɪs'teɪk] *n*
faute *f*, erreur *f*

model

model
['mɒdl] *n*
1. modèle *m* réduit, maquette *f*

he likes building model aeroplanes (Am: airplanes) il aime faire des maquettes d'avion

...model

2. modèle *m*
this car is the latest model c'est une voiture du dernier modèle

3. mannequin *m*
my sister wants to be a model ma sœur veut être mannequin

modern

modern
['mɒdən] *adj*
moderne

moment

moment
['məʊmənt] *n*
moment *m*, instant *m*

she's out at the moment elle est absente en ce moment

* *Wait for me, I'll be back in a moment.* Attendez-moi, je reviens dans un instant.
OK. O.K. *

Wait for me, I'll be back in a moment.
O.K.

Monday

Monday
['mʌndɪ] *n*
lundi *m*

he's arriving on Monday il arrive lundi

they don't work on Mondays ils ne travaillent pas le lundi

money

money
['mʌnɪ] *n*
argent *m*

I've got no money left il ne me reste plus d'argent

monkey

monkey
['mʌŋkɪ] *n*
singe *m*

* *The monkeys have taken the Captain's gun...* Les singes ont pris le fusil du capitaine... *

The monkeys have taken the Captain's gun...

month

month
[mʌnθ] *n*
mois *m*

...month

last/next month le mois dernier/prochain

monument

monument
['mɒnjʊmənt] *n*
monument *m*

mood

mood
[mu:d] *n*
humeur *f*

* *Blistering barnacles!!!* Mille sabords ! ! ! *The Captain's in a bad mood...* Le capitaine est de mauvaise humeur... *

...mood

Blistering barnacles!!!
BANG
BANG
The Captain's in a bad mood...

moon

moon
[mu:n] *n*
lune *f*
full/new moon pleine/nouvelle lune

► **moonlight**
['mu:nlaɪt] *n*
clair *m* de lune

* *The "Unicorn" in the moonlight...* La « Licorne » au clair de lune... *

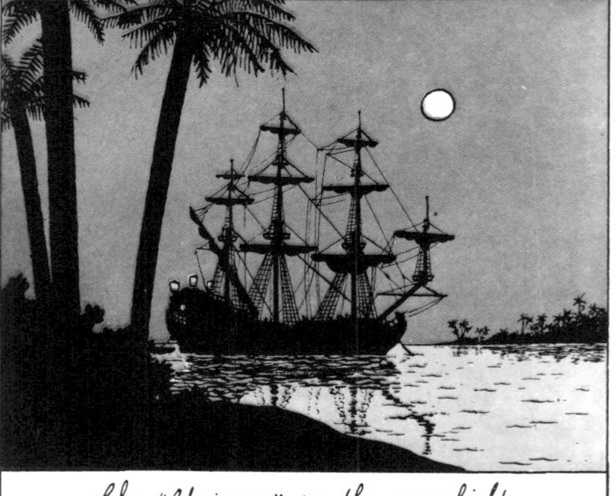
The "Unicorn" in the moonlight...

more

more
[mɔ:ʳ]
I. *adj*
1. plus de, davantage de

they've got more money than us ils ont plus d'argent que nous

there's no more cake il n'y a plus de gâteau

2. encore de
would you like some more toast? voudriez-vous encore des toasts ?

...more

II. *pron*
1. plus, davantage

not more than £50 pas plus de 50 livres

2. encore
do you want any more? en voulez-vous encore ?

III. *adv*
1. plus

this is more difficult than I thought! c'est plus difficile que je ne pensais !

2. plus, davantage
she talks even more than you elle parle encore plus que vous

3. Idiom
they don't live here any more ils n'habitent plus ici

he's more or less fifty, I'd say il a environ cinquante ans, à mon avis

more and more interesting de plus en plus intéressant

morning

morning
['mɔ:nɪŋ] *n*
1. matin *m*

* *Let's start with a few exercises as we do every morning...* Comme chaque matin, commençons par quelques exercices... *

the morning papers les journaux du matin

early in the morning de bon matin

Let's start with a few exercises as we do every morning...

2. matinée *f*
I've been working all morning j'ai travaillé toute la matinée

most

most
[məʊst]
I. *adj*
1. le plus de

who's got (the) most money? qui a le plus d'argent ?

2. la plupart de
most children go to school la plupart des enfants vont à l'école

II. *pron*
1. le plus
they always have a lot of work but in summer they have the most ils ont toujours beaucoup de travail mais c'est en été qu'ils en ont le plus

2. la plupart
most of my friends la plupart de mes amis

3. Idiom
at the most au maximum

III. *adv*
1. le plus, la plus, les plus

that was the most delicious meal I've ever eaten! c'était le repas le plus délicieux que j'aie jamais mangé !

2. très
you are most kind vous êtes très gentil

mother

mother
['mʌðəʳ] *n*
mère *f*

motor

motor
['məʊtəʳ] *n*
moteur *m*

an electric motor un moteur électrique

...motor

► **motorbike, motorcycle**
['məʊtəbaɪk], ['məʊtəsaɪkl] *n*
moto *f*

* *I'll go faster on this motorbike!...* J'irai plus vite avec cette moto !... *

► **motorway**
['məʊtəweɪ] *n*
(*Am:* **freeway**)
autoroute *f*

...motor

I'll go faster on this motorbike!...

mountain

mountain
['maʊntɪn] *n*
montagne *f*

* *In the mountains...* En montagne... *

In the mountains...

moustache

moustache
[mə'stɑːʃ] *n*
(*Am:* **mustache**)
moustache *f*

mouth

mouth
[maʊθ] *n*
bouche *f*

move

move
[muːv]
I. *v t*
1. déplacer
help me move this crate aidez-moi à déplacer cette caisse

...move

2. bouger
I can't move my legs je ne peux pas bouger les jambes

3. Idiom
to move (house) déménager

II. *v i*
1. bouger

* *Don't move or I'll fire! I'll count up to ten!* Ne bougez pas ou je tire ! Je compte jusqu'à dix ! *

Don't move or I'll fire! I'll count up to ten!

2. jouer
whose turn is it to move? c'est à qui de jouer ?

► **movement**
['muːvmənt] *n*
mouvement *m*

Mr

Mr
['mɪstəʳ] *n*
Monsieur *m*

...Mr

good morning, Mr Jones bonjour, monsieur Jones

Mrs

Mrs
['mɪsɪz] *n*
Madame *f*

have you met Mrs Harrison? connaissez-vous madame Harrison ?

much

much
[mʌtʃ]
I. *adj*
1. beaucoup de

I haven't got much money on me je n'ai pas beaucoup d'argent sur moi

2. Idiom
take as much cheese as you like prenez autant de fromage que vous voulez

...much

how much money have you got? combien d'argent avez-vous ?

he's got so much money he doesn't know how to spend it il a tellement d'argent qu'il ne sait pas comment le dépenser

we haven't got too much time nous n'avons pas trop de temps

II. *pron*
1. beaucoup

is there any cake left? – not much reste-t-il du gâteau ? – pas beaucoup

2. Idiom
take as much as you like prenez-en autant que vous en voulez

how much is it? combien ça coûte ?

how much is that ring? combien coûte cette bague ?

don't eat too much! ne mangez pas trop !

III. *adv*
beaucoup

how are you? – much better, thank you comment allez-vous ? – beaucoup mieux, merci

Mum

Mum, Mummy
[mʌm], [ˈmʌmɪ] *n*
(*Am:* **Mom, Mommy)**
maman *f*

murder

murder
[ˈmɜːdəʳ]
I. *vt*
tuer, assassiner

they tried to murder Tintin ils ont essayé d'assassiner Tintin

...murder

II. *n*
meurtre *m*

museum

museum
[mjuːˈzɪəm] *n*
musée *m*

* *The museum is closing!* Le musée ferme !
It's already five o'clock... Il est déjà cinq heures... *

...museum

music

music
[ˈmjuːzɪk] *n*
musique *f*

▸ **musician**
[mjuːˈzɪʃ(ə)n] *n*
musicien *m*, musicienne *f*

* *Boom Boom Boom Boom* Boum Boum Boum Boum
The musicians are coming... Les musiciens arrivent... *

The musicians are coming...

must

must
[mʌst] *v aux*
devoir, falloir

you must hurry! vous devez vous dépêcher !

* *They mustn't see us!* Il ne faut pas qu'ils nous voient ! *

he's late, he must have missed his train il est en retard, il a dû manquer son train

...must

mutton

mutton
[ˈmʌt(ə)n] *n*
mouton *m*

a mutton chop une côtelette de mouton

my

my
[maɪ] *adj*
mon, ma, mes

my father and my mother mon père et ma mère

where have I put my keys? où est-ce que j'ai mis mes clés ?

▸ **myself**
[maɪˈself] *pron*
1. me, m'

ouch! I've hurt myself! aïe ! je me suis fait mal !

2. moi-même
I intend to speak to him myself j'ai l'intention de lui parler moi-même

3. Idiom
I did it (all) by myself je l'ai fait tout seul

mystery

mystery
[ˈmɪstərɪ] *n*
pl mysteries
mystère *m*

▸ **mysterious**
[mɪsˈtɪərɪəs] *adj*
mystérieux

nail

nail
[neɪl]
I. *n*
1. clou *m*

a hammer and nails un marteau et des clous

2. ongle *m*
you should cut your nails tu devrais te couper les ongles

II. *vt*
clouer

name

name
[neɪm] *n*
1. nom *m*

* *Calculus has lost his memory...* Tournesol a perdu la mémoire... *But, Professor, you remember your name... your name... Calculus...* Mais, professeur, vous vous souvenez bien de votre nom... votre nom... Tournesol... *

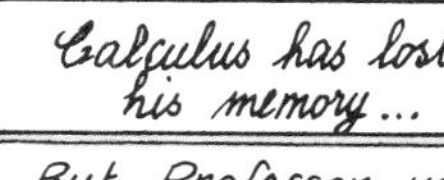

2. Idiom
what's your name? comment vous appelez-vous ?

my name is Tintin je m'appelle Tintin

first/Christian name prénom

narrow

narrow
['nærəʊ] *adj*
étroit

...narrow

a narrow road une route étroite

nasty

nasty
['nɑːstɪ] *adj*
nastier, nastiest
1. méchant

I think those men are nasty je crois que ces hommes sont méchants

...nasty

2. désagréable, sale
what a nasty smell! quelle odeur désagréable !

nationality

nationality
[næʃə'nælɪtɪ] *n*
pl nationalities
nationalité *f*

natural

natural
['nætʃ(ə)rəl] *adj*
naturel

► **naturally**
['nætʃ(ə)rəlɪ] *adv*
1. naturellement, bien sûr

can I come too? – naturally! puis-je venir aussi ? – bien sûr !

2. naturellement
my hair curls naturally mes cheveux frisent naturellement

nature

nature
['neɪtʃəʳ] *n*
nature *f*

* *Nature in Scotland is very beautiful...* La nature en Ecosse est très belle... *

naughty

naughty
['nɔ:tɪ] *adj*
naughtier, naughtiest
1. méchant, vilain

you naughty boy! méchant garçon !

2. Idiom
to be naughty faire des bêtises

* *I bet it's Abdullah being naughty again!* Je parie que c'est Abdallah qui a encore fait des bêtises ! *

I bet it's Abdullah being naughty again!

navy

navy
['neɪvɪ]
pl navies
['neɪvɪz]
marine *f*

near

near
[nɪəʳ]
I. *adj*
1. proche

...near

where's the nearest filling (Am: gas) station? où est la station-service la plus proche ?

2. Idiom
that was a near thing! on l'a échappé belle !

II. *adv*
près, proche

she lives quite near elle habite tout près

III. *prep*
près de, proche de

Croydon is near London Croydon est près de Londres

► **nearly**
['nɪəlɪ] *adv*
presque

what time is it? – it's nearly five o'clock quelle heure est-il ? il est presque cinq heures

necessary

necessary
['nesɪs(ə)rɪ] *adj*
1. nécessaire

* *We can go, Snowy, I have the necessary equipment now!...* Nous pouvons y aller, Milou, j'ai l'équipement nécessaire à présent !... *

2. Idiom
count on me to do what is necessary comptez sur moi pour faire ce qu'il faut

We can go, Snowy, I have the necessary equipment now!...

neck

neck
[nek] *n*
cou *m*

need

need
[ni:d] *vt*
1. avoir besoin de

* *I need your help, Chang, do you understand?* J'ai besoin de ton aide, Tchang, tu comprends ?

...need

I need your help, Chang, do you understand?
Yes, yes, Tintin, I do...

Yes, yes, Tintin, I do... Oui, oui, Tintin, je comprends... *

2. Idiom
you needn't come if you don't want to vous n'êtes pas obligé de venir si vous ne voulez pas

neighbour

neighbour
['neɪbəʳ] *n*
(*Am:* **neighbor)**
voisin *m*, voisine *f*

our next-door neighbours nos voisins à côté

neither

neither
['naɪðəʳ]
I. *pron*

...neither

Neither you nor I can make it across this gap!...

ni l'un ni l'autre, aucun (des deux)

neither of them is very bright aucun des deux n'est très intelligent

II. *adv*
ni

* *Neither you nor I can make it across this gap!...* Ni toi ni moi ne pouvons franchir cette crevasse !... *

III. *conj*
non plus

I don't like onions – neither do I je n'aime pas les oignons – moi non plus

nervous

nervous
['nɜ:vəs] *adj*
nerveux

I'm always nervous before exams je suis toujours nerveux avant les examens

nest

nest
[nest] *n*
nid *m*

never

never
['nevəʳ] *adv*
1. jamais

* *I've no more strength... I'll never manage it...* Je n'ai plus de

...never

I've no more strength... I'll never manage it...

force... je n'y arriverai jamais... *

2. Idiom
never mind! ça ne fait rien !

new

new
[nju:] *adj*
1. nouveau

have you seen the new teacher? as-tu vu le nouveau professeur ?

...new

2. neuf
they sell new and second-hand cars ils vendent des voitures neuves et d'occasion

what's new? quoi de neuf ?

news

news
[nju:z] *n pl*
1. nouvelle(s) *f (pl)*

...news

is the news good? les nouvelles sont-elles bonnes ?

a piece of news une nouvelle

2. informations *f pl*
* *Clic* Click
Tintin's listening to the news... Tintin écoute les informations... *

► **newspaper**
['nju:zpeɪpəʳ] *n*
journal *m*

CLIC

Tintin's listening to the news...

New Zealand

New Zealand
[nju:'zi:lənd] *n*
Nouvelle-Zélande *f*

next

next
[nekst]
I. *adj*
1. prochain

I'll see you next week! à la semaine prochaine !

...next

take the next street on the left prenez la prochaine rue à gauche

2. Idiom
* *The next day...* Le lendemain... *

II. *adv*
1. ensuite

I don't know what to do next je ne sais pas quoi faire ensuite

2. à côté
come and sit next to me venez vous asseoir à côté de moi

The next day...

► **next door**
[nekst dɔ:ʳ] *adv*
à côté

they live next door to us ils habitent dans la maison à côté de chez nous

nice

nice
[naɪs] *adj*
1. gentil, agréable, sympathique

...nice

he's a very nice man c'est un homme très sympathique

2. joli
what a nice dress! quelle jolie robe !

3. bon
I'd like a nice cup of tea! j'aimerais une bonne tasse de thé !

4. Idiom
it's nice weather il fait beau

...nice

we had a nice time nous nous sommes bien amusés

it's nice and warm in here il fait bon ici

night

night
[naɪt] *n*
1. nuit *f*

...night

it's very cold at night il fait très froid la nuit

* *Good night, Zorrino!* Bonne nuit, Zorrino !
Good night, señor Tintin! Bonne nuit, señor Tintin ! *

2. soir *m*
I went to the cinema (Am: movies) last night je suis allé au cinéma hier soir

Good night, Zorrino!
Good night, señor Tintin!

nine

nine
[naɪn]
I. *adj*
neuf

II. *n*
neuf *m*

nineteen

nineteen
[naɪn'ti:n]
I. *adj*
dix-neuf

...nineteen

II. *n*
dix-neuf *m*

ninety

ninety
['naɪntɪ]
I. *adj*
quatre-vingt-dix

my grandfather is ninety mon grand-père a quatre-vingt-dix ans

...ninety

ninety-one quatre-vingt-onze

II. *n*
pl nineties
quatre-vingt-dix *m*

in the nineties dans les années quatre-vingt-dix

no

no
[nəʊ]
I. *adv*

...no

1. non

can you swim? – no, I can't savez-vous nager ? – non

2. ne... pas
this car is no faster than mine cette voiture n'est pas plus rapide que la mienne

II. *adj*
1. ne... pas de / d'

I've got no money je n'ai pas d'argent

2. Idiom

* *It says: "no entry"...* C'est écrit « accès interdit »...
Let's go in anyway! Entrons quand même !
No entry Accès interdit *

nobody

nobody
['nəʊbɒdɪ] *pron*
personne

...nobody

that's funny, there's nobody in c'est bizarre, il n'y a personne à la maison

noise

noise
[nɔɪz] *n*
bruit *m*

* *I heard a noise!* J'ai entendu un bruit !
So did I... Moi aussi... *

...noise

► **noisy**
['nɔɪzɪ] *adj*
noisier, noisiest
bruyant

none

none
[nʌn] *pron*
1. aucun

none of them recognized Tintin

...none

aucun d'entre eux n'a reconnu Tintin

2. Idiom
how much money have you got? – none combien d'argent avez-vous ? – je n'en ai pas du tout

nonsense

nonsense
['nɒnsəns]

...nonsense

I. *n*
sottises *f pl*, absurdités *f pl*

don't talk nonsense! arrêtez de dire des sottises

no one

no one
['nəʊwʌn] *pron*
personne

...no one

there's no one in il n'y a personne à la maiso

nor

nor
[nɔ:ʳ] *conj*
1. ni

I'm neither rich nc famous je ne suis riche ni célèbre

...nor

2. Idiom
help! I can't swim! – nor can I! au secours ! je ne sais pas nager ! – moi non plus !

normal

normal
['nɔ:m(ə)l] *adj*
normal

* *Don't worry, the situation is perfectly*

...normal

normal! Ne vous inquiétez pas, la situation est tout à fait normale ! *

north

north
[nɔ:θ]
I. *n*
nord *m*

they live in the north of Scotland ils habitent dans le nord de l'Écosse

...north

II. *adj*
nord

North America Amérique du Nord

III. *adv*
vers le nord, au nord

► **Northern**
['nɔ:ðən] *adj*
nord

Northern Ireland Irlande du Nord

nose

nose
[nəʊz] *n*
nez *m*

...nose

* *What have I got on my nose?* Mais qu'est-ce que j'ai sur le nez ? *

not

not
[nɒt] *adv*
forme abrégée : n't
ne... pas

wait a minute, I'm not ready attendez un instant, je ne suis pas prêt

note

note
[nəʊt] *n*
1. note *f*

to take notes prendre des notes

2. billet *m*
a ten-pound note (Am: bill) un billet de dix livres

3. note *f*
I can't sing the high notes je n'arrive pas à chanter les notes aiguës

nothing

nothing
['nʌθɪŋ] *pron*
rien

* *But... there's nothing in this box!... Nothing at all!...* Mais... il n'y a rien dans ce coffret !... Rien du tout !... *

nothing interesting has happened rien d'intéressant ne s'est passé

notice

notice
['nəʊtɪs]
I. *n*
1. affiche *f*

what does that notice say? que dit cette affiche ?

2. attention *f*
take no notice of him, he's had a knock on the head ne faites pas attention à lui, il a reçu un coup sur la tête

noun

noun
[naʊn] *n*
nom *m*

common noun nom commun

proper noun nom propre

November

November
[nəʊ'vembəʳ] *n*
novembre *m*

now

now
[naʊ]
I. *adv*
1. maintenant

2. Idiom
now and then de temps en temps

by now à l'heure qu'il est

in a month from now dans un mois

up till now jusqu'ici

II. *interj*
allons !

* *I am playing the fool, am I?* Ah, je fais le zouave ? *Now, now! Don't get angry!* Allons, allons ! Ne vous fâchez pas ! *

► **nowadays**
['naʊədeɪz] *adv*
de nos jours

nowhere

nowhere
['nəʊweəʳ] *adv*
nulle part

where are you going? – nowhere où allez-vous ? – nulle part

nuisance

nuisance
['nju:s(ə)ns] *n*
1. peste *f*

...nuisance

my brother is a little nuisance mon frère est une petite peste

2. Idiom
what a nuisance! cela m'ennuie !

* *These mosquitoes are a nuisance!* Ces moustiques sont embêtants ! *

number

number
['nʌmbəʳ] *n*
1. numéro *m*

we live at number 80 nous habitons au numéro 80

2. nombre *m*
a large number of people were waiting outside un grand nombre de personnes attendait dehors

nurse

nurse
[nɜ:s] *n*
1. infirmière *f*

my sister wants to be a nurse ma sœur veut être infirmière

2. Idiom
male nurse infirmier *m*

► **nursery school**
['nɜ:sərɪ'sku:l] *n*
école *f* maternelle

obey

obey

obey
[ə'beɪ] *vt*
obéir à

you must obey your parents tu dois obéir à tes parents

object

object
['ɒbʒekt] *n*
1. objet *m*, chose *f*

he put all the valuable objects in his bag and left il mit tous les objets de valeur dans son sac et partit

2. but *m*
with the object of dans le but de

obvious

obvious
['ɒbvɪəs] *adj*
évident

it's obvious he's lying! il est évident qu'il ment !

occur

occur
[ə'kɜː^{r}] *vi*
occurred, occurred
1. avoir lieu, se passer

where did the accident occur? où l'accident a-t-il eu lieu ?

2. venir à l'esprit
it occurred to me that something was wrong il m'est venu à l'esprit que quelque chose n'allait pas

ocean

ocean
['əʊʃ(ə)n] *n*
océan *m*

the Atlantic/Pacific Ocean l'océan Atlantique/Pacifique

o'clock

o'clock
[ə'klɒk] *adv*

* *Let's see, what time is it? It's ten o'clock, I have some time left before I go.* Voyons, quelle heure est-il ? Il est dix heures, il me reste un moment avant d'y aller. *

Let's see, what time is it? It's ten o'clock, I have some time left before I go.

October

October
[ɒk'təʊbə^{r}] *n*
octobre *m*

the first/second of October (Am: October first/second) le premier/deux octobre

come on the 6th of October (Am: on October 6) venez le 6 octobre

odd

odd
[ɒd] *adj*
1. étrange, bizarre

* *That's odd... I heard a noise... Let's go in carefully.* C'est étrange... J'ai entendu un bruit... Entrons doucement. *

2. impair
7 is an odd number 7 est un nombre impair

That's odd... I heard a noise... Let's go in carefully.

of

of
[əv] *prep*
de

look, here's a photo of Tintin regardez voici une photo de Tintin

a lot of people beaucoup de monde

at the top of the hill en haut de la colline

off

off
[ɒf]
I. *prep*
1. de

the vase fell off the table le vase est tombé de la table

2. Idiom
a little cafe just off the main street un petit café à deux pas de la rue principale

II. *adv*
we're off to London tomorrow nous partons pour Londres demain

tomorrow is my day off c'est mon jour de congé demain

take your coat/shoes off enlève ton manteau/tes chaussures

to switch the light/television off éteindre la lumière/télévision

all the lights are off toutes les lumières sont éteintes

turn the tap (Am: faucet) off fermez le robinet

special offer: £10 off offre spéciale : réduction de 10 livres

offer

offer
['ɒfəʳ]
I. *v t*
offrir

* *Can I offer you something to drink?* est-ce que je peux vous offrir quelque chose à boire ? *

II. *n*
proposition *f*, offre *f*

they made me an offer ils m'ont fait une proposition

office

office
['ɒfɪs] *n*
bureau *m*

he's in his office il est dans son bureau

officer

officer
['ɒfɪsəʳ] *n*
officier *m*

often

often
['ɒfən] *adv*
souvent

oil

oil
[ɔɪl] *n*
1. pétrole *m*

they are drilling for oil ils font un forage pour trouver du pétrole

...oil

2. huile *f*
there's too much oil in this salad il y a trop d'huile dans cette salade

an oil painting une peinture à l'huile

OK, okay

OK, okay
[əʊ'keɪ]
I. *interj*
d'accord

...OK

shall we go? – OK! on y va ? – d'accord !

II. *adj*
Idiom

* *Are you OK, Captain?* Ça va, capitaine ? *Yes.* Oui. *

is it OK if I come with you? est-ce que je peux venir avec vous ?

old

old
[əʊld] *adj*
1. vieux, âgé

he's very old il est très âgé

an old car une vieille voiture

2. Idiom
my sister is nine years old ma sœur a neuf ans

how old are you? quel âge as-tu ?

hi! old pal! salut, mon vieux !

▸ **old-fashioned**
adj
démodé

her shoes are really old-fashioned! ses chaussures sont vraiment démodées !

on

on
[ɒn]
I. *prep*
1. sur

put it on the table mettez-le sur la table

* *Look, there's an article on Signora Castafiore in the newspaper!* Regardez, il y a un article sur la Castafiore dans le journal ! *

2. à
it's a long way on foot c'est loin à pied

he was playing a tune on the guitar il jouait un air à la guitare

3. Idiom
are you here on business? – no, I'm on holiday (Am: vacation) vous êtes là pour affaires ? – non, je suis en vacances

we're leaving on Tuesday nous partons mardi

do you work on Saturdays? est-ce que vous travaillez le samedi ?

II. *adv*
Idiom

to put the kettle on mettre de l'eau à chauffer

put your coat on, it's cold outside mets ton manteau, il fait froid dehors

he had nothing on il était tout nu

switch the lamp/television on allumez la lampe/télévision

* *My word! The radio's on!...* Ça par exemple ! La radio est allumée !...
That's certainly surprising! C'est surprenant en effet ! *

the tap (Am: faucet) is on le robinet est ouvert

from next week on à partir de la semaine prochaine

we walked on for another hour nous avons continué à marcher pendant une heure

once

once
[wʌns]
I. *adv*
1. une fois

I go riding once a week je fais de l'équitation une fois par semaine

2. autrefois, une fois
he reminds me of somebody I once knew il me rappelle quelqu'un que je connaissais autrefois

once upon a time il était une fois

3. Idiom
Snowy, come here at once! Milou, viens ici tout de suite !

don't all speak at once! ne parlez pas tous à la fois !

II. *conj*
une fois que

what shall we do once we're there? qu'est-ce que nous ferons une fois que nous serons là-bas ?

one

one
[wʌn]
I. *adj*
1. un *m*, une *f*

how many lumps of sugar? – just one please combien de morceaux de sucre ? – un seul, s'il vous plaît

2. Idiom
her baby is one son bébé a un an

II. *n*
1. un *m*, une *f*

2. Idiom
one and one are two un et un font deux

she started walking at (the age of) one elle a commencé à marcher à un an

III. *pron*
1. on

* *One must take one's shoes off in the mosque.* On doit enlever ses chaussures dans la mosquée. *

2. Idiom
this one celui-ci *m*, celle-ci *f*

that one celui-là *m*, celle-là *f*

these ones ceux-ci *m pl*, celles-ci *f pl*

which one? lequel ? *m*, laquelle ? *f* *which ones?* lesquels ? *m pl* lesquelles ? *f pl*

► **one another**
pron
se, l'un l'autre

they hate one another ils se détestent

we should all help one another nous devrions tous nous aider les uns les autres

► **one's**
[wʌnz] *adj*
son, sa, ses

it's hard to find one's way in this fog c'est dur de trouver son chemin dans ce brouillard

One can easily hurt oneself doing that...

...one

▸ **oneself**
[wʌn'self] *pron*
oneselves *pl*
[wʌn'selvz]
1. se

* *Quick! Quick! I must unjam this mechanism...* Vite ! Vite ! Il faut débloquer cette mécanique...
One can easily hurt oneself doing that... On peut facilement se faire mal en faisant ça... *

2. soi-même

it's always best to do it oneself c'est toujours mieux de le faire soi-même

3. Idiom
(all) by oneself tout seul

only

only
['əʊnlɪ]
I. *adv*

...only

1. seulement, ne... que

it's only five o'clock il n'est que cinq heures

* *Two weeks later...* Quinze jours plus tard...
If only we could stop pumping... Si seulement on pouvait s'arrêter de pomper...
If only... Si seulement... *

2. Idiom
only just tout juste

II. *adj*
seul, unique

it's the only food we have left c'est la seule nourriture qui nous reste

he's an only child il est enfant unique

onto

onto
['ɒntʊ] *prep*
sur

climb onto my shoulders monte sur mes épaules

open

open
['əʊpən]
I. *vt*
ouvrir

...open

I can't open the door je n'arrive pas à ouvrir la porte

II. *v i*
1. s'ouvrir

the box won't open la boîte ne s'ouvre pas

2. ouvrir
do they open on Sundays? est-ce qu'ils ouvrent le dimanche ?

III. *adj*
ouvert

* *In Marlinspike...* A Moulinsart...
Nestor has left the door open... Nestor a laissé la porte ouverte... *

operation

operation
[ɒpə'reɪʃn] *n*
opération *f*

...operation

the operation was successful, he's cured l'opération a réussi, il est guéri

opportunity

opportunity
[ɒpə'tju:nɪtɪ] *n*
pl opportunities
occasion *f*

you'll never have an opportunity like this again! vous n'aurez jamais plus une occasion comme celle-ci !

opposite

opposite
['ɒpəzɪt]
I. *prep*
en face de

he's sitting opposite me il est assis en face de moi

II. *adj*
1. d'en face

the house opposite la maison d'en face

2. autre
the opposite side of the road l'autre côté de la route

III. *n*
contraire *m*

when I say something you always say the opposite! quand je dis quelque chose, vous dites toujours le contraire !

or

or
[ɔ:ʳ] *conj*
ou

* *Shall I put my beard on top...* Vais-je mettre ma barbe dessus...
or... underneath?... Blistering barnacles! That's no better!... ou... dessous ?... Mille sabords ! Ce n'est pas mieux !... *

orange

orange
[ˈɒrɪndʒ]
I. *n*
orange *f*

orange juice jus d'orange

II. *adj*
orange

who's that man in the orange shirt? qui est cet homme à la chemise orange ?

order

order
[ˈɔːdəʳ]
I. *n*
1. ordre *m*, commande *f*

they've carried out my orders ils ont exécuté mes ordres

2. commande *f*
the waiter has taken our order le serveur a pris notre commande

3. ordre *m*
alphabetical order ordre alphabétique

4. Idiom
out of order en panne

I only came in order to see you je suis venu seulement pour vous voir

II. *v t*
1. ordonner

he ordered them to be quiet il leur a ordonné de se taire

2. commander
I ordered steak and chips (Am: French fries) j'ai commandé un steak frites

ordinary

ordinary
[ˈɔːdɪn(ə)rɪ] *adj*
ordinaire

organize

organize
[ˈɔːgənaɪz] *v t*
organiser

we should organize a party nous devrions organiser une fête

original

original
[əˈrɪdʒɪn(ə)l] *adj*
1. original

...original

yes, I find his painting very original oui, je trouve sa peinture très originale

2. premier
* *We have had to alter our original plan, now everything's settled.* Nous avons dû modifier notre premier projet, maintenant tout est au point.
Very well, Wolf, thank you very much... C'est très bien, Wolf, je vous remercie... *

other

other
[ˈʌðəʳ]
I. *adj*
autre

the other car is catching us up l'autre voiture nous rattrape

the other day l'autre jour

II. *pron*
autre

Snowy, you stay here with the others Milou, tu restes ici avec les autres

ought

ought
[ɔːt] *v aux*
devoir

* *You ought to go to the dentist's, my dear Haddock...* Vous devriez aller chez le dentiste, mon cher Haddock... *

...ought

he ought to have told me! il aurait dû me le dire !

our

our
[aʊəʳ] *adj*
notre, nos

this is our ship voici notre navire

we went with our parents nous y sommes allés avec nos parents

...our

► **ours**
[aʊəz] *pron*
1. le nôtre, la nôtre, les nôtres

their car is faster than ours leur voiture est plus rapide que la nôtre

2. Idiom
a friend of ours un de nos amis

► **ourselves**
[aʊəˈselvz] *pron*
1. nous

we really enjoyed ourselves nous nous sommes vraiment amusés

2. nous-mêmes
we made it ourselves nous l'avons fait nous-mêmes

3. Idiom
(all) by ourselves tout seuls

out

out
[aʊt] *adv*
1. dehors

it's very hot out il fait très chaud dehors

2. sorti
the Captain is out at the moment le capitaine est sorti en ce moment

3. Idiom
he ran out il est sorti en courant

the fire is out le feu est éteint

we are out of coffee nous n'avons plus de café

► **out of**
prep
1. hors de

have no fear, you're out of danger rassurez-vous, vous êtes hors de danger

...out

2. de
he came running out of the house il est sorti de la maison en courant

3. sur
I got 18 out of 20 in French j'ai eu 18 sur 20 en français

► **outdoor**
[aʊt'dɔ:ʳ] *adj*
en plein air

an outdoor swimming pool une piscine en plein air

► **outdoors**
[aʊt'dɔ:z] *adv*
dehors

it's a nice day, let's have lunch outdoors il fait beau, déjeunons dehors

► **outside**
[aʊt'saɪd]
I. *adv*
dehors

where's Abdullah? – he's outside in the garden où est Abdallah ? – il est dehors dans le jardin

II. *prep*
devant

I'll meet you outside the post office je vous retrouverai devant la poste

III. *n*
extérieur *m*

the outside of the house l'extérieur de la maison

oven

oven
['ʌvən] *n*
four *m*

over

over
['əʊvəʳ]
I. *adv*
1. partout

I'm aching all over j'ai mal partout

...over

2. fini
it's all right, the storm is over ça va, l'orage est fini

3. plus
children of 12 and over les enfants de 12 ans et plus

4. Idiom
over here ici

over there là-bas

* *Over there!... Look... Water!... Water!...* Là-

...over

bas !... Regardez... De l'eau !... De l'eau !... *

he does it over and over again il n'arrête pas de le faire

II. *prep*
1. au-dessus de

there is a lamp over the desk il y a une lampe au-dessus du bureau

2. par-dessus
the ball went over the wall la balle est passée par-dessus le mur

3. sur
he spilt his tea over the table il a renversé son thé sur la table

4. de l'autre côté de
who's that over the street? qui y a-t-il de l'autre côté de la rue ?

5. plus de
it must cost over £100 ça doit coûter plus de 100 livres

6. pendant, au cours de
what are you doing over the summer? qu'est-ce que vous faites pendant l'été ?

► **overcoat**
['əʊvəkəʊt] *n*
pardessus *m*, manteau *m*

► **overtake**
[əʊvə'teɪk] *v t*
(*Am:* **pass**)
overtook [əʊvə'tʊk],

...over

overtaken
[əʊvə'teɪk(ə)n]
doubler

* *I'll try to overtake that car!...* Je vais essayer de doubler cette voiture !... *

owe

owe
[əʊ] *v t*
devoir

...owe

you owe me £10 vous me devez 10 livres

own

own
[əʊn]
I. *adj*
propre

* *The Yeti!... Up there!... I saw it!... I saw it with my own eyes!...* Le yéti !... Là-

...own

haut !... Je l'ai vu !... Je l'ai vu de mes propres yeux !... *

II. *n*
Idiom
a home of my own une maison à moi

III. *v t*
1. posséder, être propriétaire de

does he own the house? est-il le propriétaire de la maison ?

2. Idiom
who owns that big house? à qui est cette grande maison ?

PQPQP

pack

pack
[pæk]
I. *v t*
1. mettre dans une valise

I forgot to pack my toothbrush j'ai oublié de mettre ma brosse à dents dans ma valise

2. Idiom
* ***Have you packed your bags?*** Avez-vous fait vos valises ?
Not yet, I've got to finish this letter!... Pas encore, je dois finir cette lettre !... *

II. *v i*
1. faire ses valises

I'm packing for the trip je fais mes valises pour le voyage

2. s'entasser
we all packed into his car nous nous sommes tous entassés dans sa voiture

▸ **package** *(Am)*
→ PARCEL

page

page
[peɪdʒ] *n*
page *f*

open your books at page 33 ouvrez vos livres à la page 33

* ***There are only a few pages left of this newspaper...*** Il ne reste que quelques pages de ce journal... *

pain

pain
[peɪn] *n*
douleur *f*

I've a pain in my shoulder j'ai une douleur à l'épaule

paint

paint
[peɪnt]
I. *n*
peinture *f*

* ***Caution! Wet paint!*** Attention ! Peinture fraîche ! *

II. *v t*
peindre

he's painting a picture il peint un tableau

we painted the bookcase red nous avons peint la bibliothèque en rouge

▸ **painter**
['peɪntəʳ] *n*
peintre *m*

▸ **painting**
['peɪntɪŋ] *n*
tableau *m*

it's a painting of my grandfather c'est un tableau de mon grand-père

pair

pair
[peəʳ] *n*
1. paire *f*

I'd like a pair of boots, please j'aimerais une paire de bottes, s'il vous plaît

2. Idiom
a pair of trousers (Am: pants) un pantalon

a pair of pliers une pince

pajamas

pajamas *(Am)*
→ PYJAMAS

pale

pale
[peɪl] *adj*
pâle

* *You look very pale, are you all right?... What's the matter?... Answer me!...* Tu es très pâle, tu vas bien ?... Qu'y a-t-il ?... Réponds-moi !... *

pan

pan
[pæn] *n*
1. casserole *f*

2. Idiom
frying pan poêle *f*

► **pancake**
['pænkeɪk] *n*
crêpe *f*

pants

pants *(Am)*
→ TROUSERS

paper

paper
['peɪpəʳ] *n*
1. papier *m*

give me a piece of paper donnez-moi une feuille de papier

let me see your papers! montrez-moi vos papiers !

2. journal *m*
I saw it in this morning's paper je l'ai vu dans le journal de ce matin

parcel

parcel
['pɑ:s(ə)l] *n*
(*Am:* **package**)
colis *m*, paquet *m*

* *Where does this parcel come from?* D'où vient ce paquet ? *Why don't you open it?* Et si tu l'ouvrais ? *

...parcel

pardon

pardon
['pɑ:d(ə)n]
I. *n*
pardon *m*

I beg your pardon je vous demande pardon

II. *interj*
comment

I think it's going to rain – pardon? je crois qu'il va pleuvoir – comment ?

parents

parents
['peərənts] *n pl*
parents *m pl*

* *I'll tell my parents and they'll punish you!...* Je le dirai à mes parents et ils te puniront !...
Good idea!... Bonne idée !... *

park

park
[pɑ:k]
I. *n*
1. parc *m*, jardin *m* public

* *He couldn't possibly have left the park...* Il n'a pourtant pas pu sortir du parc... *

2. Idiom
car park (Am: parking lot) parking *m*

II. *v t*
garer

...park

* *Can we park our car in front of the gates?* Pouvons-nous garer notre voiture devant les grilles ?
Yes, of course... Oui, bien sûr... *

III. *v i*
se garer

you can park there tu peux te garer là

► **parking**
['pɑ:kɪŋ] *n*
stationnement *m*

no parking stationnement interdit

part

part
[pɑ:t] *n*
1. partie *f*

I've saved you part of the cake je vous ai gardé une partie du gâteau

...part

2. pièce *f*
spare parts pièces de rechange

3. rôle *m*
the actor who played the part of Hamlet l'acteur qui a joué le rôle de Hamlet

4. Idiom
to take part participer

did the Professor take part in the discussion? le professeur a-t-il participé au débat ?

particular

particular
['pəˈtɪkjʊləʳ]
I. *adj*
particulier

did anything happen? – nothing particular est-ce que quelque chose est arrivé ? – rien de particulier

II. *n*
in particular en particulier

► **particularly**
[pəˈtɪkjʊləlɪ] *adv*
particulièrement

* *... and there's one point I'd particularly like to stress...* ... et je voudrais insister particulièrement sur un point... *

party

party
[ˈpɑ:tɪ] *n*

...party

... and there's one point I'd particularly like to stress...

pl parties [ˈpɑ:tɪz]
1. fête *f*, soirée *f*

we're having a party, would you like to come? nous faisons une fête, aimeriez-vous venir ?

2. groupe *m*
a party of tourists un groupe de touristes

3. parti *m*
the Labour/Republican Party le parti travailliste/républicain

pass

pass
[pɑ:s]
I. *n*
1. passe *f*

a long pass to the goalkeeper une longue passe au gardien de but

2. laissez-passer *m inv*
* *Your passes are perfectly in order... I'll take you there...* Vos laissez-passer sont tout à fait en règle... Je vais vous y conduire... *

Your passes are perfectly in order... I'll take you there...

II. *v t*
1. passer

could you pass me the salt, please? pourriez-vous me passer le sel, s'il vous plaît ?

he passed the ball to the centre (Am: center) forward il a passé la balle à l'avant-centre

2. passer
we played cards to pass the time nous avons joué aux cartes pour passer le temps

3. passer devant
we passed a castle on the way here nous sommes passés devant un château en venant ici

4. doubler
the car is trying to pass us la voiture essaie de nous doubler

5. être reçu à, réussir
did you pass your history exam? as-tu été reçu à ton examen d'histoire ?

III. *v i*
1. passer

he stepped aside to let me pass il s'est écarté pour me laisser passer

2. passer
time passes slowly le temps passe lentement

3. être reçu

...pass

only two students passed deux étudiants seulement ont été reçus

4. Idiom
to pass out s'évanouir

passenger

passenger
[ˈpæsɪndʒəʳ] *n*
passager *m*, passagère *f*

passer-by

passer-by
[ˈpɑ:səˈbaɪ] *n*
pl passers-by
passant *m*, passante *f*

* *What are the passers-by looking at?...* Que regardent les passants ?... *

What are the passers-by looking at?...

passport

passport
[ˈpɑ:spɔ:t] *n*
passeport *m*

past

past
[pɑ:st]
I. *prep*
1. passé

...past

it's past midnight already! il est déjà minuit passé !

2. devant
we came past a castle yesterday nous sommes passés devant un château en venant hier

3. après
* *The hospital is past the mosque, a little further along to your left...* L'hôpital est après la mosquée, un peu plus loin sur votre gauche...

Alright, thank you... Ah bon, merci... *

4. Idiom
it's five/quarter/half past seven il est sept heures cinq /et quart/ et demie

to go past something passer devant quelque chose

he ran past me il est passé devant moi en courant

II. *adv*
Idiom

she ran past elle est passée en courant

III. *adj*
1. passé

the past events les événements passés

what is the past tense of this verb? quel est le passé de ce verbe ?

2. dernier
where have you been for the past two weeks? où étiez-vous ces deux dernières semaines ?

IV. *n*
passé *m*

tell me about your past racontez-moi votre passé

what is the past of this verb? quel est le passé de ce verbe ?

path

path
[pɑ:θ] *n*
sentier *m*, chemin *m*, allée *f*
* *I'm sure he went along this path...* Je suis sûr qu'il est passé par cette allée... *

patience

patience
['peɪʃ(ə)ns] *n*
patience *f*

...patience

* *I'm beginning to run out of patience!...* Je commence à être à bout de patience !... *

► **patient**
['peɪʃ(ə)nt]
I. *adj*
patient

be patient, we're nearly there soyez patient, nous sommes presque arrivés

II. *n*
malade *m f*

the doctor is examining a patient le docteur est en train d'examiner un malade

pavement

pavement
['peɪvmənt] *n*
(*Am:* **sidewalk**)
trottoir *m*

walk on the pavement, Snowy! marche sur le trottoir, Milou !

pay

pay
[peɪ]
paid, paid [peɪd]

...pay

I. *vt*
1. payer

the workers are paid every Friday les ouvriers sont payés tous les vendredis

2. Idiom
why don't you pay us a visit in Marlinspike? pourquoi ne venez-vous pas nous rendre visite à Moulinsart ?

II. *vi*
payer

* *Well then, do you think it'll be alright?* Alors, vous croyez que ça ira ?
Yes it's perfect. How much did you pay for this diving suit?... Oui, c'est très bien. Combien avez-vous payé ce scaphandre ?... *

blistering barnacles, they'll pay for this! tonnerre de Brest, ils me payeront ça !

pea

pea
[pi:] *n*
petit pois *m*

peace

peace
[pi:s] *n*
paix *f*

peach

peach
[piːtʃ] *n*
pêche *f*

pear

pear
[peəʳ] *n*
poire *f*

pedestrian

pedestrian
[pəˈdestrɪən] *n*
1. piéton *m*, piétonne *f*

slow down, there are a lot of pedestrians ralentissez, il y a beaucoup de piétons

2. Idiom
* *It's lucky there is a pedestrian crossing (Am: crosswalk)!...* Heureusement qu'il y a un passage clouté !... *

It's lucky there is a pedestrian crossing!...

pen

pen
[pen] *n*
stylo *m*

there's no ink in my pen il n'y a plus d'encre dans mon stylo

pence

pence
[pens] *n pl*
pence *m pl*

...pence

it costs 99 pence cela coûte 99 pence

pencil

pencil
[ˈpens(ə)l] *n*
crayon *m*

I always write in pencil j'écris toujours au crayon

penny

penny
[ˈpenɪ] *n*
penny *m*
pl pennies & pence

I've a lot of pennies in my pocket j'ai plein de pennies dans ma poche

it cost me 20 pence ça ma coûté 20 pence

people

people
[ˈpiːp(ə)l] *n*
1. *pl* personnes *f pl*, gens *m pl*

how many people were there at the meeting? il y avait combien de personnes à la réunion ?

2. *pl* monde *m*
* *It's lucky there are a lot of people... In this crowd, we'll pass unnoticed...* Heureusement qu'il y a beaucoup de monde... Dans cette foule, nous passerons inaperçus... *

3. peuple *m*
the Syldavians are a strange people les Syldaves sont un peuple étrange

4. Idiom
English people les Anglais

French people les Français

It's lucky there are a lot of people... In this crowd, we'll pass unnoticed...

pepper

pepper
[ˈpepəʳ] *n*
poivre *m*

performance

performance
[pəˈfɔːməns] *n*
représentation *f*
Signora Castafiore is giving a performance tonight la Castafiore donne une représentation ce soir

perhaps

perhaps
[pəˈhæps] *adv*
peut-être
where's Tintin? perhaps he's had an accident où est Tintin ? peut-être a-t-il eu un accident

period

period
[ˈpɪərɪəd] *n*
1. période *f*

...period

he has periods of depression il a des périodes de dépression

2. cours *m*, leçon *f*
during the history period pendant le cours d'histoire

person

person
[ˈpɜːs(ə)n] *n*
1. personne *f*

...person

who is that person with Calculus? qui est cette personne avec Tournesol ?

I've never seen her in person je ne l'ai jamais vue en personne

2. Idiom
I'm more of a town person than a country person je suis plutôt de la ville que de la campagne

► **personal**
[ˈpɜːsən(ə)l] *adj*
personnel

* *A personal message for you, Tintin!* Un message personnel pour vous, Tintin ! *

A personal message for you, Tintin!

pet

pet
[pet] *n*
animal *m* familier

* *Two pets...* Deux animaux familiers... *

Two pets...

petrol

petrol
['petrəl] *n*
(Am: **gas(oline)**)
essence *f*

we're nearly out of petrol nous n'avons presque plus d'essence

phone

phone
[fəʊn]
I. *n*
téléphone *m*

there's somebody on the phone for you il y a quelqu'un qui vous demande au téléphone

they're not on the phone (Am: they have no phone) ils n'ont pas le téléphone

II. *v t*
téléphoner à, appeler

* *Great, a telephone box, I'll phone the Captain straight-away!* Chic, une cabine, je vais appeler le capitaine tout de suite ! *

Great, a telephone box, I'll phone the Captain straight-away!

III. *v i*
téléphoner, appeler

the Captain phoned while you were out le capitaine a appelé pendant que vous étiez sorti

▸ **phone box** (*Am:* **phone booth**) *n*
cabine *f* téléphonique

photo

photo
['fəʊtəʊ] *n*
photo *f*

he took a photo of Snowy il a pris Milou en photo

▸ **photograph**
['fəʊtəgrɑ:f] *n*
photographie *f*

Tintin's photograph is in the paper il y a la photographie de Tintin dans le journal

▸ **photographer**
[fə'tɒgrəfə^r] *n*
photographe *m, f*

piano

piano
[pɪ'ænəʊ] *n*
piano *m*

to play the piano jouer du piano

pick

pick
[pɪk] *v t*
1. choisir

pick the one you like best choisissez celui que vous préférez

2. cueillir
they are picking apples/cherries ils cueillent des pommes/cerises

▸ **pick up**
1. ramasser

he picked up a coin in the street il a ramassé une pièce dans la rue

2. passer prendre
I'll pick you up at the airport je passerai vous prendre à l'aéroport

picnic

picnic
['pɪknɪk] *n*
pique-nique *m*

let's go for a picnic faisons un pique-nique

picture

picture
['pɪktʃə^r] *n*
1. tableau *m*

* *Look... a globe!...* Regardez... un globe terrestre !...

Look... a globe!...
Yes, it was hidden by the picture!...

Yes, it was hidden by the picture!... Oui, il était caché par le tableau !... *

2. photo *f*
I've seen his picture in the papers j'ai vu sa photo dans les journaux

▸ **pictures**
(*Am:* **movies**) *n pl*
cinéma *m*

let's go to the pictures allons au cinéma

pie

pie
[paɪ] *n*
tarte *f*

another slice of apple pie? encore une part de tarte aux pommes ?

piece

piece
[pi:s] *n*
1. morceau *m*

...piece

the mirror is smashed to pieces le miroir est cassé en mille morceaux

2. Idiom
a piece of advice un conseil

a piece of news une nouvelle

a piece of information un renseignement

pig

pig
[pɪg] *n*
cochon *m*, porc *m*

pile

pile
[paɪl] *n*
tas *m*, pile *f*

* *Calculus knocked a pile of plates over and lots of other things...* Tournesol a fait

...pile

Calculus knocked a pile of plates over and lots of other things...

...pile

tomber une pile d'assiettes et beaucoup d'autres choses... *

pillar-box

pillar-box
['pɪləbɒks] *n*
(*Am:* **mailbox**)
boîte *f* aux lettres

pilot

pilot
['paɪlət] *n*
pilote *m*

pink

pink
[pɪŋk]
I. *adj*
rose

who's that lady in the pink dress? qui est cette femme avec une robe rose ?

...pink

II. *n*
rose *m*

pink is my favourite colour (Am: favorite color) le rose est ma couleur préférée

pipe

pipe
[paɪp] *n*
1. tuyau *m*

...pipe

There, I've managed to repair my pipe...

the water runs down these pipes l'eau coule dans ces tuyaux

2. pipe *f*
* *There, I've managed to repair my pipe...* Ça y est, j'ai réussi à réparer ma pipe... *

pity

pity
['pɪtɪ] *n*

...pity

1. pitié *f*

don't expect me to have any pity for you n'espérez pas que j'éprouve de la pitié pour vous

2. dommage *m*
what a pity! quel dommage !

it's a pity Tintin isn't here c'est dommage que Tintin ne soit pas là

place

place
[pleɪs] *n*
1. endroit *m*, lieu *m*

I can't find the place where we are on the map je ne trouve pas l'endroit où nous sommes sur la carte

2. place *f*
is this place taken? cette place est-elle prise ?

everything is in its place tout est à sa place

plain

plain
[pleɪn]
I. *adj*
1. simple

we had a good plain meal nous avons fait un bon repas tout simple

2. clair, évident
it's plain he doesn't believe us il est évident qu'il ne nous croit pas

II. *n*
plaine *f*

a vast arid plain une vaste plaine aride

plan

plan
[plæn]
I. *n*
1. projet *m*, plan *m*

* *What can we do?* Que pouvons-nous faire ? *Wait!... I've got a plan... Listen care-*

...plan

fully... Attendez ! J'ai un plan... Ecoutez bien... *Yes, we're listening. You always have good ideas!...* Oui, nous vous écoutons. Vous avez toujours de bonnes idées !... *

2. plan *m*
here is a plan of the building voici un plan du bâtiment

II. *vt*
projeter, prévoir

...plan

What can we do ?
Wait!... I've got a plan ... Listen carefully...
Yes, we're listening You always have good ideas!...

what are you planning to do next? que projetez-vous de faire ensuite ?

plane

plane
[pleɪn] *n*
avion *m*

the plane is coming in to land l'avion va atterrir

plant

plant
[plɑ:nt] *n*
plante *f*

plastic

plastic
['plæstɪk]
I. *n*
plastique *m*

...plastic

it seems to be made of plastic on dirait que c'est en plastique

II. *adj*
en plastique

plastic toys jouets en plastique

plate

plate
[pleɪt] *n*
1. assiette *f*

he ate a big plate of spaghetti il a mangé une grande assiette de spaghetti

2. plaque *f*
* *His name is on the plate...* Son nom est sur la plaque... *

number plate plaque d'immatriculation

...plate

Dr J.W. MÜLLER
His name is on the plate...

platform

platform
['plætfɔ:m] *n*
quai *m*

which platform does our train leave from? de quel quai notre train part-il ?

play

play
[pleɪ]
I. *vt*
1. jouer à

...play

they are playing football ils jouent au football

2. jouer de
can you play the guitar? savez-vous jouer de la guitare ?

3. jouer le rôle de
who played Hamlet? qui a joué le rôle de Hamlet ?

II. *vi*
jouer

Snowy is playing in the water Milou joue dans l'eau

III. *n*
pièce *f* (de théâtre)

we went to see a play last night nous sommes allés voir une pièce hier soir

► **player**
['pleɪəʳ] *n*
joueur *m*, joueuse *f*

► **playground**
['pleɪgraʊnd] *n*
cour *f* (de récréation)

all the children are in the playground tous les enfants sont dans la cour de récréation

pleasant

pleasant
['plez(ə)nt] *adj*
agréable

we've had a very pleasant evening nous avons passé une soirée très agréable

please

please
[pli:z] *interj*
s'il vous plaît,
s'il te plaît

...please

* *Pass me the binoculars, please!* Passez-moi les jumelles, s'il vous plaît ! *

► **pleased**
[pli:zd] *adj*
1. content, heureux

he doesn't look very pleased il n'a pas l'air très content

2. Idiom
pleased to meet you! enchanté (de faire votre connaissance) !

Pass me the binoculars please!

plenty

plenty
['plentɪ] *n*
1. abondance *f*

2. Idiom
he's got plenty of money il a beaucoup d'argent

* *There's no need to hurry, we've got plenty of time.* Ce n'est pas la peine de nous presser, nous avons largement assez de temps. *

There's no need to hurry, we've got plenty of time.

plum

plum
[plʌm] *n*
prune *f*

plural

plural
['plʊərəl] *n*
pluriel *m*

pocket

pocket
['pɒkɪt] *n*
poche *f*

* *Wait, I've got a gun in my pocket...* Attendez, j'ai un revolver dans ma poche...
Quick, give it to me... Vite, donnez-le moi... *

► **pocket money** (*Am:* **allowance)** *n*
argent *m* de poche

poem

poem
['pəʊɪm] *n*
poème *m*

► **poetry**
['pəʊɪtrɪ] *n*
poésie *f*

point

point
[pɒɪnt]
I. *n*
1. pointe *f*

I pricked myself with the point of a needle je me suis piqué avec la pointe d'une aiguille

2. point *m*
* *We're back to the point we started from, what shall we do?* Nous sommes revenus à notre point de départ, que faisons-nous ?

...point

I don't know. Je n'en sais rien. *

3. virgule *f*
decimal point virgule décimale

seven point five sept virgule cinq

4. point *m*
the winner scores ten points le gagnant marque dix points

5. Idiom

there's no point in worrying il n'y a pas de raison de s'inquiéter

what's the point of doing this? à quoi ça sert de faire ceci ?

II. *v i*
montrer du doigt

why is that man pointing at us? pourquoi cet homme nous montre-t-il du doigt ?

III. *v t*
braquer

* *Don't point that gun at him!* Ne braquez pas ce fusil sur lui ! *

► **point out**
signaler

I would like to point out that it wasn't my idea j'aimerais signaler que ce n'était pas mon idée

poison

poison
['pɒɪz(ə)n]
I. *n*
poison m

II. *v t*
empoisonner

* *Somebody's tried to poison Snowy!* Quelqu'un a essayé d'empoisonner Milou ! *

police

police
[pə'li:s] *n pl*
police *f*

* *We've been sent by the French police to help you... We've put on disguise, so we won't be noticed.* Nous sommes envoyés par la police française pour vous aider... Nous nous sommes déguisés pour passer inaperçus.
To be precise, so we won't be noticed... Je dirais même plus, inaperçus... *

► **policeman**
[pə'li:smən] *n*
pl policemen
policier *m*, agent *m* de police

► **policewoman**
[pə'li:swʊmən] *n*
pl policewomen
femme *f* policier

We've been sent by the French police to help you... We've put on disguise, so we won't be noticed.
To be precise, so we won't be noticed...

polite

polite
[pə'laɪt] *adj*
poli

be polite sois poli

political

political
[pə'lɪtɪk(ə)l] *adj*
politique

a political party un parti politique

...political

▶ **politics**
['pɒlɪtɪks] *n*
politique *f*

he isn't interested in politics il ne s'intéresse pas à la politique

pollute

pollute
[pə'lu:t] *vt*
polluer

...pollute

look, the river is all polluted regardez, la rivière est toute polluée

▶ **pollution**
[pə'lu:ʃ(ə)n] *n*
pollution *f*

pool

pool
[pu:l] *n*
1. mare *f*

...pool

ducks are swimming in the pool des canards nagent dans la mare

2. piscine *f*
they have an outdoor (swimming) pool ils ont une piscine en plein air

poor

poor
[pʊəʳ] *adj*
1. pauvre

...poor

it is one of the poorest countries in the world c'est l'un des pays les plus pauvres du monde

2. médiocre
* *This knife is really poor quality!...* Ce couteau est vraiment de qualité médiocre !... *

3. pauvre
poor Snowy, he's hurt his paw! pauvre Milou, il s'est fait mal à la patte !

...poor

This knife is really poor quality!...

popular

popular
['pɒpjʊləʳ] *adj*
1. populaire

popular music musique populaire

2. fréquenté
it's a very popular place with tourists c'est un endroit très fréquenté par les touristes

3. aimé
he was popular with his pupils il était aimé par ses élèves

4. à la mode
red is very popular this year le rouge est très à la mode cette année

pork

pork
[pɔ:k] *n*
porc *m*

a pork chop une côte de porc

port

port
[pɔ:t] *n*
port *m*

* *The boat is leaving port...* Le bateau quitte le port... *

The boat is leaving port...

possible

possible
['pɒsɪb(ə)l] *adj*
possible

...possible

* *I'll do everything possible to help you...* Je ferai tout mon possible pour vous aider... *

come as quickly as possible venez aussi vite que possible

▶ **possibly**
['pɒsɪblɪ] *adv*
1. peut-être

this is possibly the worst storm we've ever had ceci est peut-être la tempête la plus mauvaise que nous ayons jamais connue

I'll do everything possible to help you...

2. Idiom
I'll do everything I possibly can je ferai tout mon possible

I can't possibly finish by tomorrow! il m'est absolument impossible de finir d'ici demain !

post

post
[pəʊst]
I. *n*
1. poteau *m*

tie the rope to that post attachez la corde à ce poteau

2. courrier *m*
the post (Am: mail) comes at nine o'clock le courrier arrive à neuf heures

3. poste *f*
this parcel came by post (Am: mail) ce colis est arrivé par la poste

4. poste *m*
stay at your posts! restez à vos postes !

II. *vt*
mettre à la poste

could you post (Am: mail) this letter for me? pourriez-vous mettre cette lettre à la poste pour moi ?

...post

► **postcard**
['pəʊstkɑ:d] *n*
carte *f* postale

goodbye! send us a postcard! au revoir ! envoyez-nous une carte postale !

► **postman**
['pəʊstmən] *n*
(*Am:* **mailman)**
pl postmen
facteur *m*

Look what the postman's just brought!...

* *Look what the postman's just brought!...* Regarde ce que le facteur vient d'apporter !... *

► **post office**
['pəʊstɔfis] *n*
bureau de poste *m*

poster

poster
['pəʊstəʳ] *n*
affiche *f*, poster *m*

a poster announcing Signora Castafiore's concert une affiche qui annonce le concert de la Castafiore

potato

potato
[pə'teɪtəʊ] *n*
pl potatoes
pomme *f* de terre

pound

pound
[paʊnd] *n*
1. livre *f*

* *How much is this boat?* Combien, ce bateau ?
I'll let you have it for ten pounds!... Je vous le vends dix livres !... *

2. livre *f* (= 453 grammes)
a pound of onions, please une livre d'oignons, s'il vous plaît

How much is this boat?
I'll let you have it for ten pounds!...

pour

pour
[pɔ:ʳ]
I. *vt*
1. verser

he poured the water down the sink il a versé l'eau dans l'évier

2. servir
can I pour you another cup of tea? puis-je vous servir une autre tasse de thé ?

II. *vi*
Idiom

After the show...

The audience comes pouring out of the theatre...

...pour

water came pouring in through the porthole l'eau est entrée à flots par le hublot

* *After the show...* Après le spectacle...
The audience comes pouring out of the theatre (Am: theater)... Le public sort du théâtre en grand nombre... *

it's pouring (with rain)! il pleut à verse !

► **pour down**
pleuvoir à verse

take your umbrella, it's pouring down prenez votre parapluie, il pleut à verse

power

power
['paʊəʳ] *n*
1. pouvoir *m*

...power

Hurray for Alcazar!
Hurray!
What enthusiasm!

General Alcazar has just seized power...

* *Hurray for Alcazar!* Vive Alcazar !
Hurray! Hourra !
What enthusiasm! Quel enthousiasme !
General Alcazar has just seized power... Le général Alcazar vient de prendre le pouvoir... *

2. puissance *f*
there's no power in the engine! le moteur n'a pas de puissance !

practice
['præktɪs] *n*
1. entraînement *m*

he could be a good player with practice il pourrait devenir un bon joueur avec de l'entraînement

2. exercices *m pl*
have you done your piano practice? as-tu fait tes exercices de piano ?

3. pratique *f*
to put a theory into practice mettre une théorie en pratique

► **practise** (*Am:* **practice**)
['præktɪs] *vt*
1. s'entraîner à, s'exercer à

she practises her tennis every day elle s'entraîne au tennis tous les jours

2. pratiquer
he's a practising Catholic c'est un catholique pratiquant

precious

precious
['preʃəs] *adj*
1. précieux

** Thundering typhoons! Precious stones! Diamonds! Oh my word!...* Tonnerre de Brest ! Des pierres précieuses ! Des diamants ! Ça alors !... *

2. Idiom
Snowy is very precious to me je suis très attaché à Milou

prefer
[prɪ'fɜːʳ] *vt*
préférer, aimer mieux

prepare

prepare
[prɪ'peəʳ]
I. *vt*
1. préparer

** And the next morning...* Et le lendemain matin...
We have prepared a room for you... Nous avons préparé une chambre pour vous... *

2. Idiom
be prepared! soyez prêt !

II. *vi*
se préparer

we are preparing to leave tomorrow nous nous préparons à partir demain

prescription

prescription
[prɪ'skrɪpʃn] *n*
ordonnance *f*

the doctor made me out a prescription le médecin m'a fait une ordonnance

present

present
['prez(ə)nt]
I. *n*
1. cadeau *m*

here's a present for you, Snowy voici un cadeau pour toi, Milou

2. présent *m*
what is the present of this verb? quel est le présent de ce verbe ?

3. Idiom
I'm living in London at present j'habite Londres actuellement

II. *adj*
1. actuel

please signal your present position veuillez signaler votre position actuelle

2. présent
only a few people were present quelques personnes seulement étaient présentes

3. Idiom
the present tense le présent

president

president
['prezɪdənt] *n*
président *m*, présidente *f*

press

press
[pres]
I. *vt*
1. appuyer sur

** What happens if I press these buttons?... I wonder!... Never mind, I'll try! I'll see then!...* Qu'est-ce qui se passe si j'appuie sur ces boutons ?... Je me le demande !... Tant pis, j'essaie ! Je verrai bien ! *

...press

2. repasser
he pressed his trousers (Am: pants) il a repassé son pantalon

II. *n*
1. presse *f*

the freedom of the press la liberté de la presse

2. Idiom
the story isn't in the press yet l'affaire n'est pas encore dans les journaux

pretend

pretend
[prɪ'tend] *v i*
1. faire semblant

he isn't really hurt, he's only pretending il n'a pas vraiment mal, il fait semblant

2. Idiom
he pretended to be a policeman il s'est fait passer pour un policier

pretty

pretty
['prɪtɪ]
I. *adj*
prettier, prettiest
joli

* *Their costumes are really pretty, aren't they?* Leurs costumes sont vraiment très jolis, n'est-ce-pas ? *

II. *adv*
assez, plutôt

...pretty

I'm pretty tired! je suis plutôt fatigué !

prevent

prevent
[prɪ'vent] *v t*
empêcher

try to prevent the Captain from drinking essayez d'empêcher le capitaine de boire

price

price
[praɪs] *n*
prix *m*

the price is too high le prix est trop élevé

prime minister

prime minister
[praɪm'mɪnɪstəʳ] *n*
premier ministre *m*

prison

prison
['prɪzn] *n*
prison *f*

* *How am I possibly going to escape from this prison?* Comment vais-je pouvoir m'échapper de cette prison ? *

the culprit has been put into prison le coupable a été mis en prison

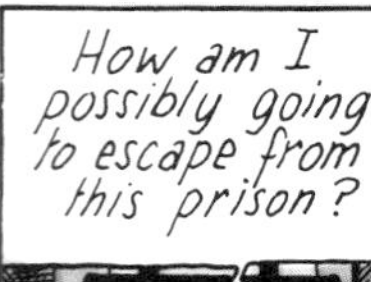

private

private
['praɪvət]
I. *adj*
1. privé

this is private property c'est une propriété privée

2. Idiom
could I speak to you in private? pourrais-je vous parler en privé ?

probable

probable
['prɒbəbl] *adj*
probable

it is probable that other forms of life exist in the universe il est probable que d'autres formes de vie existent dans l'univers

▶ **probably**
['prɒbəblɪ] *adv*
probablement

* *Tintin has probably got lost! We must look for him!...* Tintin s'est probablement perdu ! Nous devons le chercher !... *

problem

problem
['prɒbləm] *n*
problème *m*

what's the problem, Tintin? quel est le problème, Tintin ?

produce

produce
[prə'dju:s] *v t*
produire

this is where we produce the gas voici l'endroit où nous produisons le gaz

▶ **product**
['prɒdʌkt] *n*
produit *m*

▶ **production**
[prə'dʌkʃ(ə)n] *n*
production *f*

professor

professor
[prə'fesəʳ] *n*
professeur *m*

programme

programme
['prəʊgræm] *n*
(*Am:* **program**)
1. émission *f*

I saw a programme on television about whales j'ai vu une émission à la télévision sur les baleines

2. programme *m*
what's on the programme for tomorrow? quel est le programme de demain ?

progress

progress
['prəʊgres] *n*
progrès *m*

you've made progress tu as fait des progrès

promise

promise
['prɒmɪs]
I. *n*
promesse f

II. *vt*
promettre

* *Foreigners, you must promise me that you will say nothing!...* Etrangers, il faut me promettre de ne rien dire !...
Son of the Sun, I promise you that we'll keep the secret.... Fils du Soleil, je te promets que nous garderons le secret... *

protect

protect
[prə'tekt] *vt*
protéger

wear a hat to protect you from the sun mettez un chapeau pour vous protéger du soleil

protest

protest
[prə'test] *vi*
protester

the Captain protested loudly le capitaine a protesté bruyamment

proud

proud
[praʊd] *adj*
fier

* *Well done, Tintin! You've made it! I'm proud of you!* Bravo, Tintin ! Tu as réussi ! Je suis fier de toi ! *

prove

prove
[pru:v]
I. *vt*
prouver

* *Can you prove what you claim?... I need proof, you know!* Pouvez-vous prouver ce que vous prétendez ?... J'ai besoin de preuves, moi, vous savez ! *

II. *vi*
se révéler

the bomb scare proved to be a hoax l'alerte à la bombe s'est révélée être un canular

provide

provide
[prə'vaɪd] *vt*
fournir

they provide us with food ils nous fournissent de la nourriture

► **provided that**
conj
pourvu que
Snowy can come provided that he behaves himself Milou peut venir pourvu qu'il soit sage

pub

pub
[pʌb] *n*
bar *m*

they had a drink in a pub ils ont bu un verre dans un bar

public

public
['pʌblɪk]
I. *adj*
public

a public place un lieu public

II. *n*
public *m*

his novels have a very wide public ses romans ont un très large public

you shouldn't do that in public! vous ne devriez pas faire ça en public !

► **publicity**
[pʌb'lɪsɪtɪ] *n*
publicité *f*

pudding

pudding
['pʊdɪŋ] *n*
1. pudding *m*

Christmas pudding pudding de Noël

2. dessert *m*
what's for pudding (Am: dessert)? – chocolate ice cream qu'est-ce qu'il y a comme dessert ? – de la glace au chocolat

pull

pull
[pʊl]
I. *vt*
tirer
pull the rope tirez la corde

II. *vi*
1. tirer

when I say so, all pull! quand je le dirai, tirez tous !

2. Idiom
pull yourself together ressaisissez-vous

► **pull down**
démolir

the old house has been pulled down la vieille maison a été démolie

► **pull up**
1. remonter

he pulled his socks up il a remonté ses chaussettes

2. approcher
pull your chair up approchez votre chaise

3. s'arrêter
a car pulled up outside the bank une voiture s'est arrêtée devant la banque

► **pullover**
['pʊləʊvəʳ] *n*
pull *m*, pull-over *m* (*Am:* sweater)

he's wearing a red pullover il porte un pull rouge

punish

punish
['pʌnɪʃ] *vt*
punir

pupil

pupil
['pju:p(ə)l] *n*
élève *mf*

how many pupils are there in your class? il y a combien d'élèves dans ta classe ?

purple

purple
['pɜ:p(ə)l]
I. *adj*
violet, pourpre

II. *n*
violet *m*, pourpre *m*

dressed in purple habillé de violet

purpose

purpose
['pɜ:pəs] *n*
I. *n*
but *m*

what is your purpose in life? quel est votre but dans la vie ?

II. Idiom
on purpose exprès

you broke the window on purpose! tu as cassé la vitre exprès !

purse

purse
[pɜ:s] *n*
porte-monnaie *m*

push

push
[pʊʃ]
I. *vt*
1. pousser

help me push the car aidez-moi à pousser la voiture

...push

2. appuyez sur
* *Quick, push the red button!* Vite, appuyez sur le bouton rouge ! *

II. *vi*
pousser

don't push, there's room for everybody! ne poussez pas, il y a de la place pour tout le monde !

put

put
[pʊt] *vt*
put, put
1. mettre

I've put the keys in this drawer j'ai mis les clés dans ce tiroir

2. exprimer
let me put it another way si je peux m'exprimer autrement

► **put away**
ranger

...put

help me put the dishes away aidez-moi à ranger la vaisselle

► **put back**
remettre

put that book back where you found it remettez ce livre là où vous l'avez trouvé

► **put off**
1. remettre

* *The launch has been put off until tomorrow.* Le lancement a été remis à demain. *

2. déranger
he put me off just as I was going to fire il m'a dérangé juste au moment où j'allais tirer

3. Idiom
to put somebody off their food couper l'appétit à quelqu'un

► **put on**
1. mettre

put your coat on, it's raining mets ton manteau, il pleut

2. allumer
put the television on, it's time for the news allumez la télévision, c'est l'heure des informations

► **put out**
éteindre

* *Oh! They've put the lights out!...* Oh ! Ils ont éteint la lumière !... *

...put

► **put up**
héberger, loger

I'll put you up for the night je vous hébergerai pour la nuit

► **put up with**
supporter

I'll not put up with such behaviour (Am: behavior)! je ne supporterai pas un tel comportement !

pyjamas

pyjamas
[pɪ'dʒɑ:məz] *n pl*
(*Am:* **pajamas)**
pyjama *m*

a pair of pyjamas un pyjama

* *Tintin is in pyjamas...* Tintin est en pyjama...
Come on, Snowy, let's go to bed now... Allez, Milou, allons dormir maintenant...
That's a good idea! Ça, c'est une bonne idée ! *

quarrel

quarrel
['kwɒrəl]
I. *n*
querelle *f*, dispute *f*

he started the quarrel c'est lui qui a provoqué la dispute

II. *vi*
quarrelled, quarrelled (*Am:* quarreled)
se quereller, se disputer

...quarrel

he's always quarrelling with his sister il se dispute sans cesse avec sa sœur

quarter

quarter
['kwɔ:tər] *n*
quart *m*

I'll be back in a quarter of an hour je serai de retour dans un quart d'heure

queen

queen
[kwi:n] *n*
reine *f*

question

question
['kwestʃ(ə)n] *n*
1. question *f*

* *Can I ask you a question, Professor?*

...question

Puis-je vous poser une question, professeur ?
Do you have something to ask me?... Avez-vous quelque chose à me demander ?... *

2. question *f*, affaire *f*

that's a different question ça, c'est une autre affaire

queue

queue
[kju:]
(*Am:* **line)**
I. *n*
queue *f*, file *f*

they stood in a queue ils ont fait la queue

II. *vi*
faire la queue

we had to queue (Am: line up) for the tickets nous avons dû faire la queue pour les billets

quick

quick
[kwɪk]
I. *adj*
rapide

it's quicker by plane c'est plus rapide en avion

II. *adv*
vite

* *Quick, Tintin!... Come and have a look, it's extraordinary!* Vite, Tintin!... Venez voir, c'est extraordinaire ! *

► **quickly**
['kwɪklɪ] *adv*
vite, rapidement

quiet

quiet
['kwaɪət] *adj*
1. calme, tranquille

a very quiet street une rue très calme

2. Idiom
be quiet! taisez-vous !

quite

quite
[kwaɪt] *adv*
1. assez, plutôt

the weather's quite nice il fait assez beau

2. tout à fait
you're quite right, Captain vous avez tout à fait raison, capitaine

3. Idiom
quite a lot of pas mal de

rabbit

rabbit
['ræbɪt] *n*
lapin *m*

race

race
[reɪs] *n*
1. course *f*

let's have a race faisons une course

* *I wonder who's going to win this*

...race

race!... Je me demande qui va gagner cette course !... *

2. race *f*
the human race la race humaine

radio

radio
['reɪdɪəʊ] *n*
radio *f*

railway

...railway

railway
['reɪlweɪ] *n*
(*Am:* **railroad)**
chemin *m* de fer

* *Ah! There's the railway!... Let's follow the track and we'll get to the station...* Ah! Voilà la ligne de chemin de fer !... Nous allons suivre la voie et nous arriverons à la gare...
Great! You've found the solution again. Bravo! Tu as encore trouvé la solution. *

▸ **railway (***Am:* **railroad) station** *n*
gare *f*

rain

rain
[reɪn]
I. *n*
pluie *f*

...rain

don't stay out in the rain, you'll catch cold ne reste pas dehors sous la pluie, tu vas attraper froid

II. *vi*
pleuvoir

it has been raining for a week il pleut depuis une semaine

* *That's it! It's raining! Let's put the hood (Am: top) up!...* Ça y est ! Il pleut ! Mettons la capote!... *

▸ **raincoat**
['reɪnkəʊt] *n*
imperméable *m*

▸ **rainy**
['reɪnɪ] *adj*
rainier, rainiest
pluvieux

rapid

rapid
['ræpɪd] *adj*
rapide

I made a rapid calculation j'ai fait un calcul rapide

rare

rare
[reəʳ] *adj*
1. rare

...rare

I hope we'll be able to film some rare species...

** I hope we'll be able to film some rare species...* J'espère que nous allons pouvoir filmer des espèces rares... *

2. saignant
how would you like your steak? – rare, please comment aimeriez-vous votre steak ? – saignant, s'il vous plaît

► **rarely**
['reəlɪ] *adv*
rarement

rat

rat
[ræt] *n*
rat *m*

rather

rather
['rɑ:ðəʳ] *adv*
1. plutôt

I'm rather tired je suis plutôt fatigué

2. Idiom

...rather

I'd rather go tomorrow je préférerais y aller demain

would you rather have tea or coffee? préférez-vous du thé ou du café ?

raw

raw
[rɔ:] *adj*
1. cru

I can't eat that meat, it's raw! je ne peux pas manger cette viande, elle est crue !

2. Idiom
raw materials matières premières

reach

reach
[ri:tʃ] *vt*
1. atteindre

I'm not tall enough to reach the top shelf je ne suis pas assez grand pour atteindre l'étagère du haut

2. arriver à, atteindre
** I wonder whether we'll reach the island today...* Je me demande si nous atteindrons l'île aujourd'hui...

I wonder whether we'll reach the island today...
I'm beginning to doubt it...

I'm beginning to doubt it... Je commence à douter... *

read

read
[ri:d]
read, read [red]
I. *vt*
lire

what does that sign say? I can't read it

...read

que dit ce panneau ? je n'arrive pas à le lire

II. *vi*
lire

my little sister's learning to read ma petite sœur apprend à lire

► **reading**
['ri:dɪŋ] *n*
lecture *f*

** I love reading, I need these peaceful moments to rest after*

...read

I love reading, I need these peaceful moments to rest after my adventures!

my adventures! J'adore la lecture, j'ai besoin de ces moments de calme pour me reposer de mes aventures ! *

ready

ready
['redɪ] *adj*
prêt

** Are you ready? I'll throw you the rope...*

...ready

Etes-vous prêt ? Je vous lance la corde...
Go ahead!... Allez-y !... *

real

real
[rɪəl] *adj*
vrai, véritable

are those pearls real? ces perles sont-elles vraies ?

Are you ready? I'll throw you the rope...
Go ahead!...

...real

► **really**
['rɪəlɪ] *adv*
vraiment

I'm sorry, Tintin, I'm really sorry! je suis désolé, Tintin, je suis vraiment désolé !

realize

realize
['rɪəlaɪz] *vt*
se rendre compte de

...realize

* *You don't realize the difficulties, Captain!...* Vous ne vous rendez pas compte des difficultés, capitaine !... *

reason

reason
['ri:z(ə)n] *n*
raison *f*

the reason why I'm late is that I missed

...reason

the train j'ai raté le train, c'est pour cette raison que je suis en retard

receive

receive
[rɪ'si:v] *vt*
recevoir

I received his letter this morning j'ai reçu sa lettre ce matin

recent

recent
['ri:s(ə)nt] *adj*
récent

it's a very recent model c'est un modèle très récent

► **recently**
['ri:s(ə)ntlɪ] *adv*
récemment, dernièrement

have you seen the Captain recently?

...recent

avez-vous vu le capitaine récemment ?

recess

recess (*Am*)
→ BREAK

recognize

recognize
['rekəgnaɪz] *vt*
reconnaître

...recognize

* *Cuthbert, don't you recognize me? It's me, Haddock!* Tryphon, vous me reconnaissez ? C'est moi, Haddock ! *

record

record
[rɪ'kɔ:d]
I. *n*
1. disque *m*

we listened to re-

...record

cords nous avons écouté des disques

2. record *m*
she's broken the world record elle a battu le record du monde

II. [rɪ'kɔ:d] *vt*
enregistrer

I've managed to record their conversation j'ai réussi à enregistrer leur conversation

► **record player** *n*
tourne-disque *m*

red

red
[red]
I. *adj*
redder, reddest
1. rouge

* *He's red with anger.* Il est rouge de colère. *

2. roux
she's got red hair elle a les cheveux roux

II. *n*
1. rouge *m*
dressed in red habillé en rouge

He's red with anger.

when he said that I saw red! quand il a dit cela, j'ai vu rouge

reduce

reduce
[rɪ'dju:s] *vt*
réduire

reduced prices prix réduits

refuse

refuse
[rɪ'fju:z] *vt*
refuser

* *It's no good, he refuses to talk, we must find some other way!* Cela ne sert à rien, il refuse de parler, il faut trouver un autre moyen ! *

relation

relation
[rɪ'leɪʃ(ə)n] *n*
1. parent *m*, parente *f*

is he a relation of yours? est-ce l'un de vos parents ?

2. rapport *m*, relation *f*
there is no relation between the two events il n'y a aucun rapport entre les deux événements

relative

relative
['relətɪv] *n*
parent *m*, parente *f*

* *But... where are we going?...* Mais... où allons-nous ?...
Come in, I'd like you to meet a relative of mine... Entrez, j'aimerais vous présenter un parent à moi... *

relax

relax
[rɪ'læks] *vi*
se détendre

sit down and relax, Professor asseyez-vous et détendez-vous, professeur

religion

religion
[rɪ'lɪdʒən] *n*
religion *f*

remain

remain
[rɪ'meɪn] *vi*
rester

the temple is all that remains of this civilization le temple est tout ce qui reste de cette civilisation

what remains to be done? qu'est-ce qu'il reste à faire ?

remember

remember
[rɪ'membər]
I. *vt*
se souvenir de, se rappeler

what happened? I can't remember anything! qu'est-ce qui s'est passé ? je ne me souviens de rien !

II. *vi*
se souvenir

if I remember rightly si je me souviens bien

remind

remind
[rɪmaɪnd] *vt*
rappeler

* *You'll see. He's a great chap (Am: guy)!* Vous allez voir. C'est un type formidable !
He reminds me of somebody, but I can't remember who it is... Il me rappelle quelqu'un, mais je ne sais plus qui... *

rent

rent
[rent]
I. *n*
loyer *m*

we pay the rent every month nous payons le loyer tous les mois

II. *vt*
louer

we can rent a car here nous pouvons louer une voiture ici

repair

repair
[rɪ'peər] *vt*
réparer

repeat

repeat
[rɪ'pi:t] *vt*
répéter

...repeat

* *Careful, it's a secret, don't repeat it to anybody.* Attention, c'est un secret, ne le répétez à personne. *

replace

replace
[rɪ'pleɪs] *vt*
1. remplacer

* *We'll have to replace this broken*

...replace

...replace

mirror... Il faudra remplacer ce miroir cassé... *Yes... I'll do it myself...* Oui... Je le ferai moi-même... *

2. remettre
he replaced the book carefully on the shelf il a soigneusement remis le livre sur l'étagère

reply

reply
[rɪ'plaɪ]
I. *vi*
replied, replied
répondre

he hasn't replied to my letter il n'a pas répondu à ma lettre

II. *n*
pl replies
réponse *f*

in reply to your letter en réponse à votre lettre

reporter

reporter
[rɪ'pɔ:təʳ] *n*
reporter *m*, journaliste *m/f*

republic

republic
[rɪ'pʌblɪk] *n*
république *f*

rescue

rescue
['reskju:] *vt*
sauver

* *Wooaaah! Let's hope I'll get there in time to rescue Snowy!* Wouaah ! Pourvu que j'arrive à temps pour sauver Milou ! *

reserve

reserve
[rɪ'zɜ:v] *vt*
réserver

hello, I'd like to reserve a table for four, please bonjour, j'aimerais réserver une table pour quatre, s'il vous plaît

▸ **reservation**
[rezə'veɪʃ(ə)n] *n*
1. réservation *f*

I've made all the reservations for the journey j'ai fait toutes les réservations pour le voyage

2. réserve *f*
they accepted without reservation ils ont accepté sans réserve

responsible

responsible
[rɪs'pɒnsɪb(ə)l] *adj*
responsable

* *Well, I'm waiting for an explanation.*

...responsible

What do you have to say? Alors, j'attends vos explications. Qu'avez-vous à dire ?
Yes, I'm responsible for what has happened. Oui, je suis responsable de ce qui est arrivé. *

rest

rest
[rest]

...rest

I. *vi*
se reposer

* *Let's rest here for a moment.* Reposons-nous ici un instant. *

II. *vt*
appuyer

rest the ladder against the wall appuyez l'échelle contre le mur

III. *n*
1. repos *m*

...rest

you look tired, you need a rest vous avez l'air fatigué, vous avez besoin de repos

2. reste *m*
this is for me but the rest is for you celui-ci est pour moi, mais le reste est pour vous

3. Idiom
the rest of them are arriving later les autres arrivent plus tard

restaurant

restaurant
['rest(ə)rɒnt] *n*
restaurant *m*

result

result
[rɪ'zʌlt] *n*
résultat *m*

have you seen the exam results? as-tu vu les résultats de l'examen ?

return

return
[rɪ'tɜ:n]
I. *vi*
revenir, retourner

* *He wonders whether he'll ever return to America.* Il se demande s'il retournera un jour en Amérique. *

II. *vt*
rendre

thank you, I'll return it to you as soon as I've read it merci, je vous le rendrai dès que je l'aurai lu

III. *n*
1. retour *m*

we are looking forward to your return nous attendons votre retour avec impatience

2. aller et retour *m*
one return (Am: round trip) to New York please un aller et retour

...return

He wonders whether he'll ever return to America

pour New York, s'il vous plaît

3. Idiom
many happy returns (of the day) bon anniversaire

revolution

revolution
[revə'lu:ʃ(ə)n] *n*
révolution *f*

...revolution

the French Revolution la Révolution française

rice

rice
[raɪs] *n*
riz *m*

rice pudding riz au lait

rich

rich
[rɪtʃ] *adj*
riche

Mr Carreidas is very rich M. Carreidas est très riche

rid

rid
[rɪd] *vt*

to get rid of some-

...rid

thing se débarrasser de quelque chose

ride

ride
[raɪd]
rode [rəʊd], ridden ['rɪdn]
I. *vt, vi*
1. monter à, monter sur

I've never ridden a

...ride

camel je ne suis jamais monté à dos de chameau

let me ride your bicycle laisse-moi monter sur ta bicyclette

2. monter à cheval
* *The Captain is riding a horse... well... the Captain is trying to ride a horse...* Le capitaine monte à cheval... enfin... le capitaine essaie de monter à cheval... *

The Captain is riding a horse... well... the Captain is trying to ride a horse...

3. aller (à cheval/à bicyclette/etc.)
he rode into town on his bicycle il est allé en ville à bicyclette

II. *n*
promenade *f*

let's go for a ride in the car/on our bikes allons faire une promenade en voiture/à bicyclette

right

right
[raɪt]
I. *adj*
1. droit

I've hurt my right leg je me suis fait mal à la jambe droite

2. bon, juste
your answer is right votre réponse est juste

are you sure this is the right address? êtes-vous sûr que c'est la bonne adresse ?

...right

3. Idiom
you are right vous avez raison

II. *n*
1. droite *f*

take the next turning on the right prenez la prochaine rue à droite

2. droit *m*
* *You have no right to keep me here!* Vous n'avez pas le droit de me garder ici !

You should have minded your own business! Tu n'avais qu'à te mêler de tes affaires ! *

3. Idiom
the ambulance has the right of way l'ambulance a la priorité

III. *adv*
1. à droite

turn right after the church tournez à droite après l'église

2. bien, correctement
I can't pronounce his name right je n'arrive pas à bien prononcer son nom

3. droit, directement
it's right in front of you c'est droit devant vous

4. tout à fait, complètement
right at the end of the tunnel tout à fait au bout du tunnel

...right

5. Idiom
right away tout de suite

right in the middle en plein milieu

► **right-hand**
adj
droit

the right-hand side of the road le côté droit de la route

ring

ring
[rɪŋ]
I. *n*
1. bague *f*, anneau *m*

she has rings on her fingers elle a des bagues aux doigts

2. cercle *m*
sit in a ring around me mettez-vous en cercle autour de moi

3. coup *m* de fil

I'll give you a ring tomorrow morning je vous passerai un coup de fil demain matin

4. Idiom
there was a ring at the door on a sonné à la porte

II. *v i*
rang [ræŋ], rung [rʌŋ]
sonner

is that the telephone ringing? est-ce le téléphone qui sonne ?

RRRRING
?
Someone's ringing the door bell!...

III. *v t*
1. sonner

* *Rrrring* Drrring *Someone's ringing the door bell!...* Quelqu'un sonne à la porte !... *

2. appeler, passer un coup de fil à
* *Quick, ring (Am: call) the police! Hurry up!* Vite, appelez la police! Dépêchez-vous ! *No! You go and I'll wait for you here!*

...ring

Quick, ring the police! Hurry up!
No! You go and I'll wait for you here!

Non ! Allez-y... et je vous attends ici ! *

3. Idiom
his name rings a bell son nom me dit quelque chose

► **ring up** (*Am:* **call**)
appeler, passer un coup de fil à

I'll ring you up as soon as I arrive je vous appelerai dès que j'arriverai

ripe

ripe
[raɪp] *adj*
mûr

these bananas aren't ripe ces bananes ne sont pas mûres

rise

rise
[raɪz]
I. *v i*
rose [rəʊz], risen ['rɪz(ə)n]

...rise

The sun is rising...

1. se lever
* *The sun is rising...* Le soleil se lève... *

2. augmenter
prices rise all the time! les prix augmentent tout le temps !

II. *n*
augmentation *f*

she asked her boss for a rise (Am: raise) elle a demandé une augmentation à son patron

risk

risk
[rɪsk]
I. *n*
risque *m*

don't take too many risks! ne prenez pas trop de risques !

II. *v t*
risquer

thank you, Tintin, you risked your life to save me! merci, Tintin, vous avez risqué votre vie pour me sauver !

river

river
['rɪvəʳ] *n*
rivière *f*, fleuve *m*

we'll have to swim across the river il nous faudra traverser la rivière à la nage

* *There now, we can get across the river...* Ça y est, maintenant nous pouvons traverser la rivière... *

There now, we can get across the river...

road

road
[rəʊd] *n*
route *f*

rob

rob
[rɒb] *v t*
robbed, robbed
dévaliser

he robbed the bank il a dévalisé la banque

...rob

► **robbery**
['rɒbərɪ] *n*
pl robberies ['rɒbərɪz]
vol *m*

fifty pounds for that! that's robbery! cinquante livres pour ça! c'est du vol !

rocket

rocket
['rɒkɪt] *n*
fusée *f*

roof

roof
[ru:f] *n*
toit *m*

I'll try and climb onto the roof je vais essayer de monter sur le toit

room

room
[ru:m] *n*
1. pièce *f*

there are five rooms

...room

on this floor il y a cinq pièces à cet étage

2. chambre *f*
I'll show you to your room je vais vous montrer votre chambre

3. place *f*
move over, there's enough room for two poussez-vous, il y a assez de place pour deux

rope

The rope has broken!...

...rope

rope
[rəʊp] *n*
corde *f*

* *The rope has broken!...* La corde a cassé !... *

rose

rose
[rəʊz] *n*
rose *f*

rough

rough
[rʌf] *adj*
1. violent, brutal

those men look very rough ces hommes ont l'air très violent

2. rugueux
his hands are rough ses mains sont rugueuses

3. agité, houleux
we can't leave now, the sea is too rough nous ne pouvons pas partir maintenant, la mer est trop agitée

4. approximatif
it's only a rough estimate ce n'est qu'un calcul approximatif

5. Idiom
a rough copy un brouillon

round

round
[raʊnd]
I. *adj*
rond

a round table une table ronde

II. *adv*
Idiom

all the year round toute l'année

the wheels go round les roues tournent

don't look round (Am: around), I think we're being followed ne vous retournez pas, je pense qu'on nous suit

► **round** *(Am: around)*
prep

* *There's a wall all round the garden...* Il y a un mur tout autour du jardin... *

2. Idiom
it's just round the

round

There's a wall round the garden...

corner c'est juste après le coin de la rue

I'll show you round the house je vais vous faire visiter la maison

► **round trip** (*Am*)
→ RETURN

row

row
[rəʊ] *n*
rang *m*,
rangée *f*

all stand in a row mettez-vous tous en rang

row

row
[raʊ] *n*

...row

1. vacarme *m*
* *Stop that row, I'm trying to sleep!... Blistering barnacles!... Stop it!...* Arrêtez ce vacarme, j'essaie de dormir !... Mille sabords !... Arrêtez !... *

2. Idiom
to have a row with somebody se disputer avec quelqu'un

royal

royal
['rɔɪəl] *adj*
royal

the Royal Family la famille royale

rubber

rubber
['rʌbə^{r}] *n*
1. caoutchouc *m*

tyres (Am: tires) are made of rubber les pneus sont en caoutchouc

2. gomme *f*
I've made a mistake, where's my rubber (Am: eraser)? j'ai fait une faute, où est ma gomme ?

ruin

ruin
['ru:ɪn]
I. *n*
ruine *f*

the town is in ruins la ville est en ruine

II. *vt*
ruiner, gâcher

the bad weather ruined our holiday (Am: vacation) le mauvais temps a gâché nos vacances

rule

rule
[ru:l]
I. *n*
1. règle *f*, règlement *m*

* *That dog can't come in here with that protective suit on... That's the rule!* Ce chien ne peut pas entrer ici avec cette combinaison... C'est le règlement !
Oh, I didn't know!... Ah, je ne savais pas !... *

2. Idiom
as a rule en règle générale

II. *vt*
gouverner

► **ruler**
['ru:lə^{r}] *n*
1. règle *f*

draw a straight line with a ruler tracez une ligne droite avec une règle

2. chef *m* d'Etat

run

run
[rʌn]
ran [ræn], run [rʌn]
I. *vi*
1. courir

run faster, they're catching up with us! courez plus vite, ils nous rattrapent !

2. circuler
this train only runs on Mondays ce train ne circule que le lundi

3. couler
I can hear water running j'entends couler de l'eau

4. marcher, fonctionner
that's it, the machines are running! ça y est, les machines fonctionnent !

5. Idiom
to run up/down the stairs monter/descendre l'escalier en courant

she ran out of the house elle est sortie de la maison en courant

II. *vt*
1. diriger, gérer

she runs the business now that her father has retired elle dirige la société maintenant que son père est à la retraite

2. conduire
I'll run (Am: drive) you into town je vais vous conduire en ville

► **run away**
se sauver, fuir

look, they're frightened, they're running away! regardez, ils ont peur, ils se sauvent !

► **run over**
écraser

be careful not to get run over fais attention de ne pas te faire écraser

rush

rush
[rʌʃ]
I. *n*
1. ruée *f*

there was a rush for the exit il y a eu une ruée vers la sortie

2. Idiom
I'm in a rush je suis pressé

II. *vi*
se précipiter

* *The shark rushed towards our heroes...* Le requin s'est précipité sur nos héros... *

The shark rushed towards our heroes ...

sad

sad
[sæd] *adj*
sadder, saddest
triste

* ***What's wrong with this dog? He's been there all day!...*** Qu'a donc ce chien ? Il est resté là toute la journée... ***He looks so sad!... I don't know why!...*** Il a l'air tellement triste !... Je ne sais pas pourquoi !... *

safe

safe
[seɪf] *adj*
1. en sécurité

don't worry, we're safe here ne vous inquiétez pas, nous sommes en sécurité ici

2. sûr
keep the money in a safe place gardez l'argent en lieu sûr

3. Idiom
safe and sound sain et sauf

► **safety**
['seɪftɪ] *n*
sécurité *f*

safety belt ceinture de sécurité

sail

sail
[seɪl]
I. *n*
voile *f*

...sail

* ***Up sails! I said up sails!... Do you hear?... Up sails!...*** Hissez les voiles ! J'ai dit hissez les voiles !... Vous entendez ?... Hissez les voiles !... *

II. *vi*
1. naviguer

where did you learn to sail, Captain? où avez-vous appris à naviguer, capitaine ?

2. Idiom

...sail

to go sailing faire de la voile

III. *vt*
piloter

I've never sailed a boat as big as this je n'ai jamais piloté un aussi grand bateau

► **sailor**
['seɪləʳ] *n*
marin *m*

salad

salad
['sæləd] *n*
salade *f*

a tomato/fruit salad une salade de tomates/de fruits

sale

sale
[seɪl] *n*
1. vente *f*

these appliances are

...sale

on sale in all supermarkets ces appareils sont en vente dans tous les supermarchés

2. soldes *m pl*
the January sales have started les soldes de janvier ont commencé

3. Idiom
* ***Castle for sale*** Château à vendre *

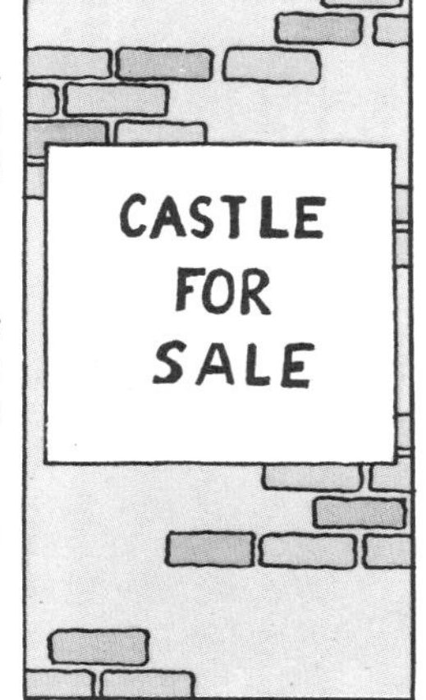

salt

salt
[sɒlt] *n*
sel *m*

same

same
[seɪm]
I. *adj*
même

* *They're both wearing the same clothes.* Ils portent tous les deux les mêmes vêtements... *

II. *pron*
le même, la même, les mêmes

their car is the same as ours ils ont la même voiture que nous

They're both wearing the same clothes.

sand

sand
[sænd] *n*
sable *m*

* *In the desert...* Dans le désert...
There's nothing but miles and miles of sand. Il n'y a rien que des kilomètres et des kilomètres de sable. *

In the desert ...
There's nothing but miles and miles of sand.

sandwich

sandwich
['sændwɪtʃ] *n*
sandwich *m*

Saturday

Saturday
['sætədɪ] *n*
samedi *m*

he's coming on Saturday il vient samedi

saucepan

saucepan
['sɔ:spən] *n*
casserole *f*

saucer

saucer
['sɔ:sər] *n*
soucoupe *f*

look, a flying saucer! regardez, une soucoupe volante !

sausage

sausage
['sɒsɪdʒ] *n*
saucisse *f*

save

save
[seɪv] *v t*
1. sauver

you saved my lif vous m'avez sauvé la vi

2. économiser
I try to save a littl money j'essaie d'économiser un peu d'argent

3. Idiom
to save time/spac gagner du temps/de l place

say

say
[seɪ] *v t*
said, said [sed]
1. dire

* *What did you say?* Qu'est-ce que tu as dit ?
I said that I can't hear what you're saying. J'ai dit que je n'entends pas ce que tu dis !... *

the notice says that it's forbidden le panneau dit que c'est interdit

What did you say?
I said that I can't hear what you're saying.

2. Idiom
I say! (Am: say!) dites donc !

scared

scared
[skeəd] *adj*
Idiom
to be scared avoir peur

scarf

scarf
[skɑ:f] *n*
pl scarves [skɑ:vz]
écharpe *f*

put your scarf on, it's cold mets ton écharpe, il fait froid

school

school
[sku:l] *n*
1. école *f*

we don't go to schoo on Saturdays nous n'allons pas à l'école l samedi

what did you do a school today? qu'est-ce que tu as fait à l'écol aujourd'hui ?

* *There's th school... And ove there is the hospital..* Voici l'école... Et là-bas c'est l'hôpital... *

2. Idiom

...school

*secondary school (Am: **high school**)* collège *m*, lycée *m*

▶ **schoolboy**
['sku:lbɔɪ] *n*
écolier *m*

▶ **schoolchildren**
['sku:ltʃɪldrən] *n pl*
écoliers *m pl*

▶ **schoolgirl**
['sku:lgɜ:l] *n*
écolière *f*

science

science
['saɪəns] *n*
science *f*

▶ **scientist**
['saɪəntɪst] *n*
scientifique *m f*, savant *m*

Professor Calculus is a famous scientist le professeur Tournesol est un scientifique célèbre

score

score
[skɔ:ʳ]
I. *n*
score *m*

what's the score ? quel est le score ?

II. *v t*
marquer

he scored a goal il a marqué un but

Scotland

Scotland
['skɒtlənd] *n*
Ecosse *f*

▶ **Scot**
[skɒt] *n*
Ecossais *m*, Ecossaise *f*

▶ **Scottish**
['skɒtɪʃ] *adj*
écossais

scratch

scratch
[skrætʃ] *v t*
égratigner

ouch, I've scratched my hand! aïe ! je me suis égratigné la main !

sea

sea
[si:] *n*
mer *f*

the sea is very rough la mer est très agitée

...sea

▶ **seasick**
['si:sɪk] *adj*
Idiom
* *They are seasick...* Ils ont le mal de mer... *

▶ **seaside**
['si:saɪd] *n*
bord *m* de la mer

we went to the seaside nous sommes allés au bord de la mer

They are seasick...

search

search
[sɜ:tʃ]
I. *v t*
fouiller

* *Military police: we're going to search your cabin.* Police militaire : nous allons fouiller votre cabine. *

...search

II. *v i*
chercher

I've searched everywhere but I can't find my glasses j'ai cherché partout, mais je ne trouve pas mes lunettes

season

season
['si:z(ə)n] *n*
saison *f*

the four seasons les quatre saisons

seat

seat
[si:t] *n*
1. siège *m*

...seat

front/back seat of the car siège avant/arrière de la voiture

2. place *f*
excuse me, is this seat taken ? excusez-moi, cette place est-elle prise ?

3. Idiom
take a seat asseyez-vous

second

second
['sekənd]
I. *n*
1. seconde *f*

in fifteen seconds dans quinze secondes

2. instant *m*, seconde *f*
I'll be ready in a second je serai prêt dans un instant

II. *adj*
deuxième, second

...second

The mummy's second victim !...

* *The mummy's second victim!...* La seconde victime de la momie !... *

a second-class ticket un billet de deuxième classe

secret

secret
['si:krɪt]
I. *adj*
secret

...secret

he's a secret agent c'est un agent secret

II. *n*
secret *m*

it's a secret c'est un secret

see

see
[si:] *v t*
saw [sɔ:], seen [si:n]

...see

1. voir

it's dark, I can't see anything il fait noir, je n'y vois rien

2. voir, comprendre
do you see what I mean ? est-ce que vous voyez ce que je veux dire ?

3. reconduire, raccompagner
I'll see you home je vais vous raccompagner

4. veiller
stay outside the door and see that nobody comes in! restez devant la porte et veillez à ce que personne n'entre !

5. Idiom
(I'll) see you tomorrow! à demain !

see you later! à tout à l'heure !

▶ **see off**
dire au revoir à

...see

they came to the station to see me off ils sont venus à la gare me dire au revoir

▶ **see to**
1. s'occuper de

I'll see to the lunch je vais m'occuper du déjeuner

2. réparer
you should get the brakes seen to vous devriez faire réparer les freins

seem

seem
[si:m] *v i*
sembler, paraître, avoir l'air

it seems a very long way cela semble très loin

Snowy doesn't seem to like that man Milou n'a pas l'air d'aimer cet homme

selfish

selfish
['selfɪʃ] *adj*
égoïste

sell

sell
[sel] *v t*
sold, sold [səʊld]
vendre

* *Do you want to sell me your boat?...* Voulez-vous me vendre votre bateau ?... *

...sell

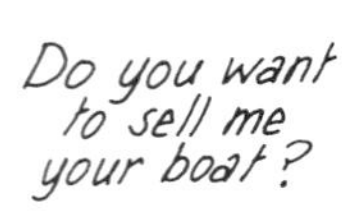
Do you want to sell me your boat?

send

send
[send] *v t*
sent, sent [sent]
envoyer

I sent the letter yesterday j'ai envoyé la lettre hier

...send

▶ **send back**
renvoyer

if the goods are faulty you must send them back si les marchandises sont défectueuses, vous devez les renvoyer

▶ **send for**
appeler, faire venir

* *He's not well, we must send for the doctor.* Il n'est pas bien, il faut faire venir le médecin. *

He's not well, we must send for the doctor.

sense

sense
[sens] *n*
1. sens *m*

sixth sense sixième sens

* *Snowy has a very keen sense of smell!*

...sense

Snowy has a very keen sense of smell!

...sense

Milou a un sens de l'odorat très développé ! *

where's your sense of humour (Am: humor) où est votre sens de l'humour ?

2. bon sens *m*
he didn't have the sense to say no il n'a pas eu le bon sens de dire non

3. Idiom
it doesn't make sense ça n'a pas de sens

sentence

sentence
['sentəns]
I. *n*
phrase *f*

* *What does this message mean? I can't make out the last sentence...* Que signifie ce message ? La dernière phrase est incompréhensible... *

II. *v t*
condamner

they have sentenced him to death ils l'ont condamné à mort

separate

separate
['sepərət]
I. *adj*
séparé

they asked for separate bills in the restaurant ils ont demandé des additions séparées au restaurant

II. *v t*
['sepəreɪt]
séparer

* *I've lost the Professor, we were separated in the crowd. Come with me, we'll try to find him...* J'ai perdu le professeur, nous avons été séparés dans la foule. Venez avec moi, nous allons essayer de le retrouver... *

...separate

September

September
[sep'tembəʳ] *n*
septembre *m*

serious

serious
['sɪərɪəs] *adj*
1. sérieux

this is a very serious matter c'est un problème très sérieux

...serious

2. grave
is the injury serious? la blessure est-elle grave ?

serve

serve
[sɜːv] *v t*
servir

the waiter who served us le garçon qui nous a servis

...serve

► **service**
['sɜːvɪs] *n*
service *m*

set

set
[set]
I. *n*
1. jeu *m*

a chess set un jeu d'échecs

2. service *m*

...set

a tea set un service à thé

3. poste *m*
we've got a new TV set nous avons un nouveau poste de télévision

II. *v t*
set, set [set]
1. mettre

they set it upright ils l'ont mis debout

help me set the table aide-moi à mettre la table

...set

2. régler
let's set our watches réglons nos montres

3. donner
the teacher didn't set (Am: assign) us any homework le professeur ne nous a pas donné de devoirs

4. Idiom
to set free libérer

to set fire to a house mettre le feu à une maison

► **set about**
se mettre à

they set about repairing the car ils se sont mis à réparer la voiture

III. *v i*
1. se coucher

* *We must hurry, Snowy, the sun will be setting soon...* Dépêchons-nous, Milou, le soleil va bientôt se coucher... *

2. prendre
wait for the glue to set attendez que la colle prenne

► **set off**
partir, se mettre en route

he's setting off for America tomorrow il part pour l'Amérique demain

► **set out**
partir, se mettre en route

it's late, we must be setting out il est tard, il faut que nous partions

settle

settle
['set(ə)l]
I. *v t*
1. installer

she settled the baby in the car elle a installé le bébé dans la voiture

...settle

2. calmer
drink this, it'll settle your nerves buvez ceci, ça vous calmera les nerfs

3. régler
that settles it, I'm leaving cela règle le problème, je pars

4. régler
to settle the bill régler la note

II. *vi*
1. s'installer

they've settled in Spain ils se sont installés en Espagne

2. se poser
the butterfly settled on a leaf le papillon s'est posé sur une feuille

3. retomber
wait for the dust to settle attendez que la poussière retombe

► **settle down**
s'installer

* *Let me settle down in my armchair and read me Abdullah's letter...* Laissez-moi m'installer dans mon fauteuil et lisez-moi la lettre d'Abdallah... *

seven

seven
['sevn]
I. *adj*
sept

II. *n*
sept *m*

► **seventeen**
[sev(ə)n'tiːn]
I. *adj*
dix-sept

II. *n*
dix-sept *m*

► **seventy**
['sev(ə)ntɪ]
I. *adj*
soixante-dix

seventy-one soixante et onze

seventy-two soixante-douze

II. *n*
pl seventies
['sev(ə)ntiz]
soixante-dix *m*

in the seventies dans les années soixante-dix

several

several
['sev(ə)rəl] *adj & pron*
plusieurs

* *Abdullah, I've told you several times not to do that!...* Abdallah, je t'ai dit plusieurs fois de ne pas faire ça !...
Waaaah! Waaah!... Wouin !... Wouin !... *

severe

severe
[sɪ'vɪəʳ] *adj*
1. sévère, strict

our teacher is very severe notre professeur est très sévère

2. grave
* *I must have a very severe illness.* Je dois avoir une maladie très grave.
No, you are seasick... Non, tu as le mal de mer... *

...severe

sew

sew
[səʊ] *vt*
sewed, sewn [səʊn]
coudre

shadow

shadow
['ʃædəʊ] *n*
ombre *f*

I saw his shadow on the wall j'ai vu son ombre sur le mur

shake

shake
[ʃeɪk]
shook [ʃʊk], shaken ['ʃeɪkn]
I. *vt*
1. secouer, agiter

shake the bottle well secouez bien la bouteille

2. serrer
I shook his hand je lui ai serré la main

* *Let's forget it and shake hands!* Oublions ça et serrons-nous la main ! *

...shake

Okay! D'accord ! *

II. *vi*
trembler

Snowy, you're shaking, are you frightened? Milou, tu trembles, tu as peur ?

shall

shall
[ʃæl] *v aux*
(forme négative :

...shall

shan't
[ʃɑ:nt])
1. *(employé pour former le futur)*

I shall be back tomorrow je serai de retour demain

I shan't see you je ne vous verrai pas

2. *(employé pour faire une suggestion)*
shall I open the window? voulez-vous que j'ouvre la fenêtre ?

shame

shame
[ʃeɪm] *n*
1. honte *f*

* *Shame on you!... I wonder whether you'll ever be sensible...* Tu devrais avoir honte !... Je me demande si tu deviendras raisonnable un jour... *

2. dommage *m*
what a shame Tintin isn't here! quel dommage que Tintin ne soit pas là !

shan't

shan't → SHALL

shape

shape
[ʃeɪp] *n*
forme *f*

a cloud in the shape of an elephant un nuage en forme d'éléphant

share

share
[ʃeəʳ] *vt*
partager

we'll have to share a cabin nous devrons partager une cabine

▸ **share out**
partager, distribuer

she shared out the toys among the children elle a distribué les jouets aux enfants

sharp

sharp
[ʃɑ:p] *adj*
1. tranchant

this knife isn't sharp enough ce couteau n'est pas assez tranchant

2. brusque, raide
a sharp fall in prices une chute brusque des prix

3. aigu, perçant
a sharp cry un cri aigu

4. Idiom
* *Look sharp Snowy...* Dépêche-toi Milou... *

she

she
[ʃi:] *pron*
elle

she's an opera singer elle est chanteuse d'opéra

sheep

sheep
[ʃi:p] *n inv*
mouton *m*

sheet

sheet
[ʃi:t] *n*
1. drap *m*

a fitted sheet un drap-housse

...sheet

2. feuille *f*
* *What's written on this sheet of paper?* Qu'est-ce qui est écrit sur cette feuille de papier ? *

shelf

shelf
[ʃelf] *n*
pl shelves [ʃelvz]
étagère *f*, rayon *m*

shell

shell
[ʃel] *n*
1. coquille *f*

boil the eggs and remove the shells faites bouillir les œufs et enlevez les coquilles

2. coquillage *m*
* *Let's go and gather shells on the beach...* Allons ramasser des coquillages sur la plage... *

3. obus *m*
the shell didn't ex-

...shell

plode l'obus n'a pas explosé

shelter

shelter
['ʃeltə^{r}] *n*
abri *m*

quick, let's take shelter under that rock! vite, mettons-nous à l'abri sous ce rocher !

shine

shine
[ʃaɪn] *vi*
shone, shone [ʃɒn]
briller

* *Look, something's shining over there! Can't you see? It's straight ahead of us.* Regardez, il y a quelque chose qui brille là-bas ! Vous ne voyez pas ? C'est juste en face de nous. *

ship

ship
[ʃɪp] *n*
navire *m*

I'm the captain of this ship! c'est moi le capitaine de ce navire !

shirt

shirt
[ʃɜ:t] *n*
chemise *f*

shock

shock
[ʃɒk] *n*
1. choc *m*

Tintin, it's you! what a shock you gave me! Tintin, c'est vous ! quel choc vous m'avez fait !

2. décharge *f*
* *Look out! An electric ray!* Attention ! Un poisson torpille !
Oh! He's got an electric shock from the fish!... Oh ! Il a reçu une

...shock

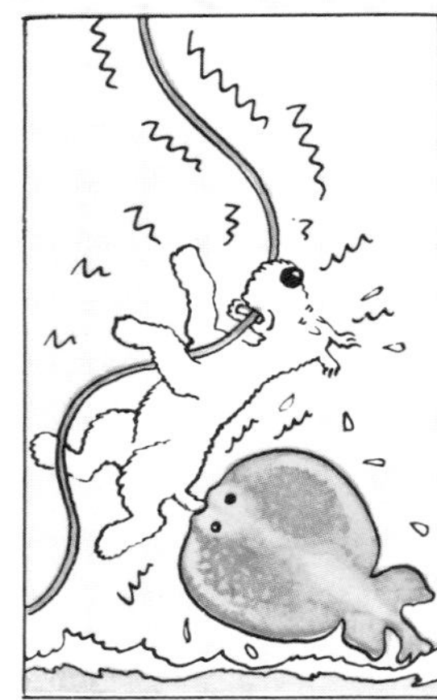

décharge électrique à cause du poisson !... *

shoe

shoe
[ʃu:] *n*
chaussure *f*

shoot

shoot
[ʃu:t]
shot, shot [ʃɒt]
I. *vi*
1. tirer

* *Hands up!... Don't move!... Don't try to escape or I'll shoot!...* Mains en l'air !... Ne bougez pas !... N'essayez pas de vous enfuir ou je tire !... *

2. se précipiter
they all shot into the room ils se sont tous

...shoot

précipités dans la pièce

II. *vt*
1. tuer, abattre

he shot three rabbits il a tué trois lapins

2. Idiom
help me, I've been shot in the leg aidez-moi, j'ai reçu un coup de fusil dans la jambe

shop

shop
[ʃɔp] *n*
1. magasin *m*, boutique *f*

2. Idiom
at the butcher's shop à la boucherie

the chemist's shop (Am: the drugstore) la pharmacie

► **shopkeeper**
['ʃɒpki:pə^{r}] *n*
commerçant *m*

...shop

commerçante *f*

* *Good gracious, that shopkeeper (Am: storekeeper) is Senhor Oliveira da Figueira!* Mais ce commerçant, c'est le senhor Oliveira da Figueira ! *

► **shopping**
['ʃɒpɪŋ] *n*
courses *f pl*

I'm going shopping je vais faire les courses

shore

shore
[ʃɔːʳ] *n*
1. côte *f*

I can see shore ahead, Captain je vois la côte devant, capitaine

2. rive *f*, rivage *m*
the shores of the lake les rivages du lac

short

short
[ʃɔːt] *adj*
1. court

this rope is too short cette corde est trop courte

we had a short holiday (Am: vacation) nous avons pris de courtes vacances

2. petit
he's a rather short man c'est un homme plutôt petit

3. Idiom

a short cut un raccourci

we're short of water nous manquons d'eau

Bill is short for William Bill est le diminutif de William

► **shorts**
[ʃɔːts] *n pl*
short *m*

he's wearing (a pair of) khaki shorts il porte un short kaki

shot

shot
[ʃɒt] *n*
coup *m* de feu

* *I heard shots!...* J'ai entendu des coups de feu !... *

...shot

should

should
[ʃʊd] *v aux*
1. devoir
(au conditionnel)

* *You shouldn't drink so much, Captain!* Vous ne devriez pas boire autant, Capitaine ! *Boohoo... Boo... hoo... hoo... Booh... hoo... Booh... hoo...* Bou-ouh... Bou-ou-ouh... Bou-ou-ou-ouh... Bou-ouh... *

I should have known! j'aurais dû le savoir !

2. *(employé pour former le conditionnel)*
I should like another cup of tea j'aimerais une autre tasse de thé

shoulder

shoulder
['ʃəʊldəʳ] *n*
épaule *f*

shout

shout
[ʃaʊt]
I. *vi*
crier

listen, somebody's shouting outside écoutez, quelqu'un crie dehors

II. *n*
cri *m*

show

show
[ʃəʊ]
I. *n*
1. spectacle *m*

there's a good show on at the theatre (Am: theater) il y a un bon spectacle au théâtre

2. exposition *f*
a flower show une exposition de fleurs

II. *vt*
showed, shown [ʃəʊn]
montrer

* *Again! This is the third check! We have to show our passports again...* Encore ! C'est le troisième contrôle ! Il faut encore montrer nos passeports... *

I'll show you the way je vais vous montrer le chemin

► **show off**
faire l'intéressant

he always shows off

...show

in front of adults il fait toujours l'intéressant devant les adultes

► **show up**
1. se présenter, arriver

most of the guests showed up early la plupart des invités sont arrivés tôt

2. se voir
it shows up in the dark cela se voit dans le noir

shower

shower
[ˈʃaʊəʳ] *n*
1. averse *f*

* *Ugh, there's going to be a shower! We must take cover... Come along...* Aïe, il va y avoir une averse ! Il faut nous mettre à l'abri... Venez...
You're right, Chang... Tu as raison, Tchang... *

2. douche *f*
I have a shower every morning je prends une douche tous les matins

shut

shut
[ʃʌt]
I. *adj*
fermé

all the windows are shut toutes les fenêtres sont fermées

...shut

II. *vt*
shut, shut
fermer

* *And don't forget to shut the doors!* Et n'oubliez pas de fermer les portes ! *

III. *vi*
1. fermer

the shops (Am: stores) shut at 6 pm les magasins ferment à 18 h

...shut

2. se fermer
the lid won't shut le couvercle ne ferme pas

► **shut up**
se taire

shut up, I'm listening to the radio! taisez-vous, j'écoute la radio !

sick

sick
[sɪk] *adj*
1. malade

what's the matter, Captain, are you sick? qu'est-ce qu'il y a, capitaine, êtes-vous malade ?

2. Idiom
to be sick vomir

I feel sick j'ai envie de vomir

side

...side

side
[saɪd] *n*
1. côté *m*

lie on your side couchez-vous sur le côté

the other side of the road l'autre côté de la route

* *There!... I'm on the other side of the river!...* Ça y est !... Je suis de l'autre côté de la rivière !... *

whose side are you on? vous êtes de quel côté ?

2. équipe *f*
our side lost again notre équipe a encore perdu

► **sidewalk** (*Am*)
→ PAVEMENT

sight

sight
[saɪt] *n*
1. vue *f*

my sight isn't as good as it used to be ma vue n'est plus aussi bonne qu'avant

2. spectacle *m*
it was a sad sight c'était un triste spectacle

3. Idiom
to see the sights faire du tourisme

to catch sight of something apercevoir quelque chose

sign

sign
[saɪn]
I. *n*
1. signe *m*

* *Why are they making signs? What's happening?* Pourquoi

...sign

...sign

font-ils des signes ? Que se passe-t-il ? *

2. panneau *m*
follow the signs to the cathedral suivez les panneaux jusqu'à la cathédrale

* *The Thompsons didn't see the sign!...* Les Dupondt n'ont pas vu le panneau !... *

3. signe *m*, indication *f*
those clouds are a

The Thompsons didn't see the sign!...

sign of rain ces nuages sont un signe de pluie

II. *vi & vt*
signer

sign here, please signez ici, s'il vous plaît

silence

silence
['saɪləns] *n*
silence *m*

...silence

What a strange place... No trees, no life... Nothing that might disturb the silence...

...silence

* *What a strange place... No trees, no life... Nothing that might disturb the silence...* Quel étrange endroit... Pas d'arbre, pas de vie... Rien qui pourrait troubler le silence... *

▸ **silent**
['saɪlənt] *adj*
1. silencieux

you must remain silent vous devez rester silencieux

2. Idiom
to keep silent (about something) garder le silence (sur quelque chose)

silly

silly
['sɪlɪ] *adj*
sillier, silliest
bête, idiot

don't ask silly questions! ne posez pas de questions idiotes !

similar

similar
['sɪmɪlər] *adj*
semblable

simple

simple
['sɪmp(ə)l] *adj*
1. facile, simple

* *Come on, Thompson, you can do it, it's simple!* Allez, Dupond, tu peux le faire, c'est facile ! *

...simple

Come on, Thompson, you can do it, it's simple!

2. simple
they lead a very simple life ils mènent une vie très simple

▸ **simply**
['sɪmplɪ] *adv*
1. simplement

she was dressed very simply elle était vêtue très simplement

2. absolument
that was simply delicious! c'était absolument délicieux !

since

since
[sɪns]
I. *prep*
depuis

I've been waiting for you since midday! je vous attends depuis midi !

II. *conj*
1. depuis que

we haven't seen them since we arrived nous ne les avons pas vus depuis que nous sommes arrivés

2. puisque
since you don't want to do it, I'll do it myself! puisque vous ne voulez pas le faire, je vais le faire moi-même !

sing

sing
[sɪŋ] *vi & vt*
sang [sæŋ],
sung [sʌŋ]
chanter

...sing

WOW-OW

!
!
WOW-OW - WOW-OW - OW-WOWWW!
?

Snowy is singing with Signora Castafiore...

...sing

* *Wow-ow* Wou-ou *Wow-ow!* Wou-ou ! *Snowy is singing with Signora Castafiore...* Milou chante avec la Castafiore... *

▶ **singer**
['sɪŋəʳ] *n*
chanteur *m*, chanteuse *f*

Signora Castafiore is a famous opera singer la Castafiore est une célèbre chanteuse d'opéra

single

single
['sɪŋg(ə)l] *adj*
1. seul

there wasn't a single car on the road il n'y avait pas une seule voiture sur la route

2. simple
a single (*Am:* *one-way*) *ticket to London, please* un aller simple pour Londres, s'il vous plaît

3. pour une personne

a single room/bed une chambre/un lit pour une personne

4. célibataire
are you married or single? êtes-vous marié ou célibataire ?

sink

sink
[sɪŋk]
I. *n*

...sink

1. évier *m*

the sink was full of dirty dishes l'évier était plein de vaisselle sale

2. lavabo *m*
he washed his hands in the bathroom sink il s'est lavé les mains dans le lavabo de la salle de bains

II. *vi*
sank [sæŋk], sunk [sʌŋk]
couler, sombrer

The boat is sinking!...

...sink

* *The boat is sinking!...* Le bateau coule !... *

sir

sir
[sɜːʳ] *n*
1. monsieur *m*

here is the menu, sir voici la carte, monsieur

2. sir *m*

...sir

Sir Walter Raleigh sir Walter Raleigh

sister

sister
['sɪstəʳ] *n*
sœur *f*

I have two brothers and two sisters j'ai deux frères et deux sœurs

sit

sit
[sɪt] *vi*
sat, sat [sæt]
s'asseoir

come and sit next to me venez vous asseoir à côté de moi

they were sitting on the floor ils étaient assis par terre

▶ **sit down**
s'asseoir

* *Please sit down,*

Please sit down, Colonel!

Colonel! Colonel, asseyez-vous, je vous en prie ! *

▶ **sitting room** (*Am:* **living room**) *n*
salon *m*

six

six
[sɪks]
I. *adj*
six

II. *n*
six *m*

▶ **sixteen**
[siːks'tiːn]
I. *adj*
seize

II. *n*
seize *m*

▶ **sixty**
['sɪkstɪ]
I. *adj*
soixante

II. *n*
pl sixties
soixante *m*

in the sixties dans les années soixante

size

size
[saɪz] *n*
1. taille *f*

it's the size of a tennis ball c'est de la taille d'une balle de tennis

what size do you take? quelle est votre taille ?

* *You're dressed now!...* Vous voilà habillé !...
I've got a space suit too, but I don't think

You're dressed now!...
I've got a space suit too, but I don't think it's my size ...

it's my size... Moi aussi, j'ai une combinaison, mais je ne pense pas qu'elle soit à ma taille... *

2. pointure *f*
what size shoe do you take? quelle est votre pointure (de chaussure) ?

skate

skate
[skeɪt] *n*
patin *m*

ice/roller skate patin à glace/à roulettes

ski

ski
[ski:]
I. *n*

...ski

ski *m*

II. *v i*
1. skier

he's learning how to ski il apprend à skier

water skiing ski nautique

2. Idiom
to go skiing faire du ski

skin

skin
[skɪn] *n*
peau *f*

my skin is dry j'ai la peau sèche

* *Tintin is coming on that boat... You'll see, his skin isn't black like ours...* Tintin arrive sur ce bateau... Tu verras, il n'a pas la peau noire comme nous !... *

skirt

skirt
[skɜ:t] *n*
jupe *f*

sky

sky
[skaɪ] *n*
pl skies
ciel *m*

...sky

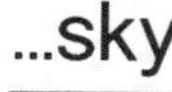

The sky is lovely.

* *The sky is lovely.* Le ciel est magnifique. *

sleep

sleep
[sli:p]
I. *n*
1. sommeil *m*

I was woken from a deep sleep j'ai été tiré d'un profond sommeil

...sleep

2. somme *m*
* *Captain! I think I'll have a little sleep!* Capitaine ! Je crois que je vais faire un petit somme !... *

3. Idiom
to go to sleep s'endormir

II. *v i*
slept, slept [slept]
dormir

good night, sleep well! bonne nuit, dormez bien !

slice

slice
[slaɪs] *n*
tranche *f*

would you like a slice of cake? voulez-vous une tranche de gâteau ?

slide

slide
[slaɪd]
I. *n*
1. toboggan *m*

...slide

the children are playing on the slide les enfants jouent sur le toboggan

2. diapositive *f*, diapo *f*
would you like to see my slides of London? veux-tu voir mes diapositives de Londres ?

II. *v i*
slid, slid [slɪd]
glisser

the table tipped and all the plates slid onto the floor la table a basculé et toutes les assiettes ont glissé par terre

slight

slight
[slaɪt] *adj*
petit, léger

we have a slight problem nous avons un petit problème

slip

slip
[slɪp] *v i*
slipped, slipped
glisser

* *The vase slipped out of my hands!...* Le vase m'a glissé des mains !... *

slope

slope
[sləʊp] *n*
pente *f*

they're skiing down the snowy slopes ils font du ski sur les pentes neigeuses

slow

slow
[sləʊ] *adj*
1. lent

can't you accelerate? this car is too slow! vous ne pouvez pas accélérer ? cette voiture est trop lente !

2. Idiom
my watch is five minutes slow ma montre retarde de cinq minutes

► **slowly**
['sləʊlɪ] *adv*
lentement

Drive more slowly, Tintin, you're going to kill us !...

* *Drive more slowly, Tintin, you're going to kill us!...* Conduis plus lentement, Tintin, tu vas nous tuer !... *

small

small
[smɔ:l] *adj*
petit

* *The submarine is really small!...* Le sous-marin est vraiment petit !... *

...small

The submarine is really small!...

smell

smell
[smel]
I. *n*
1. odeur *f*

there's a funny smell in this room il y a une drôle d'odeur dans cette pièce

2. Idiom
there's a smell of burning ça sent le brûlé

II. *vt*
smelt, smelt [smelt]
sentir

* *Captain, can you smell anything?* Capitaine, vous ne sentez rien ?
Sniff... Sniff... Sniff... Sniff...
Yes... there's a smell of burning in here... Oui... il y a une odeur de brûlé ici...
Where is it coming from? D'où vient-elle ? *

III. *vi*
sentir

that soup smells very good! cette soupe sent très bon !

it smells of fish ça sent le poisson

Captain, can you smell anything ?
Sniff... Sniff...

Yes... there's a smell of burning in here...
Where is it coming from ?

smile

smile
[smaɪl]
I. *vi*
sourire

...smile

I'm so happy to see a smile on your face again...

she smiled at me elle m'a souri

II. *n*
sourire *m*

* *I'm so happy to see a smile on your face again...* Je suis si heureux de revoir un sourire sur ton visage... *

smoke

smoke
[sməʊk]
I. *vi & vt*
fumer

he smokes a pipe il fume la pipe

II. *n*
fumée *f*

* *What's that smoke over there?* Qu'est-ce que cette fumée là-bas ? *It's a fire!* Mais c'est un incendie ! *

What's that smoke over there ?
It's a fire !

smooth

smooth
[smu:ð] *adj*
lisse

this rock is very smooth cette roche est très lisse

snack

snack
[snæk] *n*
casse-croûte *m*

we had a snack in a

...snack

café nous avons mangé un casse-croûte dans un café

snake

snake
[sneɪk] *n*
serpent *m*

* *What's this snake doing?* Que fait ce serpent ? *

sneeze

sneeze
[sni:z] *vi*
éternuer

* *Atchooo!* Tchoum! *He's sneezing!* Il éternue ! *

snow

snow
[snəʊ]
I. *vi*
neiger

He's sneezing!

...snow

* *Oh! It's snowing again!* Oh ! il se remet à neiger ! *

II. *n*
neige *f*

► **snowball**
['snəʊbɔ:l] *n*
boule *f* de neige

► **snowman**
['snəʊmæn] *n*
pl snowmen
['snəʊmen]
bonhomme *m* de neige

...snow

so

so
[səʊ] *adv*
1. si, tellement

it isn't usually so cold here il ne fait pas si froid ici d'habitude

2. aussi
I'm hungry! – so am I! j'ai faim ! – moi aussi !

3. Idiom
is the Professor all right? – I think so le professeur va-t-il bien ? – je crois que oui

I hope so je l'espère

* *Do you think it's this way?* Tu crois que c'est par là ?
I hope so!... Je l'espère !... *

so far jusqu'ici

so long! au revoir !

► **so that**
conj
pour que

speak loudly so that everyone can hear parlez fort pour que tout le monde puisse entendre

soap

soap
[səʊp] *n*
savon *m*

soccer

soccer
[sɒkəʳ], *n*
football *m*

► **soccer field**
terrain de football

► **soccer ball**
ballon de football

sock

sock
[sɒk] *n*
chaussette *f*

soft

soft
[sɒft] *adj*
doux *m*, douce *f*

► **softly**
['sɒftlɪ] *adv*
doucement

soldier

soldier
['səʊldʒəʳ] *n*
soldat *m*, militaire *m*

some soldiers have arrested the Captain des soldats ont arrêté le capitaine

some

some
[sʌm]
I. *adj*
1. du, de la, des

do you want some tea/some peas? voulez-vous du thé/des petits pois ?

...some

2. certains
some people wouldn't agree with me certaines personnes ne seraient pas d'accord avec moi

II. *pron*
1. en

if you like the cake have some more si vous aimez le gâteau, reprenez-en

2. quelques-uns, quelques-unes

some of the apples were rotten quelques-unes des pommes étaient pourries

► **somebody, someone**
['sʌmbɒdɪ], ['sʌmwʌn] *pron*
quelqu'un

look! there's someone in the house! regardez ! il y a quelqu'un dans la maison !

...some

* *Listen, the noise is getting nearer... Somebody's coming!...* Écoutez, le bruit se rapproche... Quelqu'un vient !... *

▶ **something** ['sʌmθɪŋ] *pron* quelque chose

I think I heard something je crois que j'ai entendu quelque chose !

▶ **sometimes** ['sʌmetaɪmz] *adv* quelquefois, parfois

* *It's true, I'm sometimes absent-minded, but it's rare!* C'est vrai, quelquefois je suis distrait, mais c'est rare ! *

▶ **somewhere** ['sʌmweəʳ] *adv*
1. quelque part

* *I've seen that face somewhere before...*

...some

It's Müller!... J'ai déjà vu cette tête quelque part... C'est Müller !... *

2. Idiom
somewhere else ailleurs

son

son [sʌn] *n* fils *m*

* *And this is my son*

...son

Chang Lin-Yi... Et voici mon fils Tchang Lin-Yi... *

song

song [sɒŋ] *n* chanson *f*

soon

soon [su:n] *adv*
1. bientôt

* *Goodbye, Tintin!* Au revoir, Tintin ! *Goodbye, I'll see you soon!* Au revoir, à bientôt ! *

2. Idiom
phone me as soon as you arrive téléphonez-moi dès que vous arriverez

...soon

sorry

sorry ['sɒrɪ]

I. *adj* sorrier, sorriest
1. désolé

I'm sorry to disturb you je suis désolé de vous déranger

2. Idiom
to feel sorry for someone plaindre quelqu'un

to feel sorry for oneself s'apitoyer sur son sort

II. *interj*
1. pardon, excusez-moi

ouch, my foot! – sorry! aïe, mon pied ! – excusez-moi !

* *Oh! Sorry!* Oh ! Excusez-moi !... *Wooah!* Wouah !... *

2. Idiom
say sorry to the lady! excuse-toi auprès de la dame !

sort

sort [sɔ:t] *n* sorte *f*, genre *m*

what sort of man is the Captain? quel genre d'homme est le capitaine ?

soul

soul [səʊl] *n* âme *f*

sound

sound
[saʊnd]
I. *n*
1. bruit *m*

it's a quiet night, there isn't a sound c'est une nuit calme, il n'y a pas de bruit

2. son *m*
I love the sound of bagpipes! j'adore le son de la cornemuse !

II. *vt*
sonner

* ***Blistering barnacles!... A periscope!... Sound the alarm...*** Mille sabords !... Un périscope !... Sonnez l'alerte... *

III. *vi*
Idiom
he sounds worried on dirait qu'il est inquiet

it sounds like a thunderstorm on dirait un orage

Blistering barnacles !... A periscope!... Sound the alarm...

soup

soup
[su:p] *n*
soupe *f*

fish/tomato soup soupe au poisson/à la tomate

sour

sour
[saʊəʳ] *n*
aigre

it tastes very sour cela a un goût très aigre

south

south
[saʊ:θ]
I. *n*
sud *m*

they live in the south of Spain ils habitent dans le sud de l'Espagne

II. *adj*
sud

the south coast la côte sud

South America l'Amérique du Sud

the South Pole le pôle Sud

III. *adv*
au sud, vers le sud

* ***There's an oasis 50 kilometres (Am: kilometers) south of here, in this direction...*** Il y a une oasis à 50 kilomètres au sud d'ici, dans cette direction... *

► **southern**
['sʌðən] *adj*
sud

There's an oasis 50 kilometres south of here, in this direction...

the southern hemisphere l'hémisphère sud

souvenir

souvenir
[su:və'nɪəʳ] *n*
souvenir *m*

this is a souvenir of our visit to Paris ceci est un souvenir de notre visite à Paris

space

space
['speɪs] *n*
1. espace *m*

write your answers in the spaces provided écrivez vos réponses dans les espaces prévus à cet effet

2. espace *m*
the first man in space le premier homme dans l'espace

* ***We're floating in space... It's a good thing I'm tied!*** Nous flottons dans l'espace... Heureusement que je suis attaché ! *

We're floating in space... It's a good thing I'm tied!

spade

spade
[speɪd] *n*
1. pelle *f*

pass me the spade, I'll dig a hole passez-moi la pelle, je creuserai un trou

...spade

2. *pl* spades
pique *f*
the ace of spades l'as de pique

spare

spare
[speəʳ] *adj*
1. de rechange

I always take spare clothes with me je prends toujours des vêtements de rechange avec moi

...spare

2. Idiom
the spare room la chambre d'amis

spare time temps libre

spare wheel roue de secours

speak

speak
[spiːk] *vi*
spoke [spəʊk],
spoken ['spəʊk(ə)n]
parler

hello, could I speak to Tintin, please? allô, pourrais-je parler à Tintin, s'il vous plaît ?

▸ **speak up**
parler plus fort

* *I'm asking you your name...* Je vous demande votre nom...

...special

Speak up, I can't hear you! Parlez plus fort, je ne vous entends pas ! *

special

special
['speʃ(ə)l] *adj*
spécial

* *You need a special permit to enter here. Have you got one?* Pour pénétrer ici, il faut une autorisation spéciale. L'avez-vous ? *

spectacles

spectacles
['spektək(ə)lz] *n pl*
lunettes *f pl*

I can't see very well without my spectacles (Am: eyeglasses) je vois mal sans mes lunettes

speech

speech
[spiːtʃ] *n*
discours *m*

...speech

* *Attention, please !... Mr Baxter is about to make a short speech!...* Votre attention s'il vous plaît !... Monsieur Baxter va faire un petit discours !... *

speed

speed
[spiːd] *n*
vitesse *f*

...speed

...speed

* *The train is gathering speed, why doesn't Tintin jump out now?* le train va prendre de la vitesse, pourquoi Tintin ne saute-t-il pas maintenant ? *

spell

spell
[spel] *vt*
spelt, spelt [spelt]
1. écrire, orthographier

...spell

how do you spell that word ? comment ce mot s'écrit-il ?

2. épeler
could you spell your name to me, please? pourriez-vous m'épeler votre nom, s'il vous plaît ?

▸ **spelling**
['spelɪŋ] *n*
orthographe *f*

she's good at spelling elle est forte en orthographe

spend

spend
[spend] *vt*
spent, spent [spent]
1. dépenser

I don't want to spend too much money je ne veux pas dépenser trop d'argent

2. passer
we spent the summer in California nous avons passé l'été en Californie

spider

spider
['spaɪdəʳ] *n*
araignée *f*

* *It's a spider...* C'est une araignée... *

It's a spider...

spill

spill
[spɪl] *vt*
spilt, spilt [spɪlt]
renverser

be careful not to spill your coffee faites attention de ne pas renverser votre café

spite

spite
[spaɪt] *n*
Idiom

...spite

in spite of malgré

we had a good time in spite of the rain nous nous sommes bien amusés malgré la pluie

* *We must go on in spite of the snow...* Nous devons continuer malgré la neige... *

spoil

spoil
[spɔɪl] *vt*
spoilt, spoilt [spɔɪlt]
1. gâcher, gâter

the bad weather spoilt our picnic le mauvais temps a gâché notre pique-nique

2. gâter
he's a spoilt child c'est un enfant gâté

sponge

sponge
[spʌndʒ] *n*
éponge *f*

spoon

spoon
[spu:n] *n*
cuillère *f*

he ate his vegetables with a spoon il a mangé ses légumes avec une cuillère

sport

sport
[spɔ:t] *n*
sport *m*

* *The Captain has always done a lot of sport, that's why he can walk so fast!* Le capitaine a toujours fait beaucoup de sport, c'est pourquoi il peut marcher si vite ! *

▶ **sports car** *n*
voiture *f* de sport

▶ **sportsman**
['spɔ:tsmən] *n*
pl sportsmen
sportif *m*

▶ **sportswoman**
['spɔ:tswʊmən] *n*
pl sportswomen
sportive *f*

spot

...spot

spot
[spɒt] *n*
1. endroit *m*

* *This is the spot where the plane crashed...* Voici l'endroit où l'avion s'est écrasé... *

2. goutte *f*
I felt a spot of rain j'ai senti une goutte de pluie

3. tache *f*
you've got a spot of grease on your tie vous avez une tache de graisse sur votre cravate

4. pois *m*
a pink dress with yellow spots une robe rose à pois jaunes

spread

spread
[spred]
spread, spread
I. *vt*
1. étaler

...spread

she spread jam on her bread elle a étalé de la confiture sur son pain

2. répandre
they are spreading false rumours (Am: rumors) ils répandent des rumeurs sans fondement

II. *vi*
s'étendre,
se répandre

the fog spread over the town le brouillard s'est étendu sur la ville

spring

spring
[sprɪŋ] *n*
1. printemps *m*

it's always quite warm here in (the) spring il fait toujours assez chaud ici au printemps

2. ressort *m*
there are springs in the mattress il y a des ressorts dans le matelas

3. source *f*
we drank water from a spring nous avons bu de l'eau à une source

square

square
[skweəʳ]
I. *adj*
carré

the room is square la pièce est carrée

II. *n*
carré *m*

staff

staff
[stɑ:f] *n*
personnel *m*

only staff are admitted into this part of the building seul le personnel a le droit d'entrer dans cette partie du bâtiment

stage

stage
[steɪdʒ] *n*

...stage

scène *f*

the actors were all on stage tous les acteurs étaient sur (la) scène

stairs

stairs
[steəz] *n*
escalier *m*

* *Here are your keys, your room is up the stairs...* Voici vos clés,

...stairs

Here are your keys, your room is up the stairs...

votre chambre est en haut de l'escalier... *

► **staircase**
['steəkeɪs] *n*
escalier *m*

stamp

stamp
[stæmp] *n*
timbre *m*

...stamp

would you like to see my stamp collection? veux-tu voir ma collection de timbres ?

stand

stand
[stænd]
stood, stood [stʊd]
I. *vi*
1. rester debout, se tenir debout

...stand

I'm so tired I can hardly stand! je suis tellement fatigué que j'ai du mal à rester debout !

2. se mettre
all stand in a circle around me mettez-vous tous en cercle autour de moi

II. *vt*
1. poser, mettre

he stood the vase on the table il a posé le vase sur la table

2. supporter
stop that noise, I can't stand it! je ne supporte pas ce bruit, arrêtez !

► **stand up**
1. se lever

he stood up to offer her his seat il s'est levé pour lui offrir sa place

2. se tenir
stand up straight! tiens-toi droit !

star

star
[stɑ:^{r}] *n*
1. étoile *f*

* *There are no clouds, you can see the stars! How lovely!...* Il n'y a pas de nuages, on voit les étoiles ! Comme c'est beau !... *

2. vedette *f*
she's a film (Am: movie) star c'est une vedette de cinéma

There are no clouds, you can see the stars! How lovely! ...

stare

stare
[steə^r] *vi*
1. regarder fixement

Professor Calculus was staring at the test tube le professeur Tournesol regardait fixement l'éprouvette

2. Idiom
it's rude to stare dévisager les gens est impoli

start

start
[stɑ:t]
I. *n*
début *m*, commencement *m*

the start of the lesson le début du cours

II. *vi*
1. commencer

what time does the concert start? à quelle heure commence le concert ?

2. démarrer
the car won't start la voiture ne démarre pas

III. *vt*
1. commencer

I haven't started my work je n'ai pas commencé mon travail

2. mettre en marche
everything's ready, start the engines! tout est prêt, mettez les moteurs en marche !

► **start out**
partir, se mettre en route

we'll start out early tomorrow morning nous partirons tôt demain matin

state

state
[steɪt]
I. *n*
1. état *m*

...state

your room is in a terrible state ta chambre est dans un état épouvantable

2. Etat *m*
the European heads of state les chefs d'Etat européens

the United States of America les Etats-Unis d'Amérique

II. *vt*
déclarer

he stated that he had

...state

never spoken to her il a déclaré qu'il ne lui avait jamais parlé

station

station
['steɪʃ(ə)n] *n*
gare *f*

the Captain will be waiting for us at the station le capitaine nous attendra à la gare

...station

bus station gare routière

stay

stay
[steɪ]
I. *n*
séjour *m*

have a nice stay! bon séjour !

II. *vi*
1. rester

...stay

* *How long are you staying in this country?* Combien de temps allez-vous rester dans ce pays ?
Only a few days, why? Quelques jours seulement, pourquoi ? *

2. loger
he's staying at a friend's house il loge chez un ami

► **stay in**
rester à la maison

it's raining, let's stay in il pleut, restons à la maison

► **stay out**
ne pas rentrer

he stayed out all night il n'est pas rentré de la nuit

steak

steak
[steɪk] *n*
bifteck *m*, steak *m*

I'd like a steak and chips (Am: French fries), please donnez-moi un steak frites, s'il vous plaît

steal

steal
[sti:l] *vt*
stole [stəʊl], stolen ['stəʊl(ə)n]
voler

my wallet has been stolen on a volé mon portefeuille

* *The magpie* La pie
... it has... elle a...
... stolen the key!... volé la clé !... *

steam

steam
[sti:m] *n*
vapeur *f*

* *A steam engine...* Une locomotive à vapeur... *

steel

steel
[sti:l] *n*
acier *m*

A steam engine ...

...steel

it's as hard as steel c'est dur comme de l'acier

steep

steep
[sti:p] *adj*
raide

* *It's a steep climb!* Cette montée est raide ! *

...steep

step

step
[step]
I. *n*
1. marche *f*

mind the step! faites attention à la marche !

2. pas *m*

he took two steps forward il a avancé de deux pas

try and keep in step essayez de marcher au pas

3. mesure *f*
the government should take steps to ban it le gouvernement devrait prendre des mesures pour interdire cela

II. *v i*
stepped, stepped
marcher

I stepped in a puddle j'ai marché dans une flaque d'eau

stick

stick
[stɪk]
I. *n*
1. morceau *m* de bois

collect some sticks to make a fire ramassez des morceaux de bois pour faire un feu

2. bâton *m*
he hit the dog with a stick il a frappé le chien avec un bâton

3. canne *f*
a blind man with a white stick un aveugle avec une canne blanche

a walking stick une canne

II. *v t*
stuck, stuck [stʌk]
1. coller

stick the stamp on the envelope collez le timbre sur l'enveloppe

2. enfoncer
he stuck a pin in the balloon il a enfoncé une épingle dans le ballon

3. mettre, fourrer
stick all the toys in that box mets tous les jouets dans cette boîte

► **sticking plaster** *n*
(*Am:* **band-aid)**
pansement *m* adhésif, sparadrap *m*

► **stuck**
[stʌk] *adj*
coincé

still

still
[stɪl]
I. *adv*
1. encore, toujours

is it still raining? est-ce qu'il pleut encore ?

2. encore, même
we could take a bus, or better still a taxi nous pourrions prendre un bus, ou encore mieux, un taxi

3. quand même
* *It might be dangerous, but I'll still do it!* C'est peut-être dangereux, mais je le ferai quand même ! *

II. *adj*
tranquille

can't you stand still for one minute? tu ne peux pas rester tranquille une seule minute ?

stir

stir
[stɜːʳ] *v t*
stirred, stirred
remuer

she stirred her tea elle a remué son thé

stocking

stocking
['stɒkɪŋ] *n*
bas *m*

a pair of stockings une paire de bas

stomach

stomach
['stʌmək] *n*
estomac *m*

I've got a stomach ache j'ai mal à l'estomac

stone

stone
[stəʊn] *n*
pierre *f*

they're throwing stones ils lancent des pierres

...stone

* *The Captain is throwing stones into the water!...* Le capitaine jette des pierres dans l'eau !... *Hello!* Hello ! *

a stone wall un mur en pierre

► **stone** *n inv*
6,35 kg
he weighs 11 stone il pèse 70 kilogrammes

stop

stop
[stɒp]
stopped, stopped
I. *v i*
s'arrêter, arrêter

a car stopped outside the house une voiture s'est arrêtée devant la maison

my watch has stopped ma montre est arrêtée

we're waiting for the rain to stop nous attendons que la pluie s'arrête

II. *v t*
1. arrêter

* *Hey you!...* Eh vous !... *Stop that man !* Arrêtez cet homme ! *What's happening?* Que se passe-t-il ? *

2. cesser, arrêter
you ought to stop drinking, Captain! vous devriez arrêter de boire, capitaine !

...stop

stop that noise, children! arrêtez de faire du bruit, les enfants !

3. empêcher
he wants to go back and I can't stop him il veut y retourner et je ne peux pas l'en empêcher

III. *n*
Idiom
to come to a stop s'arrêter

a full stop un point

store

store
[stɔːʳ] *n*
1. provision *f*, réserve *f*
we've got in a large store of food nous avons fait d'importantes réserves de nourriture

2. grand magasin *m* *(Am: magasin, boutique)*

a furniture store un magasin de meubles

storm

storm
[stɔːm] *n*
1. orage *m*

I heard thunder, there must be a storm coming j'ai entendu le tonnerre, il va certainement y avoir un orage

* *They're going back to avoid the storm.* Ils rentrent pour éviter l'orage... *

2. tempête *f*
the ship has been

...storm

They're going back to avoid the storm...

caught in a storm le navire a été pris dans une tempête

story

story
['stɔːrɪ] *n*
pl stories
histoire *f*

tell us a story, Captain racontez-nous une histoire, capitaine

stove

stove (*Am*)
→ COOKER

straight

straight
[streɪt]
I. *adj*
droit

the road is very straight la route est très droite

...straight

II. *adv*
1. directement

I went straight home after school je suis rentré directement chez moi après l'école

2. Idiom
straight on tout droit

* *Where shall I go?* Où dois-je aller ?
Go straight on until you come to the village! Continuez tout droit jusqu'à ce que vous arriviez au village ! *

straight away tout de suite

strange

strange
[streɪndʒ] *adj*
1. étrange, bizarre

* *What strange people!* Quels étranges personnages ! *

...strange

2. inconnu
we are lost in a strange country nous sommes perdus dans un pays inconnu

► **stranger**
['streɪndʒəʳ] *n*
inconnu *m*, inconnue *f*

don't talk to strangers ne parle pas à des inconnus

strawberry

strawberry
['strɔ:bərɪ] *n*
pl strawberries
fraise *f*

strawberries and cream des fraises à la crème

street

street
[stri:t] *n*
rue *f*

strength

strength
[streŋθ] *n*
force *f*

* *Here they come. Tintin seems to have no strength left. The Captain is having to carry him...* Les voici qui arrivent. Tintin semble à bout de forces. Le capitaine doit le porter... *

strike

strike
[straɪk]
I. *v t*
struck, struck [strʌk]
1. frapper

he struck the ball as hard as he could il a frappé la balle de toutes ses forces

2. frotter
it's dark, let's strike a match il fait noir, frottons une allumette

3. sonner
* *The clock has just struck 8, I'm late !...* La pendule vient de sonner 8 heures, je suis en retard !... *

II. *v i*
faire (la) grève

the workmen are threatening to strike les ouvriers menacent de faire (la) grève

III. *n*
grève *f*

the factory is on strike l'usine est en grève

string

string
[strɪŋ] *n*
1. ficelle *f*

she tied up the box with string elle a fermé la boîte avec de la ficelle

2. corde *f*
a guitar string une corde de guitare

strong

strong
[strɒŋ] *adj*
fort

you're stronger than me, Captain, can you lift it? vous êtes plus fort que moi, capitaine, pouvez-vous le soulever ?

this coffee is too strong! ce café est trop fort !

stubborn

stubborn
['stʌbən] *adj*
têtu

study

study
['stʌdɪ] *v t*
studied, studied
étudier

she's studying biology elle étudie la biologie

► **student**
['stju:d(ə)nt] *n*
étudiant *m*, étudiante *f*

she's a biology student elle est étudiante en biologie

stupid

stupid
['stju:pɪd] *adj*
stupide, bête

* *Don't be stupid, Thompson, maybe it's not a mirage!...* Ne sois pas stupide, Dupond, ce n'est peut-être pas un mirage !... *

subject

subject
['sʌbdzekt] *n*
1. sujet *m*

the subject of the sentence le sujet de la phrase

2. matière *f*
which is your favourite (Am: favorite) subject, mathematics or French? quelle est ta matière préférée, les mathématiques ou le français ?

3. sujet *m* de conversation
let's change the subject changeons de sujet de conversation

4. sujet *m*, sujette *f*
he's a British subject il est sujet britannique

suburb

suburb
['sʌbɜ:b] *n*
banlieue *f*

they live in the suburbs ils habitent en banlieue

subway

subway (*Am*)
→ UNDERGROUND

succeed

succeed
[sək'si:d] *v i*
réussir

how to succeed in business comment réussir dans les affaires

* *We've succeeded!... The "Unicorn" is here!...* Nous avons réussi !... La « Licorne » est là !... *

We've succeeded!... The « Unicorn » is here!...

▸ **success**
[sək'ses] *n*
succès *m*, **réussite** *f*

Signora Castafiore was a great success la Castafiore a eu un grand succès

such

such
[sʌtʃ] *adj*
1. **tellement, si**

it's such a nice day, let's go for a picnic c'est une si belle journée, faisons un pique-nique

2. **tel**
I'd never do such a thing! je ne ferais jamais une telle chose !

3. Idiom
such as comme

take a country such as France prenez un pays comme la France

there's no such thing! des choses comme ça n'existent pas !

sudden

sudden
['sʌd(ə)n] *adj*
1. **soudain, subit**

there was a sudden silence il y a eu un silence subit

2. Idiom
all of a sudden tout à coup

▸ **suddenly**
['sʌd(ə)nlɪ] *adv*
soudain, tout à coup

he suddenly started to run soudain, il s'est mis à courir

suffer

suffer
['sʌfəʳ] *v i*
souffrir

did you suffer much ? avez-vous beaucoup souffert ?

sugar

sugar
['ʃʊgəʳ] *n*
sucre *m*

a lump of sugar un morceau de sucre

suggest

suggest
[sə'dʒest] *v t*
suggérer, proposer

* *I suggest that we stop here for a short rest...* Je suggère que nous nous arrêtions ici pour nous reposer un moment... *Excellent idea!...* Excellente idée !... *

▸ **suggestion**
[sə'dʒestʃ(ə)n] *n*
suggestion *f*, **proposition** *f*

I suggest that we stop here for a short rest...
Excellent idea!...

suit

suit
[su:t]
I. *n*
1. **costume** *m*

he was wearing a blue suit il portait un costume bleu

2. **tailleur** *m*
she was wearing a red suit elle portait un tailleur rouge

3. **couleur** *f*
in cards, the four suits are hearts, clubs, diamonds and spades aux cartes, les quatre couleurs sont cœur, trèfle, carreau et pique

II. *v t*
1. **aller à**

* *Does this coat suit me ?* Ce manteau me va-t-il bien ? *

2. **convenir à**
come when it suits you venez quand cela vous convient

?
Does this coat suit me ?

▸ **suitcase**
['su:tkeɪs] *n*
valise *f*

put the suitcases in the car mettez les valises dans la voiture

sum

sum
[sʌm] *n*
1. **calcul** *m*

I can't do this sum je n'arrive pas à faire ce calcul

2. **somme** *f*
it costs a large sum of money cela coûte une grosse somme

summer

summer
['sʌməʳ] *n*
été *m*

it's very hot here in (the) summer il fait très chaud ici en été

summer holidays (Am: vacation) vacances d'été

sun

sun
[sʌn] *n*
soleil *m*

► **sunny**
['sʌnɪ] *adj*
sunnier, sunniest
1. **ensoleillé**

a sunny day une journée ensoleillée

2. Idiom
it is sunny il y a du soleil

► **sunrise**
['sʌnraɪz] *n*
lever *m* **du soleil**

► **sunset**
['sʌnset] *n*
coucher *m* **du soleil**

at sunset au coucher du soleil

► **sunstroke**
['sʌnstrəʊk] *n*
insolation *f*

Sunday

Sunday
['sʌndɪ] *n*
dimanche *m*

come and see me on Sunday venez me voir dimanche

they don't work on Sundays ils ne travaillent pas le dimanche

supermarket

supermarket

...supermarket

['su:pəmɑ:kɪt] *n*
supermarché *m*

supper

supper
['sʌpəʳ] *n*
souper *m*

supply

supply
[sə'plaɪ]

...supply

I. *n*
pl supplies
1. **provision** *f*

their supplies are delivered by helicopter leurs provisions sont livrées par hélicoptère

2. **réserve** *f*, **stock** *m*, **provision** *f*

* *Our supply of oxygen is running low...* Notre réserve d'oxygène commence à s'épuiser... *

II. *vt*
supplied, supplied
fournir

they will supply us with fuel ils nous fourniront du carburant

suppose

suppose
[sə'pəʊz] *vt*
1. **supposer, imaginer**

...suppose

* *I suppose you are Tintin...* J'imagine que vous êtes Tintin...
Yes, I am. Oui, c'est moi. *

2. Idiom
supposing it rains? et s'il pleut ?

you're supposed to be in bed tu es censé être au lit

sure

sure
[ʃʊəʳ] *adj*
1. **sûr, certain**

* *I'm sure the treasure is there!* Je suis sûr que le trésor est là-bas ! *

2. Idiom
Tintin is sure to know the answer Tintin connaît sûrement la réponse

► **surely**
['ʃʊəlɪ] *adv*
1. **sûrement, certainement**

there's surely been a mistake il y a sûrement eu une erreur

2. **tout de même**
you surely don't expect me to do it all by myself? vous ne vous attendez tout de même pas à ce que je le fasse tout seul ?

surname

surname
['sɜ:neɪm] *n*
nom *m* **de famille**

write your name and surname écrivez votre prénom et votre nom (de famille)

surprise

surprise
[sə'praɪz]
I. *n*
surprise *f*

...surprise

* *Hurray! Here he is!.* Hourra! Le voilà !...
Captain, what a nic surprise!... Capitaine quelle bonne sur prise !... *

II. *vt*
surprendre

the noise surprise me le bruit m'a surpri

surround

surround
[sə'raʊnd] *vt*
entourer

suspect

suspect
[səs'pekt] *vt*
soupçonner

I suspect that they're spies je les soupçonne d'être des espions

▸ **suspicious**
[səs'pɪʃəs] *adj*
1. soupçonneux, méfiant

* *You seem suspicious, Tintin, don't you trust him?* Vous avez l'air soupçonneux, Tintin, n'avez-vous pas confiance en lui ?
I don't know! Je ne sais pas ! *

2. suspect, louche
who is that suspicious character? qui est cet individu louche ?

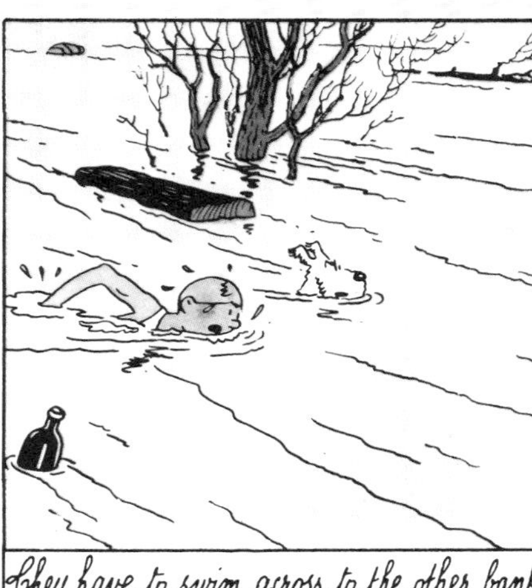

swallow

swallow
['swɒləʊ] *vt*
avaler

sweep

sweep
[swi:p] *vt*
swept, swept [swept]
balayer

I'll sweep the floor je vais balayer par terre

sweet

sweet
[swi:t]
I. *adj*
sucré

this coffee is too sweet ce café est trop sucré

II. *n*
bonbon *m*

do you want a sweet (Am: some candy)? veux-tu un bonbon ?

swim

swim
[swɪm]
I. *vi*
swam [swæm],
swum [swʌm]
1. nager

* *They have to swim across to the other bank.* Ils doivent nager jusqu'à l'autre rive. *

2. Idiom
to go swimming aller se baigner

II. *n*
Idiom
to go for a swim aller se baigner

They have to swim across to the other bank.

I had a swim before breakfast je me suis baigné avant le petit déjeuner

▸ **swimming pool**
n
piscine *f*

swing

swing
[swɪŋ]
I. *vi*
swung, swung [swʌŋ]
se balancer

the monkey swung from a creeper le singe se balançait au bout d'une liane

II. *vt*
balancer

he was swinging his satchel il balançait son cartable

III. *n*
balançoire *f*

the children are playing on the swings les enfants jouent sur les balançoires

switch

switch
[swɪtʃ] *n*
interrupteur *m*

I can't find the light switch je ne trouve pas l'interrupteur

▸ **switch on**
allumer

* *I'll switch on the radio and listen to the news...* Je vais allumer la radio et écouter les nouvelles... *

▸ **switch off**
éteindre

don't forget to switch the lamp off n'oublie pas d'éteindre la lampe

Switzerland

Switzerland
['swɪtsələnd] *n*
Suisse *f*

▸ **Swiss**
[swɪs]
I. *adj*
suisse

II. *n*
the Swiss les Suisses

T

table

table
['teɪb(ə)l] *n*
1. table *f*

help me set the table aide-moi à mettre la table

2. table *f*
multiplication tables tables de multiplication

tail

tail
[teɪl] *n*

...tail

Snowy is wagging his tail...

queue *f*

* *Wooah! Wooah!* Wouah ! Wouah !
Snowy is wagging his tail... Milou remue la queue... *

take

take
[teɪk] *v t*
took [tʊk],
taken ['teɪk(ə)n]
1. prendre

somebody's taken my pen quelqu'un a pris mon stylo

do you take sugar? prenez-vous du sucre ?

don't move, I'll take a photo of you ne bougez pas, je vais vous photographier

2. amener
he takes the children to school every morning il amène les enfants à l'école tous les matins

3. passer
to take an exam passer un examen

4. accepter
do you take traveller's cheques (Am: traveler's checks)? acceptez-vous les chèques de voyage ?

5. mettre
it took me all day to clean the house j'ai mis la journée à nettoyer la maison

...take

6. Idiom
to take place avoir lieu

where did the accident take place? où l'accident a-t-il eu lieu ?

how long does it take to fly to New York? combien de temps faut-il pour aller à New York en avion ?

► **take away**
emporter

they sell pizzas to take away (Am: to take out) ils vendent des pizzas à emporter

► **take off**
1. enlever

come in and take your coat off entrez et enlevez votre manteau

2. décoller
* *The plane is taking off...* L'avion est en train de décoller... *

The plane is taking off...

► **take over**
1. racheter

his business has been taken over by a big company son affaire a été rachetée par une grande société

2. remplacer
I'll take over from you at the wheel if you're tired je te remplacerai au volant si tu es fatigué

talk

talk
[tɔ:k] *vi*
parler

* *I'd like to talk to you in private... Is it possible?...* J'aimerais vous parler en privé... Est-ce possible ?... *

tall

tall
[tɔ:l] *adj*

...tall

1. grand

he's a very tall man c'est un homme très grand

* *The gorilla is taller than Tintin...* Le gorille est plus grand que Tintin... *

2. Idiom
how tall are you? combien mesurez-vous ?

he's 6 feet tall il mesure 1,83 m

The gorilla is taller than Tintin...

tap

tap
[tæp] *n*
(*Am:* **faucet)**
robinet *m*

somebody left the tap on quelqu'un a laissé le robinet ouvert

tap water eau du robinet

tape

tape
[teɪp] *n*
1. ruban *m*

the present was done up with green tape le cadeau était attaché avec un ruban vert

2. bande *f* (magnétique), cassette *f*
we listened to records and tapes nous avons écouté des disques et des cassettes

▸ **tape recorder** *n*
magnétophone

taste

taste
[teɪst]
I. *n*
goût *m*

what is it? it has no taste at all qu'est-ce que c'est ? ça n'a aucun goût

...taste

II. *vt*
goûter

have you tasted this cheese? avez-vous goûté ce fromage ?

III. *vi*
avoir un goût

this cheese tastes of soap ce fromage a un goût de savon

taxi

...taxi

taxi
['tæksɪ] *n*
taxi *m*

* *Taxi, to the station!...* Taxi, à la gare !... *Taxi! Follow that car!* Taxi ! Suivez cette voiture ! *

tea

tea
[ti:] *n*
1. thé *m*

* *Tintin is drinking tea...* Tintin boit du thé... *

I'd like a nice hot cup of tea! j'aimerais une tasse de thé bien chaud !

2. goûter *m*
the children have tea at five les enfants prennent leur goûter à cinq heures

Tintin is drinking tea...

▸ **teapot**
['ti:pɒt] *n*
théière *f*

▸ **teaspoon**
['ti:spu:n] *n*
petite cuillère *f*

▸ **teatime**
['ti:taɪm] *n*
heure *f* du thé

come tomorrow at teatime venez demain à l'heure du thé

teach

teach
[ti:tʃ] *vt*
taught, taught [tɔ:t]
1. enseigner

she teaches mathematics elle enseigne les mathématiques

2. apprendre
I'll teach you how to drive je t'apprendrai à conduire

► **teacher**
['ti:tʃəʳ] *n*
professeur *m*, enseignant *m*, enseignante *f*

she's an English teacher elle est professeur d'anglais

team

team
[ti:m] *n*
équipe *f*

tear

tear
[teəʳ] *vt*
tore [tɔ:ʳ], torn [tɔ:n]
déchirer

I've torn my jacket j'ai déchiré ma veste

► **tear out**
arracher

some of the pages have been torn out quelques-unes des pages ont été arrachées

This piece of paper has been torn up...

► **tear up**
déchirer (en petits morceaux)

* *This piece of paper has been torn up...* Ce papier a été déchiré en petits morceaux... *

tear

tear
[tɪəʳ] *n*
larme *f*

tears ran down her cheeks des larmes coulaient sur ses joues

teeth

teeth → TOOTH

telegram

telegram
['telɪgræm] *n*
télégramme *m*

telephone

telephone
['telɪfəʊn]
I. *n*
téléphone *m*

the telephone's ringing, who can it be? le téléphone sonne, qui cela peut-il être ?

be quiet, I'm on the telephone! taisez-vous, je suis au téléphone !

II. *vt & vi*
téléphoner à, appeler

quick, telephone the doctor! vite, téléphonez au médecin !

III. *vi*
téléphoner

* *Thank you.* Merci. *Who's telephoning at this time?* Qui téléphone à cette heure ? *

Thank you.
Who's telephoning at this time ?

► **telephone box (***Am:* **telephone booth)**
n
cabine *f* téléphonique

► **telephone number**
n
numéro *m* de téléphone

television

Oh, the television is on!...
The plane is taking off...

television
[telɪ'vɪʒ(ə)n] *n*
télévision *f*

* *Oh, the television is on!...* Oh ! la télévision est allumée !...
The plane is taking off... L'avion décolle... *

tell

tell
[tel] *vt*
told, told [təʊld]
1. dire

tell him to be careful dites-lui de faire attention

are you telling the truth? est-ce que tu dis la vérité ?

2. raconter
if you're good, I'll tell you a story si tu es sage, je te raconterai une histoire

3. voir
but you can easily tell it's a forgery! mais on voit bien que c'est un faux !

► **tell off**
gronder

* *Abdullah, your father will tell you off, come here!...* Abdallah, ton père va te gronder, viens !...
No!!!!!... Non ! ! ! ! !... *

...tell

Abdullah, your father will tell you off, come here!...
No !!!!!...

temper

temper
['tempəʳ] *n*
1. humeur *f*

to be in a good/bad temper être de bonne/mauvaise humeur

2. colère *f*
in a temper en colère

don't lose your temper! ne vous mettez pas en colère !

temperature

temperature
['temp(ə)rətʃəʳ] *n*
1. température *f*

* *It's so hot! The temperature is so high that everything's melting...* Quelle chaleur ! La température est tellement élevée que tout se met à fondre... *

2. fièvre *f*
have you got a temperature? est-ce que tu as de la fièvre ?

It's so hot! The temperature is so high that everything's melting...

ten

ten
[ten]
I. *adj*
dix

II. *n*
dix *m*

tennis

tennis
['tenɪs] *n*
tennis *m*

tense

tense
[tens] *adj*
I. tendu

why are you so tense? relax! pourquoi est-tu si tendu ? détends-toi !

II. *n*
temps *m*

the different tenses of the verb « to be » les différents temps du verbe « être »

tent

tent
[tent] *n*
tente *f*

we can pitch our tent here nous pouvons dresser notre tente ici

term

term
[tɜːm] *n*
1. trimestre *m*

we have a new teacher next term (Am: quarter) nous aurons un

...term

nouveau professeur le trimestre prochain

2. Idiom
to be on good/bad terms with somebody être en bons/mauvais termes avec quelqu'un

terrible

terrible
['terɪb(ə)l] *adj*
affreux

what terrible weather! quel temps affreux !

test

test
[test] *n*
1. interrogation *f*

we have a history test tomorrow nous avons une interrogation d'histoire demain

2. essai *m*, test *m*
here are the results of the first tests on the new rocket voici les résultats des premiers essais de la nouvelle fusée

textbook

textbook
['tekstbʊk] *n*
manuel *m*, livre *m*

a geography textbook un manuel de géographie

than

than
[ðən] *conj*
que

...than

* *Their motorcycles are faster than our car!...* Leurs motos sont plus rapides que notre voiture !... *

Their motorcycles are faster than our car!

thank

thank
[θæŋk] *v t*
remercier

you've saved my life, how can I ever thank you? vous m'avez sauvé

...thank

la vie, comment vous remercier ?

▶ **thanks**
[θæŋks]
I. *n pl*
remerciements *m pl*

please accept our sincere thanks veuillez accepter nos sincères remerciements

II. *interj*
merci

thanks very much merci beaucoup

...thank

another cup of tea? – no, thanks une autre tasse de thé ? – (non) merci

► **thanks to**
prep
grâce à

we're safe now, thanks to you, Tintin nous sommes hors de danger maintenant, grâce à vous, Tintin

► **thank you**
interj
merci

* *Thank you!* Merci ! *

thank you very much merci beaucoup

thank you for this lovely present! merci pour ce joli cadeau !

another cup of tea? – no thank you une autre tasse de thé ? – (non) merci

that

...that

that
[ðæt]
I. *adj*
pl those [ðəʊz]
ce, cette, ces

that book is mine ce livre est à moi

those cakes look delicious ces gâteaux ont l'air délicieux

II. *pron dem*
pl those [ðəʊz]
1. ce, ça, cela

that's the best meal I've eaten in a long time c'est le meilleur repas que j'aie mangé depuis longtemps

* *Haaaah!* Haaaah !... *What's that?* Qu'est-ce que c'est que ça ?... *

that's enough! ça suffit !

2. celui-là *m*, celle-là *f*, ceux-là *m pl*, celles-là *f pl*
do you prefer these or those? préférez-vous ceux-ci ou ceux-là ?

III. *pron rel*
1. qui

the train that has just left le train qui vient de partir

2. que
the book that I read last night le livre que j'ai lu hier soir

IV. *conj*
que

I told you that I was busy! je vous ai dit que j'étais occupé !

I'm so tired that I could sleep for two days! je suis tellement fatigué que je pourrais dormir deux jours !

V. *adv*
si, aussi

I didn't think it was that difficult! je ne pensais pas que c'était si difficile que ça !

the

the
[ðə] *art def*
1. le, la, l', les

your pen is on the desk/the table ton stylo est sur le bureau/la table

* *Quick, get in the plane...* Vite, montez dans l'avion... *

...the

2. Idiom
the sooner we leave the more chance we have of succeeding plus tôt nous partirons, plus nous aurons de chances de réussir

theatre

theatre
['θɪətə^r] *n*
(*Am:* **theater)**
théâtre *m*

their

their
[ðeə^r] *adj*
leur, leurs

they're getting into their car ils montent dans leur voiture

...their

► **theirs**
[ðeəz] *pron*
1. le leur, la leur, les leurs

our house is bigger than theirs notre maison est plus grande que la leur

2. Idiom
a friend of theirs un de leurs amis

that car is theirs cette voiture est à eux

them

them
[ðem] *pron*
1. les

can you see them est-ce que vous le voyez ?

2. leur
give them something to eat donnez leur à manger

► **themselves**
[ðəm'selvz] *pron*
1. se

...them

have they hurt themselves? est-ce qu'ils se sont fait mal ?

2. eux-mêmes *m pl*, elles-mêmes *f pl*
they say they can do it themselves ils disent qu'ils peuvent le faire eux-mêmes

3. Idiom
(all) by themselves tout seuls

then

then
[ðen]
I. *adv*
1. alors, à ce moment-là

I was just a young boy then je n'étais qu'un petit garçon alors

2. puis, ensuite
we went first to London, then to Oxford nous sommes allés d'abord à Londres, et ensuite à Oxford

II. *conj*
donc, alors

what's the matter with you then? qu'as-tu donc ?

there

there
[ðeəʳ]
I. *adv*
1. là

is Tintin there, please? est-ce que Tintin est là, s'il vous plaît ?

the village is over there, behind that hill le village est là-bas, derrière cette colline

2. y
I'm going there tomorrow j'y vais demain

3. Idiom
there is/are voilà

look, there's the Professor! regardez, voilà le professeur !

there is/are il y a

** There are five men in the car...* Il y a cinq hommes dans la voiture... *

is there anything to eat? est-ce qu'il y a quelque chose à manger ?

pass the salt, please – there you are passez le sel, s'il vous plaît – tenez

...there

There are five men in the car...

II. *interj*
allons

there, there, don't cry allons, allons ne pleure pas

these

these → THIS

they

they
[ðeɪ] *pron*
1. ils *m pl*, elles *f pl*

the boys say that they want to come les garçons disent qu'ils veulent venir

the girls say that they want to come les filles disent qu'elles veulent venir

2. on
they say the Marquis of Gorgonzola is the richest man in the world! on dit que le marquis de Gorgonzola est l'homme le plus riche du monde !

thick

thick
[θɪk] *adj*
épais, épaisse

she cut herself a thick slice of bread elle s'est coupée une épaisse tranche de pain

the fog is very thick le brouillard est très épais

thief

thief
[θi:f] *n*
pl thieves [θi:vz]
voleur *m*, voleuse *f*

** You thief! My wallet!!!... I've got you this time!...* Voleur ! Mon portefeuille ! ! !... Cette fois, je te tiens !... *

thin

thin
[θɪn]
thinner, thinnest
1. mince

a very thin slice for me, please une tranche très mince pour moi, s'il vous plaît

2. maigre, mince
the poor children, they're so thin! les pauvres enfants, ils sont tellement maigres !

thing

thing
[θɪŋ] *n*
1. chose *f*, objet *m*

there are many things on his desk il y a beaucoup de choses sur son bureau

2. Idiom
the best thing would be to get a taxi le mieux serait de prendre un taxi

he didn't say a thing il n'a pas dit un mot

► **things**
[θɪŋz] *n pl*
affaires *f pl*

don't leave your things lying all over the house! ne laisse pas traîner tes affaires dans toute la maison !

think

think
[θɪŋk]
thought, thought [θɔ:t]

...think

I. *v i*
penser, réfléchir

what are you thinking about? à quoi pensez-vous ?

I often think of you je pense souvent à toi

I'm trying to think j'essaie de réfléchir

II. *v t*
penser, croire

don't you think we'd better go? – I think so Ne pensez-vous pas que nous devrions partir ? – Je pense que oui

I don't think so je crois que non

third

third
[θɜ:d]
I. *adj*
troisième

...third

II. *n*
troisième *m f*

thirsty

thirsty
['θɜ:stɪ] *adj*
thirstier, thirstiest
Idiom
to be thirsty avoir soif

* *Be brave, Captain, we must go on...* Courage, capitaine, il faut continuer...

...thirsty

I'm so thirsty!... J'ai tellement soif !... *

thirteen

thirteen
[θɜ:'ti:n]
I. *adj*
treize

II. *n*
treize *m*

thirty

thirty
['θɜ:tɪ]
I. *adj*
trente

II. *n*
pl thirties ['θɜ:tɪz]
trente *m*

this

this
[ðɪs]
pl these [ði:z]

...this

I. *adj*
ce, cette, ces

this cake is delicious! ce gâteau est délicieux !

what are all these people doing here? que font tous ces gens ici ?

II. *pron*
1. ce, ceci, cela, ça

what's this? qu'est-ce que c'est que ça ?

...this

this is a very interesting book c'est un livre très intéressant

2. celui-ci *m*, celle-ci *f*, ceux-ci *m pl*, celles-ci *f pl*
do you prefer these or those? préférez-vous ceux-ci ou ceux-là ?

those

those → THAT

though

though
[ðəʊ]
I. *conj*
1. bien que, quoique

* *I'll try to catch up with them though they're almost there!...* Je vais essayer de les rattraper bien qu'ils soient presque arrivés !... *

2. Idiom
he staggered as though he was drunk

il titubait comme s'il était ivre

you look as though you're tired! vous avez l'air fatigué !

I'm going out, even though it's raining je sors, même s'il pleut

II. *adv*
pourtant

I like Scotland; it's cold there, though j'aime bien l'Écosse ;

...though

pourtant il y fait froid

thousand

thousand
['θaʊzənd]
I. *adj*
mille

it costs two thousand dollars cela coûte deux mille dollars

...thousand

II. *n*
1. mille *m*

fifty times forty makes two thousand cinquante fois quarante font deux mille

2. millier *m*
there were thousands of people in the streets il y avait des milliers de gens dans les rues

threaten

threaten
['θret(ə)n] *vt*
menacer

three

three
[θri:]
I. *adj*
trois

II. *n*
trois *m*

throat

throat
[θrəʊt] *n*
gorge *f*

I've got a sore throat j'ai mal à la gorge

through

through
[θru:]
I. *prep*
1. à travers

* ***They went through the wall!...*** Ils sont passés à travers le mur !... *

...through

2. par
I was looking through the window je regardais par la fenêtre

3. par
why don't you send it through the post (Am: mail)? pourquoi ne pas l'envoyer par la poste ?

II. *adv*
1. à travers

...through

They went through the wall!...

the bullet went right through la balle est passée à travers

2. Idiom
can I have a look at the newspaper when you're through with it? pourrai-je regarder le journal quand vous l'aurez terminé ?

3. *Am:*
Tuesday through Saturday de mardi à samedi

throw

throw
[θrəʊ] *vt*
threw [θru:], thrown [θrəʊn]
jeter, lancer

* ***Quick, let's throw him a rope!*** Vite, lançons-lui une corde ! *

► **throw away**
jeter

I've thrown all those old newspapers

...throw

Quick, let's throw him a rope!

away j'ai jeté tous ces vieux journaux

thumb

thumb
[θʌm] *n*
pouce *m*

I've hurt my thumb je me suis fait mal au pouce

thunder

thunder
['θʌndə^r] *n*
tonnerre *m*

* ***Bom Brom Bobom*** Bom Brom Bobom ***The thunder's rumbling.*** Le tonnerre gronde. *

► **thunderstorm**
['θʌndəstɔ:m] *n*
orage *m*

BOM BROM BOBOM

The thunder's rumbling.

Thursday

Thursday
['θɜ:zdɪ] *n*
jeudi *m*

come and see me on Thursday venez me voir jeudi

they don't work on Thursdays ils ne travaillent pas le jeudi

ticket

ticket
['tɪkɪt] *n*
billet *m*, ticket *m*

I've lost the theatre (Am: theater) tickets j'ai perdu les billets de théâtre

a bus ticket un ticket d'autobus

tide

tide
[taɪd] *n*
marée *f*

the tide is coming in/going out la marée monte/descend

tidy

tidy
['taɪdɪ]
I. *adj*
tidier, tidiest
bien rangé

your room is very tidy ta chambre est très bien rangée

II. *vt*
tidied, tidied
ranger

help me tidy the house aide-moi à ranger la maison

tie

tie
[taɪ]
I. *n*
cravate *f*

II. *vt*
1. attacher, lier

he tied his horse to a tree il a attaché son cheval à un arbre

2. nouer
she tied a ribbon in her hair elle a noué un ruban dans ses cheveux

3. Idiom
to tie a knot faire un nœud

► **tie up**
1. attacher

tie up your shoelaces! attache tes lacets !

2. ligoter
* *Tied up as they are, they'll keep still!* Ainsi ligotés, ils resteront tranquilles ! *

tight

tight
[taɪt]
I. *adj*
étroit, serré

these shoes are too tight ces chaussures sont trop étroites

II. *adv*
1. bien

the jar is shut tight le bocal est bien fermé

2. Idiom
hold tight! tenez bon !

till

till
[tɪl]
I. *prep*
jusqu'à

Tintin will be away till next Monday Tintin sera absent jusqu'à lundi prochain

II. *conj*
jusqu'à ce que

don't move till I give the signal ne bougez pas jusqu'à ce que je donne le signal

time

time
[taɪm] *n*
1. temps *m*

* *Hurry up, we haven't got much time!* Dépêchez-vous, nous n'avons pas beaucoup de temps ! *

I met him a short time ago je l'ai rencontré il y a peu de temps

I can't do three things at the same time! je ne peux pas faire trois choses en même temps !

2. heure *f*
what time is it? – it's half past five quelle heure est-il ? – il est cinq heures et demie

it's time to go to bed il est l'heure de se coucher

the train arrived on time le train est arrivé à l'heure

3. fois *f*
is this the first time you have been to our country? est-ce que c'est la première fois que vous visitez notre pays ?

six times seven is forty-two six fois sept font quarante-deux

4. Idiom
have you been waiting for a long time? est-ce que vous attendez depuis longtemps ?

did you have a good time at the circus? est-ce que vous vous êtes amusés au cirque ?

► **timetable**
['taɪmteɪb(ə)l] *n*
1. horaire *m*

have you looked at the train timetable? avez-vous consulté l'horaire des trains ?

2. emploi *m* du temps

on the first day the teacher gave us our new timetable le premier jour, le professeur nous a donné notre nouvel emploi du temps

tin

tin
[tɪn] *n*
(*Am:* **can**) boîte

* *Let's open a tin of crab...* Ouvrons un

...tin

boîte de crabe... *

Let's open a tin of crab...

▶ **tinned**
[tɪnd] *adj*
(*Am:* **canned)**
en boîte

tinned peas petits pois en boîte

tiny

tiny
['taɪnɪ] *adj*

...tiny

tinier, tiniest
minuscule

tip

tip
[tɪp] *n*
pourboire *m*

tire

tire (*Am*) → TYRE

tired

tired
[taɪəd] *adj*
1. fatigué

I'm tired, can we rest? je suis fatigué, pouvons-nous nous reposer ?

2. Idiom
to be tired of en avoir assez de

▶ **tiring**
['taɪərɪŋ] *adj*
fatigant

title

title
['taɪt(ə)l] *n*
1. titre *m*

what's the title of that book? quel est le titre de ce livre ?

2. titre *m*
his official title is general secretary son titre officiel est secrétaire général

to

to
[tu:] *prep*
1. à

* ***We're going to Brest!*** Nous allons à Brest ! *

?
We're going to Brest!

I'd like to speak to Tintin j'aimerais parler à Tintin

from Monday to Friday de lundi à vendredi

2. moins
it's ten/twenty to six il est six heures moins dix/vingt

3. pour
I'm here to help you je suis là pour vous aider

4. chez
let's go to the Captain's! allons chez le capitaine !

5. *(indiquant l'infinitif)*
Snowy wants to come with you Milou veut venir avec vous

toast

toast
[təʊst] *n*
1. toast *m*, pain *m* grillé

would you like a slice of toast? voudriez-vous un toast ?

2. toast *m*
let's drink a toast to Tintin and the Captain! portons un toast à Tintin et au capitaine !

tobacco

tobacco
[tə'bækəʊ] *n*
tabac *m*

today

today
[tə'deɪ] *adv & n*
aujourd'hui *m*

what are you doing today? qu'est-ce que vous faites aujourd'hui ?

toe

toe
[təʊ] *n*
orteil *m*

together

together
[tə'geðə^r] *adv*
ensemble

the Thompsons always arrive together les Dupondt arrivent toujours ensemble

toilet

toilet
['tɔɪlɪt] *n*
toilettes *f pl*

where is the toilet? où sont les toilettes ?

tomato

tomato
[tə'mɑ:təʊ] *n*
tomate *f*

tomato sauce sauce tomate

tomorrow

tomorrow
[tə'mɒrəʊ] *adv & n*
demain *m*

goodbye, see you tomorrow! au revoir, à demain !

the day after tomorrow après-demain

tongue

tongue

...tongue

[tʌŋ] *n*
langue *f*

put your tongue out tirez la langue

tonight

tonight
[tə'naɪt] *adv*
1. ce soir

what's on television tonight? qu'est-ce qu'il y a à la télévision ce soir ?

...tonight

2. cette nuit
I'll sleep well tonight! je vais bien dormir cette nuit !

too

too
[tu:] *adv*
1. aussi

can I come too? est-ce que je peux venir aussi ?

...too

2. trop
I'm not going out, it's too cold je ne sors pas, il fait trop froid

don't eat too much ne mange pas trop

tool

tool
[tu:l] *n*
outil *m*

tooth

tooth
[tu:θ] *n*
pl teeth [ti:θ]
dent *f*

I had a tooth out je me suis fait arracher une dent

▸ **toothache**
['tu:θeɪk] *n*
mal *m* aux dents

have you got a toothache? avez-vous mal aux dents ?

* *Blistering barnacles!... I have a toothache!...* Mille sabords !... J'ai mal aux dents !... *

▸ **toothbrush**
['tu:θbrʌʃ] *n*
brosse *f* à dents

▸ **toothpaste**
['tu:θpeɪst] *n*
dentifrice *m*

top

top
[tɒp] *n*
1. sommet *m*

I've reached the top of the mountain je suis arrivé au sommet de la montagne

2. haut *m*
a bird was sitting on the top of the tree un oiseau était perché en haut de l'arbre

3. dessus *m*
the top of the box is marked with a cross le dessus de la boîte est marqué d'une croix

4. couvercle *m*
put the top back on the saucepan remettez le couvercle sur la casserole

5. Idiom
on top of the cupboard sur le placard

torch

torch
[tɔ:tʃ] *n*
(*Am:* **flashlight)**
lampe *f* de poche, lampe *f* électrique

total

total
['təʊt(ə)l]
I. *n*
total *m*

the total is more than 300 le total fait plus de 300

II. *adj*
total

the total cost is quite expensive le coût total est assez élevé

touch

touch
[tʌtʃ] *vt*
toucher (à)

don't touch that lever! ne touchez pas à ce levier !

▸ **touch down**
atterrir, se poser

* *Hallo, this is the moon rocket... In a few minutes, we'll be touching down on the Moon...* Allô, ici la fusée lunaire... Dans quelques minutes, nous allons atterrir sur la Lune... *

tour

tour
[tʊəʳ] *n*
excursion *f*, voyage *m*, visite *f*

we went on a coach (Am: bus) tour nous avons fait une excursion en autocar

▸ **tourist**
['tʊərɪst] *n*
touriste *m f*

towards

towards
[tə'wɔ:dz] *prep*
(*Am:* **toward)**
1. vers

* *They're heading towards the east...* Ils se dirigent vers l'est. *

2. vers
he's coming back towards the end of next week il revient vers la fin de la semaine prochaine

...towards

3. envers, à l'égard de
this doesn't change my feelings towards him cela ne change pas mes sentiments envers lui

towel

towel
['taʊəl] *n*
serviette *f* (de toilette)

tower

tower
['taʊəʳ] *n*
tour *f*

hallo, this is flight 713 calling the control tower allô, ici le vol 713, nous appelons la tour de contrôle

town

town
[taʊn] *n*
ville *f*

toy

toy
[tɔɪ] *n*
jouet *m*

track

track
[træk] *n*
1. chemin *m*, piste *f*

this track leads to the village ce chemin mène au village

...track

2. trace *f*
let's follow these tyre (Am: tire) tracks suivons ces traces de pneus

3. voie *f*
railway (Am: railroad) track voie ferrée

traffic

traffic
['træfɪk] *n*
circulation *f*

...traffic

▶ **traffic jam** *n*
embouteillage *m*, bouchon *m*

▶ **traffic lights** (*Am* : **traffic light**) *n pl*
feux *m pl* (de circulation)

turn right at the next traffic lights tournez à droite aux prochains feux

train

train
[treɪn]
I. *n*
train *m*

* *The train has been running for several hours.* Le train roule depuis plusieurs heures... *

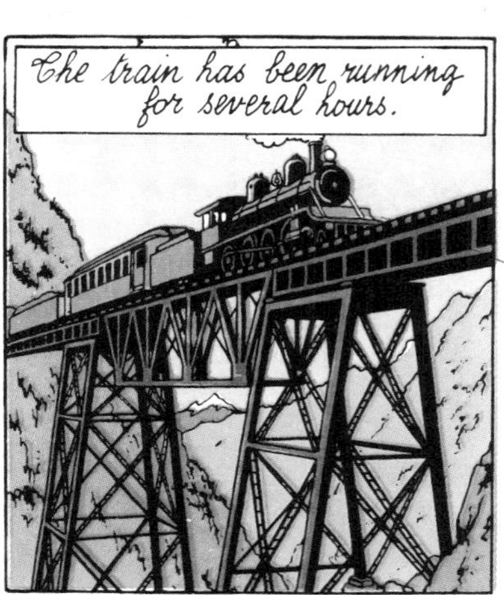
The train has been running for several hours.

II. *vt*
1. entraîner

he trains our rugby team il entraîne notre équipe de rugby

2. dresser
your dog is very well-trained votre chien est très bien dressé

III. *vi*
s'entraîner

the football team trains every day l'équipe de football s'entraîne tous les jours

translate

translate
[træns'leɪt] *vt*
traduire

translate the following passage into French traduisez le passage suivant en français

▶ **translation**
[træns'leɪʃ(ə)n] *n*
traduction *f*

trap

trap
[træp] *n*
piège *m*

travel

travel
['trævəl]
I. *vi*
travelled, travelled (*Am:* traveled)
voyager

I prefer to travel by

...travel

train je préfère voyager en train

II. *n*
voyage *m*

travel agent agent de voyage

▶ **traveller**
['trævləʳ] *n*
(*Am:* **traveler**)
voyageur *m*, voyageuse *f*

▶ **traveller's cheque** (*Am* : **traveler's check**)
chèque *m* de voyage

tray

tray
[treɪ] *n*
plateau *m*

the waiter dropped his tray le serveur a laissé tomber son plateau

treasure

treasure
['treʒəʳ] *n*
trésor *m*

* *The treasure may be here!* Le trésor est peut-être là ! *

The treasure may be here !

tree

tree
[triː] *n*
1. arbre *m*

2. Idiom
pine tree pin

apple tree pommier

trick

trick
[trɪk] *n*
tour *m*

he played a trick on the Captain il a joué un tour au Capitaine

magic trick tour de magie

trip

trip
[trɪp] *n*
voyage *m*

goodbye, have a good trip! au revoir, et bon voyage !

trouble

trouble
[ˈtrʌb(ə)l] *n*
1. ennuis *m pl,* difficulté *f*

* *You're going to get into trouble! You'd better hide!* Vous allez vous attirer des ennuis ! Il faut vous cacher ! *

2. mal *m,* peine *f*
they've gone to a lot of trouble to help us ils se sont donné beaucoup de mal pour nous aider

trousers

trousers
[ˈtraʊzəz] *m*
(*Am:* pants)
pantalon *m*

a pair of trousers un pantalon

truck

truck
[trʌk] *n*
camion *m*

true

true
[truː] *adj*
vrai

is it true that Müller is behind all this? est-ce vrai que Müller est derrière tout cela ?

trunk

trunk
[trʌŋk] *n*
1. malle *f*

pack all your belongings in this trunk mettez toutes vos affaires dans cette malle

2. *Am:* coffre *m*
your bags are in the trunk of the car vos valises sont dans le coffre de la voiture

3. tronc *m*
a tree trunk un tronc d'arbre

4. trompe *f*
an elephant's trunk une trompe d'éléphant

truth

truth
[truːθ] *n*
vérité *f*

you'd better tell me the truth vous feriez mieux de me dire la vérité

try

try
[traɪ]
I. *n*
pl tries [traɪz]

1. tentative *f,* essai *m*

* *Let's go!* Allons-y ! *Hurray! That's it!* Hourra ! Ça y est !
He succeeded at the first try... Il a réussi à sa première tentative... *

2. Idiom
let me have a try laissez-moi essayer

II. *vt*
tried, tried
essayer, tenter

stay here, I'll try to knock the guards out restez ici, je vais essayer d'assommer les gardes

to try one's luck tenter sa chance

► **try on**
essayer

here, try these shoes on tenez, essayez ces chaussures

He succeeded at the first try...

Tuesday

Tuesday
[ˈtjuːzdɪ] *n*
mardi *m*

tune

tune
[tʃuːn] *n*
air *m*

I've had that tune in my head all day j'ai eu cet air dans la tête toute la journée

turn

turn
[tɜːn]
I. *n*
1. virage *m*

there is a sharp turn in the road la route fait un virage brusque

2. tour *m*
wait your turn attendez votre tour

I want you all to read in turn je veux que vous lisiez tous, chacun à votre tour

* *Now, Thompson it's my turn to drive...* Maintenant, Dupond, c'es à mon tour d conduire... *

3. Idiom
whose turn is it (t play)? c'est à qui (d jouer) ?

it's my turn c'est à mc

II. *v i*
1. tourner

the wheels are turn

...turn

- Now, Thompson, it's my turn to drive...

ing les roues tournent

turn left at the next crossroads tournez à gauche au prochain carrefour

2. se retourner
she turned to look at me elle s'est retournée pour me regarder

3. Idiom
to turn yellow/red jaunir/rougir

III. *vt*
1. tourner

turn the knob/the page tournez le bouton/la page

2. transformer, changer
she'll turn you into a frog! elle vous transformera en grenouille !

► **turn back**
rebrousser chemin

it's too late, we can't turn back now il est trop tard, nous ne pouvons plus rebrousser chemin

► **turn down**
1. refuser

they turned down my offer ils ont refusé mon offre

2. baisser
turn the radio down, I want to sleep baissez la radio, je veux dormir

► **turn off**
éteindre, fermer

don't forget to turn the heating off n'oubliez pas d'éteindre le chauffage

► **turn on**
allumer

turn the television on, it's time for the news allumez la télévision, c'est l'heure des informations

...turn

The car turned over!...

► **turn over**
1. se retourner

* *The car turned over!...* La voiture s'est retournée !... *

2. tourner
turn over the page tournez la page

twelve

twelve
[twelv]
I. *adj*
1. douze

2. Idiom
I have lunch at twelve o'clock je déjeune à midi

at twelve o'clock at night à minuit

II. *n*
douze *m*

twenty

twenty
['twentɪ]
I. *adj*
vingt

II. *n*
pl twenties ['twentɪz]
vingt *m*

in the twenties dans les années vingt

twice

twice
[twaɪs] *adv*
deux fois

I've read this book twice j'ai lu ce livre deux fois

twin

twin
[twɪn] *n*
jumeau *m*, jumelle *f*

...twin

Thomson and Thompson look alike but they are not twins.

* *Thomson and Thompson look alike but they are not twins.* Dupont et Dupond se ressemblent, mais ils ne sont pas jumeaux. *

two

two
[tu:]
I. *adj*
deux

...two

II. *n*
deux *m*

tyre

tyre
[taɪəʳ] (*Am :* **tire**)
n
pneu *m*

ugly

ugly
['ʌglɪ] *adj*
uglier, ugliest
laid, vilain

he's the ugliest man I've ever seen! c'est l'homme le plus laid que j'aie jamais vu !

umbrella

umbrella
[ʌm'brelə] *n*
parapluie *m*

...umbrella

* ***My umbrella!... My dear old umbrella! I've found it at last!*** Mon parapluie !... Mon cher vieux parapluie ! Je le retrouve enfin ! *

uncle

uncle
['ʌŋk(ə)l] *n*
oncle *m*

under

under
['ʌndə^{r}] *prep*
1. sous

* ***Tintin is swimming under water...*** Tintin nage sous l'eau... *

2. moins de
children under 8 travel free les enfants de moins de 8 ans voyagent gratuitement

► **underground**
['ʌndəgraʊnd]
I. *adj*
souterrain

an underground passage leads to the castle un passage souterrain mène au château

II. *n*
métro *m*
***she goes to work by underground** (Am: **subway**)* elle va à son travail en métro

...under

Tintin is swimming under water.

understand

understand
[ʌndə'stænd] *v t*
understood, understood [ʌndə'stʊd]
comprendre

* ***I don't understand what you're saying!...*** Je ne comprends pas ce que vous dites !... *

unhappy

unhappy
[ʌn'hæpɪ] *adj*
unhappier, unhappiest
triste

you look unhappy, Snowy, what's the matter? tu as l'air triste, Milou, qu'est-ce qu'il y a ?

united

united
[jʊ'naɪtɪd] *adj*
uni

...united

► **United Kingdom** *n*
Royaume-Uni *m*

► **United States** *n pl*
Etats-Unis *m pl*

university

university
[ju:nɪ'vɜ:sɪtɪ] *n*
pl universities
université *f*

...university

my sister goes to (Am: to the) university ma sœur va à l'université

unless

unless
[ʌn'les] *conj*
à moins que

* *Don't move from here unless I tell you to!* Ne bougez pas d'ici à moins que je ne vous le dise ! *

...unless

Don't move from here unless I tell you to!

until

until
[ʌn'tɪl]
I. *prep*
jusqu'à

Tintin will be away until next month Tintin sera absent jusqu'au mois prochain

II. *conj*
jusqu'à ce que

stay here until I come back restez ici jusqu'à ce que je revienne

unusual

unusual
[ʌn'ju:ʒʊəl] *adj*
1. rare

it is unusual for it to rain here il est rare qu'il pleuve ici

2. étrange
* *Call me if anything unusual happens.* Appelez-moi s'il se passe quelque chose d'étrange. *Alright, chief, I'll stay here!* D'accord, chef, je reste là ! *

...unusual

Call me if anything unusual happens.
Alright, chief, I'll stay here!

up

up
[ʌp]
I. *adv*
1. en haut

there's a village up on that hill il y a un village en haut sur cette colline

2. en l'air
he jumped up to catch it il a sauté en l'air pour l'attraper

3. levé, debout
I've been up since five o'clock this morning je suis levé depuis cinq heures ce matin

4. Idiom
to get up se lever

to go up monter

the temperature is going up la température monte

II. *prep*
1. en haut de

her office is up the stairs son bureau est en haut de l'escalier

2. Idiom
he climbed up the stairs il a monté l'escalier

he climbed up the cliff il a escaladé la falaise

* *Woooaah!* Wouaaah! *It's climbing up the tree.* Il grimpe à l'arbre. *

► **up to**
prep
1. jusqu'à

I'll be working up to seven o'clock je vais travailler jusqu'à sept heures

2. Idiom
it's up to you c'est à vous de décider

what are they up to? qu'est-ce qu'ils manigancent ?

up to date moderne

...up

Woooaah!
It's climbing up the tree.

upset

upset
[ʌp'set]
I. *adj*
1. vexé

she's upset because she's broken her glass elle est vexée d'avoir cassé son verre

2. contrarié
* *The Captain looks upset, what did you say to him?* Le capitaine a l'air contrarié, qu'est-ce que vous lui avez dit ? *

The Captain looks upset, what did you say to him?

3. dérangé
I've got an upset stomach j'ai l'estomac dérangé

II. *v t*
upset, upset
1. peiner

it upset me to hear of his accident cela m'a peiné d'apprendre qu'il a eu un accident

2. contrarier
the Captain's in a bad mood, don't upset him any more le

...upset

capitaine est de mauvaise humeur, ne le contrariez pas davantage

3. renverser
I upset my coffee on the table j'ai renversé mon café sur la table

upstairs

upstairs
[ʌp'steəz] *adv*
1. en haut (de l'escalier)

...upstairs

Tintin is coming upstairs.

the bedrooms are upstairs les chambres sont en haut

2. Idiom
* *Tintin is coming upstairs.* Tintin monte l'escalier. *

urgent

urgent
['ɜːdʒənt] *adj*
urgent

us

us
[ʌs] *pron*
nous

do you want to come with us? voulez-vous venir avec nous ?

use

use
I. [juːs] *n*
1. emploi *m*, utilisation *f*

...use

the use of the future tense in English l'emploi du futur en anglais

2. Idiom
these old tools are (of) no use ces vieux outils ne servent à rien

it's no use shouting ça ne sert à rien de crier

what's the use of working so hard? à quoi ça sert de travailler autant ?

II. [juːz] *v t*

...use

1. utiliser, se servir de

* *I'll use this rope to tie myself to the ladder...* Je vais utiliser cette corde pour m'attacher aux échelons... *

2. consommer
this car uses too much petrol (Am: gas) cette voiture consomme trop d'essence

► **use up**
finir

I'll use this rope to tie myself to the ladder...

we've used up all the butter nous avons fini le beurre

► **used** *adj*
1. [juːzd]
d'occasion

a used car une voiture d'occasion.

2. [juːst]
habitué

I'm not used to getting up so early je ne suis pas habitué à me lever si tôt

3. Idiom
to get used to something s'habituer à quelque chose

► **used to**
['juːstuː] *v aux*
Idiom
when I was young I used to walk to school quand j'étais jeune, j'allais à l'école à pied

he used to be a teacher autrefois il était professeur

we don't see them as much as we used to nous les voyons moins souvent qu'avant

► **useful**
['juːsfʊl] *adj*
utile

* *These binoculars are very useful!* Ces jumelles sont très utiles ! *

...use

These binoculars are very useful!

useless

useless
['juːslɪs] *adj*
1. inutile

this knife is blunt, it's useless! ce couteau ne coupe pas, il est inutile !

2. nul
I'm useless at sport je suis nul en sport

usual

usual
['juːʒʊəl] *adj*
1. habituel, normal

I'll come at the usual time je viendrai à l'heure habituelle

Snowy is not his usual self Milou n'est pas dans son état normal

2. Idiom
as usual comme d'habitude

► **usually**
['juːʒʊəlɪ] *adv*
d'habitude

that's funny, Tintin isn't usually late! c'est bizarre, d'habitude Tintin n'est jamais en retard !

vacant

vacant
['veɪkənt] *adj*
libre

...vacant

excuse me, is this seat vacant? excusez-moi, cette place est-elle libre ?

vacation

vacation (*Am*)
→ HOLIDAY

valley

valley
['vælɪ] *n*
vallée *f*

the village is at the bottom of this valley le village est au fond de cette vallée

van

van
[væn] *n*
1. camionnette *f*

...van

* *Hurry up! Follow that van!... Hurry up!...* Dépêchez-vous ! Suivez cette camionnette !... Dépêchez-vous ! *

2. Idiom
removal (Am: moving) van camion de déménagement

vegetable

vegetable
['vedʒtəb(ə)l] *n*

...vegetable

légume *m*

vehicle

vehicle
['vi:ɪk(ə)l] *n*
véhicule *m*

verb

verb
[vɜ:b] *n*
verbe *m*

very

very
['verɪ] *adv*
1. très

* *It's very hot!* Il fait très chaud ! *

2. Idiom
very much beaucoup

I enjoyed myself very much je me suis beaucoup amusé

...very

victory

victory
['vɪktərɪ] *n*
victoire *f*

view

view
[vju:] *n*
1. vue *f*, panorama *m*

* *The next morning.* Le lendemain matin.
There's a nice view from the summit! Il y

...view

a une belle vue du sommet ! *

2. avis *m*, vue *f*
in my view, we ought to sleep à mon avis, nous devrions dormir

point of view point de vue

village

village
['vɪlɪdʒ] *n*
village *m*

violence

violence
['vaɪələns] *adj*
violence *f*

the violence of the storm la violence de l'orage

▶ **violent**
['vaɪələnt] *adj*
violent

he's a violent man il est un homme violent

visit

visit
['vɪzɪt]
I. *n*
1. visite *f*

let's go and pay him a visit si on allait lui rendre visite ?

2. séjour *m*
is this your first visit to our country? est-ce votre premier séjour dans notre pays ?

II. *vt*
1. rendre visite à

I decided to visit an old friend of mine j'ai décidé de rendre visite à un vieil ami

2. visiter
have you visited the cathedral? avez-vous visité la cathédrale ?

▶ **visitor**
['vɪzɪtə[r]] *n*
visiteur *m*,
visiteuse *f*

voice

voice
[vɔɪs] *n*
voix *f*

vote

vote
[vəʊt]
I. *n*
1. voix *f*

the motion was adopted by 25 votes to 17 la motion a été

...vote

adoptée par 25 voix contre 17

2. vote *m*
everyone has the vote in this country tout le monde a le droit de vote dans ce pays

II. *vi*
voter

vote for me! votez pour moi !

W

wage

wage
[weɪdʒ] *n*
salaire *m*

she's got a new job with a better wage elle a un nouveau travail avec un meilleur salaire

wait

wait
[weɪt] *vi*
1. attendre

...wait

they're waiting for the bus ils attendent l'autobus

**** I've been waiting here for over an hour! Why doesn't the boat come back?*** J'attends ici depuis plus d'une heure ! Pourquoi le bateau ne revient-il pas ? *

2. servir
to wait at table servir à table

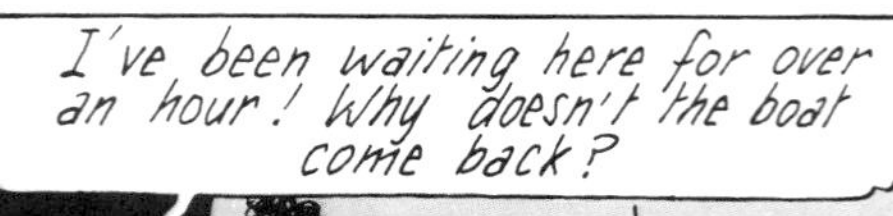
I've been waiting here for over an hour! Why doesn't the boat come back?

► **waiter**
['weɪtəʳ] *n*
serveur *m*, **garçon** *m*

► **waiting room** *n*
salle *f* **d'attente**

► **waitress**
['weɪtrɪs] *n*
serveuse *f*

wake

wake
[weɪk] *vt*
woke [wəʊk],
woken [wəʊk(ə)n]
réveiller

**** A loud noise woke me!... It came from there!...*** Un grand bruit m'a réveillé !... Ça venait de là !... *

► **wake up**
1. réveiller
wake me up at half past six réveillez-moi à six heures et demie

...wake

A loud noise woke me!... It came from there!...

2. se réveiller
wake up, it's time to go réveillez-vous, il est l'heure de partir

Wales

Wales
[weɪlz] *n*
pays *m* **de Galles**

► **Welsh**
[welʃ]
I. *adj*
gallois

II. *n*
1. gallois *m*

do you speak Welsh? parlez-vous le gallois ?

2. ***the Welsh*** les Gallois

► **Welshman, Welshwoman**
['welʃmən], ['welʃwʊmən]
Gallois *m*, **Galloise** *f*

walk

walk
[wɔːk]
I. *n*
1. promenade *f*

we had a lovely walk nous avons fait une belle promenade

2. Idiom
to go for a walk aller se promener

I'll take the dog for a walk je vais promener le chien

it's a ten minute walk from here c'est à dix minutes d'ici à pied

II. *vi*
1. marcher

he's hurt his leg, he can't walk il s'est fait mal à la jambe, il n'arrive pas à marcher

2. aller à pied
I always walk to work je vais toujours au travail à pied

...walk

I like walking in the park!

3. se promener
* *I like walking in the park!* J'aime me promener dans le parc ! *

wall

wall
[wɔ:l] *n*
mur *m*

I'll climb over this wall je vais escalader ce mur

wallet

wallet
['wɒlɪt] *n*
portefeuille *m*

* *Let's have a look!...* Faites voir !...
And now nobody can steal my wallet! Et maintenant, personne ne peut plus voler mon portefeuille ! *

Let's have a look!...
And now nobody can steal my wallet!

want

want
[wɒnt] *v t*
1. vouloir

* *Snowy wants to show me something!* Milou veut me montrer quelque chose !
Woof! Woof! Wouah ! Wouah ! *

2. rechercher
these men are wanted by the police ces hommes sont recherchés par la police

Snowy wants to show me something!
Woof! Woof!

war

war
[wɔ:ʳ] *n*
guerre *f*

why are all these soldiers in the street? is the country at war? pourquoi tous ces soldats sont-ils dans la rue ? le pays est-il en guerre ?

warder

warder
['wɔ:dəʳ] *n*
(*Am:* **guard**)
gardien *m*

warm

warm
[wɔ:m]
I. *adj*
chaud

the tea is still warm le thé est encore chaud

...warm

are you warm enough? avez-vous assez chaud ?

it's warmer today il fait plus chaud aujourd'hui

II. *v t*
réchauffer

come and warm yourself by the fire venez vous réchauffer près du feu

warn

warn
[wɔ:n] *v t*
avertir

how can we warn Tintin of the danger? comment avertir Tintin du danger ?

wash

wash
[wɒʃ]
I. *n*
Idiom

...wash

to have a wash se laver

II. *v t*
laver, se laver

go and wash your hands va te laver les mains

III. *v i*
se laver

we had to wash in cold water nous avons dû nous laver à l'eau froide

► **wash up**
faire la vaisselle

you clear the table and I'll wash up (Am: do the dishes) débarrasse la table, et moi je ferai la vaisselle

► **washing**
['wɒʃɪŋ] *n*
lessive *f*

to do the washing faire la lessive

waste

waste
[weɪst]
I. *n*
1. perte *f*

it's a waste of time! c'est une perte de temps !

2. gaspillage *m*
all that food thrown away, what a waste! toute cette nourriture jetée, quel gaspillage !

II. *v t*
1. perdre

...waste

don't waste your time talking to him, he won't listen ne perdez pas votre temps à lui parler, il n'écoutera pas

2. gaspiller
I've wasted a lot of money/energy j'ai gaspillé beaucoup d'argent/d'énergie

watch

watch
[wɒtʃ]
I. *n*
1. montre *f*

my watch has stopped, what time is it? ma montre s'est arrêtée, quelle heure est-il ?

2. Idiom
* *And that night...* Et ce soir-là...
Keep watch here, I'll try to get into the building... Fais le guet ici, je vais essayer d'entrer dans le bâtiment...
OK!... D'accord !... *

II. *vt*
1. regarder

they are watching television ils regardent la télévision

2. surveiller
* *The police are watching the house!* La police surveille la maison ! *

...watch

► **watch out**
faire attention

watch out, Tintin, he's got a gun! (faites) attention Tintin, il est armé !

water

water
['wɔ:təʳ] *n*
eau *f*

...water

a glass of water un verre d'eau

wave

wave
[weɪv]
I. *n*
vague *f*

the waves are as high as the boat! les vagues sont aussi hautes que le bateau !

...wave

II. *vt*
agiter

she stood on the platform waving her handkerchief elle est restée sur le quai à agiter son mouchoir

III. *vi*
saluer, faire un signe de la main

look, there's Tintin, he's waving to us! regardez, voilà Tintin, il nous salue de la main !

way

way
[weɪ] *n*
1. chemin *m*

could you tell me the way to the station? pourriez-vous m'indiquer le chemin de la gare ?

get out of my way! ôtez-vous de mon chemin !

2. direction *f*, sens *m*

* *Are you sure we're going the right way, Captain?* Etes-vous sûr que nous allons dans la bonne direction, capitaine ? *

3. manière *f*, façon *f*
I always do it this way je le fais toujours de cette façon

4. moyen *m*
* *We must find a way out of here...* Nous devons trouver un moyen de sortir d'ici... *

5. Idiom
it's a long way c'est loin

the way in l'entrée

the way out la sortie

come this way, please venez par ici, s'il vous plaît

by the way à propos

we

we
[wi:] *pron*
nous

I think we're lost j'ai l'impression que nous sommes perdus

weak

weak
[wi:k] *adj*
1. faible

I'm feeling weak... je me sens faible...

...weak

2. léger
this coffee is very weak ce café est très léger

weapon

weapon
['wep(ə)n] *n*
arme *f*

I can use this stick as a weapon je peux me servir de ce bâton comme arme

wear

wear
[weəʳ] *vt*
wore [wɔ:],
worn [wɔ:n]
porter

* *Tintin is wearing a cowboy hat...* Tintin porte un chapeau de cow-boy... *

► **wear out**
user

you'll wear out the batteries tu vas user les piles

Tintin is wearing a cowboy hat...

...wear

my shoes are worn out mes chaussures sont usées

weather

weather
['weðəʳ]
1. temps *m*

what's the weather like? quel temps fait-il ?

2. Idiom
the weather is very

...weather

hot/cold il fait très chaud/froid

► **weather forecast** *n*
prévisions *fpl* météorologiques

wedding

wedding
['wedɪŋ] *n*
mariage *m*

Wednesday

Wednesday
['wenzdɪ] *n*
mercredi *m*

week

week
[wi:k] *n*
semaine *f*

I saw him last week je l'ai vu la semaine dernière

...week

► **weekend**
[wi:'kend] *n*
week-end *m*

weigh

weigh
[weɪ] *vt*
peser

weigh the flour and the sugar pesez la farine et le sucre

...weigh

► **weight**
[weɪt] *n*
poids *m*

* *Snowy, you're eating too much, you're going to put on weight!* Milou, tu manges trop, tu vas prendre du poids ! *

...weigh

Snowy, you're eating too much, you're going to put on weight!

welcome

welcome
['welkəm]
I. *adj*
1. bienvenu

you'll always be welcome in my house vous serez toujours le bienvenu chez moi

2. Idiom
welcome to France bienvenue en France

II. *n*
accueil *m*

they gave us a warm welcome ils nous ont réservé un accueil chaleureux

III. *vt*
accueillir, souhaiter la bienvenue

they were at the airport to welcome us ils étaient à l'aéroport pour nous accueillir

well

well
[wel]
I. *adv*
1. bien

Signora Castafiore sings very well la Castafiore chante très bien

it's well after midnight il est largement plus de minuit

2. Idiom
as well aussi

can I come as well? est-ce que je peux venir aussi ?

as well as aussi bien que

II. *adj*
1. en bonne santé

all the family is well toute la famille est en bonne santé

2. Idiom
how are you? – I'm very well comment allez-vous ? je vais très bien

...well

III. *interj*
ça alors, eh bien

* *Drat! I've given myself away!...* Zut ! Je me suis trahi !... *Well! What a surprise!* Ça alors ! Quelle surprise ! *

west

west
[west]
I. *n*
ouest *m*

* *It keeps pointing towards the west...* Il montre toujours l'ouest... *

II. *adj*
ouest

the west coast la côte ouest

West Germany l'Allemagne de l'Ouest

III. *adv*
à l'ouest, vers l'ouest

there's a village a few miles west of here il y a un village à quelques kilomètres à l'ouest d'ici

► **western**
['westən]
I. *adj*
de l'ouest, occidental

...west

Western Europe l'Europe de l'Ouest

II. *n*
western *m*

there's a good western on television tonight il y a un bon western à la télévision ce soir

wet

wet
[wet] *adj*
wetter, wettest
1. mouillé

you're all wet, come and sit by the fire vous êtes tout mouillé, venez vous asseoir à côté du feu

2. pluvieux
the weather is very wet le temps est très pluvieux

3. Idiom
wet paint peinture fraîche

the paint is still wet la peinture n'est pas encore sèche

what

what
[wɒt]
I. *adj*
1. quel, quelle

what time is it? quelle heure est-il ?

2. quel, quelle

...what

what a pity! quel dommage !

what a lovely day! quelle belle journée !

II. *pron*
1. qu'est-ce qui, que

what's happening? qu'est-ce qui se passe ?/que se passe-t-il ?

2. qu'est-ce que, que
what are you doing? qu'est-ce que vous faites ?/que faites-vous ?

3. ce qui
I wonder what's going to happen next? je me demande ce qui va se passer maintenant ?

4. ce que
can you see what they are doing? est-ce que vous voyez ce qu'ils font ?

5. Idiom
what about me? et moi ?

...what

what about a game of chess? si on faisait une partie d'échecs ?

what's this lever for? à quoi sert ce levier ?

what did you do that for? pourquoi as-tu fait ça ?

III. *interj*
quoi

what! did you say the Thompsons are here! quoi ! vous avez dit que les Dupondt étaient là !

► **whatever**
[wɒt'evəʳ]
I. *conj*
1. ce que

you can do whatever you like vous pouvez faire (tout) ce que vous voulez

2. Idiom
whatever happens, don't tell anybody quoi qu'il arrive, ne le dites à personne

II. *pron*
1. qu'est-ce qui

whatever's happening here? mais qu'est-ce qui se passe ici ?

2. qu'est-ce que
* *Whatever are you doing, Captain?* Mais qu'est-ce que vous faites, capitaine ? *

wheel

wheel
[wi:l] *n*
1. roue *f*

2. Idiom
steering wheel volant *m*

when

when
[wen]
I. *adv*
quand

...when

when are you coming back ? quand revenez-vous?

II. *conj*
quand, lorsque

* *Mind my beard!* Attention à ma barbe ! *Tell me when you're ready.* Dites-moi quand vous serez prêt. *

I was about to go out when the telephone rang j'étais sur le point de sortir lorsque le téléphone a sonné

▶ **whenever**
[wen'evəʳ] *conj*
1. quand

come and see us whenever you like venez nous voir quand vous voudrez

2. chaque fois que
whenever I go to England, it rains chaque fois que je vais en Angleterre, il pleut

where

where
[weəʳ]
I. *adv*
où

II. *conj*
où, là où

stay where you are! don't move! restez où vous êtes ! ne bougez pas !

▶ **wherever**
[weər'evəʳ]
I. *conj*
1. où, là où

you can go wherever you like vous pouvez aller où vous voulez

2. partout où
he follows me wherever I go il me suit partout où je vais

II. *adv*
où

wherever have you been? mais où donc êtes-vous allé ?

whether

whether
['weðəʳ] *conj*
si

* *I don't know whether I'll make it...* Je ne sais pas si je vais y arriver... *

which

which
[wɪtʃ]
I. *adj*
quel, quelle

...which

which way did they go? dans quelle direction sont-ils partis ?

II. *pron interr*
1. lequel *m*,
laquelle *f*,
lesquels *m pl*,
lesquelles *f pl*

I wonder which of these cars is theirs je me demande laquelle de ces voitures est la leur

III. *pron rel*
1. qui

the vase which was on the table le vase qui était sur la table

2. que
* *There's the car which I saw in the street!* Voilà la voiture que j'ai vue dans la rue ! *Yes, that's it!* Oui, c'est elle ! *

while

while
[waɪl]
I. *conj*
1. pendant que

has he been good while I was away? a-t-il été sage pendant que j'étais absent ?

2. tandis que, alors que
my brother's good at German while I'm hopeless mon frère est fort en allemand alors que moi je suis nul

II. *n*
Idiom

it happened a long while ago ça s'est passé il y a longtemps

it's worth (your) while cela vaut la peine

whisper

whisper
['wɪspəʳ] *v t*
chuchoter

whistle

whistle
['wɪsl]
I. *n*
sifflet *m*

II. *v i & v t*
siffler

* *Are you coming, Snowy?* Tu viens, Milou ? *Tintin is whistling to Snowy.* Tintin siffle Milou. *

white

white
[waɪt]
I. *adj*
blanc *m*, blanche *f*

follow that white car suivez cette voiture blanche

II. *n*
blanc *m*

white suits you le blanc vous va bien

who

who
[huː]
I. *pron interr*
qui

who is that man in the orange shirt? qui est cet homme à la chemise orange ?

II. *pron rel*

1. qui
the man who came to see us l'homme qui est venu nous voir

2. que
the man who I saw yesterday l'homme que j'ai vu hier

► **whoever**
[huː'evəʳ] *pron*
qui

you can invite whoever you like vous pouvez inviter qui vous voulez

whole

whole
[həʊl] *adj*
entier

he's eaten the whole cake! il a mangé le gâteau entier !

whose

whose
[huːz]
I. *pron interr*
à qui

* *But Snowy, whose umbrella is that?* Mais

But Snowy, whose umbrella is that?
GENEVE

Milou, à qui est ce parapluie ? *

II. *pron rel*
dont

the woman whose son is in your class la femme dont le fils est dans ta classe

why

why
[waɪ] *adv*
pourquoi

why are the Thompsons here? pourquoi les Dupondt sont-ils là ?

why not? pourquoi pas ?

wide

wide
[waɪd] *adj*
large

the river is very wide la rivière est très large

wife

wife
[waɪf] *n*
pl wives [waɪvz]
femme *f*

wild

wild
[waɪld] *adj*
1. sauvage

* *All the wild animals are running away... Let's do the same!...* Tous les animaux sau-

All the wild animals are running away... Let's do the same!...

vages fuient... Faisons comme eux !... *

2. furieux
the Captain will be wild if we tell him le capitaine sera furieux si nous le lui disons

will

will
[wɪl] *v aux*
1. *(s'emploie pour former le futur)*

what will they do next? que feront-ils ensuite ?

I don't think it will rain je ne pense pas qu'il va pleuvoir

2. *(s'emploie dans une formule de politesse)*
will you open the window, please? voulez-vous ouvrir la fenêtre, s'il vous plaît ?

willing

willing
['wɪlɪŋ] *adj*
1. prêt, disposé

I'm always willing to help you je suis toujours prêt à vous aider

2. obligeant
he's a very willing boy c'est un garçon très obligeant

win

win
[wɪn] *vi & vt*
won, won [wʌn]
gagner

who won the match? qui a gagné le match ?

wind

wind
[wɪnd] *n*
vent *m*

* *There's a very strong wind blowing...* Il souffle un vent très fort... *

There's a very strong wind blowing...

► **windy**
['wɪndɪ] *adj*
windier, windiest
Idiom
it's windy il y a du vent

window

window
['wɪndəʊ] *n*
1. fenêtre *f*

close the window, it's cold fermez la fenêtre, il fait froid

2. vitrine *f*
I like looking at the shop (Am: store) windows j'aime bien regarder les vitrines des magasins

wine

wine
[waɪn] *n*
vin *m*

red/white wine vin rouge/blanc

wing

wing
[wɪŋ] *n*
aile *f*
the bird has hurt its wing l'oiseau s'est blessé à l'aile

winter

winter
['wɪntəʳ] *n*
hiver *m*

wipe

wipe
[waɪp] *vt*
essuyer

he wiped his glasses il a essuyé ses lunettes

wish

wish
[wɪʃ]
I. *n*
vœu *m*

the fairy granted him three wishes la fée lui a accordé trois vœux

best wishes! meilleurs vœux !

II. *vt*
1. désirer, souhaiter

he wishes to be alone il désire être seul

2. souhaiter
wish me good luck! souhaitez-moi bonne chance !

3. Idiom
I wish I'd known! si seulement j'avais su !

I wish the sun would shine! ce serait bien s'il y avait du soleil !

I wish you'd be careful! j'aimerais bien que vous fassiez attention !

with

with
[wɪð] *prep*
1. avec

I agree with you je suis d'accord avec vous

2. à
the man with the white beard l'homme à la barbe blanche

3. de
he was trembling with fear il tremblait de peur

without

without
[wɪ'ðaʊt] *prep*
sans

she talks for hours without stopping elle parle pendant des heures sans s'arrêter

woman

woman
['wʊmən] *n*
pl women ['wɪmɪn]
femme *f*

wonder

wonder
['wʌndəʳ] *vt*
se demander

* *I wonder what they're doing...* Je me demande ce qu'ils sont en train de faire... *

► **wonderful**
['wʌndəfʊl] *adj*
merveilleux, magnifique

wood

wood
[wʊd] *n*
1. bois *m*

we went in the woods nous sommes allés dans les bois

2. bois *m*
the table is made of wood la table est en bois

wool

wool
[wʊl] *n*
laine *f*

word

word
[wɜ:d] *n*
1. mot *m*

I can't read this word je n'arrive pas à lire ce mot

2. parole *f*
do you know the words of this song? connaissez-vous les paroles de cette chanson ?

3. Idiom
I'd like a word with you j'aimerais te parler

work

work
[wɜ:k]
I. *n*
1. travail *m*

he goes to work by bus il va à son travail en autobus

2. œuvre *f*
the complete works of Shakespeare les œuvres complètes de Shakespeare

3. Idiom
to be out of work être au chômage

II. *vi*
1. travailler

he doesn't work hard enough il ne travaille pas assez

2. marcher, fonctionner

* *Heck!... Nothing works in this plane!...* Zut !... Rien ne marche dans cet avion !... *

3. réussir
I hope my plan works

...work

j'espère que mon plan va réussir

► **work out**
calculer

I'm trying to work out how much it will cost j'essaie de calculer combien ça va coûter

► **worker**
[ˈwɜːkəʳ] *n*
travailleur *m*, travailleuse *f*, ouvrier *m*, ouvrière *f*

world

world
[wɜːld] *n*
monde *m*

worry

worry
[ˈwʌrɪ] *v i*
worried, worried
s'inquiéter

don't worry, I'm sure Tintin is safe and sound ne vous inquiétez pas, je suis sûr que Tintin est sain et sauf

worse

worse
[wɜːs]
I. *adj*
1. pire, plus mauvais

the weather is worse than yesterday le temps est pire qu'hier

2. plus mal
the patient is worse le malade va plus mal

II. *adv*
plus mal

he sings even worse than you! il chante encore plus mal que vous !

► **worst**
[wɜːst]
I. *adj*
pire, plus mauvais

* *This is the worst sand-storm I've ever seen!* C'est la pire tempête de sable que j'aie jamais vue !
What wind! Quel vent ! *

II. *adv*
le plus mal

...worse

Peter behaved the worst c'est Peter qui s'est le plus mal conduit

worth

worth
[wɜːθ] *adj*
Idiom
to be worth valoir

these jewels must be worth a fortune! ces bijoux doivent valoir une fortune !

...worth

it's not worth (while) waiting cela ne vaut pas la peine d'attendre

would

would
[wʊd] *v aux*
1. *(s'emploie pour former le conditionnel)*

I would help you if I could je vous aiderais si je pouvais

...would

he said he would come this evening il a dit qu'il viendrait ce soir

2. *(s'emploie dans une formule de politesse)*
would you open the window, please? voulez-vous ouvrir la fenêtre, s'il vous plaît ?

3. *(indique une répétition dans le passé)*
I would often come here when I was young je venais souvent ici quand j'étais jeune

4. Idiom
would you like a cup of tea? aimeriez-vous une tasse de thé ?

it's cold, I would rather stay in il fait froid, je préférerais rester à la maison

wrap

wrap
[ræp] *v t*
wrapped, wrapped

...wrap

1. envelopper

you're cold, wrap yourself in this blanket vous avez froid, enveloppez-vous dans cette couverture

2. emballer, empaqueter
help me wrap these presents aidez-moi à emballer ces cadeaux

wrist

wrist
[rɪst] *n*
poignet *m*

write

write
[raɪt] *v i & v t*
wrote [rəʊt], written [ˈrɪt(ə)n]
écrire

she often writes to her parents elle écrit souvent à ses parents

...write

► **write down**
noter, écrire

I wrote down the number on the back of an envelope j'ai noté le numéro sur le dos d'une enveloppe

► **writer**
[ˈraɪtəʳ] *n*
écrivain *m*

► **writing**
[ˈraɪtɪŋ] *n*
écriture *f*

wrong

wrong
[rɒŋ]
I. *adj*
1. faux

the answer is wrong la réponse est fausse

2. Idiom
to be wrong avoir tort

* *No, this is not Mr Cutts the butcher's, you've got the wrong number!... I'm telling you, this is not Mr Cutts the butcher's!...*

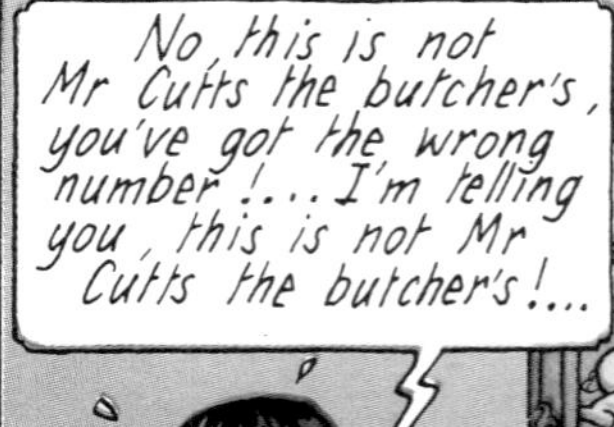

Non, ce n'est pas la boucherie Sanzot ici, vous vous êtes trompé de numéro!... Je vous dis que ce n'est pas la boucherie Sanzot !... *

it's the wrong road ce n'est pas la bonne route

II. *adv*
mal

they've spelt my name wrong ils ont mal écrit mon nom

YZYZY

yard

yard
[jɑ:d] *n*
1. 0,914 mètre

it's about a hundred yards away c'est à cent mètres environ

2. cour *f*
the children are playing in the yard les enfants jouent dans la cour

year

year
[jɪəʳ] *n*
an *m*, année *f*

she's twelve years old elle a douze ans

* ***Is he a general?*** C'est un général ?
Yes, General Alcazar... He is an old friend of mine, we've known each other for years... I met him in South America... Oui, le général Alcazar... C'est

un vieil ami à moi, nous nous connaissons depuis des années... Je l'ai rencontré en Amérique du Sud... *

happy New Year! bonne année !

yellow

yellow
['jeləʊ]
I. *adj*
jaune

...yellow

* ***The Captain's car is yellow.*** La voiture du capitaine est jaune. *

II. *n*
jaune *m*

yellow suits you le jaune te va bien

...yellow

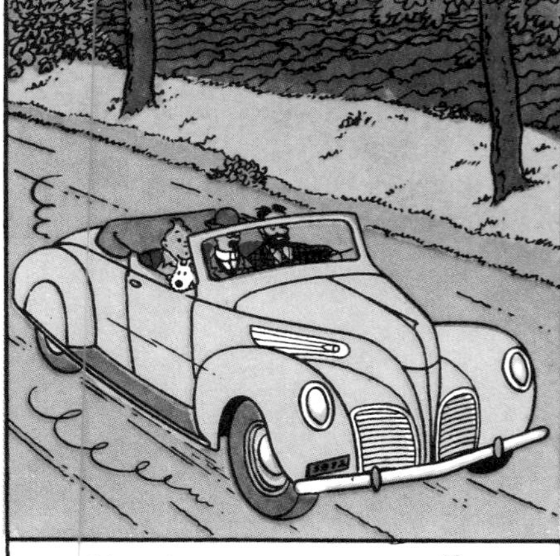

The Captain's car is yellow.

yes

yes
[jes] *adv*
1. oui

do you speak English? – yes, I do parlez-vous anglais ? – oui

2. si
aren't you pleased to see me? – yes, I am! vous n'êtes pas content de me voir ? – si, je le suis !

yesterday

yesterday
['jestədeɪ] *adv*
hier

I saw him yesterday morning je l'ai vu hier matin

the day before yesterday avant-hier

you

you
[ju:] *pron*

...you

1. tu, vous

what are you doing, Snowy? qu'est-ce que tu fais, Milou ?

* ***Good morning, Professor Calculus!*** Bonjour, professeur Tournesol !
Tintin, are you all right? Tintin, est-ce que vous allez bien ? *

2. te, vous
your father's going to tell you off, Abdul-

...you

lah! ton père va te gronder, Abdallah !

3. on
you have to be careful when driving at night on doit faire attention quand on roule la nuit

young

young
[jʌŋ] *adj*
jeune

* *Let's go...* Allons-y...

...young

Let's go...
The young reporter Tintin at work!...

The young reporter Tintin at work!... Le jeune reporter Tintin en pleine action !... *

your

your
[jɔːʳ] *adj*
ton, ta, tes, votre, vos

have you done your homework? as-tu fait tes devoirs ?

...your

don't forget your umbrella, Professor n'oubliez pas votre parapluie, professeur

open your books at page 33 ouvrez vos livres à la page 33

► **yours**
[jɔːz] *pron*
1. le tien, la tienne, les tiens, les tiennes, le vôtre, la vôtre, les vôtres

...your

this is my hat, and that is yours voici mon chapeau, et voilà le vôtre

2. Idiom
is this pen yours? est-ce que ce stylo est à toi ?

a friend of yours un de vos amis

► **yourself**
[jɔːˈself] *pron*
1. te, vous

be careful not to hurt yourself, Snowy fais attention à ne pas te faire mal, Milou

* *How awful!... Look at yourself in the mirror, Tintin!...* Quelle horreur ! Regardez-vous dans la glace, Tintin !... *

2. toi-même, vous-même
can you do it yourself? est-ce que tu peux le faire toi-même ?

How awful!... Look at yourself in the mirror, Tintin!...

3. Idiom
(all) by yourself tout seul

► **yourselves**
[jɔːˈselvz] *pron*
1. vous

did you enjoy yourselves at the party? est-ce que vous vous êtes amusés à la fête ?

2. vous-mêmes
try and do it yourselves essayez de le faire vous-mêmes

3. Idiom
(all) by yourselves tout seuls

youth

youth
[juːθ] *n*
pl youths [juːðz]
1. jeune *m*, jeune homme *m*

some youths were waiting at the bus-stop des jeunes attendaient à l'arrêt d'autobus

2. jeunesse *f*
in my youth dans ma jeunesse

► **youth club** *n*
maison *f* des jeunes

► **youth hostel** *n*
auberge *f* de jeunesse

zero

zero
[ˈzɪərəʊ] *n*
zéro *m*

...zero

Later...
It's cold... The temperature is well below zero...

* *Later...* Plus tard...
It's cold... The temperature is well below zero... Il fait froid... La température est bien en dessous de zéro... *

zoo

zoo
[zuː] *n*
zoo *m*

FRENCH GRAMMAR

VERBS

Present

Though English has two types of present tense, there is only one in French:

*Aujourd'hui, il **joue** dans le jardin.*
Today, he is playing in the garden.

*Tous les jours, il **joue** dans le jardin.*
Every day he plays in the garden.

Perfect

This is a past tense which describes completed actions.

• The perfect can be translated two ways in English:

*Il **a pris**.*
He took / He has taken.

• To form the perfect tense, most verbs use the present tense of *avoir*, followed by the past participle:
J'ai regardé partout.
I have looked everywhere.
*Il **a mangé** une pêche.*
He ate a peach.

• A few verbs (*aller, venir, partir, arriver, entrer, sortir, naître, mourir, tomber, rester*) use the present tense of *être*, followed by the past participle:
*Je **suis** parti à dix heures.*
I left at ten o'clock.

*Il **est** allé au parc.*
He has gone to the park.

• Reflexive (or pronominal) verbs (which contain *me, te, se, nous* or *vous* referring back to the subject) also use the present tense of *être*, followed by the past participle:
*Je me **suis réveillé** à sept heures.*
I woke up at seven o'clock.
*Il s'**est** occupé de tout.*
He took care of everything.

• Past participles end with *é, i, u, it,* or *rt.*

• Agreements (adding *e, s, es* to the past participle).
If the verb uses *être* + past participle, the past participle agrees with the subject:
*Elle **est** sortie.*
She went out.
*Ils **sont** arrivés.*
They arrived.
*Elles **sont** tombées.*
They fell.

• With the reflexive verbs and the verbs using *avoir*, the past participle agrees with a direct object that comes before in the sentence:
*Il les **a** rencontrés* (with an object pronoun).
He met them.
*Les émissions qu'elle **a** regardées* (relative pronoun).
The programmes that she watched.
*Quelles questions **a**-t-il posées ?* (a question)
What questions did he ask ?

Imperfect

This is a past tense which describes:
• either how something was:
*Le château **était** beau.*
The castle was beautiful.
• or an action that happened many times:
*Il **passait** toujours ses vacances à la montagne.*
He always used to spend his holidays in the mountains.
• or an action that was happening when something else happened:
*Il est arrivé quand je **regardais** la télévision.*
He arrived when I was watching television.
All the verbs have the same endings:
*je regard**ais**, tu regard**ais**, il/elle regard**ait**, nous regard**ions**, vous regard**iez**, ils/elles regard**aient**.*

Future

• As in English, the verb *aller* (go) can be used :
*Je **vais** partir demain.*
I'm going to leave tomorrow.
• But the future tense expresses the English 'will/shall + verb' in one word:
*Je partir**ai** demain.*
I will leave tomorrow.
• All verbs in French have the same endings, which are usually added to the infinitive:
*Je partir**ai**, tu partir**as**, il/elle partir**a**, nous partir**ons**, vous partir**ez**, ils/elles partir**ont**.*
• But there are a number of common exceptions :
*Elle **sera** en retard.*
She will be late.
*Nous **irons** à Paris.*
We will go to Paris.
*Il **aura** un nouveau vélo.*
He will have a new bike.
*Il **fera** froid ce soir.*
It will be cold tonight.
(For other irregular futures, refer to verb conjugations page VI.)

Pluperfect

This is a step farther back into the past than the perfect. Instead of using the present of *avoir* or *être*, it uses the imperfect + the past participle:

*Il **avait** refusé de chanter.*
He had refused to sing.

*J'**étais** arrivé avant vous.*
I had arrived before you.

The rules concerning the agreement of the past participle with the subject or preceding direct object are the same as for the perfect.

Past historic

This tense describes completed actions, but is never used when speaking and is not found in books and newspapers as often as it was:
*Napoléon **mourut** en 1821.*
Napoleon died in 1821.

Conditional

This tense expresses the English 'would or should + verb' in one word:
*Je **voudrais** six petits pains.*
I would like six rolls.
*S'il gagnait à la loterie, il **partirait** en Amérique.*
If he won the lottery, he would go to America.

Infinitive

All French verbs have an infinitive that ends in *er, ir,* or *re*, whereas in English 'to' is usually put in front.
• Its most common use is after another verb:
*Il veut **partir**.*
He wants to leave.
• Some verbs have *à* and some *de* to link to an infinitive:
*Il a appris **à faire** du ski.*
He learned to ski.
*Il a essayé **de trouver** un emploi.*
He tried to find a job.

Present participle

The French present participle, which always ends in *ant*, is often translated by a word ending in 'ing':

*Elle a gagné beaucoup en travaill**ant** dur.*
She earned a lot by working hard.
It also occurs in some idiomatic expressions:
*Je suis sorti en **courant**.*
I ran out.

But very often English uses words ending in 'ing' as part of a 'continuous' tense:
I am/was watching TV.
As we have seen, French uses just one word in these cases:
*Je **regarde** la télévision.*
I am watching TV.
*Je **regardais** la télévision.*
I was watching TV.

Commands (imperative)

Commands can be given to *tu* or *vous*. The usual form of the verb should be used: *Sors !* or *Sortez !* (Get out !) – unless the verb's infinitive ends in *er*, when the final *s* of the *tu* form should be left off:
***Mange** ton dîner.*
Eat your dinner.
***Prenez** la première rue à gauche.*
Take the first on the left.
The *nous* form can also be used alone :
***Allons** au cinéma.*
Let's go to the pictures.

Passive

• In English, the object of the most usual active verbs becomes the subject and is followed by a part of the verb 'to be' + the past participle. The same method is used in French:
*Brown **a écrit** le livre → Le livre **a été écrit** par Brown.*
Brown wrote the book → The book was written by Brown.
• But often the active is used with the subject *on* to translate an English passive:
***On** a trouvé un portefeuille.*
A wallet has been found.
• The subject *on* is also used when in English an indirect object is turned into the subject:
***On** m'a donné un nouveau vélo.*
I was given a new bike.

Negatives

• To turn a positive idea into a negative idea, French adds two words : *ne* or *n'* before the verb and *pas, rien, jamais, plus,* or *personne* etc. after the verb:
*Je l'aime bien → Je **ne** l'aime **pas**.*
I like him → I don't like him.
*Tu **n'**aimes **personne**.*
You don't like anyboby.
There is no need to translate the extra 'do, does, did' of the English:
***N'**entre **pas** maintenant.*
Don't come in now.
*Je **ne** travaille **plus**.*
I don't work any more
*Ce **n'**est **rien**.*
It's nothing.
*Elle **n'**a **jamais** joué.*
She has never played.
• Usually, the negative comes before the past participle, but not with *personne* and *que*:
*Nous **n'**avons rencontré **personne**.*
We didn't meet anybody.
*Je **n'**ai lu **que** deux pages.*
I've only read two pages.

Questions (interrogatives)

• The most formal way to ask a question is to invert subject and verb:

***Est-il** là ?*
Is he there?
• To avoid the inversion, the phrase *est-ce que* can be put in front:

***Est-ce qu'**il est là ?*
Is he there?
• Often in speaking, the only change is in the intonation of the voice which rises towards the end:
***Il est** là ?*
Is he there?

Depuis

• With *depuis* (meaning 'for/since') the tense in French is different from English:
*Il **apprend** le français depuis cinq ans.*
He has been learning French for five years.
*Il **apprend** le français depuis 1986.*
He has been learning French since 1986.
This is the present tense because he still is learning French.
• Similarly when talking about the past:

*Elle habit**ait** là depuis deux ans quand son fils est né.*
She had been living there for two years when her son was born.
French uses the imperfect *elle habitait* because she was still living there when her son was born.

Venir de + infinitive

• French uses this expression to talk about something which has just happened:
*Le train **vient de** partir.*
The train has just left.

Note that French uses the present tense of *venir* although the English equivalent is a past tense: The train has just left.
• Similarly French uses the imperfect where English uses the pluperfect:

*Elle **venait de** pleurer.*
She had just been crying.

NOUNS

Gender

All French nouns are either masculine or feminine, even if they are things and not people.

Singular and plural

• Most nouns add *s* for the plural, as in English.
chambre → ***chambres*** (bedrooms)
• But nouns ending in *eau, eu* and most ending in *ou* add *x* for the plural:
bateau → ***bateaux*** (boats).
jeu → ***jeux*** (games).
bijou → ***bijoux*** (jewels).
• Most nouns endings in *al* and *ail* change this to *aux*:
animal → ***animaux*** (animals).
travail → ***travaux*** (works).
• Nouns ending *s, x* and *z* do not change:
repas → *repas* (meals).
prix → *prix* (prices/prizes).
nez → *nez* (noses).
• The plural of *œil* (eye) must just be learnt:
oeil → *yeux* (eyes).

Definite article (the)

• Before a masculine noun: ***le*** *bateau.*
• Before a feminine noun: ***la*** *chambre.*
• Before a masculine or feminine noun that begins with a vowel or a mute 'h': ***l'****école.*
• Before any plural noun: ***les*** *prix.*
• Note also that: *à* + *le* is *au*, and *à* + *les* is *aux*:
au *bateau,* NOT ***à le*** *bateau.*
aux *enfants,* NOT ***à les*** *enfants.*
• Similarly *de* + *le* is *du*, and *de* + *les* is *des*:
du *bateau,* NOT ***de le*** *bateau.*
des *enfants,* NOT ***de les*** *enfants.*

Indefinite article (a, an)

• Before a masculine noun: ***un*** *oiseau.*
• Before a feminine noun: ***une*** *maison.*

Partitive article (some, any)

• Before a masculine noun: ***du*** *pain.*
• Before a feminine noun: ***de la*** *viande.*
• Before a masculine or a feminine noun that begins with a vowel or a mute 'h': ***de l'****eau.*
• Before a plural: ***des*** *frites.*
• Note that after a negative word, all the articles become simply *de/d'*:
*Il n'y a pas **de** pain.*
There isn't any bread.
*Elle n'achète plus **d'**oranges.*
She doesn't buy oranges any more.
• If an adjective is put before a plural noun, *des* become *de/d'*:
De *belles poires.*
Some beautiful pears.
D'*autres villes.*
Some other towns.

ADJECTIVES AND ADVERBS

Adjectives

Adjectives must agree with what they describe by ending *e* if feminine, *es* if feminine plural, and usually *s* if masculine plural:

Un petit chien.
A small dog.
*Trois petit**s** chiens.*
Three small dogs.
*Une petit**e** voiture.*
A small car.
*Trois petit**es** voitures.*
Three small cars.
• Care must be taken with some feminine forms:
– Ending *er*:
cher → *ch**è**re* (dear).
– Ending *x*:
délicieux → *délicieu**se*** (delicious).
– Doubling the last letter:
bon → *bo**nne*** (good).
gros → *gro**sse*** (big).
– Some are rather irregular, for example:
blanc → *blan**che*** (white).
long → *long**ue*** (long).
beau → ***belle*** (beautiful).
nouveau → *nouv**elle*** (new).
vieux → *vie**ille*** (old).

• Note also these forms that are used before a masculine singular noun beginning with a vowel or a mute 'h':
bel *oiseau* NOT *beau oiseau.*
nouvel *an* NOT *nouveau an.*
• Plural masculine adjectives usually add *s* unless
– If the adjective ends with *s* or *x* it does not change in the masculine plural:
heureux → *heureux* (happy).
– If the adjective ends whith *eau* it adds *x* :
beau → *beau**x*** (beautiful).
• Most adjectives follow the noun, but there are a few common ones which can go in front: *beau, bon, gentil, grand, gros, haut, jeune, joli, long, mauvais, nouveau, petit, vieux.*
*Un **grand** livre rouge.*
A large red book.
• A small number of adjectives are found either in front or after the noun, but with a different meaning:
*Sa **propre** maison.*
His/her own house.
*Une maison **propre**.*
A clean house.

Adverbs

• Adverbs can be made from many adjectives.
– Usually, *ment* is added to the feminine form:
heureuse → *heureuse**ment*** (happily).
lente → *lente**ment*** (slowly).
– If the adjective ends with a vowel, *ment* is added to the masculine form:
vrai → *vrai**ment*** (really).
– If the adjective ends with *ent, ant,* the adverb is formed like this:
évident → *évide**mment*** (evidently).
– These two are irregular:
bien = well.
mal = badly.

Comparatives and superlatives

• Comparisons can be made in four ways:
*Il est **plus grand que** son frère.*
He is taller than his brother.
*Il est **aussi grand que** son cousin.*
He is as tall as his cousin.
*Il est **moins grand que** son père.*
He is less tall than his father.
*Il n'est pas **aussi grand que** son père.*
He isn't as tall as his father.

• Adverbs work in the same way:
Elle voyage plus souvent que moi.
She travels more often than me.
– The comparative for 'good' (*bon*) is irregular:
Tintin est un meilleur détective que les Dupondt (adjective).
Tintin is a better detective than the Thompsons.
Il joue mieux que moi (adverb).
He plays better than me.
• Superlatives are very similar to comparatives:
Alain est le plus grand de la classe.
Alain is the tallest in the class.
Paul est le moins intelligent.
Paul is the least intelligent.

Expressing quantity

• Expressions of quantity are followed by *de, d'*:
Combien de bananes ?
How many bananas?
Beaucoup de fromage.
A lot of cheese.
Assez d'argent.
Enough money.
Plus de livres.
More books.
Moins de café.
Less coffee.

POSSESSIVES

Possessive adjectives

• There are three ways of saying 'my', 'your', 'his', etc. in French. It depends on the gender and the number of the thing you are talking about:
– with masculine nouns:
Mon, ton, son, notre, votre, leur livre.
My, your, his or her, our, your, their book.
– with feminine nouns:
Ma, ta, sa, notre, votre, leur voiture.
My, your, his or her, our, your, their car.
– with plural nouns (masculine or feminine):
Mes, tes, ses, nos, vos, leurs parents.
My, your, his or her, our, your, their parents.
Note that in French, the possessive adjective agrees with the thing possessed and not with the owner of the thing:
La Castafiore a perdu sa valise.
Signora Castafiore has lost her suitcase.
Tintin a perdu sa valise.
Tintin has lost his suitcase.

Note that before a feminine singular beginning with a vowel the masculine is used:
son école = his or her school.
• 'Its' is translated by *son, sa,* or *ses*, again depending on the gender and the number of the thing you are talking about.
C'est le yéti ! J'ai vu ses yeux.
It's the Yeti ! I saw its eyes.

Possessive pronouns

• These words are *mien, tien, sien, nôtre, vôtre* and *leur.*
They follow *le, la,* or *les* and must agree in number and gender with the noun that they refer back to:
– masculine singular:
Ce chien est plus grand que le mien/ tien/ sien/ nôtre/ vôtre/ leur.
The dog is bigger than mine/ yours/ his or hers/ ours/ yours/ theirs.
– feminine singular:
Cette maison est plus grande que la mienne/ tienne/ sienne/ nôtre/ vôtre/ leur.
That house is bigger than mine/ yours/ his or hers/ ours/ yours/ theirs.
– plural (with *les*) take an *s*:
masculine plural:
Tes pieds sont plus grands que les miens.
Your feet are bigger than mine.
feminine plural:
Tes notes sont meilleures que les miennes.
Your marks are better than mine.
• But to show that something belongs to somebody, you can often use *à* and a disjunctive pronoun (see under «disjunctive pronouns»):
La voiture bleue est à moi.
The blue car is mine.

You must use *de* to translate 's.

As there is no **'s** in French, link the words with *de*:
Le vélo de la fille.
The girl's bike.

DEMONSTRATIVES

Adjectives

• Before a masculine noun beginning with a consonant, *ce :*
ce bateau = this/that boat.
• Before a masculine noun beginning with a vowel or mute h, *cet :*
cet arbre = this/that tree.
cet homme = this/that man.
• Before a feminine noun, *cette :*
cette femme = this/that woman.
• Before a plural noun, *ces :*
ces enfants = these/those children.
Only if it is necessary to distinguish between 'this' and 'that' or 'these' and 'those', the demonstrative adjectives are : *-ci* for 'this', 'these', and *-là* for 'that', 'those' added after the noun:
Cette voiture-ci est plus grande que cette voiture-là.
This car is larger than that car.

Pronouns

• *C'* is used with the singular *est* and *ce* with the plural *sont*:
C'est un voleur.
He is a thief.
C'est une chanteuse.
She is a singer.
Ce sont des voleurs.
They are thieves.
Ce is also used with *qui, que, qu',* and *dont* to mean 'what' as a relative pronoun (see under «relative pronouns»):
Je ne comprends pas ce qu'il dit.
I don't understand what he is saying.
• *Ceci* (this) and *cela* or *ça* (that) are used when the identity of something is unknown or vague:
Qu'est-ce que cela ?
What is that ?
• *Celui* (masculine singular), *ceux* (masculine plural), *celle* (feminine singular), *celles* (feminine plural) are used to replace known nouns:
Celui qui arrive le premier est le vainqueur.
The one who arrives first is the winner.
Ce sont celles de Tintin.
They are Tintin's.

PRONOUNS

Subject of the verb: *je, tu, il, elle, on, nous, vous, ils, elles*

• *Tu* and *vous* both mean 'you', but *tu* can only be used when speaking

to someone you know well or to a child.
• *Ils* means 'they' when 'they' are all masculine or a mixture of masculine and feminine, but *elles* means 'they' only when 'they' are all feminine.
• *On* literally means 'one', but can be translated as a vague 'they' or 'people' and when spoken is often used to mean 'we'. (See also paragraph under «verbs»):
***On** dit qu'elle est riche.*
They say she's rich.

Direct object of the verb: *me, te, le, la, nous, vous, les*

In French these come before the verb :
*Il **nous** regarde.*
He is watching us.
*Nous **la** vendrons.*
We will sell it.
*Elle va **l'**essayer.*
She is going to try it on.

Indirect object of the verb: *me, te, lui, nous, vous, leur*

• In this example, *me* is the indirect object pronoun:
*Il va **me** donner un cadeau.*
He is going to give me a present.
The other forms are as follows:
*Il va **te/lui/nous/vous/leur** donner un cadeau.*
He is going to give you/him or her/us/you/them a present.
Notice how *me* and *te* become *m'* and *t'* in front of a vowel:
*Il **m'a** donné un cadeau.*
He has given me a present.
*Il **t'a** donné un cadeau.*
He has given you a present.
• Indirect object pronouns only follow the verbs in commands that do not contain a negative:
*Parlez-**leur** de ce problème.*
Talk to them about this problem.
• In this position, *me* changes to *moi*:
*Passe-**moi** le pain.*
Pass me the bread.

Reflexive: *me, te, se, nous, vous*

• *Se* refers back to *il, elle, ils, elles, on* or any noun used as the subject. Reflexive pronouns mean 'myself', 'yourself', etc. in English, but they are not always translated literally:
*Jean-Paul **se** lève à sept heures.*
Jean-Paul gets up at seven o'clock.
*Il **se** dirige lentement vers l'école.*
He slowly makes his way to school.

The pronoun *en*

En means 'some', 'any' ('of it/them') and refers to a quantity:
*Combien **en** voulez-vous ?*
How many of them do you want?
*Tu **en** veux ?*
Do you want any?

The pronoun *y*

Y means 'there' and replaces a phrase indicating a place:
*Vas-tu au cinéma ? – Oui, j' **y** vais ce soir.*
Are you going to the pictures? – Yes, I'm going there tonight.

Order of pronouns

• If there are two object pronouns before a verb, they come in this order:

me				
te	le	lui		
se	la	leur	y	en
nous	les			
vous				

*Il **nous les** envoie.*
He is sending them to us.
*Je **le lui** ai envoyé.*
I sent it to him.
*Il **y en** a trois.*
There are three of them.

Disjunctive pronouns: *moi, toi, lui, elle, nous, vous, eux, elles*

They are used mainly after the phrase *c'est*, after prepositions or for emphasis:
*c'est **elle*** = it's her.
*chez **lui*** = at his house.
*sans **moi*** = without me.
***lui**, il ne vient jamais* = him, he never comes.

Relative pronouns: *qui, que, dont*

They link a relative clause describing somebody or something to the main clause.
• As a subject:
*Les hommes **qui** travaillent là sont bien payés.*
The men who work here are well paid.
• As an object :
*Le film **que** j'ai vu hier était ennuyeux.*
The film (that) I saw yesterday was boring.
• To show possession:
*Tintin, **dont** le chien s'appelle Milou, est reporter.*
Tintin, whose dog is called Snowy, is a reporter.
• After a preposition:
*Le garçon, **avec qui**...*
The boy, with whom...
*La table, **sur laquelle**...*
The table, on which...
This last word has the forms *lequel, laquelle, lesquels, lesquelles*, as it must agree in gender and number with the word that it refers back to.

INTERROGATIVES

These are words that ask questions.

• *Qui* = who:
***Qui** est là ?*
Who is there?
***Qui** avez-vous choisi ?*
Who(m) have you chosen?
*Avec **qui** est-elle allée au cinéma ?*
Who has she gone to the pictures with?

• *Quoi, que, qu'* = what:
***Qu'**est-ce qui s'est passé ?*
What has happened?
***Qu'**est-ce que vous avez fait ?*
What have you done?
*Avec **quoi** a-t-il écrit ?*
What did he write with?

• *Quel, quelle, quels, quelles* = what, which:
***Quel** parfum veux-tu ?*
Which flavour do you want?
***Quelle** heure est-il ?*
What time is it?

• *Lequel, laquelle, lesquels, lesquelles* = which one(s).

• *Quand* = when.

• *Où* = where.

• *Pourquoi* = why.

• *Comment* = how.
Comment can also be used to ask what something is like:
***Comment** est ton jardin ?*
What is your garden like?

FRENCH VERB CONJUGATIONS

REGULAR VERBS

	-ER Verbs	-IR Verbs	-RE Verbs
Infinitive	*donn/er*	*fin/ir*	*vend/re*
1. Present	je donne tu donnes il donne nous donnons vous donnez ils donnent	je finis tu finis il finit nous finissons vous finissez ils finissent	je vends tu vends il vend nous vendons vous vendez ils vendent
2. Imperfect	je donnais tu donnais il donnait nous donnions vous donniez ils donnaient	je finissais tu finissais il finissait nous finissions vous finissiez ils finissaient	je vendais tu vendais il vendait nous vendions vous vendiez ils vendaient
3. Past historic	je donnai tu donnas il donna nous donnâmes vous donnâtes ils donnèrent	je finis tu finis il finit nous finîmes vous finîtes ils finirent	je vendis tu vendis il vendit nous vendîmes vous vendîtes ils vendirent
4. Future	je donnerai tu donneras il donnera nous donnerons vous donnerez ils donneront	je finirai tu finiras il finira nous finirons vous finirez ils finiront	je vendrai tu vendras il vendra nous vendrons vous vendrez ils vendront
5. Subjunctive	je donne tu donnes il donne nous donnions vous donniez ils donnent	je finisse tu finisses il finisse nous finissions vous finissiez ils finissent	je vende tu vendes il vende nous vendions vous vendiez ils vendent
6. Imperative	donne donnons donnez	finis finissons finissez	vends vendons vendez
7. Present participle	donnant	finissant	vendant
8. Past participle	donné	fini	vendu

IRREGULAR VERBS

1. = Present 2. = Imperfect 3. = Past Historic 4. = Future
5. = Subjunctive 6. = Imperative 7. = Present Participe
8. = Past Participle

accueillir *like* **cueillir**
aller 1. je vais, tu vas, il va, nous allons, vous allez, ils vont – 4. j'irai – 5. j'aille, nous allions, ils aillent – 6. va, allons, allez (*but note* vas-y)
appartenir *like* **tenir**
apprendre *like* **prendre**
s'asseoir 1. je m'assieds, nous nous asseyons, ils s'asseyent – 2. je m'asseyais – 3. je m'assis – 4. je m'assiérai – 5. je m'asseye – 7. asseyant – 8. assis
avoir 1. j'ai, tu as, il a, nous avons, vous avez, ils ont – 2. j'avais – 3. j'eus – 4. j'aurai – 5. j'aie, il ait, nous ayons, ils aient – 6. aie, ayons, ayez – 7. ayant – 8. eu
battre 1. je bats, nous battons – 5. je batte
boire 1. je bois, nous buvons, ils boivent – 2. je buvais – 3. je bus – 5. je boive, nous buvions – 7. buvant – 8. bu
comprendre *like* **prendre**
conduire 1. je conduis, nous conduisons – 3. je conduisis – 5. je conduise – 8. conduit
connaître 1. je connais, il connaît, nous connaissons – 3. je connus – 5. je connaisse – 7. connaissant – 8. connu
construire *like* **conduire**
contenir *like* **tenir**
convenir *like* **tenir**
coudre 1. je couds, nous cousons, ils cousent – 3. je cousis – 5. je couse – 7. cousant – 8. cousu
courir 1. je cours, nous courons – 3. je courus – 4. je courrai – 5. je coure – 8. couru
couvrir 1. je couvre – 2. je couvrais – 5. je couvre – 8. couvert
croire 1. je crois, nous croyons, ils croient – 2. je croyais – 3. je crus – 5. je croie, nous croyions – 7. croyant – 8. cru
cueillir 1. je cueille, nous cueillons – 2. je cueillais – 4. je cueillerai – 5. je cueille – 7. cueillant
cuire 1. je cuis, nous cuisons – 2. je cuisais – 3. je cuisis – 5. je cuise – 7. cuisant – 8. cuit
décevoir *like* **recevoir**
découvrir *like* **couvrir**
décrire *like* **écrire**
détruire *like* **conduire**
devenir *like* **tenir**
devoir 1. je dois, nous devons, ils doivent – 2. je devais – 3. je dus – 4. je devrai – 5. je doive, nous devions – 6. *not used* – 7. devant – 8. dû, due, *pl* dus, dues
dire 1. je dis, nous disons, vous dîtes – 2. je disais, – 3. je dis – 5. je dise – 7. disant – 8. dit
disparaître *like* **connaître**
dormir *like* **mentir**

écrire 1. j'écris, nous écrivons – 2. j'écrivais – 3. j'écrivis – 5. j'écrive – 7. écrivant – 8. écrit

endormir *like* **mentir**

envoyer 4. j'enverrai

éteindre 1. j'éteins, nous éteignons, ils éteignent – 2. j'éteignais – 3. j'éteignis – 4. j'éteindrai – 5. j'éteigne – 7. éteignant – 8. éteint

être 1. je suis, tu es, il est, nous sommes, vous êtes, ils sont – 2. j'étais – 3. je fus – 4. je serai – 5. je sois, nous soyons, vous soyez – 7. étant – 8. été

faire 1. je fais, nous faisons, vous faites, ils font – 2. je faisais – 3. je fis – 4. je ferai – 5. je fasse – 7. faisant – 8. fait

falloir *(impersonal)* 1. il faut – 2. il fallait – 3. il fallut – 4. il faudra – 5. il faille – 6. *none* – 7. fallu

fuir 1. je fuis, nous fuyons, ils fuient – 2. je fuyais – 3. je fuis – 5. je fuie – 7. fuyant – 8. fui

interdire *like* **dire** *except* 1. vous interdisez

lire 1. je lis, nous lisons – 2. je lisais – 3. je lus – 5. je lise – 7. lisant – 8. lu

mentir 1. je mens, nous mentons – 2. je mentais – 5. je mente – 7. mentant – 8. menti

mettre 1. je mets, nous mettons – 2. je mettais – 3. je mis – 5. je mette – 7. mettant – 8. mis

mourir 1. je meurs, nous mourons, ils meurent – 2. je mourais – 3. je mourus – 4. je mourrai – 5. je meure, nous mourions – 7. mourant – 8. mort

naître 1. je nais, il naît, nous naissons – 2. je naissais – 3. je naquis – 4. je naîtrai – 5. je naisse – 7. naissant – 8. né

offrir *like* **couvrir**

ouvrir *like* **couvrir**

paraître *like* **connaître**

partir *like* **mentir**

peindre *like* **éteindre**

permettre *like* **mettre**

plaindre *like* **éteindre**

plaire 1. je plais, nous plaisons – 2. je plaisais – 3. je plus – 5. je plaise – 7. plaisant – 8. plu

pleuvoir *(impersonal)* 1. il pleut – 2. il pleuvait – 3. il plut – 4. il pleuvra – 5. il pleuve – 6. *none* – 7. pleuvant – 8. plu

pouvoir 1. je peux *or* je puis, tu peux, il peut, nous pouvons, ils peuvent – 2. je pouvais – 3. je pus – 4. je pourrai – 5. je puisse – 6. *not used* – 7. pouvant – 8. pu

prendre 1. je prends, nous prenons, ils prennent – 2. je prenais – 3. je pris – 5. je prenne – 7. prenant – 8. pris

prévenir *like* **tenir**

prévoir *like* **voir** *except* 4. je prévoirai

promettre *like* **mettre**

recevoir 1. je reçois, nous recevons, ils reçoivent – 2. je recevais – 3. je reçus – 4. je recevrai – 5. je reçoive, nous recevions, ils reçoivent – 7. recevant – 8. reçu

reconnaître *like* **connaître**

rejoindre *like* **éteindre**

renvoyer *like* **envoyer**

reprendre *like* **prendre**

revenir *like* **tenir**

revoir *like* **voir**

rire 1. je ris, nous rions – 2. je riais – 3. je ris – 5. je rie, nous riions – 7. riant – 8. ri

savoir 1. je sais, nous savons, ils savent – 2. je savais – 3. je sus – 4. je saurai – 5. je sache – 6. sache, sachons, sachez – 7. sachant – 8. su

sentir *like* **mentir**

servir *like* **mentir**

sortir *like* **mentir**

souffrir *like* **couvrir**

sourire *like* **rire**

soutenir *like* **tenir**

se souvenir *like* **tenir**

suffir 1. je suffis, nous suffisons – 2. je suffisais – 3. je suffis – 5. je suffise – 7. suffisant – 8. suffi

suivre 1. je suis, nous suivons – 2. je suivais – 3. je suivis – 5. je suive – 7. suivant – 8. suivi

taire 1. je tais, nous taisons – 2. je taisais – 3. je tus – 5. je taise – 7. taisant – 8. tu

tenir je tiens, nous tenons, ils tiennent – 2. je tenais – 3. je tins, tu tins, il tint, nous tînmes, vous tîntes, ils tinrent – 4. je tiendrai – 5. je tienne – 7. tenant – 8. tenu

traduire *like* **conduire**

valoir 1. je vaux, nous valons – 2. je valais – 3. je valus – 4. je vaudrai – 5. vaille – 6. *not used* – 7. valant – 8. valu

venir *like* **tenir**

vivre 1. je vis, nous vivons – 2. je vivais – 3. je vécus – 5. je vive – 7. vivant – 8. vécu

voir 1. je vois, nous voyons – 2. je voyais, nous voyions – 3. je vis – 4. je verrai – 5. je voie – 7. voyant – 8. vu

vouloir 1. je veux, nous voulons, ils veulent – 2. je voulais – 3. je voulus – 4. je voudrai – 5. je veuille – 6. veuille, veuillons, veuillez – 7. voulant – 8. voulu

GRAMMAIRE ANGLAISE

ABREVIATIONS

S = sujet
Aux = auxiliaire (modal, *do, does, did...*)
V = base verbale (infinitif sans *to*)
Ved = base verbale + *ed* pour les verbes réguliers ou deuxième colonne de la liste pour les verbes irréguliers (prétérit)
Ven = base verbale + *ed* pour les verbes réguliers ou troisième colonne de la liste pour les verbes irréguliers (participe passé)
Ving = base verbale et terminaison *ing* (participe présent)
Adj = adjectif
COD = complément d'objet direct
∅ = ce signe indique qu'il n'y a pas de mot à cet endroit dans la phrase

Voir la liste des verbes irréguliers à la fin de la grammaire.

LE GROUPE VERBAL

LES STRUCTURES

La structure affirmative

Be et *have got*

I am, you are, he/she/it is, we/you/they are. I/you have got, he/she/it has got, we/you/they have got.

• S + *be* + Adj + nom
He is happy.
Il est heureux.
Tintin is a reporter.
Tintin est reporter.

• S + *have got* + nom
He has got a camera.
Il a un appareil photo.

S + *have* + Ven

He has played football in the park.
Il a joué au football dans le parc.
He has taken his umbrella.
Il a pris son parapluie.

S + Aux + V

• S + Aux + Ving
He is playing in the garden.
Il joue dans le jardin.

• S + Aux + V
He can swim very well.
Il sait très bien nager.

• S + ∅ + V
They get up at seven o'clock every morning.
Ils se lèvent à sept heures tous les matins.

La structure interrogative

Be et *have got*

• *Be* + S + Adj ou nom
Is he happy?
Est-il heureux ?

• *Have* + S + got + nom
Has Tintin got a camera?
Est-ce que Tintin a un appareil photo ?

Have + S + Ven

Has he played football?
Est-ce qu'il a joué au football ?

Aux + S + V

• *Be* + S + Ving
Is he playing football?
Est-ce qu'il est en train de jouer au football ?

• Aux + S + V
Can he swim?
Sait-il nager ?

• Dans le cas des structures S + ∅ + V, on fait apparaître l'auxiliaire *do* + S + V. Cet auxiliaire s'accorde en temps et en personne avec le verbe. Présent simple = *does* à la troisième personne
Ved = *did*
Ven = *done*
Ving = *doing*
Do they get up at seven o'clock?
Est-ce qu'ils se lèvent à sept heures ?

La structure négative

Be et *have got*

• S + *be* + not
I am not, you are not (you aren't), he/she/it is not (he/she/it isn't), we/you/they are not (we/you/they aren't)
Captain Haddock is not a reporter.
Le capitaine Haddock n'est pas reporter.

• S + *haven't/hasn't* + *got*
Snowy hasn't got a camera.
Milou n'a pas d'appareil photo.

S + *haven't* + Ven

***He hasn't taken** his umbrella.*
Il n'a pas pris son parapluie.

S + Aux + *not* + V

• S + be + *not* + Ving
***Abdullah isn't playing** in the garden.*
Abdallah n'est pas en train de jouer dans le jardin.
• S + Aux + *not* + V
***He can't** (cannot) **swim** very well.*
Il ne sait pas très bien nager.
• Dans le cas des structures S + ∅ + V, on emploie l'auxiliaire *do* à la forme négative – *don't, doesn't* (troisième personne), *didn't* (passé) : S + *don't/doesn't/didn't* + V.
***They don't get up** at seven o'clock.*
Ils ne se lèvent pas à sept heures.

TEMPS ET ASPECTS

Pour traduire les temps français, l'anglais utilise des auxiliaires ; seuls le présent (*present*) et le prétérit (*preterit*) ont une conjugaison particulière. Cependant, pour chacun de ces deux temps, il existe deux formes – la forme simple et la forme en *ing* – qui leur apportent une nuance supplémentaire.

Les formes simples

Le présent simple

• V à toutes les personnes sauf à la troisième personne du singulier qui devient V + *s* :
I give, you give, she gives.
Je donne, tu donnes, elle donne.
(Pour les verbes *to be* et *to have*, voir plus haut.)
Il s'utilise pour des actions habituelles, des généralités et avec des adverbes de fréquence tels que *always, never, usually...*
*Captain Haddock **lives** in Marlinspike.*
Le capitaine Haddock habite à Moulinsart.

Le prétérit simple

• V + *ed* ou deuxième colonne des verbes irréguliers. Il exprime une action passée, datée et révolue :
*When he was young, John **lived** in London.*
Lorsqu'il était jeune, John habitait à Londres.

• Pour la forme négative et interrogative, on utilise la même structure qu'au présent simple mais on met l'auxiliaire au prétérit :
***Did** you **play** football yesterday? No, I **didn't**, I played tennis.*
As-tu joué au football, hier ? Non, j'ai joué au tennis.

Les formes en *ing*

Le présent en *ing* ou présent continu

Se forme avec *be* au présent + Ving.
• L'action se déroule actuellement :
*What **are** you **doing**? – **I'm having** a bath.*
Que fais-tu ? – Je prends un bain.
• Il peut aussi exprimer le futur :
*Tomorrow **I'm going** to London.*
Demain je vais à Londres.

Le prétérit en *ing*

Se forme avec *be* au prétérit + Ving. L'action a lieu dans le passé et a été interrompue :
*I **was reading** when he came in.*
Je lisais quand il est entré.
L'entrée a eu lieu à un moment précis du passé.
*What **were** you **doing** yesterday at 8 o'clock?*
Que faisais-tu hier à 8 heures ?
Pour la forme négative et interrogative, voir ci-dessus dans le paragraphe « les structures ».

Have + Ven

Present perfect: Have + Ven

On utilise cette forme
• lorsqu'une action passée a encore un lien avec le présent :
*I can't open the door. I **have lost** my key.*
Je ne peux pas ouvrir la porte. J'ai perdu ma clef.
• lorsque l'action a commencé dans le passé et se poursuit dans le présent (avec *since* et *for*) :
*He's **worked** in this factory **since** 1965.*
Il travaille dans cette usine depuis 1965.
• avec certains adverbes tels que : *already, never, recently, lately...*
***I've already read** this book.*
J'ai déjà lu ce livre.

Pluperfect: Had + Ven

On l'emploie lorsqu'on parle du passé et qu'on veut situer une action antérieure :
*After they **had gone** to the pictures, they went to the pub.*
Après être allés au cinéma, ils sont allés au pub.

Present perfect continu et *pluperfect* continu : *Have* + *been* + Ving, *had* + *been* + Ving

• La première forme s'utilise beaucoup avec *for* et *since* lorsque l'action se poursuit dans le présent :
***He's been working** here **for** five years.*
Il travaille ici depuis cinq ans.
***He's been working** here **since** 1985.*
Il travaille ici depuis 1985.
• Elle s'emploie également pour expliquer un état de fait présent :
*Her eyes are red. She **has been crying**.*
Ses yeux sont rouges. Elle a pleuré.
• *Had* + *been* + Ving apparaît dans un contexte passé :
*When I saw her, her eyes were red. She **had been crying**.*
Quand je l'ai vue, ses yeux étaient rouges. Elle avait pleuré.

LES MODAUX

On appelle modaux une série d'auxiliaires qui ne prennent pas de *s* à la troisième personne. Pour leur forme interrogative et négative, voir le paragraphe « les structures ».

L'obligation = *must* + V

*You **must visit** your grand-parents.*
Tu dois rendre visite à tes grands-parents.
• *Have to*, bien qu'il ne soit pas un modal (il se conjugue normalement), exprime aussi l'obligation :

*I've got an appointment at the dentist: I **have to** go now.*
J'ai un rendez-vous chez le dentiste : je dois partir maintenant.
• *Must* ne s'utilise qu'au présent et exprime une obligation intérieure tandis que *have to* exprime une obligation extérieure. *Have to* remplace *must* aux autres temps.
• L'interdiction se marque avec *mustn't* + V :
*You **mustn't park** here.*
Il ne faut pas stationner ici.

• L'absence d'obligation se marque par : *don't have to, don't need* to + V ou *needn't* + V :
*You **don't have** to cut the grass. I've already done it.*
Tu n'es pas obligé de couper l'herbe. Je l'ai déjà fait.

Le conseil = *should* + V ou *ought to* + V

*You **should take** your umbrella. It's going to rain.*
Tu devrais prendre ton parapluie. Il va pleuvoir.
• Le reproche se marque par *should* + *have* + Ven :
*You **should have told** him before.*
Tu aurais dû lui dire avant.

La capacité = *can* + V

*He **can swim** very well.*
Il sait très bien nager.
• Au passé et au conditionnel, on emploie *could*; aux autres temps, on remplace *can* par *be able to*.

La permission = *may* + V

*Now you've finished your homework, you **may go out**.*
Maintenant que tu as fini tes devoirs, tu peux sortir.
• *May* ne s'utilise qu'au présent ; aux autres temps, on emploie *be allowed to* + V :
*I don't think I'll **be allowed to come** tomorrow.*
Je ne crois pas que je pourrai venir demain.

L'idée de futur = *will* + V

*You'**ll get** a nice present for your birthday.*
Tu auras un joli cadeau pour ton anniversaire.
• La négation = *won't* + V
• *Be going to* + V, bien que ce ne soit pas un modal, exprime également l'idée de futur.
• *Will* s'utilise lorsque l'action est inévitable ou lorsque l'on vient de prendre une décision :
*There's a knock at the door. I'**ll** answer.*
On a frappé. Je vais répondre.
• En revanche, *be going to* indique que l'action a été prévue depuis long-temps :
*Tomorrow I'**m going to** buy a present for my mother's birthday.*
Demain, je vais acheter un cadeau pour l'anniversaire de ma mère.

La condition = *would* + V

*If I could, I **would go** with you.*
Si je pouvais, j'irais avec toi.
• *Would* + *have* + Ven
*If I had known, I **wouldn't have told** you.*
Si j'avais su, je ne te l'aurais pas dit.

La suggestion = *shall* + V

***Shall** we **go** to the pictures tonight?*
Si on allait au cinéma ce soir ?

La probabilité = *must* + *be* + Ving

*He **must be working** in the garden.*
Il doit travailler dans le jardin.
• L'incertitude, le doute = *may* / *might* + V :
*He **may work** a lot but his results aren't good enough.*
Il se peut qu'il travaille beaucoup mais ses résultats ne sont pas assez bons.
• *Must* / *may* / *might* + *have* + Ven :
*He **must have lost** his wallet.*
Il a dû perdre son portefeuille.

LA NOMALISATION DU VERBE

En anglais, on peut donner à un verbe les fonctions d'un nom : sujet, objet, etc. Cette nomalisation se fait en lui ajoutant *ing* :
• Sujet :
Skiing is my favourite sport.
Le ski est mon sport favori.
• Objet :
I like playing football.
J'aime jouer au football.
• Après une préposition :
He is very good at jumping.
Il est très bon en saut.

LE PASSIF = *be* + Ved

Le passif se forme comme en français avec le verbe *to be* (être).
• Le complément d'agent est intro-duit par *by* :
*The house **has been** built **by** his father.*
La maison a été construite par son père.
• L'agent n'est pas toujours exprimé :
*The house **was** sold yesterday.*
La maison a été vendue hier / On a vendu la maison hier.
Le passif s'utilise en effet fréquem-ment pour traduire le 'on' français.
• Le verbe *be* peut se mettre à tous les temps et être précédé d'un modal :
*He **must be driven** to hospital.*
On doit le conduire à l'hôpital.
• Avec les verbes à deux complé-ments (*give/tell*, etc.), le complément d'objet indirect peut-être sujet :
*Somebody gave him a present → He **was given** a present.*
Quelqu'un lui a donné un cadeau → On lui a donné un cadeau.

LE GROUPE NOMINAL

LE NOM

Le nombre

• On classe les noms en dénombra-bles et indénombrables. Les noms dénombrables sont les noms de choses et de personnes que l'on peut compter : *a house* → *two houses*.
Les noms indénombrables désignent des concepts, des substances qu'on ne peut pas diviser : *butter, money*, etc.
• Le pluriel régulier :
– Les noms prennent un *s* au pluriel ou *es* lorsque le mot se termine par *ch, sh, ss, o* ou *x*.
– Les noms se terminant par le son [f] donnent [vz] :
leaf (feuille) → *leaves.*
– Les noms se terminant par *y* don-nent *ies*.
• Le pluriel irrégulier :
Certains noms ont un pluriel irrégulier :
child (enfant) → *children*
man (homme) → *men*
foot (pied) → *feet.*
Ils sont indiqués dans le dictionnaire.

Le genre

• Sont au masculin : les noms d'hom-mes, d'animaux mâles.
• Sont au féminin : les noms de femmes, d'animaux femelles ainsi que les noms de bateaux et de pays.
• Sont neutres : les noms de choses, et d'animaux si le sexe n'est pas important, ainsi que le mot *baby*.

LA DETERMINATION DU NOM

L'article défini *the*

• Absence de l'article *the* :
On omet l'article lorsqu'il s'agit de noms propres : *Christmas* (Noël), *Daddy* (papa), ou de généralisations :
I'm interested in history.
Je m'intéresse à l'histoire.

L'article indéfini *a, an, some*

• Avec les dénombrables, on emploie *a* pour désigner une unité :
*There is **a** dog in the street.*
Il y a un chien dans la rue.
• On emploie *a* devant une consonne, *an* devant une voyelle.
• On emploie *some* pour désigner le multiple dans une situation particulière :
*There are **some** apples in the fridge.*
Il y a des pommes dans le réfrigérateur.
• Avec les indénombrables, on utilise *some* dans une situation particulière :
*I bought **some** milk at the supermarket.*
J'ai acheté du lait au supermarché.
• L'article *a* s'utilise également pour la qualification :
*Tintin is **a** reporter.*
Tintin est reporter.

L'absence de déterminant

Lorsque les dénombrables ou indénombrables sont pris dans un sens général :
Apples are good for you.
Les pommes sont bonnes pour toi.

Les démonstratifs

• *This* (pluriel *these*)/*that* (pluriel *those*). *This* s'utilise pour désigner un objet proche dans l'espace et *that* dans les autres cas :
***This** dress is nice but I prefer **that** one.*
Cette robe-ci est jolie mais je préfère celle-là.
• *This* et *that* peuvent également marquer une opposition dans le temps :
*In **those** days they lived in huts.*
A cette époque-là ils vivaient dans des cabanes.

Les quantificateurs

• Pour les noms dénombrables :
too many = trop
lots of, plenty of, many = beaucoup
some, a few = quelques
some more = plus de
• Pour les noms indénombrables :
too much = trop
lots of, plenty of, much = beaucoup
some, some more = plus de
a little = un peu de
• Notez que *much* et *many* sont surtout employés dans les phrases affirmatives ou interrogatives.
• *Any* s'emploie dans des phrases interrogatives ou négatives :
*Did you buy **any** vegetables? No I didn't buy **any** vegetables.*
Est-ce que tu as acheté des légumes ? Non, je n'ai pas acheté de légumes.
• *Some* s'utilise en général dans les phrases affirmatives. Il apparaît également dans des questions, lorqu'on attend la réponse oui (invitations, requêtes) :
*Would you like **some** tea?*
Voulez-vous du thé ?

Les possessifs

• Les adjectifs (*my, your, his, her, its, our, their*).
L'adjectif possessif est invariable. A la troisième personne du singulier, il s'accorde avec le possesseur :
*Tintin and **his** dog.*
Tintin et son chien.
• Notez que pour les parties du corps, l'adjectif possessif anglais apparaît là où seul l'article français est utilisé :
*She broke **her** arm.*
Elle s'est cassé le bras.
• Le cas possessif ou génétif :
La possession est indiquée par *'s* : à gauche on trouve le possesseur et à droite l'objet possédé.
*The boy**'s** car.*
La voiture du garçon.
Au pluriel, on ajoute simplement l'apostrophe :
*The boys**'** car.*
La voiture des garçons.
Le cas possessif s'utilise aussi avec les noms exprimant le temps :
Yesterday's newspaper.
Le journal d'hier.
It's an hour's drive from here.
C'est à une heure d'ici en voiture.

Les adjectifs qualificatifs

En anglais, l'adjectif est toujours invariable et l'adjectif épithète se place toujours avant le nom.

• Formation, dérivation.
– On peut former un adjectif à partir d'un nom en ajoutant *ful*:
*use → **useful*** (usage, utile)
– En ajoutant *less*, on obtient le contraire :
*use → **useless*** (usage, inutile)
– Remarque : tous les adjectifs qui se terminent en *ful* n'ont pas nécessairement un contraire en *less*.
– On peut également obtenir le contraire d'un adjectif en ajoutant le préfixe *un* :
*able → **unable*** (capable, incapable)

• Les adjectifs composés
On peut composer des adjectifs de deux façons différentes :
Adj + nom-Adj + *ed* :
*A **dark-haired** girl.*
Une fille brune.
Adj-Ving :
*A **nice-looking** girl.*
Une jolie fille.

• La comparaison
– Pour les adjectifs courts (une ou deux syllabes), on emploie la forme Adj + *er* (...) *than*:
*He's tall**er than** me.*
Il est plus grand que moi.
Les adjectifs terminés par *y* prennent *ier* :
*pretty → **prettier*** (joli, plus joli)
– Pour les adjectifs longs (plus de deux syllabes), on emploie la forme :
more + Adj (...) *than*:
*This book is **more interesting than** that one.*
Ce livre-ci est plus intéressant que celui-là.
– Il existe des comparatifs irréguliers tels que :
good (bon) → ***better*** (meilleur)
bad (mauvais) → ***worse*** (pire)
– Le comparatif d'égalité se forme avec *as* + Adj + *as*:
*He is **as clever as** his brother.*
Il est aussi intelligent que son frère.
– Le comparatif d'infériorité se forme avec *not so* + Adj + *as* ou *not as* + Adj + *as* ou *less* + Adj + *than*:
*The chair is **not so comfortable as** the sofa / The chair is **not as comfortable as** the sofa.*
La chaise est moins confortable que le sofa.
*The bus is **less expensive than** a taxi.*
L'autobus est moins cher que le taxi.

• Le superlatif
– Pour les adjectifs courts Adj + *est* :

He is the* tallest *boy of the classroom.
C'est le garçon le plus grand de la classe.
Les adjectifs terminés en *y* deviennent *iest*.
– Pour les adjectifs longs, on emploie : *the most* + Adj :
This book is* the most *interesting in the library.
Ce livre est le plus intéressant de la bibliothèque.

LES PRONOMS

Le substitut *one*

• On utilise *one* pour éviter de répéter un nom au singulier. Au pluriel on emploie *ones* :
***I like this jacket but I prefer the blue* one.**
J'aime cette veste mais je préfère la bleue.
• Avec un adjectif, on reprend l'article *a* :
***How many dogs have you got ? Two:* a *black* one *and* a *white* one.**
Combien de chiens as-tu ? Deux : un noir et un blanc.

Les pronoms personnels

• Sujets : *I, you, he, she, it, we, you, they*.
• Compléments : *me, you, him, her, it, us, you, them*.
Le complément d'objet indirect se place souvent avant le complément d'objet direct :
I told* him *a story.
Je lui ai raconté une histoire.

Les pronoms possessifs

Mine, yours, his, hers, its, ours, theirs.
***John likes his job but Helen doesn't like* hers.**
John aime son travail mais Helen n'aime pas le sien.

Les pronoms réfléchis

Myself, yourself, himself, herself, itself, ourselves, yourselves, themselves.
***You're going to hurt* yourself.**
Tu vas te faire mal.

Les quantificateurs

Some, any et leurs composés

• Les règles observées pour *any* et *some* sont valables pour leurs composés (voir plus haut) :
Some, somebody/someone, something, somewhere.
Any, anybody/anyone, anything, anywhere.
No, nobody/no one, nothing, nowhere.
Every, everybody/everyone, everything, everywhere.
• Every est singulier :
Every child.
Chaque enfant.

Les interrogatifs

Pour les personnes : *who, who(m), whose*

• *Who* est sujet :
Who are you?
Qui es-tu ?
• *Who(m)* est complément :
Who(m) are you calling?
Qui appelles-tu ?
• *Whose* exprime la possession :
Whose book is this?
A qui est ce livre ?

Pour les choses : *what*

• *What* peut être sujet et complément
– Sujet :
What is happening?
Qu'arrive-t-il ?
– Complément :
What are you doing?
Qu'est-ce que tu fais ?

Pour les personnes et les choses : *which*

Which est pronom et adjectif et implique un choix :
Which book do you want?
Quel livre veux-tu ?

LA PHRASE

LA PHRASE IMPÉRATIVE

• Pour la deuxième personne = V :
Put down this book!
Pose ce livre !
• Pour la première personne du pluriel = *Let's* + V :
Let's go!
Allons-y !
• Aux autres personnes = *Let* + COD + V :
Let him play!
Qu'il joue !

Les formes emphatiques

Pour insister ou persuader, on peut utiliser *do* + V :
Do come!
Viens, je t'en prie !
On peut utiliser *do* + *be* :
Do be good!
Sois gentil !
Avec la même nuance, on peut faire suivre la phrase à l'impératif de *will you*?
***Stop shouting,* will you?**
Arrête de crier, je te prie !

LA PHRASE EXCLAMATIVE

• *What* + *a* + Adj + dénombrable au singulier :
What a *lovely day!*
Quelle belle journée !
• *What* + Adj + dénombrable pluriel :
What *nice pictures!*
Quels jolis tableaux !
• *What* + Adj + indénombrable :
What *beautiful weather!*
Quel temps magnifique !
• *How* + Adj
How *delicious (they are)!*
Comme ils sont délicieux !
• *Such* + *a* + Adj (+ nom)
He's* such a *liar!
Quel menteur !
She is* such a *nice girl!
Quelle gentille fille !
• *So* + Adj
He looks* so *old!
Comme il a l'air vieux !

LES ADVERBES

Formation

• La plupart des adverbes se forment en ajoutant *ly* à l'adjectif :
slow → ***slowly*** (lent, lentement)
• Si l'adjectif se termine par un *y*, celui-ci devient *i*.
pretty → ***prettily*** (joli, joliment)
• *Good* a un adverbe irrégulier : *well*.

Place de l'adverbe

• Les adverbes de temps
Ils se placent en général en fin de phrase quand il s'agit d'un temps précis. Les adverbes de fréquence (*always, often, sometimes, never*) se placent avant le verbe :
*I **always** fall asleep in the train.*
Je m'endors toujours dans le train.
• Les adverbes de lieu se placent après le verbe (et son complément) :
*Tintin takes Snowy **everywhere**.*
Tintin emmène Milou partout.
• Les adverbes de manière se placent généralement à la fin de la phrase :
*I like tea **very much**.*
J'aime beaucoup le thé.
• Les adverbes tels que *once, twice* (une fois, deux fois) se placent également en fin ou en début de phrase.

LA PHRASE COMPLEXE

Les complétives

• *That* ou ∅
*I know **(that)** you're right.*
Je sais que tu as raison.
• *What to, how to*
*Could you tell me **what to** do?*
Pourriez-vous me dire ce que je dois faire ?

Les circonstancielles

Les circonstancielles de temps

Elles sont introduites par *when, till, as soon as, while, whenever, after, before*. On n'y emploie jamais le futur. On le remplace par le présent :
***When I am** 16, I'll leave school.*
Quand j'aurai 16 ans, je quitterai l'école.

Les conditionnelles

• *If* + sujet + V, S + *will* + V :
***If** it **rains**, I'll **stay** indoors.*
S'il pleut, je resterai à la maison.
• *If* + S + Ved, S + *would* + V :
***If** I **bought** this computer, I **would spend** my time playing with it.*
Si j'achetais cet ordinateur, je passerais tout mon temps à jouer avec.
• *If* + S + *had* + Ven, S + *would* + *have* + Ven :
***If** I **had met** him, I **would have told** him.*
Si je l'avais rencontré je lui aurais dit.
• *Unless* = *if not* :
***Unless** it stops raining, I won't be able to go out.*
A moins qu'il s'arrête de pleuvoir, je ne vais pas pouvoir sortir.

Concession

Although (bien que), *even if* (même si) :
***Although** he is very young, he is very tall.*
Bien qu'il soit très jeune, il est très grand.

Les relatives

• L'antécédent est un animé : sujet (*who*), complément (*that* ou ∅), complément du nom (*whose*) :
*The man **who** came yesterday.*
L'homme qui est venu hier.
• L'antécédent est un inanimé : sujet (*which, that*), complément (*which, that* ou ∅), complément du nom (*whose*) :
*The house **(that)** I visited yesterday was too expensive.*
La maison que j'ai visitée hier était trop chère.
• *Where* et *when* peuvent s'utiliser avec un antécédent :
*This is the place **where** I met him.*
Voici l'endroit où je l'ai rencontré.

Les infinitives

Certains verbes (*tell, ask, want, expect,* etc.) se construisent avec une proposition infinitive V + COD + to + V :
*I **want him to take** this present.*
Je veux qu'il prenne ce cadeau.

Les propositions en *ing*

Après certaines prépositions (*after, before, instead of, without*), le verbe prend *ing* (voir ci-dessus, le paragraphe sur la nomalisation des verbes)
*Instead of **playing**, you'd better work.*
Au lieu de jouer, tu ferais mieux de travailler.

VERBES IRRÉGULIERS ANGLAIS

be	**was, were**	**been**
beat	**beat**	**beaten**
become	**became**	**become**
begin	**began**	**begun**
bet	**bet (betted)**	**bet (betted)**
bite	**bit**	**bitten**
blow	**blew**	**blown**
break	**broke**	**broken**
bring	**brought**	**brought**
build	**built**	**built**
burn	**burnt (burned)**	**burnt (burned)**
buy	**bought**	**bought**
catch	**caught**	**caught**
choose	**chose**	**chosen**
come	**came**	**come**
cost	**cost**	**cost**
creep	**crept**	**crept**
cut	**cut**	**cut**
deal	**dealt**	**dealt**
dig	**dug**	**dug**
dive	**dived (*Am* dove)**	**dived**
do	**did**	**done**
draw	**drew**	**drawn**
dream	**dreamed (dreamt)**	**dreamed (dreamt)**
drink	**drank**	**drunk**
drive	**drove**	**driven**
eat	**ate**	**eaten**
fall	**fell**	**fallen**
feed	**fed**	**fed**
feel	**felt**	**felt**
fight	**fought**	**fought**
find	**found**	**found**
fly	**flew**	**flown**
forget	**forgot**	**forgotten**
forgive	**forgave**	**forgiven**
freeze	**froze**	**frozen**
get	**got**	**got (*Am* gotten)**
give	**gave**	**given**
go	**went**	**gone**
grow	**grew**	**grown**
have	**had**	**had**
hear	**heard**	**heard**
hide	**hid**	**hidden**
hold	**held**	**held**
hurt	**hurt**	**hurt**
keep	**kept**	**kept**
know	**knew**	**known**
lay	**laid**	**laid**
lead	**led**	**led**

lean	leant	leant
	(leaned)	(leaned)
learn	learnt	learnt
	(learned)	(learned)
leave	left	left
lend	lent	lent
lie	lay	lain
lose	lost	lost
make	made	made
mean	meant	meant
meet	met	met
pay	paid	paid
put	put	put
quit	quit	quit
	(quitted)	(quitted)
read	read	read
ride	rode	ridden
ring	rang	rung
rise	rose	risen
run	ran	run
say	said	said
see	saw	seen
sell	sold	sold
send	sent	sent
set	set	set
sew	sewed	sewn
		(sewed)
shake	shook	shaken
shine	shone	shone
shoot	shot	shot
show	showed	shown
		(showed)
shut	shut	shut
sing	sang	sung
sink	sank	sunk
sit	sat	sat
sleep	slept	slept
slide	slid	slid
smell	smelt	smelt
	(smelled)	(smelled)
speak	spoke	spoken
speed	sped	sped
	(speeded)	(speeded)
spell	spelt	spelt
	(spelled)	(spelled)
spend	spent	spent
spill	spilt	spilt
	(spilled)	(spilled)
spoil	spoilt	spoilt
	(spoiled)	(spoiled)
spread	spread	spread
spring	sprang	sprung
stand	stood	stood
steal	stole	stolen
stick	stuck	stuck
strike	struck	struck
swim	swam	swum
swing	swung	swung
take	took	taken
teach	taught	taught
tear	tore	torn
tell	told	told
think	thought	thought
throw	threw	thrown
understand	understood	understood
upset	upset	upset
wake	woke	woken
wear	wore	worn
win	won	won
write	wrote	written

NUMERALS — LES NOMBRES

Cardinal numbers — Les nombres cardinaux

nought	0	zéro
one	1	un
two	2	deux
three	3	trois
four	4	quatre
five	5	cinq
six	6	six
seven	7	sept
eight	8	huit
nine	9	neuf
ten	10	dix
eleven	11	onze
twelve	12	douze
thirteen	13	treize
fourteen	14	quatorze
fifteen	15	quinze
sixteen	16	seize
seventeen	17	dix-sept
eighteen	18	dix-huit
nineteen	19	dix-neuf
twenty	20	vingt
twenty-one	21	vingt et un
twenty-two	22	vingt-deux
thirty	30	trente
forty	40	quarante
fifty	50	cinquante
sixty	60	soixante
seventy	70	soixante-dix
seventy-five	75	soixante-quinze
eighty	80	quatre-vingts
eighty-one	81	quatre-vingt-un
ninety	90	quatre-vingt-dix
ninety-one	91	quatre-vingt-onze
a *or* one hundred	100	cent
a hundred and one	101	cent un
a hundred and two	102	cent deux
a hundred and fifty	150	cent cinquante
two hundred	200	deux cents
two hundred and one	201	deux cent un
two hundred and two	202	deux cent deux
a *or* one thousand	1,000 (1 000)	mille
a thousand and two	1,001 (1 001)	mille un
a thousand and two	1,002 (1 002)	mille deux
two thousand	2,000 (2 000)	deux mille
a *or* one million	1,000,000 (1 000 000)	un million

Ordinal numbers — Les nombres ordinaux

first	1st	1er	premier
second	2nd	2[e]	deuxième
third	3rd	3[e]	troisième
fourth	4th	4[e]	quatrième
fifth	5th	5[e]	cinquième
sixth	6th	6[e]	sixième
seventh	7th	7[e]	septième
eighth	8th	8[e]	huitième
ninth	9th	9[e]	neuvième
tenth	10th	10[e]	dixième
eleventh	11th	11[e]	onzième
twelfth	12th	12[e]	douzième
thirteenth	13th	13[e]	treizième
fourteenth	14th	14[e]	quatorzième
fifteenth	15th	15[e]	quinzième
twentieth	20th	20[e]	vingtième
twenty-first	21st	21[e]	vingt et unième
twenty-second	22nd	22[e]	vingt-deuxième
thirtieth	30th	30[e]	trentième

à

à
[a] *prép*
1. in

ils sont à Moulinsart they are in Marlinspike

2. at
nous y serons à midi we'll be there at noon

3. to
ils vont à Klow they're going to Klow

4. to
Abdallah a écrit au capitaine Abdullah has written to the Captain

5. by
nous irons à vélo we'll go by bike

6. with
le capitaine ? c'est l'homme à la barbe the Captain? he's the man with the beard

7. Loc
cette pipe est à moi/à toi this pipe is mine/yours

à bientôt/demain see you soon/tomorrow

abeille

abeille
[abɛj] *n f*
bee

abord

abord
[abɔr] *n m*

au premier abord, cela semble facile at first glance, it looks easy

d'abord, je ne l'ai pas cru at first, I didn't believe him

* *Qui êtes-vous ? Détachez-moi d'abord, je vous expliquerai ensuite...* Who are you? Untie me first, and then I'll explain... *

aboyer

aboyer
[abwaje] *v i*
to bark

* *Pourquoi Milou aboie-t-il ainsi ?* Why is Snowy barking like that? *Wouah ! Wouah !* Woof! Woof! *

absent

absent, e
[apsɑ̃, ɑ̃t]

...absent

I. *adj*
1. absent

trois élèves sont absents three pupils are absent

2. away, out
* *Monsieur Fan Se-Yeng, s'il vous plaît ?...* Mr Fan Se-Yeng, please?...
Il est absent, mais il va bientôt rentrer. Voulez-vous entrer et l'attendre ?... He's away, but he'll soon be back. Would you like to come in and wait for him?... *

II. *n*
absentee

► **absence**
[apsɑ̃s] *n f*
absence

je ne m'explique pas son absence I can't account for his absence

absolument

absolument
[apsɔlymɑ̃] *adv*
1. absolutely

il faut absolument que je le voie it is absolutely vital that I see him

2. completely
non, docteur Müller, c'est absolument faux ! no, Doctor Müller, it's completely untrue!

accélérer

accélérer
[akselere] *v i*
to accelerate

accepter

accepter
[aksɛpte] *v t*
to accept

allons, capitaine, acceptez cette invitation come on, Captain, do accept this invitation

accident

accident
[aksidɑ̃] *n m*
1. accident

* *Chic ! On a eu un accident !...* Great! We've had an accident!... *

2. Loc
accident d'avion plane crash

accompagner

accompagner
[akɔ̃paɲe] *v t*
1. to come with

* *Capitaine, je vais dans le parc, voulez-vous m'accompagner ?* Captain, I'm going in the park, will you come with me? *

2. to accompany
M. Wagner accompagne la Castafiore au piano Mr Wagner accompanies Signora Castafiore on the piano

accord

accord
[akɔr] *n m*
1. consent

il faut que nous ayons l'accord des autorités we must have the authorities' consent

2. Loc
d'accord all right, OK

je suis d'accord avec toi I agree with you

ils ne sont pas d'accord they disagree

accrocher

Tournesol a accroché un gardien au portemanteau...

...accrocher

accrocher
[akrɔʃe]
I. *v t*
1. to hang

* *Calmez-vous, voyons, calmez-vous !* Calm down now, do calm down!
Tournesol a accroché un gardien au porte-manteau... Calculus has hung a guard on the coat rack... *

2. to catch
il a accroché ses vêtements dans les ronces he caught his clothes in the brambles

II. *v pr*
to hang on

il s'est accroché à la branche pour ne pas tomber he hung on to the branch so as not to fall

accueillir

accueillir
[akœjir] *v t*
to welcome

▸ **accueillant, e**
[akœjɑ̃, ɑ̃t] *adj*
1. hospitable

* *Ici, les gens sont vraiment très accueillants !... Bonjour !...* Here, people are really very hospitable!... Hello!
Venez chez nous ! Come to our place! *

2. Loc
peu accueillant unfriendly

accuser

accuser
[akyze] *v t*
to accuse

▸ **accusé, e**
[akyse] *n*
accused

acheter

acheter
[aʃte] *vt*
to buy

où avez-vous acheté cette statuette? where did you buy that statuette?

▸ **achat**
[aʃa] *n m*
faire des achats to go shopping

voyons vos achats let's see what you've bought

▸ **acheteur, euse**
[aʃtœr, øz] *n*
buyer

acteur

acteur
[aktœr] *n m*
actor

▸ **actrice**
[aktris] *n f*
actress

actif

actif, ive
[aktif, iv] *adj*
active

* *Au centre spatial...* At the space centre (*Am:* center)... *Tonnerre de Brest, je suis un homme actif, je ne peux pas rester enfermé ici!* Thundering typhoons, I'm an active man, I can't stay locked in here! *

actualité

actualité
[aktɥalite] *n f*

les actualités régionales the local news

être d'actualité to be in the news

addition

addition
[adisjɔ̃] *n f*
1. addition

non, 4 et 3 ne font pas 6, ton addition est fausse no, 4 and 3 don't make 6, your addition is wrong

2. bill (*Am:* check)
demandez l'addition au serveur ask the waiter for the bill

admirer

admirer
[admire] *vt*
to admire

* *Oh! Milou, j'admire ton courage... Sans toi, ce lion m'aurait dévoré...* Oh! Snowy, I admire your courage... If it hadn't been for you, that lion would have eaten me... *Oh! tu sais, ce lion n'était pas aussi méchant qu'il en avait l'air...* Oh! you know that lion wasn't as nasty as it looked... *

adolescent

adolescent, e
[adɔlɛsɑ̃, ɑ̃t] *n*
adolescent, teenager

adorer

adorer
[adɔre] *vt*
1. to worship

les Incas adorent le Soleil the Incas worship the Sun

...adorer

2. to love
* *Ah, c'est toi Tintin? J'adore les os que les oiseaux gardent dans leur nid!* Oh, it's you, Tintin? I just love the bones the birds keep in their nests! *

...adorer

adresse

adresse
[adrɛs] *n f*
address

* *Ah, voilà son adresse, je vais pouvoir lui rendre visite, tout à l'heure... Allons-y!* Ah, here's his address, I'll be able to pay him a visit later... Let's go!... *

▸ **adresser**
[adrɛse]
I. *vt*
1. to send

qui m'a adressé ce colis? who sent me this parcel (*Am:* package)?

2. Loc
adresser la parole à quelqu'un to speak to somebody

II. *v pr*
to ask

adressez-vous au capitaine, il s'y connaît en bateaux ask the Captain: he knows a lot about boats

adulte

adulte
[adylt] *n*
grown-up, adult

les adultes the grown-ups

aéroglisseur

aéroglisseur
[aerɔglisœr] *n m*
hovercraft

aéroport

aéroport
[aerɔpɔr] *n m*
airport

affaire

affaire
[afɛr] *n f*
1. matter, case

réglons d'abord cette affaire let's settle this matter first

...affaire

2. thing
range tes affaires put your things away

3. bargain
* *A ce prix, c'était une bonne affaire !* At that price, it was a bargain! *

4. business
Rastapopoulos est dans les affaires Rastapopoulos is in business

affiche

affiche
[afiʃ] *n f*
bill, poster

* *Les Japonais ont mis des affiches partout pour me faire arrêter !...* The Japanese have posted bills everywhere to have me arrested!... *

...affiche

affreux

affreux, euse
[afrø, øz] *adj*
awful, ghastly

quel homme affreux ! what an awful man!

le temps est affreux, nous ne pouvons pas partir the weather is ghastly: we cannot leave

âge

âge
[ɑʒ] *n m*
1. age

Abdallah n'a pas encore l'âge de raison Abdullah has not yet reached the age of reason

2. Loc
quel âge as-tu ? how old are you?

► **âgé, e**
[ɑʒe] *adj*
1. old

* *Le prophète Philippulus est très âgé.* Philippulus the prophet is very old. *

2. Loc
les personnes âgées the elderly

...âge

Le prophète Philippulus est très âgé.

agence

agence
[aʒɑ̃s] *n f*
agency

agence de voyages travel agency

s'agenouiller

s'agenouiller
[saʒnuje] *v pr*
to kneel down

agent

agent
[aʒɑ̃] *n m*
1. agent

c'est un agent de l'ennemi he's an enemy agent

2. policeman
l'agent nous fait signe de passer the policeman is waving us on

agir

agir
[aʒir]
I. *v i*
1. to act

* *Vite, chauffeur, nous devons agir rapidement !...* Hurry, driver, we must act quickly!... *

2. to work
le médicament agit lentement the medicine works slowly

...agir

Vite, chauffeur, nous devons agir rapidement!...

II. *v pr*
de quoi s'agit-il ?
what's the matter?

agneau

agneau
[aɲo] *n m*
pl agneaux
lamb

agrandir

agrandir
[agrɑ̃dir]
I. *v t*
to enlarge

j'aimerais faire agrandir ces photos I would like to have these photos enlarged

II. *v pr*
to get bigger

* ***Le trou s'agrandit, continuons...*** The hole's getting bigger, let's keep going... *

Le trou s'agrandit, continuons...

agréable

agréable
[agreabl] *adj*
1. nice

votre maison est très agréable you have a very nice house

2. pleasant
mais non, le capitaine est en fait un homme très agréable no, in fact the Captain is a very pleasant man

aider

aider
[ɛde] *v t*
to help

* ***Aidez-moi à ouvrir cette boîte...*** Help me open this box... *

▸ **aide**
[ɛd] *n f*
help

j'ai besoin de ton aide I need your help

à l'aide ! help!

Aidez-moi à ouvrir cette boîte...

aigu

aigu, aiguë
[ɛgy] *adj*
high-pitched

la Castafiore a une voix aiguë Signora Castafiore has a high-pitched voice

ailleurs

ailleurs
[ajœr] *adv*
1. elsewhere, somewhere else

...ailleurs

allons, Abdallah, va jouer ailleurs ! come on, Abdullah, go and play somewhere else!

2. Loc
par ailleurs otherwise, moreover

aimable

aimable
[ɛmabl] *adj*
friendly

...aimable

Tu verras, M. et Mme Wang sont des gens très aimables...

* ***Tu verras, M. et Mme Wang sont des gens très aimables...*** You'll see, Mr and Mrs Wang are very friendly people... *

aimer

aimer
[ɛme] *v t*
1. to like

le capitaine n'aime pas être dérangé

...aimer

Milou aime beaucoup Tintin...

quand il se repose the Captain doesn't like to be disturbed when he's having a rest

2. to be fond of
* ***Milou aime beaucoup Tintin...*** Snowy's very fond of Tintin... *

3. to love
je t'aime I love you

4. Loc
j'aimerais mieux ne pas y aller I'd rather not go

aîné

aîné, e
[ɛne]
I. *adj*
1. elder

j'ai un frère aîné I have an elder brother

2. eldest

II. *n*
1. elder (child)
2. eldest (child)
l'aînée de mes trois filles va à l'université the eldest of my three daughters goes to university

ainsi

ainsi
[ɛ̃si] *adv*
like this, like that

non, regardez, il faut s'y prendre ainsi no, look, you have to do it like this

air

air
[ɛr] *n m*
1. air

...air

* *Vite, un peu d'air, j'étouffe !* Quick, some air, I'm stifling! *

2. Loc
en plein air outdoors

regarder en l'air to look up

air

air
[ɛr] *n m*
1. appearance, look

...air

son air bizarre nous a fait rire his strange appearance made us laugh

2. Loc
vous avez l'air fatigué you look tired

air

air
[ɛr] *n m*
tune

...air

oh, mais je reconnais l'air que tu siffles oh, I recognize the tune you're whistling

alarme

alarme
[alarm] *n f*
Loc
tirez le signal d'alarme pour arrêter le train pull the communication (*Am:* alarm) cord to stop the train

allée

allée
[ale] *n f*
path

* *Je suis sûr qu'il est passé par cette allée...* I'm sure he went along this path... *

allemand

allemand, e
[almɑ̃, ɑ̃d] *adj*
German

...allemand

► **Allemand, e**
[almɑ̃, ɑ̃d] *n*
German

► **allemand**
[almɑ̃] *n m*
German
j'apprends l'allemand I'm learning German

► **Allemagne**
[almaɲ] *n f*
Germany

aller

aller
[ale] *n m*
single (ticket) (*Am:* one-way ticket)

deux allers pour Nyon, s'il vous plaît two singles to Nyon, please

aller

aller
[ale] *v aux*
to be going to

* *Le lendemain matin...* The next morning... *Drring Drring Drring* Ring Ring Ring *Quelle surprise, j'allais vous téléphoner !* What a surprise, I was going to phone you! *

il va neiger it's going to snow

aller

aller
[ale]
I. *v i*
1. to go

* *Et deux heures plus tard...* Two hours later... *Allons-y !... J'espère que je ne suis pas trop lourd.* Let's go!... I hope I'm not too heavy for you. *

va faire tes devoirs go and do your homework

2. to be
bonjour, mon cher Hippolyte, comment

...aller

vas-tu ? hello, my dear Hercules, how are you?

3. to suit

ces longs cheveux vous vont très bien this long hair suits you very well

II. s'en aller
[sãale] *v pr*
to go

au revoir, je m'en vais good bye, I'm going

va-t-en ! go away!

allô

allô
[alo] *interj*
hello, hallo

allô, allô, mademoiselle, nous avons été coupés hello, hello, operator, we've been cut off

allonger

allonger
[alɔ̃ʒe]
I. *v t*
to make longer

prenons un bateau, cela allongerait le trajet de faire le tour du lac let's take a boat–it will make the journey longer if we go around the lake

II. *v i*
to grow longer

les jours allongent the days are growing longer

...allonger

III. *v pr*
to lie down

* *Nous allons nous allonger sur nos matelas, mais avant nous avons mis nos pyjamas...* We're going to lie down on our mattresses but first we've put on our pyjamas (*Am:* pajamas)... *

allumer

allumer
[alyme] *v t*
1. to switch on

allumer la radio to switch the radio on

2. to light
je vais allumer un feu pour nous réchauffer I'll light a fire to warm us up

allumette

allumette
[alymɛt] *n f*
match

alors

alors
[alɔr] *adv*
1. then

...alors

* *Vous vous souvenez, j'étais alors commandant du Karaboudjan ?...* Do you remember, I was Captain of the Karaboudjan then?... *

2. then
et alors, qu'est-il arrivé ensuite ? and then what happened?

3. Loc
alors que while

ambiance

ambiance
[ãbjãs] *n f*
atmosphere

l'ambiance est très sympathique the atmosphere is very friendly

ambulance

ambulance
[ãbylãs] *n f*
ambulance

...ambulance

L'ambulance est en route...

...ambulance

* *L'ambulance est en route...* The ambulance is on its way... *

s'améliorer

s'améliorer
[sameljɔre] *v pr*
to improve

j'espère que le temps va s'améliorer I hope the weather will improve

aménager

aménager
[amenaʒe] *v t*
to fit out

* *Le deuxième étage de la fusée est aménagé en coin couchettes...* The second floor of the rocket has been fitted out as a sleeping area... *

amende

amende
[amɑ̃d] *n f*
fine

* *Je suis désolé, mais vous devez payer une amende ! C'est écrit, n'est-ce pas ! Baignade interdite, vous ne savez pas lire ?* I'm sorry, but you'll have to pay a fine! It's written on the sign, isn't it? No bathing–can't you read? *

...amende

amener

amener
[amne] *v t*
1. to take

mais oui, amenez Dupont avec vous yes of course, take Thomson with you

2. to bring
bonjour, qu'est-ce qui vous amène ? hello, what brings you here?

américain

américain, e
[amerikɛ̃, ɛn] *adj*
American

► **Américain, e**
[amerikɛ̃, ɛn] *n*
American

► **Amérique**
[amerik] *n f*
America

États-Unis d'Amérique United States of America

ami

ami, e
[ami] *n*
friend

► **amitié**
[amitje] *n f*
1. friendship

pour aider à l'amitié entre les hommes to help to establish friendship between men

2. Loc
avec mes amitiés with my best regards

amour

amour
[amur] *n m*
love

Abdallah, amour de ma vie ! Abdullah, the love of my life!

* *Pour l'amour de Dieu, tenez bon ! Si vous lâchez... Je... vous entendez ?...* For the love of God, hold on! If you let go... I... do you hear?... *

ampoule

ampoule
[ɑ̃pul] *n f*
1. bulb

cette ampoule est grillée this bulb has blown

2. blister
nous avons trop marché, j'ai des ampoules aux pieds we've been walking for too long, I've got blisters on my feet

amuser

amuser
[amyze]
I. *v t*
to amuse

je suis sûr que cette plaisanterie vous a beaucoup amusé I'm sure that joke amused you very much

II. *v pr*
1. to play

* *Mais où est-il ? Tout à l'heure il s'amusait dans le jardin...* Where is he? A moment ago he was playing in the garden... *

Mais où est-il ? Tout à l'heure il s'amusait dans le jardin...
?

2. to enjoy oneself
je me suis bien amusé I enjoyed myself

an

an
[ã] *n m*
year

j'y ai travaillé pendant un an I've worked there for a year

le jour de l'an New Year's Day

ancien

ancien, enne
[ãsjɛ̃, ɛn] *adj*
1. old

* *Certains des meubles de ce château sont très anciens, ils appartenaient déjà à votre ancêtre...* Some of the furniture in this castle is very old: it even belonged to your ancestor... *

Certains des meubles de ce château sont très anciens, ils appartenaient déjà à votre ancêtre ...

2. former
c'est un ancien colonel he is a former colonel

âne

âne
[an] *n m*
donkey

anglais

anglais, e
[ãglɛ, ɛz] *adj*
English

► **Anglais, e**
[ãglɛ, ɛz] *n*
Englishman *n m*, Englishwoman *n f*

les Anglais English people, the English

► **anglais**
[ãglɛ] *n m*
English

elle apprend l'anglais she's learning English

► **Angleterre**
[ãglətɛr] *n f*
England

animal

animal, aux
[animal, o] *n m*
1. animal

* *Hourrah !* Hurray! *Les lamas sont des animaux très susceptibles.* Llamas are very touchy animals. *

Hourrah !

Les lamas sont des animaux très susceptibles.

2. Loc
animal familier pet

animé

animé, e
[anime] *adj*
1. busy

c'est un quartier très animé it's a very busy part of town

2. lively
la fête est très animée it's a very lively party

3. Loc
dessin animé cartoon

année

année
[ane] *n f*
year

il y a douze mois dans une année there are twelve months in a year

bonne année ! happy New Year!

anniversaire

anniversaire
[anivɛrsɛr] *n m*
1. birthday

bon anniversaire, Tintin ! happy birthday, Tintin!

2. anniversary
c'est leur vingtième anniversaire de mariage it's their twentieth wedding anniversary

annoncer

annoncer
[anɔ̃se] *v t*
to announce

* *Nous avons de mauvaises nouvelles, ils ont annoncé que vous étiez recherché...* We have bad news. They've announced that you're wanted... *

▶ **annonce**
[anɔ̃s] *n f*
advertisement

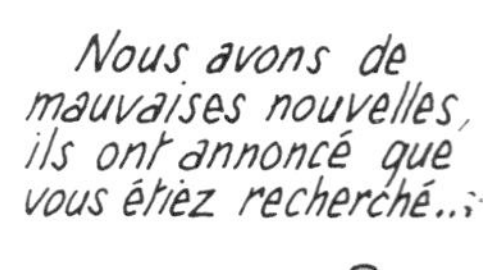

petites annonces classified advertisements (*Am:* want ads)

annuler

annuler
[anyle] *v t*
to cancel

* *Mauvaises nouvelles, capitaine ?* Bad news, Captain? *Nous devons annuler notre voyage !* We must cancel our trip! *

...annuler

antique

antique
[ɑ̃tik] *adj*
ancient

la Grèce antique ancient Greece

août

août
[u(t)] *n m*
August

Le premier/deux août the first/second of

...août

August (*Am:* August first/second)
Venez le 6 août come on the 6th of August (*Am:* on August 6)

appareil

appareil
[aparɛj] *n m*
1. device

* *Et à quoi sert cet appareil ?* And what's this device for? *

...appareil

...appareil

2. Loc
appareil photo camera

appareil dentaire brace

allô, qui est à l'appareil ? hello, who's speaking?

appartement

appartement
[apartəmɑ̃] *n m*

...appartement

flat (*Am:* apartment)

l'appartement de Tintin est au premier étage Tintin's flat is on the first (*Am:* second) floor

appartenir

appartenir
[apartənir] *v t ind*
to belong

...appartenir

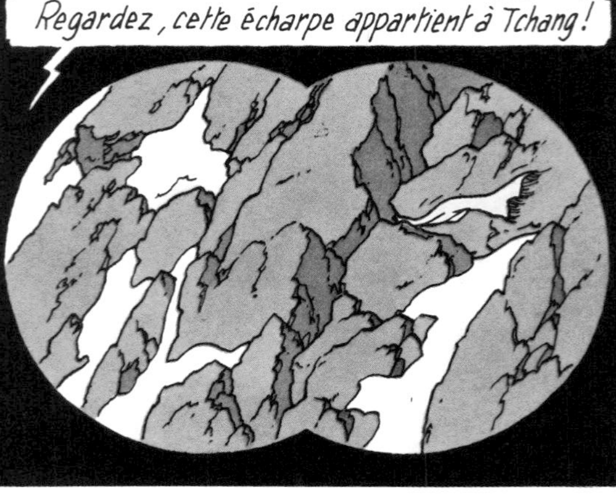

* *Regardez, cette écharpe appartient à Tchang !* Look, this scarf belongs to Chang! *

appeler

appeler
[aple]
I. *v t*
1. to call

* *Chut, écoute, Tintin nous appelle !* Sshh, listen, Tintin's calling to us!

...appeler

Chut, écoute, Tintin nous appelle !
Wouah ! Wouah !
Je suis en bas, descendez ...

Wouah ! Wouah ! Wooah! Wooah!
Je suis en bas, descendez... I'm down here, come down... *

2. to phone, to call
le capitaine a appelé ce matin the Captain phoned this morning

II. *v pr*
1. to be called

comment s'appelle cet animal ? what's this animal called?

2. Loc
je m'appelle Zorrino my name's Zorrino

appétit

appétit
[apeti] *n m*
appetite

cette promenade m'a ouvert l'appétit the walk has whetted my appetite

apporter

apporter
[apɔrte] *v t*
to bring

* ***Heureusement que j'ai apporté un pique-nique !*** It's a good thing I brought a picnic! ***Oh oui !*** Oh yes! *

Heureusement que j'ai apporté un pique-nique !
Oh oui !

apprécier

apprécier
[apresje] *v t*
to appreciate

apprendre

apprendre
[aprɑ̃dr] *v t*
1. to learn

j'apprends mes leçons I'm learning my lessons

2. to teach

...apprendre

je vais t'apprendre à nager I'll teach you to swim

3. to hear
* ***Ils apprendront peut-être que je suis en prison, et ils viendront me délivrer...*** Maybe they'll hear I'm in prison and they'll come and rescue me... *

4. to tell
je ne sais comment lui apprendre la nouvelle I don't know how to tell him the news

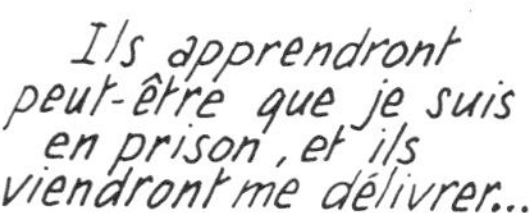
Ils apprendront peut-être que je suis en prison, et ils viendront me délivrer...

approcher

approcher
[aprɔʃe]
I. *v t*
to bring near

approchez le document de la lumière bring the document near the light

II. *v i*
to draw near

Noël approche Christmas is drawing near

III. *v pr*
to go near

approchez-vous de la fenêtre go near the window

approuver

approuver
[apruve] *v t*
to approve of

appuyer

appuyer
[apɥije]
I. *v t*
to press, to push

* ***Vite, appuyez sur le bouton rouge, sinon la fusée est perdue...*** Quick, press the red button, otherwise the rocket will be lost... *

II. *v pr*
to lean

ne vous appuyez pas sur la balustrade don't lean on the railing

Vite, appuyez sur le bouton rouge, sinon la fusée est perdue...

après

après
[aprɛ] *prép*
1. after

le capitaine est arrivé après Tintin the Captain arrived after Tintin

février vient après janvier February comes after January

2. past
* ***L'hôpital est après la mosquée, un peu plus loin, sur votre gauche...*** The hospital is past

L'hôpital est après la mosquée, un peu plus loin, sur votre gauche...
Ah bon, merci...

...après

the mosque, a little further down on your left...
Ah bon, merci... I see, thank you... *

3. Loc
alors, d'après toi, il y a une oasis là-bas so, according to you, there's an oasis over there

► **après-demain**
[aprɛdmɛ̃] *adv*
the day after tomorrow

► **après-midi**
[aprɛmidi]
n m inv ou n f inv
afternoon

nous viendrons cet(te) après-midi we'll come this afternoon

en fin d'après-midi late in the afternoon

araignée

Milou a peur de l'araignée...

araignée
[arɛɲe] *n f*
spider

* *Milou a peur de l'araignée...* Snowy's afraid of the spider... *

arbitre

arbitre
[arbitr] *n m*
1. referee

...arbitre

l'arbitre siffle la fin du match the referee's blowing the final whistle

2. umpire
l'arbitre du match de tennis the umpire of the tennis match

arbre

arbre
[arbr] *n m*
tree

* *Il est peut-être encore là-haut...* He may still be up there...
Oui, je vais grimper en haut de cet arbre... Yes, I'll climb to the top of this tree... *

Il est peut-être encore là-haut...
Oui, je vais grimper en haut de cet arbre...

argent

argent
[arʒɑ̃] *n m*
1. silver

cette bague est en argent this ring is made of silver

2. money
je n'ai pas assez d'argent pour l'acheter I haven't got enough money to buy it

argent de poche pocket money

armoire

armoire
[armwar] *n f*
1. wardrobe (*Am:* closet)

les vêtements sont dans l'armoire the clothes are in the wardrobe

2. Loc
armoire à pharmacie medicine cabinet

arracher

arracher
[araʃe] *v t*
to pull out

le dentiste lui a arraché une dent the dentist pulled out one of his teeth

arranger

arranger
[arɑ̃ʒe]
I. *v t*
to straighten

...arranger

arrange ta cravate straighten your tie

II. *v pr*
1. to manage

* *Nous nous sommes arrangés pour vous faire évader!* We managed to help you escape! *

2. Loc
cela s'arrangera things will turn out all right

Nous nous sommes arrangés pour vous faire évader !

arrêter

arrêter
[arete]
I. *v t*
1. to stop

regardez, il a arrêté sa voiture au coin de la rue look, he's stopped his car at the corner of the street

2. to arrest
les Dupondt ont arrêté le voleur the Thompsons have arrested the thief

...arrêter

3. to give up
* *Heuh... Non merci, lieutenant... J'ai arrêté de boire du whisky...* Er... No thank you, Lieutenant... I've given up drinking whisky... *Ah bon, je n'insiste pas alors !...* All right, I won't insist then!... *

4. Loc
les Dupondt n'arrêtent pas de tomber the Thompsons keep falling down

II. *v pr*
to stop

la pluie s'est arrêtée the rain has stopped

le train s'arrête à la gare de Moulinsart the train stops at Marlinspike station

► **arrêt**
[arɛ] *n m*
1. stop

l'arrêt du bus the bus stop

2. Loc
sans arrêt constantly, non-stop

arrière

arrière
I. *n m*
[arjɛr]
1. back

je vais m'asseoir à l'arrière de la voiture I'll sit in the back of the car

...arrière

2. Loc
en arrière backwards

II. *adj inv*
1. rear, back

les pneus arrière the rear tyres (*Am:* tires)

2. Loc
marche arrière reverse

arriver

arriver
[arive] *v i*
1. to arrive

leur train arrive à 17 heures their train arrives at 5 p.m.

2. to happen
* *Ils ne répondent plus, il a dû leur arriver quelque chose...* They're not answering any more. Something must have happened to them... *Essayez encore...* Try again... *

► **arrivée**
[arive] *n f*
1. arrival

à son arrivée, Tintin a été accueilli par des cris de joie on his arrival, Tintin was greeted with cheers

2. Loc
la ligne d'arrivée the finishing line

arroser

arroser
[aroze] *v t*
to water

artichaut

artichaut
[artiʃo] *n m*
artichoke

artiste

artiste
[artist] *n*
1. artist

la Castafiore est une grande artiste Signora Castafiore is a great artist

2. Loc
entrée des artistes stage door

ascenseur

ascenseur
[asɑ̃sœr] *n m*
lift (*Am:* elevator)

* *Allons, messieurs, l'ascenseur nous attend.* Come along, gentlemen, the lift is waiting for us. *

aspirateur

aspirateur
[aspiratœr] *n m*
1. vacuum cleaner

...aspirateur

2. Loc
passer l'aspirateur dans la chambre to vacuum the bedroom

s'asseoir

s'asseoir
[saswar] *v pr*
1. to sit down

* *Colonel, asseyez-vous, je vous en prie.* Colonel, do sit down. *

2. Loc
être assis to be sitting

nous étions assis par terre we were sitting on the ground

assez

assez
[ase] *adv*
1. enough

* *Il n'y a pas assez d'oxygène... J'étouffe... Je...* There isn't enough oxygen... I'm suffocating... I... *

2. fairly
c'est un homme assez gros he's a fairly fat man

3. Loc
j'en ai assez de tout ça, je veux rentrer à

Moulinsart I've had enough of all this, I want to go back to Marlinspike

assiette

assiette
[asjɛt] *n f*
plate

j'ai tout mangé, mon assiette est vide I've eaten everything: my plate is empty

assister

assister
[asiste] *v t ind*
to attend

* *Allons, capitaine, vous devez assister à la réunion. C'est très important...* Come on, Captain, you must attend the meeting. It's very important... *

assommer

assommer
[asɔme] *v t*
to knock out

* *Le coup a dû l'assommer...* The blow must have knocked him out... *

assurance

assurance
[asyrɑ̃s] *n f*
insurance

* *Je me présente : Séraphin Lampion, des Assurances « Mondass » !...* May I introduce myself : I'm Jolyon Wagg of the "Rock Bottom Insurance"!... *

police d'assurance insurance policy

astronaute

astronaute
[astrɔnot] *n*
astronaut

atelier

atelier
[atəlje] *n m*
workshop

attacher

attacher
[ataʃe]
I. *v t*
1. to tie up

qui vous a attaché ? who tied you up?

2. to fasten
* *Dans l'avion...* On the plane...
Attachez vos ceintures... Fasten your seat belts... *

II. *v i*
1. to attach
je suis très attaché

à Milou I'm very much attached to Snowy

attendre

attendre
[atɑ̃dr]
I. *v t*
1. to wait for

où étiez-vous ? je vous attends depuis dix minutes where were you? I've been waiting for you for ten minutes

...attendre

2. to expect
nous les attendons d'un moment à l'autre we're expecting them any minute now

II. *v pr*
to expect

* *Général Alcazar, quelle surprise, je ne m'attendais pas à vous rencontrer ici !* General Alcazar, what a surprise, I wasn't expecting to meet you here!
Et pourquoi ? Why? *

...attendre

Général Alcazar, quelle surprise, je ne m'attendais pas à vous rencontrer ici !
Et pourquoi ?

attention

attention
[atɑ̃sjɔ̃] *n f*
1. attention

faites bien attention à ce que je vais dire pay particular attention to what I am going to say

2. care
Milou, fais attention à ce qu'ils ne s'échappent pas Snowy, take care that they don't run away

Faites attention, Tintin, il est armé ! Restez caché !

3. Loc
* ***Faites attention, Tintin, il est armé ! Restez caché !*** Look out, Tintin, he's got a gun! Don't show yourself! *

atterrir

atterrir
[aterir] *v i*
1. to land

...atterrir

mesdames et messieurs... l'avion va atterrir dans cinq minutes ladies and gentlemen... the plane will be landing in five minutes

2. to touch down
la fusée atterrira dans vingt minutes in twenty minutes, the rocket will touch down

▶ **atterrissage**
[aterisaʒ] *n m*
landing

attirer

attirer
[atire] *v t*
1. to attract

un aimant attire le fer a magnet attracts iron

2. to attract
l'idée de ce voyage ne m'attire pas beaucoup the idea of this journey doesn't attract me much

▶ **attirant**
[atirɑ̃] *adj*
attractive

attraper

attraper
[atrape] *v t*
1. to catch

* ***Je n'arrête pas d'éternuer, j'ai attrapé un rhume !*** I keep sneezing – I've caught a cold! *

2. to tell off
Abdallah a dit une bêtise et il va se faire attraper Abdullah said something silly and he's going to get told off

Je n'arrête pas d'éternuer, j'ai attrapé un rhume !
?

auberge

auberge
[obɛrʒ] *n f*
1. inn

voici une auberge here's an inn

2. Loc
auberge de jeunesse youth hostel

aucun

aucun, e
[okœ̃, yn] *adj*
no

mais vous n'avez aucune preuve but you have no proof

augmenter

augmenter
[ogmɑ̃te]
I. *v i*
to rise, to go up

...augmenter

* ***La température augmente... J'étouffe... Je n'en peux plus...*** The temperature is rising... I'm suffocating... I can't stand it any more... *

II. *v t*
to increase

ils vont augmenter le prix de l'essence they're going to increase the price of petrol (*Am:* gas)

La température augmente... J'étouffe... Je n'en peux plus...

aujourd'hui

aujourd'hui
[oʒurdɥi] *adv*
today

et si nous y allions aujourd'hui ? why don't we go today?

aussi

aussi
[osi] *adv*
1. too, as well

invitez Tournesol et les Dupondt aussi invite Calculus and the Thompsons too

le capitaine ira aussi the Captain will go as well

2. also
les Dupondt peuvent aussi se déguiser en Syldaves the Thompsons can also dis-

...aussi

guise themselves as Syldavians

3. as
** Faites attention en entrant...* When you go in, mind...
A la marche ? The step?
Non, à la porte... No, the door...
Dupond est aussi étourdi que Dupont... Thompson is as scatterbrained as Thomson... *

Dupont est aussi étourdi que Dupond...

autobus

autobus
[otobys] *n m*
bus

autocar

autocar
[otokar] *n m*
coach (*Am:* bus)

nous ferons le voyage en autocar we'll travel by coach

autocollant

autocollant
[otokɔlɑ̃] *n m*
sticker

auto-école

auto-école
[otoekɔl] *n f*
pl auto-écoles
driving school

autographe

autographe
[otograf] *n m*
autograph

automatique

automatique
[otomatik] *adj*
automatic

** Allô, fusée lunaire, ici la Terre... Préparez-vous à régler le pilotage automatique... Vous m'entendez ?...* Hello, moon rocket, this is ground control... Get ready to set the automatic pilot... Can you hear me?... *

...automatique

automne

automne
[otɔn] *n m*
autumn (*Am:* fall)

autoriser

autoriser
[ɔtɔrize] *v t*
1. authorize
2. to allow
Tintin, tu m'autorises à prendre cet os ? Tintin, will you allow me to take this bone?

autorité

autorité
[ɔtɔrite] *n f*

...autorité

authority

vous devez vous adresser aux autorités locales you have to apply to the local authorities

autoroute

autoroute
[otorut] *n f*
motorway (*Am:* freeway)

auto-stop

auto-stop
[otostɔp] *n m*
hitchhiking

autour

autour
[otur] *adv*
around

** Regarde, Milou, il y a des montagnes tout autour.* Look, Snowy, there are mountains all around. *

...autour

► **autour de**
[oturdə] *prép*
around

ils se sont tous rassemblés autour de Tournesol they all gathered around Calculus

autre

autre
[otr]
I. *adj*
1. other

...autre

mais non, c'est l'autre bras qui me fait mal ! no, it's my other arm which hurts !

2. another
nous allons faire une autre tentative we'll make another attempt

II. *pron*
another
another one

* *Plusieurs heures après...* Several hours later...

Encore une autre, ça fait la septième trace... Another one, that makes the seventh set of tracks... *

► **autrement**
[otrəmɑ̃] *adv*
otherwise

mais Tintin, je n'ai pas pu faire autrement ! but Tintin, I couldn't do otherwise!

autrefois

autrefois
[otrəfwa] *adv*
1. once

* *Des momies... Autrefois il y avait un tombeau ici...* Mummies... Once there was a grave here... *

2. Loc
autrefois je naviguais sur le « Karaboudjan » I used to navigate on the "Karaboudjan"

avaler

avaler
[avale] *v t*
to swallow

avance

avance
[avɑ̃s] *n f*
Loc
vous êtes arrivés en avance you have come early

...avance

le train a quelques minutes d'avance the train is a few minutes early

avancer

avancer
[avɑ̃se]
I. *v i*
1. to move

* *Qu'allons-nous faire ? La voiture n'avance plus...* What

...avancer

are we going to do? The car won't move... *

2. to advance, to progress
oui, M. Baxter, mon travail avance yes, Mr Baxter, my work is progressing

3. to be fast
votre montre avance your watch is fast

II. *v t*
Loc
à quoi cela les avance-t-il ? what good will that do them ?

avant

avant
[avɑ̃]
I. *prép*
before

* *Mille sabords, je savais que j'arriverais avant vous !* Blistering barnacles, I knew

...avant

I would get there before you! *

II. *adv*
beforehand

d'accord, mais prévenez-nous avant it's OK, but let us know beforehand

► **avant de**
[avɑ̃də] *prép*
before

nous devons faire un plan avant de partir we must make a plan before we leave

avantage

avantage
[avɑ̃taʒ] *n m*
advantage

quels sont les avantages du voyage par le train ? what are the advantages of travelling by train ?

avant-hier

avant-hier
[avɑ̃tjɛr] *adv*
the day before yesterday

avec

avec
[avɛk] *prép*
1. with

voici le capitaine avec les Dupondt here comes the Captain with the Thompsons

...avec

2. with
mais enfin, Tintin, êtes-vous avec nous ou contre nous ? but Tintin, are you with us or against us?

3. to
Milou, sois gentil avec lui Snowy, be nice to him

avenir

avenir
[avnir] *n m*
future

que nous réserve l'avenir ? what does the future hold in store for us?

aventure

aventure
[avɑ̃tyr] *n f*
adventure

...aventure

* *Mille millions de mille sabords de tonnerre de Brest !... J'en ai assez de toutes ces aventures...* Billions of blistering blue barnacles!... I've had enough of all these adventures... *

avenue

avenue
[avny] *n f*
avenue

averse

averse
[avɛrs] *n f*
shower

* *Aïe, une averse ! Il faut nous mettre à l'abri !* Oh no, here's a shower! We must take shelter!
Tu as raison, Tchang... You're right, Chang... *

avion

avion
[avjɔ̃] *n m*
plane, aircraft

l'avion viendra-t-il ce soir ? will the plane come tonight?

aviron

aviron
[avirɔ̃] *n m*
oar

avis

avis
[avi] *n m*
1. opinion

Tintin, j'ai besoin d'avoir votre avis à ce sujet Tintin, I need your opinion on this matter

2. Loc
changer d'avis to change one's mind

avocat

avocat, e
[avɔka, at] *n*
lawyer

avoir

avoir
[avwar] *v t*
1. to have (got)

Milou a un pelage blanc Snowy has white fur

...avoir

Tintin a beaucoup d'amis Tintin has got many friends

pauvre capitaine, il a la grippe poor Captain, he's got the flu

2. to have
ils ont eu un accident they had an accident

3. Loc
j'ai chaud/faim/froid I'm hot/hungry/cold

* *Cette tour a bien vingt mètres de hauteur.* This tower is at least twenty metres (*Am:* meters) high. *

quel âge a le professeur ? how old is the Professor?

...avoir

avoir

avoir
[avwar] *v aux*
1. to have

* *Voilà, j'ai presque fini les plans de la fusée lunaire, qu'en pensez-vous ?...* There, I've nearly finished the plans of the moon rocket, what do you think?... *

non merci, j'ai déjà mangé no thanks, I've already eaten

2. Loc

tu n'avais qu'à obéir ! you should have obeyed!

avril

avril
[avril] *n m*
April

le premier/deux avril the first/second of April (*Am:* April first/second)

venez le 6 avril come on the 6th of April (*Am:* on April 6)

bac

bac
[bak] *n m*
ferry

le bac traverse la rivière the ferry crosses the river

bac

bac, baccalauréat
[bak], [bakalorea] *n m*
A levels (*Am:* high-school diploma)

bagages

bagages
[bagaʒ] *n m pl*
luggage

* *Allons récupérer nos bagages...* Let's go and get our luggage back... *Ils sont déjà dans l'auto...* It's already in the car... *

bague

bague
[bag] *n f*

...bague

ring

une bague en or a gold ring

baguette

baguette
[bagɛt] *n f*
1. French loaf

2. Loc
baguette de tambour drumstick

baguette magique magic wand

baigner

baigner
[beɲe]
I. *v t*
to bath (*Am:* to bathe)

Milou est très sale, je dois le baigner Snowy is very dirty, I've got to bath him

II. *v pr*
1. to bathe

j'aimerais bien me baigner dans le lac I'd like to bathe in the lake

...baigner

2. Loc
allons nous baigner ! let's go for a swim!

► **baignoire**
[bɛɲwar] *n f*
bath (*Am:* bathtub)

la baignoire va déborder the bath is going to overflow

bain

bain
[bɛ̃] *n m*
1. bath

je prends un bain tous les matins I take a bath every morning

2. swim
* *Que dirais-tu d'un bon bain ?* What would you say to a nice swim? *Hourra !... c'est une bonne idée !* Hurray!... That's a good idea! *

baiser

baiser
[beze] *n m*
kiss

donne-moi un baiser give me a kiss

baisser

baisser
[bɛse]
I. *v t*
1. to pull down, to wind down

...baisser

Baissez la radio, je veux dormir! Vous avez compris?

baisse la vitre, il fait chaud wind the window down, it's hot

2. to turn down
* *Baissez la radio, je veux dormir! Vous avez compris?* Turn the radio down, I want to sleep! Do you understand? *

II. *v i*
1. to drop

la température a baissé the temperature has dropped

2. to go down
dépêchons-nous, le soleil baisse let's hurry, the sun's going down

III. *v pr*
to stoop

il s'est baissé pour ramasser le papier he stooped to pick up the paper

bal

bal
[bal] *n m*
dance

ce soir, il y a un bal au village tonight there's a dance in the village

balayer

balayer
[balɛje] *v t*
to sweep

...balayer

n'oubliez pas de balayer le couloir don't forget to sweep the corridor

► **balai**
[balɛ] *n m*
broom

balcon

balcon
[balkɔ̃] *n m*
balcony

du balcon, on a une belle vue the view from the balcony is splendid

balle

balle
[bal] *n f*
1. ball

...balle

Il a reçu une balle dans l'épaule.

une balle de tennis a tennis ball

2. bullet
* *Il a reçu une balle dans l'épaule.* He's been hit by a bullet in the shoulder. *

ballon

ballon
[balɔ̃] *n m*
1. ball

un ballon de rugby a rugby ball

2. balloon
ils se sont envolés en ballon they went up in a balloon

3. Loc
ballon de football football (*Am:* soccer ball)

banane

banane
[banan] *n f*
banana

bande

bande
[bɑ̃d] *n f*
1. bandage

je vais mettre une bande à votre cheville I'll put a bandage round your ankle

...bande

Enfin Tintin, vous me prenez pour un personnage de bande dessinée ou quoi?
Ne partez pas!

2. strip
je n'ai trouvé que cette bande de papier all I found is this strip of paper

3. gang
une bande de copains a gang of friends

4. Loc
bande dessinée comic strip

* *Enfin Tintin, vous me prenez pour un personnage de bande dessinée ou quoi?* For goodness' sake, Tintin, do you take me for a character out of a comic strip? *Ne partez pas!* Don't go! *

banlieue

banlieue
[bɑ̃ljø] *n f*
suburbs

banque

banque
[bɑ̃k] *n f*
bank

* *Trois heures après, la première...* Three hours later, the first... *banque de la ville...* bank in the town... *était construite...* was built... *

...banque

Trois heures après, la première...

banque de la ville...

était construite...

barbe

barbe
[barb] *n f*
beard

* *Ma barbe est prise dans la fermeture Eclair !* My beard's caught in the zip (*Am:* zipper)!
Un petit coup sec, peut-être ?... Just one quick pull?...
Ça y est ! That's it!
Aïe ! Ouch! *

► **barbu**
[barby] *n m*
bearded man

bas

bas, basse
[ba, bɑs]
I. *adj*
1. low

...bas

La porte est basse...

* *La porte est basse...* The door is low... *

2. low
je vous en supplie, parlez à voix basse I beg you, speak in a low voice

3. low
nous passerons à marée basse we'll get across at low tide

II. *n m*
1. bottom
regardez au bas de l'armoire look in the bottom of the wardrobe (*Am:* closet)

2. Loc
en bas de la montagne at the foot of the mountain

III. *adv*
low

l'avion vole trop bas the plane's flying too low

bateau

bateau
[bato] *n m*
pl bateaux
1. boat

* *Voulez-vous me vendre votre bateau ?* Will you sell me your boat?
Oui, si... vous m'en donnez un bon prix. Yes, I will... if you give me a good price for it. *

...bateau

2. ship
* *Quelque part sur l'océan...* Somewhere on the ocean...
L'« Aurore » est un bon bateau, nous arriverons sûrement à temps... The "Aurora" is a good ship: we're sure to get there on time... *

bâtiment

bâtiment
[batimɑ̃] *n m*
building

battre

battre
[batr]
I. *v t*
to hit

mais enfin, vous n'allez pas me battre ! look, you're not going to hit me, are you?

...battre

II. *v pr*
to fight

arrêtez de vous battre stop fighting

bavarder

bavarder
[bavarde] *v i*
to talk, to chatter

cessez de bavarder et écoutez, c'est très important stop talking and listen now, it's very important

...bavarder

► **bavard, e**
[bavar, ard] *n*
chatterbox

beau

beau, belle
[bo, bɛl] *adj*
Note : the form bel *is used in front of a masculine noun beginning with a vowel or a mute* h
pl beaux, belles
1. beautiful

voici la Castafiore, quelle belle femme ! here comes Signora Castafiore – what a beautiful woman!

2. handsome
le capitaine est un bel homme the Captain is a handsome man

3. fine
* *Quel beau temps !...* What fine weather!... *

4. nice
Abdallah, ce n'est pas beau de mentir Abdullah, it's not nice to tell lies

► **beau**
[bo] *adv*

1. nice

il va faire beau the weather's going to be nice

2. Loc
* *Allons, Milou, ne te laisse pas tenter...* Come on, Snowy, don't yield to temptation...
Tu as beau essayer, tu ne peux pas t'empêcher de déterrer les os... However hard you try, you can't help digging up bones... *

...beau

beaucoup

beaucoup
[boku] *adv*
1. much, a lot

c'est beaucoup plus difficile que la première fois it's much more difficult than the first time

2. very much
Milou aime beaucoup les os Snowy likes bones very much

► **beaucoup de**
[bokudə] *prép*
1. a lot of

j'ai gagné beaucoup d'argent I earned a lot of money

2. many
beaucoup de gens ont vu ce film many people have seen that film

3. much
y a-t-il beaucoup de lait ? is there much milk?

beau-fils

beau-fils
[bofis] *n m*
pl beaux-fils
1. son-in-law

le mari de ma fille est mon beau-fils my daughter's husband is my son-in-law

2. stepson
le fils de ma seconde femme est mon beau-fils my second wife's son is my stepson

...beau-fils

belle-fille
[bɛlfij] *n f*
pl belles-filles
1. daughter-in-law

2. stepdaughter

▶ **beau-père**
[bopɛr] *n m*
pl beaux-pères
1. father-in-law

le père de mon mari est mon beau-père my husband's father is my father-in-law

2. stepfather
le second mari de ma mère est mon beau-père my mother's second husband is my stepfather

▶ **belle-mère**
[bɛlmɛr] *n f*
pl belles-mères
1. mother-in-law

2. stepmother

bébé

bébé
[bebe] *n m*
baby
* *Pourquoi ce bébé crie-t-il si fort ?* Why is the baby crying so loudly? *

bel

bel, belle → BEAU

▶ **belle-fille, belle-mère** → BEAU-FILS

Belgique

Belgique
[bɛlʒik] *n f*
Belgium

▶ **Belge**
[bɛlʒ] *n m, f*
Belgian

▶ **belge**
[bɛlʒ] *adj*
belgian

besoin

besoin
[bəzwɛ̃] *n m*
1. need

en cas de besoin, téléphonez-moi if the need arises, telephone me

2. Loc
* *J'ai besoin de ton aide, Tchang, tu comprends ?* I need your help, Chang, do you understand?
Tu peux compter sur moi, Tintin. You can count on me, Tintin. *

bête

bête
[bɛt] *adj*
silly

comme tu peux être bête, parfois ! you can be so silly sometimes!

▶ **bêtise**
[bɛtiz] *n f*
1. stupidity

ce n'est pas de la bêtise, c'est de l'étourderie

...bête

it's not stupidity, it's absent-mindedness

2. silly thing
cessez de dire des bêtises stop saying silly things

3. Loc
* *Je parie que c'est Abdallah qui a encore fait des bêtises !* I bet Abdullah's been naughty again! *

beurre

beurre
[bœr] *n m*
butter

bibliothèque

bibliothèque
[biblijɔtɛk] *n f*
1. bookcase

* *Oh !... Ils ont entièrement vidé ma bibliothèque.* Oh!... they

...bibliothèque

have completely emptied my bookcase. *

2. library
vous trouverez ce livre à la bibliothèque municipale you'll find this book in the public library

bicyclette

bicyclette
[bisiklɛt] *n f*
bicycle, bike

...bicyclette

sais-tu monter à bicyclette ? can you ride a bike?

bien

bien
[bjɛ̃]
I. *adv*
1. well

oui, je vous entends très bien yes, I can hear you very well

...bien

2. well
vous avez bien fait d'attendre you did well to wait

3. far
* *Zorrino est bien trop jeune pour faire une aussi longue marche...* Zorrino is far too young to walk such a long way...
Mais non, je vous assure, je peux continuer ! Not at all! I assure you, I can go on! *

4. Loc
c'est bien fait pour toi ! it serves you right!

II. *adj inv*
1. decent, nice

ce sont des gens très bien they are very decent people

2. Loc
les Dupondt essaient toujours d'être bien avec les gens du coin the Thompsons always try to be on good terms with the locals

III. *n m*
1. good

c'est pour ton bien it's for your own good

2. Loc
dire du bien de quelqu'un to speak highly of somebody

prenez ce médicament, cela vous fera du bien take this medicine – it will do you good

bientôt

bientôt
[bjɛ̃to] *adv*
1. soon

nous y serons bientôt we'll soon be there

2. Loc
* *Au revoir, Tintin...* Good bye, Tintin...
A bientôt ! So long! *

...bientôt

bienvenue

bienvenue
[bjɛ̃vny] *n f*
1. welcome

2. Loc
je suis heureux de vous souhaiter la bienvenue I'm happy to welcome you

bière

bière
[bjɛr] *n f*
beer

bifteck

bifteck
[biftɛk] *n m*
steak

bijou

bijou
[biʒu] *n m*
pl bijoux
jewel

* *Je suis désolée... ce soir, exceptionnellement, je ne porte*

...bijou

pas mes bijoux, on me les a volés... I'm sorry... On this particular evening, I'm not wearing my jewels – they've been stolen... *

bille

bille
[bij] *n f*
marble

jouer aux billes to play marbles

billet

billet
[bijɛ] *n m*
1. (bank) note
(*Am:* bill)

...billet

* *Oh, j'ai trouvé des billets !* Oh, I've found some bank notes! *

un billet de cent francs a hundred-franc note

2. ticket
il nous faut des billets pour le train we need tickets for the train

bizarre

bizarre
[bizar] *adj*
1. peculiar

quel homme bizarre ! what a peculiar man!

2. odd
pas de réponse ? c'est bizarre, il devrait être chez lui ! no answer? that's odd, he should be in!

blanc

blanc, blanche
[blɑ̃, blɑ̃ʃ] *adj*
1. white

2. Loc
nuit blanche sleepless night

page blanche blank page

► **Blanc, Blanche**
[blɑ̃, blɑ̃ʃ] *n*
white (person)

► **blanc**
[blɑ̃] *n m*
1. white
ils sont habillés de blanc they're dressed in white
2. white
blanc d'œuf egg white

blesser

blesser
[blese]
I. *v t*
1. to wound
la balle l'a blessé à la tête the bullet wounded him in the head
2. to injure
capitaine, êtes-vous blessé ? Captain, are you injured?
II. *v pr*
to hurt oneself
attention, vous allez vous blesser avec cette épée be careful, you're going to hurt yourself with that sword

► **blessé, e**
[blese] *n*
injured person
* *Avez-vous trouvé d'autres blessés ?* Have you found any other injured people?
Il y en a encore deux. There are two more. *

► **blessure**
[blesyr] *n f*
1. wound

sa blessure se cicatrise his wound is healing
2. injury
ses blessures sont graves he suffered severe injuries

bleu

bleu, e
[blø] *adj*
blue
le ciel est bleu the sky is blue
bleu marine navy blue

► **bleu**
[blø] *n m*
1. blue
le bleu te va bien blue suits you
2. bruise
* *Aïe, j'ai des bleus partout !* Ouch, I'm covered in bruises! *

bloc

bloc
[blɔk] *n m*
1. block
un gros bloc de pierre est tombé de la falaise a huge block of stone fell from the cliff
2. pad
un bloc de papier à lettres a writing pad
3. Loc
bloc opératoire operating theatre (*Am:* operating room)

blond

blond, e
[blɔ̃, ɔ̃d] *adj*
blond, fair
la Castafiore est blonde Signora Castafiore is blond
elle a des cheveux blonds she has fair hair

blouson

blouson
[bluzɔ̃] *n m*

jacket
blouson en cuir leather jacket

bocal

bocal
[bɔkal] *n m*
pl bocaux [bɔko]
jar
un bocal de confiture a jar of jam

bœuf

bœuf
[bœf] *n m*
pl bœufs [bø]
1. ox
les bœufs tirent la charrette the oxen are pulling the cart
2. beef
un ragoût de bœuf a beef stew

boire

boire
[bwar] *v t*
to drink
* *Mais j'ai dit que je ne boirai plus de whisky !...* But I said I wouldn't drink any more whisky!... *

► **boisson**
[bwasɔ̃] *n f*
drink
boisson non alcoolisée soft drink

bois

bois
[bwa] *n m*
1. wood

ce coffre est en bois this chest is made of wood

2. wood
nous nous sommes perdus dans les bois we got lost in the woods

3. antler
les bois du cerf the stag's antlers

boisson

boisson → BOIRE

boîte

boîte
[bwat] *n f*
box

* ***Qu'y a-t-il dans cette boîte ?*** What's in this box? *

boîte à lettres letter-box (*Am:* mailbox)

...boîte

Qu'y a-t-il dans cette boîte ?

boîte d'allumettes matchbox

boiter

boiter
[bwate] *v i*
to limp

Milou s'est fait mal, il boite Snowy has hurt himself, he's limping

bol

bol
[bɔl] *n m*
bowl

bon

bon, bonne
[bɔ̃, bɔn] *adj*
1. good

ce gâteau est très bon this cake is very good

...bon

Les Dupondt !... Pourvu qu'ils apportent de bonnes nouvelles !

2. good
* ***Les Dupondt !... Pourvu qu'ils apportent de bonnes nouvelles !*** The Thompsons!... I hope they're bringing us good news! *

3. good
elle est bonne en maths she's good at maths (*Am:* math)

4. kind
le capitaine est un homme très bon the Captain is a very kind man

5. right
vais-je savoir donner la bonne réponse ? will I be able to give the right answer?

6. Loc
bon anniversaire happy birthday

bon marché cheap

* ***Ce n'est pas bon marché ici...*** It isn't cheap here...
Je dirais même plus : ce n'est pas bon marché... To be precise it isn't cheap...
C'est meilleur marché à côté... It's cheaper next door... *

Ce n'est pas bon marché ici...
Je dirais même plus : ce n'est pas bon marché...
C'est meilleur marché à côté...

bonbon

bonbon
[bɔ̃bɔ̃] *n m*
sweet (*Am:* candy)

j'ai acheté des bonbons I bought some sweets

bondir

bondir
[bɔ̃dir] *v i*
to leap

...bondir

en voyant Tintin, Milou a bondi de joie when he saw Tintin, Snowy leapt for joy

► **bond**
[bɔ̃] *n m*
leap

je vais franchir la crevasse d'un bond I'll jump over the crevasse in one leap

bonheur

bonheur
[bɔnœr] *n m*
1. happiness

le bonheur d'une vie paisible the happiness of a quiet life

2. luck
* ***Prends, c'est un talisman... Il te portera bonheur et te protègera de tous les dangers.*** Take this talisman... It'll bring you luck and protect you from danger. *

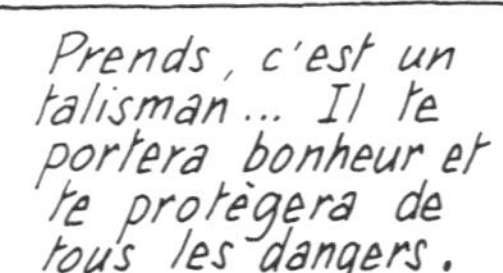
Prends, c'est un talisman... Il te portera bonheur et te protègera de tous les dangers.

3. Loc
quel bonheur de vous trouver ici ! how nice to find you here!

bonjour

bonjour
[bɔ̃ʒur] *interj*
hello, good morning, good afternoon

bonjour, avez-vous bien dormi ? good morning, did you sleep well?

...bonjour

dire bonjour à quelqu'un to say hello to somebody

bonne

bonne → BON

bonnet

bonnet
[bɔnɛ] *n m*

...bonnet

1. bonnet

2. cap
bonnet de bain bathing cap

bonsoir

bonsoir
[bɔ̃swar] *interj*
1. good evening

bonsoir mes amis, entrez je vous prie

...bonsoir

good evening, my friends, come in please

2. good night
bonsoir, à demain! good night, see you tomorrow!

bord

bord
[bɔr] *n m*
1. edge

...bord

...bord

la maison est au bord de l'eau the house is on the water's edge

2. rim
le bord du verre est cassé the rim of the glass is chipped

3. board
* *Allez capitaine, il faut monter à bord!* Come on Captain, you must come on board! *J'arrive, j'arrive!* I'm coming, I'm coming! *

botte

botte
[bɔt] *n f*
1. boot

le docteur Müller a des bottes noires Doctor Müller's wearing black boots

2. Loc
bottes de caoutchouc wellingtons (*Am:* rubber boots)

bouche

bouche
[buʃ] *n f*
1. mouth

ne parle pas la bouche pleine don't speak with your mouth full

2. Loc
bouche de métro metro entrance

boucher

boucher
[buʃe] *v t*
to cork

boucher une bouteille to cork a bottle

▶ **bouché, e**
[buʃe] *adj*
blocked up (*Am:* stopped up)

la baignoire est bouchée the bath (*Am:* bathtub) is blocked up

il a le nez bouché his nose is blocked up

boucher

boucher, ère
[buʃe, ɛr] *n*
butcher

▶ **boucherie**
[buʃri] *n f*
butcher's (shop)

bouchon

bouchon
[buʃɔ̃] *n m*
1. cork

remettez le bouchon sur la bouteille put the cork back in the bottle

2. traffic jam
il y a un bouchon sur la route there's a traffic jam on the road

bouclé

bouclé, é
[bukle] *adj*
curly

des cheveux bouclés curly hair

bouger

bouger
[buʒe] *v i*
to move

* *Arrête de bouger, il va nous entendre.*

...bouger

Stop moving, he'll hear us. *

bougie

bougie
[buʒi] *n f*
candle

le vent a éteint les bougies the wind blew the candles out

boulanger

boulanger, ère
[bulɑ̃ʒe, ɛr] *n*
baker

▶ **boulangerie**
[bulɑ̃ʒri] *n f*
baker's (shop) (*Am:* bakery)

boule

Le capitaine s'est transformé en boule de neige.

boule
[bul] *n f*
1. ball

2. Loc
* *Le capitaine s'est transformé en boule de neige.* The Captain has turned into a snowball. *

bousculer

bousculer
[buskyle] *v t*
to bump into

quelqu'un m'a bousculé et je suis tombé somebody bumped into me and I fell down

boussole

boussole
[busɔl] *n f*
compass

bout

bout
[bu] *n m*
1. piece

veux-tu un morceau de pain ? do you want a piece of bread?

2. end
ce n'est pas loin, c'est au bout de la rue it's not very far: it's at the end of the street

3. Loc
* *Les voici qui arrivent. Tintin semble à*

...bout

Les voici qui arrivent. Tintin semble à bout de forces. Le capitaine le porte presque ...

bout de forces. Le capitaine le porte presque ... Here they come. Tintin has no strength left. The Captain is almost carrying him... *

bouteille

bouteille
[butɛj] *n f*
bottle

boutique

boutique
[butik] *n f*
shop (*Am:* store)

entrez dans ma boutique, vous trouverez tout ce qu'il vous faut come into my shop, you'll find everything you need

bouton

bouton
[butɔ̃] *n m*

...bouton

J'appuie sur le bouton vert pour déclencher le moteur auxiliaire ...

...bouton

1. button

* *J'appuie sur le bouton vert pour déclencher le moteur auxiliaire...* I press the green button to start the auxiliary engine... *

2. button
il manque un bouton à ta veste there's a button missing from your jacket

3. spot
oh, j'ai un bouton sur le nez ! oh, I've got a spot on my nose!

4. bud
un bouton de rose a rosebud

branche

branche
[brɑ̃ʃ] *n f*
branch

j'ai reçu la branche sur la tête the branch fell on my head

brancher

brancher
[brɑ̃ʃe] *v t*
to plug in

* *Ah, je vois ce que c'est, l'appareil n'est pas branché.* Ah, I see what it is: the machine isn't plugged in.
Et voilà... There we are... *

Ah, je vois ce que c'est, l'appareil n'est pas branché.
Et voilà...

bras

bras
[bra] *n m*
arm

le capitaine a croisé les bras the Captain folded his arms

bravo

bravo
[bravo] *interj*
well done

* *Quoi!...* What!... *Bravo, Milou!* Well done, Snowy! *

bricoler

bricoler
[brikɔle] *v i*
to potter around (*Am:* to putter)

Tournesol aime bien bricoler Calculus likes pottering around

briller

briller
[brije] *v i*
1. to shine

...briller

le soleil brille the sun is shining

2. to sparkle
ses bijoux brillent her jewels sparkle

brique

brique
[brik] *n f*
brick

le mur est en briques it's a brick wall

britannique

britannique
[britanik] *adj*
British

les îles Britanniques the British Isles

brochure

brochure
[brɔʃyr] *n f*
booklet

* *Tout est expliqué dans cette bro-*

...brochure

chure... Everything is explained in this booklet... *

bronzer

bronzer
[brɔ̃ze] *v i*
to get a tan

▶ **bronzage**
[brɔ̃zaʒ] *n m*
suntan

brosser

brosser
[brɔse]
I. *v t*
to brush

elle brosse ses chaussures she's brushing her shoes

II. *v pr*
to brush

* *Le capitaine est en train de se brosser les dents.* The Captain is brushing his teeth. *

Le capitaine est en train de se brosser les dents.

▶ **brosse**
[brɔs] *n f*
1. brush

brosse à dents tooth-brush

brosse à cheveux hair-brush

2. Loc
j'ai donné un coup de brosse à ma veste I gave my jacket a brush

brouillard

brouillard
[brujar] *n m*
fog

* *Voilà ce que je craignais : le brouillard !...* This is what I feared: fog!... *

bruit

bruit
[brɥi] *n m*
1. noise

* *Clang Clang* Clang Clang
Vous entendez ce bruit ? Do you hear that noise? *

2. sound
j'entends un bruit de moteur I can hear the sound of an engine

3. Loc
marchons sans bruit let's walk quietly

► **bruyant, e**
[brɥjɑ̃, ɑ̃t] *adj*
noisy

que cette ville est bruyante ! what a noisy town!

* *Wouin ! Wouin ! Wouin !* Waaah! Waaah! Waaah!
Abdallah est un enfant bruyant. Abdullah's a noisy child. *

Abdallah est un enfant bruyant.

brûler

brûler
[bryle]
I. *v t*
to burn

ils ont essayé de brûler les documents they tried to burn the documents

II. *v i*
1. to burn down

* *La maison du docteur Müller a brûlé...* Doctor Müller's house was burnt down... *

...brûler

2. to burn
le feu brûle dans la cheminée the fire's burning in the fireplace

III. *v pr*
to burn oneself

attention, tu vas te brûler ! careful, you're going to burn yourself!

brume

brume
[brym] *n f*
mist

► **brumeux, euse**
[brymø, øz] *adj*
misty, hazy

brun

brun, e
[brœ̃, yn] *adj*
brown

elle a les cheveux bruns she has brown hair

bruyant

bruyant, e
→ BRUIT

buisson

buisson
[bɥisɔ̃] *n m*
bush

il s'est caché derrière un buisson he hid behind a bush

bureau

bureau
[byro] *n m*
pl bureaux
1. desk

tous les plans sont sur mon bureau all the plans are on my desk

2. office
* *Il est peut-être dans l'un de ces bureaux !* He may be in one of these offices! *

bureau des objets trouvés lost property (*Am:* lost-and-found) office

3. Loc
bureau de poste post office

bureau de tabac tobacconist's (*Am:* tobacco shop)

bureau de change bureau de change

but

but
[by(t)] *n m*
1. aim

mon but est de faciliter votre recherche my aim is to make your search easier

2. goal
il a marqué trois buts he scored three goals

ça

ça
[sa] *pron*
1. it
non, ça ne sert à rien no, it's no use
2. this
je vais lui dire ça I'm going to tell him this
3. that
vite, donnez-moi ça ! quick, give me that!
4. Loc
ça alors, quelle surprise ! well I never, what a surprise!

cabine

cabine
[kabin] *n f*

1. cabin
je dois trouver la cabine du commandant I have to find the Captain's cabin

2. box
* *Enfin, une cabine téléphonique !* At last, a telephone box (*Am:* phone booth)! *

cabinet

cabinet
[kabinɛ] *n m*
surgery (*Am:* office)

le médecin m'a reçu dans son cabinet the doctor saw me in his surgery

▶ **cabinets**
[kabinɛ] *n m pl*
toilet

les cabinets sont au fond du couloir the toilet is at the end of the corridor

cacher

cacher
[kaʃe]
I. *v t*
to hide

où a-t-il pu cacher ce papier ? where the devil did he hide this paper?

II. *v pr*
to hide

* *Cachez-vous derrière la porte !* Hide behind the door! *

cachet

cachet
[kaʃɛ] *n m*
1. tablet

je dois prendre un cachet avant chaque repas I have to take one tablet before each meal

2. stamp
* *Oui, ces papiers sont en règle, ils portent le cachet du ministère. Nous pouvons vous remettre le professeur Tournesol.* Yes, these documents are in order, they bear the ministry stamp. We can hand Professor Calculus over to you. *

cadeau

cadeau
[kado] *n m*
pl cadeaux
present

cadet

cadet, ette
[kadɛt, ɛt]
I. *adj*
1. younger

j'ai une sœur cadette I have a younger sister

2. youngest

II. *n*
1. younger child

2. youngest child

café

café
[kafe] *n m*
coffee

* *Le matin...* In the morning...
Bonjour, Tintin, voulez-vous une tasse de café ? Good morning, Tintin, would you like a cup of coffee?
Bonjour, capitaine, volontiers... Good morning, Captain, I'd love one... *

café au lait white coffee

café crème coffee with cream

caisse

caisse
[kɛs] *n f*
1. crate

* *Tournesol a failli être écrasé par une grosse caisse.* Calculus was nearly squashed by a heavy crate. *

...caisse

Tournesol a failli être écrasé par une grosse caisse.

2. cash desk (*Am:* checkout counter)
passez à la caisse payer vos achats go to the cash desk to pay for what you've bought

calculer

calculer
[kalkyle] *v t*
to calculate

...calculer

► **calcul**
[kalkyl] *n m*
sums, arithmetic

tu as fait une erreur de calcul you made a mistake in your sums

calmer

calmer
[kalme]
I. *v t*
to ease, to soothe

...calmer

ce médicament va calmer la douleur this medicine will ease the pain

II. *v pr*
to calm down

* *Aaah ! Je fais le zouave !...* So, I'm playing the fool, am I?...
Allons, calmez-vous ! Come on, calm down! *

► **calme**
[kalm]
I. *adj*
1. quiet

c'est une rue calme it's a quiet street

2. calm
allons, capitaine, restez calme ! come on, Captain, keep calm!

II. *n m*
peacefulness, calm(ness)

le calme de la campagne the peacefulness of the countryside

camarade

camarade
[kamarad] *n*
friend

c'est une de mes camarades d'école she's one of my school friends

cambrioler

cambrioler
[kɑ̃brijɔle] *v t*
to burgle (*Am:* to burglarize)

...cambrioler

Les bandits !... Ils ont cambriolé ma maison !

* *Les bandits !... Ils ont cambriolé ma maison !* Rascals!... They've burgled my house! *

► **cambrioleur**
[kɑ̃brijɔlœr] *n m*
burglar

► **cambriolage**
[kɑ̃brijɔlaʒ] *n m*
burglary

caméra

caméra
[kamera] *n f*
movie camera

camion

camion
[kamjɔ̃] *n m*
lorry (*Am:* truck)

campagne

campagne
[kɑ̃paɲ] *n f*
1. country, country-side

quelques jours à la campagne et je serai remis ! a few days in the country and I'll be all right!

2. campaign
une campagne publicitaire an advertising campaign

camper

Le lendemain soir ...
Nous camperons ici .
Voilà les premières neiges...

...camper

camper
[kɑ̃pe] *v i*
to camp

* *Le lendemain soir...* The next evening... *Nous camperons ici.* We'll camp here. *Voilà les premières neiges...* This is where the snow starts... *

► **campeur, euse**
[kɑ̃pœr, øz] *n*

► **camping**
[kɑ̃piŋ] *n m*
1. camping
faire du camping to go camping

2. Loc
(terrain de) camping campsite

canard

canard
[kanar] *n m*
duck

cantine

cantine
[kɑ̃tin] *n f*
dining hall (*Am:* cafeteria)

la cantine de l'école the school dining hall

capable

capable
[kapabl] *adj*
capable

...capable

il est capable de le faire he is capable of doing it

capitale

capitale
[kapital] *n f*
capital

Paris est la capitale de la France Paris is the capital of France

car

car
[kar] *conj*
because

je mange car j'ai faim I eat because I'm hungry

car

car
[kar] *n m*
coach (*Am:* bus)

une excursion en car a coach tour

caractère

caractère
[karaktɛr] *n m*
1. character

la Castafiore est une femme de caractère Signora Castafiore is a woman of character

2. Loc
avoir bon/mauvais caractère to be good/bad-tempered

caravane

caravane
[karavan] *n f*
1. caravan

* *Dans le désert...* In the desert... *La caravane de chameaux quitte le fort.* The caravan of camels is leaving the fort. *

2. caravan (*Am:* trailer)
nous partons dans notre caravane we're going in our caravan

Dans le désert...
La caravane de chameaux quitte le fort.

carnet

carnet
[karnɛ] *n m*
1. book

voici son carnet d'adresses here's his address book

2. report
carnet de notes school report (*Am:* report card)

3. book
carnet de chèques chequebook (*Am:* checkbook)

carnet de tickets book of tickets

carotte

carotte
[carɔt] *n f*
carrot

carré

carré
[kare] *n m*
square

un carré a quatre côtés égaux a square has four equal sides

...carré

► **carré, e**
[kare] *adj*
square

ma chambre est carrée my room is square

carreau

...carreau

carreau
[karo] *n m*
pl carreaux
windowpane

* *Oh, les carreaux!* Oh, the windowpanes! *

carrefour

carrefour
[karfur] *n m*
crossroads

carrière

carrière
[karjɛr] *n f*
1. quarry

carrière de marbre marble quarry

2. career
ma carrière de professeur my career as a teacher

carte

carte
[kart] *n f*
1. map

voici une carte de la région here's a map of the area

2. card
carte de visite/de crédit visiting (*Am:* calling)/credit card

carte postale postcard

3. card
jouer aux cartes to play cards

carton

carton
[kartɔ̃] *n m*
1. cardboard

un morceau de carton a piece of cardboard

2. cardboard box
je l'ai mis dans un carton I put it in a cardboard box

cas

cas
[kɑ] *n m*
case

en tout cas, je n'irai pas in any case, I won't go

c'est souvent le cas it's often the case

en cas d'urgence in case of emergency

casque

Les pompiers portent un casque.

casque
[kask] *n m*
helmet

* *Les pompiers portent un casque.* Firemen wear helmets. *

casser

casser
[kɑse]
I. *v t*
to break

...casser

...casser

il a cassé ma montre he broke my watch

II. *v pr*
to break

* *Cette pauvre bête s'est cassé le bras en tombant dans l'escalier.* This poor animal broke its arm falling down the stairs. *

casserole

casserole
[kasrɔl] *n f*
saucepan

cassette

cassette
[kasɛt] *n f*
cassette

cathédrale

cathédrale
[katedral] *n f*
cathedral

cause

cause
[koz] *n f*
1. cause

c'est la cause de l'accident it's the cause of the accident

...cause

2. Loc
à cause de because of

cave

cave
[kav] *n f*
cellar

* *Ils descendent à la cave...* They're going down into the cellar... *

...cave

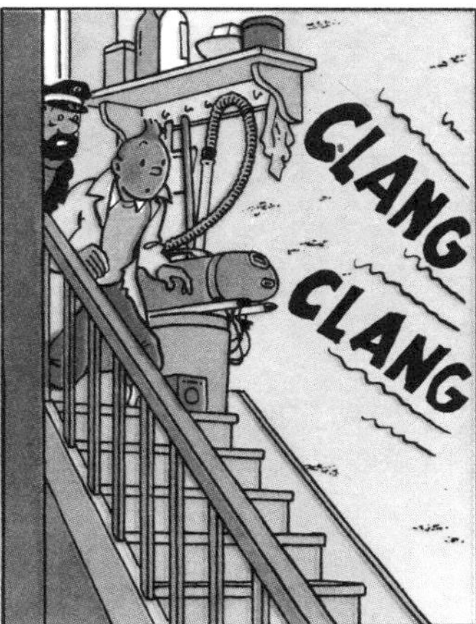
CLANG
CLANG
Ils descendent à la cave...

ceinture

ceinture
[sɛ̃tyr] *n f*
1. belt

la ceinture de mon pantalon the belt of my trousers (*Am:* pants)

ceinture de sécurité safety/seat belt

2. Loc
j'ai de l'eau jusqu'à la ceinture I'm waist-deep in water

célèbre

VIVE TINTIN ET MI OU
L'arrivée du célèbre reporter Tintin.

célèbre
[selɛbr] *adj*
famous

* *Vive Tintin et Milou !* Long live Tintin and Snowy!
L'arrivée du célèbre reporter Tintin. The arrival of Tintin, the famous journalist. *

célibataire

célibataire
[selibatɛr]
I. *adj*
unmarried

la Castafiore est célibataire Signora Castafiore is unmarried

II. *n m*
bachelor

le capitaine est un célibataire endurci the Captain is a confirmed bachelor

cent

cent
[sɑ̃] *adj num*
a hundred

cent francs a hundred francs

► **centime**
[sɑ̃tim] *n m*
centime

► **centimètre**
[sɑ̃timɛtr] *n m*
centimetre
(*Am:* centimeter)

centre

centre
[sɑ̃tr] *n m*
centre (*Am:* center)

centre commercial shopping centre
(*Am:* shopping mall)

cependant

Quelque part au Tibet ...
Il y a du soleil et cependant il fait froid !

...cependant

cependant
[səpɑ̃dɑ̃] *adv*
yet

* *Quelque part au Tibet...* Somewhere in Tibet...
Il y a du soleil et cependant il fait froid ! The sun is shining and yet it's cold! *

cerise

cerise
[səriz] *n f*
cherry

certain

certain, e
[sɛrtɛ̃, ɛn] *adj*
1. sure

* *Je suis certain que c'est le général Alcazar !* I'm sure it's General Alcazar! *

...certain

2. certain, *pl* some
certains enfants ont des idées extraordinaires some children have extraordinary ideas

► **certainement**
[sɛrtɛnmɑ̃] *adv*
1. surely

Tintin va certainement nous aider à nous échapper Tintin will surely help us to escape

2. certainly
demandons au capitaine, il connaît certainement leur adresse let's ask the Captain, he certainly knows their address

chacun

chacun, e
[ʃakœ̃, yn] *pron*
each, each one

chacun de vous sortira de la fusée each one of you will get out of the rocket

* *Doucement ! Vous en aurez chacun un !* Easy does it! Each of you will get one! *

chaîne

chaîne
[ʃɛn] *n f*
1. chain

si je pouvais me libérer de ces chaînes ! if I could free myself from these chains!

2. channel
la deuxième chaîne de télévision channel two

3. system
une chaîne stéréo a stereo system

chaise

...chaise

chaise
[ʃɛz] *n f*
chair

* *Excusez-moi, M. Baxter... Cette chaise n'était pas très solide... Je vais vous en donner une autre...* Excuse me, Mr Baxter... That chair wasn't very strong... I'll give you another one... *

chaleur

chaleur
[ʃalœr] *n f*
heat

* *Cette chaleur me donne soif !...* This heat is making me thirsty!... *

chambre

chambre
[ʃɑ̃br] *n f*
1. bedroom

* *La fumée sort de la chambre du capitaine !...* The smoke is coming from the Captain's bedroom!... *

2. Loc
chambre d'amis spare/guest room

chameau

chameau
[ʃamo] *n m*
pl chameaux
camel

champ

champ
[ʃɑ̃] *n m*
field

* *Regardez, capitaine, regardez ! L'avion se pose dans*

...champ

le champ !... Look, Captain, look! The plane is landing in the field!... *

champignon

champignon
[ʃɑ̃piɲɔ̃] *n m*
mushroom

champion

...champion

champion, onne
[ʃɑ̃pjɔ̃, ɔn] *n*
champion

* *Voici Billy Bolivar, champion du monde de l'arraché à une main.* Here's Billy Bolivar, world champion of the one-handed snatch.
Hop ! Hup! *

► **championnat**
[ʃɑ̃pjɔna] *n m*
championship

chance

chance
[ʃɑ̃s] *n f*
1. luck

tenter sa chance to try one's luck

bonne chance ! good luck!

oh, pas de chance ! oh, hard luck!

2. Loc
* *Milou a eu la chance de pouvoir se raccrocher à une*

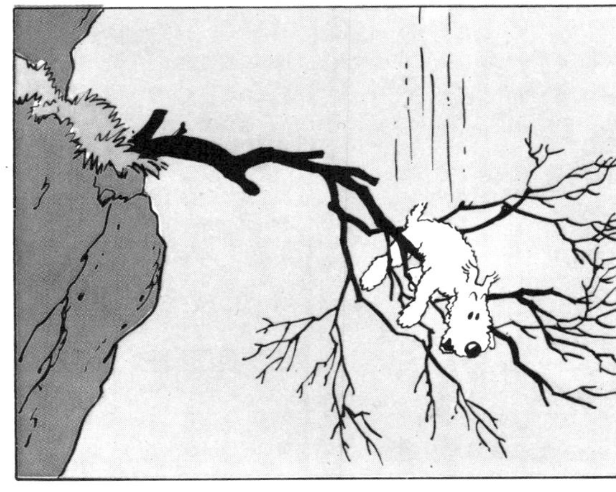

Milou a eu la chance de pouvoir se raccrocher à une branche.

...chance

branche. Snowy had the good luck to get caught on a branch. *

changer

changer
[ʃɑ̃ʒe]
I. *v t*
1. to change

* *Avez-vous changé d'avis ?* Have you changed your mind?
Jamais ! Never! *

...changer

2. to change
je dois changer de vêtements, ceux-ci sont mouillés I have to change my clothes – these are wet

II. *v i*
to change

oh, que les Dupondt ont changé ! golly, how the Thompsons have changed!

III. *v pr*
to change

un instant, je me change et je suis prête one moment, I'll change (my clothes) and I'll be ready

► **changement**
[ʃɑ̃ʒmɑ̃] *n m*
change

la radio a annoncé un changement de temps the radio's announced a change in the weather

chanter

chanter
[ʃɑ̃te]
I. *vi*
to sing

* *Wou-ou-oou-ouh-woouu!* Woow-wooow-ow-ow-ow-ooow!
Milou chante avec la Castafiore. Snowy is singing with Signora Castafiore. *

la Castafiore chante juste Signora Castafiore sings in tune

Milou chante avec la Castafiore.

tu chantes faux you sing out of tune

II. *vt*
to sing

elle chante toujours le même air! she always sings the same tune!

► **chanson**
[ʃɑ̃sɔ̃] *nf*
song

j'ai oublié les paroles de cette chanson I've

...chanter

forgotten the words of this song

► **chant**
[ʃɑ̃] *nm*
song

le chant des oiseaux the song of the birds

► **chanteur, euse**
[ʃɑ̃tœr, øz] *n*
singer

c'est une chanteuse connue she's a famous singer

chapeau

chapeau
[ʃapo] *nm*
pl chapeaux
hat

nos chapeaux sont tout neufs our hats are brand new

chaque

chaque
[ʃak] *adj indéf*
1. each

...chaque

chaque passager de la fusée a un rôle à jouer each passenger in the rocket has a part to play

2. every
je vais à Moulinsart chaque dimanche I go to Marlinspike every Sunday

3. Loc
* *Chaque fois que vous êtes là, il y a une catastrophe!... C'est incroyable!...*

Incroyable!... Whenever you're around, a catastrophe is bound to happen!... It's incredible!... Incredible! *

charcutier

charcutier, ière
[ʃarkytje, ɛr] *n*
pork butcher
(*Am:* delicatessen dealer)

...charcutier

► **charcuterie**
[ʃarkytri] *nf*
1. (cooked) pork meats

manger des charcuteries to eat pork meats

2. pork butcher's (shop)
(*Am:* delicatessen)

charger

charger
[ʃarʒe] *vt*
1. to load

* *Ce sont les dernières?...* Are these the last?...
Non, il faut encore charger ces deux caisses... No, we've still got to load these two crates... *

2. Loc
le bateau est trop chargé the boat is overloaded

chariot

chariot
[ʃarjo] *nm*
trolley (*Am:* cart)

charmant

charmant, e
[ʃarmɑ̃, ɑ̃t] *adj*
charming

c'est un homme charmant he's a charming man

chasser

chasser
[ʃase] *v t*
1. to hunt

* *Tintin va chasser le lion...* Tintin is going to hunt lions... *

2. to chase away
Milou a chassé les bandits Snowy chased the gangsters away

► **chasse**
[ʃas] *n f*
hunting

Tintin va chasser le lion ...

chat

chat, chatte
[ʃa, ʃat] *n*
cat

Milou, laisse le chat tranquille ! Snowy, leave the cat alone!

château

château
[ʃato] *n m*
pl châteaux
castle

...château

Moulinsart est un beau château Marlinspike is a beautiful castle

chaud

chaud, e
[ʃo, ʃod] *adj*
1. hot

* *Milou, l'eau est très chaude, tu vas te brûler !* Snowy, the water's very hot, you're going to scald yourself! *Wouaah !* Wooaah! *

...chaud

2. hot
son front est chaud, il a de la fièvre his forehead is hot, he's running a temperature

3. warm
prenez des vêtements chauds take some warm clothes with you

...chaud

Milou, l'eau est très chaude, tu vas te brûler !
Wouaaah !

► **chaud**
[ʃo] *adv*
hot

j'ai chaud I'm hot

il fait chaud it's hot

chauffer

chauffer
[ʃofe]
I. *v t*
to heat

...chauffer

le feu de la cheminée chauffe la pièce the fire heats the room

II. *v pr*
to warm oneself

venez vous chauffer come and warm yourself

► **chauffage**
[ʃofaʒ] *n m*
heating

chauffage central central heating

chauffeur

chauffeur
[ʃofœr] *n m*
driver

j'ai reconnu le chauffeur de cette voiture I recognized the driver of that car

chaussée

chaussée
[ʃose] *n f*
road (way)

...chaussée

Oh ! La chaussée...
... est glissante ...

* *Oh ! La chaussée...* Oh! The road... *... est glissante...* ... is slippery... *

chaussette

chaussette
[ʃosɛt] *n f*
sock

où sont mes chaussettes ? where are my socks?

chaussure

chaussure
[ʃosyr] *n f*
shoe

une paire de chaussures a pair of shoes

chef

chef
[ʃɛf] *n m*
1. leader

...chef

Le chef de l'expédition.

* *Le chef de l'expédition.* The leader of the expedition. *

2. superior
nous devons d'abord parler à nos chefs ! we must ask our superiors first

chemin

chemin
[ʃəmɛ̃] *n m*
1. path, lane

ce chemin nous conduira au château this path will lead us to the castle

2. way
demandons notre chemin let's ask the way

3. Loc
chemin de fer railway (*Am:* railroad)

cheminée

cheminée
[ʃəmine] *n f*
1. chimney

* *La cheminée de l'« Aurore » est orange.* The "Aurora's" chimney is orange. *

2. fireplace
il a brûlé des papiers dans la cheminée he burnt some papers in the fireplace

La cheminée de l'"Aurore" est orange.

chemise

chemise
[ʃəmiz] *n f*
1. shirt

une chemise blanche a white shirt

2. folder
elle a mis des papiers dans une chemise she put some papers in a folder

chèque

chèque
[ʃɛk] *n m*
cheque (*Am* check)

cher

cher, ère
[ʃɛr] *adj*
1. expensive

...cher

* *Le matériel pour l'expédition sur la Lune a coûté très cher, mais maintenant tout est au point.* The equipment for the Moon expedition was very expensive, but now everything's set. *

2. dear
ah, mon cher Tintin, que je suis heureux de vous revoir ! ah, my dear Tintin, how happy I am to see you again!

chercher

chercher
[ʃɛrʃe] *v t*
1. to look for

* *Où est ma pipe ? Je l'ai cherchée partout.* Where's my pipe? I've looked everywhere for it. *

2. to fetch
Dupond, va chercher ton chapeau Thompson go and fetch your hat

3. to look up
cherche ce mot dans ton dictionnaire look up this word in your dictionary

cheval

cheval
[ʃəval] *n m*
pl chevaux [ʃəvo]
1. horse

* *C'est le cheval du capitaine.* It's the Captain's horse. *

2. Loc
Tintin est à cheval sur une branche Tintin's sitting astride a branch

C'est le cheval du capitaine.

cheveu

cheveu
[ʃəvø] *n m*
pl cheveux
1. hair

il y a un cheveu dans mon assiette there's a hair in my plate

2. hair
ils ont des cheveux longs they have long hair

chèvre

chèvre
[ʃɛvr] *n f*
goat

chez

chez
[ʃe] *prép*
1. at

nous sommes chez lui we're at his place

2. to
* *Allons chez le capitaine !* Let's go to the Captain's! *

aller chez le coiffeur to go to the hairdresser's

3. Loc
chez nous, tous les gens rêvent d'aller à

...chez

Allons chez le capitaine !

La Mecque in our country, everybody dreams of going to Mecca

...chic

2. nice
c'est très chic de votre part it's very nice of you

chic

chic
[ʃik] *adj inv*
1. smart

vous êtes chic dans ce costume you look smart in that suit

chien

chien
[ʃjɛ̃] *n m*
dog

* *Milou, tu es un chien très intelligent !* Snowy, you are a very clever dog! *

...chien

Milou, tu es un chien très intelligent !

...chien

▸ **chienne**
[ʃjɛn] *n f*
bitch

chiffre

chiffre
[ʃifr] *n m*
figure

* *Regarde bien ces chiffres, Milou : 160891...* Look at these figures carefully, Snowy : 160891...

...chiffre

Regarde bien ces chiffres, Milou : 160891...
160 891

Je retourne et ça fait... 168091 !
168 091

Je retourne et ça fait... 168091! I turn them upside down and that makes... 168091 ! *

chirurgien

chirurgien, ienne
[ʃiryrʒjɛ̃, ɛn] *n*
surgeon

le chirurgien les a opérés the surgeon operated on them

chocolat

chocolat
[ʃɔkɔla] *n m*
chocolate

choisir

choisir
[ʃwazir] *v t*
to choose

* *Il faut que je porte ce billet... Il faut que...* I must carry this note... I must...

...choisir

Que va choisir Milou ? Which will Snowy choose? *

▸ **choix**
[ʃwa] *n m*
choice

je n'ai pas le choix I've no choice

...choisir

Il faut que je porte ce billet... Il faut que ...

Que va choisir Milou ?

chômage

chômage
[ʃomaʒ] *n m*
1. unemployment

2. Loc
il est au chômage he's unemployed

▸ **chômeur, euse**
[ʃomœr, øz] *n*
unemployed person

chose

chose
[ʃoz] *n f*
1. thing

à quoi sert cette chose ? what's this thing for?

2. thing
* *Venez, mon cher Tintin, j'ai beaucoup de choses à vous raconter !* Come along, dear Tintin, I've got many things to tell you! *

Venez, mon cher Tintin, j'ai beaucoup de choses à vous raconter!

chou

chou
[ʃu] *n m* (*pl* choux)
cabbage

▸ **chou-fleur**
[ʃuflœr] *n m*
pl choux-fleurs
cauliflower

chouette

chouette
[ʃwɛt] *n f*
owl

chouette

chouette
[ʃwɛt] *adj*
great

* ***Ça marche !... Maintenant ça marche !*** It works!... It works now ! ***Ah, vous êtes vraiment chouette !*** Hey, you're great! *

ciel

ciel
[sjɛl] *n m*
pl cieux [sjø]
sky

cigarette

cigarette
[sigarɛt] *n f*
cigarette

cinéma

cinéma
[sinema] *n m*
1. cinema
(*Am:* movie theater)

* ***J'adore le cinéma... Pas toi, Milou ?...*** I love going to the cinema... Don't you, Snowy?... ***Assis !*** Sit down! ***Chut !*** Sh! *

2. film (*Am:* movie)
une vedette de cinéma a film star

...cinéma

cinq

cinq
[sɛ̃k] *adj num & n m inv*
five

▸ **cinquième**
[sɛ̃kjɛm] *adj num, n m & f*
fifth

▸ **cinquante**
[sɛ̃kɑ̃t] *adj num & n m inv*
fifty

cintre

cintre
[sɛ̃tr] *n m*
coat hanger

mettez votre veste sur un cintre put your jacket on a coat hanger

circulation

circulation
[sirkylasjɔ̃] *n f*
traffic

...circulation

...circulation

* ***Avec cette circulation, nous ne serons jamais à l'aéroport à temps.*** With this traffic, we'll never reach the airport in time. *

cirque

cirque
[sirk] *n m*
circus

cité

cité
[site] *n f*
city

Avignon est une cité médiévale Avignon is a medieval city

citron

citron
[sitrɔ̃] *n m*
lemon

citron pressé fresh lemon juice

clair

clair, e
[klɛr] *adj*
1. bright

une pièce très claire a very bright room

...clair

...clair

2. light
** Le ciel est bleu clair* The sky is light blue. *

3. clear
l'eau de la rivière est claire the river water is clear

4. clear
essayez d'être clairs, nous n'avons rien compris try to be clear, we didn't understand a thing

► **clair**
[klɛr] *adv*
1. light

avec la lune, il fait clair dehors with the moon, it's light outside

2. clearly
on y voit clair we can see clearly

► **clair**
[klɛr] *n m*

au clair de lune in the moonlight

classe

classe
[klas] *n f*
1. form (*Am:* grade)

en quelle classe es-tu ? what form are you in?

2. class
dans ma classe, il y a 20 élèves in my class, there are 20 pupils

3. classroom
les élèves sont dans leur classe the pupils are in their classroom

4. class
un billet de première classe a first-class ticket

classer

classer
[klase]
I. *v t*
1. to file

** Est-ce que je dois classer ces documents ?* Do I have to file these documents?
Oui, et c'est très pressé ! Yes, and it's very urgent! *

2. to grade
on les a classés par taille they've been graded according to size

II. *v pr*
to come

il s'est classé premier he came first

...classer

clé

clé, clef
[kle] *n f*
1. key

** Voyez ce qui est tombé de la poche de l'inconnu : un paquet de cigarettes et une clé.* Look what's fallen out of the stranger's pocket: a packet of cigarettes and a key. *

...clé

2. spanner (*Am:* wrench)
il me faut une clé pour serrer ces boulons I need a spanner to tighten these bolts

client

client, e
[klijɑ̃, ɑ̃t] *n*
1. customer

ce magasin attire beaucoup de clients this shop (*Am:* store) attracts a lot of customers

...client

2. Loc
ce parking est réservé à nos clients this carpark (*Am:* parking lot) is for patrons only

► **clientèle**
[klijɑ̃tɛl] *n f*
customers

avis à la clientèle : le magasin sera fermé demain notice to customers: the shop will be closed tomorrow

clignoter

clignoter
[kliɲɔte] *v i*
to flash

** Là-bas, commandant... Vous voyez ?* There, Sir... Do you see it?
Oui, il y a une lumière qui clignote ! Yes, there's a light flashing! *

climat

climat
[klima] *n m*
climate

ce pays a un climat très froid this country has a very cold climate

clinique

clinique
[klinik] *n f*
clinic

* *Mais que faites-vous ?* What are you doing?
Je vais mieux, je quitte la clinique ! I'm better. I'm leaving the clinic! *

clouer

clouer
[klue] *v t*
to nail

je vais clouer ces planches I'm going to nail these planks together

► **clou**
[klu] *n m*
nail

il me faut un marteau pour enfoncer ce clou I need a hammer to drive this nail in

clown

clown
[klun] *n m*
clown

les clowns ont beaucoup fait rire les enfants the clowns amused the children a lot

club

club
[klœb] *n m*
club

...club

un club sportif a sports club

cochon

cochon
[kɔʃɔ̃] *n m*
1. pig

les cochons sont dans la porcherie the pigs are in the pigsty

2. Loc

...cochon

cochon d'Inde guinea pig

code

code
[kɔd] *n m*
code

le Code de la route the Highway Code

code postal postcode (*Am:* zip code)

cœur

cœur
[kœr] *n m*
1. heart

* *Alors, docteur, vous croyez que...* Well, doctor, do you think that...
Hélas, son cœur bat très faiblement. Alas, his heart is very weak. *

2. heart
nous voici au cœur de la forêt here we are in the heart of the forest

3. Loc

il a bon cœur he's kind-hearted

j'ai mal au cœur I feel sick

coffre

coffre
[kɔfr] *n m*
1. safe

* *Et quelques instants plus tard...* And a few moments later...

...coffre

...Et ce matin, en ouvrant le coffre, voilà ce que j'ai trouvé : de vieux journaux à la place des plans. ...And this morning when I opened the safe, look what I found : old newspapers instead of the plans. *

2. boot (*Am:* trunk)
la roue de secours est dans le coffre the spare wheel is in the boot

cogner

cogner
[kɔɲe]
I. *v i*
to bang

mais qui cogne à la porte comme ça ? but who's banging on the door like that?

II. *v pr*
to knock, to bang

aïe, je me suis cogné la tête ouch, I knocked my head

coiffeur

coiffeur, euse
[kwafœr, øz] *n*
hairdresser

coin

coin
[kwɛ̃] *n m*
1. corner

le coin de la page est plié the corner of the page is folded

...coin

2. spot
leur village est un petit coin charmant their village is a nice little spot

3. corner
* *Il ne va quand même pas surgir comme ça au coin de la rue...* He's not going to pop up at the street corner like that... *

tu n'es pas sage, va au coin ! you won't behave: go and stand in the corner!

colère

colère
[kɔlɛr] *n f*
1. anger

il a dit ça sous le coup de la colère he said that in anger

2. rage
* *Mille sabords !* Blistering barnacles!
Il s'est mis dans une colère terrible. He flew into a terrible rage. *

...colère

Il s'est mis dans une colère terrible.

colis

colis
[kɔli] *n m*
parcel (*Am:* package)

* *J'ai une lettre et un colis recommandés à remettre à monsieur Hornet...* I've got to deliver a registered letter and a parcel to Doctor Midge...
C'est bon... Entrez... All right... Come in... *

collant

collant
[kɔlɑ̃] *n m*
1. tights

mon collant a filé I've got a ladder (*Am:* run) in my tights

2. leotard
les danseurs portent des collants dancers wear leotards

collectionner

collectionner
[kɔlɛksjɔne] *v t*
to collect

je collectionne les timbres I collect stamps

▶ **collection**
[kɔlɛksjɔ̃] *n f*
collection

* *C'est un papillon pour sa collection.* It's a butterfly for his collection. *

C'est un papillon pour sa collection.

collège

collège
[kɔlɛʒ] *n m*
1. secondary (*Am:* high) school
2. Loc
collège technique technical college (*Am:* technical school)

colline

colline
[kɔlin] *n f*
hill

...colline

le monument est en haut de la colline the monument is at the top of the hill

collision

collision
[kɔlizjɔ̃] *n f*
collision

comment éviter la collision ? how can we avoid a collision?

combien

combien
[kɔ̃bjɛ̃] *adv interr*

1. how much
combien coûte ce sac? how much does this bag cost?

* *Allô, allô, ici la Terre. Combien d'oxygène vous reste-t-il? Répondez...* Hello, hello, this is ground control. How much oxygen have you got left? Answer...

Presque plus! Hardly any! *

2. how many
combien de fois l'avez-vous vu? how many times did you see him?

comédie

comédie
[kɔmedi] *n f*
1. comedy

je préfère la comédie à la tragédie I prefer comedy to tragedy

2. Loc
il n'a pas mal, il joue la comédie it doesn't hurt, he's just pretending

comique

comique
[kɔmik] *adj*
1. funny

* *Je proteste énergiquement...* I protest vigorously...
Voici les suspects, Monsieur le Directeur... Here are the suspects, Sir...
Ce qu'ils sont comiques habillés ainsi! Aren't they funny dressed like that! *

2. comic
film comique
comic film

commander

commander
[kɔmɑ̃de] *v t*
1. to command

il commande la police he commands the police

2. to order
commandons un bon repas let's order a good meal

► **commande**
[kɔmɑ̃d] *n f*
1. order

le serveur a pris notre commande the waiter took our order

2. control
* *Il faut absolument que j'arrive aux commandes.* I must reach the controls. *

comme

comme
[kɔm]
I. *conj*

1. like

de grands policiers comme eux ne peuvent se tromper great detectives like them can't be mistaken

2. as
tout se passera comme je l'ai dit everything will happen as I told you

3. as
il te regarde comme s'il te connaissait he's looking at you as if he knew you

4. since, as
comme il y a eu une tempête de sable, je l'ai perdu de vue since there was a sandstorm, I lost sight of him

II. *adv*

* *Je vais l'attacher. Comme ça, il se tiendra tranquille!* I'll tie him up. That way he'll keep quiet! *

commencer

commencer
[kɔmɑ̃se]
I. *vt*
to begin

le professeur a commencé ses travaux il y a plusieurs mois the Professor began his research several months ago

II. *vi*
1. to start

il commence à neiger it's starting to snow

2. to begin
la nouvelle année commence le 1er janvier the new year begins on January 1st

► **commencement**
[kɔmɑ̃smɑ̃] *n m*
beginning

* ***Oui, c'est une affaire très compliquée...*** Yes, it's a very complicated case...
Je vous écoute, expliquez-moi tout, mais commencez par le commencement. I'm listening, explain everything to me, but begin at the beginning. *

comment

comment
[kɔmɑ̃] *adv interr*
1. how

mais comment faites-vous pour tomber à chaque fois ? but how do you manage to fall down every time?

* ***Bonjour, capitaine!*** Good morning, Captain !
Ah ! Bonjour, Tintin, comment allez-vous ? Oh, good morning, Tintin, how are you? *

2. Loc
comment t'appelles-tu ? what's your name?

comment ? je n'ai pas entendu, vous pouvez répéter ? I beg your pardon? I didn't hear you, could you repeat what you said?

commerce

commerce
[kɔmɛrs] *n m*
1. trade

le commerce avec le Nuevo-Rico est en pleine expansion et nous espérons doubler notre chiffre d'affaires trade with Nuevo-Rico is booming and we hope to double our turnover

2. shop (*Am:* store)
ses parents tiennent un commerce his parents run a shop

► **commerçant, e**
[kɔmɛrsɑ̃, ɑ̃t] *n*
shopkeeper (*Am:* storekeeper)

commissariat

commissariat
[kɔmisarja] *n m*
police station

commission

commission
[kɔmisjɔ̃] *n f*
message

* ***Ah, il n'est pas là ? Pouvez-vous lui faire une commission ?*** Oh, he isn't in? Could you give him a message? *

► **commissions**
[kɔmisjɔ̃] *n f pl*
shopping

faire les commissions to go shopping

communication

communication
[kɔmynikasjɔ̃] *n f*
(telephone) call

compagnie

compagnie
[kɔ̃paɲi] *n f*
company

heureusement que Milou nous tient compagnie it's a good thing Snowy is keeping us company

compartiment

compartiment
[kɔ̃partimɑ̃] *n m*
compartment

* ***Malédiction, Tintin n'est plus dans le compartiment !*** Drat, Tintin's no longer in the compartment!
Où est-il passé ? Where has he gone? *

compétition

compétition
[kɔ̃petisjɔ̃] *n f*
competition

va-t-il participer à la compétition ? is he going to enter the competition?

complet

complet, ète
[kɔ̃plɛ, ɛt] *adj*
1. complete

...complet

le jeu d'échecs n'est pas complet, il manque une pièce the chess set isn't complete, there is a piece missing

2. full
le bus est complet, nous ne pouvons pas monter the bus is full, we can't get in

▸ **complètement**
[kɔ̃plɛtmɑ̃] *adv*
completely

ma parole, ils sont complètement fous ! upon my word, they're completely mad!

compliment

compliment
[kɔ̃plimɑ̃] *n m*
compliment

* *Mes compliments, madame !* My compliments, Madam!

...compliment

Irma, débarrassez le colonel de son manteau. Irma, will you help the colonel off with his coat. *

faire des compliments à quelqu'un to pay somebody compliments

compliqué

compliqué, e
[kɔ̃plike] *adj*
complicated

c'est vraiment trop compliqué, je ne comprends rien it's really too complicated, I don't understand anything

composer

composer
[kɔ̃poze] *v t*
1. to compose

qui a composé cette musique ? who composed this music?

2. to dial
* *Non, madame, ce n'est pas la boucherie Sanzot ! Vous avez composé un mauvais numéro...* No, Madam, it's not Mr Cutts the butcher! You've dialled (*Am:* dialed) the wrong number! *

composter

composter
[kɔ̃pɔste] *v t*
to punch

composter un billet de train to punch a train ticket

comprendre

comprendre
[kɔ̃prɑ̃dr] *v t*
to understand

* *Je ne comprends pas votre langue...* I don't understand your language... *

je ne comprends pas les Dupondt, où vont-ils chercher des idées pareilles ? I don't understand the Thompsons, where do they get such ideas?

...comprendre

comprimé

comprimé
[kɔ̃prime] *n m*
tablet

* *C'est l'heure de prendre nos comprimés...* It's time to take our tablets...
Hop ! There !
Hop ! There ! *

compris

compris, e
[kɔ̃pri, iz] *adj*
1. including

j'ai cherché partout, y compris dans la chambre I searched everywhere, including the bedroom

2. included
service compris service included

service non compris service not included

compter

compter
[kɔ̃te]
I. *vt*
to count

* *Dans la prison...* In prison...
J'ai compté les jours, il n'en reste plus que deux. I've counted the days, there are only two left. *

II. *vi*
to count up

Dans la prison...
J'ai compté les jours, il n'en reste plus que deux.

sais-tu compter jusqu'à cent ? can you count up to a hundred?

III. *vt ind*
to count

soyez tranquilles, vous pouvez compter sur Tintin don't worry, you can count on Tintin

► **compte**
[kɔ̃t] *nm*
1. total

dix plus dix égale vingt, le compte est bon ten plus ten is twenty – the total is right

2. Loc
compte à rebours countdown

tenir compte de quelque chose to take something into account

comptoir

comptoir
[kɔ̃twar] *nm*
counter

elle a laissé l'argent sur le comptoir she left the money on the counter

concert

concert
[kɔ̃sɛr] *nm*
concert

concierge

concierge
[kɔ̃sjɛrʒ] *n*
caretaker (*Am:* janitor)

* *Rue de Londres...* London Street...
Pardon, madame, êtes-vous la concierge ? Je cherche M. Balthazar. Excuse me, Madam, are you the caretaker ? I'm looking for Mr Balthazar. *

Rue de Londres...
Pardon, madame, êtes-vous la concierge ? Je cherche M. Balthazar.

concombre

concombre
[kɔ̃kɔ̃br] *nm*
cucumber

condamner

condamner
[kɔ̃dane] *vt*
to sentence

* *Clac.* Thwack.
Ils l'ont condamné à mort. They have sentenced him to death. *

...condamner

CLAC
Ils l'ont condamné à mort.

conduire

conduire
[kɔ̃dɥir]
I. *vt*
1. to drive

c'est l'homme qui conduisait la voiture marron it's the man who was driving the brown car

2. to take
* *Pouvez-vous me conduire à l'aéroport ?* Could you take me to the airport?
Oui, montez... Yes, get in... *

...conduire

Pouvez-vous me conduire à l'aéroport ?
Oui, montez...

II. *vpr*
to behave

il se conduit bien/mal he's behaving well/badly

► **conducteur, trice**
[kɔ̃dyktœr, tris] *n*
driver

confiance

confiance
[kɔ̃fjɑ̃s] *nf*
confidence

j'ai toute confiance en lui I've complete confidence in him

confiserie

confiserie
[kɔ̃fizri] *nf*
sweets (*Am:* candy)

tu manges trop de confiseries you eat too many sweets

confiture

confiture
[kɔ̃fityr] *nf*
jam

...confiture

confiture de fraises strawberry jam

confort

confort
[kɔ̃fɔr] *nm*
comfort

le capitaine aime le confort the Captain likes his comfort

...confort

▶ **confortable**
[kɔ̃fɔrtabl] *adj*
comfortable

* *Ils sont conforta-bles, vos fauteuils... Moi, j'aime mieux le moderne, mais je re-connais que c'est bien !* Your armchairs are comfortable... I personally prefer modern design but I admit these are nice! *

congé

congé
[kɔ̃ʒe] *n m*
leave

être en congé to be on leave

congélateur

congélateur
[kɔ̃ʒelatœr] *n m*
freezer, deep freeze

connaître

connaître
[kɔnɛtr] *v t*
1. to know

connaissez-vous le professeur Tournesol ? do you know Professor Calculus?

2. to know
* *Tu es sûr que tu connais le chemin, Zorrino ?* Are you sure you know the way, Zorrino? *Oui, Tintin, c'est par là.* Yes, Tintin, it's this way. *

...connaître

▶ **connaissance**
[kɔnɛsɑ̃s] *n f*
1. knowledge

le professeur a une bonne connaissance de l'astronautique Calculus has a good knowledge of space travel

2. acquaintance
j'ai fait de nouvelles connaissances I made new acquaintances

3. Loc
faire la connaissance de quelqu'un to meet somebody

conseiller

conseiller
[kɔ̃seje] *v t*
to advise

je vous avais conseillé d'attendre I'd advised you to wait

...conseiller

▶ **conseil**
[kɔ̃sɛj] *n m*
advice

* *Suivez mon conseil, partez !* Take my advice and leave! *

conséquence

conséquence
[kɔ̃sekɑ̃s] *n f*
consequence

...conséquence

et voilà la conséquence de votre étourderie ! now you see the consequence of your absent-mindedness!

conserver

conserver
[kɔ̃sɛrve] *v t*
1. to keep

* *Ma famille a conservé dans ce vieux coffre tout ce qui appartenait au chevalier de Hadoque...* My family has kept in this old chest everything that belonged to Sir Francis Haddock... *

...conserver

2. to preserve
le château est bien conservé the castle is well preserved

▶ **conserve**
[kɔ̃sɛrv] *n f*

petits pois en conserve tinned (*Am:* canned) peas

▶ **conserves**
[kɔ̃sɛrv] *n f pl*
tinned (*Am:* canned) food

consigne

consigne
[kɔ̃siɲ] *n f*
left-luggage office (*Am:* baggage check-room)

ma valise est à la consigne my suitcase is in the left-luggage office

construire

construire
[kɔ̃strɥir] *vt*
to build

* *Tonnerre de Brest ! Je ne rêve pas !... Ce sont mes ancêtres qui ont construit ce château !* Thundering typhoons! I'm not dreaming!... My ancestors built this castle! *

Tonnerre de Brest ! Je ne rêve pas !... Ce sont mes ancêtres qui ont construit ce château !

► **construction**
[kɔ̃stryksjɔ̃] *nf*
building

la construction du palais a pris des années the building of the palace took years

vous ne pouvez pas vous tromper, c'est la construction blanche après l'église you can't mistake it, it's the white building after the church

consulat

consulat
[kɔ̃syla] *nm*
consulate

consulter

consulter
[kɔ̃sylte] *vt*

1. to consult

* *Avez-vous remarqué comme il a l'air fatigué ? Son état est inquiétant.* Have you noticed how tired he looks? His condition is worrying.
Il faut peut-être consulter un médecin. Perhaps we should consult a doctor. *

2. to look up
non, je ne sais pas ce que ça veut dire, consulte le dictionnaire no, I don't know what it means, look it up in the dictionary

Avez-vous remarqué comme il a l'air fatigué ? Son état est inquiétant.
Il faut peut-être consulter un médecin.

contacter

contacter
[kɔ̃takte] *vt*
to get in touch with

je n'ai pas pu les contacter I couldn't get in touch with them

contenir

contenir
[kɔ̃tnir] *vt*
to contain

* *Le coffret ne contient que de vieux documents !* The casket only contains old documents!
De vieux documents ?... C'était bien la peine de se donner tant de mal ! Old documents?... It was a waste of time going to so much trouble! *

Le coffret ne contient que de vieux documents !
De vieux documents ?... C'était bien la peine de se donner tant de mal !

content

content, e
[kɔ̃tɑ̃, ɑ̃t] *adj*
pleased, glad, happy

j'étais sûr que vous seriez content de venir avec nous I knew you'd be pleased to come with us

je serais content que vous veniez vous installer à Moulinsart I'd be glad if you came and lived in Marlinspike

* *Victoire !...* Hurray!... *Le capitaine et les savants ont l'air très content.* The Captain and the scientists look very happy. *

Victoire !...

Le capitaine et les savants ont l'air très content.

continuer

continuer
[kɔ̃tinɥe] *vi*
1. to go on

...continuer

si ça continue comme ça, je pars if it goes on like this, I'm leaving

2. to carry on
je suis trop fatigué, continuez sans moi I'm too tired, carry on without me

3. to keep
* *Dépêchez-vous, ils arrivent !* Quick, they're coming!
Continuez à courir... Vite ! Keep running... Quick! *

contre

contre
[kɔ̃tr]
I. *prép*
1. against

appuyez l'échelle contre le mur lean the ladder against the wall

2. for
je t'échange ce disque contre une cassette I'll swap this record with you for a cassette

II. *adv*
against it

ah, non, je suis tout à fait contre ! no, no, I'm completely against it!

contrôler

contrôler
[kɔ̃trole] *v t*
1. to inspect

* *Nous voudrions contrôler vos papiers.* We would like to inspect your papers. *

...contrôler

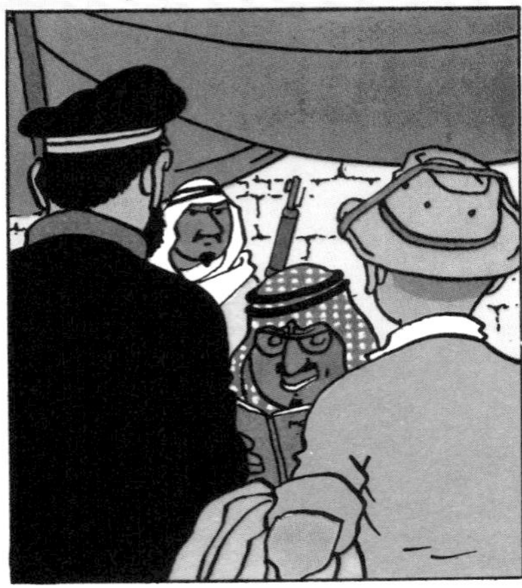

2. to check
il faut que je contrôle ce circuit électrique I must check this electrical circuit

► **contrôle**
[kɔ̃trol] *n m*
1. checking

contrôle des résultats checking of results

2. control
le conducteur a perdu le contrôle de la voiture the driver lost control of the car

convenir

convenir
[kɔ̃vnir] *v t ind*
to suit

si cela convient à tout le monde if it suits everybody

copain

copain, copine
[kɔpɛ̃, in] *n*
pal, mate (*Am:* buddy)

coq

coq
[kɔk] *n m*
cock (*Am:* rooster)

coquillage

coquillage
[kɔkijaʒ] *n m*
1. seashell

nous avons ramassé des coquillages sur la plage we picked up seashells on the beach

2. shellfish
manger des coquillages to eat shellfish

corde

corde
[kɔrd] *n f*
rope

tenez bon la corde ! hold the rope tight!

cordonnier

cordonnier
[kɔrdɔnje] *n m*
cobbler (*Am:* shoe repairer)

...cordonnier

► **cordonnerie**
[kɔrdɔnri] *n f*
cobbler's (*Am:* shoe repair store)

corps

corps
[kɔr] *n m*
body

* *Mon Dieu ! Son corps est glacé... Vite, dégageons-le !...*

...corps

Oh no! His body is frozen... Quick, let's free him!... *

correct

correct, e
[kɔrɛkt] *adj*
correct

tous mes calculs sont corrects all my calculations are correct

...correct

► **correctement**
[kɔrɛktəmɑ̃] *adv*
correctly

écris-le correctement spell it correctly

correction

correction
→ CORRIGER

correspondant

correspondant, e
[kɔrɛspɔ̃dɑ̃, ɑ̃t] *n*
pen friend (*Am:* pen pal)

mon correspondant anglais habite à Leicester my English pen friend lives in Leicester

► **correspondance**
[kɔrɛspɔ̃dɑ̃s] *n f*
1. correspondence

ma secrétaire s'occupe de ma correspondance my secretary deals with my correspondence

2. connection (*Am:* transfer)
j'ai manqué la correspondance I missed the connection

corriger

corriger
[kɔriʒe] *v t*
1. to correct

...corriger

tu as fait beaucoup de fautes, il faut les corriger you have made a lot of mistakes, you must correct them

2. to thrash
si tu n'obéis pas, je vais te corriger if you don't obey, I'm going to thrash you

► **correction**
[kɔrɛksjɔ̃] *n f*
1. correction

Allô... Compris... Mais je dois d'abord faire quelques corrections de trajectoire.

...corriger

* *Allô... Compris... Mais je dois d'abord faire quelques corrections de trajectoire.* Hello... Roger... But, first I have to make some corrections to the trajectory. *

2. thrashing
si tu n'arrêtes pas, tu vas recevoir une bonne correction if you don't stop, you'll get a good thrashing

costume

costume
[kɔstym] *n m*
suit

je dois acheter un nouveau costume I have to buy a new suit

côte

côte
[kot] *n f*
1. rib

...côte

je crois que j'ai une côte cassée I think I have a broken rib

2. slope
je me demande si je vais pouvoir monter la côte I wonder if I'll be able to get up the slope

3. coast
* *A Kiltoch, la côte est rocheuse.* In Kiltoch, the coast is rocky. *

4. Loc
côte à côte side by side

KI5

A Kiltoch, la côte est rocheuse.

côté

côté
[kote] *n m*
1. side

il a une douleur dans le côté droit he has a pain in his right side

2. side
* *Attention ! Tirez la manette qui est du côté gauche ! Cinq ! Quatre ! Trois ! Deux ! Un... Zéro !* Careful! Pull the lever on the left-hand side! Five! Four! Three! Two! One... Zero! *

Attention ! Tirez la manette qui est du côté gauche ! Cinq ! Quatre ! Trois ! Deux ! Un... Zéro !

► **à côté de**
[akotedə] *prép*
next to

Dupont est assis à côté de Dupond Thomson is sitting next to Thompson

coton

coton
[kɔtɔ̃] *n m*
cotton

coucher

coucher
[kuʃe]
I. *v i*
to sleep

vous coucherez dans la chambre à côté you'll sleep in the next room

II. *v pr*
to go to bed

ils étaient fatigués, ils sont allés se coucher they were tired: they went to bed

couchette

Sapristi ! Il y a quelqu'un dans cette couchette !...

couchette

couchette
[kuʃɛt] *n f*
1. bunk, sleeping berth

* *Sapristi ! Il y a quelqu'un dans cette couchette !...* Great snakes! There's someone in that bunk! *

2. couchette
il n'y a pas de couchettes dans ce train there are no couchettes on this train

coudre

coudre
[kudr] *v t*
1. to sew

Irma, avez-vous cousu ma robe ? Irma, have you sewn my dress?

2. Loc
machine à coudre sewing machine

couleur

couleur
[kulœr] *n f*
colour (*Am:* color)

quelle est ta couleur préférée ? – le rouge what is your favourite colour? – red

couloir

couloir
[kulwar] *n m*
corridor

* *Mais... je vois quelqu'un au fond du couloir...* Hey... I can see someone at the end of the corridor... *

coup

coup
[ku] *n m*
1. blow

il lui a donné un coup sur la tête he gave him a blow on the head

2. Loc
un coup de pied a kick

un coup de poing a punch

un coup de sonnette a ring at the door

un coup de téléphone a phone call

un coup de feu a shot

prendre un coup de soleil to get sunburnt

couper

couper
[kupe]
I. *v t*
to cut

* *Qu'allez-vous faire ?* What are you going to do?
Je vais leur couper la barbe... I'm going to cut their beards... *

II. *v pr*
to cut oneself

aïe, je me suis coupé ouch, I cut myself

elle s'est coupé le doigt she has cut her finger

cour

cour
[kur] *n f*
1. courtyard

2. Loc
cour de récréation playground

courage

courage
[kuraʒ] *n m*
1. courage

* *Allez au diable ! Et ne revenez pas !* Go to the devil! And don't come back!
Il fallait du courage pour les mettre en fuite tout seul. It took courage to chase them away on your own. *

2. heart
perdre courage to lose heart

► **courageux, euse**
[kuraʒø, øz] *adj*
brave

le capitaine est un homme courageux the Captain is a brave man

courir

courir
[kurir] *v i*
1. to run

il court plus vite que moi he runs faster than I do

2. Loc
courir un grand danger to be in great danger

courrier

courrier
[kurje] *n m*
post (*Am:* mail)

* *Vous m'avez appelé, mon général ?* Did you call for me, Sir?

...courrier

Vous m'avez appelé, mon général ?
Oui, c'est tout ce qu'il y a eu comme courrier ce matin ?

Oui, c'est tout ce qu'il y a eu comme courrier ce matin ? Yes, is this all the post that came this morning? *

cours

cours
[kur] *n m*
1. lesson

c'est l'heure de mon cours d'anglais it's time for my English lesson

...cours

2. rate
le cours officiel de la livre sterling the official rate of the pound

3. Loc
cours d'eau stream

au cours de in the course of, during

au cours de sa vie in the course of his life

course

course
[kurs] *n f*
race

qui a gagné la course ? who won the race?

► **courses**
[kurs] *n f pl*
shopping

faire des courses to go shopping

court

court, e
[kur, kurt] *adj*
short

* *Zut, la corde est trop courte, je ne peux atteindre le fond !...* Darn, the rope is too short – I can't reach the bottom!... *

...court

Zut, la corde est trop courte, je ne peux pas atteindre le fond !...

cousin

cousin, e
[kuzɛ̃, in] *n*
cousin

coussin

coussin
[kusɛ̃] *n m*
cushion

couteau

couteau
[kuto] *n m*
pl couteaux
knife

attention, il a peut-être un couteau careful, he might have a knife

coûter

coûter
[kute] *v i & v t*
1. to cost

...coûter

Combien ?
Cela coûte deux cents francs...

* *Combien ?* How much?
Cela coûte deux cents francs... It costs two hundred francs... *

2. Loc
cela coûte cher it's expensive

cela ne coûte pas cher it's cheap

couture

couture
[kutyr] *n f*
1. sewing

Irma aime la couture Irma likes sewing

2. seam
cette couture est mal faite this seam is badly done

couvert

couvert
[kuvɛr] *n m*
Loc
mettre le couvert to lay the table

une table de six couverts a table set for six

couvrir

couvrir
[kuvrir]
I. *v t*
to cover

...couvrir

je vais te couvrir avec ce drap, personne ne te verra I'll cover you with this sheet, nobody will see you

* *La montagne est couverte de neige...* The mountain is covered with snow... *

II. *v pr*
to wrap oneself up

il fait froid, couvre-toi bien it's very cold, wrap yourself up well

La montagne est couverte de neige ...

► **couvert, e**
[kuvɛr, ɛrt] *adj*
overcast

le ciel est couvert the sky is overcast

► **couverture**
[kuvɛrtyr] *n f*
1. blanket

il risque de faire froid, prenez des couvertures it might get cold, take some blankets with you

...couvrir

2. cover
la couverture du livre est abîmée the cover of the book is damaged

crabe

crabe
[krab] *n m*
crab

* *Oh ! un crabe te pince le pied !* Oh! there's a crab nipping your foot! *Aïe !* Ouch! *

cravate

cravate
[kravat] *n f*
tie

cette cravate ne va pas avec votre costume that tie doesn't go with your suit

crayon

crayon
[krɛjɔ̃] *n m*
pencil

crème

crème
[krɛm] *n f*
1. cream

mets un peu de crème sur tes fraises put some cream on your strawberries

crème au chocolat chocolate cream

2. cream
mets un peu de crème sur ton visage, sinon tu auras un coup de soleil put

...crème

some cream on your face, or you'll get sunburnt

crêpe

crêpe
[krɛp] *n f*
pancake

► **crêperie**
[krɛpri] *n f*
pancake shop

crever

crever
[krəve]
I. *v t*

un clou a crevé le pneu a nail punctured the tyre (*Am:* tire)

II. *v i*
to have a puncture (*Am:* a flat tire)

* *Il ne faudrait pas que nous crevions !* We'd better not get a puncture! *

► **crevaison**
[krəvɛzɔ̃] *n f*
puncture (*Am:* flat tire)

crevette

crevette
[krəvɛt] *n f*
shrimp

crier

crier
[krije] *v i*
1. to shout

* *Ohé !... Dupont !...* Hey!... Thomson!...
J'ai beau crier, ils ne m'entendent pas !... However loud I shout, they can't hear me!... *

2. to scream
il crie de douleur he's screaming with pain

► **cri**
[kri] *n m*
1. shout

* *Hawaaouuh !* Hawaaouuh!
Avez-vous entendu ces cris ? Est-ce le yéti ? Did you hear those shouts? Is it the Yeti? *

2. scream
pousser un cri to let out a scream

crise

crise
[kriz] *n f*
1. crisis

crise économique economic cris

2. attack
avoir une cris d'appendicite t have an attack appendicitis

critiquer

critiquer
[critike] *vt*
to criticize

capitaine, cessez de critiquer les Dupondt! Captain, stop criticizing the Thompsons!

▸ **critique**
[kritik] *nf*
criticism

ils sont blessés par vos critiques they're hurt by your criticisms

croire

croire
[krwar]
I. *vt*
1. to believe

oui, Milou, je te crois, c'est le chat qui a commencé yes, Snowy, I believe you, it's the cat that started it

2. to think
* *Je crois que c'est Tournesol que j'aperçois là-bas...* I think it's Calculus I can see over there... *

II. *vi*
to believe
ils croient en Dieu
they believe in God

croissant

croissant
[krwasɑ̃] *nm*
1. crescent

* *Ce soir, la lune n'est qu'un croissant...* Tonight the moon is only a crescent... *

2. croissant
Tintin mange des croissants au petit déjeuner Tintin has croissants for breakfast

...croissant

Ce soir, la lune n'est qu'un croissant...

croix

croix
[krwa] *nf*
cross

* *Quelle belle croix!*
What a lovely cross! *

croquer

croquer
[krɔke] *vt*
to crunch

croquer une pomme
to crunch an apple

...croquer

▸ **croque-monsieur**
[krɔkmøsjø] *nm inv*
toasted ham and cheese sandwich

cru

cru, e
[kry] *adj*
raw

* *Milou aime la viande crue, mais il préfére le poulet!* Snowy likes

...cru

Milou aime la viande crue, mais il préfère le poulet!

raw meat, but he prefers chicken! *

▸ **crudités**
[krydite] *nfpl*
assorted raw vegetables

cueillir

cueillir
[kœjir] *vt*
to pick

...cueillir

allons cueillir des fruits let's go and pick some fruit

► **cueillette**
[kœjɛt] *n f*
picking

cuillère

cuillère, cuiller
[kɥijɛr] *n f*
spoon

cuir

cuir
[kɥir] *n m*
leather

cuire

cuire
[kɥir] *v t*
1. to cook

* *Que faites-vous ?* What are you doing ? *Je vais allumer le camping-gaz pour cuire le porridge.* I'm going to light the camping stove to cook the porridge. *

2. Loc
viande trop cuite overdone meat

viande pas assez cuite underdone meat

cuisine

cuisine
[kɥizin] *n f*
1. kitchen

il est entré dans la cuisine he went into the kitchen

2. Loc
faire la cuisine to cook

► **cuisiner**
[kɥizine] *v t*
to cook

ma mère cuisine bien my mother cooks well

► **cuisiné, e**
[kɥizine] *adj*
Loc
plats cuisinés ready-cooked dishes

► **cuisinier, ère**
[kɥizinje, ɛr] *n*
cook

sa femme est une bonne cuisinière his wife is a good cook

► **cuisinière**
[kɥizinjɛr] *n f*
cooker (*Am:* stove)

une cuisinière électrique/à gaz an electric/a gas cooker

cultiver

cultiver
[kyltive] *v t*
1. to grow

ici, on cultive le blé here, they grow wheat

2. Loc
elle est très cultivée she is highly cultured

► **culture**
[kyltyr] *n f*
growing

la culture du blé wheat growing

curieux

curieux, euse
[kyrjø, øz] *adj*

1. inquisitive, curious

* *Vous êtes trop curieux, tant pis pour vous !* You're too inquisitive, too bad for you! *

2. curious
c'est curieux, je n'ai pas remarqué cette maison hier it's curious, I didn't notice that house yesterday

► **curiosité**
[kyrjozite] *n f*
1. inquisitiveness, curiosity

Milou, ta curiosité te jouera un mauvais tour ! Snowy, your inquisitiveness will get you into trouble!

2. curiosity
* *Tous ces objets sont des curiosités.* All these objects are curiosities. *

Tous ces objets sont des curiosités.

cyclisme

cyclisme
[siklism] *n m*
cycling

faire du cyclisme to go cycling

► **cycliste**
[siklist] *n*
cyclist

danger

danger
[dɑ̃ʒe] *n m*
1. danger

Tournesol est en danger Calculus is in danger

il est maintenant hors de danger he's out of danger now

2. Loc
en cas de danger, tirez la poignée in an emergency, pull the handle

► **dangereux, euse**
[dɑ̃ʒərø, øz] *adj*
dangerous

non, Tintin, n'y allez pas, c'est dangereux ! no, Tintin, don't go, it's dangerous!

ce chien est fou furieux, il est dangereux ! that dog is mad, it's dangerous!

dans

dans
[dɑ̃] *prép*
1. in

* *Est-il dans sa chambre ?* Is he in his bedroom?
Oui, il est là... Yes, he is... *

2. into
venez, entrons dans la maison come on, let's go into the house

3. in
le capitaine sera là dans une heure the Captain will be back in an hour

danser

danser
[dɑ̃se] *v i*
to dance

* *Venez danser avec moi !...* Come and dance with me!... *

...danser

► **danse**
[dɑ̃s] *n f*
dance

quelle est cette nouvelle danse ? what is this new dance?

date

date
[dat] *n f*
date

...date

* *Une date est écrite sur le parchemin !* There's a date written on the parchment! *

► **dater**
[date]
I. *v t*
to date

il n'a pas daté la lettre he didn't date the letter

II. *v t ind*
to date from

...date

ce temple date du onzième siècle this temple dates from the eleventh century

de

de, des, du
[də, de, dy] *prép*
(Note : de + le = du ; de + les = des)
1. of
le roi de Syldavie the king of Syldavia

...de

2. 's, *pl* '
le pelage de Milou Snowy's coat

les chapeaux des Dupondt the Thompsons' hats

3. from
c'est un télégramme de Tintin it's a telegram from Tintin

4. by
un livre du professeur Calys a book by Professor Phostle

Milou est le chien le plus fort du monde !

5. of
une tasse de café a cup of coffee

6. in
* *Milou est le chien le plus fort du monde !* Snowy is the strongest dog in the world! *

débarquer

débarquer
[debarke] *v i*
to land

...débarquer

Nous débarquerons les uns après les autres...
D'accord !... Les plus jeunes d'abord...

* *Nous débarquerons les uns après les autres...* We'll land one after the other... *D'accord !... Les plus jeunes d'abord...* OK!... The youngest first... *

débarrasser

débarrasser
[debarase] *v t*
to clear

...débarrasser

je vais débarrasser la table I'll clear the table

▸ **débarras**
[debara] *n m*
1. lumber room (*Am:* storeroom)
les valises sont dans le débarras the suitcases are in the lumber room

2. Loc
enfin, les Lampion s'en vont, bon débarras ! the Waggs are leaving at last, good riddance!

debout

debout
[dəbu] *adv*
1. standing

il y a beaucoup de gens debout devant la maison there are a lot of people standing in front of the house

2. Loc
allons, debout, le soleil brille ! come on, get up, the sun's shining!

début

début
[deby] *n m*
1. beginning

je n'ai pas entendu le début de votre phrase I didn't hear the beginning of your sentence

2. Loc
au début, je ne voulais pas la croire at first, I didn't want to believe her

décembre

décembre
[desɑ̃br] *n m*
December

le premier/deux décembre the first/second of December (*Am:* December first/second)

venez le 6 décembre come on the 6th of December (*Am:* on December 6)

décevoir

décevoir
[desvwar] *v t*
to disappoint

capitaine, vous me décevez ! Captain, you disappoint me!

▸ **déçu, e**
[desy] *adj*
disappointed

tu as l'air déçu you look disappointed

déchirer

déchirer
[deʃire] *v t*
to tear

* *Ah, mais bravo ! Votre machine a déchiré mon costume !* Well done! Your machine tore my suit! *

Ah, mais bravo ! Votre machine a déchiré mon costume !

décider

décider
[deside]
I. *v t*
to decide

j'ai décidé de rester à la maison I've decided to stay at home

II. *v pr*
to make up one's mind

* ***Alors, Dupont, tu te décides, oui ou non ?*** Well, Thomson, are you going to make up your mind or not? *

▸ **décision**
[desizjɔ̃] *n f*
decision

a-t-il pris sa décision ? has he made his decision?

déclarer

déclarer
[deklare] *v t*
1. to claim

...déclarer

il a déclaré qu'il était innocent he claimed he was innocent

2. to declare
* ***La guerre est déclarée !... La guerre est déclarée !*** War has been declared!... War has been declared! *

▸ **déclaration**
[deklarasjɔ̃] *n f*
1. statement

...déclarer

l'émir va faire une déclaration à la presse the Emir is going to make a statement to the press

2. declaration
déclaration de guerre declaration of war

décoller

décoller
[dekɔle] *v i*
to take off

...décoller

* ***Regarde, Milou !*** Look, Snowy!
L'avion a décollé !... The plane has taken off!... *

▸ **décollage**
[dekɔlaʒ] *n m*
take-off

découvrir

découvrir
[dekuvrir]
1. to find

...découvrir

...découvrir

* ***Oh ! Je suis sûr que j'ai découvert le trésor !...*** Oh! I'm certain I've found the treasure!... *

2. to discover
j'ai découvert un médicament qui les guérira I've discovered a drug which will cure them

▸ **découverte**
[dekuvɛrt] *n f*
1. discovery

il est l'auteur de nombreuses découvertes scientifiques he has made many scientific discoveries

2. Loc
aller à la découverte de to go in search of

décrire

décrire
[dekrir] *v t*
to describe

...décrire

▸ **description**
[dɛskripsjɔ̃] *n f*
description

décrocher

décrocher
[dekrɔʃe] *v t*
1. to pick up

* ***Le téléphone sonne...*** The phone's ringing...

...décrocher

Drring Drring Rrring Rrring
Milou décroche le combiné. Snowy picks up the receiver. *

2. to take down
aidez-moi à décrocher le tableau help me take the picture down

déçu

déçu, e
→ DÉCEVOIR

dedans

dedans
[dədɑ̃] *adv*
1. inside

* *Le trésor de Rackham le Rouge est peut-être dedans !* Red Rackham's treasure may be inside! *

Le trésor de Rackham le Rouge est peut-être dedans !

2. indoors
restons dedans, il pleut trop ! let's stay indoors, it's raining too hard!

défendre

défendre
[defɑ̃dr]
I. *vt*
1. to defend

* *Merci Milou, tu nous as courageusement*

Merci Milou, tu nous as courageusement défendus, tu as été merveilleux !
Je t'en prie ...

défendus, tu as été merveilleux ! Thank you, Snowy, you defended us bravely – you've been wonderful!
Je t'en prie... Don't mention it... *

2. to forbid
on nous a défendu d'entrer ici we have been forbidden to enter this place

II. *v pr*
il s'est courageusement défendu he defended himself bravely

► **défendu, e**
[defɑ̃dy] *adj*
forbidden

c'est défendu it's forbidden

► **défense**
[defɑ̃s] *n f*
1. defence (*Am:* defense)

l'accusé a-t-il quelque chose à dire pour sa défense ? has the accused anything to say in his defence?

2. tusk
les défenses d'un éléphant an elephant's tusks

3. Loc
défense d'entrer/de fumer no entry/smoking

prendre la défense de quelqu'un to take someone's side

dégoûtant

dégoûtant, e
[degutɑ̃, ɑ̃t] *adj*
disgusting

* *Oh ! cette boue est dégoûtante !* Oh! this mud is disgusting! *

Oh ! cette boue est dégoûtante !
PLOUF

degré

degré
[dəgre] *n m*
degree

Quelle chaleur ! La température a encore augmenté de plusieurs degrés !

* *Quelle chaleur ! La température a encore augmenté de plusieurs degrés !* It's so hot! The temperature has gone up a few more degrees! *

se déguiser

se déguiser
[sədegize] *v pr*
to disguise oneself, to dress up

Pourquoi êtes - vous déguisés en Grecs ?
Pour que l'on ne nous reconnaisse pas !

* *Pourquoi êtes-vous déguisés en Grecs ?* Why did you dress up as Greeks?
Pour que l'on ne nous reconnaisse pas ! So that we wouldn't be recognized! *

dehors

dehors
[dəɔr] *adv*
1. outside

...dehors

sortez de la chambre, attendez-moi dehors leave the room and wait for me outside

2. outdoors
Abdallah, va jouer dehors Abdullah, go and play outdoors

déjà

déjà
[deʒa] *adv*
1. already

...déjà

La fusée a déjà décollé ? Mais ce n'est pas possible !...

* *La fusée a déjà décollé ? Mais ce n'est pas possible !...* The rocket has already taken off? But that's not possible!... *

2. before
j'ai déjà vu sa tête, mais où ? I've seen his face before, but where?

déjeuner

déjeuner
[deʒøne]
I. *v i*
to have lunch

venez, allons déjeuner come on, let's go and have lunch

II. *n m*
1. lunch

Nestor prépare le déjeuner Nestor's cooking lunch

2. Loc
petit déjeuner breakfast

prendre le petit déjeuner to have breakfast

délicieux

délicieux, euse
[delisjø, øz] *adj*
delicious

...délicieux

ce gâteau est délicieux ! this cake is delicious!

demain

demain
[dəmɛ̃] *adv*
tomorrow

demain après-midi tomorrow afternoon

demain matin tomorrow morning

...demain

demain soir tomorrow evening

demander

demander
[dəmɑ̃de]
I. *v t*
1. to ask

nous lui avons demandé de nous suivre we asked him to follow us

...demander

Je me demande s'ils ont reçu notre message !

2. to ask for
Abdallah a demandé une auto à pédales à son père Abdullah asked his father for a pedal car

II. *v pr*
to wonder

* *Je me demande s'ils ont reçu notre message !* I wonder if they've received our message! *

déménager

déménager
[demenaʒe]
I. *v i*
to move

le professeur a déménagé et s'est installé à Moulinsart the Professor moved and settled in Marlinspike

II. *v t*
to remove

ils ont déménagé tous les meubles they removed all the furniture

demeurer

demeurer
[dəmœre] *v i*
to live

* *Savez-vous où le trouver ?* Do you know where to find him? *Mais oui, je le connais, il demeure rue du Château...* Yes, I know him, he lives in Castle street... *

Savez-vous où le trouver ?
Mais oui, je le connais, il demeure rue du Château...

demi

demi, e
[dəmi] *adj*
half

j'ai attendu une heure et demie I waited for an hour and a half

il est quatre heures et demie it's half past four

▸ **demi-journée**
[dəmiʒurne] *n f*
pl demi-journées
half-day

▸ **demi-litre**
[dəmilitr] *n m*
pl demi-litres
half-litre (*Am:* half-liter)

▸ **demi-tarif**
[dəmitarif] *n m*
pl demi-tarifs
half-fare

▸ **demi-tour**
[dəmitur]
Loc
faire demi-tour to turn back

dent

dent
[dɑ̃] *n f*
tooth

* ***Attention !*** Careful! ***Aïe, j'ai failli me casser les dents !*** Ouch, I nearly broke my teeth! *

▶ **dentrifrice**
[dɑ̃tifris] *n m*
toothpaste

▶ **dentiste**
[dɑ̃tist] *n*
dentist

dépanner

dépanner
[depane] *v t*
to repair

j'ai téléphoné pour qu'ils viennent dépanner notre voiture I've phoned and asked them to come and repair our car

▶ **dépannage**
[depanaʒ] *n m*
(emergency) repairing

...dépanner

▶ **dépanneuse**
[depanøz] *n f*
breakdown lorry (*Am:* tow truck)

départ

départ
[depar] *n m*
departure

notre départ a été retardé our departure has been delayed

département

département
[departmɑ̃] *n m*
department

la France est divisée en départements France is divided into departments

dépasser

dépasser
[depase] *v t*

...dépasser

1. to overtake (*Am:* to pass)

* ***Essayez de rattraper la voiture qui vient de nous dépasser !*** Try and catch up with the car which has just overtaken us! *

2. Loc
regarde, je te dépasse d'une tête look, I'm taller than you by a head

se dépêcher

se dépêcher
[sədepeʃe] *v pr*
to hurry

* ***Il faut nous dépêcher ou nous manquerons l'avion !...*** We'd better hurry or we'll miss the plane!... *

dépendre

dépendre de
[depɑ̃dr də] *v t ind*
to depend on

cela dépend du temps it depends on the weather

dépenser

dépenser
[depɑ̃se] *v t*
to spend

...dépenser

j'ai dépensé sept cents francs I spent seven hundred francs

▶ **dépenses**
[depɑ̃s] *n f pl*
expenses

pouvez-vous payer mes dépenses ? je n'ai plus d'argent could you pay my expenses? I have no money left

déplacer

déplacer
[deplase]
I. *vt*
to move

* *J'avais posé ce livre ici, qui l'a déplacé ?* I put the book here, who moved it? *

II. *v pr*
to walk (about)

elle a du mal à se déplacer depuis son accident she's having trouble walking since her accident

J'avais posé ce livre ici, qui l'a déplacé ?

dépliant

dépliant
[deplijɑ̃] *n m*
leaflet, brochure

un dépliant sur l'Inde a brochure about India

déposer

déposer
[depoze] *vt*
1. to leave

Quelqu'un a déposé un paquet pour vous...

* *Quelqu'un a déposé un paquet pour vous...* Somebody left a parcel (*Am:* package) for you... *

2. to drop
je vais vous déposer à la gare I'll drop you at the station

depuis

depuis
[dəpɥi] *prép*
1. since

je l'ai laissé et je ne l'ai pas revu depuis ce moment I left him and I've not seen him since that moment

il neige depuis hier it's been snowing since yesterday

2. for
il neige depuis une semaine it's been snowing for a week

3. from
il est venu à pied depuis Paris he walked from Paris

► **depuis que**
[dəpɥikə] *conj*
since

* *Je vais beaucoup mieux depuis que je ne bois plus de whisky.* I feel much better since I gave up drinking whisky. *

Je vais beaucoup mieux depuis que je ne bois plus de whisky.

déranger

déranger
[derɑ̃ʒe]
I. *vt*
1. to disturb

le professeur est occupé, ne le dérangez pas the Professor's busy, don't disturb him

2. to upset
qui a dérangé mes papiers ? who's upset my papers?

II. *v pr*
to bother

ne vous dérangez pas, nous prendrons un taxi don't bother, we'll take a taxi

dernier

dernier, ère
I. *adj*
[dɛrnje, ɛr]
1. last

je l'ai rencontré l'année dernière I met him last year

2. latest
as-tu entendu les dernières nouvelles ? have you heard the latest news?

3. top
M. Balthazar habitait au dernier étage Mr Balthazar used to live on the top floor

II. *n*
last one

Dupond, tu es toujours le dernier à comprendre Thompson, you're always the last one to understand

derrière

derrière
[dɛrjɛr]
I. *prép*
behind

elle est restée derrière la voiture she stayed behind the car

Les Dupondt sont derrière...

...derrière

II. *adv*
behind

* *Les Dupondt sont derrière...* The Thompsons are behind... *

III. *n m*
bottom

ah, mon pauvre Dupont, tu es tombé sur le derrière ! my poor Thomson, you fell on your bottom!

dès

dès
[dɛ] *prép*
from

dès le début, il m'a paru suspect he looked suspicious to me from the start

▶ **dès que**
[dɛkə] *conj*
as soon as

téléphonez-nous dès que vous arriverez phone us as soon as you arrive

désagréable

désagréable
[dezagreabl] *adj*
1. unpleasant

* *Quel drôle de goût !* What a funny taste!
Oui, le goût de ce médicament est désagréable... Yes, this medicine tastes unpleasant... *

2. disagreeable
oh, ce que vous êtes désagréable aujourd'hui ! oh, how disagreeable you are today!

descendre

descendre
[desɑ̃dr]
I. *v i*
1. to go down

* *Chut !* Shh!
Ils descendent à la cave. They're going down to the cellar. *

2. to get off
Tintin est descendu à la gare de Moulinsart Tintin got off at Marlinspike station

...descendre

3. to slope down
la colline descend jusqu'à la mer the hill slopes down to the sea

II. *v t*
1. to take down

Nestor va descendre nos bagages Nestor's going to take our luggage down

2. Loc
ne descends pas l'escalier en courant don't run down the stairs

Ils descendent à la cave.

▶ **descente**
[desɑ̃t] *n f*
slope

la voiture est garée dans une descente the car is parked on a slope

description

description
→ DÉCRIRE

se déshabiller

se déshabiller
[sədezabije] *v pr*
to undress

déshabillez-vous pour que le docteur vous examine undress so that the doctor can examine you

désirer

désirer
[dezire] *v t*
1. to want

nous désirons voir le professeur Tournesol tout de suite we want to see Professor Calculus at once

2. to wish
* *Désirez-vous vous reposer un peu ?* Do you wish to rest for a while?
Volontiers... I'd love to... *

...désirer

désolé

désolé, e
[dezɔle] *adj*
sorry

nous sommes vraiment désolés d'avoir oublié de venir we're so sorry that we forgot to come

dessert

dessert
[desɛr] *n m*
dessert

...dessert

il y aura de la crème au chocolat au dessert there'll be chocolate cream for dessert

dessiner

dessiner
[desine] *v t*
to draw

attendez, je vais vous dessiner un plan de la maison wait a moment, I'll draw you a plan of the house

...dessiner

▶ **dessin**
[desɛ̃] *n m*
1. drawing

je me demande ce que représente ce dessin I wonder what this drawing represents

2. Loc
dessin animé cartoon

▶ **dessinateur, trice**
[desinatœr, tris] *n*
Loc
dessinateur industriel draughtsman (*Am:* draftsman)

dessous

Il n'y a rien sur la commode...
Regardons dessous...

dessous
[dəsu] *adv*
underneath

* *Il n'y a rien sur la commode... Regardons dessous...* There's nothing on the chest of drawers (*Am:* dresser)... Let's look underneath... *

► **au-dessous de**
[odəsudə] *prép*
below

* *Il fait au moins dix degrés au-dessous de zéro !* It's at least ten degrees below zero! *Et le vent se lève !* And the wind is rising! *

► **par-dessous**
[pardəsu] *adv*
from underneath

soulevons le coffre par-dessous let's lift the chest from underneath

Il fait au moins dix degrés au-dessous de zéro !
Et le vent se lève !

dessus

dessus
[dəsy] *adv*
over it

Milou a renversé de l'eau dessus Snowy spilt water over it

► **au-dessus de**
[odəsydə] *prép*
on top of

je l'ai caché au-dessus de l'armoire I hid it on top of the wardrobe

► **par-dessus**
[pardəsy] *adv*
over it

je vais sauter par-dessus I'll jump over it

destination

destination
[dɛstinasjɔ̃] *n f*
destination

* *Arriverons-nous jamais à destination ?*

...destination

Arriverons-nous jamais à destination ?

Will we ever arrive at our destination? *

détail

détail
[detaj] *n m*
detail

donnez-nous plus de détails, sinon nous ne le retrouverons jamais give us more details, or we'll never be able to find him

se détendre

se détendre
[sədetɑ̃dr] *v pr*
to relax

je suis très inquiet, je n'arrive pas à me détendre I'm very worried, I can't relax

détester

détester
[detɛste] *v t*
to hate

...détester

je déteste qu'on m'observe I hate being watched

détruire

détruire
[detrɥir] *v t*
to destroy

l'incendie a tout détruit the fire destroyed everything

deux

deux
[dø] *adj num*
1. two

voici deux policiers français here are two French policemen

2. Loc
le 2 mai May 2nd

► **deuxième**
[døzjɛm] *adj*
second

c'est la deuxième fois it's the second time

devant

devant
[dəvɑ̃]
I. *prép*
1. in front of

* *Le capitaine marche devant les autres...* The Captain is walking in front of the others... *

n'en parlez surtout pas devant Abdallah you mustn't mention it in front of Abdullah

Le capitaine marche devant les autres...

...devant

2. opposite
sa maison est devant la gare his house is opposite the station

3. outside
je t'attendrai devant la banque I'll wait for you outside the bank

II. *adv*
1. ahead

Tintin est parti devant Tintin went ahead

2. in the front

?
?
755543
Ils sont assis devant.

* *Ils sont assis devant.* They're sitting in the front. *

III. *n m*
front

le devant de sa robe est sale the front of her dress is dirty

développer

développer
[devlɔpe]

...développer

I. *v t*
1. to develop

la gymnastique développe les muscles gymnastics develops your muscles

2. to enlarge (up)on, to develop
très intéressant, pouvez-vous développer votre idée ? very interesting, could you enlarge upon your idea?

II. *v pr*
to develop

...développer

les plantes se développent mieux au soleil plants develop better in the sun

devenir

devenir
[dəvnir] *v i*
1. to become

Abdallah est devenu grand Abdullah's become a big boy

...devenir

2. to get, to grow
il est devenu très coléreux he has got very quick-tempered

3. to grow into
la chenille est devenue papillon the caterpillar has grown into a butterfly

deviner

deviner
[dəvine] *v t*

...deviner

Devinez qui j'ai invité ! La Castafiore ! C'est drôle, non ?

to guess
* *Devinez qui j'ai invité ! La Castafiore ! C'est drôle, non ?* Guess who I have invited! Signora Castafiore! It's funny, isn't it? *

devoir

devoir
[dəvwar]
I. *v aux*
1. must

...devoir

Il est tard, je dois partir.
Au revoir, monsieur.

...devoir

* *Il est tard, je dois partir.* It's late, I must go. *Au revoir, monsieur.* Good bye, Sir. *

2. to have (got) to
je dois refuser I have (got) to refuse

3. must
elle a dû oublier she must have forgotten

4. should, ought to
tu devrais rester you should stay, you ought to stay

II. *v tr*
1. to owe

Dupont, tu me dois cent francs Thomson, you owe me a hundred francs

2. to owe
merci, Tintin, nous vous devons la vie thank you, Tintin, we owe our lives to you

III. *n m*
1. duty

tous les citoyens ont le devoir de voter every citizen has a duty to vote

2. homework
fais tes devoirs, tu joueras après do your homework first, then you can go and play

diable

diable
[djabl] *n m*
devil

* *Le diable a perdu...* The devil has lost... *

dieu

dieu
[djø] *n m*
pl dieux
god

Le diable a perdu...

différence

différence
[diferɑ̃s] *n f*
difference

* *Y a-t-il une différence entre eux ?* Is there a difference between them? *

▶ **différent, e**
[diferɑ̃, ɑ̃t] *adj*
different

leurs moustaches sont différentes their moustaches are different

Y a-t-il une différence entre eux ?

difficile

difficile
[difisil] *adj*
difficult, hard

* *La grotte est difficile à trouver, nous essayons quand même ?... Bien sûr !* The cave is difficult to find – shall we try all the same?... Of course! *

▶ **difficulté**
[difikylte] *n f*
difficulty

...difficile

il marche avec/sans difficulté he walks with/without difficulty

dimanche

dimanche
[dimɑ̃ʃ] *n m*
Sunday

viens me voir dimanche come and see me on Sunday

diminuer

diminuer
[diminɥe]
I. *v t*
to reduce

* *Il faut que je diminue la vitesse du train !... Mais comment ?...* I must reduce the speed of the train!... But how?...

II. *v i*
to get shorter

les jours diminuent the days are getting shorter

dîner

dîner
[dine]
I. *v i*
to have dinner

ils sont en train de dîner they're having dinner

II. *n m*
dinner

qu'y a-t-il pour dîner ce soir ? what's for dinner tonight?

diplôme

diplôme
[diplom] *n m*
diploma

dire

dire
[dir] *v t*
1. to say

qu'a dit le professeur ? nous n'avons pas compris what did the Professor say? we didn't understand

2. to tell
surtout ne lui dites pas la vérité above all don't tell him the truth

3. Loc
vouloir dire to mean

* *Tintin, que veut dire ce message ?* Tintin, what does this message mean? *

on dirait un avion it looks like a plane

...dire

on dirait du chocolat it tastes like chocolate

si nous faisions une promenade ? – ça ne me dit rien what about a walk? – I don't feel like it

direct

direct, e
[dirɛkt] *adj*
1. direct

quel est le chemin le plus direct pour atteindre Moulinsart ? what is the most direct way to get to the Marlinspike?

2. Loc
train direct through train, non-stop train

directeur

directeur, trice
[dirɛktœr, tris] *n*
1. headmaster *m*, headmistress *f*, (*Am:* principal *m & f*)

...directeur

elle est directrice d'école she's a headmistress

2. manager *m/f*
le directeur de l'hôtel the hotel manager

direction

direction
[dirɛksjɔ̃] *n f*
1. direction, way

...direction

dans quelle direction sont-ils partis ? which way did they go?

2. management
la direction de l'usine the management of the factory

discours

discours
[diskur] *n m*
speech

...discours

Attention !... Monsieur Baxter va faire un petit discours !...

* *Attention !... Monsieur Baxter va faire un petit discours !...* Attention!... Mr Baxter is about to make a short speech!... *

discuter

discuter
[diskyte]
I. *v tr*
to discuss, to talk about

...discuter

II. *v i*
to argue

Abdallah, cesse de discuter et obéis ! Abdullah, stop arguing and do as you're told!

► **discussion**
[diskysjɔ̃] *n f*
1. discussion, talk

nous avons eu une discussion intéressante sur le tunnel sous la Manche we had an interesting discus-

...discuter

sion about the Channel Tunnel

2. argument
le capitaine a eu une violente discussion avec les Dupondt the Captain had a heated argument with the Thompsons

disparaître

disparaître
[disparɛtr] *v i*
to disappear

...disparaître

le soleil a disparu, c'est une éclipse the sun's disappeared, it's an eclipse

► **disparition**
[disparisjɔ̃] *n f*
disappearance

la disparition de Milou m'inquiète I'm worried about Snowy's disappearance

disponible

disponible
[disponibl] *adj*
1. free

le capitaine n'est pas disponible ce soir the Captain isn't free tonight

2. available
il reste des places disponibles pour le concert there are still seats available for the concert

se disputer

se disputer
[sədispyte] *v pr*
to quarrel

* *Pourquoi vous disputez-vous ?* Why are you quarrelling (*Am:* quarreling)? *

► **dispute**
[dispyt] *n f*
quarrel

Pourquoi vous disputez-vous ?
!
!

disque

disque
[disk] *n m*
record

veux-tu écouter un disque ? do you want to listen to a record?

disque compact compact disc

distance

distance
[distɑ̃s] *n f*
1. distance

il est difficile de juger des distances quand on conduit la nuit it is difficult to judge distances when you're driving at night

2. Loc
quelle est la distance d'ici à Moulinsart ? how far is it from here to Marlinspike?

distinguer

distinguer
[distɛ̃ge] *v t*
1. to make out

* *J'ai distingué une silhouette dans la tempête de neige !* I made out a figure through the snowstorm! *

2. to distinguish, to tell
qui peut distinguer Dupont de Dupond ? who can tell Thomson from Thompson?

J'ai distingué une silhouette dans la tempête de neige !
GRRR

...distinguer

ils sont difficiles à distinguer l'un de l'autre it's difficult to tell them apart

distraction

distraction
[distraksjɔ̃] *n f*
amusement

* *La distraction favorite de Milou est de déterrer les os.* Snowy's favourite (*Am:* favorite) amusement is digging up bones. *

...distraction

?

La distraction favorite de Milou est de déterrer les os.

distribuer

distribuer
[distribɥe] *v t*
1. to distribute, to share out

je vais distribuer les rations de nourriture I'll distribute the food rations

...distribuer

2. to deal
à toi de distribuer les cartes it's your turn to deal the cards

diviser

diviser
[divize] *v t*
1. to divide

divisez les jouets entre vous divide the toys among you

...diviser

2. to divide
divise 15 par 3 divide 15 by 3

► **division**
[divizjɔ̃] *n f*
division

divorcer

divorcer
[divɔrse] *v i*
to divorce

...divorcer

► **divorce**
[divɔrs] *n m*
divorce

docteur

docteur
[dɔktœr] *n m*
doctor

appelle le docteur send for the doctor

document

document
[dɔkymɑ̃] *n m*
document

* *Ce document est d'une importance capitale.* This document is of vital importance. *

► **documentaire**
[dɔkymɑ̃tɛr] *n m*
documentary

Ce document est d'une importance capitale.

doigt

doigt
[dwa] *n m*
1. finger

je me suis pincé le doigt dans la porte I caught my finger in the door

2. Loc
montrer quelqu'un du doigt to point at somebody

domicile

domicile
[dɔmisil] *n m*
home

elle travaille à domicile she works at home

dommage

dommage
[dɔmaʒ] *n m*
1. damage

...dommage

l'orage a causé des dommages dans le parc the storm caused damage in the park

2. a pity, a shame
quel dommage qu'il ne soit pas là ! what a pity he isn't here!

(c'est) dommage ! it's a shame!

donc

donc
[dɔ̃k] *conj*
1. so, therefore

* *Je ne suis pas d'accord, donc je n'irai pas avec toi !... Je veux rester ici !...* I don't agree, so I won't go with you!... I want to stay here!...
Mais... But... *

2. Loc
mais où est donc Milou ? where on earth can Snowy be?

Je ne suis pas d'accord, donc je n'irai pas avec toi !... Je veux rester ici !...
Mais ...

donner

donner
[dɔne] *v t*
1. to give

je te donnerai ce livre I'll give you this book

2. to produce
le pommier a donné beaucoup de fruits cette année the apple tree produced a lot of fruit this year

3. Loc
ça m'a donné faim/soif it made me hungry/thirsty

pouvez-vous me donner l'heure ? can you tell me the time?

* *Viens, Milou, je vais te donner à manger !...* Come, Snowy, I'll feed you!...
Bonne idée ! Good idea! *

dont

dont
[dɔ̃] *pron rel*
1. whose

Tournesol est un savant dont les inventions sont connues dans le monde entier Calculus is a scientist whose inventions are known all over the world

2. Loc
voici les policiers dont je vous ai parlé here are the policemen whom I told you about

dormir

dormir
[dɔrmir] *v i*
to sleep, to be asleep

il dort au lieu de faire le guet he's sleeping instead of keeping watch

* *Il est si fatigué qu'il dort debout.* He's so tired he's asleep on his feet. *

...dormir

Il est si fatigué qu'il dort debout.

dortoir

dortoir
[dɔrtwar] *n m*
dormitory

dos

dos
[do] *n m*
back

allongez-vous sur le dos lie on your back

...dos

Le chat fait le gros dos !

* *Le chat fait le gros dos !* The cat is arching its back! *

douane

douane
[dwan] *n f*
customs

▸ **douanier**
[dwanje] *n m*
customs officer

double

double
[dubl]
I. *adj*
double

il a un double menton he's got a double chin

II. *n m*
double

c'est le double du prix habituel it's double the usual price

▸ **doubler**
[duble] *v t*
to overtake (*Am:* to pass)

je vais essayer de doubler cette voiture I'll try to overtake this car

doucement

doucement
→ DOUX

douche

douche
[duʃ] *n f*
shower

va prendre une douche go and have a shower

douleur

douleur [dulœr] *n f*
pain

douter

douter
[dute]
I. *v t ind*
to doubt

je commence à douter de sa sincérité I'm beginning to doubt his sincerity

je doute qu'il vienne I doubt whether he'll come

II. *v pr*
to suspect

c'était donc vous ? je m'en doutais ! so it was you? I suspected as much!

doux

doux, douce
[du, dus] *adj*
1. soft

le bébé a la peau douce the baby's skin is soft

...doux

2. gentle
Milou est un animal très doux Snowy's a very gentle animal

3. soft
la Castafiore a une voix très douce Signora Castafiore has a very soft voice

▶ **doucement**
[dusmɑ̃] *adv*
1. gently

caresse le chat doucement stroke the cat gently

2. slowly
* *Roule plus doucement, Tintin, tu vas nous tuer !* Drive more slowly, Tintin, you'll kill us! *

3. softly
parlez doucement, les enfants dorment speak softly, the children are asleep

Roule plus doucement, Tintin, tu vas nous tuer !

douze

douze
[duz] *adj num inv*
twelve

▶ **douzaine**
[duzɛn] *n f*
dozen

une douzaine d'œufs a dozen eggs

▶ **douzième**
[duzjɛm] *adj, n*
twelfth

drap

drap
[dra] *n m*
sheet

elle a changé les draps de son lit she changed the sheets on her bed

drapeau

drapeau
[drapo] *n m*
pl drapeaux
flag

dresser

dresser
[drɛse] *v t*
1. to train

le dompteur dresse les lions the lion tamer trains the lions

2. to prick up
Milou dresse les oreilles Snowy's pricking up his ears

droit

droit
[drwa] *n m*
1. right

nous avons le droit d'atterrir ici we have the right to land here

2. law
il fait du droit he's studying law

droit

droit, e
[drwa, at] *adj*
1. right

il s'est cassé le bras droit he broke his right arm

2. straight
* *Ah ! Les voilà !* Ah! There they are!
La route est droite, nous allons les rattraper ! The road's straight, we'll catch up with them! *

Ah ! Les voilà !
La route est droite, nous allons les rattraper !

▶ **droite**
[drwat] *n f*
1. right

faites attention, roulez à droite be careful, drive on the right

2. straight line
dessinez une droite draw a straight line

drôle

drôle
[drol] *adj*
funny

pourquoi disent-ils que nous sommes drôles, habillés ainsi ? why do they say we look funny dressed like this?

dur

dur, e
[dyr] *adj*

...dur

1. hard

ce lit est dur this bed is hard

2. tough
de la viande dure tough meat

3. hard, difficult
cet exercice est dur this exercise is hard

4. harsh
le capitaine est dur avec l'équipage the Captain is harsh with the crew

durant

durant
[dyrɑ̃] *prép*
during

il a neigé durant la nuit it snowed during the night

durer

durer
[dyre] *v i*
1. to last

...durer

Combien de temps cette tempête va-t-elle durer ?

* *Combien de temps cette tempête va-t-elle durer ?* How long will this storm last? *

2. Loc
ça ne peut plus durer ! this can't go on!

▶ **durée**
[dyre] *n f*
length

la durée du film the length of the film

eau

eau
[o] *n f*
pl eaux
water

* *Le capitaine a bu de l'eau...* The Captain drank some water... *

l'eau de la rivière est très froide the river water is very cold

eau minérale mineral water

Le capitaine a bu de l'eau...

échanger

échanger
[eʃɑ̃ʒe] *v t*
to exchange

* *Echangeons nos chapeaux !* Let's exchange hats! *D'accord !* OK! *

► **échange**
[eʃɑ̃ʒ] *n m*
exchange

en échange de ma montre in exchange for my watch

s'échapper

s'échapper
[seʃape] *v pr*
to escape

* *Tintin a réussi à s'échapper de la prison...* Tintin has managed to escape from prison... *

écharpe

écharpe
[eʃarp] *n f*
scarf

Tintin a réussi à s'échapper de la prison...

échecs

échecs
[eʃɛk] *n m pl*
chess

* *Vous n'aimez pas les échecs ?* Don't you like chess? *

échelle

échelle
[eʃɛl] *n f*
ladder

...échelle

Woooah!

Il a grimpé à l'échelle pour entrer par la fenêtre...

* ***Il a grimpé à l'échelle pour entrer par la fenêtre...*** He climbed the ladder to get in through the window... *

échouer

échouer
[eʃwe] *v i*
to fail

l'opération a échoué the operation has failed

éclair

éclair
[eklɛr] *n m*
flash of lightning

* ***Un éclair...*** A flash of lightning... *

éclairer

éclairer
[eklɛre] *v t*
to light up

Un éclair...

...éclairer

* ***Leurs phares éclairent la route, nous les suivrons facilement !*** Their headlights are lighting up the road, we'll be able to follow them easily! *

éclater

éclater
[eklate] *v i*
to burst

Leurs phares éclairent la route, nous les suivrons facilement !
F-VRDC

...éclater

voyez, les pneus ont éclaté look, the tyres (*Am:* tires) have burst

école

école
[ekɔl] *n f*
school

école primaire primary school

...école

► **écolier, ère**
[ekɔlje, ɛr] *n*
schoolboy n m, schoolgirl n f

économies

économies
[ekɔnɔmi] *n f pl*
1. savings

toutes mes économies sont dans le

...économies

coffre all my savings are in the safe

2. Loc
faire des économies to save

► **économique**
[ekɔnɔmik] *adj*
1. economical

une petite voiture est plus économique qu'une grosse a small car is more economical than a big one

2. economic
une crise economique an economic crisis

écouter

écouter
[ekute] *v t*
to listen to

* ***Je vais écouter les informations...*** I'll listen to the news... *

...écouter

Je vais écouter les informations...

écraser

Les Dupondt vont écraser quelqu'un...

...écraser

écraser
[ekraze] *v t*
1. to run over

* *Les Dupondt vont écraser quelqu'un...* The Thompsons are going to run somebody over... *

2. to crush
ils ont écrasé les fleurs en s'enfuyant they crushed the flowers when they ran away

écrire

écrire
[ekrir]
I. *v t*

* *Abdallah m'a écrit une lettre!* Abdullah has written me a letter! *A mon cher Milsabor* To my dear Blistering Barnacles *

II. *v pr*
to be spelt

comment s'écrit son nom ? how is his name spelt?

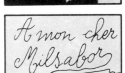

► **écriture**
[ekrityr] *n f*
handwriting

arrivez-vous à déchiffrer son écriture ? can you read his handwriting?

► **écrivain**
[ekrivɛ̃] *n m*
writer

éducation

éducation
[edykasjɔ̃] *n f*
1. upbringing

Abdallah n'a pas reçu une éducation très sévère Abdullah's upbringing has not been very strict

2. education
éducation physique physical education

effet

effet
[efɛ] *n m*
1. effect

* *Est-ce que le médicament vous a fait de l'effet ? Vous sentez-vous mieux ?* Has the medicine had any effect on you? Are you feeling better? *

2. impression
il m'a fait un bon/mauvais effet he made a good/bad impression on me

3. Loc
en effet indeed

efficace

efficace
[efikas] *adj*
effective

professeur, votre médicament est très efficace Professor, your medicine is very effective

effort

effort
[efɔr] *n m*
effort

fais un effort, tu y arriveras ! make an effort and you'll succeed!

effrayer

effrayer
[efreje] *v t*
to frighten

...effrayer

* *Wouah* Wooah
Milou a effrayé le gorille ! Snowy frightened the gorilla! *

► **effrayant, e**
[efrɛjɑ̃, ɑ̃t] *adj*
frightening

...effrayer

Milou a effrayé le gorille !

égal

égal, e
pl égaux
[egal, o] *adj*
1. equal

essaie de le découper en parts égales try to cut it up into equal portions

2. Loc
ça m'est égal I don't care

s'égarer

s'égarer
[segare] *v pr*
to lose one's way

* *Tintin s'est égaré dans la jungle...* Tintin has lost his way in the jungle... *

Tintin s'est égaré dans la jungle...

église

église
[egliz] *n f*
church

électricité

électricité
[elɛktrisite] *n f*
electricity

► **électricien, enne**
[elɛkrisjɛ̃, ɛn] *n*
electrician

► **électrique**
[elɛktrik] *adj*
electric

une voiture électrique an electric car

électronique

électronique
[elɛktrɔnik]
I. *adj*
electronic

une calculatrice électronique an electronic calculator

II. *n f*
electronics

je m'intéresse à l'électronique I am interested in electronics

électrophone

électrophone
[elɛktrɔfɔn] *n m*
record player

élégant

élégant, e
[elegɑ̃, ɑ̃t] *adj*
smart, elegant

tu es très élégant aujourd'hui you're very smart today

éléphant

éléphant
[elefɑ̃] *n m*
elephant

élève

élève
[elɛv] *n*
pupil

les élèves sont dans leur classe the pupils are in their classroom

élever

élever
[elve]
I. *v t*
1. to breed

il élève des chevaux he breeds horses

2. to bring up
maintenant M. et Mme Wang vont élever Tchang now Mr and Mrs Wang will bring up Chang

3. Loc
être bien/mal élevé to be well-mannered/bad-mannered

II. *v pr*
to rise

la température s'est élevée the temperature has risen

elle

elle
[ɛl] *pron pers sing*
1. she

la Castafiore est célèbre, elle chante bien Signora Castafiore is famous, she sings well

2. it
* *Et la radio ?* What about the radio?
Elle ne fonctionne pas, elle est cassée ! it doesn't work, it's broken! *

► **elles**
[ɛl] *pron pers pl*
they

où sont vos filles ? – elles sont à l'école where are your daughters? – they are at school

où sont les assiettes ? – elles sont dans le placard where are the plates? – they are in the cupboard

embarquer

embarquer
[ɑ̃barke] *v i*
to board

les passagers commencent à embarquer the passengers are beginning to board

embouteillage

embouteillage
[ɑ̃butɛjaʒ] *n m*
traffic jam

embrasser

embrasser
[ɑ̃brase] *v t*
1. to kiss

il a embrassé sa femme he kissed his wife

2. to embrace, to hug
* *Tintin !... Il faut que je vous embrasse !...* Tintin!... I must embrace you!... *

émission

émission
[emisjɔ̃] *nf*
programme (*Am:* program)

une émission pour enfants a children's programme

emmener

emmener
[ɑ̃mne] *vt*
to take

...emmener

je ne peux pas emmener Milou I can't take Snowy (with me)

empêcher

empêcher
[ɑ̃peʃe]
I. *vt*
to prevent

* *Nous devons l'empêcher de s'enfuir!* We must prevent him from running away! *

...empêcher

Nous devons l'empêcher de s'enfuir!

II. *v pr*
Milou ne peut s'empêcher de déterrer les os Snowy can't help digging up bones

emploi

emploi
[ɑ̃plwa] *nm*
1. job, employment
il essaie de trouver un emploi he's looking for a job

...emploi

2. Loc
emploi du temps timetable

► **employer**
[ɑ̃plwaje] *vt*
to use

j'ai employé un levier pour soulever le rocher I used a lever to lift the rock

► **employé, e**
[ɑ̃plwaje] *n*
employee

► **employeur, euse**
[ɑ̃plwajœr, øz] *n*
employer

emporter

emporter
[ɑ̃pɔrte]
I. *vt*
to take

n'oubliez pas d'emporter une carte de la région don't forget to take a map of the area

...emporter

Mais voyons, ne vous emportez pas comme ça!
Je dirais même plus: ne vous emportez pas!

II. *v pr*
to lose one's temper

* *Mais voyons, ne vous emportez pas comme ça!* Look here, don't lose your temper like that!
Je dirais même plus: ne vous emportez pas! To be precise: don't lose your temper! *

empoisonner

Quelqu'un a essayé d'empoisonner Milou!

...empoisonner

empoisonner
[ɑ̃pwazɔne] *vt*
to poison

* *Quelqu'un a essayé d'empoisonner Milou!* Somebody has tried to poison Snowy! *

emprunter

emprunter
[ɑ̃prœ̃te] *vt*
to borrow

...emprunter

pouvons-nous emprunter votre voiture? can we borrow your car?

en

en
[ɑ̃] *prép*
1. in

* *Tintin est en prison...* Tintin is in prison... *

...en

Tintin est en prison...

2. to
nous devons partir en Suisse we have to go to Switzerland

3. in
en été, il fait beau in summer, the weather is fine

4. by
nous irons en train we'll go by train

5. in
est-ce que le capitaine est en bonne santé? is the Captain in good health?

6. made of
est-ce en cuir ou en plastique? is it made of leather or plastic?

7. while
il est tombé en traversant la rivière he fell while crossing the river

8. Loc
Milou est entré/sorti en courant Snowy ran in/out

enchanté

enchanté, e
[ɑ̃ʃɑ̃te] *adj*
1. delighted

* *Je suis enchanté de vous revoir !...* I'm delighted to see you again!... *

2. pleased
je vous présente Tintin – enchanté (de faire votre connaissance) may I introduce you to Tintin? – pleased to meet you

encombré

encombré, e
[ɑ̃kɔ̃bre] *adj*
1. blocked

toutes les rues sont encombrées all the streets are blocked

2. littered
le bureau du professeur est encombré de plans the Professor's desk is littered with drawings

encore

encore
[ɑ̃kɔr] *adv*
1. more

voulez-vous encore du thé ? do you want some more tea?

2. another (one)
veux-tu encore un gâteau ? do you want another cake?

3. again
Tintin a encore réussi Tintin has succeeded again

4. still
* *Non, Milou, ne me dis pas que tu as encore faim !* No, Snowy, don't tell me you're still hungry! *

5. yet
non, ils n'ont pas encore téléphoné no, they haven't phoned yet

...encore

s'endormir

s'endormir
[sɑ̃dɔrmir] *v pr*
to fall asleep

* *Rron Rron* zzzzzz *Ils se sont endormis !...* They've fallen asleep!... *

Ils se sont endormis !...

endroit

endroit
[ɑ̃drwa] *n m*
1. place

* *Voilà l'endroit où la fusée va se poser...* This is the place where the rocket will land... *

2. right side
l'endroit du tissu the right side of the cloth

3. Loc
mettez votre manteau à l'endroit put your coat on right side out

...endroit

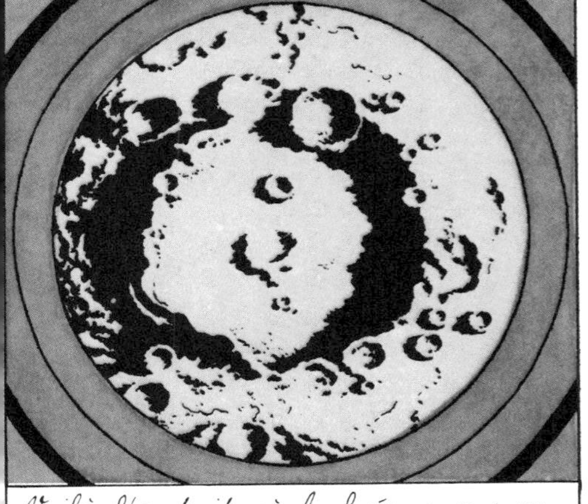

Voilà l'endroit où la fusée va se poser...

énergie

énergie
[enɛrʒi] *n f*
energy

eh bien capitaine, vous êtes plein d'énergie ! well, Captain, you're full of energy!

▸ **énergique**
[enɛrʒik] *adj*
energetic

énerver

énerver
[enɛrve] *v t*
to get on Someone's nerves

elle m'énerve quelquefois she sometimes gets on my nerves

▸ **énervant, e**
[enɛrvɑ̃, ɑ̃t] *adj*
irritating

▸ **énervé, e**
[enɛrve] *adj*
edgy

Tournesol est parfois très énervé Calculus is sometimes very edgy

enfant

enfant
[ɑ̃fɑ̃] *n m*
child

Abdallah n'est qu'un enfant Abdullah is just a child

...enfant

combien d'enfants ont les Lampion ? how many children do the Waggs have?

enfermer

enfermer
[ɑ̃fɛrme] *v t*
to lock up
enfermez les documents dans le coffre lock the documents up in the safe

...enfermer

* *Clac* Slam
Ils m'ont enfermé... They locked me up... *

enfin

enfin
[ɑ̃fɛ̃] *adv*
at last
* *Le trésor !... Nous avons enfin trouvé le trésor de Rackham le Rouge !...* The treasure!... We've found Red

...enfin

Rackham's treasure at last!... *

enlever

enlever
[ɑ̃lve] *v t*
1. to take off
enlevez votre veste si vous avez chaud take your jacket off if you're hot
2. to kidnap
on a enlevé votre fils your son's been kidnapped

ennuyer

ennuyer
[ɑ̃nɥije]
I. *v t*
to bother
cela m'ennuie de ne pas les avoir avertis it bothers me that I didn't warn them
II. *v pr*
to get bored
* *J'espère qu'Abdallah ne s'ennuie pas loin de moi !* I hope

Abdullah won't get bored away from me! *

► **ennui**
[ɑ̃nɥi] *n m*
trouble
voici les Dupondt, c'est la fin de nos ennuis here come the Thompsons, our troubles are over

► **ennuyeux, euse**
[ɑ̃nɥijø, øz] *adj*
boring
ils sont ennuyeux, ils répètent toujours la même chose they're boring: they're always saying the same thing

énorme

énorme
[enɔrm] *adj*
enormous, huge
* *Aïe !... Quel énorme requin !... Il va m'attaquer !...* Crikey!... What

...énorme

...énorme

an enormous shark!... It's going to attack me!... *

enquête

enquête
[ɑ̃kɛt] *n f*
investigation
* *Je dirais même plus... Nous allons faire une enquête...* To be precise... We're going to make an investigation... *

...enquête

enregistrer

enregistrer
[ɑ̃rəʒistre] *v t*
to record
avez-vous enregistré leur dernier concert ? did you record their last concert?

s'enrhumer

s'enrhumer
[sɑ̃ryme] *v pr*
to catch a cold

...s'enrhumer

je sens que je m'enrhume I can feel I'm catching a cold
* *AAAA...* AAAA...
Tchoum !... Tchoo!
Il s'est enrhumé... He has caught a cold... *

enseigner

enseigner
[ɑ̃seɲe] *v t*
to teach

...enseigner

mon père enseigne le français my father teaches French

ensemble

ensemble
[ɑ̃sɑ̃bl] *adv*
together

* *Les Dupondt arrivent toujours ensemble...* The Thompsons always arrive together... *

Les Dupondt arrivent toujours ensemble...

ensoleillé

ensoleillé, e
[ɑ̃sɔleje] *adj*
sunny

une belle journée ensoleillée a fine sunny day

ensuite

ensuite
[ɑ̃sɥit] *adv*
1. next

...ensuite

et qu'ont-ils fait ensuite ? and what did they do next?

2. then
j'ai sonné, ensuite je suis entré I rang the bell, then I went in

entendre

entendre
[ɑ̃tɑ̃dr]
I. *v t*
to hear

...entendre

Parlez plus fort, je ne vous entends pas !

avez-vous entendu ce qu'il a dit ? did you hear what he said?

* *Parlez plus fort, je ne vous entends pas !* Speak up, I can't hear you! *

II. *v pr*
to get on (*Am:* to get along)

Milou ne s'entend pas avec les chats Snowy doesn't get on with cats

entier

entier, ière
[ɑ̃tje, ɛr] *adj*
1. whole

* *Regardez ! Une ville entière est rayée de la carte du monde !* Look! A whole city is being wiped from the face of the earth! *

2. Loc
dans le monde entier throughout the world

Regardez ! Une ville entière est rayée de la carte du monde !

...entier

▸ **entièrement**
[ɑ̃tjɛrmɑ̃] adv
entirely

nous sommes entièrement d'accord avec le professeur we entirely agree with the Professor

entourer

entourer
[ɑ̃ture] *v t*
to surround

la police a entouré l'immeuble the police surrounded the building

entracte

entracte
[ɑ̃trakt] *n m*
interval (*Am:* intermission)

entraîner

entraîner
[ɑ̃trene]
I. *v t*
1. to carry away

* *Le courant entraîne Milou !* The current is carrying Snowy away! *

2. to lead
vous m'avez entraîné dans une aventure dangereuse you have led me into a dangerous adventure

Le courant entraîne Milou !

...entraîner

Entraînez-vous à marcher avec votre combinaison.

Ce n'est pas si difficile ...

II. *v pr*
1. to practise

* *Entraînez-vous à marcher avec votre combinaison.* Practise walking in your spacesuit. *Ce n'est pas si difficile...* It's not that difficult... *

2. to train
les vrais sportifs s'entraînent tous les jours real sportsmen train everyday

entre

Assis entre nous, il ne peut pas s'échapper!
Parfait!

...entre

entre
[ɑ̃tr] *prép*
1. between

* *Assis entre nous, il ne peut pas s'échapper!* Seated between us, he can't get away!
Parfait! Excellent! *

2. among
qu'est-ce qui brille là-bas entre les cailloux? what's that shining over there among the pebbles?

entrer

entrer
[ɑ̃tre] *v i*
1. to go in
il est entré he went in

2. to come in
entrez, je vous en prie please, come in

3. Loc
il est entré dans ma chambre pendant que je dormais he came into my room while I was sleeping
tu peux entrer dans sa chambre pendant qu'il dort you can go into his room while he's sleeping

► **entrée**
[ɑ̃tre] *n f*
1. entrance
il attend dans l'entrée de l'immeuble he's waiting in the entrance to the building

2. admission
l'entrée du musée est gratuite admission to the museum is free

envelopper

envelopper
[ɑ̃vlɔpe] *v t*
to wrap

* *J'ai enveloppé la bouteille dans un papier. Remettez-la au professeur dès son retour.* I have wrapped the bottle in a piece of paper. Hand it over to the Professor as soon as he comes back. *

► **enveloppe**
[ɑ̃vlɔp] *n f*
envelope

J'ai enveloppé la bouteille dans un papier. Remettez-la au professeur dès son retour.

...envelopper

vite, ouvrez l'enveloppe et lisez sa lettre quick, open the envelope and read his letter

envers

envers
[ɑ̃vɛr] *n m*
1. back
l'envers du tissu est uni the back of the material is plain

2. Loc

...envers

professeur, vous avez mis votre manteau à l'envers Professor, you've put your coat on inside out

envie

envie
[ɑ̃vi] *n f*
1. envy
on peut lire l'envie dans ses yeux envy shows in his eyes

...envie

Je n'ai pas envie de les voir maintenant.
Très bien mon général.

2. Loc
* *Je n'ai pas envie de les voir maintenant.* I don't feel like seeing them just now.
Très bien, mon général. Very well, Sir. *

environ

environ
[ɑ̃virɔ̃] *adv*
about

...environ

ils arriveront à 18 heures environ they'll arrive about 6 p.m.

► **environnement**
[ɑ̃virɔnmɑ̃] *n m*
environment

environs

environs
[ɑ̃virɔ̃] *n m pl*
1. surroundings

...environs

* *Les environs de Moulinsart sont boisés...* The surroundings of Marlinspike are woody... *

2. Loc
ça va coûter aux environs de deux cents francs it will cost about two hundred francs

nous partirons aux environs du 23 avril we'll leave around April 23rd

Les environs de Moulinsart sont boisés...

envoyer

envoyer
[ɑ̃vwaje] *vt*
1. to send

* *Cette lettre a été envoyée de Chine.* This letter was sent from China. *

2. to throw
envoie-moi le ballon throw me the ball

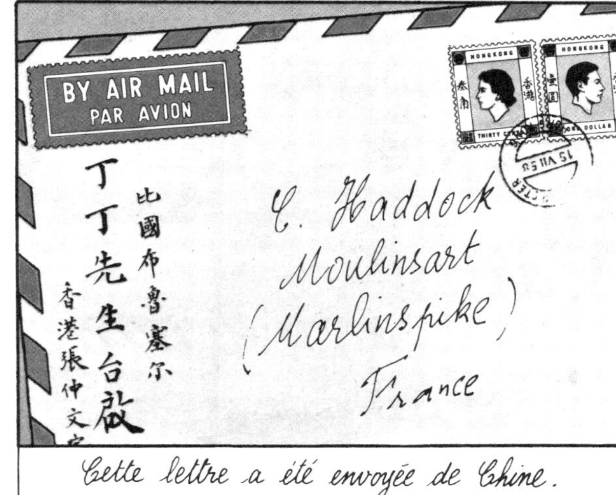
BY AIR MAIL
PAR AVION
丁丁先生台啟
比國布魯塞尔
香港張仲文
C. Haddock
Moulinsart
(Marlinspike)
France
Cette lettre a été envoyée de Chine.

épaule

épaule
[epol] *n f*
shoulder

qu'a répondu le capitaine ? – il a haussé les épaules what was the Captain's answer? – he shrugged his shoulders

épicerie

épicerie
[episri] *n f*
grocery

...épicerie

l'épicerie est fermée the grocery's closed

► **épicier, ère**
[episje, ɛr] *n*
grocer

éplucher

éplucher
[eplyʃe] *vt*
to peel

...éplucher

éplucher des pommes de terre to peel potatoes

éponge

éponge
[epɔ̃ʒ] *n f*
sponge

prends une éponge pour essuyer l'eau que tu as renversée take a sponge and mop up the water you spilt

époque

époque
[epɔk] *n f*
1. time

* *A cette époque, j'étais le commandant du bateau !* At that time, I was captain of the ship! *

2. Loc
à notre époque in this day and age

A cette époque, j'étais le commandant du bateau !

épouser

épouser
[epuze] *vt*
to marry

► **époux**
[epu] *n m inv*
1. husband

voici mon époux, M. Lampion here's my husband, Mr Wagg

2. Loc
les jeunes époux the newlyweds

► **épouse**
[epuz] *n f*
wife

voici mon épouse, Mme Lampion here's my wife, Mrs Wagg

épouvante

épouvante
[epuvɑ̃t] *n f*
horror

...épouvante

film d'épouvante horror film (*Am:* horror movie)

► **épouvantable**
[epuvɑ̃tabl] *adj*
terrible

* *Que s'est-il passé ?* What's happened?
Il y a eu un accident épouvantable ! There has been a terrible accident! *

Que s'est-il passé ?
Il y a eu un accident épouvantable !

époux

époux
→ ÉPOUSER

équipe

équipe
[ekip] *n f*
team

l'équipe de recherche du professeur Tournesol Professor Calculus' research team

...équipe

une équipe de football a football team

équipe**r**

équiper
[ekipe] *v t*
to equip

* *L'observatoire est bien équipé...* The observatory is well equipped... *

...équiper

L'observatoire est bien équipé...

▶ **équipement**
[ekipmɑ̃] *n m*
equipment

avez-vous l'équipement nécessaire ? have you got the necessary equipment?

erreur

erreur
[erœr] *n f*
mistake

je n'ai pourtant pas fait d'erreurs, les chiffres sont bons and yet I haven't made any mistake, the figures are right

* *Attendez, nous avons fait une erreur !...* Wait, we've made a mistake!... *

...erreur

Attendez, nous avons fait une erreur !...

escalier

escalier
[ɛskalje] *n m*
1. staircase, stairs

il est en haut/en bas de l'escalier he's at the top/at the bottom of the stairs

2. Loc
escalier roulant escalator

escargot

escargot
[ɛskargo] *n m*
snail

espace

espace
[ɛspas] *n m*
1. gap

laissez un espace suffisant entre les mots leave a sufficient gap between the words

...espace

Ce sera la première fusée lancée dans l'espace ...

...espace

2. space
* *Ce sera la première fusée lancée dans l'espace...* It will be the first rocket launched into space... *

3. room
on manque d'espace ici there's not enough room here

Espagne

Espagne
[ɛspaɲ] *n f*
Spain

▶ **espagnol, e**
[ɛspaɲɔl] *adj*
Spanish

▶ **Espagnol, e**
[ɛspaɲɔl] *n*
Spaniard

les Espagnols the Spanish

▶ **espagnol**
[ɛspaɲɔl] *n m*
Spanish

j'apprends l'espagnol I'm learning Spanish

espérer

espérer
[ɛspere] *v t*
to hope

* *Entrez, Messieurs !* Go in, gentlemen!

...espérer

Entrez, Messieurs !
Allons-y, Milou, j'espère que tout va bien se passer !..

...espérer

Allons-y, Milou, j'espère que tout va bien se passer !... Let's go Snowy, I hope everything goes well!... *

▶ **espoir**
[ɛspwar] *n m*
1. hope

ils avaient perdu tout espoir de le retrouver they had lost all hope of finding him

2. Loc
sans espoir hopeless

espionner

espionner
[ɛspjɔne] *v t*
to spy on

ils nous espionnent they are spying on us

▶ **espion, onne**
[ɛspjɔ̃, ɔn] *n*
spy

▶ **espionnage**
[ɛspjɔnaʒ] *n m*
spying, espionnage

nous l'avons arrêté pour espionnage we arrested him for spying

espoir

espoir
→ ESPÉRER

essayer

essayer
[eseje] *v t*
1. to try

* *Mon pauvre Milou ! Je vais essayer de te sortir de là...* My poor Snowy! I'll try to get you out of there... *

2. to try on
la Castafiore essaie sa nouvelle robe Signora Castafiore is trying on her new dress

essence

essence
[esɑ̃s] *n f*
petrol (*Am:* gas)

* *Nous n'avons presque plus d'essence...* We're nearly out of petrol... *

essuyer

essuyer
[esɥije] *v t*
to wipe

n'oubliez pas d'essuyer vos pieds avant d'entrer don't forget to wipe your feet before you go in

▶ **essuie-glace**
[esɥiglas] *n m*
pl essuie-glaces
windscreen (*Am:* windshield) wiper

est

est
[ɛst]
I. *n m*
east

la Syldavie est à l'est de notre pays Syldavia is east of our country

II. *adj*
la côte est the east coast

estomac

estomac
[ɛstɔma] *n m*
stomach

et

et
[e] *conj*
1. and

* *Voici Tintin et Milou qui arrivent.* Here come Tintin and Snowy. *

2. Loc
deux heures et demie half past two

vingt et un twenty-one

Voici Tintin et Milou qui arrivent.

étage

étage
[etaʒ] *n m*
floor, storey (*Am:* story)

* *Monsieur Tintin ?* Mr Tintin?
Premier étage. First (*Am:* second) floor. *

étagère

étagère
[etaʒɛr] *n f*
shelf

...étagère

le livre que vous cherchez est sur l'étagère du haut the book you are looking for is on the top shelf

état

état
[eta] *n m*
1. condition

l'avion est en bon/mauvais état the plane is in good/bad condition

...état

2. state
* *Regardez dans quel état ils ont laissé ma chambre !...* Look what a state they left my bedroom in!... *

État

État
[eta] *n m*
state

la Syldavie est un Etat indépendant Sylvania is an independent state

été

été
[ete] *n m*
summer

éteindre

éteindre
[etɛ̃dr]
I. *v t*
1. to extinguish

nous allons atterrir, veuillez éteindre vos cigarettes we're about to land, please extinguish your cigarettes

2. to switch off
* *Eteins la lumière !* Switch the light off! *

II. *v pr*
to go out

...éteindre

le feu s'est éteint the fire has gone out

étonner

étonner
[etɔne] *v t*
to astonish, to surprise

son courage nous a étonnés his courage astonished us

...étonner

► **étonnant, e**
[etɔnɑ̃, ɑ̃t] *adj*
astonishing, surprising

étrange

étrange
[etrɑ̃ʒ] *adj*
strange

avez-vous entendu ce bruit étrange ? did you hear that strange noise?

étranger

étranger, ère
[etrɑ̃ʒe, ɛr]
I. *adj*
foreign

il parle deux langues étrangères he can speak two foreign languages

II. *n*
1. foreigner
* *C'est un étranger, il ne connaît pas notre langue !* He's a foreigner, he doesn't know our language! *

2. stranger
c'était un étranger, je ne l'avais encore jamais vu he was a stranger, I had never seen him before

► **étranger**
[etrɑ̃ʒe] *n m*
Loc
à l'étranger abroad

elle est revenue de l'étranger she has come back from abroad

...étranger

être

être
[ɛtr] *n m*
being

* *Regarde, Dupont !* Look, Thomson!
Y a-t-il des êtres humains sur la Lune ? Are there human beings on the moon? *

Y a-t-il des êtres humains sur la Lune ?

être

être
[ɛtr]
I. *v i*
1. to be

les pommes sont mûres the apples are ripe

il est gentil he is nice

nous sommes contents we are happy

* *Qui est cet homme ?* Who is this man?

...être

Qui est cet homme ?
C'est mon ami, le capitaine Haddock...

C'est mon ami, le capitaine Haddock... It's my friend, Captain Haddock... *

quelle heure est-il ? what time is it?

2. Loc
à qui est ce livre ? whose book is this?

nous sommes dix there are ten of us

nous sommes le dix today is the tenth (of the month)

II. *v aux*
1. to have

ils ne sont pas encore arrivés they have not arrived yet

2. to be
voilà, le travail est fini there, the work is finished

3. Loc
Milou est toujours à pourchasser le chat Snowy is always chasing the cat

étroit

étroit, e
[etrwa, at] *adj*
narrow

il est difficile de se cacher dans ces ruelles étroites it's difficult to hide in these narrow lanes

étudier

étudier
[etydje] *v t*
to study

...étudier

* *Etudions ce document de près...* Let's study this document carefully... *

étudier la chimie to study chemistry

► **études**
[etyd] *n f pl*
il fait ses études à Paris he's studying in Paris

...étudier

Etudions ce document de près...

► **étudiant, e**
[etydjɑ̃, ɑ̃t] *n*
student

s'évader

s'évader
[sevade] *v pr*
to escape

* *Oh ! Oh !... Il ne sera pas facile de s'évader...* Oh dear!... It won't be easy to escape... *

...s'évader

Oh ! Oh !... Il ne sera pas facile de s'évader...

► **évasion**
[evazjɔ̃] *n f*
escape

événement

événement
[evɛnmɑ̃] *n m*
event

les principaux événements de l'année the major events of the year

évier

évier
[evje] *n m*
(kitchen) sink

laissez les assiettes à côté de l'évier leave the plates by the sink

exact

exact, e
[ɛgzakt] *adj*
1. exact

...exact

Vous souvenez-vous de ses paroles exactes ?

* *Vous souvenez-vous de ses paroles exactes ?* Can you remember his exact words? *

2. right, correct
avez-vous l'heure exacte ? have you got the right time?

► **exactement**
[ɛgzaktəmɑ̃] *adv*
exactly

il est exactement 3 heures it is exactly 3 o'clock

exagérer

exagérer
[ɛgzaʒere]
I. *v t*
to exaggerate

n'exagérez pas les difficultés don't exaggerate the difficulties

II. *v i*
to go too far

* *Milou, tu exagères ! Laisse ce chat tranquille !* Snowy, that's going a bit too far! Leave that cat alone! *

Milou, tu exagères ! Laisse ce chat tranquille !

examen

examen
[ɛgzamɛ̃] *n m*
exam

il a été reçu/collé à son examen he passed/failed his exam

excellent

excellent, e
[ɛksɛlɑ̃, ɑ̃t] *adj*
excellent

...excellent

* *Voilà un excellent bélier!* Here's an excellent battering ram! *Hourra ! ça y est !* Hurray! that's it! *

excursion

excursion
[ɛkskyrsjɔ̃] *n f*
excursion, outing, tour

excuser

excuser
[ɛkskyze]
I. v t
1. to forgive

excusez mon étourderie forgive me for my absent-mindedness

2. to excuse
* *Excusez-moi, je ne vous avais pas vu!* Excuse me, I didn't see you! *Tu parles aux réverbères maintenant ?*

So you talk to lampposts now, do you? *

II. *v pr*
to apologize

il s'est excusé de s'être moqué de toi he apologized for laughing at you

▸ **excuse**
[ɛkskyz] *n f*
1. excuse

il avait une bonne excuse he had a good excuse

2. *pl* apology
nous avons accepté ses excuses we accepted his apology

3. Loc
je dois faire des excuses à mon patron I must apologize to my boss

exemple

exemple
[ɛgzɑ̃pl] *n m*
example

vous devez donner l'exemple you must set an example

par exemple for example

exercice

exercice
[ɛgzɛrsis] *n m*
exercise

as-tu fait tes exercices de maths ? have you done your maths (*Am:* math) exercises?

exister

exister
[ɛgziste] *vi*
to exist

...exister

* *Le yéti !* The Yeti! *C'est... c'est... le yéti !* It's... it's... the Yeti! *Mais non, Tharkey, le yéti n'existe pas !...* No, Tharkey, the Yeti does not exist!... *Haouh* Wo-ow *

expédition

expédition
[ɛkspedisjɔ̃] *n f*
expedition

* *Le lendemain matin...* The next morning... *Nous allons assister au départ de l'expédition scientifique...* We're going to see the scientific expedition off... *

expérience

expérience
[ɛksperjɑ̃s] *n f*
1. experiment

* *Venez, capitaine, venez voir !...* Come, Captain, come and have a look!...
Des éclats de verre !... Tournesol a dû faire une expérience !... Broken glass!... Calculus must have carried out an experiment!... *

...expérience

2. experience
le capitaine Haddock a beaucoup d'expérience Captain Haddock has a lot of experience

expliquer

expliquer
[ɛksplike] *v t*
to explain

il ne comprend rien, on doit tout lui expli-

...expliquer

quer he doesn't understand anything, you have to explain everything to him

► **explication**
[ɛksplikasjɔ̃] *n f*
explanation

avez-vous compris leurs explications ? did you understand their explanations?

exposer

exposer
[ɛkspoze] *v t*
to display, to exhibit

tous ses dessins sont exposés sur les murs de sa chambre all his drawings are displayed on his bedroom walls

► **exposition**
[ɛkspozisjɔ̃] *n f*
exhibition

une exposition de peintures modernes an exhibition of modern paintings

exprès

exprès
[ɛksprɛ] *adv*
on purpose

excuse-moi, je ne l'ai pas fait exprès excuse me, I didn't do it on purpose

extérieur

extérieur
[ɛksterjœr] *n m*
1. outside

l'extérieur du bateau est noir the outside of the ship is black

2. Loc
à l'extérieur outside

extraordinaire

extraordinaire
[ɛkstraɔrdinɛr] *adj*
extraordinary

* *Nous voilà partis, Milou...* We're off, Snowy...
Tintin et Milou vivent des aventures extraordinaires... Tintin and Snowy have extraordinary adventures... *

Tintin et Milou vivent des aventures extraordinaires...

extrêmement

extrêmement
[ɛkstrɛmmɑ̃] *adv*
extremely

continuez, c'est extrêmement intéressant go on, it is extremely interesting

► **extrémité**
[ɛkstremite] *n f*
end

l'extrémité du couteau est pointue the end of the knife is pointed

face

face
[fas] *n f*
1. face

2. Loc
en face de opposite

* *Oui, il est assis en face de moi !* Yes, he's sitting opposite me! *

se fâcher

se fâcher
[fɑʃe] *v pr*
to get angry

* *S'il vous plaît, ne vous fâchez pas contre moi... c'était une erreur...* Don't get angry with me, please... it was a mistake... *

facile

facile
[fasil] *adj*
easy

ça a été facile de le trouver it was easy to find it

sa voiture est facile à conduire his car is easy to drive

facteur

facteur
[faktœr] *n m*
postman

est-ce que le facteur est passé ? has the postman been?

faible

faible
[fɛbl] *adj*
1. weak

* *Tintin se sent faible...* Tintin is feeling weak... *

2. soft
il est trop faible avec son fils he's too soft with his son

3. poor
elle est faible en anglais she's poor at English

Tintin se sent faible...

faim

faim
[fɛ̃] *n f*
j'ai faim I'm hungry

faire

faire
[fɛr]
I. *v t*
1. to do

as-tu fait ton exercice ? have you done your exercise ?

j'ai fait de l'anglais à l'école I did English at school

2. to make
mon père a fait une table my father made a table

3. Loc
faire une promenade to go for a walk

faire construire une maison to have a house built

je veux faire nettoyer cette robe I want to have this dress cleaned

* ***Il n'est pas bien, il faut faire venir le médecin...*** He's not well, we must send for the doctor... *

II. *v impers*
il fait beau the weather's fine/it's fine

il fait chaud/froid it's hot/cold

il fait jour/nuit it's daylight/dark

III. *v pr*
1. to make

je me suis fait des amis I made some friends

...faire

2. Loc
* ***Aïe !...*** Help !...
Le capitaine Haddock s'est fait renverser par une voiture. Captain Haddock's been knocked over by a car. *

Le capitaine Haddock s'est fait renverser par une voiture...

falloir

falloir
[falwar] *v imp*
must, have got to

il faut que je travaille I've got to work

* ***Il ne faut pas qu'ils nous voient !*** They mustn't see us! *

il fallait y penser plus tôt you should have thought of it before

il faudra la prévenir you'll have to tell her

famille

famille
[famij] *n f*
family

voici ma famille this is my family

une famille nombreuse a large family

farine

farine
[farin] *n f*
flour

fatigue

fatigue
[fatig] *n f*
tiredness

* ***Tintin tombe de fatigue !*** Tintin is dead tired! *

► **fatigant, e**
[fatigɑ̃, ɑ̃t] *adj*
1. tiring

la journée a été fatigante it was a tiring day

2. tiresome, annoying
elle est fatigante, elle raconte toujours la même chose she's tiresome, she always says the same thing

► **fatigué, e**
[fatige] *adj*
tired

► **fatiguer**
[fatige] *v t*
to tire

faute

faute
[fot] *n f*
1. mistake

* *Je ne peux pas lire ce message, il y a trop de fautes d'orthographe... Qui a écrit cela?* I can't read this message, there are too many spelling mistakes... Who wrote it? *

2. fault
c'est de ta faute si je suis en retard it's your fault I'm late

fauteuil

fauteuil
[fotœj] *n m*
armchair

faux

faux, fausse
[fo, fos] *adj*
1. wrong

ton addition est fausse your sum is wrong

...faux

2. Loc
fausse monnaie
forged money

faveur

faveur
[favœr] *n f*
favour *(Am:* favor)

une erreur en notre faveur a mistake in our favour

favori

favori, ite
[favɔri, it] *adj*
favourite (*Am:* favorite)

mon film favori my favourite film

féliciter

féliciter
[felisite] *v t*
to congratulate

je vous félicite pour votre succès I congratulate you on your success

► **félicitations**
[felisitasjɔ̃] *n f pl*
congratulations

bravo, mes félicitations! well done, congratulations!

* *Laissez-moi vous serrer la main, Tintin! Tintin... toutes mes félicitations... bravo... Grâce à vous, nous avons pu arrêter les coupables...* Let me shake your hand, Tintin congratulations!... well done!... Thanks to you we've arrested the culprits... *

femme

femme
[fam] *n f*
1. woman

c'est une femme médecin qui est venue a woman doctor came

2. wife
voici la femme de Séraphin Lampion here's Jolyon Wagg's wife

3. Loc
femme de ménage cleaning lady

fenêtre

fenêtre
[fənɛtr] *n f*
window

* *Tintin regarde par la fenêtre du train.* Tintin is looking out of the train window. *

Tintin regarde par la fenêtre du train.

fer

fer
[fɛr] *n m*
iron

une barre de fer an iron bar

un fer à repasser an iron

ferme

ferme
[fɛrm]
I. *n f*
farm
ils ont une ferme they have a farm

II. *adj*
firm
soyez ferme, refusez! be firm, refuse!

► **fermier, ère**
[fɛrmje, ɛr] *n*
farmer *n m,*
farmer's wife *n f*

fermer

fermer
[fɛrme] *v t*
to shut, to close

* *Vous oubliez toujours de fermer la porte !...* You always forget to close the door!... *

fermier

fermier, ère
→ FERME

fête

fête
[fɛt] *n f*
1. holiday

la fête nationale française the French national holiday

2. party
j'ai été invité à une fête I've been invited to a party

feu

feu
[fø] *n m*
pl feux
fire

feu de camp campfire

feuilleton

feuilleton
[fœjtɔ̃] *n m*
serial

février

février
[fevrije] *n m*
February

fier

fier, ère
[fjɛr] *adj*
proud

fièvre

fièvre
[fjɛvr] *n f*
temperature, fever

elle a de la fièvre she's running a temperature

▶ **fiévreux, euse**
[fjevrø, øz] *adj*
feverish

se sentir fiévreux to feel feverish

fille

fille
[fij] *n f*
1. girl

connais-tu cette fille ? do you know that girl?

2. daughter
c'est la fille de M. et Mme Lampion she's Mr and Mrs Waggs' daughter

film

film
[film] *n m*
film (*Am:* movie)

quel film passe-t-on ce soir ? which film is on tonight?

fils

fils
[fis] *n m*
son

...fils

Didi est le fils de Monsieur Wang...

...fils

* *Laisse-nous, et sois sage !* Leave us alone, and behave yourself!
Bien, papa... OK, father...
Didi est le fils de M. Wang... Didi is Mr Wang's son... *

fin

fin
[fɛ̃] *n f*
end

viens à la fin de l'après-midi come at the end of the afternoon

▶ **finalement**
[finalmɑ̃] *adv*
finally, in the end

▶ **fin, e**
[fɛ̃, in] *adj*
thin

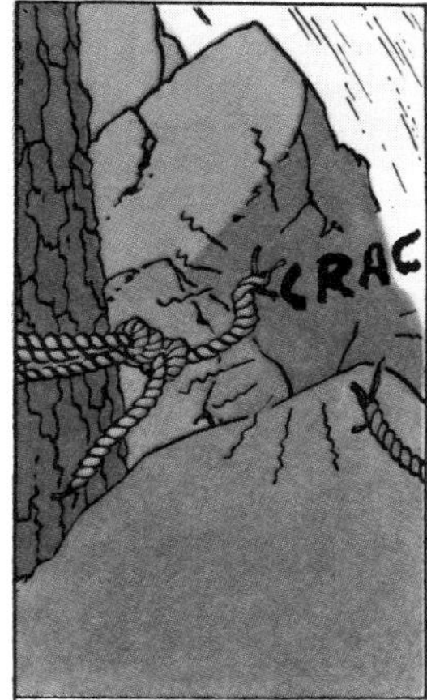

La corde était trop fine.

* *La corde était trop fine.* The rope was too thin. *

finir

finir
[finir]
I. *v t*
to finish

tu dois finir tes devoirs you have to finish your homework

...finir

II. *v i*
to end

les vacances finissent demain the holidays end tomorrow

l'histoire finit bien the story ends happily

firme

firme
[firm] *n f*
firm

...firme

il travaille pour une grande firme he works for a large firm

flamme

flamme
[flam] *n f*
flame

j'ai vu la flamme d'une bougie I saw the flame of a candle

flash

flash
[flaʃ] *n m*
pl **flashes**
flash

les flashes des photographes the photographers' flashes

fleur

fleur
[flœr] *n f*
flower

fleuve

fleuve
[flœv] *n m*
river

* *En Amazonie...* In Amazonia...
Tintin descend le fleuve. Tintin is going down the river. *

En Amazonie...
Tintin descend le fleuve.

fois

Le yéti est trois fois plus grand que Tchang !

fois
[fwa] *n f*
time

* *Le yéti est trois fois plus grand que Tchang !* The Yeti is three times bigger than Chang! *

* *Mille sabords, je dois vous couper les cheveux dix fois par jour !* Blistering barnacles, I have to cut your hair ten times a day! *

Mille sabords, je dois vous couper les cheveux dix fois par jour !

folie

folie
[fɔli] *n f*
1. **madness**

sa folie l'a égaré his madness led him astray

2. **foolish thing**
c'est une folie de dire ça it's a foolish thing to say

foncé

foncé, e
[fɔ̃se] *adj*
dark

rouge foncé dark red

fonctionner

fonctionner
[fɔ̃ksjɔne] *v i*
to work
la télévision ne fonctionne pas the television doesn't work

fond

Le capitaine est tombé au fond de la rivière.

fond
[fɔ̃] *n m*
1. **bottom**

* *Le capitaine est tombé au fond de la rivière.* The captain has fallen to the bottom of the river. *

2. Loc
* *Tintin est au fond du couloir.* Tintin is at the end of the corridor. *

au fond du placard at the back of the cupboard

Tintin est au fond du couloir.

football

football
[futbol] *n m*
football, soccer

si on jouait au football let's play football

forêt

forêt
[fɔrɛ] *n f*
forest

forme

forme
[fɔrm] *n f*
1. shape

cela a la forme d'un œuf it's in the shape of an egg

2. Loc
être en forme to be fit

* *Pour escalader cette montagne il faut être en forme.* You have to be fit to climb this mountain. *

Pour escalader cette montagne il faut être en forme...

formidable

formidable
[formidabl] *adj*
fantastic, great

le film était formidable the film was great

fort

Tintin est plus fort que lui.

fort, e
[fɔr, ɔrt] *adj*
1. strong

* *Tintin est plus fort que lui.* Tintin's stronger than him. *

le thé est fort the tea is strong

2. loud
* *La Castafiore chante trop fort !...* Signora Castafiore is singing too loud!...
Vous croyez ? Do you think so? *

AAAA
JE RIS
La Castafiore chante trop fort !...
Vous croyez ?

3. good
mon frère est fort en science my brother's good at science

fou

fou, folle
[fu, fɔl] *adj*
mad

* *Il est devenu fou !... C'est affreux !* He's gone mad! Its awful!... *

...fou

TO UNG SI NAN PEI
Il est devenu fou !... C'est affreux !

four

four
[fur] *n m*
oven

elle met le gâteau au four she's putting the cake in the oven

fourchette

fourchette
[furʃɛt] *n f*
fork

fourrure

fourrure
[furyr] *n f*
fur

la fourrure du chat the cat's fur

frais

frais, fraîche
[frɛ, frɛʃ] *adj*
1. cool, cold

* *Je boirais bien un verre d'eau fraîche !*

Je boirais bien un verre d'eau fraîche !

...frais

I could do with a glass of cold water. *

2. fresh
* *Regardez !* Look!
Ce crabe n'est pas frais ! This crab isn't fresh!
Mais si, il est frais mon crabe ! très frais, je vous assure... But my crab is fresh – very fresh – I promise you... *

fraise

fraise
[frɛz] *n f*
strawberry

framboise

framboise
[frɑ̃bwaz] *n f*
raspberry

France

France
[frɑ̃s] *n f*
France

► **français, e**
[frɑ̃sɛ, ɛz] *adj*
French

c'est une voiture française it's a French car

...France

► **Français, e**
[frɑ̃sɛ, ɛz] *n*
Frenchman *n m*
Frenchwoman *n f*
n pl the French

► **français**
[frɑ̃sɛ] *n m*
French

il parle français he speaks French

franc

franc
[frɑ̃] *n m*
(French) franc

cela coûte 300 francs it costs 300 francs

frapper

frapper
[frape] *v t*
1. to hit

* *Il frappe Milou.* He's hitting Snowy. *

...frapper

Il frappe Milou.

2. to knock
quelqu'un frappe à la porte there's somebody knocking at the door

frère

frère
[frɛr] *n m*
brother

voici mon frère cadet this is my younger brother

frigo

frigo
[frigo] *n m*
fridge (*Am:* refrigerator)

n'oublie pas de mettre le beurre au frigo don't forget to put the butter in the fridge

frites

frites
[frit] *n f pl*
chips (*Am:* French fries)

froid

froid, e
[frwa, ad]
I. *adj*
cold

...froid

en hiver le vent est froid in winter the wind is cold

mange vite, ta viande sera froide eat up or your meat will get cold

II. *n m*
il tremble de froid he's shivering with cold

III. *adv*
* *Dépêchons-nous, Milou ! Il fait très froid aujourd'hui.* Hurry up, Snowy! It's very cold today. *

fromage

fromage
[frɔmaʒ] *n m*
cheese

frontière

frontière
[frɔ̃tjɛr] *n f*
border

* *Tintin va passer la frontière.* Tintin is going to cross the border. *

Tintin va passer la frontière.

fruit

fruit
[frɥi] *n m*
fruit

voulez-vous des fruits ? would you like some fruit?

les fruits fruit

fuir

fuir
[fɥir] *v i*
to run away

* *Attention ! Ils fuient !* Look out! They're running away! *

...fuir

fumer

fumer
[fyme] *v t*
to smoke

le capitaine Haddock fume la pipe Captain Haddock smokes a pipe

je ne fume pas I don't smoke

► **fumée**
[fyme] *n f*
smoke

* *Qu'est-ce que c'est cette fumée là-bas ?* What's that smoke over there?
Mais c'est un incendie!... It's a fire!... *

► **fumeur, euse**
[fymœr, øz] *n*
smoker

compartiment non-fumeurs non-smoking compartment

furieux

furieux, euse
[fyrjø, øz] *adj*
furious

* *Attention Abdallah, cette fois je suis vraiment furieux ! !* Look out, Abdullah, this time I'm really furious!!
Ha ! ha ! ha ! ha ! Ha! ha! ha! ha! *

futur

futur, e
[fytyr] *adj*
future

il pense à son futur métier he's thinking of his future job

► **futur**
[fytyr] *n m*
future

personne ne connaît le futur nobody can see into the future

GGGGG

gagner

gagner
[gaɲe] *v t*
1. to win

Tintin a gagné la course Tintin won the race

2. to earn
gagner de l'argent to earn money

3. Loc
gagner du temps to save time

gai

gai, e
[ge] *adj*
cheerful

* *Tralalaouti ! Dzim ! Boum !... Tralalalaouti !...* Too-ra... loor-ra loor-ra-lay!...
Tintin a l'air très gai... Tintin looks very cheerful... *

Tralalaouti ! ♪ Dzim !
Boum !... Tralalaouti !...
Tintin a l'air très gai...

gant

gant
[gɑ̃] *n m*
1. glove

2. Loc
gant de toilette flannel (*Am:* washcloth)

garage

garage
[garaʒ] *n m*
garage

...garage

▶ **garagiste**
[garaʒist] *n m*
mechanic

garantir

garantir
[garɑ̃tir] *v t*
to guarantee

ils garantissent les montres un an they guarantee the watches for one year

garçon

garçon
[garsɔ̃] *n m*
1. boy

2. Loc
garçon de café waiter

garder

garder
[garde] *v t*
1. to look after

* *Tintin garde Abdal-*

...garder

WOUIN !
WOUIN !
WOUIN !
Tintin garde Abdallah.

lah. Tintin's looking after Abdullah.
Wouin ! wouin ! wouin ! Boo-hoo! Boo-hoo! *

2. to keep
* *Tu peux le garder, cela pourra peut-être te servir...* You can keep it, it might prove useful... *

Loc
garde ton manteau il fait froid keep your coat on, it's cold

Tu peux le garder, cela pourra peut-être te servir...

gardien

gardien, enne
[gardjɛ̃, ɛn] *n*

Loc
gardien d'immeuble caretaker (*Am:* janitor)

gardien de but goalkeeper

gardien de prison warder (*Am:* prison guard)

* ***Trois gardiens de prison viennent chercher Tintin.*** Three warders come to fetch Tintin. *

Trois gardiens de prison viennent chercher Tintin

gare

gare
[gar] *n f*
1. station

le train entre en gare the train is coming into the station

2. Loc
gare routière bus station

garer

garer
[gare] *v t*
to park

* ***Pouvons-nous garer notre voiture devant les grilles ?*** Can we park our car in front of the gates?
Oui, bien sûr... Yes, of course... *

gas-oil

gas-oil, gazole
[gazwal] [gazɔl] *n m*
diesel oil

gâteau

gâteau
[gato] *n m*
pl gâteaux
cake

voulez-vous encore du gâteau ? do you want some more cake?

gauche

Haddock est assis à la gauche de Tintin.

...gauche

gauche
[goʃ] *n f*
left

* ***Tchiip Tchiip Tchiip*** Creep Creep Creep
Chut ! Ssh!
Haddock est assis à la gauche de Tintin... Captain Haddock is sitting on Tintin's left... *

regarde à gauche look left

gaz

gaz
[gaz] *n m inv*
gas

l'air est un gaz air is a gas

cuisinière à gaz gas cooker (*Am:* gas stove)

geler

geler
[ʒəle]

...geler

1. *v i*
to freeze

la rivière a gelé pendant la nuit the river has frozen (over) during the night

2. *v imp*
il gèle it's freezing

* ***Vous avez remarqué ?... Il a gelé cette nuit.*** Did you notice? It froze last night. *

gendarme

gendarme
[ʒɑ̃darm] *n m*
policeman

* *Le gendarme leur signale de s'arrêter.* The policeman is signalling to them to stop. *

▸ **gendarmerie**
[ʒɑ̃darmeri] *n f*
police station

Le gendarme leur signale de s'arrêter.

général

général, e, aux
[ʒeneral, o] *adj*
1. general

une idée générale a general idea

2. Loc
en général usually, generally

en général, je me lève à huit heures I usually get up at eight o'clock

▸ **généralement**
[ʒeneralmɑ̃] *adv*
generally, usually

genou

genou
[ʒenu] *n m*
pl genoux
knee

genre

genre
[ʒɑ̃r] *n m*
1. kind, type

aimez-vous ce genre de spectacle ? do you like this kind of show?

2. Loc
le genre humain the human race

gens

gens
[ʒɑ̃] *n m pl*
people

* *Il y a beaucoup de gens !* There are a lot of people! *

gentil

gentil, ille
[ʒɑ̃ti, ij] *adj*
1. nice, kind

elle a toujours été

...gentil

gentille avec moi she's always been nice to me

2. good
est-ce qu'Abdallah a été gentil ? was Abdullah good?

▸ **gentillesse**
[ʒɑ̃tijɛs] *n f*
kindness

merci de votre gentillesse thank you for your kindness

géographie

géographie
[ʒeografi] *n f*
geography

gérant

gérant, e
[ʒerɑ̃, ɑ̃t] *n*
manager

glace

glace
[glas] *n f*
1. ice

* *Ils glissent sur la glace.* They're slipping on the ice. *

2. ice cream
j'aime la glace à la vanille I like vanilla ice cream

3. window
lavons les glaces de la voiture ! let's wash the car windows!

Ils glissent sur la glace.

...glace

4. mirror
* *Haddock se regarde dans la glace.* Captain Haddock is looking at himself in the mirror. *

gonflé

gonflé, e
[gɔ̃fle] *adj*
swollen

son pied est gonflé his foot is swollen

gorge

gorge
[gɔrʒ] *n f*
throat

goût

goût
[gu] *n m*
taste, flavour (*Am:* flavor)

* *Votre dîner, Monsieur.* Your dinner, Sir. *Hum ! Voyons s'il a un aussi drôle de goût que celui d'hier.* Hmm! Let see if it has the same strange taste as yesterday. *

Votre dîner, Monsieur.
Hum ! Voyons s'il a un aussi drôle de goût que celui d'hier.

...goût

la sauce a bon/mauvais goût the sauce tastes good/bad

* *Cette plaisanterie est de très mauvais goût.* This joke is in very bad taste. *

Tintin et la Castafiore ont des goûts différents Tintin and Signora Castafiore have different tastes

Ha ! ha ! ha ! ha !
Ha ! ha ! ha ! ha !

Cette plaisanterie est de très mauvais goût.

goûter

goûter
[gute]
1. *v t*
to taste

goûte la soupe taste the soup

2. *v i*
to have tea (*Am:* a snack)

venez goûter ! come and have tea!

gouvernement

gouvernement
[guvɛrnəmɑ̃] *n m*
government

gramme

gramme
[gram] *n m*
gramme

grand

grand
[grɑ̃, ɑ̃d] *adj*
1. tall

* *Tintin est plus grand qu'Abdallah.* Tintin is taller than Abdullah. *

2. big
voici son grand frère here's his big brother

3. large
une grande fortune a large fortune

4. great
c'est un grand homme he's great man

grands-parents

grands-parents
[grɑ̃parɑ̃] *n m pl*
grandparents

▸ **grand-père**
[grɑ̃pɛr] *n m*
pl grands-pères
grandfather

▸ **grand-mère**
[grɑ̃mɛr] *n f*
pl grand(s)-mères
grandmother

grange

grange
[grɑ̃ʒ] *n f*
barn

gratte-ciel

gratte-ciel
[gratsjɛl] *n m inv*
skyscraper

gratuit

gratuit, e
[gratɥi, it] *adj*
free

l'entrée est gratuite admission is free

nous avons eu des billets gratuits pour le cirque we got free tickets for the circus

grave

grave
[grav] *adj*
1. serious

* *Sapristi ! l'accident a l'air grave... arrêtons-nous...* Great snakes! the accident looks serious... let's stop... *

2. deep, low
sa voix est grave he's got a deep voice

Grèce

Grèce
[grɛs] *n f*
Greece

▶ **grec, grecque**
[grɛk] *adj*
Greek

▶ **Grec, Grecque**
[grɛk] *n*
Greek

▶ **grec**
[grɛk] *n m*
Greek

apprendre le grec to learn Greek

grêle

grêle
[grɛl] *n f*
hail

grenier

grenier
[grənje] *n m*
attic

le grenier est plein de vieilles choses the attic is full of old things

grenouille

grenouille
[grənuj] *n f*
frog

grève

grève
[grɛv] *n f*
strike

ils sont en grève they are on strike

grillade

grillade
[grijad] *n f*
grilled (*Am:* broiled) meat

grippe

grippe
[grip] *n f*
flu

* *Mais que se passe-t-il donc ?...* But what's happening?

...grippe

Rien, rien de grave, mais j'ai la grippe... Nothing serious, but I've got the flu... *

gris

gris, e
[gri, iz] *adj*
grey (*Am:* gray)

avez-vous vu passer une voiture grise ? did you see a grey car go past?

gros

gros, grosse
[gro, gros] *adj*
1. big

* *Oh ! quel gros léopard !...* Oh! what a big leopard! *

...gros

2. fat
* *Elle est très grosse...* She's very fat... *

groseille

groseille
[grozɛj] *n f*
red currant

groupe

groupe
[grup] *n m*
group

un groupe d'enfants a group of children

groupe sanguin blood group, blood type

guérir

guérir
[gerir]
1. *v t*
to cure, to make better

2. *v i*
to get better

* *Prends ce médicament, il va te guérir... je t'assure... avec ça tu vas guérir vite...*

...guérir

Take this medicine, it will make you better... I promise you, with this you'll soon get better... *

guerre

guerre
[gɛr] *n f*
war

guichet

guichet
[giʃɛ] *n m*
counter

* *Je suis désolé. Vous devez vous adresser à un autre guichet.* I'm sorry, you have to go to a different counter. *

guide

guide
[gid] *n m*
1. guide book

* *Et trois heures plus tard...* And three hours later...
Lisons le guide avant de nous mettre en route... Let's read the guide book before we start out.
Oui, mais nous devons partir très vite. Yes, but we have to leave very soon. *

2. guide
suivez le guide ! follow the guide!

guitare

guitare
[gitar] *n f*
guitar

gymnase

gymnase
[ʒimnaz] *n m*
gymnasium

gymnastique

gymnastique
[ʒimnastik] *n f*
gymnastics

la gymnastique développe les muscles gymnastics develops your muscles

habile

habile
[abil] *adj*
clever

* *Il est très habile de ses mains...* He's very clever with his hands... *

Il est très habile de ses mains...

s'habiller

s'habiller
[sabije] *v pr*
to get dressed

habiter

habiter
[abite] *v t*
to live

ils habitent à Moulinsart/en France they live in Marlinspike/in France

habitude

habitude
[abityd] *n f*
habit

...habitude

► **d'habitude**
[dabityd] *loc adv*
usually

Loc
comme d'habitude as usual

haricot

haricot
['ariko] *n m*
bean

...haricot

haricots verts French beans (*Am:* string beans)

haut

haut, e
['o, 'ot] *adj*
1. high

* *Dans les Andes...* In the Andes...
Cette montagne est très haute, mais il faut que nous la franchissions... That mountain is very high, but we have to climb it... *

Dans les Andes...
Cette montagne est très haute, mais il faut que nous la franchissions...

2. loud
parle à voix haute speak in a loud voice

3. Loc
en haut upstairs

la chambre est en haut the bedroom is upstairs

en haut de at the top of

hebdomadaire

hebdomadaire
[ɛbdɔmadɛr]
I. *adj*
weekly

une réunion hebdomadaire a weekly meeting

II. *n m*
weekly

il achète plusieurs hebdomadaires he buys several weeklies

heure

heure
[œr] *n f*
1. hour

il y a trois heures que Tintin attend Tintin's been waiting for three hours

2. time
quelle heure est-il ? what time is it?

3. Loc
à l'heure on time

* *Ah ! je vais être juste à l'heure !* Ah! I'll be right on time! *

de bonne heure early

le matin de bonne heure early in the morning

à tout à l'heure ! so long!/see you later!

* *A tout à l'heure, Milou, sois sage...* So long, Snowy, be good... *

heureux

heureux, euse
[œrø, øz] *adj*
happy

► **heureusement**
[œrøzmɑ̃] *adv*
fortunately, happily, luckily

Loc
* *Heureusement que je passais par là, n'est-ce pas ?...* It's lucky that I came this way, isn't it?... *

hier

hier
[(i)jɛr] *adv*
yesterday

hier matin/soir yesterday morning/evening

c'est le journal d'hier it's yesterday's newspaper

histoire

histoire
[istwar] *n f*
1. story

il raconte toujours des histoires drôles he always tells funny stories

2. history
à l'école, nous apprenons l'histoire de notre pays at school, we are learning the history of our country

hiver

hiver
[ivɛr] *n m*
winter

nous avons eu beaucoup de neige cet hiver we have had a lot of snow this winter

homme

homme
[ɔm] *n m*
man

le premier homme à marcher sur la lune the first man to walk on the moon

* *Tintin suit un homme.* Tintin is following a man. *

Tintin suit un homme.

honte

honte
['ɔ̃t] *n f*
shame

* *Tu devrais avoir honte !* Shame on you!/ You should be ashamed of yourself! *

arrête de dire des bêtises, j'ai honte de toi stop talking nonsense, I'm ashamed of you

hôpital

hôpital
[ɔpital] *n m*
pl **hôpitaux** [ɔpito]
hospital

à l'hôpital in hospital (*Am:* in the hospital)

horaire

horaire
[ɔrɛr] *n m*
timetable

horloge

horloge
[ɔrlɔʒ] *n f*
clock

l'horloge de l'église the church clock

hors de

hors de
['ɔrdə] *loc prép*
out of

* *Debout, là-dedans ! ! !* Wake up!!!

...hors de

Haddock bondit hors du lit. Haddock leaps out of the bed. *

hors-d'œuvre

hors-d'œuvre
['ɔrdœvr] *n m inv*
hors d'œuvre, starter
(*Am:* appetizer)

Haddock bondit hors du lit...

hospitalité

hospitalité
[ɔspitalite] *n f*
hospitality

hôtel

hôtel
[otɛl] *n m*
1. hotel

2. Loc
hôtel de ville town hall
(*Am:* city hall)

hôtesse

hôtesse
[otɛs] *n f*
hôtesse de l'air air hostess (*Am:* stewardess)

huile

huile
[ɥil] *n f*
oil

huître

huître
[ɥitr] *n f*
oyster

humeur

humeur
[ymœr] *n f*
mood

* *Mille sabords ! ! !* Blistering barnacles!!!

...humeur

Pan Pan Bang Bang
Il est de mauvaise humeur... He's in a bad mood... *

humide

humide
[ymid] *adj*
1. wet

le sol est humide the floor is wet

Il est de mauvaise humeur...

...humide

2. damp
le climat est humide it's a damp climate

humour

humour
[ymur] *n m*
humour

il a beaucoup d'humour he has a good sense of humour

ici

ici
[isi] *adv*
1. here

* *Viens ici, Milou !... * Come here, Snowy!...
Wouah ! Wouah ! Woof! Woof! *

2. Loc
jusqu'ici up till now

idée

idée
[ide] *n f*
idea

* *Zut ! Plus de balles... Eh bien, je vais utiliser mon fusil comme ceci...* Gosh! I'm out of bullets... Well, I'll use my rifle like this...
Tintin a toujours de bonnes idées. Tintin always has good ideas. *

Tintin a toujours de bonnes idées.

identité

identité
[idɑ̃tite] *n f*
identity

carte d'identité identity card

idiot

idiot, e
[idjo, ɔt]
I. *adj*
stupid

tu es vraiment idiot ! you're really stupid!

II. *n*
idiot

me prenez-vous pour un idiot ? do you take me for an idiot?

ignorer

ignorer
[iɲɔre] *v t*
not to know

j'ignore où il est parti I don't know where he's gone

* *J'ignore comment cet accident a pu se produire, monsieur le directeur.* I don't know how this accident happened, Sir. *

il

il
[il] *pron pers sing*
1. he

* *Mais où est-il donc ?...* Wherever is he?... *

2. it
j'aime ce livre, il est intéressant I like this book, it's interesting

il neige it's snowing

► **ils**
[il] *pron pers pl*
they

ils vont aller à Genève en avion they are going to fly to Geneva

île

île
[il] *n f*
island

* *Voilà l'Ile Noire...* Here is the Black Island... *

immédiatement

immédiatement
[imedjatmɑ̃] *adv*
at once, immediately

il faut que je voie Tintin immédiatement I must see Tintin at once

* *Capitaine, il faut que vous veniez immédiatement !... oui... oui... immédiatement... Dzingg Oh ! ...Cling Cling Cling Cling* Captain, you must come immediately!... yes... yes... immediately... Zzingg Oh! ...Cling Cling Cling Cling *

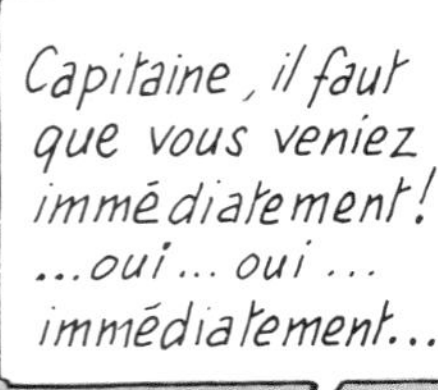

immeuble

immeuble
[imœbl] *n m*
building, block of flats (*Am:* apartment building)

son appartement est dans un vieil immeuble his flat is in an old building

immigré

immigré, e
[imigre] *adj, n*
immigrant

immobile

immobile
[imɔbil] *adj*
motionless, still

* *Tintin restait immobile.* Tintin stood still. *

...immobile

Tintin restait immobile.

imperméable

imperméable
[ɛ̃pɛrmeabl]
I. *adj*
waterproof

est-ce que ton manteau est imperméable ? is your coat waterproof?

II. *n m*
raincoat, mackintosh

il a oublié son imperméable dans le train he's left his raincoat (behind) in the train

► **imper**
[ɛ̃pɛr] *n m*
mac (*Am:* raincoat)

important

important, e
[ɛ̃pɔrtɑ̃, ɑ̃t] *adj*
1. important

* *Et pendant ce temps-là...* Meanwhile...

...important

Les Dupondt jouent un rôle important dans cette affaire. The Thompsons are playing an important part in this case. *

2. considerable
une importante somme d'argent a considerable sum of money

Et pendant ce temps-là ...
Les Dupondt jouent un rôle important dans cette affaire.

► **importance**
[ɛ̃pɔrtɑ̃s] *n f*
importance

* *Ce que j'ai à dire a une grande importance.* What I have to say is of great importance. *Oui !* Yes! *

► **n'importe où, qui...**
→ N'IMPORTE

Ce que j'ai à dire a une grande importance.
Oui !

impossible

impossible
[ɛ̃pɔsibl] *adj*
impossible

* *Ah ! Ah ! Ah !... Aller sur la lune !... Ah ! Ah !... Mais c'est impossible !... Ah ! Ah ! Ah !... Vous plaisantez !...* Ha! Ha! Ha!... Go to the moon!... Ha! Ha!... But it's impossible!... Ha! Ha! Ha!... You're joking!... *

Ah ! Ah ! Ah !... Aller sur la lune ! ... Ah ! Ah ! Mais c'est impossible !... Ah ! Ah ! Ah !... Vous plaisantez !...

impôt

impôt
[ɛ̃po] *n m*
tax

déclaration d'impôt
tax return

impressionnant

impressionnant, e
[ɛ̃prɛsjɔnɑ̃, ɑ̃t] *adj*
impressive

* *Oh ! ! !... Quel spectacle impressionnant !* Oh!!!... What an impressive sight! *

Oh !!!... Quel spectacle impressionnant !

incassable

incassable
[ɛ̃kasabl] *adj*
unbreakable

des assiettes incassables unbreakable plates

incendie

incendie
[ɛ̃sɑ̃di] *n m*
fire

* *Le capitaine lutte contre l'incendie.* The Captain is fighting the fire. *

Le capitaine lutte contre l'incendie.

inclus

inclus, e
[ɛ̃kly, yz] *adj*
inclusive (*Am:* through)

jusqu'au 23 avril inclus until April 23rd inclusive (*Am:* through April 23)

inconvénient

inconvénient
[ɛ̃kɔvenjɑ̃] *n m*
drawback

ta solution a un inconvénient, il nous faut une lime your solution has one drawback: we need a file

indépendant

indépendant, e
[ɛ̃depɑ̃dɑ̃, ɑ̃t] *adj*
independent

la Syldavie est un pays indépendant Syldavia is an independent country

indigestion

indigestion
[ɛ̃diʒɛstjɔ̃] *n f*
indigestion

indiquer

indiquer
[ɛ̃dike] *v t*
to indicate

* *Tout indique que le professeur a été enlevé.* Everything indicates that the Professor's been kidnapped. *

indispensable

indispensable
[ɛ̃dispɑ̃sabl] *adj*
essential

il est indispensable que nous prenions un peu de repos it's essential that we have a little rest

industrie

industrie
[ɛ̃dystri] *n f*
industry

infirmerie

infirmerie
[ɛ̃firmeri] *n f*
infirmary, sick bay

* *Sortez-moi de l'infirmerie !* Get me out of the infirmary! *

► **infirmière**
[ɛ̃firmjɛr] *n f*
nurse

information

information
[ɛ̃fɔrmasjɔ̃] *n f*
1. information

j'ai besoin d'une information I need some information

2. news
* *Tintin écoute les informations.* Tintin's listening to the news. *

Tintin écoute les informations.

informatique

informatique
[ɛ̃fɔrmatik] *n f*
computer science, data processing

informer

informer
[ɛ̃fɔrme] *v t*
to let someone know, to inform

vous devez nous informer de votre départ you must let us know when you're going to leave

ingénieur

ingénieur
[ɛ̃ʒenjœr] *n m*
engineer

inondation

inondation
[inɔ̃dasjɔ̃] *n f*
flood

* *La voie ferrée est coupée à cause des inondations.* The railway line is cut off because of the floods. *

La voie ferrée est coupée à cause des inondations.

inquiet

inquiet, ète
[ɛ̃kjɛ, ɛt] *adj*
worried

* *Je suis inquiet, le professeur a disparu...* I'm worried: the Professor has disappeared... *

► **s'inquiéter**
[sɛ̃kjete] *v pr*
to worry

ne vous inquiétez pas, je vais arranger tout ça don't worry, I'll sort everything out

insecte

insecte
[ɛ̃sɛkt] *n m*
insect

insolation

insolation
[ɛ̃sɔlasjɔ̃] *n f*
sunstroke

nous allons attraper une insolation we're going to get sunstroke

installation

installation
[ɛ̃stalasjɔ̃] *n f*
1. installation, putting in

2. fittings
installations sanitaires modernes modern sanitary fittings

► **s'installer**
[sɛ̃stale] *v pr*
to settle down

* *Laissez-moi m'installer dans mon fauteuil et lisez-moi la lettre d'Abdallah...* Let me settle down in my armchair, and read me Abdullah's letter... *

instant

instant
[ɛ̃stɑ̃] *n m*
moment, instant

* *Attendez-moi, je reviens dans un instant.* Wait for me, I'll be back in a moment.
O.K. OK. *

instruction

instruction
[ɛ̃stryksjɔ̃] *n f*
1. education

instruction religieuse religious education

2. Loc
instruction civique civics

instrument

instrument
[ɛ̃strymɑ̃] *n m*
instrument

instrument de musique musical instrument

insupportable

insupportable
[ɛ̃sypɔrtabl] *adj*
unbearable

cet enfant est insupportable that child is unbearable

intelligent

intelligent, e
[ɛ̃teliʒɑ̃, ɑ̃t] *adj*
clever, intelligent

* *Quel chien intelligent !* What a clever dog! *

Quel chien intelligent !

intention

intention
[ɛ̃tɑ̃sjɔ̃] *n f*
1. intention

connaissez-vous ses intentions ? do you know what his intentions are ?

2. Loc
j'ai l'intention de le lui dire I intend to tell him

interdire

interdire
[ɛ̃tɛrdir] *v t*
to forbid

* *Milou, je t'interdis de boire encore ! Tu devrais avoir honte !* Snowy, I forbid you to drink anymore! You should be ashamed of yourself! *

▸ **interdit, e**
[ɛ̃tɛrdi, it] *adj*
1. forbidden

il est strictement interdit de parler it is strictly forbidden to talk

2. Loc
interdit de fumer no smoking

...interdire

Milou, je t'interdis de boire encore ! Tu devrais avoir honte !

intéresser

intéresser
[ɛ̃terese] *v t*
to interest

ce film ne m'intéresse pas this film doesn't interest me

▸ **s'intéresser**
[sɛ̃terese] *v pr*
to be interested

Tintin s'intéresse à ce personnage étrange Tintin is interested in this strange character

▸ **intéressant, e**
[ɛ̃teresɑ̃, ɑ̃t] *adj*
interesting

* *Voilà une affaire intéressante...* This is an interesting case...
Je dirais même plus : très intéressante ! To be precise: very interesting! *

Voilà une affaire intéressante ...
Je dirais même plus : très intéressante !

internat

internat
[ɛ̃tɛrna] *n m*
boarding school

international

international, e
[ɛ̃tɛrnasjɔnal] *adj*
pl internationaux
[ɛ̃tɛrnasjɔno]
international

inutile

inutile
[inytil] *adj*
useless

il est inutile de crier it's useless to shout

inviter

inviter
[ɛ̃vite] *v t*
to invite, to ask

...inviter

je vous remercie de nous avoir invités à dîner thank you for inviting us to dinner

▸ **invitation**
[ɛ̃vitasjɔ̃] *n f*
invitation

merci de votre invitation thank you for your invitation

Italie

Italie
[itali] *n f*
Italy

▸ **italien, enne**
[italjɛ̃, ɛn] *adj*
Italian

▸ **Italien, enne**
[italjɛ̃, ɛn] *n*
Italian

les Italiens the Italians

▸ **italien**
[italjɛ̃] *n m*
Italian

apprendre l'italien to learn Italian

jaloux

jaloux, ouse
[ʒalu, uz] *adj*
jealous

il est jaloux de ma fortune he's jealous of my wealth

jamais

jamais
[ʒamɛ] *adv*
never

...jamais

* *Je n'ai plus de force... je n'y arriverai jamais...* I've no more strength... I'll never manage it... *

Je n'ai plus de force ... je n'y arriverai jamais ...

jambe

jambe
[ʒɑ̃b] *n f*
leg

il s'est cassé la jambe he broke his leg

jambon

jambon
[ʒɑ̃bɔ̃] *n m*
ham

janvier

janvier
[ʒɑ̃vje] *n m*
January

le premier/deux janvier the first/second of January (*Am:* January first/second)

venez le 6 janvier come on the 6th of January (*Am:* on January 6)

jardin

jardin
[ʒardɛ̃] *n m*
1. garden

* *Quelle belle journée!* What a lovely day!
Dans le jardin... In the garden... *

Quelle belle journée!
Dans le jardin...

2. Loc
jardin public park

▸ **jardinier**
[ʒardinje] *n m*
gardener

jaune

jaune
[ʒon] *adj*
yellow

les citrons sont jaunes lemons are yellow

jeans

jeans
[dʒinz] *n m*

un jeans a pair of jeans

jeter

jeter
[ʒəte]
I. *v t*
1. to throw

les enfants jettent des cailloux dans la rivière the children are throwing stones in the river

2. to throw away
je vais jeter ces vieux journaux I'm going to throw these old newspapers away

...jeter

II. *v pr*
to throw oneself

* *Tournesol se jeta dans les bras de Haddock.* Calculus threw himself into Haddock's arms. *

Tournesol se jeta dans les bras de Haddock.

jeu

jeu
[ʒø] *n m*
pl jeux
game

...jeu

connais-tu les règles de ce jeu? do you know the rules of this game?

les jeux Olympiques the Olympic Games

jeudi

jeudi
[ʒødi] *n m*
Thursday

...jeudi

viens me voir jeudi come and see me on Thursday

ils ne travaillent pas le jeudi they don't work on Thursdays

jeune

jeune
[ʒœn]
I. *adj*
young

...jeune

Tchang est plus jeune que Tintin Chang is younger than Tintin

II. *n*
young boy *n m*
young girl *n f*

► **jeunesse** [ʒœnɛs] *n f*
1. youth

il aime beaucoup parler de sa jeunesse he likes to talk about his youth

2. young people

une émission pour la jeunesse a programme (*Am:* program) for young people

les jeunes young people

joli

joli, e
[ʒɔli] *adj*
nice, pretty

* *Capitaine, votre costume est vrai-*

...joli

Capitaine, votre costume est vraiment très joli, vous savez ...
Je suis content qu'il vous plaise.

ment très joli, vous savez... You know, Captain, your costume is very nice...
Je suis content qu'il vous plaise. I'm glad you like it. *

c'est la plus jolie robe que j'aie jamais vue it's the prettiest dress I've ever seen

jouer

jouer
[ʒwe] *v i*
to play

si l'on jouait au football/aux cartes let's play football/cards

► **joueur, euse**
[ʒwœr, øz] *n*
player

combien de joueurs y a-t-il dans votre équipe? how many players are there in your team?

Voilà le jouet que j'ai acheté à Abdallah pour son sixième anniversaire ...

► **jouet**
[ʒwɛ] *n m*
toy

* *Voilà le jouet que j'ai acheté à Abdallah pour son sixième anniversaire...* Here's the toy I bought Abdullah for his sixth birthday... *

jour

jour
[ʒur] *n m*
1. day

quel jour sommes-nous, capitaine? what day is it today, Captain?

il y a sept jours dans une semaine there are seven days in a week

2. Loc
il fait jour it's daylight

...jour

* *Ça, par exemple ! Il fait jour. J'ai dû dormir très longtemps...* Well I never! It's daylight. I must have slept for a very long time... *

en plein jour in broad daylight

jour férié public/bank holiday (*Am:* legal holiday)

journal

journal
[ʒurnal] *n m*
pl journaux [ʒurno]
newspaper, paper

* *Regardons le journal... Peut-être y aura-t-il des détails sur cette catastrophe...* Let's look in the paper... Perhaps there'll be some details about this disaster... *

► **journaliste**
[ʒurnalist] *n*
journalist, reporter

...journal

il est journaliste à la radio he's a radio reporter

journée

journée
[ʒurne] *n f*
1. day

quelle belle journée ! what a lovely day !

* *L'épave de l'avion se trouve à cinq journées de marche d'ici...* The wreck of the plane is five days' walk from here. *

...journée

2. Loc
à longueur de journée all day long

joyeux

joyeux, euse
[ʒwajø, øz] *adj*
1. delighted

Tintin est joyeux à l'idée de revoir le capitaine Tintin is delighted at the thought of seeing the Captain again

2. merry
Joyeux Noël ! Merry Christmas!

juillet

juillet
[ʒɥijɛ] *n m*
July

le premier/deux juillet the first/second of July (*Am:* July first/second)

venez le 6 juillet come on the 6th of July (*Am:* on July 6)

juin

juin
[ʒɥɛ̃] *n m*
June

le premier/deux juin the first/second of June (*Am:* June first/second)

venez le 6 juin come on the 6th of June (*Am:* on June 6)

jumeau

jumeau, jumelle
[ʒymo, ʒymɛl] *n*
pl jumeaux, jumelles
twin

* *Dupont et Dupond se ressemblent, mais ils ne sont pas jumeaux.* Thomson and Thompson look alike, but they are not twins. *

► **jumelage**
[ʒymlaʒ] *n m*
twinning

Dupont et Dupond se ressemblent mais ils ne sont pas jumeaux.

...jumeau

le jumelage de deux villes the twinning of two towns

jupe

jupe
[ʒyp] *n f*
skirt

une jupe plissée a pleated skirt

jus

jus
[ʒy] *n m*
juice

jus de fruit fruit juice

jusqu'à

jusqu'à
[ʒyska] *prép*
1. to, as far as

* *Allez jusqu'au bout de la rue et tournez à gauche...* Go to the end of the street and turn left...
D'accord ! All right! *

2. until, till
nous devons attendre jusqu'à demain we must wait until tomorrow

...jusqu'à

3. up to
capitaine, comptez jusqu'à 10 count up to 10, Captain

juste

juste
[ʒyst]
I. *adj*
1. right

avez-vous l'heure juste ? have you got the right time ?

2. fair
ce n'est pas juste, je n'ai rien fait ! it's not fair, I haven't done anything!

3. tight
* *Bizarre, mon chapeau est trop juste...* Strange, my hat is too tight...
Je dirais même plus, mon chapeau est trop juste... to be precise, my hat is too tight... *

II. *adv*
in tune

la Castafiore chante juste Signora Castafiore sings in tune

kilogramme

kilogramme, kilo
[kilɔgram, kilo] *n m*
kilogramme (*Am:* kilogram), kilo

cette pierre pèse au moins dix kilos this stone weighs at least ten kilos

kilomètre

kilomètre
[kilɔmɛtr] *n m*
kilometre
(*Am:* kilometer)

* *Que fait-il ici ? Moulinsart est à 20 kilomètres d'ici.* What's he doing here? Marlinspike is 20 kilometres from here. *

la

la
[la] → LE

là

là
[la] *adv*
1. there

où est la pipe du capitaine ? elle est là, sur la table... where's the Captain's pipe? it's there, on the table...

...là

Là-bas !... Regardez ! ... De l'eau ! ... De l'eau ! ...
?

2. Loc
là-bas over there

* *Là-bas !... Regardez !... De l'eau !... De l'eau...* Over there!... Look!... Water!... Water!... *

laboratoire

laboratoire
[labɔratwar] *n m*
laboratory

...laboratoire

le professeur Tournesol est dans son laboratoire Professor Calculus is in his laboratory

lac

lac
[lak] *n m*
lake

ils se baignent dans le lac they're swimming in the lake

laine

laine
[lɛn] *n f*
wool

laisser

laisser
[lese] *v tr*
1. to leave

...laisser

Les cambrioleurs ont laissé des traces ...

* *Les cambrioleurs ont laissé des traces...* The burglars have left traces behind them... *

laisse-moi tranquille ! leave me alone!

2. to let
laissez-moi parler, je vous prie please, let me speak

laissez-moi entrer/sortir let me in/out

* *Laissez-moi passer, vous...* Let me past, you... *

Laissez-moi passer, vous ...

lait

lait
[lɛ] *n m*
milk

laitue

laitue
[lɛty] *n f*
lettuce

lampe

lampe
[lɑ̃p] *n f*
1. lamp, light

la lampe de chevet est allumée the bedside lamp is on

éteins la lampe switch the light off

2. Loc
lampe de poche torch (*Am:* flashlight)

langue

langue
[lɑ̃g] *n f*
1. tongue

* *Moi aussi, je sais tirer la langue !...* I can stick my tongue out too!... *

2. language
Tintin parle plusieurs langues Tintin speaks several languages

3. Loc
langue maternelle mother tongue

Moi aussi je sais tirer la langue !...

lapin

lapin
[lapɛ̃] *n m*
rabbit

large

large
[larʒ]
I. *adj*
wide

II. *n m*
open sea

...large

Le bateau gagne le large ...

...large

* *Le bateau gagne le large...* The boat is heading for the open sea... *

lavabo

lavabo
[lavabo] *n m*
wash-basin (*Am:* washbowl, sink)

laver

laver
[lave]
I. *v tr*
1. to wash

qui va laver mon pantalon, maintenant ? and who's going to wash my trousers, now?

2. Loc
laver la vaisselle to wash up (*Am:* to do the dishes)

II. *v pr*
to wash, to have a wash (*Am:* to wash up)

va te laver go and have a wash

► **lavage**
[lavaʒ] *n m*
wash

la tache partira au lavage the stain will come out in the wash

► **laverie**
[lavri] *n f*

laverie automatique launderette (*Am:* laundromat)

► **lave-vaisselle**
[lavvɛsɛl] *n m inv*
dishwasher

le

le, la, les
[lə, la, le]

...le

I. *art déf*
1. the

le chien the dog
la clé the key
les arbres the trees

2. my, his, her
j'ai mal à la main I've a pain in my hand

* *Et quelques minutes plus tard... Victoire ! Il ouvre les yeux...* And a few minutes later... Victory! He's opening his eyes... *

...le

Et quelques minutes plus tard...
Victoire ! Il ouvre les yeux...

elle a fermé la bouche she closed her mouth

II. *pron*
1. him, her, them

Tintin ? je l'ai entendu entrer Tintin? I heard him coming in

je ne la connais pas I don't know her

je les ai vus I saw them

2. it, them
* *Retenez votre chien et ne le laissez plus partir, sinon...* Hold your dog and don't let it go again, or else... *

prends ces livres et ne les perds pas take these books and don't lose them

3. Loc
je le sais I know

je l'espère I hope so

Retenez votre chien et ne le laissez plus partir, sinon ...

lécher

lécher
[leʃe] *v t*
to lick

▸ **lèche-vitrines**
[lɛʃvitrin] *n m inv*
window-shopping

faire du lèche-vitrines to go window-shopping

leçon

leçon
[ləsɔ̃] *n f*
lesson

lecture

lecture
[lɛktyr] *n f*
1. reading

Tintin aime la lecture Tintin likes reading

2. something to read

...lecture

* *Heureusement, j'ai pensé à tout : j'ai pris de la lecture pour le voyage...* Fortunately, I've thought of everything: I've brought something to read on the journey... *

léger

léger, ère
[leʒe, ɛr] *adj*
1. light

...léger

ma valise est très légère my suitcase is very light

2. weak
ce café est léger this coffee is weak

3. faint, slight
Milou a entendu un léger bruit Snowy heard a faint noise

légume

légume
[legym] *n m*
vegetable

que voulez-vous comme légumes avec votre poulet ? what vegetables would you like with your chicken?

lendemain

lendemain
[lɑ̃dəmɛ̃] *n m*

...lendemain

1. *le lendemain* the day after, the next day

* *Et le voyage sera long ?* And will the trip be long?
Non, nous partirons jeudi et nous arriverons le lendemain. No, we'll be leaving on Thursday and arriving the next day. *

2. Loc
le lendemain matin/soir the next morning/evening

lent

lent, e
[lɑ̃, lɑ̃t] *adj*
slow

dépêchez-vous, vous êtes trop lents ! hurry up, you're being too slow!

▸ **lentement**
[lɑ̃tmɑ̃] *adv*
slowly

parle lentement, je ne te comprends pas speak slowly, I can't understand what you're saying

lessive

lessive
[lesiv] *n f*
1. washing powder (*Am:* detergent)

2. washing
elle fait la lessive she's doing the washing

lettre

lettre
[lɛtr] *n f*
1. letter

écrivez en lettres majuscules/minuscules write in capital/small letters

2. letter
* *Quelques jours après...* A few days later...
Tintin, vous avez une lettre de Tournesol ! Tintin, you've got a letter from Calculus! *

levée

levée
[ləve] *n f*
collection

les heures de levée sont indiquées sur les boîtes aux lettres collection times are marked on the letter-boxes (*Am:* mailboxes)

lever

lever
[ləve]
I. *v tr*
1. to raise

* *Il lève la main.* He's raising his hand. *

2. to put up, to raise
levez les mains et vite !... le premier qui bouge... put your hands up, quickly!... the first one to move...

II. *v pr*
1. to get up

* *Le lendemain matin...* The next morning... *Allez Milou, il est l'heure de se lever...* Come on, Snowy, it's time to get up... *

2. to rise
le soleil se lève the sun is rising

liberté

liberté
[libεrte] → LIBRE

librairie

librairie
[librεri] *n f*
bookshop
(*Am:* bookstore)

libre

libre
[libr] *adj*
1. free

* *Ne fais plus jamais ça !...* Never do that again... *Te voilà libre, Milou... Tu es content ?...* You're free, Snowy... Are you pleased?... *

vous êtes libre de refuser you're free to refuse

2. free
je ne pourrai pas venir demain, je ne suis pas libre I won't be able to come tomorrow: I'm not free

► **libre-service**
[librəsεrvis] *n m*
pl libres-services
self-service

ce magasin/restaurant est un libre-service this is a self-service shop/restaurant

► **liberté**
[libεrte] *n f*
freedom, liberty

* *Etranger ! Si tu tiens à ta liberté, fais réapparaître le soleil...* Stranger! If you value your freedom... Make the sun shine again... *

...libre

licence

licence
[lisɑ̃s] *n f*
1. degree

faire une licence de français to do a French degree (*Am:* to study for a French degree)

2. licence
licence d'exportation export licence (*Am:* license)

lieu

lieu
[ljø] *n m*
pl lieux
1. place, spot

quel est votre lieu de naissance ? what is your place of birth?

2. Loc
au lieu de in place of, instead of

* *Tonnerre de Brest ! Que faites-vous là, vous deux, au lieu de travailler ?...* Thundering

...lieu

typhoons, What are you two doing, instead of working ?...
Nous nous reposons... Nous sommes fatigués. We're having a rest... We're tired... *

les dernières épreuves du rallye auront lieu à Moulinsart the last trials of the rally will take place at Marlinspike

ligne

ligne
[liɲ] *n f*
1. line

tracez une ligne droite draw a straight line

* *Les premières lignes sont illisibles...* The first lines are illegible... *

2. line
la ligne de chemin de fer est coupée the railway (*Am:* railroad) line is cut off

Les premières lignes sont illisibles...

limonade

limonade
[limɔnad] *n f*
lemonade

linge

linge
[lɛ̃ʒ] *n m*
1. cloth

frotte-le avec un linge mouillé rub it with a damp cloth

...linge

2. linen
linge de table table linen

lire

lire
[lir] *v tr*
to read

lisez cette lettre, Tintin read this letter, Tintin

lisons la carte let's read the map

liste

liste
[list] *n f*
list

j'ai dressé une liste de tous leurs noms I've drawn up a list of all their names

lit

lit
[li] *n m*
1. bed

...lit

!
Vous devriez vous mettre au lit...

* *Vous devriez vous mettre au lit...* You should go to bed... *

2. bed
le lit de la rivière est asséché the river-bed has dried up

litre

litre
[litr] *n m*
litre (*Am:* liter)

littérature

littérature
[literatyr] *n f*
literature

il est professeur de littérature anglaise he teaches English literature

livre

livre
[livr] *n m*
book

* *Capitaine, regardez*

...livre

ce livre : c'est très intéressant... cela va nous aider... nous avons eu de la chance... Captain, look at this book: it's very interesting... it will help us... we've been lucky... *

livre

livre
[livr] *n f*
1. pound, half a kilo

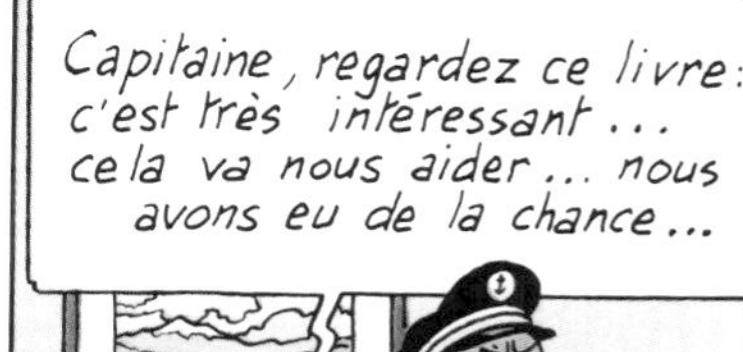
Capitaine, regardez ce livre : c'est très intéressant... cela va nous aider... nous avons eu de la chance...

...livre

une livre de beurre a pound of butter

2. pound

la livre sterling the pound sterling

combien de francs y-a-t-il dans une livre ? how many francs are there to the pound?

location

location
[lɔkasjɔ̃] *n f*
renting, hiring

la location d'une voiture hiring a car (*Am:* car rental)

loger

loger
[lɔʒe] *v tr*
1. to put up, to accommodate

...loger

le capitaine logera Tintin pour quelques jours the Captain will put Tintin up for a few days

2. to live
M. Sakharine loge ici, au deuxième étage Mr Sakharine lives here, on the second floor

logique

logique
[lɔʒik]
I. *adj*
logical

* *Des traces de pas... il y a d'autres hommes ici...* Footprints... there are other men here...
Des traces de pas... donc des hommes... c'est logique... Footprints... therefore men... that's logical... *

...logique

II. *n f*
logic

la logique du raisonnement du professeur Tournesol the logic of Calculus' reasoning

loin

loin
[lwɛ̃] *adv*
1. far

...loin

la gare n'est pas loin the station isn't far

plus loin farther, further

2. Loc
loin de a long way from

Moulinsart est loin de chez Tintin Marlinspike is a long way from Tintin's place

loisirs

loisirs
[lwazir] *n m pl*
spare time

comment occupes-tu tes loisirs ? what do you do in your spare time?

long

long, longue
[lɔ̃, lɔ̃g] *adj*
1. long

...long

elle a les cheveux longs she's got long hair

2. long
le film était long the film lasted a long time

► **long**
[lɔ̃] *n m*
1. length

* *Tintin est tombé de tout son long...* Tintin has fallen full length... *

Tintin est tombé de tout son long...

...long

2. Loc
* *Tintin marche le long du fleuve.* Tintin is walking along the river. *

longtemps

longtemps
[lɔ̃tɑ̃] *adv*
1. for a long time

2. a long time
il y a longtemps qu'il est parti he left a long time ago

Tintin marche le long du fleuve.

...longtemps

3. long
je n'en ai pas pour longtemps I won't be long

* *Pourvu que je n'attende pas trop longtemps !... Je commence à avoir des fourmis dans les jambes...* I hope I don't have to wait too long!... I'm getting pins and needles in my legs... *

louer

louer
[lwe] *v tr*
1. to let, to rent

chambre à louer room to let (*Am:* for rent)

2. to hire (*Am:* to rent)
ils ont loué une voiture they hired a car

loup

loup
[lu] *n m*
wolf

lourd

lourd, e
[lur, lurd] *adj*
heavy

* *Milou, cet os est trop lourd pour toi !...* Snowy, that bone is too heavy for you!... *

...lourd

loyer

loyer
[lwaje] *n m*
rent

le loyer de notre appartement est cher the rent on our flat (*Am:* apartment) is very high

lumière

lumière
[lymjɛr] *n f*
1. light

...lumière

venez dans cette pièce, il y a plus de lumière come in this room, there is more light

2. light
il fait nuit, allume la lumière it's dark: put the light on

* *Mille milliards de mille sabords!... Le courant est coupé : il n'y a plus de lumière...* Billions of blue blistering barnacles!... The power has been cut off: there's no more light... *

...lumière

lundi

lundi
[lœ̃di] *n m*
Monday

viens me voir lundi come and see me on Monday

ils ne travaillent pas le lundi they don't work on Mondays

lune

lune
[lyn] *n f*
1. moon

la lune se lève the moon is rising

2. Loc
* *La « Licorne », au clair de lune...* The "Unicorn" in the moonlight... *

La "Licorne" au clair de lune ...

lunettes

lunettes
[lynet] *n f pl*
glasses

* *Le professeur Tournesol porte des lunettes...* Professor Calculus wears glasses... *

Le professeur Tournesol porte des lunettes ...

luxe

luxe
[lyks] *n m*
luxury

vivre dans le luxe to live in luxury

lycée

lycée
[lise] *n m*
secondary (*Am:* high) school

machine

machine
[maʃin] *n f*
machine
* *Tournesol a inventé une machine extraordinaire pour Tintin.* Calculus has invented an amazing machine for Tintin. *

Tournesol a inventé une machine extraordinaire pour Tintin.

maçon

maçon
[masɔ̃] *n m*
builder, bricklayer

madame

madame
[madam] *n f*
pl mesdames
[medam]
1. Mrs
voici madame Lampion here is Mrs Wagg

2. lady
* *Le lendemain matin...* The next morning... *Mesdames et messieurs, bonjour, voici les nouvelles...* Ladies and gentlemen, good morning, here is the news... *

Le lendemain matin...
Mesdames et messieurs, bonjour, voici les nouvelles ...

3. Madam
Madame est servie dinner is ready, Madam

mademoiselle

mademoiselle
[madmwazɛl] *n f*
pl mesdemoiselles
[medmwazɛl]
1. Miss
mademoiselle Tartempion Miss Tartempion

2. lady
bonsoir mesdemoiselles good evening, ladies

magasin

magasin
[magazɛ̃] *n m*
1. shop (*Am:* store)
tous les magasins sont fermés aujourd'hui all the shops are closed today

2. Loc
grand magasin (department) store

magazine

magazine
[magazin] *n m*
magazine
je vais acheter un magazine avant de prendre le train I'll buy a magazine before I get on the train

magicien

magicien, enne
[maʒisjɛ̃, ɛn] *n*
magician, conjurer

magnétophone

magnétophone
[maɲetɔfɔn] *n m*
tape recorder

▸ **magnétoscope**
[maɲetɔskɔp] *n m*
videocassette recorder, VCR

mai

mai
[mɛ] *n m*
May
le premier/deux mai the first/second of May

venez le 6 mai come on the 6th of May (*Am:* on May 6)

maillot

maillot de bain
[majo] *n m*

le maillot de bain de Tintin Tintin's swimming trunks (*Am:* swimsuit)

le maillot de bain de la Castafiore Signora Castafiore's swimming costume (*Am:* bathing suit)

main

main
[mɛ̃] *n f*
1. hand

qu'est-ce que tu tiens dans la main ? what are you holding in your hand?

* *Vous... vous avez vu ?... j'avais le verre à la main et...* Did... did you see ? ... I had the glass in my hand, and... *Ça c'est rigolo !* That's funny! *

...main

2. Loc
serrons-nous la main let's shake hands

une poignée de main a handshake

maintenant

maintenant
[mɛ̃tnɑ̃] *adv*
1. now

il est trop tard maintenant it's too late now

...maintenant

2. next
* *Je ne sais pas comment nous allons nous en sortir cette fois...* I don't know how we'll get out of it this time...
Qu'allons-nous faire maintenant ?... What shall we do next?... *

3. Loc
dès maintenant from now on

maire

maire
[mɛr] *n m*
mayor

▶ **mairie**
[mɛri] *n f*
town hall (*Am:* city hall)

mais

mais
[mɛ] *conj*
1. but

...mais

* *Nous devrions être près de l'île, mais je ne vois rien...* We ought to be near the island, but I can't see anything... *

2. Loc
mais enfin, tu vas rester tranquille ! for heaven's sake, will you be quiet!

...mais

maison

maison
[mɛzɔ̃] *n f*
1. house

* *Regardez ce qu'est devenue ma maison...* Look what's happened to my house... *

2. home
aujourd'hui, Milou, nous restons à la maison today, Snowy, we're staying at home

je veux rentrer à la maison I want to go home

majeur

majeur, e
[maʒœr] *adj*
1. main, major

leur préoccupation majeure est de s'évader their main concern is to escape

2. of age
à dix-huit ans, tu seras majeur when you're eighteen, you'll be of age

3. Loc
la majeure partie de most of

mal

mal
[mal] *n m*
pl maux [mo]
1. ache, pain

j'ai mal à l'estomac I've a pain in my stomach

avoir mal aux dents/ à la tête to have a toothache/a headache

2. sickness
mal de mer seasickness

3. Loc
* *Ils ont le mal de mer...* They are seasick... *

où as-tu mal ? where does it hurt ?

il s'est fait mal en sautant du train he hurt himself when he jumped out of the train

j'ai eu du mal à te trouver I had a job to find you

Ils ont le mal de mer ...

malade

malade
[malad]
I. *adj*
ill, sick

les sept savants sont gravement malades the seven scientists are seriously ill

II. *n*
ill person, sick person

les malades ont été transportés à l'hôpital the sick people have been taken to hospital (*Am:* to the hospital)

► **maladie**
[maladi] *n f*
disease, illness, sickness

* *Nous ne comprenons pas. Ils sont atteints d'une maladie inconnue...* We don't understand. They are suffering from an unknown disease... *

Nous ne comprenons pas . Ils sont atteints d'une maladie inconnue ...

sa maladie le met de mauvaise humeur his illness makes him bad-tempered

malchance

malchance
[malʃɑ̃s] *n f*
bad luck, misfortune

il a eu la malchance d'arriver après la fermeture he had the bad luck to arrive after closing time

si tu as la malchance de perdre ton chemin if you have the misfortune to lose your way

malgré

malgré
[malgre] *prép*
in spite of, despite

* *Nous devons continuer malgré la neige...* We must go on in spite of the snow... *

Nous devons continuer malgré la neige ...

malheureux

malheureux, euse
[malørø, øz] *adj*
1. unhappy, miserable

...malheureux

* *Je suis si malheureux que tu t'en ailles...* I'm so miserable that you're leaving... *J'espère que nous nous reverrons bientôt...* I hope we'll meet again soon... *

2. unfortunate
ils ont aidé à dégager les malheureuses victimes they helped to free the unfortunate victims

Je suis si malheureux que tu t'en ailles ...
J'espère que nous nous reverrons bientôt ...

► **malheureusement**
[malørøzmɑ̃] *adv*
unfortunately

malheureusement, je ne pense pas pouvoir atterrir unfortunately, I don't think I can land

► **malheur**
[malœr] *n m*
misfortune

soyez courageux dans ce malheur you

...malheureux

must have courage to bear this misfortune

maman

maman
[mamɑ̃] *n f*
mum, mummy (*Am:* mom, mommy)

mandat

mandat
[mɑ̃da] *n m*
mandat postal postal order (*Am:* money order)

manger

manger
[mɑ̃ʒe] *v tr*
to eat

* ***Bon sang !... Quel os magnifique !... Je le mangerais bien...***

...manger

Golly!... What a magnificent bone!... I'd very much like to eat it... *

manière

manière
[manjɛr] *n f*
way, manner

ne vous inquiétez pas, je vais le faire à ma manière don't worry, I'll do it my own way

...manière

► **manières**
[manjɛr] *n f pl*
manners

* ***Mille millions de tonnerres de Brest !... Je vais t'apprendre les bonnes manières, Abdallah !...*** Ten thousand thundering typhoons!... I'll teach you good manners, Abdullah!...
Wouin !... Wouin !... Waaah!... Waaah!... *

...manière

manquer

manquer
[mɑ̃ke] *v tr*
1. to miss

* ***Dupont a manqué le train...*** Thomson has missed the train... *

2. to be short of
nous n'allons pas tarder à manquer d'eau we'll soon be short of water

Dupont a manqué le train ...

manteau

manteau
[mɑ̃to] *n m*
pl manteaux
coat

n'oubliez pas votre manteau don't forget your coat

maquereau

maquereau
[makro] *n m*
pl maquereaux
mackerel

maquillage

maquillage
[makijaʒ] *n m*
make-up

► **se maquiller**
[səmakije] *v pr*
to make oneself up (*Am:* to put on make-up)

elle s'est maquillée she's made up (*Am:* she's put on her make-up)

marchand

marchand, e
[marʃɑ̃, ɑ̃d] *n*
1. shopkeeper (*Am:* storekeeper)

mais ce marchand, c'est le senhor Oliveira da Figueira but that shopkeeper (*Am:* storekeeper) is Senhor Oliveira da Figueira

2. Loc
marchand de sable sandman

marché

marché
[marʃe] *n m*
market

* ***Tenez.*** Here.
Tintin et Milou sont au marché aux puces... Tintin and Snowy are at the flea market... *

Tintin et Milou sont au marché aux puces...

marcher

marcher
[marʃe] *v i*
1. to walk

la voiture est en panne, nous allons marcher the car's broken down, we'll have to walk

2. to work
* *Malheur !... rien ne marche dans cet avion !...* Hell! nothing works in this plane!... *

mardi

mardi
[mardi] *n m*
Tuesday

viens me voir mardi come and see me on Tuesday

ils ne travaillent pas le mardi they don't work on Tuesdays

marée

marée
[mare] *n f*
tide

à marée basse/haute at low/high tide

mari

mari
[mari] *n m*
husband

se marier

se marier
[səmarje] *v pr*
to marry, to get married

le capitaine Haddock ne s'est jamais marié Captain Haddock has never married

se marier avec quelqu'un to marry somebody

marin

marin
[marɛ̃] *n m*
sailor

le capitaine Haddock est un marin Captain Haddock is a sailor

marque

marque
[mark] *n f*
1. mark

...marque

* *Il porte une marque au cou... Le malheureux a reçu une fléchette...* He's got a mark on his neck... The poor man's been hit by a dart... *

2. make
quelle est la marque de cette voiture ? what make is this car?

marquer

marquer
[marke] *v tr*
1. to mark

je l'ai marqué d'une croix I've marked it with a cross

2. to score
marquer un but to score a goal

marron

marron
[marɔ̃] *adj inv*
brown

il a les yeux marron he has brown eyes

mars

mars
[mars] *n m*
March

le premier/deux mars the first/second of

...mars

March (*Am:* March first/second)

venez le 6 mars come on the 6th of March (*Am:* on March 6)

marteau

marteau
[marto] *n m*
pl marteaux
hammer

...marteau

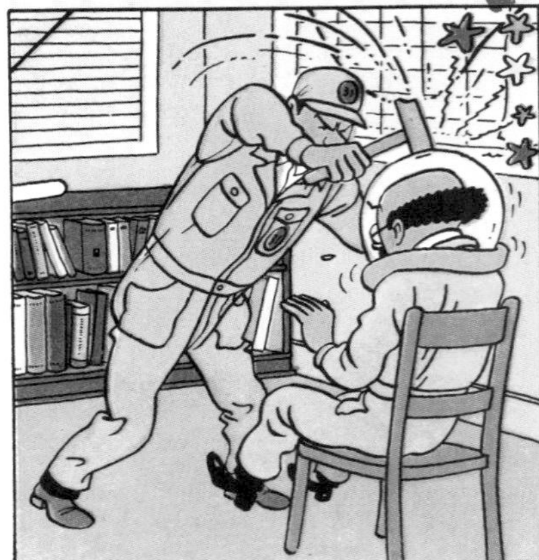

Le casque résiste aux coups de marteau ...

* *Le casque résiste aux coups de marteau...* The helmet resists hammer blows... *

masculin

masculin
[maskylɛ̃] *n m*
masculine

« cahier » est un nom masculin "cahier" is a masculine noun

match

match
[matʃ] *n m*
pl matches, matchs
match

match de football football match

matelas

matelas
[matla] *n m*
1. mattress

...matelas

* *Chacun est couché sur son matelas...* Everyone is lying on his mattress... *

2. Loc
matelas pneumatique air-bed

Chacun est couché sur son matelas...

matériel

matériel
[materjɛl] *n m*
equiment, gear

matériel de camping camping equipment

mathématiques

mathématiques
[matematik] *n f pl*
mathematics

matière

matière
[matjɛr] *n f*
material

matières premières raw materials

matin

matin
[matɛ̃] *n m*
morning

* *Comme chaque matin, commençons par quelques exercices...* Let's start with a few exercises as we do every morning... *

▸ **matinée**
[matine] *n f*
morning

...matin

Comme chaque matin, commençons par quelques exercices...

nous partirons dans la matinée we'll leave sometime in the morning

mauvais

mauvais, e
[movɛ, ɛz]
I. *adj*
1. wrong

une mauvaise adresse the wrong address

2. bad

...mauvais

de mauvaises notes bad marks (*Am:* grades)

c'est mauvais pour la santé it's bad for your health

3. poor

* *Ce couteau est vraiment de mauvaise qualité !...* This knife is really poor quality!... *

II. *adv*
bad

il fait mauvais the weather's bad

Ce couteau est vraiment de mauvaise qualité !...
!
!

maximum

maximum
[maksimɔm] *n m*
1. maximum

Tintin prend le maximum de risques pour arriver à temps Tintin's taking a maximum of risks to arrive in time

2. Loc
au maximum at the very most

mécanicien

mécanicien, enne
[mekanisjɛ̃, ɛn] *n*
mechanic

méchant

méchant, e
[meʃɑ̃, ɑ̃t] *adj*
1. nasty

c'était méchant de lui dire ça it was nasty of you to say that to him

...méchant

2. dangerous, vicious

* *Attention Milou ! Ce gorille a l'air méchant...* Be careful, Snowy! That gorilla looks dangerous!
Mon Dieu ! Oh no! *

3. Loc
chien méchant beware of the dog

Attention Milou ! Ce gorille a l'air méchant...

Mon Dieu !
RHAAH!

mécontent

mécontent, e
[mekɔ̃tɑ̃, ɑ̃t] *adj*
dissatisfied, displeased

médecin

médecin
[mɛdsɛ̃] *n m*
doctor

appelez le médecin tout de suite send for the doctor immediately

médicament

médicament
[medikamɑ̃] *n m*
medicine

avez-vous des médicaments pour me guérir rapidement ? do you have any medicine that can cure me quickly?

se méfier

se méfier
[səmefje] *v pr*
1. to distrust, not to trust

il se méfie de Rastapopoulos he doesn't trust Rastapopoulos

2. to be careful
* *Méfiez-vous, vous allez tomber !...* Be careful, you're going to fall!... *

meilleur

meilleur, e
[mɛjœr] *adj*
1. better

* *Ce whisky est meilleur que celui d'hier, n'est-ce pas, Tournesol ?* This whisky is better than yesterday's, isn't it, Calculus?
Peut-être, mais je crois plutôt que c'est du rhum... Perhaps, but I think in fact it's rum. *

2. best
Tintin est son meilleur ami Tintin's his best friend

melon

melon
[məlɔ̃] *n m*
melon

membre

membre
[mɑ̃br] *n m*
1. limb

il a les membres inférieurs cassés his lower limbs are broken

2. member
tous les membres de la famille Lampion all the members of the Wagg family

même

même
[mɛm]
I. *adj*
1. same

* *Vous voyez bien, capitaine, qu'ils ont le même chapeau...* You can see they've got the same hat, Captain... *

2. Loc
moi-même myself

nous l'avons fait nous-mêmes we did it ourselves

II. *adv*
even

il ne se rappelle même pas son nom he can't even remember his name

ménage

ménage
[menaʒ] *n m*
housework

Nestor fait le ménage Nestor's doing the housework

mentir

mentir
[mɑ̃tir] *v i*
to lie

je parie qu'il vous a menti I bet he lied to you

▸ **mensonge**
[mɑ̃sɔ̃ʒ] *n m*
lie

arrête de dire des mensonges stop telling lies

menu

menu
[məny] *n m*
menu

qu'est-ce qu'il y a au menu ? what's on the menu?

mer

mer
[mɛr] *n f*
sea

* *Sapristi !... La mer est mauvaise !...* Great snakes!... the sea is rough!... *

Sapristi !... La mer est mauvaise !...

le navire est en mer the ship is at sea

merci

merci
[mɛrsi] *interj*
thank you

merci d'être venu aussi vite thank you for coming so quickly

mercredi

mercredi
[mɛrkrədi] *n m*
Wednesday

viens me voir mercredi come and see me on Wednesday

ils ne travaillent pas le mercredi they don't work on Wednesdays

mère

mère
[mɛr] *n f*
mother

* *Eh bien, Tchang, qu'y a-t-il ?* What's the matter, Chang?
Eh bien... Je pleure à cause du départ de Tintin et je ris parce que je trouve un père et une mère !... Well... I'm crying because Tintin has left and I'm laughing because I've found a father and a mother!... *

Eh bien, Tchang, qu'y a-t-il ?
Eh bien, ... je pleure à cause du départ de Tintin et je ris parce que je trouve un père et une mère !...

merveilleux

merveilleux, euse
[mɛrvɛjø, øz] *adj*
wonderful, marvellous (*Am:* marvelous)

mesurer

mesurer
[məzyre] *v tr*
1. to measure

il faut d'abord mesurer la chambre first, we must measure the room

2. Loc
combien mesure Tintin ? – il mesure 1,70 m how tall is Tintin? – he's 5 foot 7 inches tall

métal

métal
[metal] *n m*
pl métaux [meto]
metal

le fer et l'or sont des métaux iron and gold are metals

* *Tonnerre de Brest, des plaques de métal !... A quoi cela peut-il bien servir ?* Thundering typhoons, metal plates!... What can they be for?
Regardons dans les autres caisses... Let's look in the other crates... *

Tonnerre de Brest, des plaques de métal !... A quoi cela peut-il bien servir ?
Regardons dans les autres caisses...

météo

météo
[meteo] *n f*
weather forecast

la météo annonce de la pluie the weather forecast says it's going to rain

as-tu écouté la météo ? did you listen to the weather forecast?

▶ **météorologique**
[meteɔrɔlɔʒik] *adj*
1. meteorological

2. Loc
bulletin météorologique weather report

métier

métier
[metje] *n m*
1. job, profession

il dit qu'il est reporter, est-ce vraiment son métier ? he says he's a reporter, is that really his job?

il connaît son métier he knows his job

2. Loc
il exerce encore son métier he's still in practice

mètre

mètre
[mɛtr] *n m*
metre (*Am:* meter)

métro
[metro] *n m*
underground (*Am:* subway)

en métro by underground

mettre

mettre
[mɛtr]
I. *v tr*
1. to put

* *Je mets la statuette dans la valise.* I'll put the statuette in the case. *

2. to put on
ils mettent leurs manteaux avant de sortir they put their coats on before going out

3. to take
Tintin a mis trois jours pour les rattraper it took Tintin three days to catch up with them

II. *v pr*
1. to start, to begin

* *A-a-a-a-h A-a-a-a-h A-a-a-a-h.* Aaaah Aaaah Aaaah.
Elle se met à chanter... She is starting to sing... *

2. Loc
se mettre en colère to get angry

se mettre en route to set off

Elle se met à chanter...

meuble

meuble
[mœbl] *n m*
piece of furniture

les frères Loiseau ont vraiment entassé beaucoup de meubles the Bird brothers have really collected a lot of furniture

midi

midi
[midi] *n m*
1. midday, noon

ils écoutent les informations de midi they're listening to the midday news

2. *le Midi* the south of France

mieux

mieux
[mjø] *adv*
1. better

est-ce que Tournesol se sent mieux ? is Calculus feeling any better?

personne ne chante mieux que la Castafiore nobody sings better than Signora Castafiore

* *Attention ! J'entends quelqu'un venir. Nous ferions*

mieux de nous cacher... Careful! I can hear somebody coming, we'd better hide...
Oui, venez ! Yes, come on!... *

2. best
c'est dans mon laboratoire que je travaille le mieux I work best in my laboratory

le mieux est de ne rien dire the best thing would be to say nothing

milieu

milieu
[miljø] *n m*
pl milieux
middle

* *Il y a une voiture arrêtée au milieu de la route...* There's a car stopped in the middle of the road... *

Il y a une voiture arrêtée au milieu de la route...

militaire

militaire
[militɛr] *n m*
soldier

les militaires les poursuivent soldiers are chasing them

mince

mince
[mɛ̃s] *adj*
1. thin

la corde est trop mince the rope is too thin

2. slim, slender
elle est grande et mince she's tall and slender

mineur

mineur
[minœr]
I. *n m*
miner

mineur (dans les mines de charbon) coalminer

II. *adj*
f mineure
minor

à 18 ans il ne sera plus mineur at 18 he'll no longer be a minor

minimum

minimum
[minimɔm] *n m*
1. minimum

essayez de réduire les dépenses au minimum try to keep the expenses to a minimum

2. Loc
au minimum at least

* *Une croix en or, incrustée de pierreries !... C'est un vrai trésor !... C'est magnifique !...* A gold cross, set with precious stones!... It's a real treasure!... It's magnificent!...
Ça vaut au minimum 100 000 francs !... It's worth at least 100,000 francs!... *

minuit

minuit
[minɥi] *n m*
midnight

Une croix en or, incrustée de pierreries !... C'est un vrai trésor !... C'est magnifique !...
Ça vaut au minimum 100 000 francs !...

...minuit

il est minuit, nous devons nous coucher it's midnight, we must go to bed

minute

minute
[minyt] *n f*
minute

dans quelques minutes in a few minutes

...minute

Tintin surveille l'aiguille des minutes Tintin's watching the minute hand

mixte

mixte
[mikst] *adj*
coeducational (*Am:* coed)

une école mixte a coeducational school

mode

mode
[mɔd] *n f*
1. fashion

elle s'habille à la dernière mode she's dressed in the latest fashion

2. Loc
à la mode fashionable

moderne

moderne
[mɔdɛrn] *adj*
modern

nous avons ici le matériel le plus moderne we have the most modern equipment here

moineau

moineau
[mwano] *n m*
pl moineaux
sparrow

moins

moins
[mwɛ̃]
I. *adv*
1. less

* *Bon, je suis moins fatigué qu'hier.* Well, I'm less tired than I was yesterday. *

2. least
c'est le moins que nous puissions faire pour vous it's the least we can do for you

Bon, je suis moins fatigué qu'hier.

...moins

II. *prép*
minus

7 moins 3 égale 4 7 minus 3 equals 4

mois

mois
[mwa] *n m*
month

nous serons de retour dans un mois we'll be back in a month's time

...mois

le mois prochain next month

moitié

moitié
[mwatje] *n f*
half

la moitié de 20, c'est 10 half of 20 is 10

...moitié

la moitié des passagers sont déjà à bord half the passengers are already on board

moment

moment
[mɔmɑ̃] *n m*
1. moment

* *Attendez un moment... Je reviens...* Wait a moment... I'll be back... *

...moment

Attendez un moment... Je reviens...
?
?

...moment

2. time
Milou est arrivé au bon moment Snowy arrived at the right time

monde

monde
[mɔ̃d] *n m*
1. world

Tintin a voyagé dans le monde entier Tintin's travelled (*Am:* traveled) all over the world

...monde

2. people
* *Heureusement qu'il y a beaucoup de monde... Dans cette foule, nous passerons inaperçus...* It's lucky there are a lot of people... In this crowd, nobody will see us... *

monnaie

monnaie
[mɔnɛ] *n f*
1. currency

...monnaie

le franc est la monnaie française the franc is the French currency

2. change
as-tu la monnaie de 200 francs ? have you got change for 200 francs?

je n'ai pas de monnaie I haven't got any change

monsieur

monsieur
[məsjø] *n m*
pl messieurs [mesjø]
1. Mister, Mr
voici monsieur Lampion here's Mister Wagg
M. Dupont Mr Thomson
2. Sir
bonjour monsieur good morning, Sir
3. gentleman
messieurs, veuillez vous asseoir gentlemen, please be seated

montagne

montagne
[mɔ̃taɲ] *n f*
mountain

le temple est dans les montagnes the temple is in the mountains

monter

monter
[mɔ̃te]
I. *v i*
1. to climb

...monter

* *J'y suis !...* I've made it!...
Tintin a dû monter sur le mur. Tintin had to climb up on the wall. *

2. to go up
Nestor est monté au grenier Nestor's gone up to the attic

3. to get into
vite, capitaine, montez dans la voiture ! quick, Captain, get into the car!

J'y suis!...
Tintin a dû monter sur le mur

4. to rise
sa température monte his temperature is rising

5. Loc
monter à bicyclette/à cheval to ride a bicycle/a horse

II. *v t*
to assemble

monter un appareil to assemble a machine

montre

montre
[mɔ̃tr] *n f*
watch

sa montre avance/retarde her watch is fast/slow

montrer

montrer
[mɔ̃tre] *v t*
1. to show

il faut encore montrer nos passeports we have to show our passports again

2. Loc
montrer quelque chose du doigt to point at something

monument

monument
[mɔnymɑ̃] *n m*
monument

* *A New Delhi...* In New Delhi...
Ce monument est le Qutab Minar... This monument is the Qutab Minar... *

morceau

morceau
[mɔrso] *n m*

...morceau

pl morceaux
piece

* *J'ai écrit son adresse sur ce morceau de papier...* I wrote his address on this piece of paper... *

Milou et le chat ont cassé le vase, il est en morceaux Snowy and the cat have broken the vase: it's all in pieces

J'ai écrit son adresse sur ce morceau de papier...

mordre

mordre
[mɔrdr] *v tr*
to bite

ce gros chien va me mordre that big dog is going to bite me

mort

mort
[mɔr]
I. *n f*
death

...mort

* *Vous n'avez pas le droit de nous condamner à mort !* You have no right to sentence us to death! *

II. *adj*
f morte
[mɔrt]
dead

dangereux bandits recherchés, morts ou vifs dangerous gangsters wanted, dead or alive

Vous n'avez pas le droit de nous condamner à mort !

morue

morue
[mɔry] *n f*
cod

mot

mot
[mo] *n m*
1. word

Tintin, que signifie ce mot ? Tintin, what does this word mean?

...mot

2. note
envoyez-lui un mot pour lui dire que nous arrivons send him a note to tell him we're coming

moteur

moteur
[mɔtœr] *n m*
engine

encore un moteur qui explose ! another engine has blown up!

moto

moto
[mɔto] *n f*
motorbike

j'irai plus vite avec cette moto I'll go faster on this motorbike

mouchoir

mouchoir
[muʃwar] *n m*
handkerchief

mouillé

mouillé, e
[muje] *adj*
wet

* *Les vêtements du capitaine sont mouillés.* The Captain's clothes are wet. *

moule

moule
[mul] *n f*
mussel

Les vêtements du capitaine sont mouillés .

mourir

mourir
[murir] *v i*
1. to die

il faut qu'il meure he must die

2. Loc
je meurs de faim ! I'm starving!

moutarde

moutarde
[mutard] *n f*
mustard

mouton

mouton
[mutɔ̃] *n m*
1. sheep *inv*

les moutons ont de la laine sur le dos sheep have wool on their backs

...mouton

2. mutton
des côtelettes de mouton mutton chops

mouvement

mouvement
[muvmɑ̃] *n m*
1. movement

ses mouvements sont très gracieux her movements are very graceful

...mouvement

2. Loc
faire un mouvement to move

moyen

moyen
[mwajɛ̃] *n m*
1. way

* *Nous devons trouver un moyen de*

...moyen

Nous devons trouver un moyen de sortir d'ici.

sortir d'ici. We must find a way out of here... *

2. Loc
moyens de transport means of transport

au moyen de by means of

moyen

moyen, enne
[mwajɛ̃, ɛn] *adj*
average

pouvez-vous le décrire ? – c'est un homme de taille moyenne can you describe him? – he's a man of average height

municipal

municipal, e
[mynisipal] *adj*
pl municipaux [mynisipo]
1. municipal

2. Loc
conseil municipal town council

se munir

se munir de
[səmynir də] *v pr*
to take

...se munir

* *A Katmandou, au Népal...* At Katmandu, in Nepal...
Nous devons nous munir de vêtements chauds, il fera peut-être froid... We'd better take warm clothes with us, it might get cold...
Oui, mais ne compte pas sur moi pour porter ce sac... Ok, but don't expect me to carry the rucksack... *

mur

mur
[myr] *n m*
wall

* *Tintin franchit le mur...* Tintin climbs over the wall... *

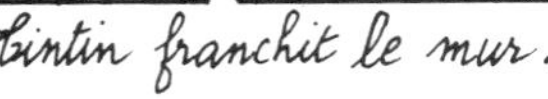
Tintin franchit le mur...

mûr

mûr, e
[myr] *adj*
ripe

mais ces bananes ne

...mûr

sont pas mûres ! but these bananas aren't ripe!

musée

musée
[myze] *n m*
museum

Tintin, on trouve des choses extraordinaires dans un musée ! Tintin, you can find wonderful things in a museum!

musicien

musicien, enne
[myzisjɛ̃, ɛn] *n*
musician

* *Boum Boum Boum Boum* Boom Boom Boom Boom
Les musiciens arrivent... The musicians are coming... *

▸ **musique**
[myzik] *n f*
music

aimez-vous la musique ? do you like music?

...musicien

Les musiciens arrivent ...

mystère

mystère
[mistɛr] *n m*
mystery

* *Ça alors !... La disparition de Tournesol est un mystère !...* How strange!... Calculus' disappearance is a mystery!...
Que lui est-il arrivé, mille sabords ? ?... Blistering barnacles, what can have happened to him??... *

▸ **mystérieux, euse**
[misterjø, øz] *adj*
mysterious

ce message est très mystérieux this note is very mysterious

nager

nager
[naʒe] *v i*
to swim

* *Ils doivent nager jusqu'à l'autre rive...* They have to swim across to the other bank... *

Ils doivent nager jusqu'à l'autre rive...

naissance

naissance
[nɛsɑ̃s] *n f*
birth

inscrivez votre date de naissance write down your date of birth

► **naître**
[nɛtr] *v i*
to be born

où es-tu né ? – en Chine where were you born? – in China

nappe

nappe
[nap] *n f*
tablecloth

natation

natation
[natasjɔ̃] *n f*
swimming

nationalité

nationalité
[nasjɔnalite] *n f*
nationality

nature

nature
[natyr] *n f*
1. nature

la nature en Ecosse est très belle nature in Scotland is very beautiful

...nature

2. Loc
Nestor est une heureuse nature Nestor is good-natured

naturel

naturel, elle
[natyrɛl] *adj*
natural

ici les animaux vivent dans leur environnement naturel here animals live in their natural

...naturel

surroundings

► **naturellement**
[natyrɛlmɑ̃] *adv*
1. naturally

* *Mais si, je vous assure... mes cheveux frisent naturellement...* Yes, I can assure you... my hair curls naturally... *

2. of course
et naturellement tu as oublié de le prévenir ! and of course, you forgot to tell him!

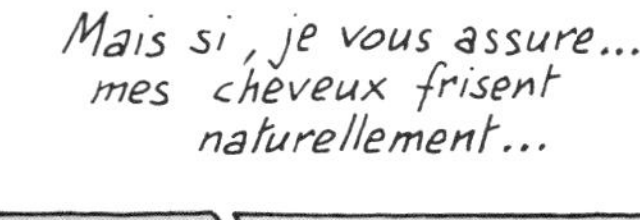

Mais si, je vous assure... mes cheveux frisent naturellement...

nautique

nautique
[notik] *adj*
1. nautical

2. Loc
ski nautique water-skiing

nécessaire

nécessaire
[nesesɛr] *adj*
necessary

neige

neige
[nɛʒ] *n f*
snow

attention, il y a beaucoup de neige ici careful, there's a lot of snow here

► **neiger**
[nɛʒe] *v imp*
to snow

il neige it's snowing

...neige

* *Oh ! Il se remet à neiger !...* Oh! it's snowing again!... *

n'est-ce pas

n'est-ce pas
[nɛspɑ] *adv*

il fait beau, n'est-ce pas ? the weather's nice, isn't it?

tu vas être bien sage, n'est-ce pas ? you're going to behave yourself, aren't you?

vous ne lui avez rien dit, capitaine, n'est-ce pas ? you didn't tell him, Captain, did you?

...n'est-ce pas ...nettoyer

nettoyer

nettoyer
[netwaje] *v t*
to clean

* *Je vais nettoyer les meubles...* I'm going to clean the furniture... *

neuf

neuf
[nœf] *adj num*
nine

il y a neuf sarcophages there are nine sarcophagi

neuf

neuf
[nœf] *n m*
I. *n m*
new

il y a du neuf there's been something new

II. *adj*
f neuve [nœv]
new

leur voiture est neuve their car is new

nez

nez
[ne] *n m*
nose

* *Mais qu'est-ce que j'ai sur le nez ?* What have I got on my nose?
Ah, c'est un pansement !... Ah, it's sticking plaster (*Am:* a band-aid)!...
Le voilà décollé... There, it's off... *

ni

ni
[ni] *conj*
neither

ni toi ni moi ne pouvons le faire neither you nor I can make it

n'importe

- **n'importe comment**
[nɛ̃pɔrtkɔmɑ̃] *adv*
anyhow

- **n'importe lequel, laquelle** [nɛ̃pɔrt ləkɛl, lɑkɛl] *pron indéf*
any (one)

- **n'importe où**
[nɛpɔrtu] *adv*
anywhere

- **n'importe quand**
[nɛpɔrtkɑ̃] *adv*
at any time

- **n'importe qui**
[nɛ̃pɔrtki] *pron indéf*
anybody, anyone

- **n'importe quoi**
[nɛ̃pɔrtkwa] *pron indéf*
anything

niveau

niveau
[nivo] *n m*
pl niveaux
1. level

* *Le niveau de l'eau a monté...* The water level has gone up... *

2. Loc
la neige leur arrive au niveau des genoux the snow comes up to their knees

Noël

Noël
[nɔɛl] *n m*
Christmas

arbre de Noël Christmas tree

Père Noël Father Christmas (*Am:* Santa Claus)

noir

noir, e
I. *adj*
[nwar]
black

* *Le « Karaboudjan » est un bateau noir.* The "Karaboudjan" is a black ship. *

nous voici en Afrique noire, Milou here we are in black Africa, Snowy

II. *n m*
1. black

c'est une vieille photographie en noir et blanc it's an old black-and-white photograph

2. dark
Milou a peur du noir Snowy's afraid of the dark

Le Karaboudjan est un bateau noir.

noix

noix
[nwa] *n f*
walnut

nom

nom
[nɔ̃] *n m*
1. name

* *Le professeur a perdu la mémoire...* Calculus has lost his memory...
Mais professeur, vous vous souvenez bien de votre nom... votre nom... Tryphon Tournesol... But Professor, you remember your name... your name... Cuthbert Calculus... *

2. noun
Dupont est un nom propre Thomson is a proper noun

nombre

nombre
[nɔ̃br] *n m*
number

j'ai un certain nombre de questions à te poser I have a number of questions to ask you

...nombre

► **nombreux, euse**
[nɔ̃brø, øz] *adj*
numerous

non

non
[nɔ̃] *adv*
1. no

pouvez-vous nous conduire à l'aéroport ? – non could you take us to the aiport? – no

...non

2. Loc
je crois que non I don't think so

ils partiront demain, moi non they'll leave tomorrow, I won't

nord

nord
[nɔr] *n m*
north

normal

normal, e
[nɔrmal] *adj*
pl normaux [nɔrmo]
usual

* *Milou n'est pas dans son état normal...* Snowy's not his usual self... *

► **normalement**
[nɔrmalmɑ̃] *adv*
normally

note

note
[nɔt] *n f*
1. mark (*Am:* grade)

ils ont eu de mauvaises notes à leur devoir they got bad marks for their homework

2. note
M. Wagner ne fait pas de fausses notes Mr Wagner doesn't play any wrong notes

notre

notre
[nɔtr] *adj poss*
our

► **nôtre**
[notr] *pron poss*
ours
leur voiture est plus rapide que la nôtre their car is faster than ours

nourrir

nourrir
[nurir] *v t*
to feed

Tintin nourrit Milou Tintin feeds Snowy

▶ **nourriture**
[nurityr] *n f*
food

* *C'est de la nourriture pour chien...* It's dog food... *

C'est de la nourriture pour chien...

nouveau

nouveau, elle
[nuvo, ɛl]
I. *adj*
pl nouveaux
1. new

voulez-vous acheter une nouvelle voiture ? do you want to buy a new car?

2. Loc
quoi de nouveau ? what's new ?

II. *n m*
Loc
* *Bonjour !... Y a-t-il du nouveau dans cette affaire ?* Hello!... Is there anything new in this case? *

à nouveau again

novembre

novembre
[nɔvɑ̃br] *n m*
November

Bonjour !... Y a-t-il du nouveau dans cette affaire ?

...novembre

le premier/deux novembre the first/second of November (*Am:* November first/second)
venez le 6 novembre come on the 6th of November (*Am:* on November 6)

se noyer

se noyer
[sənwaje] *v pr*
to drown

...se noyer

Mon Dieu, Milou nous allons nous noyer !...

* *Mon Dieu, Milou nous allons nous noyer !...* Heavens, Snowy, we're going to drown!... *

nuage

nuage
[nɥaʒ] *n m*
cloud

* *Il y a de gros nuages dans le ciel.*

...nuage

Il y a de gros nuages dans le ciel.

There are large clouds in the sky. *

▶ **nuageux, euse**
[nɥaʒø, øz] *adj*
cloudy

un ciel nuageux a cloudy sky

nuit

nuit
[nɥi] *n f*
1. night

...nuit

nous devrons voyager de nuit we'll have to travel by night

les nuits sont fraîches ici the nights are cold here

* *Bonne nuit, Zorrino !* Good night, Zorrino!
Bonne nuit, señor Tintin ! Good night, señor Tintin! *

2. Loc
il fait nuit it's dark

Bonne nuit, Zorrino !
Bonne nuit, señor Tintin !

nul

nul, nulle
[nyl] *adj*
1. hopeless

il est nul en anglais he's hopeless at English

2. Loc
faire match nul to draw

numéro

numéro
[nymero] *n m*
number

* *Mais quel numéro demandez-vous, madame ? Non, madame, ce n'est pas la boucherie Sanzot...* What number did you dial, Madam? No, Madam, this is not Mr Cutts the butcher... *

Tintin habite au numéro 26 Tintin lives at number 26

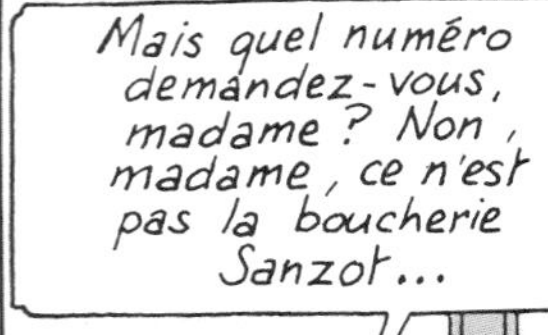
Mais quel numéro demandez-vous, madame ? Non, madame, ce n'est pas la boucherie Sanzot...

objet

objet
[ɔbʒɛ] *n m*
1. object

* *Les cambrioleurs ont emporté beaucoup d'objets de valeur !* The burglars have taken many valuable objects! *

2. Loc
objets trouvés lost property (*Am:* lost and found)

Les cambrioleurs ont emporté beaucoup d'objets de valeur !

obligatoire

obligatoire
[ɔbligatwar] *adj*
compulsory

cette visite à l'ambassade est obligatoire this visit to the embassy is compulsory

occasion

occasion
[ɔkazjɔ̃] *n f*
1. opportunity

...occasion

je cherche une occasion de parler au roi I'm looking for an opportunity to speak to the king

2. Loc
une voiture d'occasion a second-hand car

* *Une auto ?... J'en ai une ici, je l'ai achetée d'occasion mais c'est un excellent modèle...* A car?... I have one here, I bought it second-hand but it's an excellent model....

...occasion

Une auto?... J'en ai une ici, je l'ai achetée d'occasion mais c'est un excellent modèle ...

Et le lendemain matin ...
1385

Et le lendemain matin... And the following morning... *

occupé

occupé, e
[ɔkype] *adj*
1. engaged (*Am:* busy)

la ligne est occupée, vous devez patienter the line's engaged, you must hold on

...occupé

2. busy
les Dupondt sont des gens très occupés the Thompsons are very busy people

► **s'occuper**
[sɔkype] *v pr*
1. to occupy oneself

2. to deal with
qui s'occupe de cette affaire de cambriolage ? who's dealing with that burglary?

octobre

octobre
[ɔktɔbr] *n m*
October

le premier/deux octobre the first/second of October (*Am:* October first/second)

venez le 6 octobre come on the 6th of October (*Am:* on October 6)

odeur

odeur
[ɔdœr] *n f*
smell

il y a une odeur de brûlé ici there's a smell of burning in here

* *Capitaine, vous ne sentez rien ?* Captain, don't you smell anything?
Sniff... Sniff... Sniff... Sniff...
Oui... il y a une odeur de brûlé... Yes... there's a smell of burning in here...

D'où vient-elle ?... Where's it coming from?... *

œil

œil
[œj] *n m*
pl yeux [jø]
eye

ouvrez/fermez les yeux open/close your eyes

œuf

œuf
[œf] *n m*
pl œufs [ø]
egg

un œuf sur le plat, un œuf à la coque a fried egg, a boiled egg

offrir

offrir
[ɔfrir] *v t*
to offer

...offrir

* *Est-ce que je peux vous offrir quelque chose à boire ?* Can I offer you something to drink? *

oie

oie
[wa] *n f*
goose

oignon

oignon
[ɔɲɔ̃] *n m*
onion

soupe à l'oignon onion soup

oiseau

oiseau
[wazo] *n m*
pl oiseaux
bird

...oiseau

...oiseau

* *Je n'ai pas peur des gros oiseaux...* I'm not afraid of big birds... *

ombre

ombre
[ɔ̃br] *n f*
1. shade

reposez-vous un moment à l'ombre de cette dune rest for a

...ombre

while in the shade of this dune

2. shadow
on voit leur ombre sur le mur you can see their shadow on the wall

omelette

omelette
[ɔmlɛt] *n f*
omelette

omnibus

omnibus
[ɔmnibys] *n m*
local train

* *Le lendemain, à la gare...* The next day, at the station...
Est-ce l'omnibus pour Jauga ?... Is this the local train for Jauga?...
Oui, señor... It is, señor... *

on

on
[ɔ̃] *pron pers*
1. somebody, someone

on a frappé à la porte somebody's just knocked on the door

2. people
on dit que personne n'est jamais revenu de l'île Noire people say nobody has ever come back from Black Island

oncle

oncle
[ɔ̃kl] *n m*
uncle

opéra

opéra
[ɔpera] *n m*
1. opera

la Castafiore chante un opéra de Gounod Signora Castafiore is singing an opera by Gounod

...opéra

2. opera house
* *A l'opéra...* At the opera house... *

opération

opération
[ɔperasjɔ̃] *n f*
1. operation

l'addition, la soustraction, la division et la multiplication sont des opérations addition, subtraction, division

A l'opéra...

...opération

and multiplication are operations

2. operation
* *Le lendemain...* The next day...
Alors, docteur ? Well, doctor?
L'opération a réussi !... Il est sauvé !... Dans quelques jours il sera guéri... The operation was successful!... He's saved!... In a few days he'll be back on his feet... *

...opération

Alors, docteur ?
L'opération a réussi ! ... Il est sauvé ! ... Dans quelques jours il sera guéri ...

Le lendemain ...

opinion

opinion
[ɔpinjɔ̃] *n f*
opinion

capitaine, nous avons la même opinion Captain, we are of the same opinion

orage

orage
[ɔraʒ] *n m*
storm

...orage

le capitaine et Tintin rentrent pour éviter l'orage... the Captain and Tintin are going back into the house to escape the storm...

► **orageux, euse**
[ɔraʒø, øz] *adj*
stormy

le temps est orageux the weather is stormy

orange

orange
[ɔrɑ̃ʒ] *n f*
orange

* *Ah ! Ah !* Ha! Ha!
Ah! Ah! Ha! Ha!
Ils ont fait tomber ses oranges... They've tipped over his oranges... *

Ah! Ah!
Ah! Ah!

Ils ont fait tomber ses oranges ...

orchestre

orchestre
[ɔrkɛstr] *n m*
orchestra

Loc
chef d'orchestre conductor

ordinaire

ordinaire
[ɔrdinɛr]
I. *adj*
ordinary

...ordinaire

les Dupondt veulent toujours avoir l'air de gens ordinaires the Thompsons always want to look like ordinary people

II. *n m*
ordinary

cela sort de l'ordinaire it's out of the ordinary

ordinateur

ordinateur
[ɔrdinatœr] *n m*
computer

* *Il y a beaucoup d'ordinateurs dans la fusée pour faciliter le pilotage...* There are many computers in the rocket to help with the piloting... *

Il y a beaucoup d'ordinateurs dans la fusée pour faciliter le pilotage ...

ordonnance

ordonnance
[ɔrdɔnɑ̃s] *n f*
prescription

ordre

ordre
[ɔrdr] *n m*
order

ils ont exécuté mes ordres they've carried out my orders

ordre

ordre
[ɔrdr] *n m*
1. tidiness

2. Loc
une chambre en ordre a tidy bedroom

mettre de l'ordre dans la maison to tidy the house

oreille

oreille
[ɔrɛj] *n f*
ear

* *Milou dresse les oreilles.* Snowy is pricking up his ears. *

Milou dresse les oreilles.

oreiller

oreiller
[ɔreje] *n m*
pillow

organiser

organiser
[ɔrganize] *v t*
to organize

nous devons organiser notre évasion we must organize our escape

os

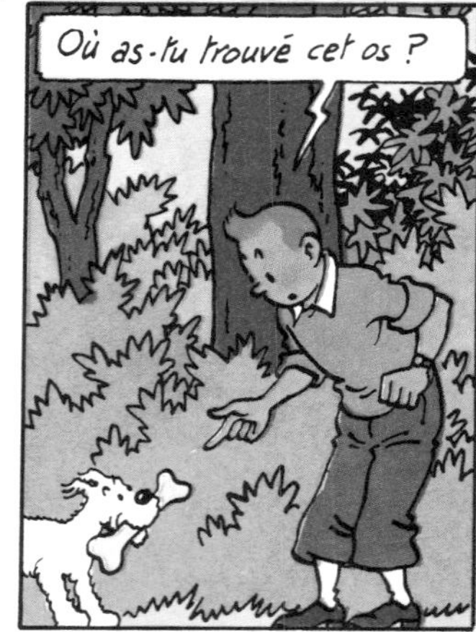

...os

os
[ɔs] *n m inv*
pl [o]
bone

* *Où as-tu trouvé cet os ?* Where did you find that bone? *

oser

oser
[oze] *v t*
dare

ou

ou
[u] *conj*
1. or

voulez-vous y aller en bateau ou en avion ? do you want to go there by boat or by plane?

* *Dessus ?...* On top?... *... Ou dessous ?...* ... Or underneath?... *

2. Loc
ou (bien) c'est Dupont qui se trompe, ou (bien) c'est Dupond it's either Thomson or Thompson who's mistaken

où

où
[u] *adv*
1. where

où est Milou ? Where's Snowy?

d'où venez-vous ? where do you come from?

2. Loc
au moment où when

oublier

oublier
[ublije] *v t*
1. to forget

les Dupondt ont oublié qu'ils devaient garder le silence the Thompsons forgot they were to keep silent

2. to leave
Dupont a oublié sa valise dans le train Thomson left his suitcase on the train

ouest

ouest
[wɛst] *n m*
west

oui

oui
[wi] *adv*
yes

ours

ours
[urs] *n m*
bear

ours en peluche teddy bear

ouvert

ouvert, e
→ OUVRIR

ouvre-boîtes

ouvre-boîtes
[uvrəbwat] *n m inv*
tin-opener (*Am:* can opener)

ouvrier

ouvrier, ère
[uvrije, ɛr] *n*
worker, (female) worker

ouvrir

ouvrir
[uvrir] *v t*
to open

▶ **ouvert, e**
[uvɛr, ɛrt] *adj*
open

* *A Moulinsart...* At Marlinspike...
Nestor a laissé la porte ouverte. Nestor left the door open... *

page

page
[paʒ] *n f*
page

pain

pain
[pɛ̃] *n m*
1. bread

partageons-nous ce morceau de pain let's share this piece of bread

...pain

2. Loc
pain grillé toast

paire

paire
[pɛr] *n f*
1. pair

voici une paire de gants here's a pair of gloves

2. Loc

...paire

* *Abdallah ! Petit vaurien !... Tu vas recevoir une paire de gifles...* Abdullah! You little rascal!... You're going to get a slap in the face...
Wouin !... Waah!... *

paisible

paisible
[pɛzibl] *adj*
peaceful, quiet

mille sabords, je suis pourtant un homme paisible blistering barnacles, I may be a peaceful man, but

paix

paix
[pɛ] *n f*
peace

pâle

pâle
[pɑl] *adj*
pale

est-ce que ça va ? tu es très pâle are you all right? you look very pale

bleu pâle pale blue

palier

palier
[palje] *n m*
landing

panier

panier
[panje] *n m*
basket

* *Oh là là !... Ces paniers sont bien lourds...* Oh dear!... These baskets are quite heavy... *

...panier

panne

panne
[pan] *n f*
1. breakdown

je crois que j'ai trouvé la cause de la panne I think I've located the cause of the breakdown

2. Loc
tomber en panne to break down

tomber en panne d'essence to run out of petrol (*Am:* gas)

panneau

panneau
[pano] *n m*
pl panneaux
1. sign

* *Les Dupondt n'ont pas vu le panneau...* The Thompsons didn't see the sign... *

2. Loc
panneau routier roadsign

panneau d'affichage notice-board (*Am:* billboard)

Les Dupondt n'ont pas vu le panneau...

pansement

pansement
[pɑ̃smɑ̃] *n m*
1. dressing, bandage

il faut refaire son pansement his dressing has to be changed

2. Loc
pansement adhésif sticking plaster (*Am:* band-aid)

pantalon

pantalon
[pɑ̃talɔ̃] *n m*
trousers
(*Am:* pants)

deux pantalons two pairs of trousers

pantoufle

pantoufle
[pɑ̃tufl] *n f*
slipper

papa

papa
[papa] *n m*
dad, daddy

papier

papier
[papje] *n m*
1. paper

je l'ai écrit sur un bout de papier I wrote it down on a piece of paper

2. Loc
* *Montrez-moi vos papiers !* Let me see your papers!
Vous êtes Tintin et le capitaine Haddock ?... Are you Tintin and Captain Haddock?...
Oui. Yes. *

Montrez-moi vos papiers !

Vous êtes Tintin et le capitaine Haddock ?...
Oui.

Pâques

Pâques
[pɑk] *n m* et *n f pl*
Easter

paquet

paquet
[pakɛ] *n m*
1. packet

un paquet d'enveloppes a packet of envelopes

...paquet

2. parcel
(*Am:* package)
d'où vient ce paquet ? where does this parcel come from?

par

par
[par] *prép*
1. by

la porte a été ouverte par Nestor the door was opened by Nestor

...par

2. through
* *Si vous passez par Las Dopicos, venez me voir !* If you happen to go through Las Dopicos, come and visit me!...
Bon voyage ! Have a good trip!
Allons ! pressons... We'd better hurry... *

3. out of
il les a trahis par haine he betrayed them out of hatred

...par

Si vous passez par Las Dopicos venez me voir !
Bon voyage !
Allons ! pressons..

4. a
trois fois par semaine three times a week

5. Loc
nous irons à Genève par avion we'll fly to Geneva

paraître

paraître
[parɛtr] *v i*
1. to seem, to look

...paraître

la Castafiore ne paraît pas son âge Signora Castafiore doesn't look her age

2. Loc
il paraît que it seems (that)

parapluie

parapluie
[paraplɥi] *n m*
umbrella

...parapluie

Regardez !... C'est le parapluie du professeur !...

...parapluie

* *Regardez !... C'est le parapluie du professeur !...* Look!... That's Calculus' umbrella!... *

parasol

parasol
[parasɔl] *n m*
sunshade

parc

parc
[park] *n m*
park

parce que

parce que
[parskə] *conj*
because

Milou aboie parce qu'il s'est fait mal Snowy is barking because he hurt himself

pardon

pardon
[pardɔ̃]
I. *n m*

demander pardon à quelqu'un to apologize to somebody

II. *exclam*
excuse me

► **pardonner**
[pardɔne] *v t*
to forgive

...pardon

* *Je suis désolé, Tintin, pourrez-vous me pardonner ? Pardonnez-moi, je vous en prie !...* I'm sorry, Tintin, won't you forgive me? Please forgive me!... *Chut !...* Ssh!... *

pare-brise

pare-brise
[parbriz] *n m inv*
windscreen
(*Am:* windshield)

pareil

pareil, eille
[parɛj] *adj*
1. same

* *Tes vêtements sont pareils que les miens.* Your clothes are the same as mine. *Je dirais même plus... Ils sont pareils...* To be precise... They are the same... *

2. Loc
tout ça, c'est pareil it's all the same thing

parent

parent, e
[parɑ̃, ɑ̃t]
I. *adj*
related

est-ce que les Dupondt sont parents ? are the Thompsons related?

II. *n*
relative

je vous présente quelques parents à moi let me introduce some of my relatives

► **parents**
[parɑ̃] *n m pl*

* *Je le dirai à mes parents... et ils te puniront !...* I'll tell my parents... and they'll punish you!... *C'est ça !...* You do that!... *

...parent

paresseux

paresseux, euse
[paresø, øz]
I. *adj*
lazy

II. *n*
lazybones

parfait

parfait, e
[parfɛ, ɛt] *adj*
1. perfect

...parfait

...parfait

Nestor, c'est parfait !

2. Loc
* *Nestor, c'est parfait !* Nestor, that's excellent! *

parfum

parfum
[parfœ̃] *n m*
1. scent

sentez ces roses, capitaine, quel parfum délicieux ! smell these roses, Captain, what a delicious scent!

2. perfume
la Castafiore se met du parfum Bianca Castafiore wears perfume

3. flavour
(*Am:* flavor)
à quel parfum est votre glace ? what flavour is your ice cream?

parisien

parisien, enne
[parizjɛ̃, ɛn] *adj*
Parisian

la mode parisienne Parisian fashion

▸ **Parisien, enne**
[parizjɛ̃, ɛn] *n*
Parisian

les Parisiens vivent à Paris Parisians live in Paris

parking

parking
[parkiŋ] *n m*
car park
(*Am:* parking lot)

parler

parler
[parle]
I. *v t*
to speak

les Dupondt ne parlent pas la langue du pays the Thompsons don't speak the language of this country

II. *v t ind*
to speak, to talk

je voudrais vous parler un instant I'd like to talk to you for a moment

III. *v pr*
to be on speaking terms

ils ne se parlent plus they are no longer on speaking terms

part

part
[par] *n f*
1. portion

partageons le pain en parts égales let's share the bread in equal portions

2. Loc
* *C'est un paquet de la part de Tournesol !...* It's a parcel from Calculus!... *

je viens vous voir de la part de Tournesol Calculus sent me to see you

nulle part nowhere

quelque part somewhere

C'est un paquet de la part de Tournesol !...

partager

partager
[partaʒe] *v t*
to share

partageons ces fruits let's share the fruit

participer

participer
[partisipe] *v t ind*
to take part

particulièrement

particulièrement
[partikyljɛrmɑ̃] *adv*
particularly

* *... et je voudrais insister particulièrement sur plusieurs points...* ... there are several points I'd particularly like to emphasize... *

... et je voudrais insister particulièrement sur plusieurs points ...

partie

partie
[parti] *n f*
1. part

la capitale est dans la partie nord du pays the capital is in the northern part of the country

2. game
* *Vous avez perdu, mon cher Tintin !... Sapristi ! c'est exact...* You have lost, my dear Tintin!... Great snakes! it's true...

Vous avez perdu mon cher Tintin !...
Sapristi ! c'est exact...
Le général Alcazar et Tintin font une partie d'échecs.

...partie

Le général Alcazar et Tintin font une partie d'échecs... General Alcazar and Tintin are playing a game of chess... *

3. Loc
en partie partly

partir

partir
[partir] *v i*
1. to leave

...partir

HERGÉ
Les Lampion partent de Moulinsart...

* *Les Lampion partent de Moulinsart...* The Waggs are leaving Marlinspike... *

le train pour Noyon vient juste de partir the Noyon train has just left

2. to come out
la tache partira au lavage the stain will come out in the wash

3. Loc
à partir de maintenant from now on

partout

partout
[partu] *adv*
everywhere

Milou suit Tintin partout Snowy goes everywhere with Tintin

pas

pas
[pɑ] *n m*
step

...pas

il a fait un pas en arrière/en avant he took a step backwards/forwards

pas

pas
[pɑ] *adv*
1. not

Milou n'a pas soif! Snowy is not thirsty!

2. Loc
pas encore not yet

pas de no

passage

passage
[pɑsaʒ] *n m*
1. passage

un passage secret a secret passage

2. Loc
* *Heureusement qu'il y a un passage clouté !...* Thank goodness there's a pedestrian crossing (*Am:* crosswalk)! *

Heureusement qu'il y a un passage clouté !...
Beaulieu

passager

passager, ère
[pɑsaʒe, ɛr] *n*
passenger

tous les passagers sont montés à bord all passengers are on board

passant

passant, e
[pɑsɑ̃, ɑ̃t] *n*
passer-by

...passant

mais que regardent les passants ? what on earth are the passes-by looking at?

passeport

passeport
[pɑspɔr] *n m*
passport

montrez-moi vos passeports let me see your passports

passer

passer
[pɑse]
I. *v t*
1. to pass

capitaine, passez-moi le journal s'il vous plaît pass me the newspaper, please, Captain

2. to cross
* *Nous devons absolument passer la frontière !* We must cross the border! *

Nous devons absolument passer la frontière !

...passer

3. to spend
ils ont passé un mois en prison they spent a month in prison

II. *v i*
1. to pass

* *Regardez, le yéti est passé par ici...* Look, the Yeti has passed this way... *

2. to call in
(*Am:* drop by)
Tintin est passé voir le capitaine Haddock Tintin called in to see Captain Haddock

3. Loc
un avion passe dans le ciel a plane is flying overhead

III. *v pr*
1. to happen

* *Capitaine, vous êtes blessé, que s'est-il passé ?...* Captain, you're hurt, what happened?... *

...passer

2. to do/go without
le capitaine ne peut pas se passer de sa pipe the Captain can't go without his pipe

passe-temps

passe-temps
[pɑstɑ̃] *n m inv*
pastime

passionnant

passionnant, e
[pasjɔnɑ̃, ɑ̃t] *adj*
thrilling

pastille

pastille
[pastij] *n f*
lozenge

des pastilles contre la toux cough lozenges

pâté

pâté
[pɑte] *n m*
pâté

patience

patience
[pasjɑ̃s] *n f*
patience

je commence à perdre patience I'm beginning to run out of patience

...patience

► **patient, e**
[pasjɑ̃, ɑ̃t] *adj*
patient

pâtisserie

pâtisserie
[pɑtisri] *n f*
1. pastry

ne mange pas trop de pâtisseries don't eat too many pastries

...pâtisserie

2. confectioner's
(*Am:* bakery)
va à la pâtisserie go to the confectioner's

patron

patron
[patrɔ̃] *n m*
1. employer

2. Loc
le patron du restaurant the manager of the restaurant

patte

patte
[pat] *n f*
1. leg

* *Allez Milou, montre-moi ta patte... il faut que je voie si elle est cassée !...* Here, Snowy, show me your leg... I must see if it's broken!... *

2. paw
le chat lui a donné un coup de patte the cat hit it with its paw

pauvre

pauvre
[povr]
I. *adj*
poor

II. *n*
poor person

les pauvres the poor

payer

payer
[pɛje] *v t*
to pay

...payer

combien avez-vous payé ce scaphandre ? how much did you pay for this diving suit?

► **payant, e**
[pɛjɑ̃, ɑ̃t] *adj*
1. paying

hôte payant paying guest

2. Loc
le spectacle est payant there is a charge for the show

pays

pays
[pei] *n m*
country

paysage

paysage
[pɛizaʒ] *n m*
landscape, scenery

* *Quel magnifique paysage !* What a magnificent landscape!... *

péage

péage
[peaʒ] *n m*
1. toll

une autoroute à péage a toll motorway (*Am:* turnpike)

2. toll-gate

peau

peau
[po] *n f*
pl peaux
1. skin

elle a la peau douce she has soft skin

2. Loc
il faut enlever la peau de ce fruit you have to peel this fruit

pêche

pêche
[pɛʃ] *n f*
peach

ces pêches sont mûres these peaches are ripe

pêche

pêche
[pɛʃ] *n f*
fishing

* *Vous allez à la pêche ?...* Are you going fishing?... *

un bateau de pêche a fishing-boat

► **pêcher**
[peʃe] *v t*
1. to fish

nous allons devoir pêcher pour nous nourrir we'll have to fish to get some food

2. to catch
quel beau poisson vous avez pêché ! what a fine fish you caught!

► **pêcheur**
[pɛʃœr] *n m*
fisherman

pédale

pédale
[pedal] *n f*
pedal

la pédale du frein ne marche plus the brake pedal doesn't work any longer

peigne

peigne
[pɛɲ] *n m*
comb

► **se peigner**
[səpɛɲe] *v pr*
to comb one's hair

peindre

peindre
[pɛ̃dr]
to paint

peine

peine
[pɛn] *n f*
1. sorrow

il s'en va et Nestor n'éprouve pas de peine he's leaving and Nestor doesn't feel much sorrow

2. difficulty
ils ont eu beaucoup de peine à arriver jusqu'au sommet they had great difficulty reaching the summit

3. Loc
* *Parlez plus fort, je vous entends à peine...* Speak up, I can hardly hear you... *

à peine dans le train, il s'est endormi no sooner was he on the train than he fell asleep

ce n'est pas la peine d'en discuter it isn't worth arguing about it

peinture

peinture
[pɛ̃tyr] *n f*
paint

il nous faut un peu de peinture bleue we need some blue paint

* *Attention ! Peinture fraîche !* Caution! Wet Paint! *

pellicule

pellicule
[pɛlikyl] *n f*
film

as-tu une pellicule dans ton appareil ? have you got any film in your camera?

pelouse

pelouse
[pəluz] *n f*
lawn

pencher

pencher
[pɑ̃ʃe]
I. *v t*
to bend

penche la tête en avant, tu le verras bend your head forward, you'll see him

II. *v pr*
to lean

ne pas se pencher par la fenêtre do not lean out of the window

pendant

pendant
[pɑ̃dɑ̃] *prép*
1. during

* *Allô ?... Allô ?... Quoi ?... J'ai horreur qu'on me dérange pendant mon bain !...* Hello?... Hello?... What?... I hate being disturbed during my bath!... *

2. for
il a été absent pendant deux mois he was away for two months

► **pendant que**
[pɑ̃dɑ̃kə] *conj*
while

soyez tranquille, Tintin, je monterai la garde pendant que vous dormirez don't worry, Tintin, I'll mount guard while you're sleeping

penser

penser
[pɑ̃se] *v t*
1. to think

que pensez-vous de cette affaire ? what do you think of this case?

2. to remember
avez-vous pensé à leur dire que nous arrivions ? did you remember to tell them we were coming?

pension

pension
[pɑ̃sjɔ̃] *n f*
1. boarding-school

* *Arrête ou je dis à ton père de te mettre en pension !...* Stop it or I'll tell your father to send you to boarding school!...
Non !... No!... *

2. board
une chambre en pension complète a room with full board

► **pensionnaire**
[pɑ̃sjɔnɛr] *n*
1. boarder

les pensionnaires mangent au réfectoire boarders have their meals in the dining hall

2. resident
les pensionnaires de l'hôtel the residents of the hotel

pente

pente
[pɑ̃t] *n f*
slope

* *Ils dévalent la pente.* They're running down the slope. *

...pente

Ils dévalent la pente.

perdre

perdre
[pɛrdr]
I. *v t*
1. to lose

* *Grands dieux, Dupond, j'ai perdu mon portefeuille !* Good grief, Thompson, I've lost my wallet! *

2. to waste
nous perdons notre temps we're wasting our time

II. *v i*
to lose

tu as perdu, moi j'ai gagné ! you lost, I won!

III. *v pr*
to get lost

nous nous sommes perdus dans le désert we got lost in the desert

père

père
[pɛr] *n m*
father

permettre

permettre
[pɛrmɛtr] *v t*
to allow

Tintin, me permets-t... d'emporter cet os Tintin, will you allow m... to take that bone with me

...permettre

▸ **permis**
[pɛrmi] *n m*

permis de conduire driving licence (*Am:* driver's license)

▸ **permission**
[pɛrmisjɔ̃] *n f*
permission

nous devons demander la permission à nos supérieurs we must ask our superiors' permission

personne

personne
[pɛrsɔn]
I. *n f*
1. person *pl* people

c'est la dernière personne qui l'a vu he's the last person who saw him

plusieurs personnes ont pu s'échapper several people managed to escape

2. Loc
les grandes personnes the grown-ups

II. *pron*
1. nobody

* *Personne ne l'a vu... Où est donc passé ce bougre de cornichon de Tournesol...* Nobody's seen him... Where has that nitwitted Calculus gone... *

2. anybody
presque personne ne la connaît hardly anybody knows her

persuader

persuader
[pɛrsɥade] *v t*
to convince

peser

peser
[pəze]
I. *v t*
to weigh
à l'aéroport, ils ont pesé nos bagages at the airport, they weighed our luggage

...peser

II. *v i*
to weigh

* *Mille sabords !... Combien ce sac peut-il bien peser ?... Si j'avais su qu'il était si lourd !... J'aurais dû le peser avant de partir !...* Blistering barnacles!... How much can this bag weigh?... If only I had known it was so heavy!... I should have weighed it before I left!... *

petit

petit, e
[pəti, it] *adj*
1. little

il montre les petits oiseaux he's pointing at the little birds

2. small
Tchang est plus petit que Tintin Chang is smaller than Tintin

3. young
quand j'étais petit when I was young

▸ **petit**
[pəti] *n m*
young
la femelle et ses petits the female and her young

▸ **petit-fils**
[pətifis] *n m*
pl petits-fils
grandson

▸ **petite-fille**
[pətitfij] *n f*
pl petites-filles
granddaughter

▸ **petits-enfants**
[pətizɑ̃fɑ̃] *n m pl*
grandchildren

peu

peu
[pø] *adv*
1. little

je mange très peu I eat very little

...peu

2. Loc
* *Le professeur Tournesol ?... Vous l'avez manqué de peu, il est parti il y a quelques minutes...* Professor Calculus?... You just missed him, he left a few minutes ago... *

soyez bref, j'ai peu de temps be brief, I haven't got much time

Tintin, nous sommes un peu fatigués Tintin, we're a bit tired

peur

peur
[pœr] *n f*
1. fear

nous avons soudain été saisis par la peur a sudden fear came over us

2. Loc
Milou a peur de l'araignée Snowy's afraid of the spider

ce gros chien m'a fait peur that big dog frightened me

* *Dupont, vite, j'ai vu un squelette, je suis mort de peur !... Mais non, n'aie pas peur, tu as cru voir un squelette !...* Thomson, quick, I saw a skeleton, I'm scared to death!... Don't be scared, you thought you saw a skeleton!... *

peut-être

peut-être
[pøtɛtr] *adv*
1. perhaps

allons sur le port, nous y trouverons peut-être le capitaine let's go to the harbour (*Am:* harbor) perhaps we'll find the Captain there

2. maybe
peut-être est-il sorti maybe he isn't in

phare

phare
[far] *n m*
1. headlight

2. lighthouse
c'est le phare de l'île it's the island lighthouse

pharmacie

pharmacie
[farmasi] *n f*
chemist's (shop) (*Am:* drugstore)

▸ **pharmacien, enne**
[farmasjɛ̃, ɛn] *n*
chemist (*Am:* druggist)

photographie

photo(graphie)
[fɔto(grafi)] *n f*
photo(graph)

▸ **photographier**
[fɔtografje] *v t*

to take a photograph of

phrase

phrase
[fraz] *n f*
sentence

* *Que signifie ce message ? La dernière phrase est incompréhensible...* What does this message

Que signifie ce message ? La dernière phrase est incompréhensible...

mean? I can't make out the last sentence... *

physique

physique
[fizik] *adj*
physical

* *Allons, Milou, un peu d'exercice physique nous fera du bien.* Come on, Snowy, some physical exercise will do us good. *

Allons, Milou, un peu d'exercice physique nous fera du bien.

piano

piano
[pjano] *n m*
piano

M. Wagner joue du piano. Mr Wagner plays the piano.

pièce

pièce
[pjɛs] *n f*
1. coin

une pièce d'argent a silver coin

2. room
il y a beaucoup de pièces dans ce château ! there are a lot of rooms in this castle!

3. piece
les pièces du jeu d'échecs sont là the pieces of the chess set are here

4. play
au théâtre, nous avons vu une pièce we saw a play at the theatre (*Am:* theater)

pied

pied
[pje] *n m*
1. foot

Tintin, j'ai mal aux pieds Tintin, my feet hurt

Allez Milou, courage, nous devons y aller à pied...

* *Allez Milou, courage, nous devons y aller à pied...* Come on, Snowy, cheer up, we'll have to go on foot... *

2. leg
les pieds de la table sont cassés the legs of the table are broken

piéton

piéton
[pjetɔ̃] *n m*
pedestrian

pile

pile
[pil] *n f*
1. pile

une pile d'assiettes a pile of plates

2. battery
cette radio marche avec des piles this radio runs on batteries

3. Loc
tu choisis, pile ou face ? you choose, heads or tails?

pilote

pilote
[pilɔt] *n m*
1. pilot

* *Ce pilote est fantastique !* This pilot is fantastic! *

2. driver
les pilotes de course gagnent beaucoup d'argent racing drivers earn a lot of money

Ce pilote est fantastique !

pilule

pilule
[pilyl] *n f*
pill

pipe

pipe
[pip] *n f*
pipe

ça y est, j'ai réussi à réparer ma pipe that's it, I managed to fix my pipe

pique-nique

pique-nique
[piknik] *n m*
pl pique-niques
picnic

faisons un pique-nique let's have a picnic

piquer

piquer
[pike]
I. *v t*
1. to prick

...piquer

Pauvre Milou, la flèche t'a piqué la queue.
WOUAAAAAH!

...piquer

* *Wouaaaah !* Wooaaah *Pauvre Milou, la flèche t'a piqué la queue !...* Poor Snowy, the arrow pricked your tail! *

2. to sting
la fumée me pique les yeux the smoke is making my eyes sting

II. *v pr*
to prick oneself

il s'est piqué avec l'aiguille he pricked himself with the needle

▶ **piqûre**
[pikyr] *n f*
1. sting

il faut désinfecter cette piqûre de guêpe this wasp sting must be disinfected

2. injection
* *N'ayez pas peur, je vous fais juste une piqûre, ça ne sera pas long !...* Don't be afraid, I'll just give you an injection... It won't take long!... *

N'ayez pas peur, je vous fais juste une piqûre, ça ne sera pas long !...

pire

pire
[pir]
I. *adj*
1. worse

c'est pire que jamais
it's worse than ever

2. worst
il est mon pire ennemi
he's my worst enemy

II. *n m*
worst

* *Maintenant, Milou, il faut s'attendre au pire !* Now, Snowy, we must expect the worst... *

Maintenant, Milou, il faut s'attendre au pire !...

piscine

piscine
[pisin] *n f*
swimming pool

piste

piste
[pist] *n f*
1. track

* *Dans le désert...* In the desert...
Ne nous écartons pas de la piste... Let's keep to the track... *

...piste

Dans le désert...
Ne nous écartons pas de la piste ...

2. runway
* *L'avion roule sur la piste...* The plane is taxiing on the runway... *

3. trail
ils sont sur la piste du voleur they're on the thief's trail

pitié

pitié
[pitje] *n f*
pity

L'avion roule sur la piste.

pittoresque

pittoresque
[pitɔresk] *adj*
picturesque

* *Regardez, Tintin, comme cet endroit est pittoresque !* Look, Tintin, how picturesque this place is!... *

placard

placard
[plakar] *n m*
cupboard

place

place
[plas] *n f*
1. square

votre hôtel donne sur la place your hotel looks on to the square

2. place
la momie n'est plus à sa place the mummy is no longer in its place

3. seat
y a-t-il une place dans ce compartiment ? is there a vacant seat in this compartment?

4. room
fais-moi une petite place make a bit of room for me

placer

placer
[plase] *v t*
to put, to place

...placer

il faut d'abord placer les pièces sur l'échiquier first you must place the pieces on the chessboard

plafond

plafond
[plafɔ̃] *n m*
ceiling

plage

plage
[plaʒ] *n f*
beach

* *Reposons-nous un moment sur la plage... Vous avez l'air bien fatigué, capitaine !* Let's rest for a moment on the beach... You look tired, Captain!... *Oui, d'accord !...* Yes. OK... *

plaindre

plaindre
[plɛ̃dr]
I. *v t*
to feel sorry for

* *Mon pauvre Milou, je te plains, comme tu dois avoir mal !... Ces moustiques t'ont piqué partout !...* My poor Snowy, I feel sorry for you, it must be very painful!... Those mosquitoes have bitten you all over!... *

...plaindre

II. *v pr*
to complain

ça ne sert à rien de se plaindre it's no use complaining

plaire

plaire
[plɛr] *v t ind*

on dirait que cet homme ne plaît pas

...plaire

à Milou Snowy doesn't seem to like that man

► **s'il te plaît, s'il vous plaît**
[siltəplɛ, silvuplɛ] *exclam*
please

* *Milou, s'il te plaît, laisse ce perroquet !* Snowy, please leave that parrot alone! *Laisse ce perroquet !* Leave that parrot alone! *

plaisir

plaisir
[plɛzir] *n m*
pleasure

quel plaisir de vous retrouver ! it's such a pleasure to see you again!

plan

plan
[plɑ̃] *n m*
1. plan

voici le plan de la maison here's the plan of the house

2. plan
* ***Attends !... J'ai un plan... Ecoute bien !...*** Wait!... I've got a plan... Listen carefully!...
Ah oui ! Oh yes! *

3. Loc
au premier plan in the foreground

* ***Tintin est au premier plan...*** Tintin's in the foreground... *

à l'arrière-plan in the background

gros plan close-up

plan de la ville city map

Tintin est au premier plan ...

planche

planche
[plɑ̃ʃ] *n f*
1. plank, board

cette planche nous servira de passerelle we'll use this plank as a footbridge

2. Loc
planche à voile sailboard

plancher

plancher
[plɑ̃ʃe] *n m*
floor

* ***Que pensez-vous de cette trappe dans le plancher ?...*** What do you think of this trap door in the floor?... *

plante

plante
[plɑ̃t] *n f*
plant

plastique

plastique
[plastik] *n m*
plastic

Milou n'aime pas les os en plastique Snowy doesn't like plastic bones

plat

plat
[pla] *n m*
dish

un plat en faïence an earthenware dish

plat

plat, e
[pla, at] *adj*
1. flat

...plat

heureusement, le terrain est plat ici fortunately the ground is flat here

2. Loc
* ***Zut !... Les pneus sont à plat !...*** Heck!... The tyres (*Am:* tires) are flat!... *

plâtre

plâtre
[plɑtr] *n m*
plaster

...plâtre

ils ont un bras dans le plâtre one of their arms is in plaster/in a (plaster) cast

plein

plein, e
[plɛ̃, ɛn] *adj*
1. full

non merci, mon verre est plein no thanks, my glass is full

...plein

2. Loc
en plein jour in broad daylight

en pleine nuit in the middle of the night

en plein air in the open air

la lune est pleine cette nuit there's a full moon tonight

...plein

Nous avons fait le plein. Partons !

► **plein**
[plɛ̃] *n m*
Loc

faire le plein to fill up (the tank)

* ***Nous avons fait le plein. Partons !*** We've filled up the tank. Let's go! *

pleurer

pleurer
[plœre] *v i*
to cry

pleuvoir

pleuvoir
[pløvwar] *v impers*
to rain

il pleut it's raining

* ***Il pleut à verse...*** It's raining cats and dogs... *

...pleuvoir

Il pleut à verse...

plier

plier
[plije]
I. *v t*
to fold

plie la feuille de papier avant de la mettre dans l'enveloppe fold the sheet of paper before putting it in the envelope

Les arbres se plient dans la tempête...

II. *v pr*
to bend

* ***Les arbres se plient dans la tempête...*** The trees are bending in the storm... *

plombier

plombier
[plɔ̃bje] *n m*
plumber

plonger

plonger
[plɔ̃ʒe] *v i*
to dive

* ***Ils ont plongé...*** They've dived... *

► **plongée**
[plɔ̃ʒe] *n f*
diving

ils font de la plongée (sous-marine) they go diving

Ils ont plongé...

pluie

pluie
[plɥi] *n f*
rain

si seulement la pluie pouvait s'arrêter ! if only the rain would stop!

plume

plume
[plym] *n f*
1. feather

les plumes de ce perroquet sont bleues this parrot's feathers are blue

2. nib
la plume de mon stylo est cassée my pen nib is broken

plupart

plupart
[plypar] *n f*
1. most

la plupart des passagers ont le mal de mer most of the passengers are seasick

2. Loc
pour la plupart, ils sont d'accord avec vous for the most part, they agree with you

plus

plus
[plys] [plyz] *before vowel*
I. *prép*
plus

deux plus deux font quatre two plus two are four

II. *adv*
[ply(s)]
1. more

* ***Tintin, je vous en prie, marchez plus lentement... Je ne***

Tintin, je vous en prie, marchez plus lentement... Je ne peux pas vous suivre...

...plus

peux pas vous suivre... Tintin, please walk a bit more slowly... I can't keep up with you... *

est-ce que Dupont est plus jeune/vieux que Dupond ? is Thomson younger/older than Thompson?

2. most
mille sabords, vous êtes la personne la plus têtue que je connaisse blistering barnacles, you're the most

Je suis en prison et en plus mon bateau s'en va!...

stubborn person I've ever met

3. Loc
on m'a donné un livre en plus I was given an extra book

* *Je suis en prison et en plus mon bateau s'en va!...* I'm in prison and on top of that my boat is leaving!... *

III. *adv*
[ply]
Loc

il ne pleut plus it's no longer raining

il n'y a plus de place there's no room left

je n'ai pas envie d'y aller – moi non plus I don't feel like going – neither do I

plutôt

plutôt
[plyto] *adv*
rather

pneu

pneu
[pnø] *n m*
pl pneus
tyre (*Am:* tire)

le pneu de la voiture a éclaté the tyre of the car burst

poche

poche
[pɔʃ] *n f*
pocket

poids

poids
[pwa] *n m*
weight

* *Milou, tu manges trop, tu vas prendre du poids !* Snowy, you're eating too much, you're going to put on weight! *

Milou, tu manges trop, tu vas prendre du poids !

point

point
[pwɛ̃] *n m*
1. dot

que signifient ces points sur ce dessin ? what is the meaning of these dots on this drawing?

2. full stop
(*Am:* period)
n'oublie pas le point à la fin de la phrase don't forget to put a full stop at the end of the sentence

3. Loc
un steak à point a medium-rare steak

* *Drrring Drrring* Rrrring Rrrring
Oh, quelle surprise, j'étais sur le point de vous téléphoner !... Oh, what a surprise, I was about to call you!... *

DRRRING
DRRRING

Oh, quelle surprise, j'étais sur le point de vous téléphoner.

pointure

pointure
[pwɛ̃tyr] *n f*
size

Dupont, quelle est la pointure de tes chaussures ? Thomson, what size shoes do you take?

poire

poire
[pwar] *n f*
pear

poireau

poireau
[pwaro] *n m*
pl poireaux
leek

pois

pois
[pwa] *n m*
pea

poisson

poisson
[pwasɔ̃] *n m*
fish

► **poissonnerie**
[pwasɔnri] *n f*
fishmonger's (*Am:* fish dealer)

poitrine

poitrine
[pwatrin] *n f*
1. chest

* *Et vlan, un coup de poing dans la poitrine !* Slap-bang, a punch in the chest! *

2. bosom, bust
la Castafiore a une grosse poitrine Signora Castafiore has a large bosom

Et vlan, un coup de poing dans la poitrine !

poivre

poivre
[pwavr] *n m*
pepper

poli

poli, e
[pɔli] *adj*
polite

un homme très poli a very polite man

police

police
[pɔlis] *n f*
police

► **policier**
[pɔlisje] *n m*
policeman

politique

politique
[pɔlitik] *n f*
politics

pollution

pollution
[pɔlysjɔ̃] *n f*
pollution

► **pollué, e**
[pɔlɥe] *adj*
polluted

pomme

pomme
[pɔm] *n f*
apple

...pomme

Cette pomme est énorme !...
BOUM

* *Cette pomme est énorme !...* This apple is enormous!... *

pomme de terre

pomme de terre
[pɔmdətɛr] *n f*
pl pommes de terre
potato

pompier

pompier
[pɔ̃pje] *n m*
fireman

pompiste

pompiste
[pɔ̃pist] *n m*
petrol-pump (*Am:* gas-station) attendant

pont

Il plonge du haut du pont.

pont
[pɔ̃] *n m*
1. bridge

* *Il plonge du haut du pont.* He's diving from the bridge. *

2. deck
* *Sur le pont...* On the deck... *

Sur le pont ...

pop

pop
[pɔp]
I. *adj inv*
pop

un chanteur pop a pop singer

II. *n f*
pop music

populaire

populaire
[pɔpylɛr] *adj*
popular

porc

porc
[pɔr] *n m*
1. pig

dans cette ferme, ils élèvent des porcs they breed pigs on this farm

...porc

2. pork
côtes de porc pork chops

port

port
[pɔr] *n m*
port, harbour (*Am:* harbor)

* *Le bateau quitte le port.* The boat is leaving port. *

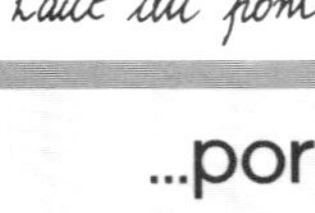

...port

Le bateau quitte le port.

porte

porte
[pɔrt] *n f*
door

quelqu'un frappe à la porte somebody's knocking at the door

* *La porte est fermée à clé !... Ils nous ont enfermés !...* The door is locked!... They've shut us in!... *

La porte est fermée à clé !... Ils nous ont enfermés !...

porte-clés

porte-clés, porte-clefs
[pɔrtəkle] *n m inv*
keyring

portefeuille

portefeuille
[pɔrtəfœj] *n m*
wallet

...portefeuille

* *Faites voir !...* Let's have a look!... *Comme ça, on ne me volera plus mon portefeuille !* And now, nobody will steal my wallet! *

porte-monnaie

porte-monnaie
[pɔrtəmɔnɛ] *n m*
purse

porter

porter
[pɔrte]
I. *v t*
1. to carry

nous pouvons porter cette caisse we can carry this crate

...porter

2. to wear
la Castafiore porte un collier Bianca Castafiore is wearing a necklace

II. *v pr*
le capitaine se porte bien/mal the Captain is well/unwell

poser

poser
[poze]
I. *v t*
1. to put down

posez vos pistolets par terre ! put your guns down!

2. to pose
* *Prêts ? Posez pour la photo...* Ready? Pose for the photo... *

II. *v pr*
1. to settle

la pie s'est posée sur la branche de l'arbre the magpie settled on the branch of the tree

2. to land
victoire ! la fusée s'est posée sur la Lune ! hurray! the rocket landed on the Moon!

possible

possible
[pɔsibl] *adj*
possible

vous est-il possible de partir tout de suite ? is it possible for you to leave at once?

autant que possible as far as possible

dès que possible as soon as possible

poste

poste
[pɔst] *n f*
1. post (*Am:* mail)

* *Ce colis est arrivé par la poste, il faut l'ouvrir tout de suite...* This parcel (*Am:* package) came by post, we must open it immediately... *

2. post office
va acheter des timbres à la poste go and buy some stamps at the post office

► **poster**
[pɔste] *v t*
to post (*Am:* to mail)

...poste

pot

pot
[po] *n m*
1. jar

un pot de confiture a jar of jam

2. pot
le pot de fleurs lui est tombé sur la tête the flower pot fell on his head

potable

potable
[pɔtabl] *adj*
1. drinkable

* *Mais que fait-il ? Il ne sait pas si l'eau est potable !...* But what's he doing? He doesn't know whether the water is drinkable! *C'est vrai !... Allons voir !...* It's true!... Let's go and see! *

2. Loc
eau non potable not drinking water

potage

potage
[pɔtaʒ] *n m*
soup

potage de légumes vegetable soup

poubelle

poubelle
[pubɛl] *n f*
dustbin (*Am:* garbage can)

poule

poule
[pul] *n f*
hen

▶ **poulet**
[pulɛ] *n m*
chicken

poupée

poupée
[pupe] *n f*
doll

pour

pour
[pur] *prép*
1. for

* *Un cadeau pour Milou.* A present for Snowy. *

2. for
Tintin part pour l'Amérique Tintin's leaving for America

3. for
peux-tu payer pour moi ? can you pay for me?

Un cadeau pour Milou

4. to
il me faut une échelle pour franchir ce mur I need a ladder to get over this wall

5. Loc
lui téléphoner ? je suis pour phone him? I'm all for it

pour cent per cent

pourboire

pourboire
[purbwar] *n m*
tip

* *Oh !... J'ai oublié de laisser un pourboire au garçon...* Oh, I nearly forgot to leave the waiter a tip... *

Oh !... J'ai oublié de laisser un pourboire au garçon...

pourquoi

pourquoi
[purkwa] *adv*
why

...pourquoi

pourquoi n'est-il pas chez lui ? why isn't he at home?

allons-y tout de suite – pourquoi pas ? let's go now – why not?

pourri

pourri, e
[puri] *adj*
rotten

pourtant

pourtant
[purtɑ̃] *adv*
yet

* *Et alors ?...* So?... *Rien !... Je n'ai rien trouvé, et pourtant j'ai exploré toute l'épave...* Nothing!... I couldn't find anything, and yet I explored the whole wreck... *

Et alors ?...
Rien !... Je n'ai rien trouvé, et pourtant j'ai exploré toute l'épave ...

pousser

pousser
[puse]
I. *v t*
1. to push

pouvez-vous m'aider à pousser la voiture ? could you help me push the car?

2. to utter
* *Ouaaaaah !...* Yeeooow!... *Le capitaine a poussé un cri terrible...* The Captain uttered a frightful cry... *

OUAAAAAH!...

Le capitaine a poussé un cri terrible ...

II. *v i*
1. to push

ne poussez pas, il n'y a plus de place don't push, there's no more room

2. to grow
l'herbe a poussé the grass has grown

III. *v pr*
to move over

poussez-vous un peu que je puisse m'asseoir move over a bit so that I can sit down

pouvoir

pouvoir
[puvwar]
I. *v aux*
1. can

je viendrai dès que je pourrai I'll come as soon as I can

2. to be able to
ne soyez pas triste, madame Wang, on pourra le guérir... don't be sad, Mrs Wang, we'll be able to cure him...

3. Loc
Milou, tu pourrais écouter ce que je dis ! Snowy, you could listen to what I say!

II. *n m*
power

le général Alcazar vient de prendre le pouvoir... General Alcazar has just seized power...

pratique

pratique
[pratik] *adj*
practical, convenient

ces combinaisons spatiales sont très pratiques these space-suits are very convenient

pratiquer

pratiquer
[pratike] *v t*
1. to practise (*Am:* to practice)

pratiquer un sport to practise a sport

2. Loc
pratiquer le football to play football

préférer

préférer
[prefere] *v t*
to prefer

maintenant, le capitaine préfère l'eau au whisky now the Captain prefers water to whisky

► **préférence**
[preferɑ̃s] *n f*
preference

premier

premier, ère
[prəmje, ɛr]
I. *adj*
first

* *Dépêchons-nous !* Hurry!
Nous prendrons le premier avion ! We'll take the first plane! *

la première fois que je l'ai vue the first time I saw her

II. *n m*
first (one)

qui de vous y a pensé le premier ? which of you thought of it first?

prendre

prendre
[prɑ̃dr]
I. *v t*
1. to take

prenez ce pistolet et soyez prêt à tirer ! take this gun and be ready to shoot!

il a pris des photos he took photos

2. to catch
Dupond et Dupont ont pris le voleur Thompson and Thomson caught the thief

Tintin a pris froid Tintin caught cold

3. to have
avez-vous pris votre petit déjeuner ? did you have your breakfast?

prendre un bain to have a bath

4. to pick up
venez me prendre à la gare come and pick me up at the station

5. to take
nous avons pris un taxi we came by taxi

II. *v i*
1. to catch

le feu commence à prendre the fire is beginning to catch

2. to start
* *Vite, le feu a pris dans le salon !...* Quick, a fire has started in the lounge!... *

3. to be busy
je serai pris toute la journée I'll be busy all day

III. *v pr*
to catch

* *Mes vêtements se sont pris dans les fils de fer barbelés !* My clothes got caught in the barbed-wire fence! *

prénom

prénom
[prenɔ̃] *n m*
first name (*Am:* given name)

mon prénom est Bianca my first name is Bianca

préparer

préparer
[prepare]
I. *v t*
to prepare

je vous ai préparé un bon repas I have prepared you a nice meal

II. *v pr*
to get ready

le capitaine se prépare à plonger the Captain is getting ready to dive

près

près
[prɛ] *adv*
1. nearby

Tintin habite tout près Tintin lives nearby

2. Loc
nous les surveillerons de près we'll keep a close watch on them

▶ **près de**
[prɛdə] *prép*
near

J'espère que l'hôtel est près de l'aéroport ...

* *J'espère que l'hôtel est près de l'aéroport...* I hope the hotel is near the airport... *

présent

présent, e
[prezɑ̃, ɑ̃t] *adj*
present

▶ **présent**
[prezɑ̃] *n m*
1. present

un verbe au présent a verb in the present (tense)

2. Loc
à présent now

présenter

présenter
[prezɑ̃te]
I. *v t*
1. to introduce

je vous présente un vieil ami let me introduce an old friend

2. to show
le malade présente des symptômes inquiétants the patient's showing worrying symptoms

II. *v pr*
to introduce oneself

permettez-moi de me présenter : Tintin, reporter please, allow me to introduce myself : Tintin, reporter

presque

presque
[prɛsk] *adv*
1. almost

Tournesol est presque sourd Calculus is almost deaf

* *Hourra ! Nous sommes presque arrivés...* Hurray, we're almost there... *

2. nearly
vite, capitaine, il est presque midi quick, Captain, it's nearly twelve o'clock

3. hardly
y avait-il beaucoup de monde ? – presque personne were there many people? – hardly anyone

Hourra ! Nous sommes presque arrivés ...

presser

presser
[prɛse]
I. *v t*
1. to squeeze

presser une orange to squeeze an orange

2. to press
pressez le bouton rouge press the red button

II. *v pr*
1. to hurry

sans se presser without hurrying

2. to hurry up
pressez-vous, nous allons rater le train hurry up or we'll miss the train

pression

pression
[prɛsjɔ̃] *n f*
pressure

prêt

prêt, e
[prɛ, ɛt] *adj*
ready

* *Etes-vous prêt ? Je vous lance la corde...* Are you ready? I'll throw the rope...
Allez-y ! Go ahead! *

Monsieur, le dîner est prêt dinner's ready, Sir

Etes-vous prêt ? Je vous lance la corde ...
Allez-y !

prêter

prêter
[prete] *vt*
to lend

Dupond, peux-tu me prêter un peigne ? Thompson, could you lend me a comb?

▶ **prêt**
[prɛ] *nm*
loan

prévenir

prévenir
[prɛvnir] *vt*
1. to warn

vous étiez prévenus du danger you were warned of the danger

2. to let someone know
* *Allô ?... Tintin... Prévenez-nous dès qu'ils seront là !* Hello, Tintin?... Let us know as soon as they arrive! *

Allô ?... Tintin ... Prévenez-nous dès qu'ils seront là !

prévision

prévision
[previzjɔ̃] *nf*
forecast

quelles sont les prévisions météorologiques ? what is the weather forecast?

prévoir

prévoir
[prevwar] *vt*
1. to foresee

...prévoir

je ne peux pas prévoir ce qu'il va décider I can't foresee what he's going to decide

2. to anticipate
* *Tiens !... Attrape ça !...* There take that!... *Attention señor !...* Watch out, señor!... *Le capitaine n'avait pas prévu cette réaction du lama...* The Captain hadn't anticipated that kind of reaction from the llama... *

...prévoir

Tiens !... Attrape ça !...
Attention señor !...

Le capitaine n'avait pas prévu cette réaction du lama ...

prier

prier
[prije] *vt*
1. to pray

prions qu'ils ne nous aient pas entendus let's pray that they didn't hear us

2. to beg

* *Milou, je t'en prie, dépêche-toi ! Dépêche-toi !* I beg you Snowy, hurry up! Hurry up!... *

3. Loc
je vous en prie please

Milou, je t'en prie, dépêche-toi ! Dépêche-toi !...

printemps

printemps
[prɛ̃tɑ̃] *nm*
spring

priorité

priorité
[prijɔrite] *nf*
right of way

* *L'ambulance a la priorité...* The ambulance has the right of way... *

...priorité

L'ambulance a la priorité ...

DING
DING DING

prise

prise
[priz] *nf*
1. plug

Ah, voici la prise de la radio ! Good, here's the plug for the radio!

2. socket (*Am:* outlet)
brancher l'aspirateur dans la prise to plug the vacuum cleaner in the socket

3. hold
je vais lui faire une prise de judo I'll get him in a judo hold

privé

privé, e
[prive] *adj*
private

propriété privée private property

prix

prix
[pri] *n m*
1. price

les prix ont augmenté prices have gone up

2. prize
Tintin a gagné le premier prix Tintin won the first prize

3. Loc
* *Quel est le prix de cette boîte ?* How much is this tin (*Am:* can)? *

Quel est le prix de cette boîte ?

probable

probable
[prɔbabl] *adj*
likely

il est probable que le professeur Tournesol a oublié Professor Calculus is likely to have forgotten

▶ **probablement**
[prɔbabləmɑ̃] *adv*
probably

ils vont probablement téléphoner they'll probably phone

problème

problème
[prɔblɛm] *n m*
1. problem

je ne sais pas faire mon problème de maths I can't solve my maths (*Am:* math) problem

2. problem
oh, tu sais, Dupond, chacun a ses problèmes well, Thompson, you know, everyone has their problems

3. Loc
le problème, c'est que nous ne connaissons pas le chinois the trouble is we can't speak Chinese

prochain

prochain, e
[prɔʃɛ̃, ɛn] *adj*
next

* *Arrête, Milou ! La prochaine fois que tu t'en prendras à un chat, je te punirai...* Stop it, Snowy! Next time you attack a cat, I'll punish you... *

nous prendrons le prochain train we'll take the next train

Arrête, Milou ! La prochaine fois que tu t'en prendras à un chat, je te punirai...

proche

proche
[prɔʃ] *adj*
1. near

allons nous renseigner dans le magasin le plus proche let's ask for information in the nearest shop

2. close
c'est un de mes proches parents he is a close relation

produit

produit
[prɔdɥi] *n m*
1. product

produits pharmaceutiques pharmaceutical products

2. liquid
produit de vaisselle washing-up liquid

3. Loc
produit de beauté cosmetic

produit chimique chemical

professeur

professeur
[prɔfesœr] *n m*
1. teacher

voici mon professeur de français here's my French teacher

2. professor
bonjour, je suis le professeur Tournesol hello, I'm Professor Calculus

profession

profession
[prɔfesjɔ̃] *n f*
1. occupation

* *Quelle est votre profession ?* What's your occupation? *

2. Loc
profession libérale (liberal) profession

Quelle est votre profession ?

profond

profond, e
[prɔfɔ̃, ɔ̃d] *adj*
1. deep

* *La rivière est bien profonde !...* The river is quite deep!...
Plouf ! Splash! *

2. Loc
la rivière est peu profonde ici the river is shallow here

La rivière est bien profonde !...
PLOUF

programme

programme
[prɔgram] *n m*
1. programme (*Am:* program)

programme de télévision TV programme

2. syllabus
le programme de maths va changer the maths (*Am:* math) syllabus is going to change

3. program
un programme d'ordinateur a computer program

► **programmeur, euse**
[prɔgramœr, øz] *n*
programmer

progrès

progrès
[prɔgrɛ] *n m*
progress

projet

projet
[prɔʒɛ] *n m*
1. plan

avez-vous des projets pour ce soir ? have you plans for tonight?

2. Loc
projet de loi bill

promenade

promenade
[prɔmnad] *n f*

1. walk, stroll

2. Loc
une promenade en bateau/à cheval/en voiture a sail/ride/drive

► **se promener**
[səprɔmne] *v pr*
1. to walk

ils se promènent dans le jardin they're walking in the garden

2. Loc
se promener en bateau/à bicyclette/en voiture to go for a sail/a ride/a drive

promettre

promettre
[prɔmɛtr] *v t*
1. to promise

il faut me promettre de ne rien dire you

must promise me that you won't say a word

2. Loc
* *Allez-y, sautez !...* Go on, Jump!...
L'arrivée de ces parachutistes ne promet rien de bon... The dropping of these parachutists is not a good sign... *

Allez-y, sautez !...

L'arrivée de ces parachutistes ne promet rien de bon...

promotion

promotion
[prɔmɔsjɔ̃] *n f*
promotion

propos

propos
[prɔpo] *n m pl*
1. remarks

il a tenu des propos inquiétants he made some worrying remarks

2. Loc
à propos de Milou, savez-vous où il est ? about Snowy, do you know where he is?

proposer

proposer
[prɔpoze] *v t*
to propose, to suggest

professeur, je vous propose de venir à Moulinsart Professor, I would suggest that you come to Marlinspike

► **proposition**
[prɔpozisjɔ̃] *n f*
proposal, suggestion

* *Mon cher Tintin, j'ai une proposition à vous faire...* Dear Tintin, I've got a suggestion to make... *

Mon cher Tintin, j'ai une proposition à vous faire...

propre

propre
[prɔpr] *adj*
1. clean

voilà, Milou, maintenant tu es propre there you are Snowy, now you're clean

2. own
* *Le yéti !... Là-haut !... je l'ai vu !... je l'ai vu de mes propres yeux !...* The Yeti!... Up there!... I saw it!... I saw it with my own eyes!... *

Le yéti !... Là-haut !... je l'ai vu !... je l'ai vu de mes propres yeux !...

propriétaire

propriétaire
[prɔprijetɛr] *n*
owner

protéger

protéger
[prɔteʒe] *v t*
to protect

ceci nous protégera du froid this will protect us from the cold

protester

protester
[prɔtɛste] *v i*
to protest

je proteste contre cette arrestation ! I protest against this arrest!

prouver

prouver
[pruve] *v t*
to prove

provenance

provenance
[prɔvnɑ̃s] *n f*

* *Je me demande quelle est la provenance de ces caisses...* I wonder where these boxes come from... *

l'avion en provenance de Paris the plane from Paris

province

province
[prɔvɛ̃s] *n f*

une ville de province a provincial town

provision

provision
[prɔvizjɔ̃] *n f*
1. stock

j'ai une bonne provision de livres pour ce long voyage I've a large stock of books for this long journey

2. Loc
faire les provisions to go shopping

provisoire

provisoire
[prɔvizwar] *adj*
temporary

proximité

proximité
[prɔksimite] *n f*
1. closeness, proximity

la proximité des mines d'uranium est un avantage the closeness of the uranium mines is an advantage

2. Loc
nous devons être à proximité de Moulinsart we must be near Marlinspike

prune

prune
[pryn] *n f*
plum

public

public, que
[pyblik] *adj*
public

la nouvelle vient juste d'être rendue publique the news has just been made public

jardin public public gardens

▶ **public**
[pyblik] *n m*
1. audience

le public a aimé ce qu'elle a chanté the audience liked what she sang

2. Loc
passage interdit au public authorized persons only

▶ **publicité**
[pyblisite] *n f*
advertisement, advert

puis

puis
[pɥi] *adv*
then

* *J'ai entendu un bruit, puis j'ai reçu un coup sur la tête !...* I heard a noise and then I was hit on the head!... *

puisque

puisque
[pɥisk] *conj*
since

* *Je vais être obligé d'employer d'autres moyens puisque vous ne voulez pas parler...* I'll have to use other means since you will not talk... *

pull-over

pull-over
[pyl(ɔvɛr)] *n m*
pl pull-overs
pullover, jumper

punir

punir
[pynir] *v t*
to punish

* *Milou, ne recommence pas, sinon tu seras puni !* Snowy, don't do it again, or you'll be punished! *

pur

pur, e
[pyr] *adj*
pure

purée

purée
[pyre] *n f*

purée de pommes de terre mashed potatoes

quai

quai
[kɛ] *n m*
1. platform

le train part du quai 2 the train leaves from platform 2

2. wharf, quay
* *Tintin marche sur le quai...* Tintin is walking along the wharf... *

Tintin marche sur le quai ...

qualité

qualité
[kalite] *n f*
1. quality

allons, capitaine, nous avons tous nos qualités et nos défauts come on, Captain, each of us has qualities as well as faults

2. quality
cette eau minérale est de bonne/mauvaise qualité this is a good/bad quality mineral water

quand

quand
[kɑ̃] *conj*
when

quand viens-tu ? when are you coming?

quart

quart
[kar] *n m*
1. quarter

2. Loc
onze heures moins le quart/et quart a quarter to/past eleven

quartier

quartier
[kartje] *n m*
district, area

que

que
[kə]
I. *pron interr*
what

que dites-vous ? what are you saying?

* *Il a eu un choc, il ne sait plus ce qu'il dit... Qu'allons-nous faire ?... Je ne sais pas si cela va durer...* He's had a shock, he doesn't know what he's saying... What shall we do next?... I don't know whether it will last... *

II. *pron rel*
that

ce n'est pas l'homme que j'ai vu it's not the man (that) I saw

c'est l'os que j'ai trouvé it's the bone (that) I found

III. *exclam*
how

Il a eu un choc, il ne sait plus ce qu'il dit... Qu'allons-nous faire ?... Je ne sais pas si cela va durer...

Zorrino, que tu es gentil ! how nice you are, Zorrino!

IV. *conj*
1. that

je crois que nous n'aurons pas fini à temps I'm afraid (that) we won't have finished in time

2. than
le capitaine est plus âgé que Tintin the Captain is older than Tintin

quel, quelle

quel, quelle
[kɛl] *adj*
1. what

quelle heure est-il ? what time is it?

2. Loc.
* *Quelle chance vous avez eue ! La balle est passée là !* How lucky you were! The bullet went through here!
Mon pauvre chapeau ! My poor hat! *

quelque

▶ **quelque chose**
[kɛlkəʃoz] *pron*
something

▶ **quelquefois**
[kɛlkəfwa] *adv*
sometimes

* *C'est vrai, quelquefois je suis distrait, mais c'est rare !* It's true, sometimes I am absent-minded, but it's rare! *

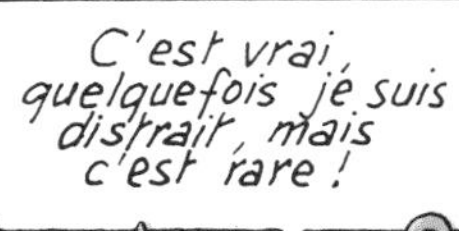

▶ **quelque part**
[kɛlkəpar] *adv*
somewhere

▶ **quelqu'un**
[kɛlkœ̃] *pron*
somebody

* *Ecoutez ce bruit... Quelqu'un vient !...* Listen to that sound... Somebody's coming!... *

...quelque

question

question
[kɛstjɔ̃] *n f*
1. question

répondez à ma question answer my question

2. Loc
* *Quelques heures plus tard...* A few hours later...
Dans ce livre, il est question des Indiens Arumbayas. This book is about the "Arumbayas" Indians. *

queue

queue
[kø] *n f*
1. tail

* *Wouaaaaaah !* Wooaaaaah!
Milou s'est coincé la queue. Snowy caught his tail. *

2. queue (*Am:* line)
il y a une longue queue devant le théâtre there's a long queue outside the theatre (*Am:* theater)

faire la queue to queue up

Milou s'est coincé la queue.

qui

qui
[ki]
I. *pron interr*
who

qui vous l'a dit ? who told you?

II. *pron rel*
who

l'homme qui voulait nous avertir est mort the man who wanted to warn us is dead

quitter

quitter
[kite]
I. *v t*
to leave

* *Le professeur a quitté Moulinsart il y a deux semaines...* Professor Calculus left Marlinspike two weeks ago...
Ah bon, il est parti ? He's gone then?... *

Loc
allô, ne quittez pas ! hello, hold the line!/hold on!

II. *v pr*
to part

nous nous sommes quittés devant cette maison et je ne l'ai plus revu we parted in front of this house and I've not seen him since

quotidien

quotidien, enne
[kɔtidjɛ̃, ɛn]
I. *adj*
everyday

la vie quotidienne everyday life

II. *n m*
daily (newspaper)

raccommoder ...raconter

raccommoder
[rakɔmɔde] *vt*
to mend

raconter

raconter
[rakɔ̃te] *vt*
to tell

* *Alors Tintin, racontez-nous ce qui s'est passé...* So, Tintin, tell us what happened...

Alors Tintin, racontez-nous ce qui s'est passé ...
Oui, je vais vous raconter...

Oui, je vais vous raconter... Yes, I'll tell you... *

radio

radio
[radjo] *nf*
radio

oui, capitaine, je l'ai entendu à la radio yes, Captain, I heard it on the radio

raide

Soyez prudent, cette pente est très raide.

...raide

raide
[rɛd] *adj*
1. straight

Tintin a les cheveux raides Tintin has straight hair

2. steep
* *Soyez prudent, cette pente est très raide.* Be careful, this slope is very steep. *

3. stiff
je suis très fatigué, mes jambes sont raides I'm tired, my legs are stiff

raisin

raisin
[rɛzɛ̃] *nm*
grape

une grappe de raisin a bunch of grapes

raison

raison
[rɛzɔ̃] *nf*
1. reason

tonnerre de Brest, il a perdu la raison! thundering typhoons, he's lost his reason!

2. reason
la raison pour laquelle j'ai choisi cette date plutôt qu'une autre the reason (why) I've chosen this date rather than another

3. Loc
oui, professeur, vous avez raison yes, Professor, you're right

ralentir

ralentir
[ralɑ̃tir] *vi*
to slow down

ralentis, Dupond, ralentis! slow down, Thompson, slow down!

ramer

ramer
[rame] *vi*
to row

maintenant, capitaine, c'est à moi de ramer now, Captain, it's my turn to row

ranger

ranger
[rɑ̃ʒe]
I. *vt*
1. to tidy up

...ranger

Maintenant, il va falloir tout ranger !

* *Maintenant, il va falloir tout ranger!* And now I have to tidy everything up! *

2. to put away
je vais ranger ce livre I'll put this book away

II. *v pr*
to line up

rangez-vous par deux devant la porte line up in twos in front of the door

rapide

rapide
[rapid] *adj*
1. quick

pourtant il nous faudra marcher d'un pas rapide and yet we'll have to walk at a quick pace

2. fast
cette voiture est très rapide this car is very fast

► **rapides**
[rapid] *n m pl*
rapids

Il faut franchir ces rapides !...

...rapide

* *Il faut franchir ces rapides !...* We've got to shoot these rapids!... *

► **rapidement**
[rapidmɑ̃] *adv*
quickly

rappeler

rappeler
[raple]
I. *v t*
1. to call back

...rappeler

non, Nestor, ne vous inquiétez pas, je le rappellerai no, Nestor, don't worry, I'll call him back

2. to remind
* *Il me rappelle quelqu'un, mais je ne sais plus qui...* He reminds me of somebody, but I can't remember who... *

II. *v pr*
to remember

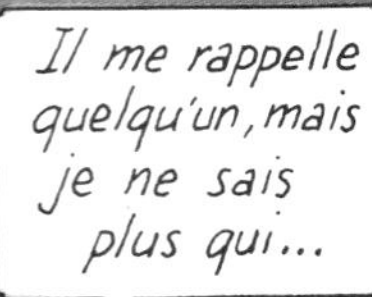
Il me rappelle quelqu'un, mais je ne sais plus qui...

je me rappelle les avoir mis dans le coffre I remember putting them away in the safe

rare

rare
[rar] *adj*
1. unusual

c'est rare de le voir en colère it's most unusual to see him angry

...rare

2. few
les rares personnes présentes l'ont entendu the few people present heard it

► **rarement**
[rarmɑ̃] *adv*
seldom

est-ce qu'ils viennent souvent vous voir ? – rarement do they often visit you? – seldom

se raser

se raser
[səraze] *v pr*
to shave

je me rase tous les matins I shave every morning

► **rasoir**
[razwar] *n m*
razor, shaver

rater

rater
[rate] *v t*
1. to miss

* *Zut ! Je les ai ratés !...* Heck! I missed them!... *

heureusement, le bandit l'a raté, il n'est que blessé fortunately, the gangster missed him, he's only wounded

2. to fail
j'ai raté mon examen I failed my exam

Zut ! Je les ai ratés !...

ravi

ravi, e
[ravi] *adj*
delighted

rayé

rayé, e
[rɛje] *adj*
1. crossed out

plusieurs mots sont rayés several words have been crossed out

2. scratched
l'aile de la voiture est rayée the car wing (*Am:* fender) is scratched

rayon

rayon
[rɛjɔ̃] *n m*
1. ray

* *Un rayon de soleil ?... Mais quelle heure est-il donc ?...* A ray of sunshine?... But what time can it be?... *

2. spoke
les rayons de la roue de mon vélo the spokes of my bicycle wheel

3. department
où est le rayon des jouets dans ce magasin ? where's the toy department in this store?

réaliser

réaliser
[realize] *v t*
1. to carry out

* *Nous avons un plan, maintenant il faut le réaliser !* We've got a plan, now we must carry it out! *

2. to realize
est-ce que vous réalisez que nous sommes leurs prisonniers ? do you realize we're their prisoners?

récent

récent
[resɑ̃, ɑ̃t] *adj*
recent

► **récemment**
[resamɑ̃] *adv*
recently

réception

réception
[resɛpsjɔ̃] *n f*
1. reception

nous donnerons une réception en votre honneur we'll give a reception in your honour

2. reception (desk)
* *Il n'a pas laissé la clé de sa chambre à la réception...* He didn't leave his room key at the reception desk...
Sapristi ! Elle est là ! Great snakes! It's there! *

recevoir

recevoir
[rəsəvwar] *v t*
1. to receive
j'ai reçu sa lettre ce matin I received his letter this morning

2. to entertain
nous recevons quelques amis we're entertaining a few friends

3. Loc
il a reçu un coup de pied/poing he was kicked/punched

réclamation

réclamation
[reklamasjɔ̃] *n f*
complaint

je veux faire une réclamation I want to make a complaint

► **réclamer**
[reklame] *v t*
to ask for

Abdallah réclame son père Abdullah's asking for his father

récolte

récolte
[rekɔlt] *n f*
harvest

la récolte de pommes a été bonne the apple harvest was good

recommander

recommander
[rəkɔmɑ̃de] *v t*
1. to recommend
je vous recommande le docteur X I recommend Doctor X to you

2. to advise
je vous recommande la prudence I advise you to be careful

3. Loc
ce n'est pas recommandé it's not advisable

lettre recommandée registered letter

récompense

récompense
[rekɔ̃pɑ̃s] *n f*
reward

* *Milou, voilà le bonnet de Zorrino. Retrouve sa trace, tu auras une récompense.* Snowy, here is Zorrino's cap. If you find his trail you'll get a reward. *

reconnaître

reconnaître
[rəkɔnɛtr] *v t*
1. to recognize

Tournesol, vous me reconnaissez ? c'est moi, Haddock ! Calculus, don't you recognize me? It's Haddock!

2. to admit
oui, je reconnais que j'ai eu tort yes, I admit I was wrong

récréation

récréation
[rekreasjɔ̃] *n f*
break (*Am:* recess)

c'est l'heure de la récréation it's break time

rectangle

rectangle
[rɛktɑ̃gl] *n m*
rectangle

reculer

reculer
[rəkyle] *v t*
1. to move back

recule un peu pour que je puisse passer move back a bit so that I can pass

2. to reverse
* *Vite, reculez Tintin, nous allons tomber dans le précipice !...* Quick, Tintin, reverse or we'll fall into the chasm!... *

réduction

réduction
[redyksjɔ̃] *n f*
discount

je vous ferai une réduction I'll give you a discount

réduit

réduit
[redɥi, it] *adj*
small-scale

...réduit

* *C'est une reproduction à échelle réduite du bateau de mon ancêtre...* It's a small-scale reproduction of my ancestor's ship... *

réfléchir

réfléchir
[refleʃir]
I. *v i*
to think

Dupont, réfléchis à ce que tu vas dire ! Thomson, think about what you're going to say!

II. *v t*
to reflect

le miroir réfléchit son visage the mirror reflects her face

refroidir

refroidir
[rəfrwadir]
I. *v i*
to cool down

il faut laisser refroidir le moteur ! you must let the engine cool down!

II. *v pr*
to get colder

le temps se refroidit it's getting colder

refuser

refuser
[rəfyze] *v t*
to refuse

allons, capitaine, c'est un cadeau, ne le refusez pas ! come on, Captain, it's a present, don't refuse it!

regarder

regarder
[rəgarde] *v t*
1. to look at

...regarder

il me regarde, mais ne me reconnaît pas he's looking at me but he doesn't recognize me

2. to watch
ils regardent la télévision they're watching television

3. to concern
non, cela ne me regarde pas no, this doesn't concern me

région

région
[reʒjɔ̃] *n f*
area

régler

régler
[regle] *v t*
1. to regulate, to adjust, to put right

ma montre avance, je dois la faire régler my watch is fast, I must put it right

...régler

...régler

2. to pay
il faut régler la facture we must pay the bill

► **règlement**
[rɛgləmɑ̃] *n m*
regulation, rule

* *Ce chien ne peut pas entrer ici, c'est le règlement !* This dog can't come in here, it's the regulation!
Ah, je ne savais pas !... Oh, I didn't know!... *

regretter

regretter
[rəgrɛte] *v t*
1. to regret

Tintin, je t'ai désobéi et je le regrette Tintin, I disobeyed you and I regret it

2. to be sorry
nous regrettons de ne pouvoir venir avec vous we're sorry that we can't come with you

3. to miss
* *Suivez-moi, capitaine !* Follow me, Captain!
Qu'est-ce que je suis venu faire dans cette galère !... Ah, comme je regrette Moulinsart !... What the devil have I come here for? How I miss Marlinspike!... *

rejoindre

rejoindre
[rəʒwɛ̃dr]
I. *v t*
to join

* *Nestor, laissez nos bagages, nous devons rejoindre le professeur en Syldavie.* Nestor, leave our luggage, we have to join Calculus in Syldavia... *

II. *v pr*
to meet

regardez, les deux sentiers se rejoignent look, the two paths meet

se réjouir

se réjouir
[sərеʒwir] *v pr*
to be delighted

nous nous réjouissons de votre succès we're delighted at your success

relations

relations
[relasjɔ̃] *n f pl*
1. relations

les relations diplomatiques sont rompues diplomatic relations have been broken

2. Loc
il n'a pas de bonnes relations avec ses voisins he isn't on friendly terms with his neighbours

relever

relever
[rələve]
I. *v t*
to raise

relève la tête raise your head

II. *v pr*
to get back on one's feet, to get up

* *Eh bien, professeur, que vous arrive-t-il ?* Well, Professor, what's the matter?

J'ai du mal à me relever... Aidez-moi et je vous expliquerai. I can't get back on my feet... Help me and I'll explain to you. *

relier

relier
[rəlje] *v t*
to link

...relier

un pont relie la rive droite à la rive gauche a bridge links the right bank to the left bank

religion

religion
[rəliʒjɔ̃] *n f*
religion

remarquer

remarquer
[rəmarke] *v t*
to notice

* *Habillés comme ça, personne ne nous remarquera !...* Nobody will notice us, dressed like this!... *

Habillés comme ça, personne ne nous remarquera !...
!

rembourser

rembourser
[rãburse] *v t*
to pay back

remède

remède
[rəmɛd] *n m*
1. medicine

n'oublie pas de prendre ton remède don't forget to take your medicine

2. remedy, cure
il n'y a pas de remède there's no remedy

remercier

C'est le capitaine qu'il faut remercier, c'est lui qui vous a guéri...
Merci, mon ami, merci...

...remercier

remercier
[rəmɛrsje] *v t*
to thank

* *C'est le capitaine qu'il faut remercier, c'est lui qui vous a guéri...* It's the Captain you must thank. It was he that cured you...
Merci, mon ami, merci... Thank you, my friend, thank you... *

remplacer

Il faudra remplacer ce miroir cassé.
Oui... Je le ferai moi-même...

remplacer
[rãplase] *v t*
to replace

* *Il faudra remplacer ce miroir cassé.* We'll have to replace this broken mirror.
Oui... Je le ferai moi-même... Yes... I'll do it myself... *

personne ne peut le remplacer nobody can replace him

remplir

remplir
[rãplir] *v t*
to fill up

Nestor, la bouteille est vide, allez la remplir Nestor, the bottle's empty, go and fill it up

renard

renard
[rənar] *n m*
fox

rencontrer

Ah, cher capitaine Karbock, je n'oublierai jamais notre première rencontre !
Haddock, madame, capitaine Haddock.

rencontrer
[rãkɔ̃tre] *v t*
to meet

quelle chance de vous rencontrer, j'allais chez vous how lucky that I met you : I was going to your place

► **rencontre**
[rãkɔ̃tr] *n f*
meeting

* *Ah, cher capitaine Karbock, je n'oublierai jamais notre première rencontre !* Ah, my dear Captain Padlock, I'll never forget our first meeting!
Haddock, madame, capitaine Haddock. Haddock, Madam, Captain Haddock. *

rendez-vous

rendez-vous
[rãdevu] *n m inv*
appointment

* *A quelle heure est votre rendez-vous avec le chef de la police ?* What time is your appointment with the chief of the police?
Dix heures. At ten o'clock. *

A quelle heure est votre rendez-vous avec le chef de la police ?
Dix heures.

rendre

rendre
[rɑ̃dr]
I. *v t*
1. to give back

rendez-moi ma pipe give me my pipe back

2. to feel sick, to vomit
oh, ces vagues ! j'ai envie de rendre oh, those waves! I feel like vomiting

3. Loc
rendre service à quelqu'un to help somebody

II. *v pr*
1. to go

nous devons nous rendre à Genève we have to go to Geneva

2. to surrender
les bandits se sont rendus the gangsters have surrendered

3. Loc
te rends-tu compte que je suis en retard ? do you realize that I'm late?

renseigner

renseigner
[rɑ̃seɲe]
I. *v t*
1. to give some information

* *Ce jeune garçon pourra nous renseigner...* This young boy

...renseigner

will be able to give us some information...
Oui, essayons... Yes, let's try... *

2. Loc
je suis bien renseigné sur vous I know a lot about you

II. *v pr*
to inquire

allô, je voudrais me renseigner sur les vols pour Klow hello, I'd like to inquire about flights to Klow

...renseigner

► **renseignement**
[rɑ̃sɛɲmɑ̃] *n m*
1. piece of information

bravo, Tchang, voilà un renseignement utile well done, Chang, that's a useful piece of information

2. Loc
avez-vous des renseignements sur cet incident ? do you have any information on this incident?

rentrer

rentrer
[rɑ̃tre]
I. *v i*
1. to go back, to return

* *Venez, rentrons vite à la maison...* Come on, let's go back home quickly... *

2. to be back
allô, Nestor, nous rentrerons la semaine prochaine hello, Nestor, we'll be back next week

3. to go in
flûte, la clé ne rentre pas dans la serrure too bad, the key won't go in the lock

II. *v t*
to put away

Il pleut, vite, capitaine, rentrons la voiture au garage it's raining, quick, Captain, let's put the car away in the garage

renverser

renverser
[rɑ̃vɛrse]
I. *v t*
to knock over

vous allez renverser ce piéton ! you're going to knock this pedestrian over!

II. *v pr*
to overturn

* *La fusée va se renverser !* The rocket is going to overturn! *

renvoyer

renvoyer
[rɑ̃vwaje] *v t*
to send away

ah non, je ne veux pas qu'ils restent, renvoyez-les ! no, no, I don't want them to stay, send them away!

réparer

réparer
[repare] *v t*
to repair, to mend

...réparer

* *Il va falloir réparer la radio...* We'll have to repair the radio... *

► **réparateur**
[reparatœr] *n m*
repairman

► **réparation**
[reparasjɔ̃] *n f*
repair

il y a beaucoup de réparations à faire there are many repairs to be done

repas

repas
[rəpa] *n m*
meal

voulez-vous un repas froid ? do you want a cold meal?

repasser

repasser
[rəpase]
I. *v i*
to call again

...repasser

Pas de réponse ?...

Pas de réponse . Le capitaine n'est pas là, nous repasserons...

* *Pas de réponse ?...* No answer?...
Pas de réponse. Le capitaine n'est pas là, nous repasserons... No answer. The Captain isn't in, we'll call again... *

II. *v t*
to iron

non, ce n'est pas la peine de repasser ma chemise ! no, don't bother to iron my shirt!

répéter

répéter
[repete] *v t*
1. to say again

je n'ai pas entendu, pouvez-vous répéter ? I didn't hear you, could you say it again?

2. to repeat
* *Attention, c'est un secret, ne le répétez à personne...* Careful, it's a secret, don't repeat it to anyone...
Ah ?... Really?...

...répéter

Attention, c'est un secret, ne le répétez à personne...
Ah?...

Je dirais même plus, c'est un secret... ne le répétez à personne...
Ah?...

Je dirais même plus, c'est un secret... ne le répétez à personne... To be precise, it's a secret... Don't repeat it to anyone...
Ah ?... Really?... *

répondre

répondre
[repɔ̃dr] *v t*
1. to answer
Allons, répondez ! Come on, answer!

...répondre

2. to reply
avez-vous répondu à sa lettre ? did you reply to his letter?

se reposer

se reposer
[sərəpoze] *v pr*
to rest

reposons-nous ici un instant let's rest here for a moment

...se reposer

► **repos**
[rəpo] *n m*
rest

reprendre

reprendre
[rəprɑ̃dr] *v t*
1. to take some more

il a repris de la soupe he took some more soup

...reprendre

Allons, Tintin, reprenez votre récit, comment êtes-vous ici ?
Eh bien ...

2. to resume
* *Allons, Tintin, reprenez votre récit, comment êtes-vous ici ?* Well, Tintin, resume your story. How do you come to be here?
Eh bien... Well... *

requin

requin
[rəkɛ̃] *n m*
shark

réserver

réserver
[rezɛrve] *v t*
1. to book

* *... Voilà, vos places sont réservées... Vous devez être à l'aéroport à huit heures...* Right, your seats are booked... You must be at the airport at 8 o'clock... *

2. to reserve
le parking est réservé aux clients the car park (*Am:* parking lot) is reserved for customers

... Voilà, vos places sont réservées ... Vous devez être à l'aéroport à huit heures...

► **réservation**
[rezɛrvasjɔ̃] *n f*
booking

respecter

respecter
[rɛspɛkte] *v t*
to respect

...respecter

je respecte votre opinion I respect your opinion

responsable

responsable
[rɛspɔ̃sabl]
I. *adj*
responsible

* *Alors, j'attends vos explications. Qu'avez-vous à dire ?* Well... I'm waiting for an explanation. What do you have to say?
Oui, je suis responsable de ce qui est arrivé. Yes, I'm responsible for what happened. *

...responsable

II. *n*
person in charge

c'est M. Baxter le responsable du centre de recherches Mr Baxter is the person in charge of the research centre (*Am:* center)

ressembler

ressembler
[rəsɑ̃ble]
I. *v t ind*
to look like

est-ce qu'il ressemble à son père ? does he look like his father?

II. *v pr*
to look alike

Dupont et Dupond se ressemblent Thomson and Thompson look alike

restaurant

restaurant
[rɛstɔrɑ̃] *n m*
restaurant

rester

rester
[rɛste] *v i*
1. to stay

Milou, reste ici, je reviens tout de suite Snowy, stay here, I'll be right back

...rester

2. to remain
* *Alors professeur, rien ne reste de cette civilisation ?...* So, Professor, nothing remains of this civilization?...
Non... Mais lisez la suite... No... But read on... *

3. to be left
reste-t-il du gâteau ? is there any cake left?

résultat

résultat
[rezylta] *n m*
result

et voilà le résultat de votre étourderie and here's the result of your absent-mindedness

retard

...retard

retard
[rətar] *n m*
1. delay

léger retard pour le train de Jauga slight delay for the train from Jauga

2. Loc
* *Dépêchez-vous, nous allons être en retard !* Hurry up or we'll be late! *

retour

retour
[rətur] *n m*
1. return

nous le verrons à notre retour we'll see him on our return

2. Loc
est-il de retour ? is he back?

allons-y, nous serons de retour demain ! let's go, we'll be back tomorrow!

retourner

retourner
[rəturne]
I. *v t*
to turn over

allez-y, retournez cette carte come on, turn this card over

II. *v i*
to go back

* *Je veux retourner à Moulinsart... Laisse-moi !...* I want to go back to Marlinspike... Leave me alone!... *

retraite

retraite
[rətrɛt] *n f*

est-ce que les Dupondt sont à la retraite ? have the Thompsons retired?

retrouver

retrouver
[rətruve]
I. *v t*
1. to find

...retrouver

Ça y est, j'ai retrouvé ma pipe !... Je me demande qui l'a mise ici ...

* *Ça y est, j'ai retrouvé ma pipe !... Je me demande qui l'a mise ici...* Here it is, I've found my pipe!... I wonder who put it here... *

2. to recover
la police a retrouvé la statuette volée the police recovered the stolen statue

II. *v pr*
1. to meet again

nous nous sommes retrouvés à Hou Kou we met again in Hukow

2. Loc
je ne m'y retrouve plus, ces papiers sont tout mélangés I'm completely at sea, these papers are all mixed up

rétroviseur

rétroviseur
[retrɔvizœr] *n m*
rearview mirror

réunion

réunion
[reynjɔ̃] *n f*
meeting

réussir

réussir
[reysir]
I. *v i*
to succeed

tu ne réussiras pas si tu ne fais pas d'effort you won't succeed if you don't make an effort

...réussir

II. *v t*
to manage

ils ont réussi à voir le yéti they managed to see the yeti

réveiller

réveiller
[revɛje]
I. *v t*
to wake up

...réveiller

n'oubliez pas de me réveiller don't forget to wake me up

II. *v pr*
to wake up

* *Drrrrrrring ! Professeur ! Professeur ! Réveillez-vous !... C'est l'heure !...* Rrrrrrrring! Professor... Wake up, Professor!... It's time...
Déjà !... Il est déjà l'heure ?... Already! Is it already time?... *

► **réveil**
[revɛj] *n m*
1. alarm clock

le réveil n'a pas sonné the alarm clock didn't go off

2. Loc
au réveil, il fait un peu de gymnastique when he gets up, he does some physical exercises

revenir

revenir
[rəvnir] *v i*
to come back

* *Non, monsieur, le capitaine n'est pas revenu de voyage !* No, Sir, the Captain hasn't come back from his trip! *Je vous dis qu'il n'y a personne. Le capitaine n'est pas revenu de voyage !* I'm telling you that nobody's in. The Captain hasn't come back from his trip! *

Non, monsieur, le capitaine n'est pas revenu de voyage !

Je vous dis qu'il n'y a personne. Le capitaine n'est pas revenu de voyage !

rêver

rêver
[rɛve] *v i*
1. to dream

* *Vous voyez ?... Personne !... Il a rêvé comme nous.* You see?... No one!... He was only dreaming like us. *

j'ai toujours rêvé de faire un grand voyage I've always dreamt of taking a long journey

Vous voyez ?... Personne !... il a rêvé comme nous.

2. to daydream
vous ne m'écoutez pas, vous rêvez ! you're not listening to me, you're daydreaming!

► **rêve**
[rɛv] *n m*
dream

réviser

réviser
[revize] *vt*
to revise

revoir

revoir
[rəvwar] *v t*
to see again

non, je ne l'ai pas revu no, I haven't seen him again

...revoir

► **au revoir**
[ɔrvwar] *interj*
goodbye

au revoir, à bientôt ! goodbye, see you soon!

rhume

rhume
[rym] *n m*
cold

riche

riche
[riʃ] *adj*
rich

rideau

rideau
[rido] *n m*
pl rideaux
curtain

ouvre/ferme les rideaux open/draw the curtains

ridicule

ridicule
[ridikyl] *adj*
ridiculous

rien

rien
[rjɛ̃] *pron*
1. nothing

* ***Voyez-vous quelque chose ?*** Can you see anything?
Non, rien... No, nothing... *

...rien

...rien

il ne reste rien there's nothing left

2. not... anything
avez-vous dit quelque chose ? – non, je n'ai rien dit did you say something? – no, I didn't say anything

3. Loc
merci beaucoup – de rien thank you very much – you're welcome

* ***Cela ne sert à rien de se mettre en colère.*** It's no use getting angry. *

rire

rire
[rir]
I. *v i*
1. to laugh

* ***Ha ! ha ! ha ! laissez-moi rire !...*** Ha! ha! ha!... You make me laugh!...
Je dirais même plus : Ha ! ha ! ha !... To be precise : Ha! ha! ha!... *

2. Loc
j'ai dit ça pour rire I was only joking when I said that

II. *n m*
laughter

risquer

risquer
[riske] *v t*
to risk

► **risque**
[risk] *n m*
risk

prendre des risques to take risks

rivière

rivière
[rivjɛr] *n f* river

riz

riz
[ri] *n m* rice

robe

robe
[rɔb] *n f* dress

robinet

robinet
[rɔbinɛ] *n m*
tap (*Am:* faucet)

tu as laissé le robinet ouvert, ferme-le you've left the tap running, turn it off

robuste

robuste
[rɔbyst] *adj*
robust

rond

rond, e
[rɔ̃, rɔ̃d] *adj*
1. round

* ***Regardez comme la terre est ronde ! C'est magnifique !*** Look how round the Earth is! It's wonderful! *

2. plump
la Castafiore est une femme un peu ronde Signora Castafiore is a rather plump woman

► **rond**
[rɔ̃] *n m*
circle

il a dessiné un rond he drew a circle

► **ronde**
[rɔ̃d] *n f*
1. rounds

les gardiens font leur ronde the watchmen are doing their rounds

2. Loc
faire la ronde to dance in a circle

rose

rose
[roz]
I. *n f*
rose

les roses sont fleuries the roses are in bloom

II. *adj*
pink

c'est ma robe rose qui me va le mieux my pink dress suits me best

rôti

rôti
[roti] *n m*
joint (*Am:* roast)

roue

roue
[ru] *n f*
wheel

* *Voilà !... Où est-il votre Tournesol ? Dans la roue de secours, peut-être ?*

...roue

Voilà !... Où est-il votre Tournesol ? Dans la roue de secours, peut-être ?

There you are! Where's Calculus? In the spare wheel...? *

rouge

rouge
[ruʒ]
I. *adj*
red

* *Il est rouge de colère !* He's red with anger! *

...rouge

Il est rouge de colère.

attention, le feu est rouge careful, the light is red

II. *n m*
1. red

il l'a écrit en rouge he wrote it in red

2. Loc
rouge à lèvre lipstick

rouler

rouler
[rule]
I. *v i*
1. to go

nous roulons trop vite, nous allons déraper we're going too fast, we're going to skid

2. to roll
le ballon a roulé jusqu'en bas de la pente the ball rolled down to the bottom of the hill

II. *v t*
to roll up

aidez-moi à rouler les plans help me to roll up the plans

III. *v pr*
to roll about

Milou, cesse de te rouler dans la neige ! Snowy, stop rolling about in the snow!

route

route
[rut] *n f*
road

route nationale main road

roux

roux, rousse
[ru, rus] *adj*
ginger, red

rue

rue
[ry] *n f*
street

* *Quel embouteillage !* What a traffic jam! *Mais comment allons-nous traverser cette rue ?...* But how are we going to cross this street?... *

Quel embouteillage !
Mais comment allons-nous traverser cette rue ?...

russe

russe
[rys] *adj*
Russian

► **Russe**
[rys] *n*
Russian

les Russes Russians

► **russe**
[rys] *n m*
Russian

apprendre le russe to learn Russian

► **Russie**
[rysi] *n f*
Russia

sac

sac
[sak] *n m*
bag

sage

sage
[saʒ] *adj*
good

* *Sois sage, Milou!* Be good, Snowy! *Wouah! Wouah!* Woof! Woof! *

...sage

saigner

saigner
[seɲe] *v i*
to bleed

regardez, il est blessé, il saigne look, he's wounded, he's bleeding

▸ **saignant, e**
[seɲɑ̃, ɑ̃t] *adj*
rare

un steak saignant a rare steak

saisir

saisir
[sezir] *v t*
1. to seize

il m'a saisi par le bras he seized my arm

2. to catch
* *Allô?... Comment?... Je n'ai pas saisi votre nom...* Hello? What?... I didn't catch your name... *

saison

saison
[sɛzɔ̃] *n f*
season

salade

salade
[salad] *n f*
salad

une salade de tomates a tomato salad

salaire

salaire
[salɛr] *n m*
wage(s), salary

sale

sale
[sal] *adj*
dirty

* *Vraiment Milou, non seulement tu as trop bu, mais en plus tu es*

...sale

sale!... Honestly, Snowy, not only have you drunk too much, but you're also dirty!... *Sale... Tu penses... hic... que... hic... je suis sale... hic...* Dirty... You think... hic... that... hic... I'm dirty... *

▸ **salir**
[salir] *v t*
to dirty

n'entrez pas, vous allez salir le plancher don't go in, you'll dirty the floor

salé

salé → SEL

salle

salle
[sal] *n f*
room

salle de classe/d'attente classroom, waiting-room

salon

salon
[salɔ̃] *n m*
1. lounge, living room

faites-les entrer dans le salon show them into the lounge

2. Loc
salon de coiffure hairdressing salon

saluer

saluer
[salɥe] *v t*
1. to greet

* *Je suis très content que tu viennes saluer ce très grand roi...* I'm very glad that you've come to greet this great king...
Salut, noble roi... Hail to you, noble king... *

2. to bow
les acteurs ont salué le public the actors bowed to the audience

...saluer

▸ **salut**
[saly]
I. *n m*
greeting

vous ne répondez pas à son salut ? don't you answer his greeting?

II. *interj*
1. hi

salut tout le monde, comment ça va ? hi everybody, how are you?

2. (good)bye
salut, je m'en vais ! bye, I'm off!

▸ **salutation**
[salytasjɔ̃] *n f*
greeting

samedi

samedi
[samdi] *n m*
Saturday

...samedi

viens me voir samedi come and see me on Saturday

ils ne travaillent pas le samedi they don't work on Saturdays

sandwich

sandwich
[sɑ̃dwitʃ] *n m*
pl sandwich(e)s
sandwich

sang

...sang

sang
[sɑ̃] *n m*
blood

* *Il y a une trace de sang sur l'arbre...* There's a blood mark on the tree... *

prise de sang blood test

sans

sans
[sɑ̃] *prép*
1. without

* *Attendez, je ne peux pas partir sans Milou...* Wait, I can't leave without Snowy...
Trop tard !... Too late!... *

2. Loc
un ciel sans nuages a cloudless sky

santé

...santé

santé
[sɑ̃te] *n f*
health

* *La santé de Milou m'inquiète, docteur... Qu'en pensez-vous ?* Snowy's health worries me, Doctor... What do you think?...
Oui, en effet... Je vais voir... Yes, indeed... I'll have a look... *

sapin

sapin
[sapɛ̃] *n m*
1. fir tree

2. Loc
sapin de Noël Christmas tree

sardine

sardine
[sardin] *n f*
sardine

satellite

satellite
[satɛlit] *n m*
satellite

satisfait

satisfait, e
[satisfɛ, ɛt] *adj*
satisfied

je suis loin d'être satisfait de toi I am far from satisfied with you

saucisson

saucisson
[sosisɔ̃] *n m*
sausage, salami

sauf

sauf
[sof] *prép*
1. except

tout le monde est prêt, sauf Tournesol everybody's ready, except Calculus

...sauf

...sauf

2. unless
* *Nous y arriverons sauf si la corde casse !* We'll do it unless the rope breaks! *

sauvage

sauvage
[sovaʒ] *adj*
1. savage
* *Vous voyez, c'était des étrangers... comme vous !...* See, they were foreigners... like you!...
C'est bien ce que je pensais, cette tribu sauvage est une tribu de coupeurs de têtes... That's what I thought, this savage tribe is a tribe of head-hunters... *

2. wild
ici on trouve des animaux/plantes sauvages here you'll see wild animals/plants

...sauvage

sauver

sauver
[sove]
I. *v t*
to save

* *Tintin, vous m'avez sauvé la vie, comment vous remercier ?* Tintin, you saved my life, how can I thank you?
Mon général, dites plutôt que j'ai sauvé nos deux vies... Or rather, Sir, I saved both our lives... *

...sauver

II. *v pr*
to run away

vite, sauvons-nous ! quick, let's run away!

savoir

savoir
[savwar] *v t*
1. to know

* *Savez-vous où est Milou ? Il vient de me voler un poulet !* Do you know where Snowy is? He's just stolen a chicken from me!
Non... No...
Milou ?... Snowy?... *

2. can, to be able to
au secours, je ne sais pas nager ! help, I can't swim!

3. Loc
je l'ai su par Nestor I heard it from Nestor

...savoir

savon ...science se

savon

savon
[savɔ̃] *n m*
soap

▶ **savonner**
[savɔne] *v t*
to soap

science

science
[sjɑ̃s] *n f*
1. science

2. Loc
sciences naturelles biology

▶ **science-fiction**
[sjɑ̃sfiksjɔ̃] *n f*
science fiction

▶ **scientifique**
[sjɑ̃tifik]
I. *adj*
scientific

II. *n*
scientist

* *Je prends l'avion pour Genève où je dois assister à un congrès de scientifiques.* I'm taking a plane to Geneva where I have to attend a congress of scientists.
Mais... mais, vous ne m'avez pas prévenu. But... You didn't tell me about it. *

se

se
[sə] *pron pers*
oneself

se couper to cut oneself

* *Oh là là, le professeur a dû se faire mal !* My goodness! the Professor must have hurt himself! *

la Castafiore se donne à son métier Signora Castafiore devotes herself to her art

...se

séance

séance
[seɑ̃s] *n f*
performance, show

dépêchez-vous, la dernière séance est à 8 heures hurry up, the last performance is at 8 o'clock

sécher

sécher
[seʃe]

...sécher

I. *v t*
to dry

* *Comment sécher nos vêtements ?* How can we dry our clothes? *

II. *v i*
to dry

le linge a séché vite the washing has dried quickly

▶ **sec, sèche**
[sɛk, sɛʃ] *adj*
dry

second

second
[səgɔ̃, ɔ̃d]
I. *adj*
second

la seconde victime de la momie the mummy's second victim

II. *n*
second

vous serez le second à marcher sur la Lune you'll be the second (person) to walk on the Moon

seconde

seconde
[səgɔ̃d] *n f*
second

le train part dans 30 secondes the train is leaving in 30 seconds

secours

secours
[səkur] *n m*
1. help

...secours

* *Vite, il faut demander du secours...* Quick, we must ask for help... *

2. rescue
ils viennent à notre secours they're coming to our rescue

3. Loc
au secours ! help!

secret

secret
[səkrɛ] *n m*
secret

sécurité

sécurité
[sekyrite] *n f*
1. safety

...sécurité

vos gardes veilleront à votre sécurité your guards will see to your safety

2. security
Sécurité sociale Social Security

3. Loc
tu es en sécurité ici, Milou you're safe here, Snowy

ceinture de sécurité safety belt

séjour

séjour
[seʒur] *n m*
stay

sel

sel
[sɛl] *n m*
salt

pouvez-vous me passer le sel, s'il vous plaît ? could you pass me the salt, please?

...sel

► **salé, e**
[sale] *adj*
1. salty

goûte, ça a un goût salé try it, it tastes salty

2. Loc
eau salée salt water

semaine

semaine
[səmɛn] *n f*
week

semblable

semblable
[sɑ̃blabl] *adj*
similar

* ***Je me suis trompé. J'ai pris ton chapeau, il est semblable au mien.*** I made a mistake.

...semblable

Je me suis trompé. J'ai pris ton chapeau, il est semblable au mien.
Je dirais même plus, mon chapeau est semblable au tien.

I took your hat, it is similar to mine.
Je dirais même plus, mon chapeau est semblable au tien. To be precise, my hat is similar to yours. *

sens

sens
[sɑ̃s] *n m*
1. sense

...sens

Milou a un sens de l'odorat très développé !

* ***Milou a un sens de l'odorat très développé !*** Snowy has a very keen sense of smell! *

2. meaning
cherche le sens de ce mot dans ton dictionnaire look up the meaning of this word in your dictionary

3. direction
dans quel sens sont-ils partis ? (in) which direction did they go?

sensible

sensible
[sɑ̃sibl] *adj*
1. sensitive

elle s'est évanouie, elle est si sensible ! she fainted, she's so sensitive!

2. perceptible, appreciable
un progrès sensible a appreciable progress

sentiment

J'ai le sentiment que quelqu'un nous regarde...

...sentiment

sentiment
[sɑ̃timɑ̃] *n m*
feeling

* ***J'ai le sentiment que quelqu'un nous regarde...*** I have a feeling somebody's watching us... *

sentir

sentir
[sɑ̃tir]

...sentir

I. *vt*
1. to smell

sentez ces fleurs smell these flowers

2. to feel
* ***J'ai senti une douleur dans le bras. J'espère que ce n'est pas grave...*** I felt a pain in my arm... I hope it's not serious...
Montre-moi, Tintin, ne bouge pas... Let me see, Tintin, don't move... *

J'ai senti une douleur dans le bras. J'espère que ce n'est pas grave...
Montre-moi, Tintin, ne bouge pas...

II. *vi*
to smell

ces fleurs ne sentent rien these flowers don't smell of anything

il sent des pieds his feet smell

III. *v pr*
to feel

* ***Elle ne se sent pas très bien...*** She doesn't feel very well... *

!

Elle ne se sent pas très bien...

séparé

séparé, e
[separe] *adj*
separate

deux chambres séparées two separate bedrooms

septembre

septembre
[sɛptɑ̃br] *n m*
September

le premier/deux septembre the first/second of September (*Am:* September first/second)

venez le 6 septembre come on the 6th of September (*Am:* on September 6)

sérieux

sérieux, euse
[serjø, øz]
I. *adj*
1. serious

Tournesol est très sérieux, il ne rit pas souvent Calculus is very serious: he doesn't often laugh

2. hard-working
c'est une élève sérieuse she's a hard-working pupil

II. *n m*
garder son sérieux to keep a straight face

serpent

serpent
[sɛrpɑ̃] *n m*
snake

* *Un serpent !...* A snake!... *

Un serpent!...

serrer

serrer
[sere] *v t*
1. to clasp

venez, que je vous serre dans mes bras ! let me clasp you in my arms!

2. Loc
* *Venez donc serrer la main de mon jeune ami Tintin...* Come and shake hands with my young friend Tintin... *Enchanté.* How do you do? *Quelle poignée de main !...* What a handshake!... *

Venez donc serrer la main de mon jeune ami Tintin ...
Quelle poignée de main !
Enchanté.

► **serré, e**
[sere] *adj*
tight

aïe, ces chaussures sont trop serrées ouch, these shoes are too tight

serrure

serrure
[seryr] *n f*
lock

serveur

Voilà, monsieur.

Le serveur apporte les boissons.

serveur, serveuse
[sɛrvœr, øz] *n*
waiter, waitress

* *Voilà, monsieur.* Here you are, Sir. *Le serveur apporte les boissons...* The waiter is bringing the drinks... *

service

service
[sɛrvis] *n m*
1. service

j'aimerais entrer à votre service comme majordome I'd like to enter your service as a butler

2. favour (*Am:* favor)

veux-tu me rendre un service ? will you do me a favour?

serviette

serviette
[sɛrvjɛt] *n f*
1. napkin

il n'y a pas de serviettes sur la table there are no napkins on the table

2. towel
où est ma serviette de bain ? where is my bath towel?

3. briefcase
* *J'ai votre contrat d'assurance dans ma serviette...* I've got your insurance policy in my briefcase... *

J'ai votre contrat d'assurance dans ma serviette ...
!

servir

servir
[sɛrvir]
I. *vt*
1. to serve

quel est le garçon qui vous a servi ? which was the waiter who served you?

2. Loc
cela ne te servira à rien de mentir lying won't do you any good

II. *vi*
1. to be useful

non, ne le jetez pas, il pourra encore servir no, don't throw it away, it might still be useful

2. Loc
* *Encore dix secondes... Neuf... Huit... Sept...* Ten more seconds... Nine... Eight... Seven...
A quoi sert ce levier ? What's this lever for?

Il commande le décollage... It controls the takeoff... *

III. *v pr*
1. to help oneself

je vous en prie, servez-vous de gâteau please, help yourself to some cake

2. to use
je ne me servirai pas de la voiture aujourd'hui I won't use the car today

seul

seul, e
[sœl]
I. *adj*
1. alone

ne me laisse pas seul don't leave me alone

2. by oneself
je n'arriverai pas à le faire tout seul I won't manage to do it by myself

...seul

II. *pron*
only one

hélas, Tournesol est le seul qui puisse le faire alas, Calculus is the only one who can do it

► **seulement**
[sœlmɑ̃] *adv*
1. only

* *Quinze jours après...* Two weeks later...

Si seulement on pouvait arrêter... If only we could stop...
... de pomper... ... pumping... *

2. only, but
vous pouvez leur parler, seulement pas trop longtemps you can speak to them, only not for too long

sévère

sévère
[sevɛr] *adj*
strict

short

short
[ʃɔrt] *n m*
(pair of) shorts

si

si
[si]
I. *conj*
1. if

s'il pleut, ne sortons pas if it rains, let's not go out

2. whether
je ne sais pas si c'est possible I don't know whether it is possible

II. *adv*
1. so

* *Ah, je fais le zouave ? Je suis si*

...si

fâché que je pourrais vous frapper ! I'm playing the fool, am I? I'm so angry I could hit you! *

2. yes
ne l'avez-vous pas prévenu ? – si didn't you tell him – yes (I did)

3. Loc
* *Je n'ai pas peur de toi, yéti, si grand que tu sois !...* I'm not afraid of you, Yeti, however big you are!... *

siècle

siècle
[sjɛkl] *n m*
century

ce tableau a été peint il y a des siècles this picture was painted centuries ago

siège

siège
[sjɛʒ] *n m*
seat

signer

signer
[siɲe] *v t*
to sign

► **signature**
[siɲatyr] *n f*
signature

silence

silence
[silɑ̃s] *n m*
1. silence

* *Quel étrange endroit... Pas d'arbre, pas de vie... Rien ne trouble le silence...* What a strange place... No trees, no sign of life... Nothing disturbs the silence... *

2. Loc
garder le silence to keep silent

s'il te plaît

s'il te plaît, s'il vous plaît
→ PLAIRE

simple

simple
[sɛ̃pl] *adj*
1. simple

allons, c'est très simple come on, it's quite simple

2. plain
je n'aime pas les robes simples I don't like plain dresses

► **simplement**
[sɛ̃pləmɑ̃] *adv*
1. simply

expliquez-le lui simplement explain it simply to him

2. plainly
il est toujours vêtu simplement he's always plainly dressed

singe

singe
[sɛ̃ʒ] *n m*
monkey

* *Les singes ont pris le fusil du capitaine.* The monkeys have taken the Captain's gun. *

Les singes ont pris le fusil du capitaine.

se situer

se situer
[səsitɥe] *v pr*
to be (situated)

où se situe Klow? where is Klow?

ski

ski
[ski] *n m*
1. ski

avec des skis, ce serait plus facile it would be easier with skis

2. skiing
faire du ski to go skiing

slip

slip
[slip] *n m*
(under)pants, briefs

société

société
[sɔsjete] *n f*
1. society

* *C'est une société primitive, je pense qu'ils vont nous couper la tête...* It's a primitive society. I think they're going to cut off our heads... *

2. company
une société d'assurance an insurance company

soeur

sœur
[sœr] *n f*
sister

soif

soif
[swaf] *n f*
1. thirst

2. Loc
* *Courage, capitaine, il faut continuer...* Be brave, Captain, we must carry on...
J'ai tellement soif!... I'm so thirsty!... *

soigner

soigner
[swaɲe]
I. *vt*
to treat

* *Ne vous inquiétez pas, on soigne votre collègue.* Don't worry, your colleague is being treated. *

II. *v pr*
to take care of
soignez-vous bien ! take good care of yourself!

soir

soir
[swar] *n m*
evening

nous l'avons rencontré hier soir we met him yesterday evening

▸ **soirée**
[sware] *n f*
evening

j'ai passé ma soirée à lire I spent my evening reading

sol

sol
[sɔl] *n m*
ground

soleil

soleil
[sɔlɛj] *nm*
1. sun

2. Loc
au coucher/lever du soleil at sunset/sunrise

solide

solide
[sɔlid] *adj*
1. strong

* *Ne vous inquiétez pas, cette passerelle est assez solide...* Don't worry, this footbridge is strong enough... *

2. solid
le fer et le bois sont des matériaux solides iron and wood are solid materials

...solide

sommeil

sommeil
[sɔmɛj] *n m*
1. sleep

je dormais d'un sommeil de plomb I was in a very deep sleep

2. Loc
nous avons sommeil we feel sleepy

sommet

sommet
[sɔmɛ] *n m*
1. summit

* *Nous avons presque atteint le sommet de la montagne !* We've almost reached the summit of the mountain! *

2. top
la pie s'est perchée au sommet de l'arbre the magpie perched on the top of the tree

son

son
[sɔ̃] *n m*
sound

* *Vous entendez, Tintin ?* Do you hear that, Tintin?
Oui, c'est un son étrange... C'est une pompe, non ?... Yes, it's a strange sound... It's a pump, isn't it? *

sonner

sonner
[sɔne] *v i*
to ring

quelqu'un a sonné à la porte somebody rang the door-bell

* *Eh bien, il était temps que nous rentrions...* Well, it was time we got back...
Le téléphone sonne, Nestor. The telephone's ringing, Nestor. *

...sonner

► **sonnerie**
[sɔnri] *n f*
ringing

Loc
pourvu qu'il entende la sonnerie du téléphone let's hope he'll hear the phone ringing

sorte

sorte
[sɔrt] *n f*
1. kind, sort

...sorte

nous avons plusieurs sortes de fruits we have several kinds of fruit

2. Loc
de sorte que so that

sortir

sortir
[sɔrtir]
I. *v i*
1. to go out

...sortir

il vient juste de sortir he's just gone out

2. to get out
* *Sortez d'ici tout de suite !* Get out of here at once! *

3. to come out
c'est la fumée qui sort de la cheminée du « Peary » it's the smoke coming out of the "Peary's" chimney

4. to leave
puis-je sortir de table ? may I leave the table?

II. Loc
ne vous inquiétez pas, ils s'en sortiront don't worry, they'll pull through

► **sortie**
[sɔrti] *n f*
1. exit

la sortie est là the exit is here

...sortir

2. Loc
je t'attendrai à la sortie de l'école I'll wait for you after school

souci

souci
[susi] *n m*
1. worry

trouver un hôtel, c'est le dernier de mes soucis finding a hotel is the least of my worries

...souci

2. Loc
je me fais beaucoup de souci pour lui I'm very worried about him

soucoupe

soucoupe
[sukup] *n f*
saucer

soucoupe volante flying saucer

soudain

soudain
[sudɛ̃] *adv*
suddenly

et soudain, la pluie s'est mise à tomber and suddenly, it began to rain

souffler

souffler
[sufle]
I. *v t*
to blow out

...souffler

...souffler

* *Ah... Enfin !...* Ah!... At last!...
On ne voit rien, le vent a soufflé la bougie... We can't see a thing, the wind has blown out the candle... *

II. *v i*
to blow

le vent souffle de l'est the wind is blowing from the east

souffrir

souffrir
[sufrir] *v i*
1. to suffer

de quoi souffrent-ils ? what are they suffering from?

2. Loc
* *Mon pauvre Milou, cette épine a dû te faire souffrir...* Poor Snowy, this thorn must have hurt you... *

souhaiter

souhaiter
[swɛte] *v t*
to wish

je vous souhaite une bonne année ! I wish you a happy New Year!

soulager

soulager
[sulaʒe] *v t*
to relieve

...soulager

je suis soulagé que vous soyez venus me délivrer I'm so relieved that you've come and set me free

soulever

soulever
[sulve] *v t*
to lift

soupe

soupe
[sup] *n f*
soup

soupe de légumes vegetable soup

souple

souple
[supl] *adj*
supple

sourire

sourire
[surir]
I. *v i*
to smile

continuez à sourire keep smiling

II. *n m*
smile

* *Tchang, je suis si content de voir ton sourire...* Chang, I'm so happy to see a smile on your face... *

souris

souris
[suri] *n f*
mouse, *pl* mice

Des souris !... Milou, ici, Milou ! Mice!... Snowy, here, Snowy!

sous

sous
[su] *prép*
under

...sous

* *Ah ! le brave Nestor... Nous allons pouvoir nous abriter sous son parapluie...* Ah! good old Nestor... We'll be able to shelter under his umbrella... *

sous-titre

sous-titre
[sutitr] *n m*
pl sous-titres
subtitle

soutenir

soutenir
[sutnir] *v t*
1. to hold up

* *Capitaine ! Capitaine ! Aidez-moi à le soutenir !* Captain! Captain! Help me hold him up! *

2. to support
nous soutenons le gouvernement ! We support the government!

souterrain

souterrain
[suterɛ̃]
I. *n m*
underground passage

* *Où conduit ce souterrain ?* Where does this underground passage lead? *

II. *adj*
underground
une rivière souterraine an underground river

souvenir

souvenir
[suvnir] *n m*
1. memory

je garderai un merveilleux souvenir de ce séjour en Amérique... I'll always have happy memories of this stay in America...

2. souvenir
allons acheter des souvenirs let's go and buy some souvenirs

► **se souvenir**
[səsuvnir] *v pr*
1. to remember

ah, mon gaillard, je me souviens de vous ! aha, my lad, I remember you!

2. Loc
c'est pour que vous vous souveniez que vous ne devez pas fumer ici that's to remind you that you can't smoke here

souvent

souvent
[suvɑ̃] *adv*
often

il oublie souvent ses promesses he often forgets his promises

sparadrap

sparadrap
[sparadra] *n m*
sticking-plaster
(*Am:* Band-Aid®)

...sparadrap

* *Vous avez un sparadrap sur votre chapeau.* You've got a piece of sticking-plaster on your hat. *

spécial

spécial, e
[spesjal] *adj*
pl spéciaux [spesjo]
1. special

* *Pour pénétrer dans cette partie du centre, il faut une autorisation spéciale.* You need a special permit to enter this part of the centre (*Am:* center)... *

2. peculiar
cette nourriture est vraiment spéciale this food is rather peculiar

▸ **spécialité**
[spesjalite] *n f*
speciality
(*Am:* specialty)

spécialités régionales regional specialities

spectacle

spectacle
[spɛktakl] *n m*
show, performance

splendide

splendide
[splɑ̃did] *adj*
splendid

il fait un temps splendide the weather's splendid

sport

sport
[spɔr] *n m*
1. sport

...sport

2. Loc
voiture de sport sports car

▸ **sportif, ive**
[spɔrtif, iv]
I. *adj*
athletic

II. *n*
sportsman *n m*,
sportswoman *n f*

stade

stade
[stad] *n m*
stadium

stage

stage
[staʒ] *n m*
training course

station

station
[stasjɔ̃] *n f*
1. stop

* *A quelle station descendrez-vous ?* What stop do you get off at? *

2. resort
station de sports d'hiver ski resort

▸ **stationnement**
[stasjɔnmɑ̃] *n m*
parking

stationnement interdit no parking

▸ **stationner**
[stasjɔne] *v i*
to park

▸ **station-service**
[stasjɔ̃sɛrvis] *n f*
pl stations-service
petrol (*Am:* gas) station

stylo

stylo
[stilo] *n m*
pen

stylo à bille ball-point pen

stylo à encre foutain pen

succès

succès
[syksɛ] *n m*
success

...succès

* *Vous allez voir le magicien : son numéro a eu beaucoup de succès !...* You're about to see the magician : his act has had great success!
Ah bon ! mais attendez, il y a beaucoup d'autres numéros avant le sien. Really! But wait, there are a lot of other acts before his... *

sucre

sucre
[sykr] *n m*
sugar

un morceau de sucre a sugar lump

▸ **sucré, e**
[sykre] *adj*
sweet

mon café n'est pas assez sucré my coffee isn't sweet enough

sud

sud
[syd] *n m*
south

* *Dis-donc, tu es sûr que nous roulons vers le sud ?* Listen, are you sure that we're driving towards the south?
Tout à fait sûr !... Absolutely certain!... *

...sud

suffire

suffire
[syfir] *vi*
to be enough

* *Est-ce que l'essence qui nous reste suffira ?* Will the petrol (*Am:* gas) that is left be enough? *

maintenant, ça suffit ! now, that's enough!

suggérer

suggérer
[sygʒere] *vt*
to suggest

capitaine, permettez-moi de vous suggérer de ne plus boire Captain, may I suggest that you stop drinking?

Suisse

Suisse
[sɥis] *nf*
Switzerland

► **suisse**
[sɥis] *adj*
Swiss

► **Suisse, Suissesse**
[sɥis, sɥisɛs] *n*
Swiss

les Suisses the Swiss

suivre

suivre
[sɥivr] *vt*
1. to follow

* *J'ai l'impression que nous sommes suivis.* I have a feeling we're being followed. *C'est sûr, on nous suit...* You're right: we're being followed... *

suivez le sentier jusqu'au village follow the path to the village

2. to keep up
quelques élèves n'arrivent pas à suivre some pupils can't keep up (with the class)

► **suivant, e**
[sɥivɑ̃, ɑ̃t] *adj*
1. following

nous les avons revus le jour suivant we saw them again the following day

2. next
attention, le mot suivant est difficile be careful, the next word is a difficult one

► **suite**
[sɥit] *nf*
1. series

c'est simplement une suite de nombres it's merely a series of numbers

2. Loc
la suite au prochain numéro to be continued

...suivre

racontez-nous la suite de l'histoire tell us what happened next

sujet

sujet
[syʒɛ] *nm*
1. topic, subject

changeons de sujet de conversation let's change the subject

...sujet

2. subject
le sujet du verbe the subject of the verb

supermarché

supermarché
[sypɛrmarʃe] *nm*
supermarket

supplément

supplément
[syplemɑ̃] *nm*
Loc.

je voudrais bien un supplément de saucisses I'd like extra sausages

► **supplémentaire**
[syplemɑ̃tɛr] *adj*

train supplémentaire relief (*Am:* extra) train

supposer

supposer
[sypoze] *vt*
to suppose

sur

sur
[syr] *prép*
1. on

* *Qu'y a-t-il sur la chaise ?* What is on the chair? *

...sur

...sur

2. onto
grimpe sur ce mur et dis-moi ce que tu vois climb up onto this wall, and tell me what you can see

3. about
c'est un livre sur l'Amérique it's a book about America

sûr

sûr, e
[syr] *adj*
1. sure, certain

* *Que le grand Cric me croque, je suis sûr que ce sont des pirates !* Ration my rum, I'm sure they are pirates! *

vous pouvez être sûr qu'ils viendront you can be certain they'll come

2. safe
cette partie de la ville n'est pas sûre this part of the town isn't safe

3. Loc
être sûr de soi to be self-assured

bien sûr of course

surgelé

surgelé, e
[syrʒəle] *adj*
frozen

surprenant

surprenant, e
[syrprənɑ̃, ɑ̃t] *adj*
surprising

* *Oui... C'est bien du crabe... Et pourtant j'ai vu les mêmes boîtes remplies d'opium.* Yes... it's crab. And yet I saw the same tins (*Am:* cans) filled with opium.
C'est surprenant !... How surprising!...

Je dirais même plus, surprenant !... To be precise, how surprising!... *

surprise

surprise
[syrpriz] *n f*
surprise

* *Oh, comme c'est drôle !... Abdallah a voulu me faire une surprise, il a mis des pétards dans mes cigares! ...* Oh, how funny!... Abdullah wanted to give me a surprise: he put firecrackers in my cigars!... *

► **surprise-partie**
[syrprizparti] *n f*
pl surprises-parties
party

surveiller

surveiller
[syrvɛje] *v t*
to watch

* *Attention, tu es surveillé ... Ecoute-moi sans regarder de mon côté...* Careful, you're being watched... Listen to me without looking my way... *

sympathique

sympathique
[sɛ̃patik] *adj*
nice

quel garçon sympathique ! what a nice boy!

syndicat

syndicat
[sɛ̃dika] *n m*
1. trade union (*Am:* labor union)

2. Loc
syndicat d'initiative tourist information bureau

système

système
[sistɛm] *n m*
system

le système solaire the solar system

tabac

tabac
[taba] *n m*
tobacco

table

table
[tabl] *n f*
1. table

mettre/débarrasser la table to set/to clear the table

...table

2. table
tables de multiplication multiplication tables

table des matières table of contents

tableau

tableau
[tablo] *n m*
pl tableaux
1. blackboard

...tableau

le professeur écrit au tableau the teacher is writing on the blackboard

2. painting
* *Vous voyez ce tableau ?* Do you see this painting?
Oui, c'est un de vos ancêtres ? Yes, is he one of your ancestors? *

3. Loc
tableau d'affichage notice (*Am:* bulletin) board

tableau de bord dashboard

tablier

tablier
[tablije] *n m*
apron

Irma, allez mettre votre tablier Irma, go and put your apron on

taille

taille
[taj] *n f*
1. size

...taille

* *Vous voilà habillé...* You're dressed now...
Moi aussi, j'ai une combinaison, mais je pense qu'elle n'est pas à ma taille... I've got a spacesuit too, but I don't think it's my size... *

2. waist
* *La corde est autour de ma taille.* The rope is around my waist. *

se taire

se taire
[sətɛr] *v pr*
1. to keep quiet

taisez-vous, il pourrait nous entendre keep quiet, he might hear us

2. to fall silent
tout le monde s'est tu quand le général est entré everybody fell silent when the General came in

tant

tant
[tɑ̃] *adv*
1. so much

Milou aime tant les os qu'il oublie parfois ses promesses Snowy likes bones so much that he sometimes forgets his promises

2. as long as
* *Tant que je n'aurai pas retrouvé Tchang, je continuerai à le chercher. Je ne veux pas l'abandonner.* As long as I have not found Chang, I'll keep looking for him. I don't want to abandon him. *

Tant que je n'aurai pas retrouvé Tchang, je continuerai à le chercher. Je ne veux pas l'abandonner.

3. Loc
vous pouvez venir ? tant mieux ! you can come? great!

il ne s'en souvient plus – tant pis ! he can't remember – too bad!

tante

tante
[tɑ̃t] *n f*
aunt

taper

taper
[tape]
I. *vi*
to hit

ne tapez pas sur ce pauvre animal ! don't hit that poor animal!

...taper

taper sur un clou to hit a nail

II. *v t*
to type

tapez cette lettre (à la machine) type this letter

tapis

Ah, quel bonheur ! Je vais pouvoir dormir confortablement sur ce tapis !

tapis
[tapi] *n m*
carpet

* *Ah, quel bonheur ! Je vais pouvoir dormir confortablement sur ce tapis !* Ah, bliss! I'll be able to sleep comfortably on this carpet! *

tard

tard
[tar] *adv*
late

c'est trop tard it's too late

tarif

tarif
[tarif] *n m*
fare

...tarif

nous pourrons voyager à demi-tarif we'll be able to travel at half fare

tarte

tarte
[tart] *n f*
1. tart

tarte à la framboise/aux pommes raspberry/apple tart

...tarte

2. pie
tarte à la crème custard pie

tasse

tasse
[tas] *n f*
cup

voulez-vous une tasse de thé ? would you like a cup of tea?

taureau

taureau
[tɔro] *n m*
pl taureaux
bull

taxi

taxi
[taksi] *n m*
taxi

* *Merci, nous irons en taxi.* Thank you, we'll get a taxi. *

...taxi

Merci, nous irons en taxi.

technicien

technicien, enne
[tɛknisjɛ̃, ɛn] *n*
technician

* *C'est à partir de ce tableau que les techniciens manœuvrent la fusée...* The technicians operate the rocket from this control panel... *Comme ça a l'air compliqué !...* It looks ever so complicated!... *

C'est à partir de ce tableau que les techniciens manœuvrent la fusée ...
Comme ça a l'air compliqué !...

télégramme

télégramme
[telegram] *n m*
telegram (*Am:* wire)

téléphoner

téléphoner
[telefɔne] *v t*
to phone, to telephone
je vous téléphonerai dès que possible I'll phone you as soon as possible

...téléphoner

► **téléphone**
[telefɔn] *n m*
phone, telephone
un coup de téléphone a phone call

télévision

télévision
[televizjɔ̃] *n f*
television, TV

tellement

tellement
[tɛlmɑ̃] *adv*
1. so much
il a tellement d'argent qu'il ne sait comment le dépenser he has so much money he doesn't know how to spend it

2. so many
* *Il y a tellement de gens que nous allons être en retard...* There are so many people that we're going to be late... *

température

température
[tɑ̃peratyr] *n f*
1. temperature
* *La température est basse, nous ne pouvons pas dormir sans tente !* The temperature is low, we can't sleep without a tent! *

2. temperature
tu as l'air malade, tu devrais prendre ta température you don't look well, you'd better take your temperature

tempête

tempête
[tɑ̃pɛt] *n f*
1. storm
pourvu que cette tempête ne dure pas ! let's hope this storm won't last!

2. Loc
tempête de neige/sable snowstorm, sandstorm

temps

temps
[tɑ̃] *n m*
1. time
Milou, dépêche-toi, nous n'avons pas beaucoup de temps ! hurry up, Snowy, we haven't got much time!
oh, que le temps passe vite ! oh, how quickly time passes!
de temps en temps from time to time

2. weather
quel temps fait-il à Moulinsart ? what's the weather like in Marlinspike?
* *Si le temps le permet...* Weather permitting...
... nous commencerons l'ascension à 8 heures... ...we'll start climbing at 8 o'clock... *

...temps

tenir

tenir
[tənir]
I. *v t*
1. to hold
je vais te tenir par la main, n'aie pas peur I'll hold your hand, don't be afraid

2. to hold up
c'est un clou qui tient le tableau a nail holds the picture up

3. to run
c'est ici que le senhor Oliveira da Figueira tient une boutique this is where Senhor Oliveira da Figueira runs a shop

II. *v pr*
to behave oneself
Milou, arrête tout de suite, tiens-toi bien ! Snowy, stop that immediately and behave yourself!

tente

tente
[tɑ̃t] *n f*
tent

nous allons dresser la tente ici we'll put up the tent here

terminer

terminer
[tɛrmine]
I. *v t*
to finish

allons, capitaine, vous terminerez votre livre demain come on, Captain, you can finish your book tomorrow

II. *v pr*
to end

le film se termine bien the film ends well

terrain

terrain
[tɛrɛ̃] *n m*
1. land

ce terrain appartient à mon père this land belongs to my father

2. Loc
terrain de camping campsite

terrain de football football field

terrasse

terrasse
[tɛras] *n f*
terrasse

la terrasse de cette maison donne sur la mer the terrace of this house looks out onto the sea

terre

terre
[tɛr] *n f*
1. Earth

* *Ici la Terre, m'entendez-vous ?... Vous êtes à 20 000 km de la Terre, tout va bien ?* This is ground control, can you hear me?.. You are 20,000 km from Earth, is everything all right?
Tout va bien. Everything's all right. *

2. soil
cette terre n'est pas bonne pour les roses roses don't grow well in this soil

3. ground
asseyons-nous par terre et attendons let's sit on the ground and wait

4. land
quand se terminera cette traversée ? j'aimerais retrouver la terre ferme when will this crossing end? I'd like to be on dry land again

tête

tête
[tɛt] *n f*
1. head

* *Je vais vous couper la tête et vous serez sauvé !* I'll cut your head off and you'll be saved! *

2. face
ne faites pas la tête, capitaine, nous retrouverons votre pipe ! don't pull such a long face, Captain, we'll find your pipe again!

3. mind
oh, excusez-moi, j'avais la tête ailleurs I'm sorry, my mind was elsewhere

4. Loc
ils sont arrivés en tête they came first

têtu

têtu, e
[tɛty] *adj*
stubborn

* *Ah, professeur, que vous êtes têtu !* Ah, Professor, how stubborn you can be!
Mais non, pas du tout, pas du tout. No, not at all, not at all. *

thé

thé
[te] *n m*
tea

* *Tintin boit du thé.* Tintin is drinking tea. *

▶ **théière**
[tejɛr] *n f*
teapot

Tintin boit du thé.

théâtre

théâtre
[teatr] *n m*
1. theatre (*Am:* theater)

ce soir, nous irons au théâtre this evening we are going to the theatre

2. Loc
une pièce de théâtre a play

ticket ...tiède

ticket
[tikɛ] *n m*
ticket

tiède

tiède
[tjɛd] *adj*
lukewarm

* *Cette soupe n'est pas bonne, elle est tiède !* This soup is no good, it's lukewarm! *

Cette soupe n'est pas bonne, elle est tiède !

timbre ...timide

timbre
[tɛ̃br] *n m*
stamp

timide

timide
[timid] *adj*
shy

* *Ne sois pas timide, Zorrino, nous sommes tes amis.* Don't be shy, Zorrino, we are your friends. *

Ne sois pas timide, Zorrino, nous sommes tes amis.

tirer ...titre ...toilette

tirer
[tire]
I. *v t*
1. to pull

il lui a tiré les cheveux he pulled his hair

2. to draw
attendez, je vais tirer les rideaux wait a minute, I'll draw the curtains

II. *v i*
to shoot

N'essayez pas de vous enfuir ou je tire !...

* *N'essayez pas de vous enfuir ou je tire !...* Don't try to escape or I'll shoot!... *

titre

titre
[titr] *n m*
1. title

j'ai oublié le titre du livre I've forgotten the title of the book

2. title
n'oubliez pas son titre, c'est un prince don't forget to use his title, he's a prince

toilette

toilette
[twalɛt] *n f*
1. wash

va faire ta toilette go and have a wash

2. outfit
la Castafiore va mettre sa plus belle toilette Signora Castafiore is going to wear her best outfit

▸ **toilettes**
[twalɛt] *n f pl*
toilet, lavatory

où sont les toilettes, s'il vous plaît ? where's the toilet, please?

toit

toit
[twa] *n m*
roof

le toit du wagon est glissant the roof of the carriage (*Am:* railcar) is slippery

tomate

tomate
[tɔmat] *n f*
tomato

tomber

tomber
[tɔ̃be] *v i*
1. to fall

tenez bon, Tintin, sinon je vais tomber hold on, Tintin, or I'll fall

2. to drop
abritons-nous et attendons que le vent tombe let's take shelter and wait for the wind to drop

La nuit tombe sur la Lune, les passagers de la fusée sont endormis...

3. to fall
* *La nuit tombe sur la Lune, les passagers de la fusée sont endormis...* Night is falling on the Moon, the rocket's passengers are asleep... *

4. Loc
tomber malade to fall ill

tomber amoureux de quelqu'un to fall in love with somebody

tonalité

tonalité
[tɔnalite] *n f*
dialling (*Am:* dial) tone

* *Le téléphone est coupé, il n'y a pas de tonalité !* The phone's been cut off, there's no dialling tone! *

tondre

tondre
[tɔ̃dr] *v t*
1. to mow

il est en train de tondre la pelouse he's mowing the lawn

2. to shear
tondre les moutons to shear the sheep

tonner

tonner
[tɔne] *v impers*
to thunder

avez-vous entendu ? il a tonné toute la nuit did you hear? it thundered all night long

► **tonnerre**
[tɔnɛr] *n m*
thunder

* *Bom Brom Bobom* Bom Brom Bobom *Le tonnerre gronde.* The thunder's rumbling. *

Le tonnerre gronde.

tort

tort
[tɔr] *n m*
1. fault

reconnaissez-vous vos torts ? do you admit your faults?

2. Loc
avoir tort to be wrong

tôt

tôt
[to] *adv*
1. early

...tôt

nous partirons tôt demain matin we're leaving early tomorrow morning

2. soon
allez le voir le plus tôt possible go and see him as soon as possible

toucher

toucher
[tuʃe]

...toucher

I. *v t*
1. to touch

* *Ne touchez pas le fils de mon maître !* Don't touch my master's son! *

2. to move
Tintin, tu ne m'as pas oublié, cela me touche ! Tintin, you've not forgotten me, I'm moved!

II. *v pr*
to be adjacent

...toucher

leurs maisons se touchent their houses are adjacent

toujours

toujours
[tuʒur] *adv*
1. always

je n'entends pas toujours ce que vous dites I can't always hear what you say

...toujours

2. still
est-ce qu'il neige toujours ? is it still snowing?

tour

tour
[tur] *n f*
tower

il s'est réfugié en haut de la tour he's taken refuge at the top of the tower

tour

tour
[tur] *n m*
1. turn

et n'oubliez pas de donner un tour de clé and don't forget to give the key a turn

2. turn
* *Maintenant, Dupond, c'est à mon tour de conduire...* Now, Thompson, it's my turn to drive... *

...tour

3. trick
ils ont voulu nous jouer un tour they wanted to play a trick on us

4. Loc
il a fait le tour du monde he has been around the world

tourner

tourner
[turne]
I. *vi*
1. to revolve

la Terre tourne autour du Soleil the Earth revolves round the Sun

2. to turn
* *Vite, tournez à droite au prochain carrefour, vite...* Quick, turn right at the next crossroads, quick... *

Vite, tournez à droite au prochain carrefour, vite ...

II. *vt*
to turn

j'ai fini de lire, tourne la page I've finished reading, turn the page

tousser

tousser
[tuse] *vi*
to cough

tout

tout, e
[tu, tut] *adj*
1. all

* *Tintin a marché toute la journée...* Tintin has been walking all day... *

est-ce que tous les prisonniers sont là ? are all the prisoners here?

2. every
il me téléphone tous les jours he phones me every day

...tout

Tintin a marché toute la journée...

3. Loc
ils ont disparu tous les deux both of them have disappeared

► **tout**
[tu] *adv*

tout à coup suddenly

tout à fait quite

tout de suite right now, immediately

c'est tout droit it's straight ahead

tout le monde everybody

traduire

traduire
[tradɥir] *vt*
to translate

train

train
[trɛ̃] *n m*
1. train

* *Le train de Shangaï va arriver.* The train from Shangaï is coming. *

...train

Le train de Shanghaï va arriver.

2. Loc
être en train de faire quelque chose to be doing something

il est en train de lire he's reading

trajet

trajet
[traʒɛ] *n m*
1. route

je ne connais pas le trajet de ce bus I don't know the route of this bus

2. distance
nous devrons faire un trajet de 12 kilomètres... we'll have to walk a distance of 12 kilometres (*Am:* kilometers)

tranche

tranche
[trɑ̃ʃ] *n f*
slice

tranquille

tranquille
[trɑ̃kil] *adj*
1. quiet

j'aimerais mener une vie tranquille I'd like to lead a quiet life

...tranquille

2. peaceful
c'est une rue tranquille it's a peaceful street

3. Loc
laisse-moi tranquille leave me alone

transformer

transformer
[trɑ̃sfɔrme] *vt*
to turn into

* *C'est facile de se transformer ...en général ...japonais !* It's easy to turn oneself... into a Japanese ...general! *

C'est facile de se transformer
... en

général

...japonais!

transport

transport
[trɑ̃spɔr] *n m*
transport

transports en commun public transport

travailler

travailler
[travaje]
I. *v i*
1. to work

...travailler

il travaille dans le laboratoire he's working in the laboratory

2. Loc
est-ce qu'il travaille bien à l'école ? is he doing well at school?

II. *v t*
to practise (*Am:* to practice)

M. Wagner travaille son piano tous les jours Mr Wagner practises the piano every day

► **travail**
[travaj] *n m*
pl travaux [travo]
1. work

nous aiderons aux travaux des champs we'll help with the farm work

travaux pratiques practical work

2. job
je cherche du travail I'm looking for a job

traverser

...traverser

traverser
[travɛrse] *v t*
1. to cross

* *Je me demande si j'arriverai à traverser la rivière sans tomber dans l'eau...* I wonder whether I'll manage to cross the river without falling into the water... *

2. Loc
bon, je dois traverser la rivière à la nage well, I'll have to swim across the river

► **traversée**
[travɛrse] *n f*
crossing

très

très
[trɛ] *adv*
very

* *Regardez !* Look! *Les Dupondt sont très malades.* The Thompsons are very ill. *

...très

Les Dupondt sont très malades.

tricher

tricher
[triʃe] *v i*
to cheat

trimestre

trimestre
[trimɛstr] *n m*
term
(*Am:* quarter)

triste

triste
[trist] *adj*
1. unhappy, sad

Ils sont tristes de partir...

* *Ils sont tristes de partir...* They're sad to leave... *

2. sad
que cette histoire est triste ! what a sad story!

tromper

tromper
[trɔ̃pe]
I. *v t*
to deceive

...tromper

le vendeur vous a trompé, cette voiture n'est pas neuve the salesman deceived you, this car is not new

II. *v pr*
to make a mistake

* *Vous vous êtes trompé dans vos calculs, ce n'est pas possible !...* You've made a mistake in your calculations, it's impossible!... *

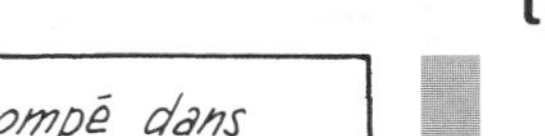

trop

trop
[tro] *adv*
1. too

...trop

Tonnerre, tu as bu trop de whisky !
LOMOND
ISKY

je suis trop sourd pour vous entendre I'm too deaf to hear you

2. too much
* *Tonnerre, tu as bu trop de whisky !* You've drunk too much whisky! *

3. too many
tu manges trop de bonbons you eat too many sweets

trottoir

trottoir
[trɔtwar] *n m*
pavement (*Am:* sidewalk)

trou

trou
[tru] *n m*
hole

* *Je vais pouvoir m'enfuir grâce à ce trou dans le mur...* I'll get away through the hole in the wall... *

...trou

Je vais pouvoir m'enfuir grâce à ce trou dans le mur...

trouver

trouver
[truve]
I. *v t*
1. to find

comment avez-vous trouvé le film ? how did you find the film?

2. to think
je trouve que tu as tort I think you're wrong

II. *v pr*
1. to find oneself

...trouver

2. Loc
où se trouve Moulinsart ? where's Marlinspike?

tuer

tuer
[tɥe]
I. *v t*
to kill

je vous tuerai ! I'll kill you!

...tuer

II. *v pr*
to kill oneself

il s'est tué pour nous sauver he killed himself to save us!

un

un
[œ̃] *adj num*
one

un plus un font deux one plus one are two

...un

► **un, une**
[œ̃, yn] *art indef*
1. a, an

j'ai acheté une cravate/un livre/une pomme I bought a tie/a book/an apple

2. Loc
j'ai en eux une confiance absolue I have complete confidence in them

un de ces jours one of these days

uni

uni, e
[yni] *adj*
1. level, even

ici le terrain est uni, ce sera plus facile pour atterrir the ground's level here, it'll be easier to land

2. plain
une chemise unie a plain shirt

unique

unique
[ynik] *adj*
1. only

je suis fils unique I'm an only child

2. unique
ce timbre est unique, il n'a pas de prix this stamp is unique, it's priceless

unité

unité
[ynite] *n f*
unit

le mètre est une unité de longueur the metre (*Am:* meter) is a unit of length

urgent

urgent, e
[yrʒɑ̃, ɑ̃t] *adj*
urgent

...urgent

► **urgence**
[yrʒɑ̃s] *n f*
emergency

en cas d'urgence in an emergency

usine

usine
[yzin] *n f*
factory

utiliser

utiliser
[ytilize] *v t*
to use

* *Je vais utiliser cette corde pour m'attacher aux échelons...* I'll use this rope to tie myself to the ladder... *

► **utile**
[ytil] *adj*
useful

Je vais utiliser cette corde pour m'attacher aux échelons...

V W V W

vacances

vacances
[vakɑ̃s] *n f pl*
holiday(s) (*Am:* vacation)

les vacances de Noël the Christmas holidays

ils sont partis en vacances they've gone on holiday

vache

vache
[vaʃ] *n f*
cow

* *Mais où cette vache va-t-elle me conduire ?...* Where on earth is this cow taking me?... *Wouah ! Wouah !* Woof! Woof! *

vaisselle

vaisselle
[vɛsɛl] *n f*

...vaisselle

1. dishes

2. Loc
faire la vaisselle to do the washing-up (*Am:* the dishes)

valable

valable
[valabl] *adj*
valid

ce billet n'est plus valable this ticket is no longer valid

valise

valise
[valiz] *n f*
suitcase

* *Capitaine, voilà l'individu...* Captain, here's the fellow...
Ouvrez votre valise ! Open your suitcase! *

vallée

vallée
[vale] *n f*
valley

...vallée

d'ici, on découvre toute la vallée from here we can see the whole valley

valoir

valoir
[valwar] *v i*
1. to be worth

* *Combien vaut ce bateau ?* How much is this boat (worth)? *

...valoir

...valoir

2. Loc
cela ne vaut rien it's worthless

il vaut mieux partir it's best to leave

il vaudrait mieux vous taire you had better say nothing

variable

variable
[varjabl] *adj*
changeable

temps variable changeable weather

► **varié, e**
[varje] *adj*
varied

mon travail est très varié my work is very varied

vase

vase
[vaz] *n f*
mud

* *Milou est là-dessous ?...* Is Snowy down there?...
Dans la vase ?... In the mud?... *

vase

vase
[vaz] *n m*
vase

elle met les fleurs dans un vase she's putting the flowers in a vase

veau

veau
[vo] *n m*
pl veaux
1. calf

...veau

une vache et son veau a cow and its calf

2. veal
une côte de veau a veal cutlet

vedette

vedette
[vədɛt] *n f*
1. launch

* *Que se passe-t-il ?* What's happening?

...vedette

Il y a deux malades très contagieux à bord de cette vedette ! N'approchez pas !... There are two people with a very contagious disease on board this launch! Don't come nearer!... *

2. star
la Castafiore est une vedette Signora Castafiore is a star

véhicule

véhicule
[veikyl] *n m*
vehicle

veille

veille
[vɛj] *n f*
1. day before

les vacances commenceront la veille de Pâques the holidays

...veille

(*Am:* vacation) will begin the day before Easter

2. Loc
la veille au soir the night before

vélo

vélo
[velo] *n m*
bike

...vélo

avec ce vélo, je vais le rattraper with this bike, I'll catch up with him

vendre

vendre
[vɑ̃dr] *v t*
to sell

le boulanger vend du pain the baker sells bread

...vendre

* *Voici votre argent...* Here is your money...
Mais que vend-il à l'ennemi ? But what is he selling to the enemy? *

► **vendeur, euse**
[vɑ̃dœr, øz] *n*
salesman *n m*, saleswoman *n f*

vendredi

vendredi
[vɑ̃drədi] *n m*
Friday

viens me voir vendredi come and see me on Friday

ils ne travaillent pas le vendredi they don't work on Friday

venir

venir
[vənir] *v i*
1. to come

les Dupondt viendront demain the Thompsons will come tomorrow

2. to come
* *Ces cigarettes viennent de Bordurie, regardez le paquet, capitaine...* These cigarettes come from Borduria, look at the packet, Captain...

Ça alors !... Good grief!... *

3. to come
l'été vient après le printemps summer comes after spring

4. Loc
il vient de téléphoner he's just phoned

vent

vent
[vɑ̃] *n m*
wind

le vent se lève the wind is rising

vente

vente
[vɑ̃t] *n f*
sale

...vente

mettre quelque chose en vente to put something on sale

ventre

ventre
[vɑ̃tr] *n m*
stomach

ils ont mal au ventre they've got stomach-ache

vérifier

vérifier
[verifje] *v t*
to check

* *Correction minime, me semble-t-il... Mais vérifions tout de même ces calculs... Vérifions encore une fois, nous ne devons pas nous tromper.* A trifling correction, I think... But we'd better just check these calculations... Let's check once more, we mustn't make a mistake. *

vérité

vérité
[verite] *n f*
truth

* *Vous feriez mieux de me dire la vérité... Sinon...* You'd better tell me the truth... Otherwise... *

verre

verre
[vɛr] *n m*
1. glass

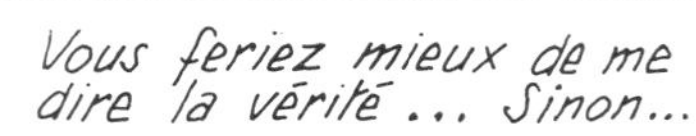

...verre

une plaque de verre a sheet of glass

2. glass
deux verres sont cassés two glasses are broken

vers

vers
[vɛr] *prép*
1. towards

* *Allô ? Allô ?... nous nous dirigeons vers la fusée...* Hallo? Hallo?... we are heading towards the rocket... *

2. around
nous arriverons vers midi we'll be there around noon

vers

vers
[vɛr] *n m*
line

apprenez les dix premiers vers du poème learn the first ten lines of the poem

version

version
[versjɔ̃] *n f*
1. version

...version

la version du deuxième témoin est différente the second witness's version is different

2. translation
version latine translation from Latin

vert

vert, e
[vɛr, vɛrt] *adj*
1. green

...vert

Voilà la forêt, elle est verte n'est-ce pas ?

* *Voilà la forêt, elle est verte n'est-ce pas ?* There is the forest, it's green, isn't it? *

2. green, unripe
ces fruits sont verts this fruit is unripe

▶ **vert**
[vɛr] *n m*
green

le vert lui va bien green suits her

veste

veste
[vɛst] *n f*
jacket

* *Vous avez vu dans quel état est ma veste ?* Have you seen what state my jacket is in? *

▶ **veston**
[vɛstɔ̃] *n m*
jacket

le veston de mon costume my suit jacket

Vous avez vu dans quel état est ma veste ?

vestiaire

vestiaire
[vɛstjɛr] *n m*
changing (*Am:* locker) room

l'équipe est encore dans les vestiaires the team hasn't left the changing room yet

vêtement

vêtement
[vɛtmã] *n m*
1. garment

...vêtement

2. clothes *n pl*
* *Vous trouverez des vêtements à côté.* You'll find some clothes in the next room.
Merci... Thank you...
Ça va ? Alright?
Ça va, j'arrive... Alright, I'm coming...
Me voilà. Here I am. *

Vous trouverez des vêtements à côté .
Merci...
?

Ça va ?
Ça va , j'arrive ...

Me voilà .

vétérinaire

vétérinaire
[veterinɛr] *n m*
vet, veterinary surgeon (*Am:* veterinarian)

viande

viande
[vjãd] *n f*
meat

* *Allons mon ami, ne vous fâchez pas. Je*

...viande

Allons mon ami, ne vous fâchez pas. Je vous demandais seulement ce que vous préparez comme viande pour ce soir...

vous demandais seulement ce que vous préparez comme viande pour ce soir... Come on, my friend, don't be angry. I was just asking you what meat you were preparing for dinner... *

victime

victime
[viktim] *n f*
1. casualty

il y a trop de victimes sur la route there are too many road casualties

2. victim
nous avons été victimes d'une mauvaise plaisanterie we've been the victims of a bad joke

vide

vide
[vid] *adj*
empty

Tintin, mon ventre est vide, il faut trouver un os Tintin, my stomach's empty, we've got to find a bone

▶ **vider**
[vide]
I. *v t*
to empty

...vide

videz cette bouteille dans l'évier empty that bottle in the sink

II. *v pr*
to empty

le théâtre s'est vidé rapidement the theatre (*Am:* theater) quickly emptied

vie

vie
[vi] *n f*
1. life

il a risqué sa vie pour nous he risked his life for us

2. life story
inutile de nous raconter votre vie no need to tell us your life story

vieux

vieux, vieille
[vjø, vjɛj] *adj*

note: vieil is used before a masculine noun beginning with a vowel or a mute h

1. old
est-ce que Dupont est plus vieux que Dupond ? is Thomson older than Thompson?

2. old
vous voyez le vieil homme là-bas ? do you see that old man over there?

3. old
nous ne devrions pas garder ces vieux chapeaux we shouldn't keep these old hats

vif

vif, vive
[vif, viv] *adj*
1. vivid

...vif

son histoire m'a fait une vive impression his story made a vivid impression on me

2. bright
* *C'est une voiture rouge vif.* It's a bright red car. *

3. lively
Abdallah est un enfant très vif Abdullah is a very lively child

...vif

C'est une voiture rouge vif.

village

village
[vilaʒ] *n m*
village

comment s'appelle ce village ? what's the name of this village?

ville

ville
[vil] *n f*
1. town

...ville

* *Quelle est la ville la plus proche ?* What's the nearest town?
Hou Kou, monsieur... Hou Kou, Sir... *

2. city
les gens de la ville city-dwellers

vin

vin
[vɛ̃] *n m*
wine

vinaigre

vinaigre
[vinɛgr] *n m*
vinegar

vingt

vingt
[vɛ̃] *adj num*
twenty

► **vingtaine**
[vɛ̃tɛn] *n f*
score, about twenty

...vingt

une vingtaine de personnes about twenty people

violence

violence
[vjɔlɑ̃s] *n f*
violence

la violence de l'orage the violence of the storm

* *Répondez !...*

...violence

Qu'avez-vous fait de Tournesol ?... Répondez !... Answer!... What have you done with Calculus?... Answer!...
Expliquons-nous calmement, je déteste la violence !... Let's discuss it calmly, I hate violence!... *

► **violent, e**
[vjɔlɑ̃, ɑ̃t] *adj*
violent

c'est un homme violent he's a violent man

violon

violon
[vjɔlɔ̃] *n m*
violin

virage

virage
[viraʒ] *n m*
bend (*Am:* curve)

* *Il y a beaucoup de virages !* There are a lot of bends! *

...virage

Il y a beaucoup de virages !

visage

visage
[vizaʒ] *n m*
face

* *Son visage est sale.* His face is dirty. *

?
Son visage est sale.

visiter

visiter
[vizite] *v t*
to go round (*Am :* around)

...visiter

allons visiter la ville let's go round the town

► **visite**
[vizit] *n f*
1. visit

si nous allions lui rendre visite let's go and pay him a visit

2. tour
la visite du musée prendra l'après-midi the museum tour will take all afternoon

vite

vite
[vit] *adv*
1. quickly

que le temps passe vite ! time flies by so quickly!

2. soon
nous reviendrons aussi vite que possible we'll be back as soon as possible

vitesse

Le train va prendre de la vitesse, pourquoi Tintin ne saute-t-il pas maintenant ?

vitesse
[vitɛs] *n f*
1. speed

...vitesse

* *Le train va prendre de la vitesse, pourquoi Tintin ne saute-t-il pas maintenant ?* The train is picking up speed, why doesn't Tintin jump now? *

2. gear
la côte est raide, changez de vitesse the slope's steep, change gear

3. Loc
faire de la vitesse to speed

vitrine

vitrine
[vitrin] *n f*
shop window

* *J'ai vu un scaphandre dans la vitrine.* I saw a diving suit in the shop window. *Ah ! oui, le scaphandre... Suivez-moi...* Oh, yes! The diving suit... Follow me... *

J'ai vu un scaphandre dans la vitrine.
Ah ! oui le scaphandre ... Suivez-moi...

vivre

vivre
[vivr]
I. *v i*
1. to be alive, to live

* *Mille sabords !... Est-ce ce qu'il est...* Blistering barnacles!... Is he...
Non, il n'est que blessé, il vit encore. No, he's only wounded – he's still alive. *

il a vécu très vieux he lived to a great age

Mille sabords !... Est-ce qu'il est...
Non, il n'est que blessé, il vit encore.

...vivre

2. to live
le capitaine vit à Moulinsart the Captain lives in Marlinspike

II. *v t*
to spend

nous avons vécu des jours heureux à Moulinsart we spent happy days in Marlinspike

► **vivant, e**
[vivɑ̃, ɑ̃t] *adj*
1. alive

* *Je sais que Tchang est vivant !* I know Chang is alive!
Vivant ? ?... Alive?? *

2. living
un être vivant a living creature

3. lively
c'est un enfant très vivant he's a very lively child

4. Loc
langue vivante modern language

vocabulaire

vocabulaire
[vɔkabylɛr] *n m*
vocabulary

voici

voici
[vwasi] *adv*
here is, here are

voici Milou here's Snowy

voici les Dupondt here are the Thompsons

voie

voie
[vwa] *n f*
1. lane

une route à deux voies a two-lane road

2. Loc
voie ferrée railway (*Am:* railroad) track

voilà

voilà
[vwala] *adv*
1. there is, there are

ah, voilà mon livre là-bas ah, there's my book over there

2. here is, here are
* *La voilà, votre grotte... Vous la cherchiez... la voilà!...* Here's your cave... You were looking for it... here it is! *

voile

voile
[vwal] *n f*
1. sail

* *Hissez les voiles ! J'ai dit hissez les voiles !... Vous entendez... Hissez les voiles !...* Hoist the sails! I said hoist the sails!... Do you hear... Hoist the sails!... *

2. Loc
faire de la voile to go sailing

...voile

voir

voir
[vwar] *v t*
1. to see

* *Que se passe-t-il mille sabords !...* What's happening blistering barnacles!...
Vous verrez mieux avec vos lunettes !... You'll see better with your glasses on!... *

je ne vois rien I can't see anything

2. to see
nous devons aller voir Tintin we must go and see Tintin

3. to see
je vous avoue que je ne vois pas ce que vous voulez dire I must confess I don't see what you mean

4. Loc
faire voir quelque chose à quelqu'un to show somebody something

voisin

voisin, e
[vwazɛ̃, in]
I. *n*
neighbour
(*Am:* neighbor)

attendez, je vais demander à ma voisine wait a minute, I'll ask my neighbour

II. *adj*
1. neighbouring
(*Am:* neighboring)

les pays voisins the neighbouring countries

2. next
la maison voisine the next house

voiture

voiture
[vwatyr] *n f*
1. car

essayez de rattraper cette voiture try to catch up with that car

...voiture

2. carriage
(*Am:* car)
* *C'est curieux... tous les compartiments de cette voiture sont vides...* It's strange... all the compartments in this carriage are empty... *

voix

voix
[vwa] *n f*
voice

la Castafiore a une voix magnifique, n'est-ce pas ? Signora Castafiore has a magnificent voice, hasn't she?

vol

vol
[vɔl] *n m*
1. flight

...vol

le vol des oiseaux the birds' flight

2. flight
nous prendrons le vol 217 pour Genève we'll take flight 217 to Geneva

▸ **voler**
[vɔle] *v i*
to fly

* *Nous volons trop bas !* We're flying too low! *C'est vrai, attendez, nous allons atterrir...*

It's true, wait, we're going to land... *

vol

vol
[vɔl] *n m*
theft

les Dupondt enquêtent sur tous ces vols the Thompsons are investigating all these thefts

...vol

▸ **voler**
[vɔle] *v t*
1. to steal

* *La pie...* The magpie... *elle a...* it has... *volé la clé...* stolen the key... *

2. to rob
je me suis fait voler dans la rue I was robbed in the street

▸ **voleur, euse**
[vɔlœr, øz] *n*
thief

...vol

volant

volant
[vɔlɑ̃] *n m*
wheel

allons Dupont, prends le volant come on, Thomson, take the wheel

vomir

vomir
[vɔmir] *v i*
to vomit

...vomir

oh, que je suis malade, je vais vomir oh, I feel sick, I'm going to vomit

vouloir

vouloir
[vulwar] *v t*
1. to want

* *Milou veut me montrer quelque chose !* Snowy wants to show me something!

...vouloir

Milou veut me montrer quelque chose !
Wouah ! Wouah !

Wouah ! Wouah ! Woof! Woof! *

2. to like
puis-je venir avec vous ? si tu veux can I go with you? if you like

3. would like
veux-tu un verre de lait ? would you like a glass of milk?

4. will
Abdallah, veux-tu arrêter de crier ? Abdullah, will you stop shouting?

5. Loc
qu'est-ce que ça veut dire ? what does it mean?

* ***Je vous demande pardon, professeur...*** I beg your pardon, Professor...
Aaah ! je fais le zouave ! Aah! I'm playing the fool, am I?
Tournesol en veut au capitaine... Calculus bears a grudge against the Captain... *

Je vous demande pardon, professeur...
Aaah ! je fais le zouave !...

Tournesol en veut au capitaine...

voyage

voyage
[vwajaʒ] *n m*
1. journey

avez-vous fait un bon voyage ? did you have a good journey?

2. trip
comment s'est passé votre voyage à Genève ? how was yout trip to Geneva?

► **voyager**
[vwajaʒe] *vi*
to travel

Tintin a beaucoup voyagé Tintin has travelled (*Am:* traveled) a lot

► **voyageur, euse**
[vwajaʒœr, øz] *n*
1. traveller
(*Am:* traveler)

le capitaine est un grand voyageur the Captain is a great traveller

2. passenger
les voyageurs sont priés de montrer leurs passeports passengers are requested to show their passports

vrai

vrai, e
[vrɛ] *adj*
1. true

eh oui, mon cher Tintin, tout ceci est vrai yes, my dear Tintin, all this is true

...vrai

2. real
quelle est la vraie cause de l'accident ? what is the real cause of the accident?

► **vraiment**
[vrɛmɑ̃] *adv*
really, truly

nous sommes vraiment désolés d'avoir mal compris we are truly sorry that we misunderstood

vue

vue
[vy] *n f*
1. eyesight

il a une mauvaise vue et doit porter des lunettes he has poor eyesight and has to wear glasses

2. view
d'ici, on a une belle vue sur la campagne you have a fine view of the countryside from here

wagon

wagon
[vagɔ̃] *n m*
1. carriage
(*Am:* car)

* ***Boum crac*** Crash Crack
Oh ! regardez le wagon dégringole... Il était temps que nous sautions... Oh! look, the carriage is tumbling down... We jumped just in time... *

BOUM CRAC
Oh ! regardez le wagon dégringole... Il était temps que nous sautions...
!

2. wagon
(*Am:* freight car)
les caisses vont être chargées dans les wagons the crates are going to be loaded onto the wagons

W.-C.

w.-c.
[vese] *n m pl*
toilet

week-end

week-end
[wikɛnd] *n m*
pl week-ends
weekend

si nous allions passer le week-end à Moulinsart ? what about going to Marlinspike for the weekend?

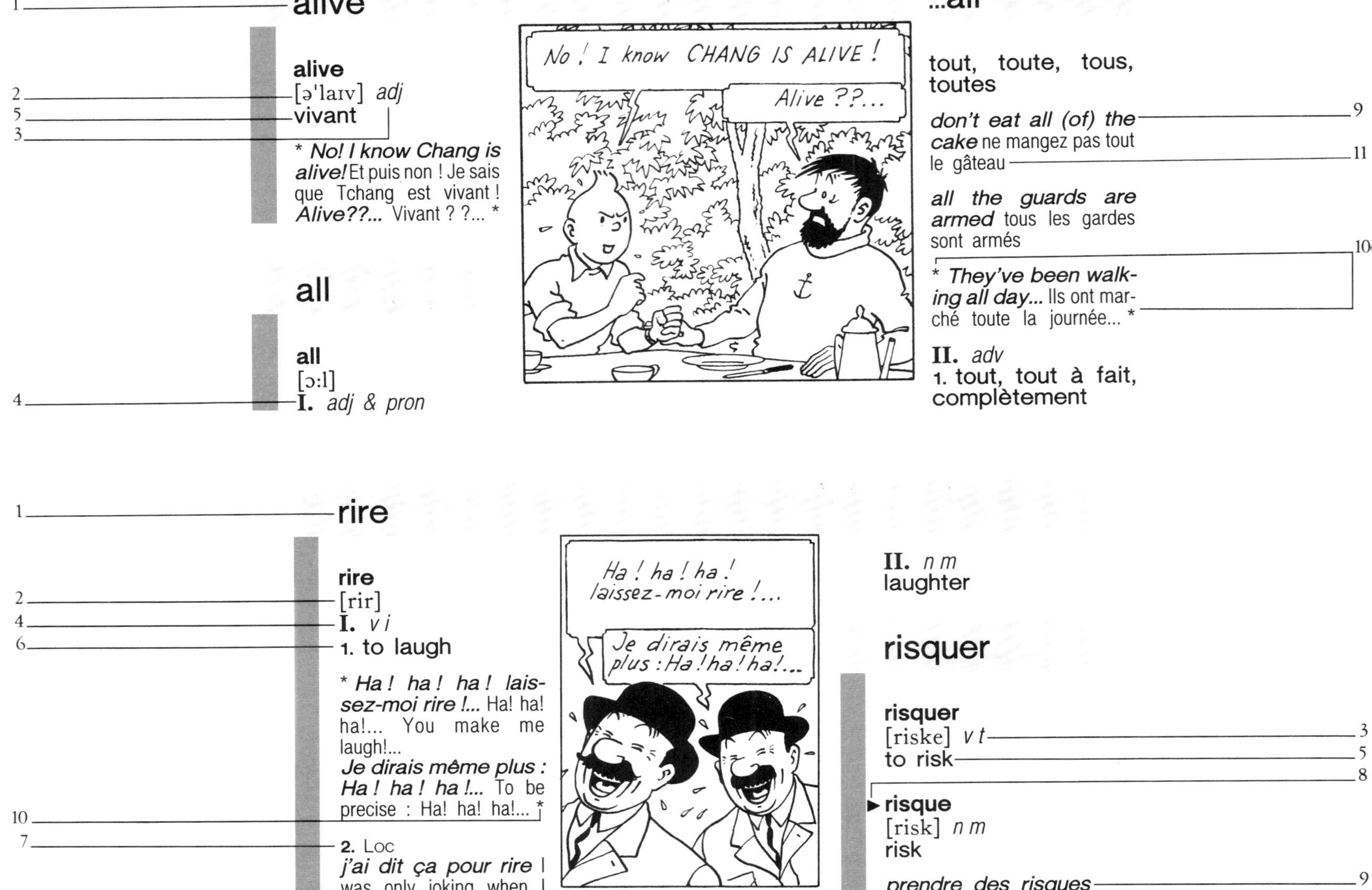

1 **alive**

alive
2 [ə'laɪv] *adj*
5 vivant
3

* ***No! I know Chang is alive!*** Et puis non ! Je sais que Tchang est vivant ! ***Alive??...*** Vivant ? ?... *

all

all
[ɔ:l]
4 **I.** *adj & pron*

...all

tout, toute, tous, toutes

don't eat all (of) the cake ne mangez pas tout le gâteau 9 11

all the guards are armed tous les gardes sont armés

* ***They've been walking all day...*** Ils ont marché toute la journée... * 10

II. *adv*
1. tout, tout à fait, complètement

1 **rire**

rire
2 [rir]
4 **I.** *v i*
6 **1.** to laugh

* ***Ha ! ha ! ha ! laissez-moi rire !...*** Ha! ha! ha!... You make me laugh!...
Je dirais même plus : Ha ! ha ! ha !... To be precise : Ha! ha! ha!... *
10

7 **2.** Loc
j'ai dit ça pour rire I was only joking when I said that

II. *n m*
laughter

risquer

risquer
[riske] *v t* 3
to risk 5
8
▸ **risque**
[risk] *n m*
risk

prendre des risques 9
to take risks 11

HOW TO USE THE DICTIONARY

1. Headword.
2. Pronunciation (see table).
3. Part of speech.
4. Figures I., II., etc. show the different parts of speech of a headword.
5. Translation of the headword.
6. Figures 1., 2., etc. show the different meanings of the word.
7. Idiom (Loc, for locution, in French) introduces idiomatic expressions.
8. Sub-entry. The main derivatives are given as sub-entries beneath the headword. The structure of the sub-entries is identical to that of the main entries.
9. Example.
10. Asterisks show that the example is illustrated. The example is identical to the text in the speech bubble.
11. Translation of example.

COMMENT UTILISER LE DICTIONNAIRE

1. Entrée.
2. Prononciation (voir tableau).
3. Catégorie grammaticale.
4. Les chiffres I., II., etc. indiquent les différentes catégories grammaticales d'un même mot.
5. Traduction du mot.
6. Les chiffres 1., 2., etc. indiquent les différentes traductions du mot.
7. Loc (en anglais Idiom) indique que le mot entre dans une expression idiomatique (ou dans plusieurs).
8. Sous-entrée. Sous le mot d'entrée ont été regroupés ses principaux dérivés. La structure de cette sous-entrée est la même que la structure de l'entrée principale.
9. Exemple.
10. L'astérisque indique que l'exemple est illustré. Le texte de l'exemple est celui qui figure dans la bulle.
11. Traduction de l'exemple.

YZYZY

yaourt

yaourt
[jaurt] *n m*
yoghurt

yeux

yeux
→ ŒIL

zéro

zéro
[zero] *n m*
1. nought (*Am:* zero)

100 s'écrit avec deux zéros 100 is written with two noughts

2. zero
* *Plus tard...* Later...
La température est très nettement en dessous de zéro... The temperature is a long way below zero... *

zone

zone
[zon] *n f*
1. area

zone vinicole wine-growing area

2. Loc
zone piétonnière pedestrian precinct

* *Arrêtons-nous, nous arrivons en zone interdite...* Let's stop, we're arriving in the forbidden zone...
Zone interdite. Forbidden zone. *

...zone

zoo

zoo
[zoo] *n m*
zoo

zut

zut
[zyt] *interj*
bother, heck

* *Zut! C'est fini!...* Heck! There's no more!... *

Achevé d'imprimer en Juin 1992
Réalisation Partenaires
Imprimé en France
Dépôt légal: Juin 1992